Numerical Analysis and Applied Mathematics

Numerical Analysis and Applied Mathematics

Guest Editor

Stoil I. Ivanov

MDPI

Basel • Beijing • Wuhan • Barcelona • Belgrade • Novi Sad • Cluj • Manchester

Guest Editor
Stoil I. Ivanov
Faculty of Physics and Technology
University of Plovdiv Paisii Hilendarski
Plovdiv
Bulgaria

Editorial Office
MDPI AG
Grosspeteranlage 5
4052 Basel, Switzerland

This is a reprint of the Special Issue, published open access by the journal *Axioms* (ISSN 2075-1680), freely accessible at: https://www.mdpi.com/journal/axioms/special_issues/W6JKVARK8L.

For citation purposes, cite each article independently as indicated on the article page online and as indicated below:

Lastname, A.A.; Lastname, B.B. Article Title. *Journal Name* **Year**, *Volume Number*, Page Range.

ISBN 978-3-7258-7687-7 (Hbk)
ISBN 978-3-7258-7688-4 (PDF)
https://doi.org/10.3390/books978-3-7258-7688-4

Cover image courtesy of Stoil I. Ivanov

Contents

Alicia Cordero, Jose A. Reyes, Juan R. Torregrosa and Maria P. Vassileva
Stability Analysis of a New Fourth-Order Optimal Iterative Scheme for Nonlinear Equations
Reprinted from: *Axioms* **2024**, *13*, 34, https://doi.org/10.3390/axioms13010034 . . . . **1**

José M. Gutiérrez and Víctor Galilea
Two Dynamic Remarks on the Chebyshev–Halley Family of Iterative Methods for Solving Nonlinear Equations
Reprinted from: *Axioms* **2023**, *12*, 1114, https://doi.org/10.3390/axioms12121114 . . . . **25**

Allaberen Ashyralyev and Ibrahim Mohammed Ibrahım
High-Order, Accurate Finite Difference Schemes for Fourth-Order Differential Equations
Reprinted from: *Axioms* **2024**, *13*, 90, https://doi.org/10.3390/axioms13020090 . . . . **41**

Safyan Mukhtar, Weaam Alhejaili, Mohammad Alqudah, Ali M.Mahnashi, Rasool Shah and Samir A. El-Tantawy
Kink Wave Phenomena in the Nonlinear Partial Differential EquationRepresenting the Transmission Line Model of Microtubules for NanoionicCurrents
Reprinted from: *Axioms* **2024**, *13*, 686, https://doi.org/10.3390/axioms13100686 . . . . **56**

Keyang Zhang, Fazlollah Soleymani and Stanford Shateyi
On the Construction of a Two-Step Sixth-Order Scheme to Find the Drazin Generalized Inverse
Reprinted from: *Axioms* **2025**, *14*, 22, https://doi.org/10.3390/axioms14010022 . . . . **68**

Nicola Apollonio
Cantelli's Bounds for Generalized Tail Inequalities
Reprinted from: *Axioms* **2025**, *14*, 43, https://doi.org/10.3390/axioms14010043 . . . . **82**

Andrej Liptaj
Round-Off Error Suppression by Statistical Averaging
Reprinted from: *Axioms* **2024**, *13*, 615, https://doi.org/10.3390/axioms13090615 . . . . **100**

Aubain Nzokem, Daniel Maposa and Anna M. Seimela
Enhanced Fast Fractional Fourier Transform (FRFT) Scheme Based on Closed Newton-Cotes Rules
Reprinted from: *Axioms* **2025**, *14*, 543, https://doi.org/10.3390/axioms14070543 . . . . **124**

Peter Junghanns
The Numerical Solution of Volterra Integral Equations
Reprinted from: *Axioms* **2025**, *14*, 675, https://doi.org/10.3390/axioms14090675 . . . . **143**

Mingming Liu and Stanford Shateyi
On the Derivationof a Fast Solver for Nonlinear Systems of Equations Utilizing Frozen Substeps with Applications
Reprinted from: *Axioms* **2025**, *14*, 77, https://doi.org/10.3390/axioms14020077 . . . . **173**

Runqi Xue, Yalin Li, Enbin Song and Tao Liu
An Enhanced Method with Memory Derived from Newton's Scheme in Solving Nonlinear Equations: Higher R-Order Convergence and Numerical Performance
Reprinted from: *Axioms* **2025**, *14*, 387, https://doi.org/10.3390/axioms14050387 . . . . **185**

Lanyin Sun, Siya Wen and Ziwei Dong
Superconvergence of Mixed Finite Element Method with Bernstein Polynomials for Stokes Problem
Reprinted from: *Axioms* **2025**, *14*, 168, https://doi.org/10.3390/axioms14030168 . . . . **200**

Jonas Šiaulys, Mantas Dirma, Neda Nakliuda and Luca Zanardelli
Asymptotic Formulas for the Haezendonck–Goovaerts Risk Measure of Sums with Consistently Varying Increments
Reprinted from: *Axioms* **2026**, *15*, 20, https://doi.org/10.3390/axioms15010020 . . . . **219**

Logapriya Balasubramaniam, Saeid Jafari, Vidhya Dhayalan and Shobana Arunachalam
Optimizing Textile Manufacturing with an $M^X/G/1$ Queueing Model: Two Heterogeneous Services, Bernoulli Vacations, and Disaster–Repair Interventions
Reprinted from: *Axioms* **2025**, *14*, 863, https://doi.org/10.3390/axioms14120863 . . . . **250**

axioms
MDPI

Article

Stability Analysis of a New Fourth-Order Optimal Iterative Scheme for Nonlinear Equations

Alicia Cordero [1,*], José A. Reyes [2], Juan R. Torregrosa [1] and María P. Vassileva [2]

[1] Multidisciplinary Mathematics Institute, Universitat Politècnica de València (UPV), 46022 Valencia, Spain; jrtorre@mat.upv.es
[2] Departamento de Ciencias Básicas, Instituto Tecnológico de Santo Domingo (INTEC), Santo Domingo 10801, Dominican Republic; 1097590@est.intec.edu.do or jreyes471@uasd.edu.do (J.A.R.); maria.penkova@intec.edu.do (M.P.V.)
* Correspondence: acordero@mat.upv.es

Abstract: In this paper, a new parametric class of optimal fourth-order iterative methods to estimate the solutions of nonlinear equations is presented. After the convergence analysis, a study of the stability of this class is made using the tools of complex discrete dynamics, allowing those elements of the class with lower dependence on initial estimations to be selected in order to find a very stable subfamily. Numerical tests indicate that the stable members perform better on quadratic polynomials than the unstable ones when applied to other non-polynomial functions. Moreover, the performance of the best elements of the family are compared with known methods, showing robust and stable behaviour.

Keywords: nonlinear equations; iterative methods; convergence order; stability; parameter plane

MSC: 65H05; 47F99

1. Introduction and Preliminary Concepts

It is widely known that fixed-point iterative methods play a fundamental role in scientific disciplines such as Celestial Mechanics (see for example [1,2]), Electrical Power Systems [3], Chemistry [4], Hydraulic Engineering [5], and Civil Engineering [6]. These algorithms provide approximate solutions when exact solutions are challenging to obtain or when problems are ill-conditioned, while offering computational efficiency in terms of both time and computational resources.

In the field of numerical analysis, a current trend involves designing families of numerical methods that generalize existing approaches. Notable examples include King's family [7] as well as the one developed by Hueso et al. in [8]. A number of these methods incorporate weight functions into their design process; see for example [9,10].

The efficiency index of an iterative method was defined by Ostrowski in [11] as $EI = p^{1/d}$, where p is the order of convergence and d is the number of functional evaluations per iteration. This concept is directly related to Kung and Traub's conjecture [12], which states the order of convergence of any iterative scheme cannot be greater than 2^{d-1} (called the optimal order).

Several authors have generalized optimal iterative schemes according to the Kung–Traub conjecture. However, because there is no difference between the number of function evaluations and the order of the members within a class of iterative procedures, it is necessary to conduct a stability study on some simple nonlinear functions, such as quadratic polynomials. It has been observed that iterative schemes stable for such functions tend to perform better when applied to more complicated functions than methods exhibiting pathologies. To this end, the tools of complex discrete dynamics are employed to analyze stability in quadratic polynomials (see for example the work of Amat et al. in [13,14], Argyros et al.

in [15], Behl et al. in [16], Chicharro et al. in [17], Rafiq et al. in [18], Kansal et al. in [19], Khirallah et al. in [20], and Moccari et al. in [21], among others).

A detailed description of the following concepts in complex dynamics appears in [22,23]. Let R be be a rational function on the Riemann sphere $\widehat{\mathbb{C}} = \mathbb{C} \cup \{\infty\}$, $R : \widehat{\mathbb{C}} \rightarrow \widehat{\mathbb{C}}$; then, we denote by $R(z)$ the operator $R(z) = \frac{P(z)}{Q(z)}$, with $P(z)$ and $Q(z)$ being complex polynomials. Usually, R is obtained by applying an iterative scheme on a quadratic polynomial $p(z) = (z-a)(z-b)$.

Given $z_0 \in \widehat{\mathbb{C}}$, the orbit of z_0 under R is the sequence of points $\{z_0, z_1 = R(z_0), z_2 = R^2(z_0), \ldots, z_n = R^n(z_0), \ldots\}$. Point z_0 is called the seed of the orbit. There are many different kind of orbits in a typical dynamical system. Undoubtedly, the most important kind of orbit is a fixed point, that is, a point z_0 that satisfies $R(z_0) = z_0$. Another important element is the periodic orbit or cycle. A point z_0 is n-periodic if $R^n(z_0) = z_0$ for some $n > 0$, with $R^p(z_0) \neq z_0$ for any $p < n$. The smallest value of n for which the orbit becomes periodic is known as the period of the orbit.

Let us suppose that z_0 is a fixed point of R; then, z_0 is an attracting fixed point if $|R'(z_0)| < 1$. The point z_0 is a repelling fixed point if $|R'(z_0)| > 1$. Finally, if $|R'(z_0)| = 1$, then the fixed point is called neutral or indifferent.

Theorem 1 ([23]). *Attracting Fixed Point Theorem. Suppose that z_0 is an attracting fixed point for R. Then, there exists a domain D contained within the Riemann sphere such that $z_0 \in D$ and in which the following conditions are satisfied: if $z \in D$, then $R^n(z) \in D$ for all n; moreover, $R^n(z) \rightarrow z_0$, as $n \rightarrow \infty$.*

Theorem 2 ([23]). *Repelling Fixed Point Theorem. Suppose that z_0 is a repelling fixed point for R. Then, there exists a domain D contained within the Riemann sphere such that $z_0 \in D$ and in which the following condition is satisfied: if $z \in D$ and $z \neq z_0$, then there is an integer $n > 0$ such that $R^n(z) \notin D$.*

Now, let us suppose that z_0 is an attracting fixed point for R. The basin of attraction of z_0 is the set of all points with orbits tending to z_0. The immediate basin of attraction of z_0 is the largest convex component containing z_0 that lies in the basin of attraction. The critical points of the operator R are those z^C that meet $R'(z^C) = 0$. A critical point is called free if it does not match the roots of the polynomial. These two concepts are closely related to the next result.

Theorem 3 ([24,25]). *If R is a rational function, then the immediate basin of attraction of a periodic (or fixed) attracting point contains at least one critical point.*

Fatou and Julia studied the iteration of rational maps $R : \widehat{\mathbb{C}} \rightarrow \widehat{\mathbb{C}}$ under the assumption that $\deg(R) \geq 2$. They focused on a disjoint invariant decomposition of $\widehat{\mathbb{C}}$ into two sets. One of these sets is often called the Julia set. The other is referred as the Fatou set [22]. The Fatou set is the union of all basins of attraction, and the Julia set is its boundary.

Per Theorem 3, all of the attracting behaviours of a rational function can be found by iterating the free critical points and classifying them by their asymptotical performance in the Fatou set. This is accomplished by means of the parameter plane in the case where the rational function R depends on a complex parameter γ. This is the graphical representation that provides information about the choice of one or another value of a parameter γ within a family of iterative methods. This graphical representation directly relates each point in the complex plane to the corresponding parameter value that specifies each member of the family. Given a free critical point of R used as the initial estimate, the parameter plane indicates which attracting periodic orbit or fixed point the orbit of the critical point converges to.

When all of the free critical points are known, we can calculate the parameter planes to determine which values of γ relate the final state of all free critical points to any of the roots of $p(z)$. According to Theorem 3, this ensures the stability (on quadratic polynomials) of the associated elements of the class, as the only basins of attraction correspond with these roots.

Given a free critical point $cr(\gamma)$ as a seed of the rational function R, we define D_{cr} as the set of values of γ where the free critical point is in the basin of attraction of any of the roots of $p(z)$.

The characteristic function of the set D_{cr} is defined as

$$F_{D_{cr}}(\gamma) = \begin{cases} 1 & \text{if} \quad \gamma \in D_{cr}, \\ 0 & \text{if} \quad \gamma \notin D_{cr}. \end{cases}$$

Therefore, we can consider the parameter plane by representing the characteristic function of D_{cr}, where a red color is assigned when $F_{D_{cr}}(\gamma) = 1$ and black when $F_{D_{cr}}(\gamma) = 0$.

Our interest is to determine the values of γ for which the final state of the orbits of all free critical points is one of the polynomial roots. Because we construct a parameter plane for each free critical point, we proceed to construct the intersection of the parameter planes, which is called the unified parameter plane [26]. In this plane, we graph $F_{\bigcap_{i=1}^{n} D_{cr_i}}(\gamma)$, where n is the number of free critical points of the rational operator. Each red-colored point corresponds to values of γ for which all members of the family of iterative schemes are stable on quadratic polynomials.

One way to validate the information obtained through parameter planes is to use dynamical planes, which graphically represent the basins of attraction of a set of initial values for a specific member of the family, that is, for a value of γ. In other words, given a parameter value for which the associated method is stable, its dynamical plane is composed only of the basins of the polynomial roots. This indicates that it will always be able to converge to one of the roots, regardless of the initial estimate of the method. On the other hand, if the parameter value is in the instability region on the parameter plane, other basins corresponding to attracting periodic or strange fixed points appear in addition to the basins of the roots. Through the dynamical planes, we can determine the attracting fixed point to which the orbit of any initial estimate z_0 converges for a specific value of γ.

The basin of attraction for the root $z = a$ is represented in orange color, while the basin for $z = b$ is represented in blue. Additionally, different colors such as green, red, etc. are assigned depending on the number of attracting strange fixed points associated with γ, and black is used to represent basins of periodic orbits. The decrease in brightness of each color is an indicator of the size of the orbit of each point, meaning that brighter colors represent points that require fewer iterations to reach the fixed or periodic point. The codes used to present the parameter and dynamical planes are defined by Chicharro et al. in [27].

Let us remark that all of the obtained information depends on the quadratic polynomial $p(z)$ used to define the rational function R by applying the class of iterative methods on it. A key tool to extend these results to any quadratic polynomial is the conjugation. Let f and g be two functions from the Riemann sphere to itself. An analytic conjugation between f and g is a diffeomorphism h of the Riemann sphere onto itself such that $h \circ f = g \circ h$, where h is called the conjugation. In [28], Blanchard introduced the conjugation map $\phi(z) = \frac{z-a}{z-b}$, which is a Möbius transformation satisfying the following properties: $\phi(\infty) = 1$, $\phi(a) = 0$, and $\phi(b) = \infty$, with a and b being the roots of the arbitrary quadratic polynomial $p(z) = (z-a)(z-b)$.

The next result was proven by [22,29] for Newton's method. In Section 3, the Scaling Theorem is proven for the rational function related to the proposed class of iterative methods.

Theorem 4. *Scaling Theorem. Let $f(z)$ be an analytic function and let $A(z) = \eta z + \beta$, with $\eta \neq 0$ as an affine application. If $\mathrm{h}(z) = \lambda(f \circ A)(z)$ with $\lambda \neq 0$, then R_f is analytically conjugate with R_h through A, i.e., $\left(A \circ R_h \circ A^{-1}\right)(z) = R_f(z)$.*

If a family of iterative methods satisfies the Scaling Theorem, then the Möbius transformation can be applied. As demonstrated by Blanchard in [22], the asymptotic behavior of the system is qualitatively equivalent under conjugation. This allows us to perform dynamical analysis on an associated operator that does not depend on the roots a and b. Instead, the dynamical study is conducted based on their corresponding values in the new operator, which are $\phi(a) = 0$ and $\phi(b) = \infty$. Additionally, the strange fixed point $z = 1$ is the divergence of the original scheme. This makes the analysis of its stability particularly important.

In the following Section 2 a one-parametric class of iterative procedures with fourth-order of convergence is designed using the weight function technique. In Section 3, the rational function resulting from the fixed point operator applied on a quadratic polynomial $p(z)$ is analyzed. More specifically, we study the dynamics of the fixed points of this rational operator R, allowing us to determine its stability. In Section 4, the numerical behavior of some of the most stable members on other non-polynomial functions is analyzed and compared with other known methods from the literature. Finally, in Section 5, conclusions highlighting the most significant findings of the research are presented.

2. Construction of a New Parametric Family of Iterative Methods

If $f(x) = 0$ is a nonlinear equation, then an iterative method, under certain conditions, generates a sequence of real numbers that converges to a solution $\bar{x}$. However, the guarantee of convergence to a solution, the convergence rate, and the solution to which an iterative scheme converges all have a direct dependence on the initial estimate. The creation of a new class of iterative methods makes sense as long as there are members of the family that are competitive compared to existing schemes with good behavior. In our study, we present a new family of iterative methods using the weight function procedure, characterized by

$$\begin{aligned} y_k &= x_k - \beta \frac{f(x_k)}{f'(x_k)}, \\ x_{k+1} &= x_k - H(\mu) \frac{f(x_k)}{f'(x_k)}, \; k = 0, 1, \ldots, \end{aligned} \tag{1}$$

where β is an arbitrary parameter and H is a real function depending on $\mu(x) = \frac{f'(x)}{f'(y)}$. Now, we prove the convergence of this class, stating the conditions on $H(\mu(x))$, to achieve fourth-order convergence.

Theorem 5. *Let $\bar{x} \in I$ be a simple zero of a sufficiently differentiable function $f : I \subset \mathbb{R} \longrightarrow \mathbb{R}$ and $\mu(x) = \frac{f'(x)}{f'(y)}$. Let us assume an initial estimation x_0 that is close enough to a zero $\bar{x}$ of f. If a weight function $H(\mu(x_k))$, $\mu(x_k) = \frac{f'(x_k)}{f'(y_k)}$ is chosen that satisfies $H(1) = 1$ in addition to $H'(1) = \frac{3}{4}$, $H''(1) = \frac{3}{4}$, and $|H'''(1)| < +\infty$, then class (1) has an order of convergence of four if and only if $\beta = \frac{2}{3}$, with the following error equation:*

$$e_{k+1} = \frac{1}{81}\Big((117 - 32H'''(1))c_2^3 - 81c_3c_2 + 9c_4\Big)e_k^4 + O\Big(e_k^5\Big),$$

where $c_j = \frac{1}{j!}\frac{f^{(j)}(\bar{x})}{f'(\bar{x})}$ for $j = 2, 3, \ldots$ and $e_k = x_k - \bar{x}$.

Proof. By applying Taylor expansion of $f(x_k)$ on $\bar{x}$,

$$f(x_k) = f'(\bar{x})\Big[e_k + c_2e_k^2 + c_3e_k^3 + c_4e_k^4 + O\Big(e_k^5\Big)\Big] \tag{2}$$

and

$$f'(x_k) = f'(\bar{x})\left[1 + 2c_2e_k + 3c_3e_k^2 + 4c_4e_k^3 + O\left(e_k^4\right)\right]. \tag{3}$$

Dividing directly (2) by (3), we obtain

$$\frac{f(x_k)}{f'(x_k)} = e_k - c_2e_k^2 + 2\left(c_2^2 - c_3\right)e_k^3 + \left(-4c_2^3 + 7c_2c_3 - 3c_4\right)e_k^4 + O\left(e_k^5\right).$$

If, in the first step of (1), we subtract $\bar{x}$ on both sides, then we have its error expression

$$\begin{aligned} y_k - \bar{x} &= e_k - \beta\frac{f(x_k)}{f'(x_k)} \\ &= (1-\beta)e_k + \beta c_2e_k^2 + 2\beta\left(c_3 - c_2^2\right)e_k^3 + \beta\left(4c_2^3 - 7c_2c_c + 3c_4\right)e_k^4 + O\left(e_k^5\right). \end{aligned}$$

Then,

$$f'(y_k) = 1 - 2(\beta - 1)c_2e_k + B_1e_k^2 + B_2e_k^3 + O\left(e_k^4\right), \tag{4}$$

with

$$\begin{aligned} B_1 &= 3(\beta-1)^2c_3 + 2\beta c_2^2, \\ B_2 &= -4(\beta-1)^3c_4 - 4\beta c_2^3 + 2(5-3\beta)\beta c_2c_3. \end{aligned}$$

Dividing (3) by (4),

$$\mu(x_k) = \frac{f'(x_k)}{f'(y_k)} = 1 + 2\beta c_2e_k + D_1e_k^2 + D_2e_k^3 + O\left(e_k^4\right),$$

where

$$\begin{aligned} D_1 &= \left((4\beta-6)c_2^2 - 3(\beta-2)c_1c_3\right)\beta, \\ D_2 &= \left(2\left(\beta^2 - 3\beta + 2\right)c_2^3 + \left(-3\beta^2 + 9\beta - 7\right)c_2c_3 + \left(\beta^2 - 3\beta + 3\right)c_4\right)4\beta. \end{aligned}$$

We expand $H(\mu(x_k))$ around one because the variable μ approaches unity as k tends to infinity:

$$\begin{aligned} H(\mu(x_k)) &= H(1) + H'(1)\nu_k + \frac{H''(1)}{2!}\nu_k^2 + \frac{H'''(1)}{3!}\nu_k^3 + O\left(\nu_k^4\right) \\ &= H(1) + 2\beta H'(1)c_2e_k + F_1e_k^2 + \frac{2\beta}{3}(F_2 + F_3)e_k^3 + O\left(e_k^4\right), \end{aligned}$$

where

$$\begin{aligned} \nu_k &= \mu(x_k) - 1, \\ F_1 &= \left(2((2\beta-3)H'(1) + \beta H''(1))c_2^2 - 3(\beta-2)H'(1)\right)\beta c_3, \\ F_2 &= 6\left(\beta^2 - 3\beta + 3\right)c_4H'(1) - 3\left(2\left(3\beta^2 - 9\beta + 7\right)H'(1) + 3(\beta-2)\beta H''(1)\right)c_2c_3, \\ F_3 &= 2\left(6\left(\beta^2 - 3\beta + 2\right)H'(1) + \beta((6\beta-9)H''(1) + \beta H'''(1))\right)c_2^3. \end{aligned}$$

Subtracting $\bar{x}$ on both sides of the second step of (1),

$$\begin{aligned} e_{k+1} &= (x_k - \bar{x}) - H\left(\frac{f'(x_k)}{f'(y_k)}\right)\frac{f(x_k)}{f'(x_k)} \\ &= (1 - H(1))e_k + (H(1) - 2\beta H'(1))c_2e_k^2 + (2H(1) + 3(\beta-2)\beta H'(1))c_3 \\ &\quad - 2\left(H(1) + \beta(2(\beta-2)H'(1) + \beta H''(1))c_2^2\right)e_k^3 + O\left(e_k^4\right). \end{aligned} \tag{5}$$

Forcing the coefficients of e_k, e_k^2, and e_k^3 to be zero, we obtain $H(1) = 1$, along with $H'(1) = \frac{3}{4}$, $H''(1) = \frac{3}{4}$, and $\beta = \frac{2}{3}$. By replacing them in (5), we have

$$e_{k+1} = \frac{1}{81}\left((117 - 32H'''(1))c_2^3 - 81c_2c_3 + 9c_4\right)e_k^4 + O\left(e_k^5\right),$$

and the optimal order of convergence of four is proven. □

Parametric Family

The proposed parametric family generalizes some existing classes of iterative methods. Let us recall the one-parameter families of fourth-order optimal iterative methods developed by Hueso et al. in [8]:

$$\begin{aligned} y_k &= x_k - \frac{2}{3}\frac{f(x_k)}{f(x_k)}, k = 0, 1, \ldots, \\ x_{k+1} &= x_k - \left[\frac{5-8\alpha}{8} + \alpha\left(\frac{f'(x_k)}{f'(y_k)}\right) + \frac{\alpha}{3}\left(\frac{f'(x_k)}{f'(y_k)}\right)^{-1} + \frac{9-8\alpha}{24}\left(\frac{f'(x_k)}{f'(y_k)}\right)^2\right]\frac{f(x_k)}{f'(x_k)} \end{aligned} \tag{6}$$

and the parametric family defined by Cordero et al. in [10]:

$$\begin{aligned} y_k &= x_k - \frac{2}{3}\frac{f(x_k)}{f'(x_k)}, k = 0, 1, \ldots, \\ x_{k+1} &= x_k - \left[1 - \frac{3}{4}\left(\frac{f'(y_k)}{f'(x_k)} - 1\right) + \frac{9}{8}\left(\frac{f'(y_k)}{f'(x_k)} - 1\right)^2 + \frac{\alpha}{6}\left(\frac{f'(y_k)}{f'(x_k)} - 1\right)^3\right]\frac{f(x_k)}{f'(x_k)}. \end{aligned} \tag{7}$$

Both families have the structure of the iterative function defined in Equation (1) for $\beta = \frac{2}{3}$, and their weight functions satisfy Theorem 5. It is evident that the weight functions of these families share similar structures, suggesting the possibility of constructing a generalized family that encompasses both.

The following result shows that, under certain conditions, the parametric weight function

$$K(\mu(x)) = a_0\mu^{k_0}(x) + a_1\mu^{k_1}(x) + a_2\mu^{k_2}(x) + a_3\mu^{k_3}(x), \tag{8}$$

where $a_i \in \mathbb{R}$ and $k_i \in \mathbb{N}$ for $i = 0, 1, 2, 3$, satisfies the conditions of Theorem 5.

Theorem 6. *The parametric weight function $K(\mu(x)) = a_0\mu^{k_0}(x) + a_1\mu^{k_1}(x) + a_2\mu^{k_2}(x) + a_3\mu^{k_3}(x)$ satisfies the conditions imposed on the weight function H of Theorem 5 if and only if*

$$\begin{aligned} & k_i \neq k_j, \text{ with } i \neq j, \\ & a_0 = \frac{(k_1 - k_2)(-3k_2 + k_1(4k_2 - 3) + 6) - \gamma\phi_0}{4\phi_3}, \\ & a_1 = \frac{(3(k_2 - 2) + k_0(3 - 4k_2))(k_0 - k_2) + \gamma\phi_1}{4\phi_3}, \\ & a_2 = \frac{(k_0 - k_1)(-3k_1 + k_0(4k_1 - 3) + 6) - \gamma\phi_2}{4\phi_3}, \\ & a_3 = \gamma, \end{aligned}$$

where

$$\phi_n = \prod_{\substack{i<j \\ i,j \neq n}} (k_i - k_j), \text{ with } i, j \text{ and } n \in \{0, 1, 2, 3\}.$$

Proof. Considering that

$$\begin{aligned} K(\mu(x)) &= a_0\mu^{k_0}(x) + a_1\mu^{k_1}(x) + a_2\mu^{k_2}(x) + a_3\mu^{k_3}(x), \\ K'(\mu(x)) &= a_0k_0\mu^{k_0-1}(x) + a_1k_1\mu^{k_1-1}(x) + a_2k_2\mu^{k_2-1}(x) + a_3k_3\mu^{k_3-1}(x), \\ K''(\mu(x)) &= a_0(k_0-1)k_0\mu^{k_0-2}(x) + a_1(k_1-1)k_1\mu^{k_1-2}(x) + a_2(k_2-1)k_2\mu^{k_2-2}(x) \\ &\quad + a_3(k_3-1)k_3\mu^{k_3-2}(x), \end{aligned}$$

we have

$$\begin{aligned} &K(1) = a_0 + a_1 + a_2 + a_3, \\ &K'(1) = a_0k_0 + a_1k_1 + a_2k_2 + a_3k_3, \\ &K''(1) = a_0(k_0-1)k_0 + a_1(k_1-1)k_1 + a_2(k_2-1)k_2 + a_3(k_3-1)k_3. \end{aligned}$$

If we equate these expressions to the conditions imposed in Theorem 5, then we have the following system:

$$\begin{aligned} a_0 + a_1 + a_2 + a_3 &= 1, \\ a_0k_0 + a_1k_1 + a_2k_2 + a_3k_3 &= \tfrac{3}{4}, \\ a_0(k_0-1)k_0 + a_1(k_1-1)k_1 + a_2(k_2-1)k_2 + a_3(k_3-1)k_3 &= \tfrac{3}{4}, \end{aligned}$$

for which the solution set for $a_3 = \gamma$ and $k_i \neq k_j$ if $i \neq j$ is

$$\begin{aligned} a_0 &= -\frac{4\gamma k_3^2 - 4\gamma k_1k_3 - 4\gamma k_2k_3 + 4\gamma k_1k_2 + 3k_1 - 4k_1k_2 + 3k_2 - 6}{4(k_0-k_1)(k_0-k_2)} = -\frac{3(k_2-2)+k_1(3-4k_2)}{4(k_0-k_1)(k_0-k_2)} + \frac{\gamma(k_1-k_3)(k_3-k_2)}{(k_0-k_1)(k_0-k_2)}, \\ a_1 &= -\frac{4\gamma k_3^2 - 4\gamma k_0k_3 - 4\gamma k_2k_3 + 4\gamma k_0k_2 + 3k_0 - 4k_0k_2 + 3k_2 - 6}{4(k_1-k_0)(k_1-k_2)} = \frac{3(k_2-2)+k_0(3-4k_2)}{4(k_0-k_1)(k_1-k_2)} + \frac{\gamma(k_0-k_3)(k_2-k_3)}{(k_0-k_1)(k_1-k_2)}, \\ a_2 &= -\frac{-4\gamma k_3^2 + 4\gamma k_0k_3 + 4\gamma k_1k_3 - 4\gamma k_0k_1 - 3k_0 + 4k_0k_1 - 3k_1 + 6}{4(k_1-k_2)(k_2-k_0)} = \frac{3(k_1-2)+k_0(3-4k_1)}{4(k_0-k_2)(k_2-k_1)} + \frac{\gamma(k_0-k_3)(k_1-k_3)}{(k_1-k_2)(k_2-k_0)}, \\ a_3 &= \gamma. \end{aligned}$$

By defining

$$\phi_n = \prod_{\substack{i<j \\ i,j\neq n}} (k_i - k_j) \text{ with } i,j \text{ and } n \in \{0,\ldots,3\},$$

then multiplying and dividing by ϕ_3, we have

$$\begin{aligned} a_0 &= \frac{(k_1-k_2)(-3k_2+k_1(4k_2-3)+6) - \gamma(k_1-k_2)(k_1-k_3)(k_2-k_3)}{4\phi_3} = \frac{(k_1-k_2)(-3k_2+k_1(4k_2-3)+6) - \gamma\phi_0}{4\phi_3}, \\ a_1 &= \frac{(3(k_2-2)+k_0(3-4k_2))(k_0-k_2) + \gamma(k_0-k_2)(k_0-k_3)(k_2-k_3)}{4\phi_3} = \frac{(3(k_2-2)+k_0(3-4k_2))(k_0-k_2) + \gamma\phi_1}{4\phi_3}, \\ a_2 &= \frac{(k_0-k_1)(-3k_1+k_0(4k_1-3)+6) - \gamma(k_0-k_1)(k_0-k_3)(k_1-k_3)}{4\phi_3} = \frac{(k_0-k_1)(-3k_1+k_0(4k_1-3)+6) - \gamma\phi_2}{4\phi_3}, \\ a_3 &= \gamma, \end{aligned}$$

and the proof is finished. □

In Theorem 6, it can be observed that the parametric weight function $K(\mu(x))$ depends on the parameters $k_0, k_1, k_2, k_3,$ and a_3; thus, we denote it as $K_{(k_0,k_1,k_2,k_3,a_3)}(\mu(x))$. It is easy to see that the families of iterative methods from the iterative expressions (6) and (7) are subfamilies of the family formed by the iterative scheme (1) when $H(\mu) = K_{(-1,0,1,2,\frac{9-8\alpha}{24})}(\mu)$ and $H(\mu) = K_{(-3,-2,-1,0,\frac{1}{6}\alpha)}(\mu)$, respectively.

3. Complex Stability Analysis

In Section 2, we have set the conditions for the following iterative scheme to be a fourth-order optimal class of iterative methods:

$$\begin{aligned} y_k &= x_k - \frac{2}{3}\frac{f(x_k)}{f'(x_k)}, \quad k = 0, 1, \ldots, \\ x_{k+1} &= x_k - \left[a_0\mu(x_k)^{k_0} + a_1\mu(x_k)^{k_1} + a_2\mu(x_k)^{k_2} + a_3\mu(x_k)^{k_3}\right]\frac{f(x_k)}{f'(x_k)}, \end{aligned} \tag{9}$$

where $\mu(x_k) = \dfrac{f'(x_k)}{f'(y_k)}$.

If we assign integer values to k_0, k_1, k_2, and k_3, all distinct from each other, and define a_i for $i \in \{0, 1, 2, 3\}$ as in Theorem 6, then the following result demonstrates that the resulting one-parametric subfamily satisfies the Scaling Theorem. As a result, the Möbius transformation can be used as an analytical conjugation to analyze the stability of its members on quadratic polynomials by means of its associated rational operator.

Theorem 7. *Let $f(z)$ be an analytic function, let R be the rational operator associated with the iterative scheme (9), and let $A(z) = \eta_1 z + \eta_2$ with $\eta_1 \neq 0$, an affine transformation. Let $h(z) = \lambda(f \circ A)(z)$; then, R_f and R_h are analytically conjugated by $A(z)$.*

Proof. Let us consider $N_f(z) = z - \frac{2}{3}\frac{f(z)}{f'(z)}$; taking into account that

$$A(x-y) = \eta_1(x-y) + \eta_2 = (\eta_1 x + \eta_2) - (\eta - 1y + \eta_2) + \eta_2 = A(x) - A(y) + \eta_2$$

and $h(z) = \lambda(f \circ A)(z) = \lambda f(A(z))$, then $h'(z) = A'(z)\lambda f'(A(z)) = \eta_1\lambda(f' \circ A)(z)$, and it can be deduced that

$$\begin{aligned} A \circ N_h \circ A^{-1} &= A\left(A^{-1}(z) - \frac{2}{3}\frac{h(A^{-1}(z))}{h'(A^{-1}(z))}\right) \\ &= A\left(A^{-1}(z) - \frac{2}{3}\frac{f(z)}{\eta_1 f'(z)}\right) \\ &= z - \frac{2}{3}\frac{f(z)}{f'(z)} = N_f(z). \end{aligned}$$

Thus, N_f and N_h are analytically conjugated by $A(z)$. Then,

$$R_h = z - \left[\sum_{i=0}^{3} a_i \left(\frac{h'(z)}{h'(N_h)}\right)^{k_i}\right]\frac{h(z)}{h'(z)}.$$

Because

$$\begin{aligned} h(z) &= \lambda(f \circ A)(z) = \lambda f(A(z)), \\ h'(z) &= \eta_1\lambda(f' \circ A)(z) \end{aligned}$$

and

$$h'(N_h) = \eta_1\lambda(f' \circ A \circ N_h)(z),$$

we have

$$R_h = z - \left[\sum_{i=0}^{3} a_i \left(\frac{f' \circ A}{f' \circ A \circ N_h}\right)^{k_i}\right] \frac{1}{\eta_1} \frac{f \circ A}{f' \circ A}.$$

Using the fact that $A \circ N_h \circ A^{-1} = N_f$,

$$R_h \circ A^{-1} = A^{-1}(z) - \left[\sum_{i=0}^{3} a_i \left(\frac{f'(z)}{f' \circ N_f}\right)^{k_i}\right] \frac{1}{\eta_1} \frac{f(z)}{f'(z)},$$

we obtain

$$A \circ R_h \circ A^{-1} = A\left[A^{-1}(z) - \left[\sum_{i=0}^{3} a_i \left(\frac{f'(z)}{f' \circ N_f}\right)^{k_i}\right] \frac{1}{\eta_1} \frac{f(z)}{f'(z)}\right].$$

Because $A(x - y) = A(x) - A(y) + \eta_2$, we have

$$A \circ R_h \circ A^{-1} = z - \left[\sum_{i=0}^{3} a_i \left(\frac{f'(z)}{f' \circ N_f}\right)^{k_i}\right] \frac{f(z)}{f'(z)} = R_f,$$

meaning that R_f and R_h are analytically conjugated by $A(z)$. □

3.1. Asymptotical Study of Fixed Points

As a consequence of Theorem 7 we know, under the conditions established for the parameters k_i and a_i for $i \in \{0,1,2,3\}$ in class (9), that the dynamical behavior of the associated rational operator remains invariant under the Möbius transformation through conjugation over quadratic polynomials.

Applying the family of iterative methods (9) on $p(z) = (z-a)(z-b)$, where $a, b \in \hat{\mathbb{C}}$, we obtain the associated rational operator $R_K = \phi \circ R_p \circ \phi^{-1}$ after conjugation with the Möbius map $\phi(z) = \frac{z-a}{z-b}$.

Now, for the dynamical analysis, distinct integer values are assigned to k_0, k_1, k_2, and k_3 and the dynamics of the rational operator R_K of the parametric family associated with these values is studied. We use the following criteria to select the class:

1. As our aim is to construct a parameter plane for each independent free critical point, the polynomial with roots that are critical points depending on γ should have a degree no higher than 4. This is because it becomes extremely laborious to construct parameter planes when the critical points that depend on γ are the roots of a high-degree polynomial.
2. It is necessary to find a radius disk where $|R'_K(1, k_0, k_1, k_2, k_3, \gamma)| > 1$ as much as is possible. By making $z = 1$ in $R'_K(z, k_0, k_1, k_2, k_3, \gamma)$, it is easy to see that $R'_K(1, k_0, k_1, k_2, k_3, \gamma) = \frac{A(k_0,k_1,k_2,k_3)}{B(k_0,k_1,k_2,k_3)+C(k_0,k_1,k_2,k_3)\gamma}$, where $A(k_0, k_1, k_2, k_3) = 8(k_0 - k_1)(k_0 - k_2)(k_1 - k_2)$,

$$\begin{aligned} B(k_0,k_1,k_2,k_3) = & - {k_0}^2 k_1 2^{2-k_2} 3^{k_2} + {k_0}^2 2^{2-k_1} 3^{k_1} k_2 - {k_0}^2 2^{-k_1} 3^{k_1+1} + 8{k_0}^2 k_1 \\ & + {k_0}^2 2^{-k_2} 3^{k_2+1} - 8{k_0}^2 k_2 + k_0 {k_1}^2 2^{2-k_2} 3^{k_2} - 2^{2-k_0} 3^{k_0} {k_1}^2 k_2 - 8 k_0 {k_1}^2 \\ & + 2^{-k_0} 3^{k_0+1} {k_1}^2 - k_0 2^{2-k_1} 3^{k_1} {k_2}^2 + 2^{2-k_0} 3^{k_0} k_1 {k_2}^2 \\ & + k_0 2^{1-k_1} 3^{k_1+1} 2^{1-k_0} 3^{k_0+1} k_1 + 8 k_0 {k_2}^2 - 2^{-k_0} 3^{k_0+1} {k_2}^2 - k_0 2^{1-k_2} 3^{k_2+1} \\ & + 2^{1-k_0} 3^{k_0+1} k_2 - {k_1}^2 2^{-k_2} 3^{k_2+1} + 8 {k_1}^2 k_2 + 2^{-k_1} 3^{k_1+1} {k_2}^2 - 8 k_1 {k_2}^2 \\ & + k_1 2^{1-k_2} 3^{k_2+1} - 2^{1-k_1} 3^{k_1+1} k_2, \end{aligned}$$

and

$$\begin{aligned}C(k_0,k_1,k_2,k_3) =& {k_0}^2k_1 2^{2-k_2}3^{k_2} - {k_0}^2 2^{2-k_1}3^{k_1}k_2 - {k_0}^2k_1 2^{2-k_3}3^{k_3} + {k_0}^2 2^{2-k_1}3^{k_1}k_3 + \\ & {k_0}^2k_2 2^{2-k_3}3^{k_3} - {k_0}^2 2^{2-k_2}3^{k_2}k_3 - k_0{k_1}^2 2^{2-k_2}3^{k_2} + 2^{2-k_0}3^{k_0}{k_1}^2k_2 + \\ & k_0{k_1}^2 2^{2-k_3}3^{k_3} - 2^{2-k_0}3^{k_0}{k_1}^2k_3 + k_0 2^{2-k_1}3^{k_1}{k_2}^2 - 2^{2-k_0}3^{k_0}k_1{k_2}^2 - \\ & k_0 2^{2-k_1}3^{k_1}{k_3}^2 + 2^{2-k_0}3^{k_0}k_1{k_3}^2 - k_0{k_2}^2 2^{2-k_3}3^{k_3} + 2^{2-k_0}3^{k_0}{k_2}^2k_3 + \\ & k_0 2^{2-k_2}3^{k_2}{k_3}^2 - 2^{2-k_0}3^{k_0}k_2{k_3}^2 - {k_1}^2k_2 2^{2-k_3}3^{k_3} + {k_1}^2 2^{2-k_2}3^{k_2}k_3 + \\ & k_1{k_2}^2 2^{2-k_3}3^{k_3} - 2^{2-k_1}3^{k_1}{k_2}^2k_3 - k_1 2^{2-k_2}3^{k_2}{k_3}^2 + 2^{2-k_1}3^{k_1}k_2{k_3}^2.\end{aligned}$$

Then, $|\frac{A(k_0,k_1,k_2,k_3)}{C(k_0,k_1,k_2,k_3)}| > |\frac{B(k_0,k_1,k_2,k_3)}{C(k_0,k_1,k_2,k_3)} + \gamma|$ when $|R'(1,k_0,k_1,k_2,k_3,\gamma)| > 1$, and now $G(k_0,k_1,k_2,k_3) = \frac{A(k_0,k_1,k_2,k_3)}{C(k_0,k_1,k_2,k_3)}$ is defined such that we choose values of k_0, k_1, k_2 and k_3 where $|G(k_0,k_1,k_2,k_3)|$ can be made as large as desired.

3. The coefficients of the rational operator must be simple in the sense that they do not exceed three digits.

Table 1 presents the degrees of those polynomials with zeros that are free critical points of the rational operator associated with 330 one-parameter families constructed with values of k_0, k_1, k_2, and k_3 taken from the set of all unique permutations of integers from -5 to 5. Within this set, nine families can be identified that meet the criteria established in the first point. Of these, eight families have an associated polynomial of degree 4, while one family has a polynomial of degree 2.

Table 1. Degrees of the polynomials with zeros that are free critical points of R_K.

Degree	Number of Families
18	36
16	56
14	63
12	60
10	50
8	30
6	26
4	8
2	1

Table 2 presents the values of k_j for $j = 0,1,2,3$, radius $|G(k_0,k_1,k_2,k_3)|$, and rational function of those classes of iterative schemes such that the polynomials generating the free critical points have a degree lower than or equal to four. It can be observed that the families by Hueso et al. (6) and Cordero et al. (7) meet our selection criteria. In the case of the first family, the radius as a function of γ of the disk where divergence is repelling is 24, and the polynomial that meets the first criterion is of degree 4. On the other hand, the second class has a radius as a function of γ of 54, and possesses the only second-degree polynomial that satisfies the first criterion among all possible formed families. In both families, the coefficients of the rational operators do not exceed three digits.

The family associated with $K_{(-4,-3,-2,-1,\gamma)}$ has a divergence radius greater than that of the two families mentioned earlier, and the polynomial degree is 4. However, the coefficients of the rational operator are not simple. On the other hand, the family associated with $K_{(-2,-1,0,1,\gamma)}$ has simple coefficients and a radius of 36, which is greater than the radius of the family studied by Hueso et al. (6). Therefore, we focus our analysis on this family. It is worth mentioning that it would be interesting to study the dynamical behavior of the family associated with $K_{(0,1,2,3,\gamma)}$ or $K_{(1,2,3,4,\gamma)}$, as well as other families, without considering the simple coefficient criterion.

Table 2. Values of k_j related to parametric families where the degree (D) of the polynomial with zeros that are free critical points of the associated rational operator does not exceed 4 and their radius (r).

(k_0, k_1, k_2, k_3)	r	D	$R_K(z,\gamma)$
$(1,2,3,4)$	$\frac{32}{3}$	4	$-\frac{z^4(-192\gamma+81z^5+135z^4+324z^3+204z^2-192\gamma z+187z-3)}{3(64\gamma+1)z^5+(192\gamma-187)z^4-204z^3-324z^2-135z-81}$
$(0,1,2,3)$	16	4	$-\frac{z^4(-64\gamma+27z^4+54z^3+90z^2+62z+39)}{(64\gamma-39)z^4-62z^3-90z^2-54z-27}$
$(-4,-3,-2,0)$	18	4	$-\frac{z^4(-256\gamma+27z^6+216z^5+729z^4+1296z^3+(1813-256\gamma)z^2-8(32\gamma-157)z+679)}{(256\gamma-679)z^6+8(32\gamma-157)z^5+(256\gamma-1813)z^4-1296z^3-729z^2-216z-27}$
$(-1,0,1,2)$	24	4	$-\frac{z^4(-64\gamma+27z^4+90z^3+138z^2+114z+63)}{(64\gamma-63)z^4-114z^3-138z^2-90z-27}$
$(-4,-3,-1,0)$	$\frac{162}{5}$	4	$-\frac{z^4(-384\gamma+81z^6+648z^5+2187z^4+3888z^3+(4839-384\gamma)z^2-8(64\gamma-421)z+1437)}{3(128\gamma-479)z^6+8(64\gamma-421)z^5+(384\gamma-4839)z^4-3888z^3-2187z^2-648z-81}$
$(-2,-1,0,1)$	36	4	$-\frac{z^4(-64\gamma+27z^4+126z^3+234z^2+198z+135)}{(64\gamma-135)z^4-198z^3-234z^2-126z-27}$
$(-4,-2,-1,0)$	$\frac{486}{11}$	4	$-\frac{z^4(-768\gamma+243z^6+1944z^5+6561z^4+11664z^3+(13629-768\gamma)z^2+(9512-1280\gamma)z+3423)}{(768\gamma-3423)z^6+8(160\gamma-1189)z^5+3(256\gamma-4543)z^4-11664z^3-6561z^2-1944z-243}$
$(-3,-2,-1,0)$	54	2	$-\frac{z^4(-64\gamma+27z^4+162z^3+378z^2+378z+319)}{(64\gamma-319)z^4-378z^3-378z^2-162z-27}$
$(-4,-3,-2,-1)$	81	4	$-\frac{z^4(-192\gamma+81z^6+648z^5+2187z^4+3888z^3+(5439-192\gamma)z^2-8(16\gamma-471)z+2037)}{3(64\gamma-679)z^6+8(16\gamma-471)z^5+3(64\gamma-1813)z^4-3888z^3-2187z^2-648z-81}$

From Table 2, we denote the rational operator of the family associated with $K_{(-2,-1,0,1,\gamma)}$ by

$$R(z,\gamma) = \frac{z^4(27z^4+126z^3+234z^2+198z+135-64\gamma)}{(135-64\gamma)z^4+198z^3+234z^2+126z+27}.$$

Now, let us analyze some properties of the rational operator R.

Theorem 8. *The fixed points of the rational function $R(z,\gamma)$ are $z=0$, $z=\infty$, and the following strange fixed points:*

- $ex_1(\gamma) = 1$, *which corresponds to divergence from the original method*
- $ex_2(\gamma) = z_{1,1} = \frac{1}{2}\left(\frac{1}{9}S(\gamma) - \sqrt{\left(-\frac{1}{9}S(\gamma) + \frac{17}{9S(\gamma)} + \frac{17}{9}\right)^2 - 4} - \frac{17}{9S(\gamma)} - \frac{17}{9}\right)$
- $ex_3(\gamma) = z_{1,2} = \frac{1}{2}\left(\frac{1}{9}S(\gamma) + \sqrt{\left(-\frac{1}{9}S(\gamma) + \frac{17}{9S(\gamma)} + \frac{17}{9}\right)^2 - 4} - \frac{17}{9S(\gamma)} - \frac{17}{9}\right)$
- $ex_4(\gamma) = z_{2,1} = \frac{1}{2}\left(-\frac{1}{9}wS(\gamma) - \sqrt{-4 + \left(\frac{1}{9}wS(\gamma) - \frac{17\overline{w}}{9S(\gamma)} + \frac{17}{9}\right)^2} + \frac{17\overline{w}}{9S(\gamma)} - \frac{17}{9}\right)$
- $ex_5(\gamma) = z_{2,2} = \frac{1}{2}\left(-\frac{1}{9}wS(\gamma) + \sqrt{-4 + \left(-\frac{1}{9}wS(\gamma) - \frac{17\overline{w}}{9S(\gamma)} + \frac{17}{9}\right)^2} + \frac{17\overline{w}}{9S(\gamma)} - \frac{17}{9}\right)$
- $ex_6(\gamma) = z_{3,1} = \frac{1}{2}\left(-\frac{1}{9}\overline{w}S(\gamma) - \sqrt{-4 + \left(\frac{1}{9}\overline{w}S(\gamma) - \frac{17w}{9S(\gamma)} + \frac{17}{9}\right)^2} + \frac{17w}{9S(\gamma)} - \frac{17}{9}\right)$
- $ex_7(\gamma) = z_{3,2} = \frac{1}{2}\left(-\frac{1}{9}\overline{w}S(\gamma) + \sqrt{-4 + \left(\frac{1}{9}\overline{w}S(\gamma) - \frac{17w}{9S(\gamma)} + \frac{17}{9}\right)^2} + \frac{17w}{9S(\gamma)} - \frac{17}{9}\right)$

where $S(\gamma) = \sqrt[3]{3\sqrt{3}\sqrt{27648\gamma^2 - 60544\gamma + 33327} - 864\gamma + 946}$ *and* $w = \frac{1}{2}\left(1 - i\sqrt{3}\right)$.

Proof. From the definition of a fixed point, we have $R(z,\gamma) = z$. Then,

$$\frac{z^4(27z^4+126z^3+234z^2+198z+135-64\gamma)}{(135-64\gamma)z^4+198z^3+234z^2+126z+27} = z.$$

Thus,

$$z\left[27\left(z^7-1\right) + 126z\left(z^5-1\right) + 234z^2\left(z^3-1\right) + (63+64\gamma)z^3(z-1)\right] = 0$$

and

$$z(z-1)\left(27z^6+153z^5+387z^4+z^3(450+64\gamma)+387z^2+153z+27\right)=0.$$

Let $J(z,\gamma)$ denote the last factor of this equation. If we substitute $u=z+\frac{1}{z}$, then $u^2-2=z^2+\frac{1}{z^2}$ and $u^3-3u=z^3+\frac{1}{z^3}$. Thus, $J(z,\gamma)=z^3\left[27u^3+153u^2+306u+(144+64\gamma)\right]$. Therefore, the factor $27u^3+153u^2+306u+(144+64\gamma)$ must be zero. Consequently, we have

$$u_1(\gamma)=\frac{1}{9}S(\gamma)-\frac{17}{9S(\gamma)}-\frac{17}{9},$$

$$u_2(\gamma)=-\frac{1}{18}\left(1-i\sqrt{3}\right)S(\gamma)+\frac{17\left(1+i\sqrt{3}\right)}{18S(\gamma)}-\frac{17}{9},$$

$$u_3(\gamma)=-\frac{1}{18}\left(1+i\sqrt{3}\right)S(\gamma)+\frac{17\left(1-i\sqrt{3}\right)}{18S(\gamma)}-\frac{17}{9},$$

where

$$S(\gamma)=\sqrt[3]{3\sqrt{3}\sqrt{27648\gamma^2-60544\gamma+33327}-864\gamma+946}.$$

Therefore, $ex_{j+k}(\gamma)=\frac{u_i(\gamma)+(-1)^{j+k}\sqrt{u_i(\gamma)^2-4}}{2}$, for $i=1,2,3$, $j=1,3,5$ and $k=1,2$. Note that the strange fixed points $ex_{i+1}(\gamma)=z_{i,2}=\frac{1}{z_{i,1}}=\frac{1}{ex_i(\gamma)}$, as $z^2-u_i(\gamma)z+1=0$ is a symmetric polynomial:

- $ex_2(\gamma)=z_{1,1}=\frac{1}{2}\left(\frac{1}{9}S(\gamma)-\sqrt{\left(-\frac{1}{9}S(\gamma)+\frac{17}{9S(\gamma)}+\frac{17}{9}\right)^2-4}-\frac{17}{9S(\gamma)}-\frac{17}{9}\right)$
- $ex_3(\gamma)=z_{1,2}=\frac{1}{2}\left(\frac{1}{9}S(\gamma)+\sqrt{\left(-\frac{1}{9}S(\gamma)+\frac{17}{9S(\gamma)}+\frac{17}{9}\right)^2-4}-\frac{17}{9S(\gamma)}-\frac{17}{9}\right)$
- $ex_4(\gamma)=z_{2,1}=\frac{1}{2}\left(-\frac{1}{9}wS(\gamma)-\sqrt{-4+\left(\frac{1}{9}wS(\gamma)-\frac{17\overline{w}}{9S(\gamma)}+\frac{17}{9}\right)^2}+\frac{17\overline{w}}{9S(\gamma)}-\frac{17}{9}\right)$
- $ex_5(\gamma)=z_{2,2}=\frac{1}{2}\left(-\frac{1}{9}wS(\gamma)+\sqrt{-4+\left(-\frac{1}{9}wS(\gamma)-\frac{17\overline{w}}{9S(\gamma)}+\frac{17}{9}\right)^2}+\frac{17\overline{w}}{9S(\gamma)}-\frac{17}{9}\right)$
- $ex_6(\gamma)=z_{3,1}=\frac{1}{2}\left(-\frac{1}{9}\overline{w}S(\gamma)-\sqrt{-4+\left(\frac{1}{9}\overline{w}S(\gamma)-\frac{17w}{9S(\gamma)}+\frac{17}{9}\right)^2}+\frac{17w}{9S(\gamma)}-\frac{17}{9}\right)$
- $ex_7(\gamma)=z_{3,2}=\frac{1}{2}\left(-\frac{1}{9}\overline{w}S(\gamma)+\sqrt{-4+\left(\frac{1}{9}\overline{w}S(\gamma)-\frac{17w}{9S(\gamma)}+\frac{17}{9}\right)^2}+\frac{17w}{9S(\gamma)}-\frac{17}{9}\right)$

where $w=\frac{1}{2}\left(1-i\sqrt{3}\right)$.

In a similar way, it can be easily checked that $z=0$ is a fixed point of $\frac{1}{R\left(\frac{1}{z},\gamma\right)}$; thus, $z=\infty$ is a fixed point of R. □

It is clear that the long-term behavior of fixed points is influenced by γ. This dependence can result in an attracting character of some strange fixed points, leading the corresponding numerical method to attract elements that are not solutions to the problem under investigation.

In order to perform a stability analysis of the fixed points, we can evaluate their derivative operator:

$$R'(z,\gamma)=-\frac{36z^3(z+1)^4N(z,\gamma)}{\left(64\gamma z^4-135z^4-198z^3-234z^2-126z-27\right)^2},$$

where $N(z,\gamma) = (192\gamma - 405)z^4 - (96\gamma + 540)z^3 + (64\gamma - 990)z^2 - (96\gamma + 540)z + (192\gamma - 405)$.

Fixed points $z = 0$ and $z = \infty$ have a superattracting character, as $|R'(z,\gamma)| = 0$ for those values. However, the stability of $z = 1$ provides important numerical information, as it indicates divergence in the original procedure. Hence, we determine the stability of these fixed points in the forthcoming results.

Theorem 9. *For $\gamma \neq \frac{45}{4}$, the fixed point $ex_1(\gamma) = 1$ has the following characteristics:*

(i) *It can not be superattracting;*

(ii) *When $\left|\frac{45}{4} - \gamma\right| < 36$, it is repelling;*

(iii) *If $\left|\frac{45}{4} - \gamma\right| = 36$, $ex_1(\gamma) = 1$ is neutral;*

(iv) *When $\left|\frac{45}{4} - \gamma\right| > 36$, then $ex_1(\gamma) = 1$ is attracting.*

Proof. (i) The derivative $R_h'(1,\gamma) = \frac{144}{45-4\gamma}$ is always different from zero; thus, $ex_1(\gamma) = 1$ cannot be superattracting. Moreover, it is not defined for $\gamma = \frac{45}{4}$; thus, $z = 1$ is not a fixed point for this value of γ.

(ii) According to the definition, $ex_1(\gamma) = 1$ is a repelling fixed point if $|R_h'(1,\gamma))| = \left|\frac{144}{45-4\gamma}\right| > 1$. Therefore, $\left|\frac{144}{45-4\gamma}\right| > 1$ is equivalent to $\left|\frac{45}{4} - \gamma\right| < \frac{144}{4} = 36$.

Let us consider an arbitrary complex number $\gamma = c + id$. Then, $\left|\frac{45}{4} - \gamma\right| < 36$ is equivalent to $(c - \frac{45}{4})^2 + d^2 < 36^2$, indicating that the divergence represents a repelling fixed point for values of $\gamma \neq \frac{45}{4}$ inside the disk D_1 centered at $C\left(\frac{45}{4}, 0\right)$ with a radius of 36. It is neutral at the circumference and attracting outside the disk; see Figure 1 for a visual representation.

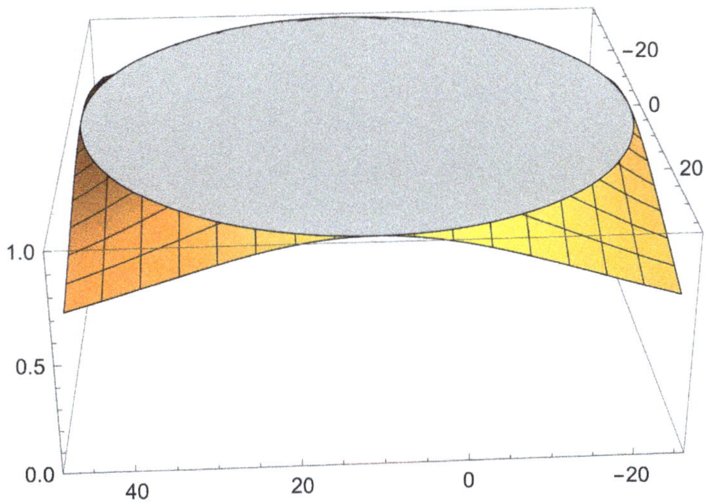

Figure 1. Stability region of $ex_1(\gamma) = 1$ in the complex plane.

The proofs for items (iii) and (iv) follow a similar approach to that for item (ii). □

We aim for the only attracting fixed points to be $z = 0$ and $z = \infty$. Therefore, the stability function $|R'(z,\gamma)|$ at the other fixed points should always be greater than one. Indeed, to prevent divergence, a stable method must be defined with a γ value from within the disk D_1.

Figure 2 displays the stability function of $ex_2(\gamma)$ and $ex_3(\gamma)$, indicating that there are only attracting fixed points inside the orange cardioid contained within the rectangular region defined by

$$B(\gamma) = \left\{ \gamma \in \mathbb{C} : \gamma = c + id, \frac{22}{5} < c < \frac{99}{8}, -\frac{83}{20} < d < \frac{83}{20} \right\}.$$

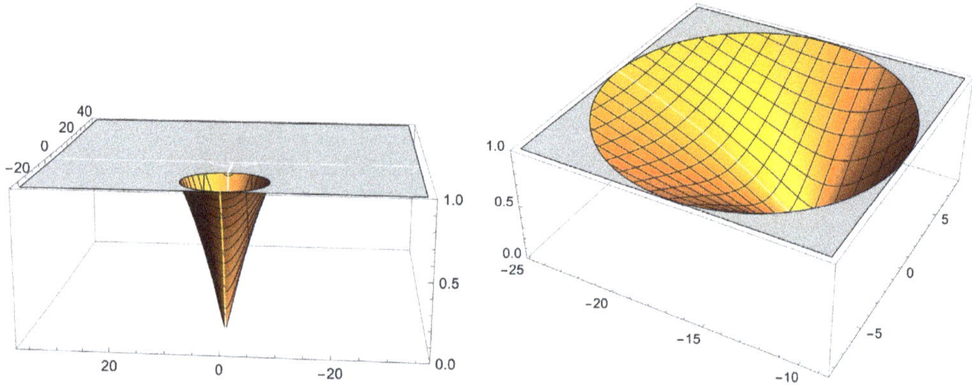

(**a**) $ex_2(\gamma)$ and $ex_3(\gamma)$ in D_1 (**b**) $ex_2(\gamma)$ and $ex_3(\gamma)$ in $B(\gamma)$

Figure 2. Stability regions of $ex_2(\gamma)$ and $ex_3(\gamma)$, in the complex plane.

Figure 3 displays the stability surfaces of the strange fixed points $ex_i(\gamma)$ for $i = 4, 5, 6, 7$, illustrating that they are always repelling for γ values inside the disk D_1.

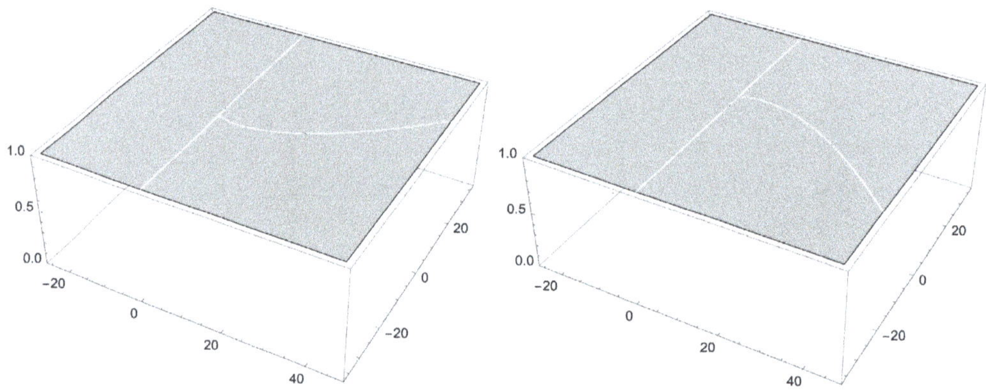

(**a**) $ex_4(\gamma)$ and $ex_5(\gamma)$ (**b**) $ex_6(\gamma)$ and $ex_7(\gamma)$

Figure 3. Stability surfaces of $ex_i(\gamma)$ for $i = 4, 5, 6, 7$, in the complex plane.

On the other hand, we know that $z = 0$ and $z = \infty$ are critical points for all values of γ. The following result identifies the critical points of the rational operator, which allows us to determine the values of γ for which the zeros of $p(z)$ are the only attracting elements.

Theorem 10. *The rational operator R has the following free critical points:*

(i) $cr_1 = -1$,

(ii) $cr_2(\gamma) = z_{1,1} = \frac{1}{2}\left(v_1(\gamma) - \sqrt{v_1^2(\gamma) - 4}\right)$,

(iii) $cr_3(\gamma) = z_{1,2} = \frac{1}{2}\left(v_1(\gamma) + \sqrt{v_1^2(\gamma) - 4}\right)$,

(iv) $cr_4(\gamma) = z_{2,1} = \frac{1}{2}\left(v_2(\gamma) - \sqrt{v_2^2(\gamma) - 4}\right)$,

(v) $cr_5(\gamma) = z_{2,2} = \frac{1}{2}\left(v_2(\gamma) + \sqrt{v_2^2(\gamma) - 4}\right)$,

where $v_1(\gamma) = \frac{2\left(-8\sqrt{3}\sqrt{83\gamma^2-90\gamma}+24\gamma+135\right)}{3(64\gamma-135)}$ *and* $v_2(\gamma) = \frac{2\left(8\sqrt{3}\sqrt{83\gamma^2-90\gamma}+24\gamma+135\right)}{3(64\gamma-135)}$.

Proof. It is straightforward that

$$R'(z,\gamma) = -\frac{36z^3(z+1)^4 M(z,\gamma)}{(64\gamma z^4 - 135z^4 - 198z^3 - 234z^2 - 126z - 27)^2},$$

where $M(z,\gamma) = (192\gamma - 405)z^4 - (96\gamma + 540)z^3 + (64\gamma - 990)z^2 - (96\gamma + 540)z + (192\gamma - 405)$. Hence, the free critical points are $cr_1 = -1$ and the solutions of the equation $M(z,\gamma) = 0$. Thus, it can be expressed as

$$z^2\left[(192\gamma - 405)z^2 - (96\gamma + 540)z + (64\gamma - 990) - (96\gamma + 540)\frac{1}{z} + (192\gamma - 405)\frac{1}{z^2}\right] = 0,$$

and we have

$$z^2\left[(192\gamma - 405)(z^2 + \frac{1}{z^2}) - (96\gamma + 540)(z + \frac{1}{z}) + (64\gamma - 990)\right] = 0.$$

By making $v = z + \frac{1}{z}$, we have $v^2 - 2 = z^2 + \frac{1}{z^2}$. Then,

$$z^2\left[(192\gamma - 405)(v^2 - 2) - (96\gamma + 540)v + (64\gamma - 990)\right] = 0$$

and

$$z^2\left[(192\gamma - 405)v^2 - (96\gamma + 540)v - (320\gamma + 180)\right] = 0.$$

Because $z \neq 0$,

$$(192\gamma - 405)v^2 - (96\gamma + 540)v - (320\gamma + 180) = 0$$

and we have

$$v_1 = \frac{2\left(-8\sqrt{3}\sqrt{83\gamma^2 - 90\gamma} + 24\gamma + 135\right)}{3(64\gamma - 135)},$$

$$v_2 = \frac{2\left(8\sqrt{3}\sqrt{83\gamma^2 - 90\gamma} + 24\gamma + 135\right)}{3(64\gamma - 135)}.$$

Thus, the free critical points are $cr_{j+k}(\gamma) = \frac{v_i(\gamma) + (-1)^{j+k}\sqrt{v_i(\gamma)^2 - 4}}{2}$ for $i = 1,2$, $j = 1,3$, and $k = 1,2$.

Note that $cr_{i+1}(\gamma) = \frac{1}{cr_i(\gamma)}$ for $i = 1,2$. Therefore, $cr_i(\gamma) = \frac{v_i(\gamma) \pm \sqrt{v_i(\gamma)^2 - 4}}{2}$,

$$cr_2(\gamma) = \frac{1}{2}\left(v_1(\gamma) - \sqrt{v_1^2(\gamma) - 4}\right),$$

$$cr_3(\gamma) = \frac{1}{2}\left(v_1(\gamma) + \sqrt{v_1^2 - 4(\gamma)}\right),$$

$$cr_4(\gamma) = \frac{1}{2}\left(v_2(\gamma) - \sqrt{v_2^2 - 4(\gamma)}\right),$$

$$cr_5(\gamma) = \frac{1}{2}\left(v_2(\gamma) + \sqrt{v_2^2 - 4(\gamma)}\right).$$

□

3.2. Parameter Plane

By means of Theorem 3, the critical points are employed to locate the basins of attraction of periodic or fixed attracting points. To achieve this, they are used as initial guesses, then the parameter planes are used to locate those values of γ where the only attracting elements are the roots of polynomial $p(z)$.

The parameter plane is plotted for values of γ in the rectangular region defined by

$$\{\gamma \in \mathbb{C} : \gamma = c + id, -\frac{99}{4} < c < \frac{198}{4}, -36 < d < 36\},$$

as it contains $\left|\frac{45}{4} - \gamma\right| = 36$. To generate the plot, we use a grid of 2000×2000 points, a maximum of 200 iterations, and a tolerance of 10^{-3}.

Given a free critical point as the initial estimate for our iterative scheme, we define D_{cr_i} as the loci of the complex plane defined by the values of γ for which the free critical point is in the basin of attraction of $z = 0$ or $z = \infty$. The parameter plane is represented by the graph of the characteristic function of set D_{cr_i}, where the color red is assigned when $F_{D_{cr_i}}(\gamma) = 1$ and black is assigned when $F_{D_{cr_i}}(\gamma) = 0$. We plot the parameter plane for γ values in the interior of the disk D_1 (defined in Theorem 9); this region guarantees the divergence, as $ex_1(\gamma) = 1$ is repelling.

Figure 4 displays the parameter planes corresponding to the critical points $cr_i(\gamma)$, where $i = 2, 3, 4, 5$. Let us remark that because conjugate critical points have the same parameter plane, only two of them are independent.

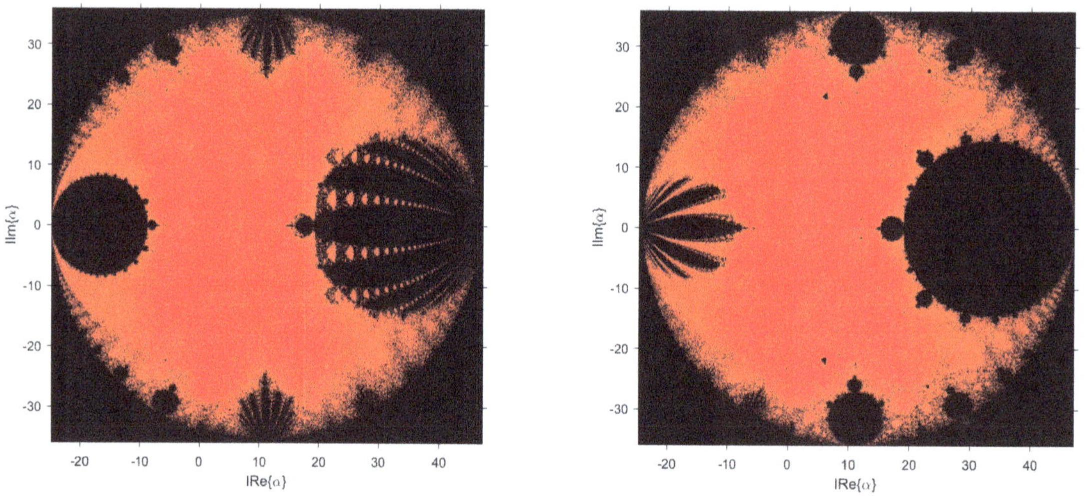

(**a**) $cr_2(\gamma)$ and $cr_3(\gamma)$ (**b**) $cr_4(\gamma)$ and $cr_5(\gamma)$

Figure 4. Parameter planes corresponding to critical points $cr_i(\gamma)$, $i = 2, 3, 4, 5$.

On the other hand, Figure 5 represents the unified parameter plane corresponding to the characteristic function $F_{\bigcap_{i=2}^{5} D_{cr_i}}(\gamma)$, where each point colored in red corresponds to values of γ for which all members of our family of iterative schemes are stable on quadratic polynomials.

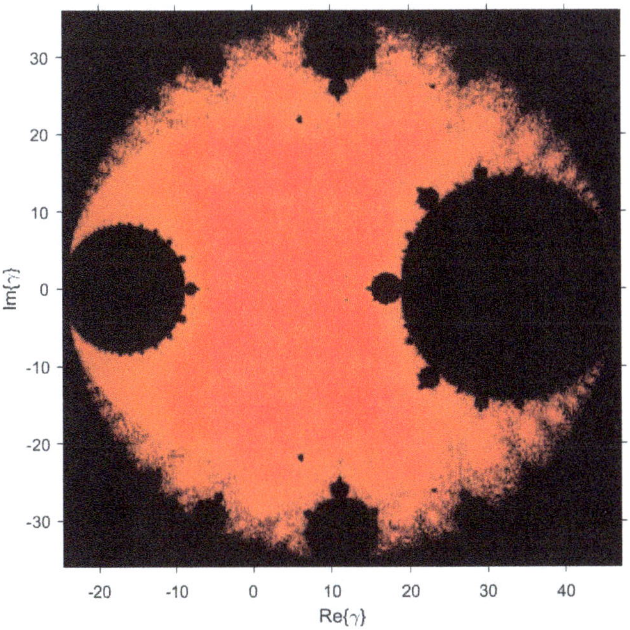

Figure 5. Unified parameter plane.

3.3. Dynamical Planes of Some Stable and Unstable Members

In Figure 5, red represents the values of γ associated with stable members. To obtain additional complementary information that allows us to verify the stability characterization obtained through the parameter planes and the stability functions of the strange fixed points, in Figure 6 we present the corresponding dynamical planes for some stable and unstable values, as per the information obtained from the intersection of parameter planes.

To construct the dynamical planes in Figure 6, we define a grid in the complex plane with 2000×2000 points, where each one corresponds to a different value of the initial estimate z_0. Each dynamical plane shows the final state of the orbit of each point in the grid, considering a maximum of 200 iterations and a tolerance of 10^{-3}. In each dynamical plane, we mark certain special points: repelling fixed points (RFP) are marked with circles ($\circ$), critical points (CP) with squares ($\square$), and attracting fixed points (AFP) with asterisks ($*$).

Through the dynamical planes, we can determine the attracting elements that the orbit of any initial estimate z_0 converge to when using the rational operator R with a specific value of γ. The basin of attraction of $z = 0$ is represented in orange, while the basin of $z = \infty$ is represented in blue. Additionally, different colors such as green, red, etc., are assigned to other attracting strange fixed points, while black is used to represent basins of periodic orbits.

We have confirmed that the values of γ in the red region of Figure 5 have only two basins of attraction, namely, $z = 0$ and $z = \infty$. This guarantees that the iterative scheme associated with these values of γ always converges to a root of $p(z)$, regardless of the initial estimate z_0. Similarly, it is validated that there are always pathologies that depend on the initial estimate z_0 for the methods associated with values of γ in the black region of the parameter plane.

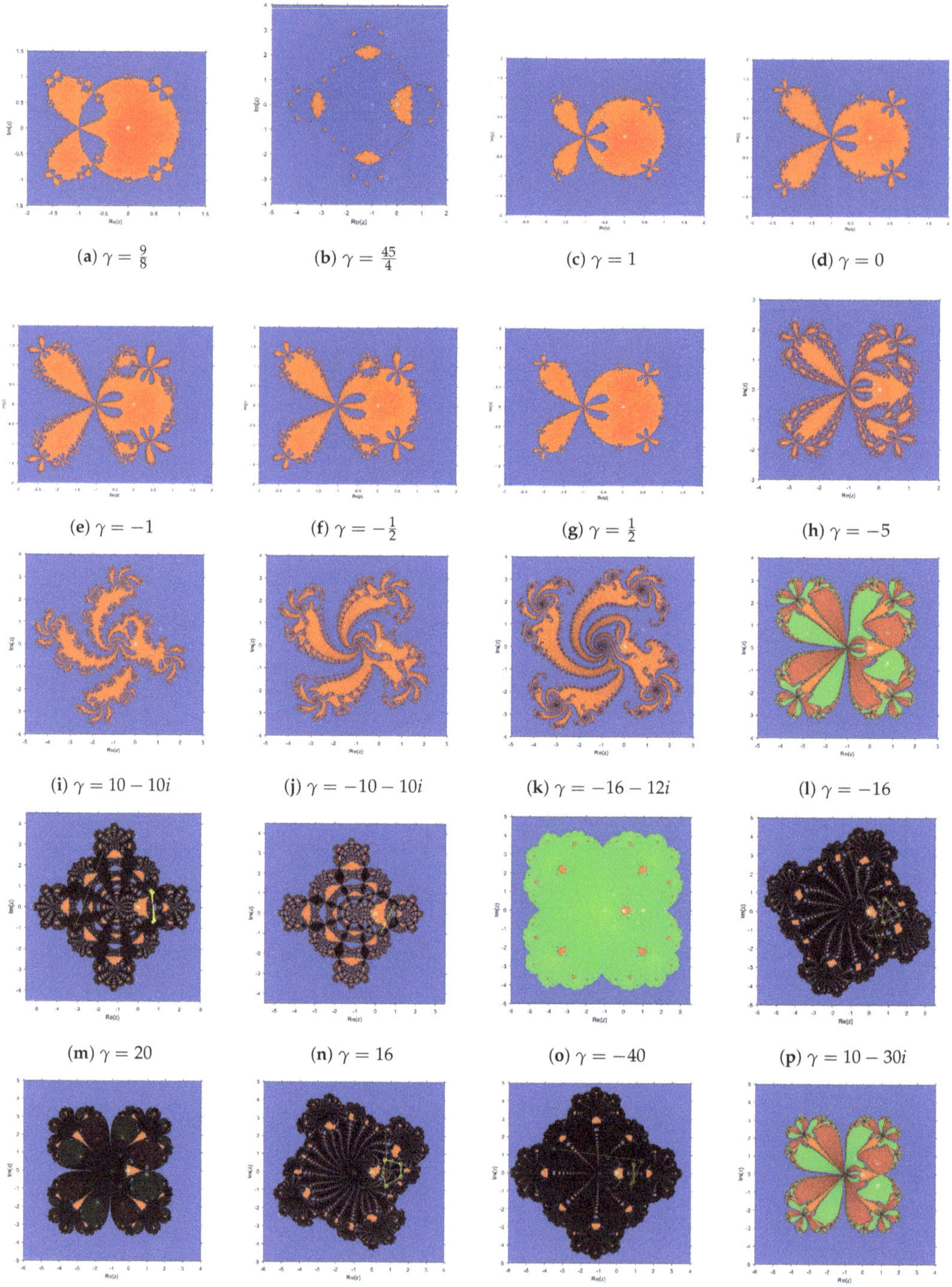

(a) $\gamma = \frac{9}{8}$ **(b)** $\gamma = \frac{45}{4}$ **(c)** $\gamma = 1$ **(d)** $\gamma = 0$

(e) $\gamma = -1$ **(f)** $\gamma = -\frac{1}{2}$ **(g)** $\gamma = \frac{1}{2}$ **(h)** $\gamma = -5$

(i) $\gamma = 10 - 10i$ **(j)** $\gamma = -10 - 10i$ **(k)** $\gamma = -16 - 12i$ **(l)** $\gamma = -16$

(m) $\gamma = 20$ **(n)** $\gamma = 16$ **(o)** $\gamma = -40$ **(p)** $\gamma = 10 - 30i$

(q) $\gamma = -24$ **(r)** $\gamma = -6 + 28i$ **(s)** $\gamma = 34$ **(t)** $\gamma = -18$

Figure 6. Dynamical planes for stable and unstable γ values.

In Table 3, we present a classification of the stability of the methods associated with the values of γ presented in Figure 6, along with the number of special points and the period of the attracting orbits found for each γ.

Table 3. Stable and unstable values of γ.

γ	**# RFP** ($\circ$)	**# CP** ($\square$)	**# AFP** ($*$)	**Period**	**Stability**
$\gamma_{(a)} = \frac{9}{8}$	7	4	2	1	Stable
$\gamma_{(b)} = \frac{45}{4}$	8	5	2	1	Stable
$\gamma_{(c)} = 1$	9	7	2	1	Stable
$\gamma_{(d)} = 0$	7	3	2	1	Stable
$\gamma_{(e)} = -1$	9	7	2	1	Stable
$\gamma_{(f)} = -\frac{1}{2}$	9	7	2	1	Stable
$\gamma_{(g)} = \frac{1}{2}$	9	7	2	1	Stable
$\gamma_{(h)} = -5$	9	7	2	1	Stable
$\gamma_{(i)} = 10 - 10i$	9	7	2	1	Stable
$\gamma_{(j)} = -10 - 10i$	9	7	2	1	Stable
$\gamma_{(k)} = -16 - 12i$	9	7	2	1	Stable
$\gamma_{(l)} = -16$	9	7	4	1	Unstable
$\gamma_{(m)} = 20$	9	7	2	2	Unstable
$\gamma_{(n)} = 16$	9	7	2	2	Unstable
$\gamma_{(o)} = -40$	9	7	3	1	Unstable
$\gamma_{(p)} = 10 - 30i$	9	7	2	4	Unstable
$\gamma_{(q)} = -24$	9	7	4	1	Unstable
$\gamma_{(r)} = -6 + 28i$	9	7	2	4	Unstable
$\gamma_{(s)} = 34$	9	7	2	2	Unstable
$\gamma_{(t)} = -18$	9	7	4	1	Unstable

4. Numerical Tests

In this section, numerical tests are conducted on some academical functions. Our goal is to determine whether methods that are stable in the previous analysis for quadratic polynomials perform better than unstable methods on non-polynomial functions. Subsequently, we compare the most effective methods on these functions with other well-known iterative methods in the field of numerical analysis, such as:

Newton's method, the iterative expression of which is

$$x_{k+1} = x_k - \frac{f(x_k)}{f'(x_k)}, \quad k = 0, 1, \ldots,$$

Chun's method, defined in [9] as

$$\begin{aligned} y_k &= x_k - \frac{f(x_k)}{f'(x_k)}, \\ x_{k+1} &= y_k - \frac{f(x_k) + 2f(y_k)}{f(x_k)} \frac{f(y_k)}{f'(x_k)}, \quad k = 0, 1, \ldots, \end{aligned}$$

Ostrowski's method, proposed in [11] and expressed as

$$
\begin{aligned}
y_k &= x_k - \frac{f(x_k)}{f'(x_k)}, \\
x_{k+1} &= y_k - \frac{f(x_k)}{f(x_k) - 2f(y_k)} \frac{f(y_k)}{f'(x_k)}, \quad k = 0, 1, \ldots,
\end{aligned}
$$

Kung-Traub's method, defined in [12] with the iterative expression

$$
\begin{aligned}
y_k &= x_k - \frac{f(x_k)}{f'(x_k)}, \\
x_{k+1} &= y_k - \frac{f(x_k)^2}{(f(x_k) - f(y_k))^2} \frac{f(y_k)}{f'(x_k)}, \quad k = 0, 1, \ldots,
\end{aligned}
$$

and Jarratt's method, constructed in [30] as

$$
\begin{aligned}
y_k &= x_k - \frac{2}{3} \frac{f(x_k)}{f'(x_k)}, \\
x_{k+1} &= x_k - \frac{1}{2} \left(\frac{3f'(y_k) + f'(x_k)}{3f'(y_k) - f'(x_k)} \right) \frac{f(x_k)}{f'(x_k)}, \quad k = 0, 1, \ldots.
\end{aligned}
$$

For our comparative analysis, we consider the best performing methods to be those iterative schemes that converge in the least number of iterations, where the estimation of the error is as small as possible, and where the theoretical order is closely approximated by the computational convergence order (ACOC) as defined by Cordero and Torregrosa in [31]:

$$
ACOC = \frac{\ln \frac{|x_{k+1} - x_k|}{|x_k - x_{k-1}|}}{\ln \frac{|x_k - x_{k-1}|}{|x_{k-1} - x_{k-2}|}}.
$$

The test functions and their zeros to be estimated are as follows:

$$
\begin{aligned}
f_1(x) &= -2 + \sqrt{x^2 + 2x + 5}\sin(x) - x^2 + 3, & \bar{x} &\approx 2.33196765588396 \\
f_2(x) &= -1 + (x-1)^3 + e^x, & \bar{x} &\approx 0.297570665698774 \\
f_3(x) &= \arctan(x) + e^{x^3}, & \bar{x} &\approx -0.757044010769526 \\
f_4(x) &= xe^{x^2} - \cos(x), & \bar{x} &\approx 0.588401776500996
\end{aligned}
$$

We present numerical results obtained using a Thinkpad T480s laptop equipped with an eighth-generation Core i7 processor (Intel(R) Core(TM) i7-8650U CPU @ 1.90 GHz 2.11 GHz) and 16 GB of RAM. We used the academic version of MATLAB R2021b, employing variable-precision arithmetics with 200 digits.

Table 4 displays the number of iterations required for each proposed method to achieve the desired convergence for each of the functions when using the parameter values specified in Table 3. It can be observed that methods associated with values of $\gamma \neq \frac{45}{4}$, which are stable for real quadratic polynomials, demonstrate good performance on these test functions. However, methods associated with stable complex γ values fail to converge in at least one of the test functions, as do methods associated with unstable γ values. For $\gamma = \frac{45}{4}$, the associated method does not converge for either f_2 or f_4. It is worth noting that the color intensity in the dynamical plane associated with this value of γ indicates the number of iterations required to ensure convergence. The latter is more intense than those associated with the other stable real values of γ, indicating that those converging in fewer iterations on quadratic polynomials are more reliable when applied to non-polynomial test functions (see Figure 6).

As shown in Table 4, seven of the methods associated with real values guarantee convergence within a maximum of nine iterations. Tables 5–8 present the results obtained when applying Newton, Chun, Ostrowski, Kung and Traub, Jarratt, and the seven proposed methods. These tables provide information about the function to which each iterative method is applied, the initial estimate used (x_0), the target root ($\bar{x}$) to which the methods are expected to converge within the stopping criterion $|x_{k+1} - x_k| + |f(x_{k+1})| < 10^{-18}$, the number of iterations (Iter) required for convergence, approximate order of computational convergence (ACOC), execution time (Time), estimation of the error in the last iteration ($|x_{k+1} - x_k|$ and $|f(x_{k+1})|$), and the approximate solution $\bar{x}$.

Table 4. Number of iterations on test functions.

Parameter Values	f_1	f_2	f_3	f_4	Stability
$\Upsilon_{(a)} = \frac{9}{8}$	4	5	4	7	Stable
$\Upsilon_{(b)} = \frac{45}{4}$	4	100	4	100	Stable
$\Upsilon_{(c)} = 1$	4	5	4	6	Stable
$\Upsilon_{(d)} = 0$	4	5	4	6	Stable
$\Upsilon_{(e)} = -1$	4	5	4	5	Stable
$\Upsilon_{(f)} = -\frac{1}{2}$	4	4	4	5	Stable
$\Upsilon_{(g)} = \frac{1}{2}$	4	5	4	6	Stable
$\Upsilon_{(h)} = -5$	4	6	4	6	Stable
$\Upsilon_{(i)} = 10 - 10i$	4	100	4	100	Stable
$\Upsilon_{(j)} = -10 - 10i$	4	64	4	100	Stable
$\Upsilon_{(k)} = -16 - 12i$	4	37	4	100	Stable
$\Upsilon_{(l)} = 16$	4	100	4	100	Unstable
$\Upsilon_{(m)} = 20$	4	100	4	100	Unstable
$\Upsilon_{(n)} = 16$	4	100	4	100	Unstable
$\Upsilon_{(o)} = -40$	4	59	5	100	Unstable
$\Upsilon_{(p)} = 10 - 30i$	4	100	4	100	Unstable
$\Upsilon_{(q)} = -24$	4	100	4	31	Unstable
$\Upsilon_{(r)} = -6 + 28i$	4	100	4	44	Unstable
$\Upsilon_{(s)} = 34$	4	100	4	100	Unstable
$\Upsilon_{(t)} = -18$	4	100	4	11	Unstable

Table 5. Comparative analysis on $f_1(x)$.

Function	Method	Iter	Time	*ACOC*	$\|x_{k+1} - x_k\|$	$\|f(x_{k+1})\|$
$f_1(x) = \sqrt{x^2+2x+5} - 2\sin(x) - x^2 + 3$, $x_0 = 1.5$, $\bar{x} \approx 2.33196765588396$	Newton	5	0.0713269	2	8.68×10^{-28}	2.11×10^{-27}
	Chun	5	0.0927903	2	1.39×10^{-27}	3.38×10^{-27}
	Ostrowski	5	0.0995647	2	1.58×10^{-27}	3.83×10^{-27}
	Kung-Traub	5	0.1000585	2	1.53×10^{-27}	3.72×10^{-27}
	Jarratt	4	0.0862121	4	1.44×10^{-55}	3.50×10^{-55}
	$\Upsilon_{(a)}$	4	0.0957585	4	5.81×10^{-57}	1.41×10^{-56}
	$\Upsilon_{(c)}$	4	0.1063336	4	2.11×10^{-57}	5.11×10^{-57}
	$\Upsilon_{(d)}$	4	0.0842142	4	7.05×10^{-58}	1.71×10^{-57}
	$\Upsilon_{(e)}$	4	0.0909392	4	2.56×10^{-55}	6.21×10^{-55}
	$\Upsilon_{(f)}$	4	0.0864402	4	3.05×10^{-56}	7.41×10^{-56}
	$\Upsilon_{(g)}$	4	0.0856559	4	1.99×10^{-62}	4.82×10^{-62}
	$\Upsilon_{(h)}$	4	0.0971327	4	2.00×10^{-52}	4.85×10^{-52}

Table 6. Comparative analysis on $f_2(x)$.

Function	Method	Iter	Time	*ACOC*	$\lvert x_{k+1} - x_k \rvert$	$\lvert f(x_{k+1}) \rvert$
$f_2(x) = (x-1)^3 - 1 + e^x$, $x_0 = 1.5$, $\bar{x} \approx 0.2975706656698774$	Newton	7	0.0590956	2	1.03×10^{-34}	2.93×10^{-34}
	Chun	6	0.0674999	2	1.05×10^{-27}	2.96×10^{-27}
	Ostrowski	8	0.1065735	2	4.74×10^{-30}	1.34×10^{-29}
	Kung-Traub	7	0.079534	2	1.61×10^{-24}	4.54×10^{-24}
	Jarratt	5	0.0657351	4	2.29×10^{-73}	6.48×10^{-73}
	$\Upsilon(a)$	5	0.0744865	4	1.70×10^{-53}	4.82×10^{-53}
	$\Upsilon(c)$	5	0.0720414	4	2.82×10^{-48}	7.98×10^{-48}
	$\Upsilon(d)$	5	0.071041	4	2.10×10^{-71}	5.93×10^{-71}
	$\Upsilon(e)$	5	0.069821	4	1.66×10^{-75}	4.68×10^{-75}
	$\Upsilon(f)$	4	0.0596417	4	3.96×10^{-38}	1.12×10^{-37}
	$\Upsilon(g)$	5	0.0698009	4	6.62×10^{-51}	1.87×10^{-50}
	$\Upsilon(h)$	6	0.1015708	4	6.70×10^{-33}	1.89×10^{-32}

Table 7. Comparative analysis on $f_3(x)$.

Function	Method	Iter	Time	*ACOC*	$\lvert x_{k+1} - x_k \rvert$	$\lvert f(x_{k+1}) \rvert$
$f_3(x) = \arctan(x) + e^{x^3}$, $x_0 = -0.5$, $\bar{x} \approx -0.7570440107695526$	Newton	5	0.0536364	2	2.94×10^{-20}	5.15×10^{-20}
	Chun	6	0.0789598	2	3.14×10^{-35}	5.49×10^{-35}
	Ostrowski	5	0.1089681	2	3.26×10^{-19}	5.70×10^{-19}
	Kung-Traub	6	0.0912986	2	7.53×10^{-38}	1.32×10^{-37}
	Jarratt	4	0.0626825	4	2.81×10^{-58}	4.92×10^{-58}
	$\Upsilon(a)$	4	0.0754623	4	5.40×10^{-44}	9.46×10^{-44}
	$\Upsilon(c)$	4	0.0704758	4	2.02×10^{-44}	3.53×10^{-44}
	$\Upsilon(d)$	4	0.0670903	4	3.62×10^{-49}	6.33×10^{-49}
	$\Upsilon(e)$	4	0.0725264	4	1.51×10^{-66}	2.64×10^{-66}
	$\Upsilon(f)$	4	0.0794614	4	1.46×10^{-53}	2.56×10^{-53}
	$\Upsilon(g)$	4	0.0924925	4	2.00×10^{-46}	3.50×10^{-46}
	$\Upsilon(h)$	4	0.0739391	4	8.47×10^{-49}	1.48×10^{-48}

Table 8. Comparative analysis on $f_4(x)$.

Function	Method	Iter	Time	*ACOC*	$\lvert x_{k+1} - x_k \rvert$	$\lvert f(x_{k+1}) \rvert$
$f_4(x) = xe^{x^2} - \cos(x)$, $x_0 = 1.5$, $\bar{x} \approx 0.5884017765009996$	Newton	9	0.0776262	2	4.38×10^{-26}	1.29×10^{-25}
	Chun	7	0.1032848	2	1.02×10^{-21}	3.01×10^{-21}
	Ostrowski	7	0.1054047	2	1.49×10^{-23}	4.39×10^{-23}
	Kung-Traub	7	0.1014812	2	3.53×10^{-22}	1.04×10^{-21}
	Jarratt	5	0.0895486	4	1.04×10^{-46}	3.05×10^{-46}
	$\Upsilon(a)$	7	0.1140201	4	3.56×10^{-65}	1.05×10^{-64}
	$\Upsilon(c)$	6	0.0925447	4	1.16×10^{-19}	3.43×10^{-19}
	$\Upsilon(d)$	6	0.1102584	4	5.51×10^{-51}	1.62×10^{-50}
	$\Upsilon(e)$	5	0.0844069	4	1.33×10^{-33}	3.92×10^{-33}
	$\Upsilon(f)$	5	0.0966304	4	1.061×10^{-20}	3.13×10^{-20}
	$\Upsilon(g)$	6	0.1174171	4	1.94×10^{-32}	5.72×10^{-32}
	$\Upsilon(h)$	6	0.1047413	4	1.04×10^{-46}	3.08×10^{-46}

The results suggest that the methods associated with γ values demonstrate competitive performance compared to Kung and Traub, Newton, Chun, Ostrowski, and Jarratt based on our measurement parameters.

5. Conclusions

In this study, we have established a set of conditions that weight functions must satisfy in order to ensure that the resulting iterative scheme has a convergence order of at least 4. Furthermore, a generalization of known uniparametric families of fourth-order optimal iterative methods has been presented and criteria for selecting the best subfamilies of these uniparametric families have been established. A dynamical analysis allowed us to identify stable members within the subfamily that exhibit good performance on quadratic polynomials; however, elements with pathological behavior were observed as well, and these should be avoided in numerical applications.

Furthermore, the performance of stable members of the subfamily was evaluated in comparison to unstable members when applied to non-polynomial functions. The results highlight the importance of stability in quadratic polynomials and its positive influence on the overall performance of iterative methods in various contexts.

Finally, stable methods within the subfamily that compete favorably with widely used iterative schemes in the literature have been identified. Through academical examples and detailed comparisons, it is shown that the proposed methods represent viable and effective alternatives for solving nonlinear equations.

Author Contributions: Conceptualization, A.C. and J.R.T.; methodology, M.P.V.; software, J.A.R.; validation, A.C., J.R.T., and M.P.V.; formal analysis, J.A.R.; investigation, J.A.R.; writing—original draft preparation, J.A.R.; writing—review and editing, A.C. and J.R.T.; supervision, M.P.V. All authors have read and agreed to the published version of the manuscript.

Funding: This research received no external funding.

Data Availability Statement: Data are contained within the article.

Acknowledgments: The authors would like to thank the anonymous reviewers for their comments and suggestions that have improved the final version of this manuscript.

Conflicts of Interest: The authors declare no conflicts of interest.

References

1. Danby, J.M.A. *Fundamentals of Celestial Mechanics*; Willmann-Bell: Richmond, VA, USA, 1992.
2. Yaseen, S.; Zafar, F.; Alsulami, H.H. An Efficient Jarratt-Type Iterative Method for Solving Nonlinear Global Positioning System Problems. *Axioms* **2023**, *12*, 562. [CrossRef]
3. Yaseen, S.; Zafar, F.; Chicharro, F.I. A Seventh Order Family of Jarratt Type Iterative Method for Electrical Power Systems. *Fractal Fract.* **2023**, *7*, 317. [CrossRef]
4. Zafar, F.; Cordero, A.; Ashraf, I.; Torregrosa, J.R. An optimal eighth order derivative free multiple root finding numerical method and applications to chemistry. *J. Math. Chem.* **2023**, *61*, 98–124. [CrossRef]
5. Bonilla-Correa, D.M.; Coronado-Hernández, O.E.; Fuertes-Miquel, V.S.; Besharat, M.; Ramos, H.M. Application of Newton–Raphson Method for Computing the Final Air–Water Interface Location in a Pipe Water Filling. *Water* **2023**, *15*, 1304. [CrossRef]
6. Padilla, J.J.; Chicharro, F.I.; Cordero, A.; Hernández-Díaz, A.M.; Torregrosa, J.R. Parametric Iterative Method for Addressing an Embedded-Steel Constitutive Model with Multiple Roots. *Mathematics* **2023**, *11*, 3275. [CrossRef]
7. King, R.F. A family of fourth-order methods for nonlinear equations. *SIAM J. Numer. Anal.* **1973**, *10*, 876–879. [CrossRef]
8. Hueso, J.L.; Martínez, E.; Teruel, C. Convergence, efficiency and dynamics of new fourth and sixth order families of iterative methods for nonlinear systems. *Appl. Math. Lett.* **2015**, *275*, 412–420. [CrossRef]
9. Chun, C. Construction of newton-like iterative methods for solving nonlinear equations. *Numer. Math.* **2006**, *104*, 297–315. [CrossRef]
10. Cordero, A.; Guasp, L.; Torregrosa, J.R. Fixed Point Root-Finding Methods of Fourth-Order of Convergence. *Symmetry* **2019**, *11*, 769. [CrossRef]
11. Ostrowski, A. *Solution of Equations in Euclidean and Banach Spaces*; Academic Press: Cambridge, MA, USA, 1973; Volume 3.
12. Kung, H.T.; Traub, J.F. Optimal order methods for nonlinear equations. *J. Assoc. Comput. Math.* **1974**, *21*, 643–651. [CrossRef]
13. Amat, S.; Busquier, S.; Plaza, S. Review of some iterative root-finding methods from a dynamical point of view. *Scientia* **2004**, *10*, 3–35.
14. Amat, S.; Busquier, S. *Advances in Iterative Methods for Nonlinear Equations Series SEMA*; SIMAI Springer Series; Springer: Cham, Switzerland, 2016.

15. Argyros, I.K.; Magreñán, Á.A. *Iterative Methods and Their Dynamics with Applications: A Contemporary Study*; CRC Press: Boca Raton, FL, USA, 2017.
16. Behl, R.; Sarría, Í.; González, R.; Magreñán, Á.A. Highly efficient family of iterative methods for solving nonlinear models. *J. Comput. Appl. Math.* **2019**, *346*, 110–132. [CrossRef]
17. Chicharro, F.I.; Contreras, R.A.; Garrido, N. A Family of Multiple-Root Finding Iterative Methods Based on Weight Functions. *Mathematics* **2020**, *8*, 2194. [CrossRef]
18. Rafiq, N.; Akram, S.; Mir, N.A.; Shams, M. Study of Dynamical Behavior and Stability of Iterative Methods for Nonlinear Equation with Applications in Engineering. *Math. Probl. Eng.* **2020**, *2020*, 3524324. [CrossRef]
19. Kansal, M.; Sharma, H. Analysis of optimal iterative methods from a dynamical point of view by studying their stability properties. *J. Math. Chem.* **2023**, 1–24. [CrossRef]
20. Khirallah, M.Q.; Alkhomsan, A.M. Convergence and Stability of Optimal two-step fourth-order and its expanding to sixth order for solving non linear equations. *Eur. J. Pure Appl. Math.* **2022**, *15*, 971–991. [CrossRef]
21. Moccari, M.; Lotfi, T.; Torkashvand, V. On the stability of a two-step method for a fourth-degree family by computer designs along with applications. *Int. J. Nonlinear Anal. Appl.* **2023**, *14*, 261–282.
22. Blanchard, P. Complex Analytic Dynamics on the Riemann Sphere. *Bull. AMS* **1984**, *11*, 85–141. [CrossRef]
23. Devaney, R. *A First Course in Chaotic Dynamical Systems, Theory and Experiment*, 2nd ed.; CRC Press/Taylor & Francis Group: Boca Raton, FL, USA, 2020.
24. Fatou, P. Sur les équations fonctionelles. *Bull. Soc. Mat. Fr.* **1919**, *47*, 161–271. [CrossRef]
25. Julia, G. Memoire sur l'iteration des fonctions rationnelles. *J. Mat. Pur. Appl.* **1918**, *8*, 47–245.
26. Chicharro, F.I.; Cordero, A.; Garrido, N.; Torregrosa, J.R. On the choice of the best members of the Kim family and the improvement of its convergence. *Math. Methods Appl. Sci.* **2020**, *43*, 8051–8066. [CrossRef]
27. Chicharro, F.I.; Cordero, A.; Torregrosa, J.R. Drawing Dynamical and Parameters Planes of Iterative Families and Method. *Sci. World J.* **2013**, *2013*, 780153. [CrossRef]
28. Blanchard, P. The Dynamics of Newton's Method. *Proc. Symp. Appl. Math.* **1994**, *49*, 139–154.
29. Curry, J.H.; Garnett, L.; Sullivan, D. On the iteration of a rational function: Computer experiment with Newton's method. *Commun. Math. Phys.* **1983**, *91*, 267–277. [CrossRef]
30. Jarratt, P. Some fourth order multipoint iterative methods for solving equations. *Math. Comput.* **1966**, *20*, 434–437. [CrossRef]
31. Cordero, A.; Torregrosa, J.R. Variants of Newton's methods using fifth-order quadrature formulas. *Appl. Math. Comput.* **2007**, *190*, 686–698. [CrossRef]

axioms MDPI

Article

Two Dynamic Remarks on the Chebyshev–Halley Family of Iterative Methods for Solving Nonlinear Equations

José M. Gutiérrez * and Víctor Galilea *

Departamento de Matemáticas y Computación, Universidad de La Rioja, Complejo Científico-Tecnológico, Madre de Dios 53, 26006 Logroño, Spain
* Correspondence: jmguti@unirioja.es (J.M.G.); victor.galilea@unirioja.es (V.G.)

Abstract: The aim of this paper is to delve into the dynamic study of the well-known Chebyshev–Halley family of iterative methods for solving nonlinear equations. Our objectives are twofold: On the one hand, we are interested in characterizing the existence of extraneous attracting fixed points when the methods in the family are applied to polynomial equations. On the other hand, we are also interested in studying the free critical points of the methods in the family, as a previous step to determine the existence of attracting cycles. In both cases, we want to identify situations where the methods in the family have bad behavior from the root-finding point of view. Finally, and joining these two studies, we look for polynomials for which there are methods in the family where these two situations happen simultaneously. The rational map obtained by applying a method in the Chebyshev–Halley family to a polynomial has both super-attracting extraneous fixed points and super-attracting cycles different from the roots of the polynomial.

Keywords: Chebyshev–Halley family of iterative methods; extraneous fixed points; critical points; parameter plane; dynamical systems

MSC: 37F10; 65H05

1. Introduction

The well-known Chebyshev–Halley family of iterative methods ($\mathcal{CH}$ from now on) for solving nonlinear scalar equations, $f(z) = 0$, was first introduced by Werner [1] in 1980. This family, initially defined for real-valued functions, has been extended to complex variables, systems of equations, or even equations defined in Banach spaces, as can be seen, for instance, in [2–5]. In this work, we focus our interest on functions defined on the complex plane $f : \mathbb{C} \to \mathbb{C}$.

Each member in $\mathcal{CH}$ is given by an iteration map, which can be seen as a modification of the Newton iteration map,

$$N(z) = z - \frac{f(z)}{f'(z)}, \tag{1}$$

with the inclusion of a parameter $\alpha \in \mathbb{C}$ and new evaluations of $f(z)$ and its derivatives up to order two. Specifically, we build a sequence $z_{n+1} = G_\alpha(z_n)$, $n \geq 0$, where

$$G_\alpha(z) = z - \left(1 + \frac{1}{2}\frac{L_f(z)}{1 - \alpha L_f(z)}\right)\frac{f(z)}{f'(z)}, \tag{2}$$

and

$$L_f(z) = \frac{f(z)f''(z)}{f'(z)^2}. \tag{3}$$

All methods in $\mathcal{CH}$ have the cubic order of convergence for simple roots. In the case of multiple roots, there exist several variants of $\mathcal{CH}$ that make it possible to recover the cubic order of convergence, as given by Ivanov [6] or Osada [7].

One of the reasons for considering the $\mathcal{CH}$ family is because it allows us to study in a unified way the most famous third-order iterative methods, such as Chebyshev's method ($\alpha = 0$), Halley's method ($\alpha = 1/2$), or super-Halley method ($\alpha = 1$). In general, it is not possible to establish a classification of the members of $\mathcal{CH}$ in terms of efficiency, velocity of convergence, and other similar numerical criteria because the behavior of $G_\alpha(z)$ depends on the considered function $f(z)$ through the asymptotic error constant (see [8] for more details). However, for particular problems, it is possible to find the optimal method in $\mathcal{CH}$ to approximate the solution. This is the case for the calculus of nth roots, (see Dubeau and Gnang [9] or Gutiérrez, Hernández, and Salanova [10] for a more detailed study), the computation of the matrix sign (Cordero et al. [11]), or the simultaneous calculus of all the roots of a polynomial (Osada [7]).

The dynamical study of the iteration maps arising from the application of the methods in $\mathcal{CH}$ (2) to polynomial equations is a problem that has attracted many researchers. For instance, Cordero, Torregrosa, and Vindel [12] studied the dynamics of the methods in $\mathcal{CH}$ applied to quadratic polynomials. In the analysis of the corresponding parameter planes appears a singular set, baptized as "the cat" by the authors, with curious similarities with the Mandelbrot set. In this same paper, the existence of members in $\mathcal{CH}$ with a pathological behavior as root-finding methods is emphasized; they can be attracted by limits that are not roots of the considered equation $f(z) = 0$, such as periodic orbits (cycles) or extraneous fixed points. In [13,14], it is proved that there exist methods in $\mathcal{CH}$ with attracting two-cycles; Campos et al. [15,16] studied the behavior of $\mathcal{CH}$ for polynomials in the form $z^n + c$, where c is a complex parameter. In particular, they characterized methods with Fatou components that are simply connected and, hence, the Julia set is connected; Gutiérrez, Magreñán, and Varona [17] characterized the universal Julia sets for the methods in $\mathcal{CH}$ applied to quadratic polynomials; in this same line, Babajee, Cordero, and Torregrosa [18] introduced the Cayley Quadratic Test as a first step in the study of the stability of families of iterative processes for solving nonlinear equations. In brief, this test allows us to check if the universal Julia set of an iterative process is conjugated with the unit circle or not.

In the rest of this work, we continue with the dynamic study of the methods of the $\mathcal{CH}$-family. Specifically, in Section 2, we characterize the existence of super-attracting fixed points for the methods in $\mathcal{CH}$. We place a special emphasis on the case of the Chebyshev and super-Halley methods. For these methods, we even prove the existence of polynomials with both super-attracting fixed points and super-attracting cycles. In Section 3, we study the number of critical points of the methods in $\mathcal{CH}$. In particular, we show that the graphical tool known as the parameter plane is useful only for two methods in the $\mathcal{CH}$ family: $\alpha = 0$ (Chebyshev's method) and $\alpha = 1/2$ (Halley's method). These two cases have been profusely studied by Gutiérrez and Varona [19] and by Roberts and Horgan-Kobelski [20], respectively. For the rest of the methods in the family, the high number of free critical points and the difficulty of obtaining them discourage the use of the parameter plane.

2. Fixed Points in the Family $\mathcal{CH}$

In this section, we apply the methods introduced in (2) to a polynomial equation

$$p(z) = 0, \quad p(z) = z^d + a_{d-1}z^{d-1} + \cdots + a_1 z + a_0, \tag{4}$$

where the coefficients a_j, $j = 0, 1, \ldots, d-1$ are constant complex numbers. We can assume, without loss of generality, that $p(z)$ is a monic polynomial. We use the notation $R_{\alpha,p}(z)$ for the rational map obtained in this case

$$R_{\alpha,p}(z) = z - \left(1 + \frac{1}{2}\frac{L_p(z)}{1 - \alpha L_p(z)}\right)\frac{p(z)}{p'(z)}, \tag{5}$$

where $L_p(z)$ is defined in (3). In addition, we consider the rational map related to Newton's method (1) in the polynomial case

$$R_p(z) = z - \frac{p(z)}{p'(z)}. \tag{6}$$

The first thing to complete for investigating the dynamics of the rational maps defined in (5) is to study its degree. Following Nayak and Pal [21], we can generalize the result they give for Chebyshev's method to all the methods in the family (5). The exact degree is given in terms of the number of distinct roots of p and in terms of certain types of critical points introduced by these authors. Indeed, given a polynomial $p(z)$, a critical point $\omega \in \mathbb{C}$ is called special if $p(\omega) \neq 0$ and $p''(\omega) = 0$.

Theorem 1. *Let $p(z)$ be the polynomial defined in (4). Let m, n, and r denote the number of its distinct simple roots, double roots, and roots of multiplicity bigger than two, respectively. Let s be the number of distinct special critical points of $p(z)$. Then, for $\alpha \neq 1/2$,*

$$\deg(R_{\alpha,p}(z)) = 3(m+n+r) - 2 - B + s,$$

where B is the sum of the multiplicities of all the special critical points. If $p(z)$ has no special critical points, then $\deg(R_{\alpha,p}(z)) = 3(m+n+r) - 2$. If $p(z)$ has no special critical points or multiple roots, then $\deg(R_{\alpha,p}(z)) = 3d - 2$.

Proof. This proof mimics the one given by Nayak and Pal [21] for the case of Chebyshev's method, $R_{0,p}(z)$ given by $\alpha = 0$ in (5). Indeed, this proof is based on the following factorization of the polynomial $p(z)$, in terms of its simple, double, and multiple (with multiplicity bigger than two) roots:

$$p(z) = \prod_{i=1}^{m}(z-\alpha_i)\prod_{j=1}^{n}(z-\beta_j)^2\prod_{k=1}^{r}(z-\gamma_k)^{a_k},$$

with $\deg(p) = m + 2n + M$, $M = \sum_{k=1}^{r} a_k$.

So, let c_j, $j = 1, \ldots, s$ be the special critical points of $p(z)$, with multiplicities b_j, then the quotient $L_p(z)$ defined in (3) can be written in the form

$$L_p(z) = \frac{\tilde{h}(z)}{\tilde{g}(z)^2}\prod_{i=1}^{m}(z-\alpha_i)\frac{1}{\prod_{j=1}^{s}(z-c_j)^{b_j+1}},$$

where $\tilde{h}(z)$ and $\tilde{g}(z)$ are functions without common roots. It can be seen (in [21]) that

$$\deg L_p(z) = 2m + 2n + 2r - 2 - B - s.$$

Note that $\deg(R_{\alpha,p}(z))$ equals the number of fixed points of $R_{\alpha,p}(z)$ minus one (see [22]), and the number of fixed points of $R_{\alpha,p}(z))$ are as follows:

1. The number of different roots of $p(z)$: $m + n + r$.
2. The roots of the equation $L_p(z) = 2/(2\alpha - 1)$, $\alpha \neq 1/2$, that is, $2m + 2n + 2r - 2 - B + s$.
3. The infinity point.

Consequently, $\deg(R_{\alpha,p}(z)) = 3(m+n+r) - 2 - B + s$. □

As a root-finder method, it would be desirable that each attracting fixed point of $R_{\alpha,p}(z)$ would be a root of $p(z)$. However, this "ideal behavior" is disturbed by the appearance of other attracting phenomena, such as periodic orbits (cycles) or extraneous fixed points, which are fixed points of $R_{\alpha,p}(z)$ that are not roots of $p(z)$.

It is well-known that the only fixed points of Newton's method in the complex plane are the roots of $p(z)$ (see the classical book of Traub [23], for instance). If we consider the extended complex plane, it is also known that the infinity point is a repelling fixed point for Newton's method, with the multiplier $d/(d-1) > 1$, where d is the degree of $p(z)$. In addition, we have that simple roots of $p(z)$ are super-attracting fixed points of $R_p(z)$, whereas roots with the multiplicity $m > 1$ are attracting fixed points with the multiplier $(m-1)/m < 1$.

For the case of Halley's method (obtained for $\alpha = 1/2$ in (5)), it is known (see Kneisl [24]) that the only attracting fixed points are the roots of $p(z)$. There exist extraneous fixed points in the complex plane, but all of them are repelling with the multiplier $1 + 2/j$ for an adequate $j \in \mathbb{N}$. The infinity point is a repelling fixed point for Halley's method, with the multiplier $(d+1)/(d-1) > 1$, where d is the degree of $p(z)$.

For the case of the Chebyshev method ($\alpha = 0$ in (5)), the existence of attracting extraneous fixed points has been proven (see [24] Theorem 2.6.4 or Vrscay–Gilbert [25] p. 12). In addition, in [19], the existence of super-attracting extraneous fixed points has been established in terms of the quotients $L_p(z)$, defined in (4), and $L_{p'}(z)$, defined by

$$L_{p'}(z) = \frac{p'(z)p'''(z)}{p''(z)^2}. \tag{7}$$

In particular, ω is an extraneous fixed point of Chebyshev's method if $L_p(z) = -2$. ω is attracting if $\left|6 - 2L_{p'}(z)\right| < 1$ and super-attracting if $L_{p'}(z) = 3$.

In this section, we are going to generalize this result by determining sufficient conditions for the existence of super-attracting extraneous fixed points for the methods in $\mathcal{CH}$. First, we establish a preliminary technical result that will help us in further theoretical development.

Lemma 1. *Let $p(z)$ be a d-degree polynomial and $L_p(z)$, $L_{p'}(z)$ be the rational functions defined in* (4) *and* (7)*, respectively. Then,*

$$L_p'(z)\frac{p(z)}{p'(z)} = L_p(z) - 2L_p(z)^2 + L_{p'}(z)L_p(z)^2. \tag{8}$$

Proof. The proof simply requires a process of derivation and the grouping of terms in an appropriate way. First,

$$L_p'(z) = \left(\frac{p(z)p''(z)}{p'(z)^2}\right)' = \frac{(p'(z)p''(z) + p(z)p'''(z))p'(z)^2 - 2p(z)p'(z)p''(z)^2}{p'(z)^4},$$

and next,

$$L_p'(z)\frac{p(z)}{p'(z)} = L_p(z) + \frac{p(z)^2 p'''(z)}{p'(z)^3} - 2L_p(z)^2.$$

Just by multiplying and dividing by $p''(z)^2/p'(z)$ in the second term, and taking (7) into account, we arrive at the result. □

Theorem 2. *For $\alpha \neq 1/2$, let $\omega \in \mathbb{C}$ be a point such that $p(\omega) \neq 0$, $p'(\omega) \neq 0$, $p''(\omega) \neq 0$. Then, if*

$$L_p(\omega) = \frac{2}{2\alpha - 1}, \quad L_{p'}(\omega) = 3 - \alpha, \tag{9}$$

ω is a super-attracting extraneous fixed point of the rational map $R_{\alpha,p}(z)$ defined in (5) *and, therefore, of the iterative method corresponding to the parameter α in $\mathcal{CH}$.*

Proof. First, as $p(\omega) \neq 0$, ω is not a root of $p(z)$. In addition, ω is a fixed point of $R_{\alpha,p}(z)$ because

$$1 + \frac{1}{2}\frac{L_p(\omega)}{1 - \alpha L_p(\omega)} = 0, \tag{10}$$

just by taking into account the first equation in (9). So, ω is an extraneous fixed point of $R_{\alpha,p}(z)$.

For ω to be a super-attractor, it must be true that $R'_{\alpha,p}(\omega) = 0$. Then, taking into account (10), we have

$$R'_{\alpha,p}(\omega) = 1 - \left(1 + \frac{1}{2}\frac{L_p(z)}{1 - \alpha L_p(z)}\right)'\Bigg|_{z=\omega} \frac{p(\omega)}{p'(\omega)}.$$

Note that

$$\left(1 + \frac{1}{2}\frac{L_p(z)}{1 - \alpha L_p(z)}\right)' = \frac{1}{2}\frac{L'_p(z)}{(1 - \alpha L_p(z))^2},$$

and then, by Lemma 1,

$$R'_{\alpha,p}(\omega) = 1 - \frac{1}{2}\frac{L_p(\omega) - 2L_p(\omega)^2 + L_{p'}(\omega)L_p(\omega)^2}{(1 - \alpha L_p(\omega))^2}.$$

As $L_p(\omega) = 2/(2\alpha - 1)$, we obtain

$$R'_{\alpha,p}(\omega) = 2(3 - \alpha - L_{p'}(\omega)).$$

Finally, as $L_{p'}(\omega) = 3 - \alpha$, the condition $R'_{\alpha,p}(\omega) = 0$ also holds and, as a consequence, ω is a super-attracting extraneous fixed point of the rational map $R_{\alpha,p}(z)$. □

The previous theorem allows us to find, as long as its conditions are met, extraneous super-attractor fixed points for all the methods in the family $\mathcal{CH}$, with the exception of Halley's method ($\alpha = 1/2$). Note that the conditions $p(\omega) \neq 0$, $p'(\omega) \neq 0$, $p''(\omega) = 0$ imply $L_p(\omega) = 0$, which makes the existence of extraneous super-attractor fixed points impossible. If $\alpha \neq 1/2$, $p(\omega) \neq 0$ and $p'(\omega) = 0$, the expression of the corresponding method in (5) is not well-defined.

For Halley's method, we can give the following result, which was also proven by Kneisl ([24] Theorem 2.6.3). Previously, we wrote the corresponding iteration function with an alternative expression:

$$R_{1/2,p}(z) = z - \left(1 + \frac{1}{2}\frac{L_p(z)}{1 - L_p(z)/2}\right)\frac{p(z)}{p'(z)} = z - \frac{2p(z)p'(z)}{2p'(z)^2 - p(z)p''(z)}. \tag{11}$$

Theorem 3. *Let us consider Halley's method, obtained for $\alpha = 1/2$ in $\mathcal{CH}$ and whose iteration function is shown in* (11). *The extraneous fixed points of the rational function $R_{1/2,p}(z)$ are the solutions of $p'(z) = 0$, with $p(z) \neq 0$. All of them are repulsors.*

Proof. The fixed points of $R_{1/2,p}(z)$ are the roots of $p(z)$ and the solutions of $p'(z) = 0$. Then, ω is an extraneous fixed point of $R_{1/2,p}(z)$ if, and only if, $p'(\omega) = 0$ and $p(\omega) \neq 0$. Let $m \in \mathbb{N}$ be the multiplicity of ω as a root of $p'(z)$. We can then write

$$p'(z) = (z - \omega)^m g(z),$$

with $g(\omega) \neq 0$. After a few calculi in (11), we obtain

$$R'_{1/2,p}(\omega) = 1 + \frac{2}{m} > 1.$$

Therefore, ω is a repelling fixed point. □

Remark 1. *In the extended complex plane, the infinity point is a fixed point for the methods in $\mathcal{CH}$, with the multiplier*

$$\frac{2d(d(\alpha-1)-\alpha)}{(d-1)(2d(\alpha-1)-2\alpha+1)}.$$

In the case of the most famous methods in the family, infinity is a repelling fixed point. Indeed, for $\alpha = 0, 1/2, 1$, that is, the Chebyshev, Halley, and super-Halley methods, the multiplier of the infinity point is $2d^2/((2d-1)(d-1))$, $(d+1)/(d-1)$, and $2d/(d-1)$, respectively. However, we can see that infinity is not always a repelling fixed point. Even more, for each degree $d \geq 2$, we can obtain a method corresponding with the value of

$$\alpha = \frac{d}{d-1},$$

for which infinity is a super-attracting fixed point. In Figure 1, we show the basins of attraction related to the method in $\mathcal{CH}$ with $\alpha = 2$ applied to $p(z) = z^2 - 1$ and related to the method in $\mathcal{CH}$ with $\alpha = 3/2$ applied to $p(z) = z^3 - 1$. Together with the basins of the roots of these polynomials, we have plotted in white the basin of attraction of the infinity point.

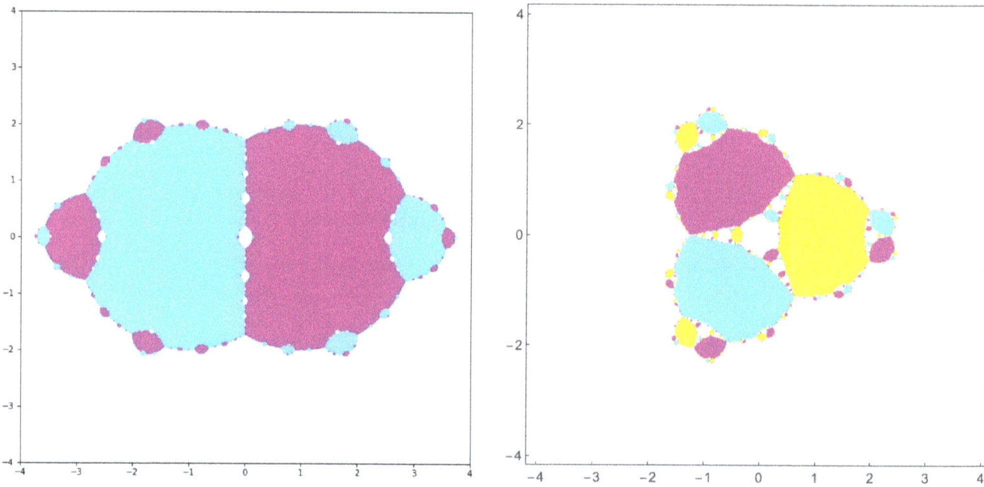

Figure 1. (On the **left**), basins of attraction of the method corresponding to $\alpha = 2$ applied to the polynomial $p(z) = z^2 - 1$. (On the **right**), basins of the method corresponding to $\alpha = 3/2$ are applied to the polynomial $p(z) = z^3 - 1$. In both cases, the basin of attraction of the infinity point can be seen in white, whereas the basins of the roots are colored cyan-magenta or cyan-magenta-yellow, respectively.

We are now going to characterize polynomials for which $z = 0$ is a strange super-attractor fixed point for the methods of the (5) family. To perform this, we consider the generic polynomial of degree d defined in (4).

Theorem 4. *Let $p(z)$ be the polynomial defined in* (4) *and $R_{\alpha,p}(z)$ be the rational map defined in* (5)*, with $\alpha \neq 1/2$. Then, if*

$$a_1 = \beta, \quad a_2 = \frac{\beta^2}{2\alpha-1}, \quad a_3 = \frac{2(3-\alpha)}{3}\frac{\beta^3}{(2\alpha-1)^2},$$

with $\beta \in \mathbb{C} \setminus \{0\}$, $z = 0$ is a super-attracting extraneous fixed point of $R_{\alpha,p}(z)$.

Proof. Note that since $z = 0$ must not be a root of $p(z)$, we can consider, without loss of generality, that $a_0 = 1$. Furthermore, for the conditions of Theorem 2 to be fulfilled, $p'(0) \neq 0$ and $p''(0) \neq 0$, it is also necessary that $a_1 \neq 0$ and $a_2 \neq 0$. The proof continues simply by solving the system given by Equation (9) which, in this case, is

$$L_p(0) = \frac{2a_2}{a_1^2} = \frac{2}{2\alpha - 1}, \quad L_{p'}(0) = \frac{3a_1 a_3}{2a_2^2} = \frac{2}{2\alpha - 1}.$$

□

In particular cases, we can obtain polynomials with $z = 0$ as an extraneous super-attracting fixed point for Chebyshev's method (already known by García-Olivo et al. [26]). In this case,

$$a_1 = \beta \neq 0, \quad a_2 = -\beta^2, \quad a_3 = 2\beta^3. \tag{12}$$

The super-Halley method is another well-known method in $\mathcal{CH}$ ([27,28]). However, its dynamical properties have been less studied. We can obtain polynomials with $z = 0$ as an extraneous super-attracting fixed point for the super-Halley method:

$$a_1 = \beta \neq 0, \quad a_2 = \beta^2, \quad a_3 = \frac{4}{3}\beta^3. \tag{13}$$

In the left side of Figure 2, we show the basins of attraction of Chebyshev's method applied to the polynomial

$$p(z) = z^3 + z^2 + 2z - 4. \tag{14}$$

It is obtained by taking $\beta = 1/2$ in (12) and, next, by multiplying by four. The basin of the root $z = 1$ appears colored in cyan, that of the root $z = -1 + \sqrt{3}i$ in yellow, and that of the root $z = -1 - \sqrt{3}i$ in magenta. The basin of attraction of the extraneous fixed point appears in white.

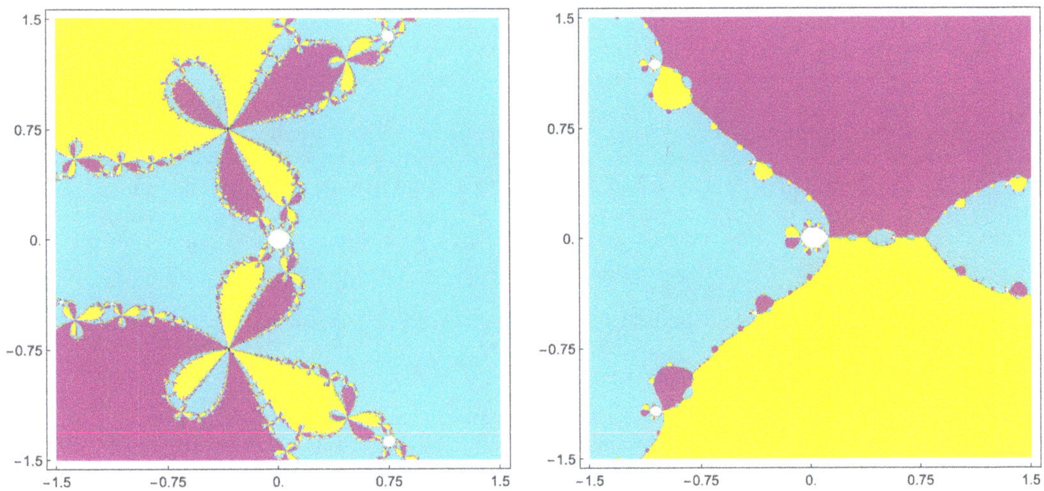

Figure 2. (On the **left**) the basins of attraction of the Chebyshev method applied to the polynomial (14). (On the **right**) the basins of attraction of the super-Halley method applied to the polynomial (15). In both cases, the basin of attraction of the extraneous fixed point at $z = 0$ can be seen in white.

In the right part of Figure 2, we show the basins of attraction of the super-Halley applied to the polynomial

$$p(z) = 4z^3 + 3z^2 + 3z + 3. \tag{15}$$

It is obtained by taking $\beta = 1$ in (13) and, next, by multiplying by three. The basin of the three roots $z = -0.873873$, $z = 0.0619363 - 0.924344i$, and $z = 0.0619363 + 0.924344i$ are colored in cyan, yellow, and magenta, respectively. The basin of attraction of the extraneous fixed point $z = 0$ appears in white.

In general, Chebyshev's method applied to polynomials in the form

$$p(z) = -1 + az + a^2z^2 + 2a^3z^3 + \sum_{j=4}^{d} a_j z^j \tag{16}$$

has a super-attracting extraneous fixed point at $z = 0$. Actually, we have

$$p(0) \neq 0, \quad L_p(0) = -2, \quad L_{p'}(0) = 3,$$

so the conditions in Theorem 2 are fulfilled.

In a similar way, the super-Halley method applied to polynomials in the form

$$p(z) = 1 + az + a^2z^2 + 4/3a^3z^3 + \sum_{j=4}^{d} a_j z^j \tag{17}$$

has a super-attracting extraneous fixed point at $z = 0$. Indeed, we have

$$p(0) \neq 0, \quad L_p(0) = L_{p'}(0) = 2,$$

so the conditions in Theorem 2 are satisfied.

3. Critical Points in the Family $\mathcal{CH}$

The parameter plane (space) is a very powerful graphical tool for better understanding the dynamic behavior of an iterative method for solving a family of nonlinear equations depending on a complex parameter. It is based on the Fatou–Julia Theorem [22], which says that the immediate basin of attraction of a (super) attractor cycle contains at least one critical point. Consequently, to determine the existence of attracting behaviors (fixed points and cycles), we must study the iterations of the critical points of the iteration function in question.

Let us restrict our interest to the case of iterative methods applied to polynomial Equation (4). In this case, a free critical point of an iterative method is a critical point of the corresponding iteration map that is not a root of the polynomial $p(z)$. Taking into account that the roots of $p(z)$ are (super) attracting fixed points of the iteration map, all of them have their own basin of attraction that is related to a critical point (the same root). Therefore, to detect attracting behaviors different from the root, we must follow the orbits of the free critical point.

For example, G. Roberts and J. Horgan-Kobelski [20] characterize cubic polynomials in the form

$$p_\lambda(z) = (z-1)(z+1)(z-\lambda), \quad \lambda \in \mathbb{C}, \tag{18}$$

for which Newton's method has super-attracting n-cycles. Specifically, they obtain (numerically) some values of the parameters $\lambda_n = \beta_n i$, with β_n given in Table 1, for which Newton's method applied to the polynomial $p_{\lambda_n}(z)$ defined in (18), with $\lambda_n = \beta_n i$ having a super-attracting n-cycle.

Table 1. Approximate values of the parameter β_n, for which Newton's method applied to the polynomial $p_{\lambda_n}(z)$ defined in (18), with $\lambda_n = \beta_n i$ having a super-attracting n-cycle (see [20]).

n	β_n	n	β_n	n	β_n
2	4.500116	6	1.982100	10	1.777227
3	2.938069	7	1.892459	20	1.732819
4	2.396385	8	1.836401	25	1.732152
5	2.131089	9	1.800522	50	1.732051

The strategy consists of coloring the parameter space $\lambda \in \mathbb{C}$ according to the convergence of the only free critical point $\lambda/3$, as performed in Figure 3. If the orbit of $\lambda/3$ converges to 1, -1, or λ, the value of the corresponding parameter λ is colored in cyan, magenta, or yellow, respectively.

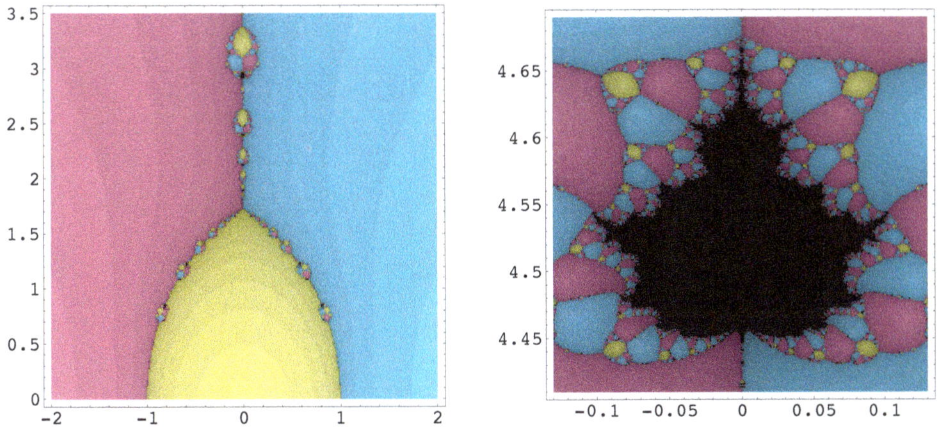

Figure 3. Graphic representation of the parameter plane of Newton's method applied to polynomials in the form (18). The figure on the right shows an enlargement of a black area where a Mandelbrot-type set can be seen.

The black-colored regions in the parameter space are formed by the values of λ, for which Newton's method applied to the corresponding polynomial $p_\lambda(z)$, have an attracting cycle that does not contain any root of the polynomial. The appearance of the Mandelbrot-type sets in the black areas of the parameter plane is a notable phenomenon.

Continuing in this line of work, Roberts and Horgan-Kobelski themselves [20] or, previously, E. R. Vrscay and W. J. Gilbert [25], prove the existence of polynomials with attracting cycles for Halley's method. Specifically, the table of values of β_n, for which Halley's method applied to the polynomial $p_{\lambda_n}(z)$ with $\lambda_n = \beta_n i$, has a super-attracting n-cycle and is shown in Table 2.

Table 2. Approximate values of the parameters β_n, for which Halley's method applied to the polynomial $p_{\lambda_n}(z)$ defined in (18) with $\lambda_n = \beta_n i$, have super-attracting n-cycle (see [20]).

n	β_n	n	β_n	n	β_n
2	1.342232060	6	1.018656160	10	1.0011575040
3	1.158338303	7	1.009291550	20	1.0000011298
4	1.076647075	8	1.004637455	25	1.0000000353
5	1.037611090	9	1.002316127	50	1.0000000011

The strategy to graphically represent the parameter space associated with Halley's method applied to polynomials of the form (18) changes slightly due to the appearance of two free critical points:

$$\rho_{\pm}(\lambda) = \frac{2\lambda \pm \sqrt{-2\lambda^2 - 6}}{6}.$$

As can be seen in [20], the range of colors in the parameter plane is expanded, according to the criteria shown in Table 3. For example, λ is colored blue if the orbit of $\rho_-(\lambda)$ converges to the root -1 and the orbit of $\rho_+(\lambda)$ converges to the root 1. The result of coloring the parameter plane of Halley's method in this way is shown in Figure 4.

Table 3. Color scheme for drawing the parameter plane associated with Halley's method applied to the polynomials defined in (18).

Color	$(\rho_-(\lambda), \rho_+(\lambda)) \to$	Color	$(\rho_-(\lambda), \rho_+(\lambda)) \to$
Yellow	$(-1, -1)$	Blue	$(-1, 1)$
Green	$(1, -1)$	Red	(λ, λ)
Brown	$(-1, \lambda)$	Pink	$(\lambda, -1)$
Orange	$(1, 1)$	Cyan	$(\lambda, 1)$
Purple	$(1, \lambda)$		

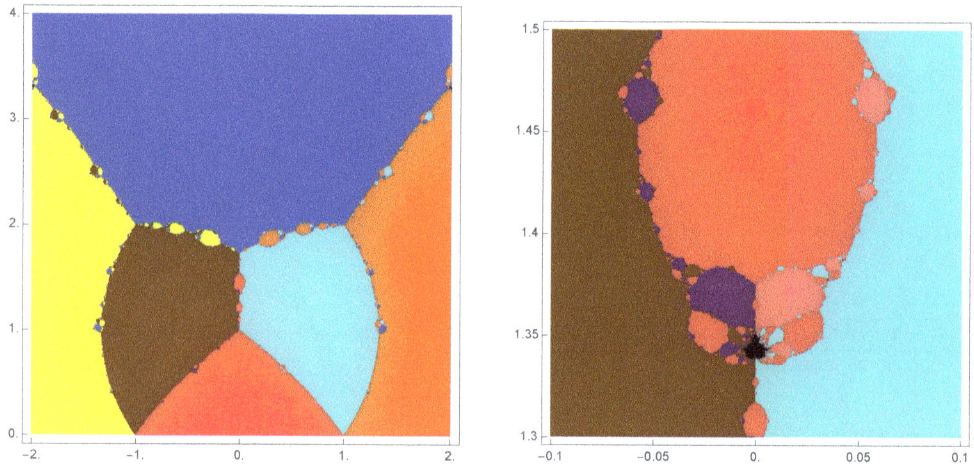

Figure 4. Parameter plane of Halley's method applied to the family of polynomials (18). In the figure on the right, we can see a Mandelbrot type set that appears in an enlargement of a black area.

The richness of the dynamic study of the methods of the family $\mathcal{CH}$ increases when we consider Chebyhev's method, as evidenced in the work of Gutiérrez and Varona [19]. With techniques similar to those used for the Newton or Halley methods, values of the parameter β_n can be given, for which Chebyshev's method applied to the polynomial $p_{\lambda_n}(z)$ defined in (18) with $\lambda_n = \beta_n i$, which have a super-attracting n-cycle (see Table 4).

Table 4. Approximate values of the parameter β_n, for which Chebyshev's method applied to the polynomial $p_{\lambda_n}(z)$ defined in (18) with $\lambda_n = \beta_n i$, have a super-attracting n-cycle (see [19]).

n	β_n	n	β_n	n	β_n
2	1.28657	6	1.48369	10	1.62056
3	1.34015	7	1.52557	20	1.72078
4	1.38943	8	1.56245	25	1.72856
5	1.43776	9	1.59405	50	1.72856

The strategy for coloring the parameter plane associated with Chebyshev's method applied to polynomials of the family (18) is the same as that followed for Halley's method (see [19] for more details), studying the orbits of the two fixed points which, in this case is

$$\rho_{\pm}(\lambda) = \frac{5\lambda \pm \sqrt{-5\lambda^2 - 15}}{15}.$$

The result is shown in Figure 5.

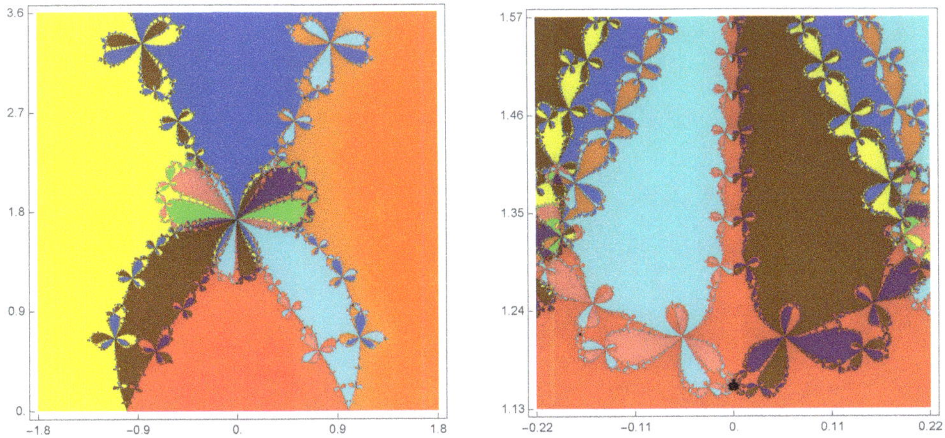

Figure 5. Parameter plane of Chebyshev's method applied to the family of polynomials (18). In the figure on the right, a channel of black holes around the imaginary axis can be seen.

Now, when analyzing the parameter plane associated with Chebyshev's method applied to the polynomials of the family (18), we have the "black holes" that appear in it, which are caused by two reasons: attracting cycles or attracting extraneous fixed points.

On the left side of Figure 5, the parameter plane of Chebyshev's method applied to the family of polynomials (18) is shown. The figure on the right shows an enlargement, around the imaginary axis, where a sort of channel of black holes can be seen. The black hole shown below is associated with a strange fixed point at $z = 2\sqrt{3}/3i$. However, the rest of the black holes in this channel are associated with attractor cycles.

Figure 6 shows two details of black holes: one associated with an extraneous fixed point (on the left) and another with an attracting two-cycle attractor (on the right).

What happens when we want to draw the parameter plane associated with other methods of the family $\mathcal{CH}$? The situation becomes considerably more complicated. The following results explain the reason.

Lemma 2. *Let $p(z)$ be a polynomial and let $L_p(z)$ and $L_{p'}(z)$ be the rational functions defined in* (4) *and* (7)*, respectively. Suppose that $p'(z) \neq 0$ and that $p''(z) \neq 0$. Then, the free critical points of the rational function $R_{\alpha,p}(z)$ defined in* (5) *are solutions of the equation*

$$L_{p'}(z) = 3(1-\alpha) + \alpha(2\alpha - 1)L_p(z). \tag{19}$$

Proof. To calculate the free critical points associated with a method in $\mathcal{CH}$, we derive the rational function $R_{\alpha,p}(z)$ that appears in (5). Taking into account (7) and Lemma 1, we obtain

$$R'_{\alpha,p}(z) = \frac{L_p(z)^2\Big(3(1-\alpha) + \alpha(2\alpha-1)L_p(z) - L_{p'}(z)\Big)}{2(1-\alpha L_p(z))^2}. \tag{20}$$

Note that $L_p(z) \neq 0$ because we are assuming that $p''(z) \neq 0$ and $p(z) \neq 0$ because z is a free critical point (it is not the root of $p(z)$). The result follows by simply solving for $L_{p'}(z)$ in the equation $R'_{\alpha,p}(z) = 0$. □

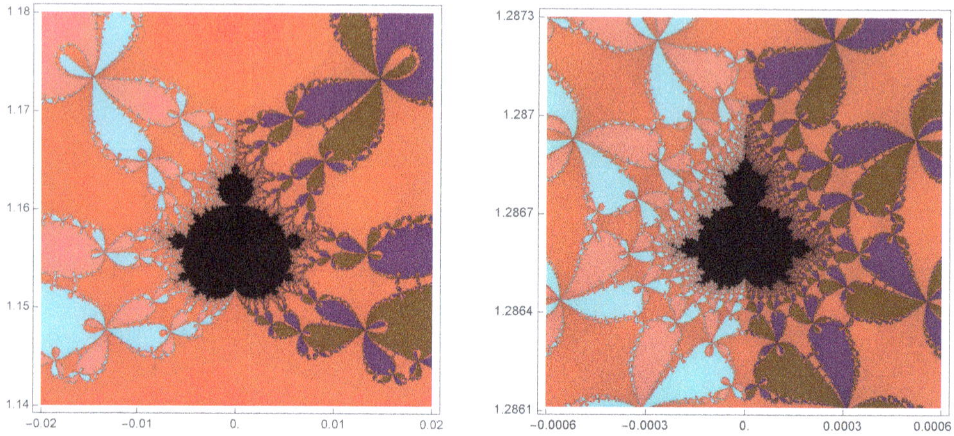

Figure 6. Two details of black holes of different nature: (on the **left**) one is associated with an extraneous fixed point and (on the **right**) one is associated with an attracting 2-cycle.

The analysis of Lemma 2 allows us to obtain some interesting conclusions about the number of free critical points in the family $\mathcal{CH}$. First, we note that there are two situations for which the Equation (19) has particularly simple solutions. These are the cases where $\alpha = 0$ (Chebyshev method) and $\alpha = 1/2$ (Halley method). In both cases, we arrive at an equation of the type $L_{p'}(z) = C$ with a constant C, which leads us to a polynomial equation of degree $2d - 4$, with d being the degree of the polynomial $p(z)$. In the case of cubic polynomials, such as those given in (18), the equation to be solved is quadratic. Consequently, to draw the parameter plane associated with Chebyshev's and Halley's methods, it is necessary to analyze the orbits of the two free critical points obtained, as has been performed, for example, in [19,20], respectively.

The number of free critical points in other methods in $\mathcal{CH}$ increases, which complicates their analysis from a dynamic point of view. For example, in another of the named methods of the family, such as the super-Halley method ($\alpha = 1$), the equation $L_{p'}(z) = L_p(z)$ is obtained. This equation leads to a polynomial equation of degree $4d - 6$. In the case of cubic polynomials (18), an equation of degree six must be solved, which greatly complicates the process. To be more specific, there is no formula that provides in an analytic way the roots in terms of the coefficients, as occurs in the cases of Chebyshev's and Halley's method, where a quadratic equation must be solved. Furthermore, with six possible free critical points and three roots, the range of colors to be handled is $3^6 = 729$, which makes it cumbersome to use, in the case of the super-Halley method, the strategy developed for Chebyshev's and Halley's methods. The situation is similar for the rest of the methods of the $\mathcal{CH}$ family, where the degree of the polynomial equation obtained to find the free critical points is also $4d - 6$.

4. Polynomials with Double Misbehavior

We have seen that some methods in $\mathcal{CH}$ can have a pathological behavior when they are applied to polynomial equations. By pathological, we mean the convergence to points or cycles that are not the roots of the polynomial. In particular, we have analyzed this bad behavior for the Chebyshev and super-Halley method. We have found polynomials for which each of these methods has extraneous fixed points or super-attracting cycles not including the roots. Now, we face the following question: is it possible to find polynomials and methods in $\mathcal{CH}$ so that the rational map obtained by applying the method to the polynomial has both extraneous fixed points and super-attracting cycles? Halley's method must be excluded from this search since it does not have attracting extraneous fixed points. Our first "candidate" is Chebyshev's method.

We follow a numerical strategy to find a polynomial in the form (16) (it has a super-attracting extraneous fixed point at zero), such that Chebyshev's method applied to it has a super-attracting two-cycle in $\{-1,1\}$. To perform this, let $R_{0,p}(z)$ be the iteration map related to Chebyshev's method (see (5), with $\alpha = 0$). We look for a solution to the system of equations

$$\begin{cases} R_{0,p}(1) &= -1, \\ R_{0,p}(-1) &= 1, \\ R'_{0,p}(1) &= 0, \\ R'_{0,p}(-1) &= 0. \end{cases} \tag{21}$$

Taking into account (see (20) in Lemma 2)

$$R'_{0,p}(z) = \frac{1}{2}(3 - L_{p'}(z))L_p(z)^2,$$

the last two equations in (21) can be substituted by $L_{p'}(1) = 3$ and $L_{p'}(-1) = 3$. As we have four equations, we take four parameters a, a_4, a_5, and a_6 in (16). So, we solve numerically the nonlinear system (21), and we obtain two solutions with real coefficients:

$$a = 0.115238, \quad a_4 = 0.00106173, \quad a_5 = 0.000786477, \quad a_6 = 0.000284636,$$

$$a = -0.115238, \quad a_4 = 0.00106173, \quad a_5 = -0.000786477, \quad a_6 = 0.000284636.$$

In Figure 7, we show the basins of attraction of Chebyshev's method applied to the polynomial

$$p(z) = -1 + az + a^2z^2 + 2a^3z^3 + a_4z^4 + a_5z^5 + a_6z^6, \tag{22}$$

where a, a_4, a_5, and a_6 are the first of the above solutions. Together with the basins of the six roots of the polynomial, we can see (in white) the basin of the super-attracting extraneous fixed point $z = 0$. In yellow, we can see the basin of the super-attracting two-cycle $\{-1,1\}$.

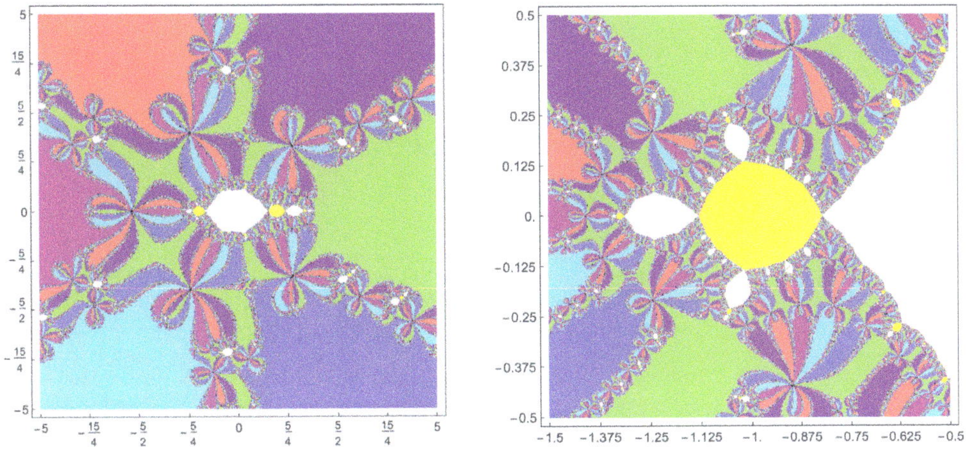

Figure 7. Two details of the basins of attraction of Chebyshev's method applied to the polynomial defined in (22), where we can see the basin of attraction of super-attracting extraneous fixed point (in white) and a super-attracting 2-cycle (in yellow). The basins of the other six roots are colored with the rest of colors (magenta, green, purple, pink, cyan, or blue).

In the case of the super-Halley method, we proceed in a similar way. In this case, we find a polynomial in the form (17) (it has a super-attracting extraneous fixed point at zero), such that the super-Halley method applied to it has a super-attracting two-cycle in $\{-1,1\}$. To perform this, let $R_{1,p}(z)$ be the iteration map related to the super-Halley method (see (5), with $\alpha = 1$). We look for a solution to the system of equations

$$\left\{\begin{array}{lcr} R_{1,p}(1) & = & -1, \\ R_{1,p}(-1) & = & 1, \\ R'_{1,p}(1) & = & 0, \\ R'_{1,p}(-1) & = & 0. \end{array}\right. \tag{23}$$

Taking into account (see (20) in Lemma 2)

$$R'_{1,p}(z) = \frac{L_p(z) - L_{p'}(z)}{2(1 - L_p(z))^2} L_p(z)^2,$$

the last two equations in (23) can be substituted by $L_p(1) = L_{p'}(1)$ and $L_p(-1) = L_{p'}(-1)$. As we have four equations, we take four parameters a, a_4, a_5, and a_6 in (17). So, we solve numerically the nonlinear system (23), and we obtain the solution (not the only one)

$$a = 0.325178, \quad a_4 = -0.009199, \quad a_5 = -0.029499, \quad a_6 = -0.011043.$$

In Figure 8, we show the basins of attraction of the super-Halley method applied to the polynomial

$$p(z) = -1 + az + a^2z^2 + 2a^3z^3 + a_4z^4 + a_5z^5 + a_6z^6, \tag{24}$$

where a, a_4, a_5, and a_6 are the above parameters. Together with the basins of the six roots of the polynomial, we can see (in white) the basin of the super-attracting extraneous fixed point $z = 0$. In yellow, we can see the basin of the super-attracting two-cycle $\{-1,1\}$.

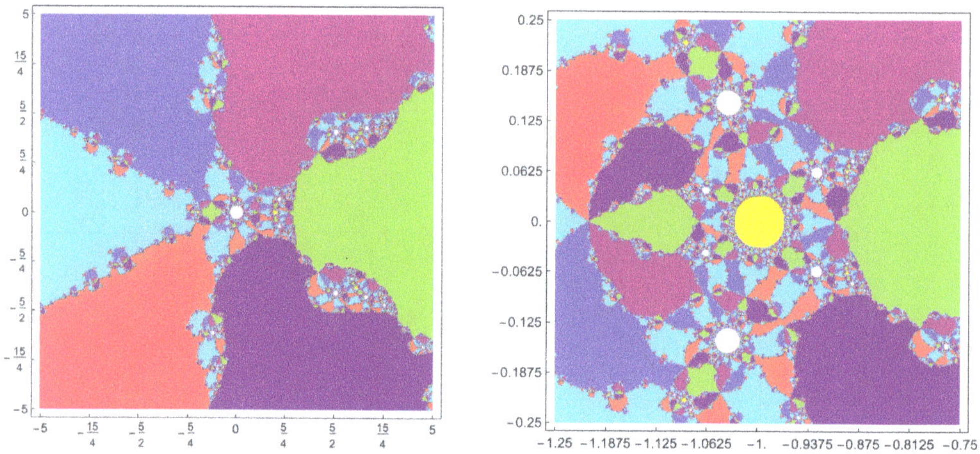

Figure 8. Two details of the basins of attraction of super-Halley method applied to the polynomial defined in (24), where we can see the basin of attraction of super-attracting extraneous fixed point (in white) and a super-attracting 2-cycle (in yellow). The basins of the other six roots are colored with the rest of colors (magenta, green, purple, pink, cyan, or blue).

5. Conclusions

In this article, we have made an incursion into the dynamic study of iterative processes for solving polynomial equations in the complex plane. We have focused our interest on the well-known Chebyshev–Halley family of root-finding methods. This is a one-parameter family, depending on the parameter $\alpha \in \mathbb{C}$, which includes the most famous third-order iterative methods, such as Chebyshev, Halley, or super-Halley methods. First, we have characterized the existence of extraneous fixed points (fixed points of the iteration map that are not roots of the corresponding polynomial) in terms of the quotients

$$L_p(z) = \frac{p(z)p''(z)}{p'(z)^2} \text{ and } L_{p'}(z) = \frac{p'(z)p'''(z)}{p''(z)^2}.$$

In addition, we have analyzed the behavior of the infinity point as an extraneous fixed point, reaching the conclusion that it is not always repulsive, as in the case of the aforementioned most famous iterative processes or even Newton's method.

The following part of this article is devoted to the study of the critical points of the methods in the family $\mathcal{CH}$. In particular, we have given a result that characterizes the existence and number of free critical points, that is, critical points that are not roots of the considered polynomial. This result plays a key role in the construction of the parameter plane related to the rational map obtained by applying the methods in $\mathcal{CH}$ to families of polynomials depending on a complex parameter (we have considered the case of cubic polynomials).As far as we know, only the parameter planes associated with the methods of Newton, Halley, or Chebyshev have been represented (see references [19,20], for instance). The main limitations for using the parameter plane with the rest of the methods in the family arise when solving the equations of critical points because there is not a "closed formula" for them. We have not managed to solve this difficulty and the problem is open for future research. Maybe, a good starting point to face this challenge is to consider the dynamic behavior of the super-Halley method, which has all the ingredients that we have not been able to solve.

Finally, we conclude with another new dynamic question: the problem of finding polynomials and methods in $\mathcal{CH}$ so that the rational map obtained by applying the method to the polynomial has both extraneous fixed points and super-attracting cycles. We have obtained some of these couples of polynomial methods by following a numerical strategy. In fact, we have found polynomials with double misbehavior for Chebyshev and super-Halley methods. In both cases, polynomials with a sixth-degree have been obtained. This problem opens a suggestive line of research, with issues such as whether it is possible to find couples of polynomial methods with double misbehavior with a lower degree. Is there a geometric, algebraic, or analytical strategy to find these polynomials?

This work can be also extended to other problems such as nonlinear systems of equations or nonlinear ordinary differential equations. For instance, in [29], we can find promising results in solving these problems using an iterative scheme.

Author Contributions: This research has been carried out in equal parts by the two authors. All authors have read and agreed to the published version of the manuscript.

Funding: This research received no external funding.

Data Availability Statement: Data is contained within the article.

Conflicts of Interest: The authors declare no conflict of interest.

References

1. Werner, W. Some improvements of classical iterative methods for the solution of nonlinear equations. In *Numerical Solution of Nonlinear Equations: Proceedings, Bremen 1980*; Lecture Notes in Mathematics; Allgower, E.L., Glashoff, K., Peitgen, H.O., Eds.; Springer: Berlin/Heidelberg, Germany, 1981; Volume 878, pp. 427–440.
2. Argyros, I.K.; Szidarovszky, F. *The Theory and Applications of Iteration Methods*; CRC Press: Boca Raton, FL, USA, 1993.
3. Argyros, I.K.; Chen, D.; Qian, Q.S. A convergence analysis for rational methods with a parameter in a Banach space. *Pure Math. Appl.* **1994**, *5*, 59–73.
4. Gutiérrez, J.M.; Hernández-Verón, M.Á. A family of Chebyshev-Halley type methods in Banach spaces. *Bull. Austral. Math. Soc.* **1997**, *55*, 113–1309. [CrossRef]

5. Hernández-Verón, M.Á.; Salanova, M.A. A family of Chebyshev-Halley type methods. *Int. J. Comput. Math.* **1993**, *47*, 59–63. [CrossRef]
6. Ivanov, S.I. Unified Convergence Analysis of Chebyshev-Halley Methods for Multiple Polynomial Zeros. *Mathematics* **2022**, *10*, 135. [CrossRef]
7. Osada, N. Chebyshev-Halley methods for analytic functions. *J. Comput. Appl. Math.* **2008**, *216*, 585–599. [CrossRef]
8. Dubeau, F. On comparisons of Chebyshev-Halley iteration functions based on their asymptotic constants. *Int. J. Pure Appl. Math.* **2013**, *85*, 965–981. [CrossRef]
9. Dubeau, F.; Gnang, C. On the Chebyshev-Halley family of iteration functions and the n-th root computation problem. *Int. J. Pure Appl. Math.* **2013**, *85*, 1051–1059. [CrossRef]
10. Gutiérrez, J.M.; Hernández-Verón, M.Á.; Salanova, M.A. Calculus of n-th roots and third order iterative methods. *Nonlinear Anal.* **2001**, *47*, 2875–2880. [CrossRef]
11. Cordero, A.; Soleymani, F.; Torregrosa, J.R.; Zaka Ullah, M. Numerically stable improved Chebyshev-Halley type schemes for matrix sign function. *J. Comput. Appl. Math.* **2017**, *318*, 189–198. [CrossRef]
12. Cordero, A.; Torregrosa, J.R.; Vindel, P. Dynamics of a family of Chebyshev-Halley type methods. *Appl. Math. Comput.* **2013**, *2019*, 8568–8583. [CrossRef]
13. Cordero, A.; Torregrosa, J.R.; Vindel, P. Bulbs of Period Two in the Family of Chebyshev-Halley Iterative Methods on Quadratic Polynomials. *Abstr. Appl. Anal.* **2013**, *2013*, 536910. [CrossRef]
14. Cordero, A.; Torregrosa, J.R.; Vindel, P. Period-doubling bifurcations in the family of Chebyshev-Halley-type methods. *Int. J. Comput. Math.* **2013**, *90*, 2061–2071. [CrossRef]
15. Campos, B.; Canela, J.; Vindel, P. Connectivity of the Julia set for the Chebyshev-Halley family on degree n polynomials. *Commun. Nonlinear Sci. Numer. Simulat.* **2020**, *82*, 508–525. [CrossRef]
16. Campos, B.; Canela, J.; Vindel, P. Convergence regions for the Chebyshev-Halley family. *Commun. Nonlinear Sci. Numer. Simulat.* **2018**, *56*, 508–525. [CrossRef]
17. Gutiérrez, J.M.; Magreñán, Á.A.; Varona, J.L. Fractal Dimension of the Universal Julia Sets for the Chebyshev-Halley Family of Methods. *AIP Conf. Proc.* **2011**, *1389*, 1061.
18. Babajee, D.K.R.; Cordero, A.; Torregrosa, J.R. Study of iterative methods through the Cayley Quadratic Test. *J. Comput. App. Math.* **2016**, *291*, 358–369. [CrossRef]
19. Gutiérrez, J.M.; Varona, J.L. Superattracting extraneous fixed points and n-cycles for Chebyshev's method on cubic polynomials. *Qual. Theory Dyn. Syst.* **2020**, *19*, 54. [CrossRef]
20. Roberts, G.E.; Horgan-Kobelski, J. Newton's versus Halley's methods: A dynamical systems approach. *Int. J. Bifurc. Chaos Appl. Sci. Eng.* **2004**, *14*, 3459–3475. [CrossRef]
21. Nayak, T.; Pal, S. The Julia sets of Chebyshev's method with small degrees. *Nonlinear Dyn.* **2022**, *110*, 803–819. [CrossRef]
22. Beardon, A.F. *Iteration of Rational Functions*; Springer: Nueva York, NY, USA, 1991.
23. Traub, J.F. *Iterative Methods for the Solution of Equations*; Prentice-Hall: Englewood Cliffs, NJ, USA, 1964.
24. Kneisl, K. Julia sets for the super-Newton method, Cauchy's method, and Halley's method. *Chaos* **2001**, *11*, 359–370. [CrossRef]
25. Vrscay, E.R.; Gilbert, W.J. Extraneous fixed points, basin boundaries and chaotic dynamics for Schröder and König rational iteration functions. *Numer. Math.* **1988**, *52*, 1–16. [CrossRef]
26. García-Olivo, M.; Gutiérrez, J.M.; Magreñán, Á.A. A complex dynamical approach of Chebyshev's method. *SeMA J.* **2015**, *71*, 57–68. [CrossRef]
27. Basto, M.; Semiao, V.; Calheiros, F.L. A new iterative method to compute nonlinear equations. *Appl. Math. Comput.* **2006**, *173*, 468–483. [CrossRef]
28. Gutiérrez, J.M.; Hernández-Verón, M.Á. An acceleration of Newton's method: Super-Halley method. *Appl. Math. Comput.* **2001**, *117*, 223–239. [CrossRef]
29. Ben-Romdhane, M.; Temimi, H.; Baccouch, M. An iterative finite difference method for approximating the two-branched solution of Bratu's problem. *Appl. Numer. Math.* **2019**, *139*, 62–76. [CrossRef]

axioms

MDPI

Article

High-Order, Accurate Finite Difference Schemes for Fourth-Order Differential Equations

Allaberen Ashyralyev [1,2,3,*] and Ibrahim Mohammed Ibrahım [4,5]

1 Department of Mathematics, Bahcesehir University, Istanbul 34353, Turkey
2 Department of Mathematics, Peoples' Friendship University of Russia RUDN University, Moscow 117198, Russia
3 Institute of Mathematics and Mathematical Modeling, Almaty 050010, Kazakhstan
4 Department of Mathematics, Near East University Nicosia, TRNC Mersin 10, Nicosia 99138, Turkey; 20194365@std.neu.edu.tr or ibrahimkalash81@gmail.com
5 Department of Mathematics, Akre University for Applied Science, Akre 42002, Duhok, Iraq
* Correspondence: aallaberen@gmail.com

Abstract: This article is devoted to the study of high-order, accurate difference schemes' numerical solutions of local and non-local problems for ordinary differential equations of the fourth order. Local and non-local problems for ordinary differential equations with constant coefficients can be solved by classical integral transform methods. However, these classical methods can be used simply in the case when the differential equation has constant coefficients. We study fourth-order differential equations with dependent coefficients and their corresponding boundary value problems. Novel compact numerical solutions of high-order, accurate finite difference schemes generated by Taylor's decomposition on five points have been studied in these problems. Numerical experiments support the theoretical statements for the solution of these difference schemes.

Keywords: Taylor's decomposition; finite difference schemes; approximation; accuracy

MSC: 65M; 65J

1. Introduction

Differential equations can be solved with highly accurate difference schemes because of modern computers. Therefore, creating and investigating highly accurate difference schemes for differential equations is a topic of current interest. A thorough investigation was conducted into the application of Taylor's decomposition on two and three points for the numerical solution of high-order approximation compact finite difference schemes of linear ordinary differential equations and partial differential equations (see, for example, [1–3]). In paper [4], the oxygen diffusion problem inside one cell is modelled by a one-dimensional time-dependent partial differential equation whose initial moving boundary value problem is the Du Fort–Frankel finite difference scheme. In [5], a partial differential equation describing oxygen diffusion in absorbing tissues was estimated analytically and numerically. An approximate analytical solution was proposed using Fourier expansion and, with limited modifications, the techniques of Crank and Gupta were employed.

There have not been enough investigations performed on Taylor's decomposition on four and five points for the numerical solution of high-order approximation compact finite difference schemes of linear ordinary differential equations and partial differential equations. In papers [6–8], three-step difference schemes of the fourth order of approximation for the numerical solutions of the local and non-local boundary-value problems for third-order ordinary differential equations and partial differential equations were investigated, and Taylor decomposition on four points was used. A method for numerically solving third-order time-varying linear dynamical systems using Taylor's decomposition on four points was presented. The procedure for the numerical examination of an up-converter applied in communication networks was explained.

In [9], the four-step difference schemes generated by Taylor decomposition on five points of the sixth order of approximation for the numerical solutions to the boundary-value problem

$$\begin{cases} \frac{d^4u(t)}{dt^4} + a(t)u(t) = f(t), 0 < t < T, \\ u(0) = \varphi, u(T) = \omega, u'(0) = \psi, u'(T) = \chi \end{cases} \quad (1)$$

for a fourth-order differential equation with a dependent coefficient were presented. Here and hereafter, $a(t)$ and $f(t)$ denote smooth given functions defined on $[0, T]$.

In theory and applications, boundary value problems for ordinary differential equations are important. Many physical, biological, and chemical phenomena are described using them. Rich areas of such applications include the elasticity work of Timoshenko [10], the deformation of structure monographs by Soedel [11], and the effects of soil settlement work by Dulacska [12].

Boundary value problems of second- and higher-order differential equations have been extensively studied; papers of Anderson and Davis [13], Baxley and Haywood [14], and Hao and Liu [15] are among the recent contributions to this field. The reader is referred to the monographs of Agarwal et al. [16,17] for surveys of known results and additional references. As far as we are aware though, the majority of the aforementioned studies as well as a large body of other literature on ordinary differential equations focused on either the two-point boundary value problem for higher-order ordinary differential equations or the multi-point boundary value problem for second-order ordinary differential equations. The boundary value problem for higher-order ordinary differential equations has been well investigated. In the present article, we investigate the ordinary differential equation of the fourth order (1).

The beam equation, or the nonlinear form of differential Equation (1), has been probed under multiple boundary conditions.

The work of Zill and Cullen ([18], pp. 237–243) provides a succinct and easily readable explanation as well as a physical interpretation of a few of the boundary conditions related to the linear beam equation. The multi-point boundary conditions that are the subject of this study deviate somewhat from those commonly encountered in the literature, such as the conjugate [19], focal [13,20], and Lidstone [21] conditions.

Some physical systems have mathematical descriptions that use linear differential equations subject to specific boundary conditions, particularly beam deflection mathematical models. These beams, which are utilised in many structures, can flex due to external forces acting on them or due to their weight. The deflection curve, also known as the elastic curve, is the curve connecting the centroids of all cross sections if a load is applied to a beam, for instance, on a vertical plane that contains the axis of symmetry. This causes the beam to undergo distortion.

In ref. [22], in the context of structural mechanics, the equation controlling the bending of a cantilever beam under a distributed load was presented and is a famous example of a fourth-order differential equation. This illustration is often known as the "Euler–Bernoulli beam equation". The beam's transverse displacement, w(x, t), as a function of position (x) and time (t) is expressed by this equation. The equation for the Euler–Bernoulli beam is as follows:

$$EIw_{xxxxx}(x,t) + pAw_{tt}(x,t) = q(x,t)$$

where:

E	is the Young's modulus of the material;
I	is the moment of inertia of the cross-sectional area;
P	is the mass density of the beam material;
A	is the cross-sectional area of the beam;
w_{xxxxx}	is the fourth spatial derivative of w with respect to x;
w_{tt}	is the second time derivative of w with respect to t;
$q(x,t)$	represents an external distributed load.

The numerical solutions of problem (1) are approximated to a high order of accuracy for the construction of the four-step difference schemes and the local boundary value problem of the form

$$\begin{cases} \frac{d^4u(t)}{dt^4} + a(t)u(t) = f(t), 0 < t < T, \\ u(0) = \varphi, u(T) = \omega, u''(0) = \psi, u''(T) = \chi \end{cases} \tag{2}$$

For a fourth-order differential equation, we consider the five points $t_{k\pm 2}$, $t_{k\pm 1}$, and t_k of the uniform grid space

$$[0,T]_\tau = \{t_k = k\tau, k = 0,1,\cdots,N, N\tau = T\}.$$

Applying the five points $t_k, t_{k\pm 1}, t_{k\pm 2} \in [0,T]_\tau$, we can present the second-order approximation four-step difference schemes as

$$\begin{cases} \tau^{-4}\{u_{k+2} + 4u_{k+1} + 6u_k + 4u_{k-1} + u_{k-2}\} + a(t_k)u_k = f(t_k), 2 \le k \le N-2, \\ u_0 = \varphi, u_N = \omega, \\ \frac{3}{2}u_0 - 2u_1 + \frac{1}{2}u_2 = \tau\psi, -\frac{3}{2}u_N + 2u_{N-1} - \frac{1}{2}u_{N-2} = \tau\chi \end{cases} \tag{3}$$

for the numerical solution of boundary value problem (1), and

$$\begin{cases} \tau^{-4}\{u_{k+2} - 4u_{k+1} + 6u_k - 4u_{k-1} + u_{k-2}\} + a(t_k)u_k = f(t_k)\,, 2 \le k \le N-2, \\ u_0 = \varphi, u_N = \omega, \\ 2u_0 - 5u_1 + 4u_2 - u_3 = \tau^2\psi, 2u_N - 5u_{N-1} + 4u_{N-2} - u_{N-3} = \tau^2\chi \end{cases} \tag{4}$$

for the numerical solution of boundary value problem (2). Note that there are two difference schemes for the numerical solutions of boundary value problems (1) and (2). It is easy to see that the order of these difference schemes is two. They are based on the formulas

$$\tau^{-4}u(t_{k+2}) - 4u(t_{k+1}) + 6u(t_k) - 4u(t_{k-1}) + u(t_{k-2}) - u^{(4)}(t_k)) = o(\tau^2),$$

$$\tau^{-1}\left(\frac{3}{2}u(0) - 2u(\tau) + \frac{1}{2}u(2\tau)\right) - u'(0) = o(\tau^2),$$

$$\tau^{-1}\left(-\frac{3}{2}u(T) + 2u(T-\tau) - \frac{1}{2}u(T-2\tau)\right) - u'(T) = o(\tau^2),$$

$$\tau^{-2}(2u(0) - 5u(\tau) + 4u(2\tau) - u(3\tau)) - u''(0) = o(\tau^2),$$

$$\tau^{-2}(2u(T) - 5u(T-\tau) + 4u(T-2\tau) - u(T-3\tau)) - u''(T) = o(\tau^2).$$

In this work, we numerically compare the results and methods of other authors. We use the fourth-order approximation of the numerical solutions of the first and second derivatives of local boundary value problems (1) and (2) at points zero and T, while in [6,7], approximations for the numerical solutions of local boundary value problems are used only for the first derivative of each problem.

We have used these different schemes with different values of τ, namely $\tau = \frac{1}{80}, \frac{1}{160}, \frac{1}{320}$. Here and hereafter, the error of the numerical solutions is defined by the formula:

$$E_N = \max_{0 \leq k \leq N} |u(t_k) - u_k|. \tag{5}$$

Remark 1. *Note that (see Table 1). If N is doubled, the value of errors between the exact solution and approximate solution decreases by a factor of approximately 1/4 for difference schemes (3) and (4). So, the order of accuracy of these difference schemes is 2.*

Table 1. Errors of difference schemes (3) and (4).

$\tau = \frac{1}{N}$	$N = 80$	$N = 160$	$N = 320$
Difference Scheme (3)	6.4210×10^{-6}	1.6149×10^{-6}	4.0506×10^{-7}
Difference Scheme (4)	1.2318×10^{-5}	3.0893×10^{-6}	7.7417×10^{-7}

The main aim of this work is the construction of highly accurate four-step difference schemes for the numerical solution of fourth-order differential equations. In the present paper, fourth- and sixth-order approximation finite difference schemes generated by Taylor decomposition on five points for solving these problems are presented. The results of numerical experiments support the theoretical statements for the solution of these difference schemes. This paper is organised as follows. Section 1 is an introduction. In Sections 2 and 3, local boundary value problems (1) and (2) are presented. A novel numerical method for the solutions to these problems is investigated. Finally, Section 4 is the conclusion and our future plans.

2. Local Boundary Value Problem (1)

Based on the following theorem, difference schemes of the fourth order of approximation for the numerical solutions of local boundary value problems (1) and (2) are constructed utilising Taylor decomposition on five points.

Theorem 1. *Let $v(t)$ be a function with a continuous eighth derivative $(0 \leq t \leq T)$. Then, the following relations hold:*

$$\begin{aligned} &\tau^{-4}(v(t_{k+2}) - 4v(t_{k+1}) + 6v(t_k) - 4v(t_{k-1}) + v(t_{k-2})) \\ &-\frac{2}{3}v^{(4)}(t_k) - \frac{1}{6}\left(v^{(4)}(t_{k+1}) + v^{(4)}(t_{k+1})\right) = o(\tau^4), \end{aligned} \tag{6}$$

$$\begin{aligned} &\tau^{-4}(v(t_{k+2}) - 4v(t_{k+1}) + 6v(t_k) - 4v(t_{k-1}) + v(t_{k-2})) \\ &-\frac{11}{12}v^{(4)}(t_k) - \frac{1}{24}\left(v^{(4)}(t_{k+2}) + v^{(4)}(t_{k+2})\right) = o(\tau^4). \end{aligned} \tag{7}$$

Proof. Using Taylor's formula, we have the following two formulas

$$v(t_{k+1}) + v(t_{k-1}) = 2v(t_k) + 2v''(t_k)\frac{\tau^2}{2!} + 2v^{(4)}(t_k)\frac{\tau^4}{4!} + 2v^{(6)}(t_k)\frac{\tau^6}{6!} + o(\tau^8),$$

$$v(t_{k+2}) + v(t_{k-2}) = 2v(t_k) + 2v''(t_k)\frac{4\tau^2}{2!} + 2v^{(4)}(t_k)\frac{16\tau^4}{4!} + 2v^{(6)}(t_k)\frac{64\tau^6}{6!} + o(\tau^8).$$

From these formulas, it follows that

$$\begin{aligned} &\tau^{-4}(v(t_{k+2}) - 4v(t_{k+1}) + 6v(t_k) - 4v(t_{k-1}) + v(t_{k-2})) \\ &= v^{(4)}(t_k) + v^{(6)}(t_k)\frac{\tau^2}{6} + o(\tau^4). \end{aligned} \tag{8}$$

Now, we will obtain α, β such that

$$\tau^{-4}(\nu(t_{k+2}) - 4\nu(t_{k+1}) + 6\nu(t_k) - 4\nu(t_{k-1}) + \nu(t_{k-2}))$$

$$-\alpha\nu^{(4)}(t_k) - \beta(\nu^{(4)}(t_{k+1}) + \nu^{(4)}(t_{k-1})) = o(\tau^4).$$

We have that

$$\nu^{(4)}(t_{k+1}) + \nu^{(4)}(t_{k-1}) = 2v^{(4)}(t_k) + 2v^{(6)}(t_k)\frac{\tau^2}{2!} + o(\tau^4).$$

Using Formula (8) and the last formula, we get

$$v^{(4)}(t_k) + v^{(6)}(t_k)\frac{\tau^2}{6} - \alpha\nu^{(4)}(t_k) - \beta(2v^{(4)}(t_k) + 2v^{(6)}(t_k)\frac{\tau^2}{2!}) + o(\tau^4) -$$

$$= (1 - (\alpha + 2\beta))v^{(4)}(t_k) + \left(\frac{1}{6} - \beta\right)v^{(6)}(t_k)\tau^2 + o(\tau^4) = 0.$$

The system of equations is then obtained by equating the coefficients of the lowest power of τ in the formula above to zero.

$$\begin{cases} 1 - (\alpha + 2\beta) = 0, \\ \frac{1}{6} - \beta = 0. \end{cases}$$

Solving this system of equations, we can obtain $\alpha = \frac{2}{3}, \beta = \frac{1}{6}$. So, relation (6) is proved. Similarly, we can prove relation (7). Theorem 1 is proved.

Let us consider boundary value problem (1). Taylor decomposition's on five points (6) and (7), as well as the fourth order of approximation for $v'(0)$ and $v'(T)$, forms a basis for the construction of the fourth order of approximation for the approximate solution of problem (1). □

Theorem 2. *Let $v(t)$ be a function with a continuous fifth derivative on $(0 \le t \le T)$. Then, the following is valid:*

$$v'(0) - \tau^{-1}\left(-\frac{25}{12}v(0) + 4v(\tau) - 3v(2\tau) + \frac{4}{3}v(3\tau) - \frac{1}{4}v(4\tau)\right) = o(\tau^4), \quad (9)$$

$$v'(T) - \tau^{-1}\left(\frac{25}{12}v(T) - 4v(T-\tau) + 3v(T-2\tau) - \frac{4}{3}v(T-3\tau) + \frac{1}{4}v(T-4\tau)\right) = o(\tau^4). \quad (10)$$

Proof. Applying the undetermined coefficients method, we will seek

$$v'(0) = \alpha v(0) + \beta v(\tau) + \gamma v(2\tau) + dv(3\tau) + pv(4\tau) + o\left(\tau^4\right). \quad (11)$$

Using Taylor's formula, we have the following two formulas

$$v'(0) = \alpha v(0) + \beta\left(v(0) + v'(0)\tau + v''(0)\frac{\tau^2}{2!} + v'''(0)\frac{\tau^3}{3!} + v^{(4)}(0)\frac{\tau^4}{4!} + o\left(\tau^5\right)\right)$$

$$+\gamma\left(v(0) + 2v'(0)\tau + 4v''(0)\frac{\tau^2}{2!} + 8v'''(0)\frac{\tau^3}{3!} + 16v^{(4)}(0)\frac{\tau^4}{4!} + o\left(\tau^5\right)\right)$$

$$+d\left(v(0) + 3v'(0)\tau + 9v''(0)\frac{\tau^2}{2!} + 27v'''(0)\frac{\tau^3}{3!} + 81v^{(4)}(0)\frac{\tau^4}{4!} + o\left(\tau^5\right)\right)$$

$$+p\left(v(0)+4v'(0)\tau+4^2v''(0)\frac{\tau^2}{2!}+4^3v'''(0)\frac{\tau^3}{3!}+4^4v^{(4)}(0)\frac{\tau^4}{4!}+o\left(\tau^5\right)\right)+o\left(\tau^4\right).$$

The system of equations is then obtained by equating the coefficients of the lowest power of τ in the formula above to zero.

$$\begin{cases} -\alpha-\beta-\gamma-d-p=0, \\ \beta+2\gamma+3d+4p=\tau^{-1}, \\ \beta+4\gamma+9d+16p=0, \\ \beta+8\gamma+27d+64p=0, \\ \beta+16\gamma+81d+256p=0. \end{cases}$$

Solving this system of equations, we can obtain $\alpha=\frac{25}{12\tau},\beta=\frac{4}{\tau},\gamma=\frac{3}{3\tau},\ d=\frac{4}{3\tau},p=\frac{11}{4\tau}$. So, relation (9) is proved. Similarly, one can obtain relation (10). Theorem 7 is proved.

We obtain the fourth order of approximation difference schemes by applying Taylor decomposition on five points (6), Equation (1), and Formulas (9) and (10), and neglecting small terms.

$$\begin{cases} \frac{1}{\tau^4}\{u_{k+2}-4u_{k+1}+6u_k-4u_{k-1}+u_{k-2}\}+\frac{2}{3}a(t_k)u_k \\ +\frac{1}{6}(a(t_{k-1})u_{k-1}+a(t_{k+1})u_{k+1}) \\ =\frac{2}{3}f(t_k)+\frac{1}{6}(f(t_{k-1})+f(t_{k+1})), 2\le k\le N-2, \\ u_0=\varphi, \tau^{-1}(-\frac{25}{12}u_0+4u_1-3u_2+\frac{4}{3}u_3-\frac{1}{4}u_4)=\psi, \\ \tau^{-1}(\frac{25}{12}u_N-4u_{N-1}+3u_{N-2}-\frac{4}{3}u_{N-3}+\frac{1}{4}u_{N-4})=\chi, u_N=\omega, \end{cases} \tag{12}$$

and

$$\begin{cases} \frac{1}{\tau^4}\{u_{k+2}-4u_{k+1}+6u_k-4u_{k-1}+u_{k-2}\}-\frac{11}{12}a(t_k)u_k \\ -\frac{1}{24}(a(t_{k-2})u_{k-2}+a(t_{k+2})u_{k+2}) \\ =\frac{11}{12}f(t_k)+\frac{1}{24}(f(t_{k-2})+f(t_{k+2})), 2\le k\le N-2, \\ u_0=\varphi, \tau^{-1}(-\frac{25}{12}u_0+4u_1-3u_2+\frac{4}{3}u_3-\frac{1}{4}u_4)=\psi, \\ \tau^{-1}(\frac{25}{12}u_N-4u_{N-1}+3u_{N-2}-\frac{4}{3}u_{N-3}+\frac{1}{4}u_{N-4})=\chi, u_N=\omega \end{cases} \tag{13}$$

for the boundary value problem's numerical solution (1). In Section 2, note that there are two difference schemes for the numerical solutions of boundary value problems (1) and (2). We consider the boundary value problem in numerical analysis

$$\begin{cases} \frac{d^4u(t)}{dt^4}+u(t)=4!-4\cdot 5!t+6\cdot\frac{6!}{2!}t^2-4\cdot\frac{7!}{3!}t^3+\frac{8!}{4!}t^4+t^4(1-t)^4, 0<t<1, \\ u(0)=u(1)=u'(0)=u'(1)=0 \end{cases} \tag{14}$$

with the exact solution

$$u(t)=t^4(1-t)^4.$$

Note that we utilised the fourth order of approximation difference schemes (12) and (13) for the approximate solution of problem (14) with different values of τ, namely $\tau=\frac{1}{80},\frac{1}{160},\frac{1}{320}$. □

Remark 2. *Note that (see Table 2). It is observed that for difference schemes (12) and (13), the value of errors between the exact solution and approximate solution decreases by a factor of about* 1/16 *if N is doubled. Thus, these difference schemes have an accuracy order of* 4.

Table 2. Errors of difference schemes (12) and (13).

$\tau=\frac{1}{N}$	$N=80$	$N=160$	$N=320$
Difference Scheme (12)	4.7729×10^{-7}	3.2983×10^{-8}	2.1517×10^{-9}
Difference Scheme (13)	3.7069×10^{-7}	2.6319×10^{-8}	1.7380×10^{-9}

We now consider the approximation difference schemes of the sixth order for the approximate solution of problem (1). It was observed that the approximate solution to problem (1) requires a sixth-order approximation difference scheme.

$$\begin{cases} \frac{1}{\tau^4}\{u_{k+2}-4u_{k+1}+6u_k-4u_{k-1}+u_{k-2}\}+\frac{237}{360}a(t_k)u_k \\ +\frac{31}{180}(a(t_{k-1})u_{k-1}+a(t_{k+1})u_{k+1})-\frac{1}{720}(a(t_{k-2})u_{k-2}+a(t_{k+2})u_{k+2}) \\ =\frac{237}{360}f(t_k)+\frac{31}{180}(f(t_{k-1})+f(t_{k+1}))-\frac{1}{720}(f(t_{k-2})+f(t_{k+2})), 2\le k\le N-2, \\ u_0=\varphi, u_N=\omega, \\ \tau^{-1}\Big(\Big(-11+\frac{1}{20}\tau^4\Big)u_0+\Big(18+\frac{11}{10}\tau^4\Big)u_1+(-9+\frac{7}{20}\tau^4)u_2+2u_3\Big)=\psi, \\ \tau^{-1}\Big(\Big(11-\frac{1}{20}\tau^4\Big)u_N-\Big(18+\frac{11}{10}\tau^4\Big)u_{N-1}+(9-\frac{7}{20}\tau^4)u_{N-2}-2u_{N-3}\Big)=\chi \end{cases}$$

was discussed in the research paper [13]. We now consider the sixth-order approximation formulas for $v'(0)$ and $v'(T)$, and Taylor decomposition on five points forms the basis for difference scheme (2)'s construction.

Theorem 3 ([13]). *Let $v(t)$ be a function with a continuous tenth derivative on $(0\le t\le T)$. Then, the following holds:*

$$\tau^{-4}(v(t_{k+2})-4v(t_{k+1})+6v(t_k)-4v(t_{k-1})+v(t_{k-2})) \tag{15}$$
$$-\frac{237}{360}v^{(4)}(t_k)-\frac{31}{180}(v^{(4)}(t_{k+1})+v^{(4)}(t_{k-1}))+\frac{1}{720}(v^{(4)}(t_{k+2})+v^{(4)}(t_{k-2}))=o(\tau^6).$$

Theorem 4 ([13]). *Let $v(t)$ be the function with a continuous seventh derivative $(0\le t\le T)$. The relation that follows thus holds:*

$$v'(0)-\tau^{-1}(-\frac{11}{6}v(0)+3v(\tau)-\frac{3}{2}v(2\tau)+\frac{1}{3}v(3\tau)) \tag{16}$$
$$+\tau^3\left\{\frac{1}{120}v^{(4)}(0)+\frac{11}{60}v^{(4)}(\tau)+\frac{7}{120}v^{(4)}(2\tau)\right\}=o(\tau^6),$$
$$v'(T)-\tau^{-1}(\frac{11}{6}v(T)-3v(T-\tau)+\frac{3}{2}v(T-2\tau)-\frac{1}{3}v(T-3\tau)) \tag{17}$$
$$+\tau^3\left\{-\frac{1}{120}v^{(4)}(T)-\frac{11}{60}v^{(4)}(T-\tau)-\frac{7}{120}v^{(4)}(T-2\tau)\right\}=o(\tau^6).$$

We used the sixth-order approximation difference scheme (2) to estimate the solution of problem (14) with different values of τ, namely $\tau=\frac{1}{40},\frac{1}{80},\frac{1}{160}$.

Remark 3. *Note that (see Table 3). It is observed that for the difference scheme (2), the value of errors between the exact solution and approximate solution decreases by a factor of about 1/8 if N is doubled. Thus, these difference schemes have an accuracy order of 3.*

Table 3. Errors of difference schemes (2).

$\tau=\frac{1}{N}$	$N=40$	$N=80$	$N=160$
Difference Scheme (2)	5.6162×10^{-7}	1.8675×10^{-7}	3.2178×10^{-8}

We obtain new sixth-order approximation formulas for $v'(0)$ and $v'(T)$ in the present paper.

Theorem 5. *Let $v(t)$ be the function with a seventh continuous derivative $(0\le t\le T)$. The relation that follows thus holds:*

$$v'(0)-\tau^{-1}\left\{-\frac{49}{20}v(0)+6v(\tau)-\frac{15}{2}v(2\tau)+\frac{20}{3}v(3\tau)\right. \tag{18}$$

$$\left.-\frac{15}{4}v(4\tau)+\frac{6}{5}v(5\tau)-\frac{1}{6}v(6\tau)\right\}=o(\tau^6),$$

$$v'(T)-\tau^{-1}\left\{\frac{49}{20}v(T)-6v(T-\tau)+\frac{15}{2}v(T-2\tau)-\frac{20}{3}v(T-3\tau)\right. \tag{19}$$

$$\left.+\frac{15}{4}v(T-4\tau)-\frac{6}{5}v(T-5\tau)+\frac{1}{6}v(T-6\tau)\right\}=o(\tau^6).$$

Proof. Applying the undetermined coefficients method, we will seek

$$v'(0)=\alpha v(0)+\beta v(\tau)+\gamma v(2\tau)+dv(3\tau) \tag{20}$$

$$+pv(4\tau)+qv(5\tau)+mv(6\tau)+o\left(\tau^6\right)$$

It can be written using Taylor's formula that

$$v'(0)=\alpha v(0)+\beta\Bigg(v(0)+v'(0)\tau+v''(0)\frac{\tau^2}{2!}+v'''(0)\frac{\tau^3}{3!}+v^{(4)}(0)\frac{\tau^4}{4!}+v^{(5)}(0)\frac{\tau^5}{5!}$$

$$+v^{(6)}(0)\frac{\tau^6}{6!}+o\left(\tau^7\right)\Bigg)$$

$$+\gamma\Bigg(v(0)+2v'(0)\tau+4v''(0)\frac{\tau^2}{2!}+8v'''(0)\frac{\tau^3}{3!}+16v^{(4)}(0)\frac{\tau^4}{4!}+32v^{(5)}(0)\frac{\tau^5}{5!}$$

$$+64v^{(6)}(0)\frac{\tau^6}{6!}+o\left(\tau^7\right)\Bigg)$$

$$+d\Bigg(v(0)+3v'(0)\tau+9v''(0)\frac{\tau^2}{2!}+27v'''(0)\frac{\tau^3}{3!}+81v^{(4)}(0)\frac{\tau^4}{4!}+243v^{(5)}(0)\frac{\tau^5}{5!}$$

$$+729v^{(6)}(0)\frac{\tau^6}{6!}+o\left(\tau^7\right)\Bigg)$$

$$+p\Bigg(v(0)+4v'(0)\tau+(4)^2v''(0)\frac{\tau^2}{2!}+(4)^3v'''(0)\frac{\tau^3}{3!}+(4)^4v^{(4)}(0)\frac{\tau^4}{4!}+(4)^5v^{(5)}(0)\frac{\tau^5}{5!}$$

$$+(4)^6v^{(6)}(0)\frac{\tau^6}{6!}+o\left(\tau^7\right)\Bigg)$$

$$+q\Bigg(v(0)+5v'(0)\tau+(5)^2v''(0)\frac{\tau^2}{2!}+(5)^3v'''(0)\frac{\tau^3}{3!}+(5)^4v^{(4)}(0)\frac{\tau^4}{4!}+(5)^5v^{(5)}(0)\frac{\tau^5}{5!}$$

$$+(5)^6 v^{(6)}(0)\frac{\tau^6}{6!}+o\left(\tau^7\right)\Big)$$

$$+m\left(v(0)+6v'(0)\tau+(6)^2 v''(0)\frac{\tau^2}{2!}+(6)^3 v'''(0)\frac{\tau^3}{3!}+(6)^4 v^{(4)}(0)\frac{\tau^4}{4!}+(6)^5 v^{(5)}(0)\frac{\tau^5}{5!}\right.$$

$$\left.+(6)^6 v^{(6)}(0)\frac{\tau^6}{6!}+o\left(\tau^7\right)\right)+o\left(\tau^6\right).$$

A system of equations is then obtained by equating the coefficients of the lowest power of τ in the formula above to zero.

$$\begin{cases} -\alpha-\beta-\gamma-d-p-q-m=0, \\ \beta+2\gamma+3d+4p+5q+6m=\tau^{-1}, \\ \frac{1}{2!}\beta+\frac{4}{2!}\gamma+\frac{9}{2!}d+\frac{(4)^2}{2!}p+\frac{(5)^2}{2!}q+\frac{(6)^2}{2!}m=0, \\ \frac{1}{3!}\beta+\frac{8}{3!}\gamma+\frac{27}{3!}d+\frac{(4)^3}{3!}p+\frac{(5)^3}{3!}q+\frac{(6)^3}{3!}m=0, \\ \frac{1}{4!}\beta+\frac{16}{4!}\gamma+\frac{81}{4!}d+\frac{(4)^4}{4!}p+\frac{(5)^4}{4!}q+\frac{(6)^4}{4!}m=0, \\ \frac{1}{5!}\beta+\frac{32}{5!}\gamma+\frac{243}{5!}d+\frac{(4)^5}{5!}p+\frac{(5)^5}{5!}q+\frac{(6)^5}{5!}m=0, \\ \frac{1}{6!}\beta+\frac{64}{6!}\gamma+\frac{729}{6!}d+\frac{(4)^6}{6!}p+\frac{(5)^6}{6!}q+\frac{(6)^6}{6!}m=0. \end{cases}$$

Solving this system of equations, we can obtain $\alpha=-\frac{49}{20\tau},\beta=\frac{6}{\tau},\gamma=-\frac{15}{2\tau}$, $d=\frac{20}{3\tau},p=-\frac{15}{4\tau},q=\frac{6}{5\tau},m=-\frac{1}{6\tau}$. So, relation (18) is proved. Similarly, relation (19) can be proved. Theorem 5 is proved.

We obtain the fourth order of approximation difference schemes by applying Taylor decomposition on five points (15), Equation (1), and Formulas (18) and (19), and neglecting small terms.

$$\begin{cases} \frac{1}{\tau^4}\{u_{k+2}-4u_{k+1}+6u_k-4u_{k-1}+u_{k-2}\}+\frac{237}{360}a(t_k)u_k \\ +\frac{31}{180}(a(t_{k-1})u_{k-1}+a(t_{k+1})u_{k+1})-\frac{1}{720}(a(t_{k-2})u_{k-2}+a(t_{k+2})u_{k+2}) \\ =\frac{237}{360}f(t_k)+\frac{31}{180}\left(f(t_{k-1})+f(t_{k+1})-\frac{1}{720}f(t_{k-2})+f(t_{k+2})\right), 2\le k\le N-2, \\ u_0=\varphi, \tau^{-1}(-\frac{49}{20}u_0+6u_1-\frac{15}{2}u_2+\frac{20}{3}u_3-\frac{15}{4}u_4+\frac{6}{5}u_5-\frac{1}{6}u_6)=\psi, \\ \tau^{-1}(\frac{49}{20}u_N-6u_{N-1}+\frac{15}{2}u_{N-2}-\frac{20}{3}u_{N-3}+\frac{15}{4}u_{N-4}-\frac{6}{5}u_{N-5}+\frac{1}{6}u_{N-6})=\chi, u_N=\omega \end{cases} \tag{21}$$

for the numerical solution of the boundary value problem (1). It can be seen that for the approximate solution of problem (14), the accuracy order of this difference method is 6. We used the sixth order of approximation difference scheme (21) with different values of τ, namely $\tau=\frac{1}{40},\frac{1}{80},\frac{1}{160}$. □

Remark 4. *Note that (see Table 4). It is observed that for difference schemes (21), the value of errors between the exact solution and approximate solution decreases by a factor of about 1/64 if N is doubled. Thus, these difference schemes have an accuracy order of 6.*

Table 4. Errors of difference schemes (21).

$\tau=\frac{1}{N}$	$N=40$	$N=80$	$N=160$
Difference Scheme (21)	1.5237×10^{-7}	2.5606×10^{-9}	4.0844×10^{-11}

3. Local Boundary Value Problem (2)

We consider the boundary value problem (2). Theorem 3 and the fourth-order approximation formulas for $v''(0)$ and $v''(T)$ form the basis for the construction of the difference schemes of the fourth order of approximation for the approximate solution of problem (2).

Theorem 6. *Let $v(t)$ be a function with a continuous sixth derivative on $(0 \leq t \leq T)$. Then, the following holds:*

$$v''(0) - \tau^{-2}\left\{\frac{15}{4}v(0) - \frac{77}{6}v(\tau) + \frac{107}{6}v(2\tau) - 13v(3\tau)\right. \quad (22)$$

$$\left.+\frac{61}{12}v(4\tau) - \frac{5}{6}v(5\tau)\right\} = o(\tau^4),$$

$$v''(T) - \tau^{-2}\left\{\frac{15}{4}v(T) - \frac{77}{6}v(T-\tau) + \frac{107}{6}v(T-2\tau) - 13v(T-3\tau)\right. \quad (23)$$

$$\left.+\frac{61}{12}v(T-4\tau) - \frac{5}{6}v(T-5\tau)\right\} = o(\tau^4).$$

Proof. Applying the undetermined coefficients method, we will seek

$$v''(0) - \alpha v(0) + \beta v(\tau) + \gamma v(2\tau) + dv(3\tau) + pv(4\tau) + qv(5\tau) + o\left(\tau^4\right). \quad (24)$$

It can be written using Taylor's formula that

$$v''(0)\tau^2 = \alpha v(0) + \beta\left(v(0) + v'(0)\tau + v''(0)\frac{\tau^2}{2!} + v'''(0)\frac{\tau^3}{3!} + v^{(4)}(0)\frac{\tau^4}{4!} + v^{(5)}(0)\frac{\tau^5}{5!} + o(\tau^6)\right)$$

$$+\gamma\left(v(0) + 2v'(0)\tau + 4v''(0)\frac{\tau^2}{2!} + 8v'''(0)\frac{\tau^3}{3!} + 16v^{(4)}(0)\frac{\tau^4}{4!} + 32v^{(5)}(0)\frac{\tau^5}{5!} + o(\tau^6)\right)$$

$$+d\left(v(0) + 3v'(0)\tau + 9v''(0)\frac{\tau^2}{2!} + 27v'''(0)\frac{\tau^3}{3!} + 81v^{(4)}(0)\frac{\tau^4}{4!} + 243v^{(5)}(0)\frac{\tau^5}{5!} + o(\tau^6)\right)$$

$$+p\left(v(0) + 4v'(0)\tau + (4)^2v''(0)\frac{\tau^2}{2!} + (4)^3v'''(0)\frac{\tau^3}{3!} + (4)^4v^{(4)}(0)\frac{\tau^4}{4!} + (4)^5v^{(5)}(0)\frac{\tau^5}{5!} + o(\tau^6)\right)$$

$$+q\left(v(0) + 5v'(0)\tau + (5)^2v''(0)\frac{\tau^2}{2!} + (5)^3v'''(0)\frac{\tau^3}{3!} + (5)^4v^{(4)}(0)\frac{\tau^4}{4!} + (5)^5v^{(5)}(0)\frac{\tau^5}{5!} + o(\tau^6)\right)$$

$$+o(\tau^4).$$

The system of equations is then obtained by equating the coefficients of the lowest power of τ in the formula above to zero.

$$\begin{cases} -\alpha - \beta - \gamma - d - p - q = 0, \\ \beta + 2\gamma + 3d + 4p + 5q = 0, \\ \frac{1}{2!}\beta + \frac{4}{2!}\gamma + \frac{9}{2!}d + \frac{(4)^2}{2!}p + \frac{(5)^2}{2!}q = \tau^{-2}, \\ \frac{1}{3!}\beta + \frac{8}{3!}\gamma + \frac{27}{3!}d + \frac{(4)^3}{3!}p + \frac{(5)^3}{3!}q + \frac{(6)^3}{3!}m + \frac{(7)^3}{3!}n = 0, \\ \frac{1}{4!}\beta + \frac{16}{4!}\gamma + \frac{81}{4!}d + \frac{(4)^4}{4!}p + \frac{(5)^4}{4!}q = 0, \\ \frac{1}{5!}\beta + \frac{32}{5!}\gamma + \frac{243}{5!}d + \frac{(4)^5}{5!}p + \frac{(5)^5}{5!}q = 0. \end{cases}$$

Solving this system of equations, we can obtain $\alpha = \frac{15}{4\tau^2}, \beta = -\frac{77}{6\tau^2}, \gamma = \frac{107}{6\tau^2}$, $d = \frac{-13}{\tau^2}$, $p = \frac{61}{12\tau^2}, q = -\frac{5}{6\tau^2}$. So, relation (22) is proved. Likewise, one can prove relation (23). This is the end of the proof of Theorem 6.

We now have the fourth order of approximation difference schemes by applying Taylor decomposition on five points (6), Equation (2), and Formulas (22) and (23), and neglecting small terms.

$$\begin{cases} \frac{1}{\tau^4}\{u_{k+2}-4u_{k+1}+6u_k-4u_{k-1}+u_{k-2}\}+\frac{2}{3}a(t_k)u_k \\ +\frac{1}{6}(a(t_{k-1})u_{k-1}+a(t_{k+1})u_{k+1}) \\ =\frac{2}{3}f(t_k)+\frac{1}{6}(f(t_{k-1})+f(t_{k+1})), 2\le k\le N-2, \\ u_0=\varphi, \tau^{-2}(\frac{15}{4}u_0-\frac{77}{6}u_1+\frac{107}{6}u_2-13u_3+\frac{61}{12}u_4-\frac{5}{6}u_5)=y''(0), \\ \tau^{-2}(\frac{15}{4}u_N-\frac{77}{6}u_{N-1}+\frac{107}{6}u_{N-2}-13u_{N-3}+\frac{61}{12}u_{N-4}-\frac{5}{6}u_{N-5})=y''(T), \\ u_N=\omega \end{cases} \tag{25}$$

and

$$\begin{cases} \frac{1}{\tau^4}\{u_{k+2}-4u_{k+1}+6u_k-4u_{k-1}+u_{k-2}\}+\frac{11}{12}a(t_k)u_k \\ +\frac{1}{24}(a(t_{k-2})u_{k-2}+a(t_{k+2})u_{k+2}) \\ =\frac{11}{12}f(t_k)+\frac{1}{24}(f(t_{k-2})+f(t_{k+2})), 2\le k\le N-2, \\ u_0=\varphi, \tau^{-2}(\frac{15}{4}u_0-\frac{77}{6}u_1+\frac{107}{6}u_2-13u_3+\frac{61}{12}u_4-\frac{5}{6}u_5)=y''(0), \\ u_0=\varphi, \tau^{-2}(\frac{15}{4}u_0-\frac{77}{6}u_1+\frac{107}{6}u_2-13u_3+\frac{61}{12}u_4-\frac{5}{6}u_5) \\ =y''(0), \\ \tau^{-2}(\frac{15}{4}u_N-\frac{77}{6}u_{N-1}+\frac{107}{6}u_{N-2}-13u_{N-3}+\frac{61}{12}u_{N-4}-\frac{5}{6}u_{N-5})=y''(T), \\ u_N=\omega \end{cases} \tag{26}$$

for boundary value problem (2)'s numerical solution. In Section 3, we consider the boundary value problem in numerical analysis

$$\begin{cases} \frac{d^4u(t)}{dt^4}+u(t)=4!-4\cdot 5!t+6\cdot\frac{6!}{2!}t^2-4\cdot\frac{7!}{3!}t^3+\frac{8!}{4!}t^4+t^4(1-t)^4, 0<t<1, \\ u(0)=u(1)=u''(0)=u''(1)=0, \end{cases} \tag{27}$$

with the exact solution

$$u(t)=t^4(1-t)^4.$$

Note that we utilised the fourth order of approximation difference schemes (25) and (26) for the approximate solution of this problem (14) with different values of τ, namely $\tau=\frac{1}{80},\frac{1}{160},\frac{1}{320}$. □

Remark 5. *Note that (see Table 5). It is observed that for difference schemes (25) and (26), the value of errors between the exact solution and approximate solution decreases by a factor of about 1/16 if N is doubled. Thus, these difference schemes have an accuracy order of* 4.

Table 5. Errors of difference schemes (25) and (26).

$\tau=\frac{1}{N}$	$N=80$	$N=160$	$N=320$
Difference Scheme (25)	8.7410×10^{-6}	5.8235×10^{-7}	3.7504×10^{-8}
Difference Scheme (26)	8.2124×10^{-6}	5.4930×10^{-7}	3.5437×10^{-8}

The approximation difference scheme of the sixth order is now under consideration for the approximate solution of problem (2). Theorem 3 and the sixth-order approximation formulas for $v''(0)$ and $v''(T)$ form the basis for the construction of the sixth-order approximation for the approximate solution of problem (1).

Theorem 7. *Let $v(t)$ be a function with a continuous eighth derivative on $(0 \le t \le T)$. Then, the following holds:*

$$v''(0) - \tau^{-2}\left\{\frac{469}{90}v(0) - \frac{223}{10}v(\tau) + \frac{879}{20}v(2\tau) - \frac{949}{18}v(3\tau)\right. \tag{28}$$

$$\left. +41v(4\tau) - \frac{201}{10}v(5\tau) + \frac{1019}{180}v(6\tau) - \frac{7}{10}v(7\tau)\right\} = o(\tau^6),$$

$$v''(T) - \tau^{-2}\left\{\frac{469}{90}v(T) - \frac{223}{10}v(T-\tau) + \frac{879}{20}v(T-2\tau) - \frac{949}{18}v(T-3\tau)\right. \tag{29}$$

$$\left. +41v(T-4\tau) - \frac{201}{10}v(T-5\tau) + \frac{1019}{180}v(T-6\tau) - \frac{7}{10}v(T-7\tau)\right\} = o(\tau^6).$$

Proof. Applying the undetermined coefficients method, we will seek

$$v''(0)\tau^2 = \alpha v(0) + \beta v(\tau) + \gamma v(2\tau) + dv(3\tau) + pv(4\tau) + qv(5\tau) + mv(6\tau) + nv(7\tau) + o\left(\tau^6\right). \tag{30}$$

Using Taylor's formula, we get

$$v''(0)\tau^2 = \alpha v(0) + \beta\left(v(0) + v'(0)\tau + v''(0)\frac{\tau^2}{2!} + v'''(0)\frac{\tau^3}{3!} + v^{(4)}(0)\frac{\tau^4}{4!} + v^{(5)}(0)\frac{\tau^5}{5!}\right.$$

$$\left. +v^{(6)}(0)\frac{\tau^6}{6!} + v^{(7)}(0)\frac{\tau^7}{7!} + o\left(\tau^8\right)\right)$$

$$+\gamma\left(v(0) + 2v'(0)\tau + 4v''(0)\frac{\tau^2}{2!} + 8v'''(0)\frac{\tau^3}{3!} + 16v^{(4)}(0)\frac{\tau^4}{4!} + 32v^{(5)}(0)\frac{\tau^5}{5!}\right.$$

$$\left. +64v^{(6)}(0)\frac{\tau^6}{6!} + 128v^{(7)}(0)\frac{\tau^7}{7!} + o\left(\tau^8\right)\right)$$

$$+d\left(v(0) + 3v'(0)\tau + 9v''(0)\frac{\tau^2}{2!} + 27v'''(0)\frac{\tau^3}{3!} + 81v^{(4)}(0)\frac{\tau^4}{4!} + 243v^{(5)}(0)\frac{\tau^5}{5!}\right.$$

$$\left. +729v^{(6)}(0)\frac{\tau^6}{6!} + 2187v^{(7)}(0)\frac{\tau^7}{7!} + o\left(\tau^8\right)\right)$$

$$+p\left(v(0) + 4v'(0)\tau + 4^2v''(0)\frac{\tau^2}{2!} + 4^3v'''(0)\frac{\tau^3}{3!} + 4^4v^{(4)}(0)\frac{\tau^4}{4!}\right.$$

$$\left. +4^5v^{(5)}(0)\frac{\tau^5}{5!} + 4^6v^{(6)}(0)\frac{\tau^6}{6!} + 4^7v^{(7)}(0)\frac{\tau^7}{7!} + o\left(\tau^8\right)\right)$$

$$+q\left(v(0) + 5v'(0)\tau + 5^2v''(0)\frac{\tau^2}{2!} + 5^3v'''(0)\frac{\tau^3}{3!} + 5^4v^{(4)}(0)\frac{\tau^4}{4!}\right.$$

$$\left. +5^5v^{(5)}(0)\frac{\tau^5}{5!} + 5^6v^{(6)}(0)\frac{\tau^6}{6!} + 5^7v^{(7)}(0)\frac{\tau^7}{7!} + o\left(\tau^8\right)\right)$$

$$+m\left(v(0) + 6v'(0)\tau + 6^2v''(0)\frac{\tau^2}{2!} + 6^3v'''(0)\frac{\tau^3}{3!} + 6^4v^{(4)}(0)\frac{\tau^4}{4!}\right.$$

$$+6^5v^{(5)}(0)\frac{\tau^5}{5!}+6^6v^{(6)}(0)\frac{\tau^6}{6!}+6^7v^{(7)}(0)\frac{\tau^7}{7!}+o\left(\tau^8\right)\Big)$$

$$+n\left(v(0)+7v'(0)\tau+7^2v''(0)\frac{\tau^2}{2!}+7^3v'''(0)\frac{\tau^3}{3!}+7^4v^{(4)}(0)\frac{\tau^4}{4!}\right.$$

$$\left.+7^5v^{(5)}(0)\frac{\tau^5}{5!}+7^6v^{(6)}(0)\frac{\tau^6}{6!}+7^7v^{(7)}(0)\frac{\tau^7}{7!}+o\left(\tau^8\right)\right)+o\left(\tau^6\right).$$

Equating the coefficients of the lowest power of τ in the last formula to zero, we obtain the system of equations

$$\begin{cases} -\alpha-\beta-\gamma-d-p-q-m-n=0, \\ \beta+2\gamma+3d+4p+5q+6m+7n=0, \\ \frac{1}{2!}\beta+\frac{4}{2!}\gamma+\frac{9}{2!}d+\frac{(4)^2}{2!}p+\frac{(5)^2}{2!}q+\frac{(6)^2}{2!}m+\frac{(7)^2}{2!}n=\tau^{-2}, \\ \frac{1}{3!}\beta+\frac{8}{3!}\gamma+\frac{27}{3!}d+\frac{(4)^3}{3!}p+\frac{(5)^3}{3!}q+\frac{(6)^3}{3!}m+\frac{(7)^3}{3!}n=0, \\ \frac{1}{4!}\beta+\frac{16}{4!}\gamma+\frac{81}{4!}d+\frac{(4)^4}{4!}p+\frac{(5)^4}{4!}q+\frac{(6)^4}{4!}m+\frac{(7)^4}{4!}n=0, \\ \frac{1}{5!}\beta+\frac{32}{5!}\gamma+\frac{243}{5!}d+\frac{(4)^5}{5!}p+\frac{(5)^5}{5!}q+\frac{(6)^5}{5!}m+\frac{(7)^5}{5!}n=0, \\ \frac{1}{6!}\beta+\frac{64}{6!}\gamma+\frac{729}{6!}d+\frac{(4)^6}{6!}p+\frac{(5)^6}{6!}q+\frac{(6)^6}{6!}m+\frac{(7)^6}{6!}n=0, \\ \frac{1}{7!}\beta+\frac{(2)^7}{7!}\gamma+\frac{(3)^7}{7!}d+\frac{(4)^7}{7!}p+\frac{(5)^7}{7!}q+\frac{(6)^7}{7!}m+\frac{(7)^7}{7!}n=0. \end{cases}$$

Solving this system of equations, we can obtain $\alpha=\frac{469}{90\tau^2},\beta=-\frac{223}{10\tau^2},\gamma=\frac{879}{20\tau^2}$, $d=-\frac{949}{18\tau^2}$, $p=\frac{41}{\tau^2},q=-\frac{201}{10\tau^2}$, $m=\frac{1019}{180\tau^2},n=-\frac{7}{10\tau^2}$. So, relation (28) is proved. Similarly, one can prove relation (29). Theorem 7 is proved.

Applying Taylor's decomposition on five points (15), Equation (2), and Formulas (28) and (29) and neglecting small terms, we get the sixth-order approximation difference scheme.

We obtain the sixth order of approximation difference schemes by applying Taylor decomposition on five points (15), Equation (2), and Formulas (28) and (29), and neglecting small terms.

$$\begin{cases} \frac{1}{\tau^4}\{u_{k+2}-4u_{k+1}+6u_k-4u_{k-1}+u_{k-2}\}+\frac{237}{360}a(t_k)u_k \\ +\frac{31}{180}(a(t_{k-1})u_{k-1}+a(t_{k+1})u_{k+1})-\frac{1}{720}(a(t_{k-2})u_{k-2}+a(t_{k+2})u_{k+2}) \\ =\frac{237}{360}f(t_k)+\frac{31}{180}\left(f(t_{k-1})+f(t_{k+1})-\frac{1}{720}(f(t_{k-2})+f(t_{k+2}))\right), 2\le k\le N-2, \\ u_0=\varphi, u_N=\omega, \\ \tau^{-2}(\frac{469}{90}u_0-\frac{223}{10}u_1+\frac{879}{20}u_2-\frac{949}{18}u_3+41u_4-\frac{201}{10}u_5+\frac{1019}{180}u_6-\frac{7}{10}u_7)=y''(0), \\ \tau^{-2}(\frac{469}{90}u_N-\frac{223}{10}u_{N-1}+\frac{879}{20}u_{N-2}-\frac{949}{18}u_{N-3}+41u_{N-4}-\frac{201}{10}u_{N-5}+\frac{1019}{180}u_{N-6}-\frac{7}{10}u_{N-7}) \\ =y''(T) \end{cases} \quad (31)$$

for the numerical solution of boundary value problem (2). It can be seen that, for the approximate solution of problem (27), the accuracy order of this difference method is 6. We used the sixth order of approximation difference scheme (31) with different values of τ, namely $\tau=\frac{1}{40},\frac{1}{80},\frac{1}{160}$. □

Remark 6. *Note that (see Table 6). It is observed that for difference schemes (31), the value of errors between the exact solution and approximate solution decreases by a factor of about* $1/64$ *if* N *is doubled. Thus, these difference schemes have an accuracy order of* 6.

Table 6. Errors of difference scheme (31).

$\tau = \frac{1}{N}$	$N = 40$	$N = 180$	$N = 160$
Difference Scheme (31)	7.8925×10^{-7}	1.2332×10^{-8}	1.8981×10^{-10}

4. Conclusions and Our Future Plans

1. Two boundary value problems for fourth-order differential equations with dependent coefficients are investigated in this article. To solve these problems, the fourth- and sixth-order approximation finite difference schemes generated by Taylor's decomposition on five points are constructed and investigated. The results of numerical experiments support the numerical results. Our results and methods can be utilised to extend nonlinear and partial differential equations in the future.

2. We established and investigated highly accurate four-step difference schemes for the numerical solution of boundary value problems related to general differential equations of the fourth order.

$$\frac{d^4u(t)}{dt^4} + d(t)\frac{d^3u(t)}{dt^3} + c(t)\frac{d^2u(t)}{dt^2} + b(t)\frac{du(t)}{dt} + a(t)u(t) = f(t), 0 < t < T.$$

Here, $a(t), b(t), c(t), d(t)$, and $f(t)$ are given smooth functions defined on $[0, T]$.

Here, we have smooth given functions $a(t), b(t), c(t), d(t)$, and $f(t)$ defined on $[0, T]$.

3. We developed and investigated highly accurate four-step difference schemes for the numerical solution of both local and non-local problems related to abstract fourth-order elliptic differential equations:

$$\frac{d^4u(t)}{dt^4} + A(t)u(t) = f(t), 0 < t < T$$

given the self-adjoint positive definite operators $A(t)$ in a Hilbert space H. Note that we will be able to determine the stability of these difference schemes via the operator approach in [16].

Author Contributions: All authors contributed equally to this work. A.A. and I.M.I. wrote the main text of the manuscript. All authors have read and agreed to the published version of the manuscript.

Funding: This research received no external funding.

Data Availability Statement: Data are contained within the article.

Acknowledgments: The publication was prepared with the support of the "RUDN University Program 5-100" and published under target program BR05236656 of the Science Committee of the Ministry of Education and Science of the Republic of Kazakhstan.

Conflicts of Interest: The authors declare no conflict of interest.

Abbreviations

The following abbreviations are used in this manuscript:

IBVP	Initial Boundary Value Problem
IVP	Initial Value Problem
BS	Bounded Solution
ODES	Ordinary Differential Equation
PDES	Partial Differential Equation
DE	Differential Equation
FSADSs	First- and Second-Order Accuracy Difference Schemes
ES	Exact Solution
FADS	First-Order Accuracy Difference Scheme
SADS	Second-Order Accuracy Difference Scheme

AS	Approximate Solution
SE	System of Equations
SLEs	System of Linear Equations
DS	Difference Scheme

References

1. Ashyralyev, A.; Sobolevskii, P.E. On the two new approaches for the construction of the high order approximation difference schemes for the second-order differential equations. *Funct. Differ. Equ.* **2003**, *10*, 333–405.
2. Ashyralyev, A.; Sobolevskii, P.E. On the two-step the High-order approximation difference schemes for the second-order differential equations. *Proc. Dyn. Syst. Appl.* **2004**, *4*, 528–535.
3. Ashyralyev, A.; Sobolevskii, P.E. *New Difference Schemes for Partial Differential Equations*; Birkhauser Verlag: Basel, Switzerland; Boston, MA, USA; Berlin, Germany, 2004.
4. Boureghda, A. Numerical solution of the oxygen diffusion in absorbing tissue with a moving boundary. *Commun. Numer. Methods Eng.* **2006**, *22*, 933–942. [CrossRef]
5. Boureghda, A.; Djellab, N. Du Fort-Frankel Finite difference scheme for solving of oxygen diffusion problem inside one cell. *J. Comput. Theor. Transp.* **2023**, *52*, 363–373. [CrossRef]
6. Ashyralyev, A.; Arjmand, D. A note on the Taylor's decomposition on four points for a third-order differential equation. *Appl. Math. Comput.* **2007**, *188*, 1483–1490. [CrossRef]
7. Ashyralyev, A.; Arjmand, D.; Koksal, M. Taylor's decomposition on four points for solving third-order linear time-varying systems. *J. Frankl. Inst. Eng. Appl. Math.* **2009**, *346*, 651–662. [CrossRef]
8. Arjmand, D. Highly Accurate Difference Schemes for the Numerical Solution of Third-Order Ordinary and Partial Differential Equations. Master's Thesis, KTH Royal Institute of Technology, Stockholm, Sweden, 2010.
9. Ashyralyeva, M.A. A note on the Taylor's decomposition on five points and its applications to differential equations. *Funct. Differ. Equ.* **2006**, *13*, 357–370.
10. Timoshenko, S.P. *Theory of Elastic Stability*; McGraw-Hill: New York, NY, USA, 1961.
11. Soedel, W. *Vibrations of Shells and Plates*; Dekker: New York, NY, USA, 1993.
12. Dulácska, E. Soil settlement effects on buildings. In *Developments in Geotechnical Engineering*; Elsevier: Amsterdam, The Netherlands, 1992; Volume 69.
13. Anderson, D.R.; Davis, J.M. Multiple solutions and eigenvalues for third-order right focal boundary value problem. *J. Math. Anal. Appl.* **2002**, *267*, 135–157. [CrossRef]
14. Baxley, J.; Haywood, L.J. Nonlinear boundary value problems with multiple solutions. *Nonlinear Anal.* **2001**, *47*, 1187–1198. [CrossRef]
15. Hao, Z.; Liu, L. A necessary and sufficient condition for the existence of positive solution of fourth-order singular boundary value problems. *Appl. Math. Lett.* **2003**, *16*, 279–285. [CrossRef]
16. Agarwal, R.P. *Focal Boundary Value Problems for Differential and Difference Equations*; Kluwer Academic: Dordrecht, The Netherlands, 1998.
17. Agarwal, R.P.; O'Regan, O.; Wong, P.J.Y. *Positive Solutions of Differential, Difference, and Integral Equations*; Kluwer Academic: Dordrecht, The Netherlands, 1998.
18. Zill, D.G.; Cullen, M.R. *Differential Equations with Boundary-Value Problems*, 5th ed.; Brooks/Cole: Pacific Grove, CA, USA, 2001.
19. Wong, P.J.Y. Triple positive solutions of conjugate boundary value problems. *Comput. Math. Appl.* **1998**, *36*, 19–35. [CrossRef]
20. Leray, J.; Schauder, J. Topologie et Equations Fonctionels. *Ann. Sci. École Norm. Sup.* **1934**, *51*, 45–78. [CrossRef]
21. Graef, J.R.; Yang, B. On a nonlinear boundary value problem for fourth order equations. *Appl. Anal.* **1999**, *72*, 439–448. [CrossRef]
22. Hibbeler, R.C.; Nolan, G. *Structural Analysis*; Prentice Hall: Upper Saddle River, NJ, USA, 1997.

axioms MDPI

Article

Kink Wave Phenomena in the Nonlinear Partial Differential Equation Representing the Transmission Line Model of Microtubules for Nanoionic Currents

Safyan Mukhtar [1,2,*], Weaam Alhejaili [3], Mohammad Alqudah [4], Ali M. Mahnashi [5], Rasool Shah [6,*] and Samir A. El-Tantawy [7,8]

1 General Administration of Preparatory Year, King Faisal University, Al-Ahsa 31982, Saudi Arabia
2 Department of Mathematics and Statistics, College of Science, King Faisal University, Al-Ahsa 31982, Saudi Arabia
3 Department of Mathematical Sciences, College of Science, Princess Nourah bint Abdulrahman University, P.O. Box 84428, Riyadh 11671, Saudi Arabia; waalhejali@pnu.edu.sa
4 Department of Basic Sciences, School of Electrical Engineering & Information Technology, German Jordanian University, Amman 11180, Jordan; mohammad.qudah@gju.edu.jo
5 Department of Mathematics, Faculty of Science, Jazan University, P.O. Box 2097, Jazan 45142, Saudi Arabia; amahnashi@jazanu.edu.sa
6 Department of Computer Science and Mathematics, Lebanese American University, Beirut 1102 2801, Lebanon
7 Department of Physics, Faculty of Science, Port Said University, Port Said 42521, Egypt; tantawy@sci.psu.edu.eg
8 Department of Physics, Faculty of Science, Al-Baha University, Al-Baha 1988, Saudi Arabia
* Correspondence: smahmad@kfu.edu.sa (S.M.); rasoolshah@awkum.edu.pk or rasool.shah@lau.edu.lb (R.S.)

Abstract: This paper provides several new traveling wave solutions for a nonlinear partial differential equation (PDE) by applying symbolic computation and a new approach, the Riccati–Bernoulli sub-ODE method, in a computer algebra system. Herein, employing the Bäcklund transformation, we solve a nonlinear PDE associated with nanobiosciences and biophysics based on the transmission line model of microtubules for nanoionic currents. The equation introduced here in this form is suitable for critical nanoscience concerns like cell signaling and might continue to explain some of the basic cognitive functions in neurons. We employ advanced procedures to replicate the previously detected solitary waves. We offer our solutions in graphical forms, such as 3*D* and contour plots, using Mathematica. We can generalize the elementary method to other nonlinear equations in physics, requiring only a few steps.

Keywords: Bäcklund transformation; soliton; microtubules; non-linear RLC transmission line; Riccatti equation; symbolic computation; traveling wave solutions

MSC: 35A24; 35C08; 35G20; 44A05

1. Introduction

Bifurcated processes are central to dynamics in applied mathematics and theoretical physics. Finding exact numerical solutions for functions of separated variables is a key part of soliton theory. In particular, traveling wave solutions for nonlinear equations in mathematical physics are very important. In recent years, the search for exact solutions to nonlinear partial differential equations (PDEs) has become a focus. Using specific software, such as MATLAB V2020, Maple V18, and Mathematica V31.1 or any above version makes the difference, as these softwares help carry out complicated algebraic manipulations. Obtaining the exact solutions to these equations is always required since they represent real-life problems in many engineering disciplines, including chemistry, biology, mechanics, and applied physics. Engineers and physicists have developed several efficient approaches to grasp the mechanisms of physical models and comprehend the fundamental issues that arise in underlying problems. Besides Hirota's bilinear method and the inverse scattering transform [1,2], there are other more effective ways to find the traveling wave explicit solitary solutions of nonlinear equations. These include the Painleve expansions method [3], the homogeneous balance method [4,5], the F-expansion method [6], and the Jacobi elliptic function method [7]. Only recently has the tanh-function method been used to find exact solutions for non-linear differential equations [8,9]. We emphasize that mathematicians have several powerful techniques to find new traveling wave solutions, among which are the Khater methods [10,11], G'/G-expansion method [12], Kudryashov method [13], exp-function method [14], Sin–Gordon method [15], and Sardar sub-equation method [16]. These approaches are pivotal for extending the research and application of solitons on non-linear fractional differential equations.

The objective of this study is to elaborate and demonstrate the effectiveness of the Ricatti–Bernoulli sub-ode approach using a new nonlinear partial differential equation (PDE). This is relevant to nanosciences, including the transmission line model for nanoionic currents along microtubules (MTs), which play a role in cellular signaling. The MTs are fibrous cytoplasmic biopolymers in nanotubes that enable cell movement, cell communication and transportation of substances and data inside neuronal extensions. Researchers have also suggested that MTs participate in higher neuronal functions such as memory and consciousness. Nevertheless, how MTs process and operate electrical signals is a mystery. For the first time, researchers formulated a concept for ionic waves along MTs based on the polyelectrolyte nature of cylindrical biopolymers. It is like an electric element, with capacitive, resistive, and negative incrementally resistive properties for each tubulin dimer protein [17]. Nanopores (NPs) between the dimers in the MT wall are given extra attention because they appear to function as ionic channels [18,19]. These stated NPs might help to describe the behavior of MTs as biomolecular transistors, which amplify electrical information in neurons. An analysis of their physical properties provides the foundation for the derivation of the following equation, which may define the ionic currents along MTs. These details are elaborated fully in [18], including the principles upon which they are based and the mathematics that underlie the process. This derivation describes in detail the mechanisms through which biopolymers contribute to the signaling events within cells, including the polyelectrolyte character of MTs, structural aspects of these proteins, and the behavior of nanoionic currents

$$r_2 c_0 l^2 \frac{\partial}{\partial t}\left(\frac{\partial^2 F}{\partial x^2}\right) + l^2 \frac{\partial^2 F}{\partial x^2} + 2 r_1 c_0 \gamma F \frac{\partial F}{\partial t} - r_1 c_0 \frac{\partial F}{\partial t}. \tag{1}$$

This study defines the transverse resistance $r_1 = 10^9\ \Omega$ and the longitudinal resistance $r_2 = 7 \times 10^6\ \Omega$ as elementary ring (ER) components. In a given MT, the parameter γ represents the nonlinearity of an ER capacitor. Here, setting the inductance $l = 8 \times 10^{-9}\ m$ and the total maximal capacitance (c_0) of the ER is $1.8 \times 10^{-15}\ F$. Sekulic et al. [20] studied the MT equation formulated in terms of the nonlinear RLC transmission line. To gain solitary wave solutions for the problem, they used the method called METF, the extended tanh-function, which was modified to analyze the behavior of ionic currents in microtubules successfully.

Nonlinear PDEs have recently gained significant attention due to their applications in science and engineering, particularly wave processes and biology. In the present work, we added to this field by applying symbolic computations and the Riccati–Bernoulli sub-ODE method with the Bäcklund transformation [21] to obtain new and multiple traveling wave solutions of nonlinear PDEs. This is crucial for nanosciences, biophysics, and applications directly related to the transmission line models of microtubules, which help transport ions in living cells. We specifically construct this nonlinear equation to solve fundamental nanoscience problems, particularly those involving cell signaling and the primary processes in neuron functioning. Thus, by presenting solutions in terms of 3D graphics and contour plots using Mathematica software, we can reproduce previously obtained solitary wave solutions employing a modern approach and present additional novel findings. One could argue that the generality of the presented method makes it more versatile in applying further nonlinear equations in physics, thereby supporting its use in tackling significant issues in complex systems. This work is timely and important because it not only contributes to the field of nonlinear dynamics but also provides opportunities for further investigation in the areas of biophysical modeling and cognitive science. Furthermore, several optional PDEs represent a problem to solve using the standard approaches. A preliminary method described in refs. [22–24] is known to resolve high-order algebraic solutions effectively and is utilized to discover standalone wave solutions. Indeed, these PDEs are transformed into algebraic equations using the Bäcklund transformation and the Riccati–Bernoulli equation. Consequently, we can apply this technique effectively to solve various issues in mathematical physics and evaluate its effectiveness to some extent. This methodology ensures finite solutions for the derived equations and gives efficient results for the investigated equations. As we know, it is a relative of PDEs, thus indicating its ability to produce infinitely many solutions, where the Bäcklund transformation is introduced as an infinite chain of solutions.

The present work employs the proposed methodology to solve nonlinear PDEs related to nanobiosciences as transmission lines and to model MTs as nonlinear RLCs. This illustrates the efficiency and utility of the proposed approach to target multifaceted biological organizations. By focusing on the nanoionic current flow, the qualitatively enhanced outcomes provide better insights into real-life physical difficulties and indicate the effective application of the introduced methods in numerous scientific disciplines. These results also provide further evidence of this approach's applicability in solving other nonlinear equations in a broad range of applications in physics and biology.

2. Methodology

The use of the Riccati–Bernoulli sub-ODE method is appropriate in solving very complex nonlinear partial differential equations (PDEs), particularly by simplifying them into simple and solvable ordinary differential equations (ODEs). This progression lessens the dimensionality of the problem by introducing traveling wave transformations. To illustrate the fundamental concept of the Ricatti–Bernoulli sub-ode method, we consider a given PDE with two variables, expressed as follows:

$$G\left(F, \frac{\partial F}{\partial x}, \frac{\partial F}{\partial t}, \frac{\partial^2 F}{\partial x^2}, \dots\right) = 0. \tag{2}$$

Making use of the traveling wave transformation $\zeta = x \pm ct$, one can transform the partial derivatives in the above PDE into ζ-derivatives, so the PDE can be expressed as an ODE. This prepares the ground for utilizing the Riccati–Bernoulli sub-ODE method, which systematically derives closed form solutions.

$$H\left(f, \frac{df}{d\zeta}, \frac{d^2 f}{d\zeta^2}, \frac{d^3 f}{d\zeta^3}, \dots\right) = 0. \tag{3}$$

Subsequently, we use the following series expansion as a solution to Equation (3):

$$f(x,t) = f(\zeta) = \sum_{i=-n}^{n} z_i R(\xi)^i, \tag{4}$$

with

$$R(\xi) = \frac{-Xk_2 + k_1\phi(\xi)}{k_1 + k_2\phi(\xi)}.$$

Here, we give a solution as the series expansion, in which $R(\xi)$ is inferred from the Bäcklund transformation, while $\phi(\xi)$ satisfies the Riccati equation, $\frac{d\phi}{d\xi} = X + \phi(\xi)^2$. It offers a systematic way to balance the nonlinear terms in the ODE and also remarkably reduces the higher-order derivatives. The Bäcklund transformation is essential in bringing in the term $R(\xi))$ in Equation (4), which requires that $\phi(\xi)$ satisfies the Riccati equation, a nonlinear ODE representing the way the newly transformed wave solutions would change. Herein lies the crucial bridge between the Bäcklund transformation and the Riccati–Bernoulli method. That is, while the Bäcklund transformation will yield new variables that will simplify the form or structure of the solution, it is the Riccati equation that describes, or dictates, how these variables would evolve. The constants (X) , (k_1) , and (k_2) are fixed parameters with $k_2 \neq 0$. Thus, the positive integer (n) can easily be balanced by equating the coefficient of the highest-order derivative term with the coefficient of the nonlinear terms in Equation (3). We substitute the series expansion, Equation (4), into the transformed ODE, Equation (2), to obtain an algebraic system of equations. The system arises naturally from the interaction of the Bäcklund transformation that represents $R(\xi)$)and the Riccati equation for $\phi(\xi)$, together with the given solution. The algebraic system leads to the constants (z_i) and wave velocity (c), which in turn give exact traveling wave solutions. Fortunately, the Riccati equation admits several types of solutions [25]:

$$\begin{aligned}
\phi(\xi) &= \begin{cases} -\sqrt{-X}\tanh(\sqrt{-X}\xi), & \text{as } X < 0, \\ -\sqrt{-X}\coth(\sqrt{-X}\xi), & \text{as } X < 0, \end{cases} \\
\phi(\xi) &= -\frac{1}{\xi}, \quad \text{as } X = 0, \\
\phi(\xi) &= \begin{cases} \sqrt{X}\tan(\sqrt{X}\xi), & \text{as } X > 0, \\ -\sqrt{X}\cot(\sqrt{X}\xi), & \text{as } X > 0. \end{cases}
\end{aligned} \tag{5}$$

3. Execution of the Problem

Next, we apply the method in the previous section to a new nonlinear PDE that is very important in nanosciences. This is the transmission line model, which shows nano-ionic currents moving along MTs and is a part of how cells communicate. To solve Equation (1), applying the proposed method, we use the traveling wave transformation

$$\chi = \frac{x}{l} - \frac{\omega t}{T},$$

where (ω) is the dimensionless velocity of the wave. The characteristic time for charging the ER capacitor is set as $T = r_1 c_0 = 1.32 \times 10^{-6}$. Thus, Equation (1) is converted into a set of ODEs:

$$\frac{d^2 f}{d\chi^2} - \frac{\kappa}{\omega}\frac{dF}{d\chi} + \frac{\nu}{2}\left(f^2\right) - \mu f = 0, \tag{6}$$

where $\kappa = \frac{T}{r_2 c_0}$, $\nu = \frac{2 r_1 \gamma}{r_2}$, $\gamma = \frac{r_1}{r_2}$, and $T = r_1 c_0 = 1.32 \times 10^{-6}$. Next, we compare the leading high-order derivative term with the leading high-order nonlinear term. By equating the order of (f) from the second equation with (f^2) in Equation (6), we obtain $n = 2$. Inserting Equation (4) into Equation (6), we obtain a system of algebraic equations. By solving the resulting system of algebraic equations using Maple, we can identify several distinct cases, as follows:

$$\begin{aligned}
&\phi^0 : \nu z_{-2}{}^2 k_2{}^8 \omega + 12 z_{-2} k_2{}^8 \omega X^2 = 0, \\
&\phi^1 : -4 z_{-1} k_2{}^8 \omega X^3 - 4\kappa z_{-2} k_2{}^8 X^2 - 2\nu z_{-2} k_2{}^8 z_{-1} \omega X = 0, \\
&\phi^2 : 2\kappa z_{-1} k_2{}^8 X^3 + 16 z_{-2} k_2{}^8 X^3 \omega - 2\mu z_{-2} k_2{}^8 \omega X^2 + \nu z_{-1}{}^2 k_2{}^8 \omega X^2 + 2\nu z_{-2} k_2{}^8 z_0 \omega X^2 = 0, \\
&\phi^3 : -2\nu z_{-1} k_2{}^8 z_0 \omega X^3 - 4 z_{-1} k_2{}^8 X^4 \omega - 4\kappa z_{-2} k_2{}^8 X^3 + 2\mu z_{-1} k_2{}^8 \omega X^3 - 2\nu z_{-2} k_2{}^8 z_1 X^3 \omega = 0, \\
&\phi^4 : \nu z_0{}^2 \omega k_2{}^8 X^4 + 2\nu z_{-2} k_2{}^8 z_2 X^4 \omega - 2\mu z_0 \omega k_2{}^8 X^4 + 2\kappa z_{-1} k_2{}^8 X^4 + 2\nu z_{-1} k_2{}^8 z_1 X^4 \omega + \\
&4 z_{-2} k_2{}^8 X^4 \omega + 4 z_2 k_2{}^8 X^6 \omega - 2\kappa z_1 k_2{}^8 X^5 = 0, \\
&\phi^5 : -4 z_1 k_2{}^8 X^6 \omega + 4\kappa z_2 k_2{}^8 X^6 - 2\nu z_0 z_1 X^5 k_2{}^8 \omega - 2\nu z_{-1} k_2{}^8 z_2 X^5 \omega + 2\mu z_1 X^5 k_2{}^8 \omega = 0, \\
&\phi^6 : 2\nu z_0 z_2 X^6 k_2{}^8 \omega - 2\kappa z_1 k_2{}^8 X^6 + 16 z_2 k_2{}^8 X^7 \omega - 2\mu z_2 X^6 k_2{}^8 \omega + \nu z_1{}^2 X^6 k_2{}^8 \omega = 0, \\
&\phi^7 : 4\kappa z_2 k_2{}^8 X^7 - 4 z_1 k_2{}^8 X^7 \omega - 2\nu z_1 X^7 k_2{}^8 z_2 \omega = 0, \\
&\phi^8 : 12 z_2 k_2{}^8 X^8 \omega + \nu z_2{}^2 X^8 k_2{}^8 \omega = 0.
\end{aligned} \tag{7}$$

Case 1:

$$z_0 = \frac{1}{2}\frac{\mu}{\nu}, z_1 = 0, z_{-1} = -\frac{1}{2}\mu\nu^{-1}\frac{1}{\sqrt{-6\,\mu^{-1}}},$$
$$z_2 = 0, z_{-2} = -\frac{1}{48}\frac{\mu^2}{\nu}, X = \frac{1}{24}\mu, \omega = \frac{1}{5}\sqrt{-6\,\mu^{-1}}\kappa. \tag{8}$$

Case 2:

$$z_0 = \frac{3}{4}\frac{\mu}{\nu}, z_1 = 12\,\nu^{-1}\frac{1}{\sqrt{-6\,\mu^{-1}}}, z_{-1} = -\frac{1}{8}\mu\nu^{-1}\frac{1}{\sqrt{-6\,\mu^{-1}}},$$
$$z_2 = -12\,\nu^{-1}, z_{-2} = -\frac{1}{768}\frac{\mu^2}{\nu}, X = \frac{1}{96}\mu, \omega = \frac{1}{5}\sqrt{-6\,\mu^{-1}}\kappa. \tag{9}$$

This study employs the Riccati–Bernoulli sub-ODE technique to simplify the solutions of nonlinear partial differential equations (PDEs) by transforming them into ordinary differential equations (ODEs). This method's strength is seen in the fact that it considers nonlinear terms analytically and thus offers multiple traveling wave solutions. However, due to the complexity of some of the nonlinear PDEs, better solutions call for further improvements, which is where the Bäcklund transformation comes into play. The Bäcklund transformation can be accomplished as a bridge between the different solutions of the PDE through the transformation of one solution into another more easily soluble solution. In this work, the transformation alters the forms of nonlinear terms in the PDE, enabling the use of the Riccati–Bernoulli technique to solve them. In fact, one can say that the Bäcklund transformation reduces the complexity of the process of combining nonlinear wave solutions by directly relating different solutions of the same equation.

Thus, the Bäcklund transformation and the Riccati–Bernoulli method function synergistically. The Riccati–Bernoulli method yields the exact solutions of the reduced ODE, while on the other hand, the Bäcklund transformation relates the solutions and further analyzes the steeper, uncharted solution profiles. This combined approach plays a crucial role in identifying the wave solutions for the given nonlinear PDE equation, which is crucial for modeling nanoionic currents and cell signaling. It provides both existing analytical solutions and new solutions for the wave solutions while also effectively addressing the nonlinearity of the system.

Solution family 1: Considering case 1 for $X < 0$, we obtain the precise traveling wave solution for Equation (1) in the following form:

$$f_1(x,t) = -\frac{1}{48}\frac{\mu^2 W_1^2}{\nu\, W_2^2} - \frac{1}{2}\mu\, W_1 \nu^{-1}\frac{1}{\sqrt{-6\,\mu^{-1}}}W_2^{-1} + \frac{1}{2}\frac{\mu}{\nu}, \tag{10}$$

with

$$W_1 = k_1 - \frac{1}{12}k_2\sqrt{-6\,\mu}\tanh\left(\frac{1}{12}\sqrt{-6\,\mu}\chi\right),$$
$$W_2 = -\frac{1}{24}\mu\, k_2 - \frac{1}{12}k_1\sqrt{-6\,\mu}\tanh\left(\frac{1}{12}\sqrt{-6\,\mu}\chi\right),$$

or

$$f_2(x,t) = -\frac{1}{48}\frac{\mu^2 W_3^2}{\nu\, W_4^2} - \frac{1}{2}\mu\, W_3 \nu^{-1}\frac{1}{\sqrt{-6\,\mu^{-1}}}W_4^{-1} + \frac{1}{2}\frac{\mu}{\nu}, \tag{11}$$

with

$$W_3 = k_1 - \frac{1}{12}k_2\sqrt{-6\,\mu}\coth\left(\frac{1}{12}\sqrt{-6\,\mu}\chi\right),$$
$$W_4 = -\frac{1}{24}\mu\, k_2 - \frac{1}{12}k_1\sqrt{-6\,\mu}\coth\left(\frac{1}{12}\sqrt{-6\,\mu}\chi\right).$$

Solution family 2: Considering case 1 for $X > 0$, we obtain the precise traveling wave solution for Equation (1) in the following form:

$$f_3(x,t) = -\frac{1}{48}\frac{\mu^2 S_1^2}{\nu\, S_2^2} - \frac{1}{2}\mu\, S_1 \nu^{-1}\frac{1}{\sqrt{-6\,\mu^{-1}}}S_2^{-1} + \frac{1}{2}\frac{\mu}{\nu}, \tag{12}$$

with

$$S_1 = k_1 + \frac{1}{12}k_2\sqrt{6}\sqrt{\mu}\tan\left(\frac{1}{12}\sqrt{6}\sqrt{\mu}\chi\right),$$
$$S_2 = -\frac{1}{24}\mu\, k_2 + \frac{1}{12}k_1\sqrt{6}\sqrt{\mu}\tan\left(\frac{1}{12}\sqrt{6}\sqrt{\mu}\chi\right),$$

or

$$f_4(x,t) = -\frac{1}{48}\frac{\mu^2 S_3^2}{\nu\, S_4^2} - \frac{1}{2}\mu\, S_3 \nu^{-1}\frac{1}{\sqrt{-6\,\mu^{-1}}}S_4^{-1} + \frac{1}{2}\frac{\mu}{\nu}, \tag{13}$$

with

$$S_3 = k_1 - \frac{1}{12}k_2\sqrt{6}\sqrt{\mu}\cot\left(\frac{1}{12}\sqrt{6}\sqrt{\mu}\chi\right),$$
$$S_4 = -\frac{1}{24}\mu\, k_2 - \frac{1}{12}k_1\sqrt{6}\sqrt{\mu}\cot\left(\frac{1}{12}\sqrt{6}\sqrt{\mu}\chi\right),$$

Solution family 3: Considering case 1 for $X = 0$, we obtain the precise traveling wave solution for Equation (1) in the following form:

$$f_5(x,t) = -\frac{1}{48}\mu^2 S_5^2 \nu^{-1} S_6^{-2} - \frac{1}{2}\mu\, S_5 \nu^{-1}\frac{1}{\sqrt{-6\,\mu^{-1}}}S_6^{-1} + \frac{1}{2}\frac{\mu}{\nu}, \tag{14}$$

with

$$S_5 = k_1 - \frac{k_2}{\chi},$$
$$S_6 = -\frac{1}{24}\mu\, k_2 - \frac{k_1}{\chi},$$

Here, $\chi = \frac{x}{l} + \frac{1}{5}\sqrt{-6\,\mu^{-1}}\kappa\, t T^{-1}$.

Solution family 4: Considering case 2 for $X < 0$, we obtain the precise traveling wave solution for Equation (1) in the following form:

$$f_6(x,t) = \frac{z_{-2}R_1^2}{R_2^2} + \frac{z_{-1}R_1}{R_2} + z_0 + \frac{z_1 R_2}{R_1} - 12\frac{R_2^2}{\nu\, R_1^2}, \tag{15}$$

with

$$R_1 = k_1 - k_2\sqrt{-X}\tanh\left(\sqrt{-X}\chi\right),$$
$$R_2 = -Xk_2 - k_1\sqrt{-X}\tanh\left(\sqrt{-X}\chi\right),$$

or

$$f_7(x,t) = \frac{z_{-2}R_3^2}{R_4^2} + \frac{z_{-1}R_3}{R_4} + z_0 + \frac{z_1 R_4}{R_3} - 12\frac{R_4^2}{\nu\, R_3^2}, \tag{16}$$

with

$$R_3 = k_1 - k_2\sqrt{-X}\coth\left(\sqrt{-X}\chi\right),$$
$$R_4 = -Xk_2 - k_1\sqrt{-X}\coth\left(\sqrt{-X}\chi\right).$$

Solution family 5: Considering case 2 for $X > 0$, we obtain the precise traveling wave solution for Equation (1) in the following form:

$$f_8(x,t) = \frac{z_{-2}G_1^2}{G_2^2} + \frac{z_{-1}G_1}{G_2} + z_0 + \frac{z_1 G_2}{G_1} - 12\,\frac{G_2^2}{\nu\, G_1^2}, \tag{17}$$

with

$$G_1 = k_1 + k_2\sqrt{X}\tan\left(\sqrt{X}\chi\right),$$
$$G_2 = -Xk_2 + k_1\sqrt{X}\tan\left(\sqrt{X}\chi\right),$$

or

$$f_9(x,t) = \frac{z_{-2}G_3^2}{G_4^2} + \frac{z_{-1}G_3}{G_4} + z_0 + \frac{z_1\left(-Xk_2 - k_1\sqrt{X}\cot\left(\sqrt{X}\chi\right)\right)}{G_3} - 12\,\frac{G_4^2}{\nu\, G_3^2}, \tag{18}$$

with

$$G_3 = k_1 - k_2\sqrt{X}\cot\left(\sqrt{X}\chi\right),$$
$$G_4 = -Xk_2 - k_1\sqrt{X}\cot\left(\sqrt{X}\chi\right).$$

Solution family 6: Considering case 2 for $X = 0$, we obtain the precise traveling wave solution for Equation (1) in the following form:

$$f_{10}(x,t) = z_{-2}G_5^2G_6^{-2} + z_{-1}G_5G_6^{-1} + z_0 + z_1G_6G_5^{-1} - 12\,G_6^2\nu^{-1}G_5^{-2}, \tag{19}$$

with

$$G_5 = k_1 - \frac{k_2}{\chi},$$
$$G_6 = -Xk_2 - \frac{k_1}{\chi}.$$

Here, $\chi = \frac{x}{l} + \frac{1}{5}\sqrt{-6\,\mu^{-1}}\kappa\, tT^{-1}, z_1 = 12\,\nu^{-1}\frac{1}{\sqrt{-6\,\mu^{-1}}}, z_{-1} = -\frac{1}{8}\,\mu\nu^{-1}\frac{1}{\sqrt{-6\,\mu^{-1}}}, z_{-2} = -\frac{1}{768}\,\frac{\mu^2}{\nu}, z_0 = \frac{3}{4}\,\frac{\mu}{\nu}$ and $X = \frac{1}{96}\,\mu,$.

4. Results and Discussion

In this paper, we describe a methodology for nonlinear PDEs that arise in nanosciences and biophysics, with a focus on microtubule transmission line models for nanoionic currents. These PDEs are then transformed into ODEs via the Bäcklund transformation, which helps to reduce the complexity of the problem and makes it easier to solve. We find the coefficients for the series solution using the Riccati–Bernoulli sub-ODE approach, enhancing our understanding of the system's integrated dynamics. The Riccati–Bernoulli sub-ODE method provides a detailed framework for solving the equation system, revealing three distinct families of solutions. There are three classes of functions, namely the hyperbolic, rational, and trigonometric functions. Despite the differences in the form and structure of these solutions, each of them has specific analytical potential to effectively reveal the system's features. This framework is especially useful in capturing such patterns as kink solitons, which are important in theoretical applications including solitons in particle physics and dislocations in solids. By identifying these solution families, the method increases the opportunities for understanding the various behaviors of complex systems, underscoring the significance of the results for contemporary biophysics and nanoscience. In our numerical analysis of the obtained solutions, the following values for all related parameters are considered [18]: $k_1 = 0.1$, $k_2 = 0.3$, $\kappa = \frac{T}{r_2 c_0}$, $\nu = \frac{2r_1\gamma}{r_2}$, $\gamma = \frac{r_1}{r_2}$, $T = r_1 c_0 = 1.32 \times 10^{-6}$, and $\gamma = -1$. We demonstrated the relationship between the kink and anti-kink dynamics by analyzing the distinct cases derived from the algebraic system. In particular, we presented the development of kink-blow dynamics by examining the solutions obtained for various parameter values and spatial distributions. The solution families, derived from Case 1 and Case 2, reflect different physical conditions, allowing for a more detailed exploration of the system stability, propagation characteristics, and interaction behaviors. Each family provides a distinct representation of how the model behaves under specific parameter configurations.

Figure 1 presents the development of anti-kink solutions through their evolution in the context of microtubules modeled by nonlinear RLC transmission lines in nanobiosciences. We presented the link between the obtained solutions and the dynamics of kinks through the details in the behavior of kink-blow dynamics with different parameters and spatial configurations. The solution provides more evidence of stability and other propagation aspects of the system. The changes in the values of the parameters may affect the interactions in such a way that the physical conditions driving the variation in wave dynamics can be interpreted, hence providing the possibility to describe the interaction processes at the nanoscale in detail.

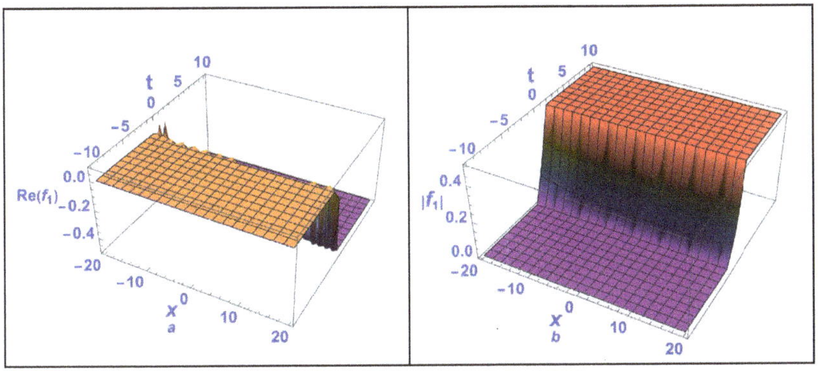

Figure 1. Three-dimensional topographical representation of (**a**) the real component to the solution f_1 in the (x, t)-plane and (**b**) the absolute to the solution f_1 in the (x, t)-plane.

Figure 2 shows the kink plot of these solutions compared to the nonlinear wave solutions previously presented. Both plots demonstrate the change in space under different parameters and distributions, with contours indicating regions where specific parameters, such as amplitude and phase, are the same. These pictures have given us essential details about how stable microtubules are, how they move, and how they interact at the nanoscale. This is critical for understanding and manipulating microtubules in biological settings.

Figure 3 indicates the dynamics of localized disturbances and nonlinear waves (kink waves) in microtubules formulated as nonlinear RLC transmission lines in nanoscience. This plot concerns how kink profiles change with respect to different parameters, and the distribution of solitons as compared to the anti-symmetric patterns of anti-kink profiles. The contour lines on the plot show areas with constant parameters such as amplitude and phase. This shows how complicated the stability, propagation, and interaction mechanisms are at the nanoscale level for microtubules, which are essential for biological functioning.

The anti-kink plot in Figure 4 shows how the anti-kink modes in microtubules move, as seen through the nonlinear RLC transmission lines used in nanosciences. This plot demonstrates a distinct interference of these solutions under the parameters and spatial distributions, as well as their symmetrical mode against the localized perturbations that could be observed in the kink solutions. This knowledge is essential for explaining the complexity of biological processes that involve microtubules in cells.

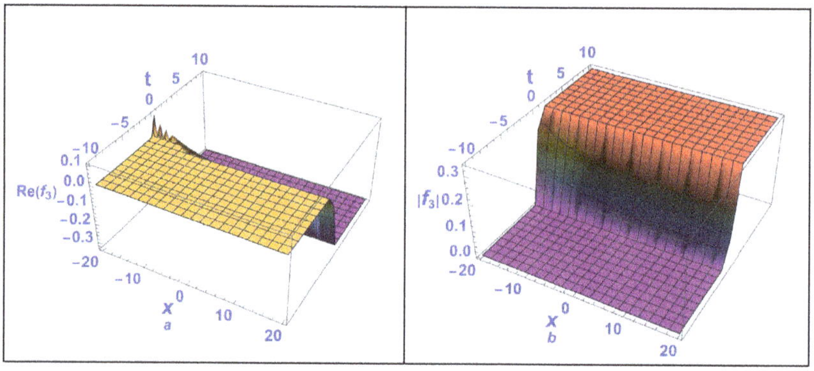

Figure 2. Three-dimensional topographical representation of (**a**) the real component to the solution f_3 in the (x, t)-plane and (**b**) the absolute to the solution f_3 in the (x, t)-plane.

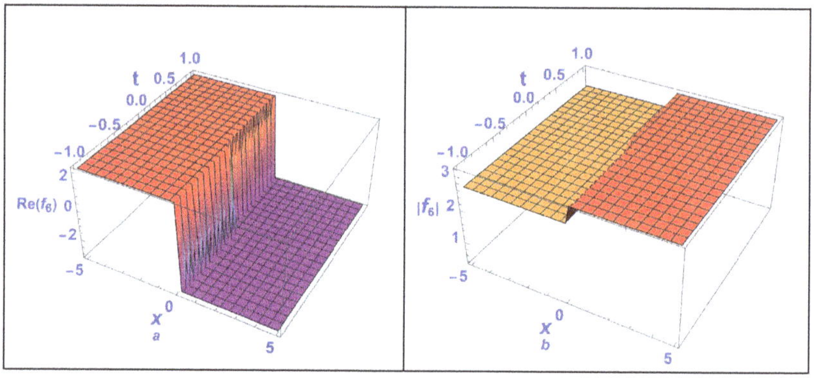

Figure 3. Three-dimensional topographical representation of (**a**) the real component to the solution f_6 in the (x, t)-plane and (**b**) the absolute to the solution f_6 in the (x, t)-plane.

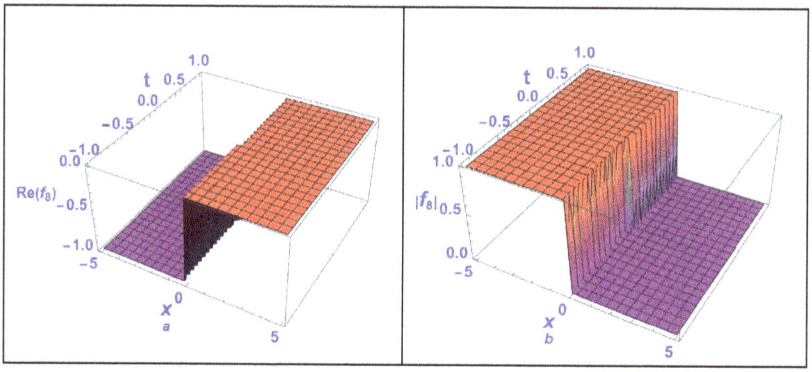

Figure 4. Three-dimensional topographical representation of (**a**) the real component to the solution f_8 in the (x, t)-plane and (**b**) the absolute to the solution f_8 in the (x, t)-plane.

Figure 5 shows the kink plot describing the velocities of local disturbances and nonlinear wave dynamics. From the kink plot, it is well evinced that kink solutions present neat velocity shooting profiles for changes in parameters and density distributions. This contrasts with the almost symmetrical speed profile observed in anti-kink solutions. Actually, in the dissimilarity of the velocity modes, interesting information about the very complex biomechanical processes and transport phenomena realized by microtubules within cells can be found. Understanding such variability is crucial for understanding how microtubules function in various dynamic cellular contexts.

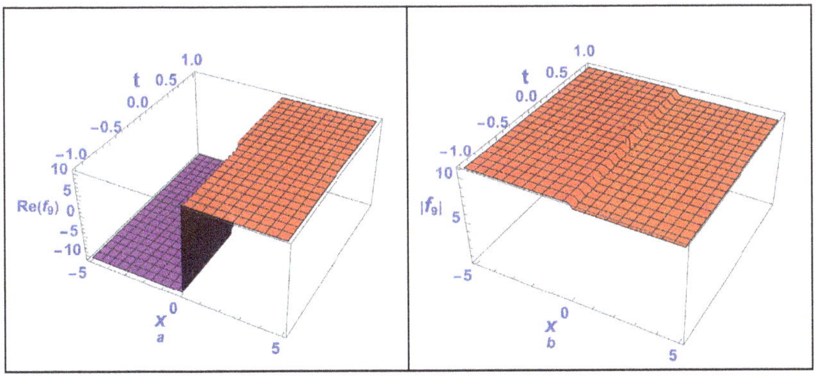

Figure 5. Three-dimensional topographical representation of (**a**) the real component to the solution f_9 in the (x,t)-plane and (**b**) the absolute to the solution f_9 in the (x,t)-plane.

To prove the effectiveness of the method used in this study over some methods in analyzing the problem under study, we made a simple comparison between the derived and derived solutions using the modified extended tanh-function method (METFM), as shown in Table 1. It is clear that there are some cases in which METFM does not provide solutions, while the technique under study does, confirming the effectiveness of the method used in this study.

Table 1. Comparison of the current approach with the alternative approach, the modified extended tanh-function method (METFM) [20].

Case I: $X < 0$	Present method	$f(x,t) = \frac{z_{-2}R_1^2}{R_2^2} + \frac{z_{-1}R_1}{R_2} + z_0 + \frac{z_1R_2}{R_1} - 12\,\frac{R_2^2}{\nu R_1^2}.$
Case I: $b < 0$	METFM	$u(x,t) = \frac{3}{4}\frac{\gamma}{\beta} - a_1\sqrt{\frac{1}{24}}\gamma\tanh(\theta_1) - \frac{\gamma}{4\beta}\tanh^2(\theta_1)$
Case II: $X > 0$	Present method	$f(x,t) = \frac{z_{-2}G_1^2}{G_2^2} + \frac{z_{-1}G_1}{G_2} + z_0 + \frac{z_1G_2}{G_1} - 12\,\frac{G_2^2}{\nu G_1^2}.$
Case II: $b > 0$	METFM	$u(x,t) = \frac{1}{4}\frac{\gamma}{\beta} + a_1\sqrt{\frac{1}{24}}\gamma\tan(\theta_1) - \frac{\gamma}{4\beta}\tan^2(\theta_1)$
Case III: $X = 0$	Present method	$f(x,t) = z_{-2}G_5^2G_6^{-2} + z_{-1}G_5G_6^{-1} + z_0 + z_1G_6G_5^{-1} - 12\,G_6^2\nu^{-1}G_5^{-2}$
Case III: $b = 0$	METFM	No solutions at $b = 0$.

5. Conclusions

- The Riccati–Bernoulli sub-ODE method has been successfully used to obtain solutions to the nonlinear PDE, the nonlinear RLC transmission line model of microtubules (MTs).
- This approach produced new traveling wave solutions of substantial importance in the nascent areas of nanotechnology, biosciences, and biophysics.
- The Riccati–Bernoulli sub-ODE method's calculated kink solutions match well with-known solutions from other methodologies, demonstrating the method's efficacy.
- The Riccati–Bernoulli sub-ODE method seems to be an effective, brief, and elegant representation for analyzing wide classes of nonlinear evolution equations in physics.
- We have established the applicability and robustness of the proposed method by demonstrating its ability to yield further solutions.

6. Future Work

Another direction that could be explored in the future would be a continuation of the studies of the usage of the Riccati–Bernoulli sub-ODE method and Bäcklund transformation on more complicated nonlinear phenomena and processes in nanosciences and other branches of science, such as analyzing different nonlinear structures in plasma physics. Future work can be expanded to examine various types of physical PDEs that describe different nonlinear structures in plasma and fluids or to include stochastic perturbations to encapsulate the noise associated with nanoionic currents.

Moreover, the methods introduced in this study can be extended to investigate wave propagation in biological structures other than microtubules, such as in protein complexes or neuronal signal transduction pathways. More experimentally verifiable scenarios involving the calculated solutions may also be another line of research interest, along with real-time integration of the solutions into nanotechnology and biophysical research. These could not only extend the current study to a wider range but also promote more developments in theoretical modeling and application. However, it is crucial to understand that the Riccati–Bernoulli sub-ODE method and Bäcklund transformation offer reliable solutions to the studied nonlinear PDEs, though there are certain shortcomings. When applied to highly nonlinear systems or systems with complex boundary conditions, the method may encounter problems. The use of symbolic computation also becomes problematic when the method runs into computational complexity issues. In addition, this approach could potentially not completely solve high-dimensional cases or variability. It is important to note this study's limitations in order to set boundaries and expectations for its applicability and further research directions.

Author Contributions: All authors (S.M., W.A., M.A., A.M.M., R.S. and S.A.E.-T.) contributed equally. All authors have read and agreed to the published version of the manuscript.

Funding: The authors express their gratitude to Princess Nourah bint Abdulrahman University Researchers Supporting Project number (PNURSP2024R229), Princess Nourah bint Abdulrahman University, Riyadh, Saudi Arabia. This work was supported by the Deanship of Scientific Research, Vice Presidency for Graduate Studies and Scientific Research, King Faisal University, Saudi Arabia (KFU241978).

Data Availability Statement: Data sharing is not applicable to this article, as no new data were created or analyzed in this study.

Acknowledgments: The authors express their gratitude to Princess Nourah bint Abdulrahman University Researchers Supporting Project number (PNURSP2024R229), Princess Nourah bint Abdulrahman University, Riyadh, Saudi Arabia. This work was supported by the Deanship of Scientific Research, Vice Presidency for Graduate Studies and Scientific Research, King Faisal University, Saudi Arabia (KFU241978).

Conflicts of Interest: The authors declare no conflicts of interest.

References

1. Drazin, P.G.; Johnson, R.S. *Solitons: An Introduction*; Cambridge University Press, Cambridge, UK, 1989.
2. Nazia Batool, W.; Masood, M.; Batool, N.; Masood, W.; Siddiq, M.; Alrowaily, A.W.; Ismaeel, S.M.; El-Tantawy, S.A. Hirota bilinear method and multi-soliton interaction of electrostatic waves driven by cubic nonlinearity in pair-ion-electron plasmas. *Phys. Fluids* **2023**, *35*, 033109. [CrossRef]
3. Cariello, F.; Tabor, M. Painleve expansions for nonintegrable evolution equations. *Phys. D* **1989**, *39*, 77–94. [CrossRef]
4. Wang, L.M. Exact solutions for a compound KdV-Burgers equation. *Phys. Lett. A* **1996**, *213*, 279–287. [CrossRef]
5. Fan, E. Two new applications of the homogeneous balance method. *Phys. Lett. A* **2000**, *265*, 353–357. [CrossRef]
6. Zhou, Y.; Wang, M.; Wang, Y. Periodic wave solutions to a coupled KdV equations with variable coefficients. *Phys. Lett. A* **2003**, *308*, 31–36. [CrossRef]
7. Yomba, E. The extended Fan's sub-equation method and its application to KdV–MKdV, BKK and variant Boussinesq equations. *Phys. Lett. A* **2005**, *336*, 463–476. [CrossRef]
8. Feng, X. Exploratory approach to explicit solution of nonlinear evolutions equations. *Int. J. Theor. Phys.* **2000**, *39*, 207–222. [CrossRef]

9. Li, Z.B.; Liu, Y.P. RATH: A Maple package for finding travelling solitary wave solutions to nonlinear evolution equations. *Comput. Commun.* **2002**, *148*, 256–266. [CrossRef]
10. Khater, M.M. Physics of crystal lattices and plasma; analytical and numerical simulations of the GilsonPickering equation. *Results Phys.* **2023**, *44*, 106193. [CrossRef]
11. Wang, F.; Salama, S.A.; Khater, M.M. Optical wave solutions of perturbed time-fractional nonlinear Schrdinger equation. *J. Ocean Eng. Sci.* **2022**. [CrossRef]
12. Sahoo, S.; Ray, S.S. Solitary wave solutions for time fractional third order modified KdV equation using two reliable techniques (G'/G)-expansion method and improved (G'/G)-expansion method. *Phys. Stat. Mech. Its Appl.* **2016**, *448*, 265–282. [CrossRef]
13. Thadee, W.; Chankaew, A.; Phoosree, S. Effects of wave solutions on shallow-water equation, optical-fibre equation and electric-circuit equation. *Maejo Int. J. Sci. Technol.* **2022**, *16*, 262–274.
14. He, J.H.; Wu, X.H. Exp-function method for nonlinear wave equations. *Chaos Solitons Fractals* **2006**, *30*, 700–708. [CrossRef]
15. Iftikhar, A.; Ghafoor, A.; Zubair, T.; Firdous, S.; Mohyud-Din, S.T. Solutions of (2 + 1) dimensional generalized KdV, Sin-Gordon and Landau-Ginzburg-Higgs Equations. *Sci. Res. Essays* **2013**, *8*, 1349–1359.
16. Cinar, M.; Secer, A.; Ozisik, M.; Bayram, M. Derivation of optical solitons of dimensionless Fokas-Lenells equation with perturbation term using Sardar sub-equation method. *Opt. Quantum Electron.* **2022**, *54*, 402. [CrossRef]
17. Sataric, M.V.; Ilic, D.I.; Ralevic, N.; Tuszynski, J.A. A nonlinear model of ionic wave propagation along microtubules. *Eur. Biophys.* **2009**, *38*, 637–647. [CrossRef]
18. Sataric, M.V.; Sekulic, D.; Zivanov, M. Solitonic ionic currents along microtubules. *J. Comput. Theor. Nanosci.* **2010**, *7*, 2281–2290. [CrossRef]
19. Sekulic, D.L.; Sataric, B.M.; Tuszynski, J.A.; Sataric, M.V. Nonlinear ionic pulses along microtubules. *Eur. Phys. J. Soft Matter* **2011**, *34*, 49. [CrossRef]
20. Sekulić, DL; Satarić, MV; Živanov, M.B. Symbolic computation of some new nonlinear partial differential equations of nanobiosciences using modified extended tanh-function method. *Appl. Math. Comput.* **2011**, *218*, 3499–3506. [CrossRef]
21. Tariq, M.S.; Masood, W.; Siddiq, M.; Asghar, S.; Alotaibi, B.M.; Sherif, M.E.; Ismaeel El-Tantawy, A. Bücklund transformation for analyzing a cylindrical Korteweg-de Vries equation and investigating multiple soliton solutions in a plasma. *Phys. Fluids* **2023**, *35*, 103105. [CrossRef]
22. Abdelrahman, M.A.E.; Sohaly, M.A. Solitary waves for the modified Korteweg-de-Vries equation in deterministic case and random case. *J. Phys. Math.* **2017**, *8*, 214.
23. Abdelrahman, M.A.E.; Sohaly, M.A. Solitary waves for the nonlinear Schrödinger problem with the probability distribution function in the stochastic input case. *Eur. Phys. J. Plus.* **2017**, *132*, 339. [CrossRef]
24. Yang, X.F.; Deng, Z.C.; Wei, Y. A ricatti-bernoulli sub-ode method for nonlinear partial differential equations and its application. *Adv. Diff. Equa.* **2015**, *1*, 117–133. [CrossRef]
25. Lu, D.; Shi, Q. New Jacobi elliptic functions solutions for the combined KdV-mKdV equation. *Int. J. Nonlinear Sci.* **2010**, *10*, 320–325.

axioms

MDPI

Article

On the Construction of a Two-Step Sixth-Order Scheme to Find the Drazin Generalized Inverse

Keyang Zhang [1], Fazlollah Soleymani [2] and Stanford Shateyi [3,*]

1 Department of Mathematical Sciences, New Jersey Institute of Technology, 323 Martin Luther King Blvd., Newark, NJ 07102, USA; kz78@njit.edu
2 Department of Mathematics, Institute for Advanced Studies in Basic Sciences (IASBS), Zanjan 45137-66731, Iran; soleymani@iasbs.ac.ir
3 Department of Mathematics and Applied Mathematics, School of Mathematical and Natural Sciences, University of Venda, P. Bag X5050, Thohoyandou 0950, South Africa
* Correspondence: stanford.shateyi@univen.ac.za

Abstract: This study introduces a numerically efficient iterative solver for computing the Drazin generalized inverse, addressing a critical need for high-performance methods in matrix computations. The proposed two-step scheme achieves sixth-order convergence, distinguishing it as a higher-order method that outperforms several existing approaches. A rigorous convergence analysis is provided, highlighting the importance of selecting an appropriate initial value to ensure robustness. Extensive numerical experiments validate the analytical findings, showcasing the method's superior speed and efficiency, making it an advancement in iterative solvers for generalized inverses.

Keywords: generalized inverse; order of convergence; numerical method; initial matrix; Drazin

MSC: 15A09; 65Y20

1. Preliminary Remarks

The computation of generalized inverses remains an area of significant research in computational mathematics (see, for example, [1,2]). Over the past 63 years, substantial advancements have been achieved in this field. Early contributions by E.H. In 1920, Moore pioneered the concept of a generalized algebraic matrix inverse, yet the field gained momentum only after 1955, as marked by the works of Penrose (1955, 1956), Golub and Kahan (1965), and Rao and Mitra (1971) as discussed in [3]. These and other significant contributions have defined much of the field, establishing foundations that allow limited scope for new developments [4].

Terms such as "the pseudo-inverse", "{2}-inverse", and "the minimum-norm least squares inverse" are widely utilized, often more so than "Drazin inverse", to denote unique matrix inverses in applications involving the resolution of linear systems and optimization [5].

Greville's foundational partitioning approach in computing generalized inverses was examined in [3]. While effective, this solver incurs a high operational cost and greater round-off errors. Many numerical solvers devised for the Drazin generalized inverse often lack computational stability, prompting the need to explore and propose new iterative approaches that address these limitations; see the discussions in [6] for more.

In numerical computation, it is essential to counteract cumulative rounding errors effectively; symbolic computation achieves this by preserving variable precision throughout the process. However, the symbolic computation of the Drazin inverse becomes computationally intensive for matrices of high dimensionality, which has led investigators to propose computationally effective iteration solvers methods for this target [7,8].

The general solution for a square singular linear system of the form

$$\Gamma y = \phi, \tag{1}$$

can be expressed as

$$y = \Gamma^D \phi + (I - \Gamma\Gamma^D)z, \tag{2}$$

utilizing the Drazin generalized inverse, whereas $z \in \mathcal{N}(\Gamma) + \mathcal{R}(\Gamma^{\iota-1})$, as investigated in [9]. For example, in control theory, the Drazin inverse helps to determine the solution of descriptor systems, which are characterized by differential–algebraic equations. These systems often model engineering processes involving constraints, such as electrical circuits with dependent components or robotic mechanisms with non-holonomic constraints. The Drazin inverse ensures that solutions respect the system's algebraic constraints, providing stability and robustness in the analysis.

We describe $\mathbb{C}^{N\times N}$ and $\mathbb{C}_r^{N\times N}$ as the sets of $N \times N$ square matrices with complex entries and those of rank r, in the respective order. Additionally, Γ^*, $\mathcal{N}(\Gamma)$, $\text{rank}(\Gamma)$, and $\mathcal{R}(\Gamma)$ represent the conjugate transpose, null space, rank, and range of $\Gamma \in \mathbb{C}^{N\times N}$.

Drazin introduced a generalized inverse, non-reflexive yet commuting with elements of associative rings and semigroups, in his seminal paper [10]. Wilkinson further elaborated on its significance and computation in [11]. The study of the Drazin inverse spans multiple domains, including matrix theory (specifically within generalized inverses) and ring theory.

A dynamical system governed by a homogeneous equation is referred to as pointwise complete if every possible terminal state of the system can be attained by appropriately selecting its initial state. Conversely, a system that fails to exhibit this property is described as pointwise degenerate. The concepts of pointwise completeness and degeneracy have been extensively studied in various contexts, including linear continuous-time systems with delays, as well as fractional linear discrete-time systems, as highlighted in the literature [12]. Furthermore, the Drazin inverse of matrices has proven to be a valuable tool for analyzing the pointwise completeness and degeneracy of descriptor fractional linear systems.

In recent years, significant advancements have been made in extending these mathematical notions. The author of [13] has generalized the concepts of the Drazin inverse, the Core–Moore–Penrose inverse, and the Drazin–Moore–Penrose inverse of finite square matrices to finite potent endomorphisms. This work has introduced numerous properties of these extended inverses, thereby broadening their applicability. Notably, all results derived for finite potent endomorphisms remain valid for the special case of finite square matrices, thereby enriching the theoretical framework and providing deeper insights into the structural characteristics of these systems.

The Drazin inverse is particularly useful in the computation of spectral projectors, which separate the behavior of a system into stable and unstable dynamics. This is essential for understanding and controlling dynamical systems in engineering fields like aerodynamics and robotics. It also has applications in network theory, where it aids in determining steady-state solutions in Markov chains with absorbing states, which is crucial for designing efficient communication or traffic flow systems.

To proceed, we first furnish some essential definitions [3].

Definition 1. *The minimum non-negative integer ι for which*

$$\text{rank}(\Gamma^{\iota+1}) = \text{rank}(\Gamma^{\iota}), \tag{3}$$

holds is known as the index of Γ, represented by $\text{ind}(\Gamma)$.

Definition 2. *Consider a complex matrix Γ of order $N \times N$. The Drazin inverse of Γ, shown via Γ^D, is the distinct matrix Θ that fulfills the conditions below*

$$(1)\ \Gamma^{\iota}\Theta\Gamma = \Gamma^{\iota}, \qquad (2)\ \Theta\Gamma\Theta = \Theta, \qquad (3)\ \Gamma\Theta = \Theta\Gamma, \tag{4}$$

where $\iota = \text{ind}(\Gamma)$, *the matrix index of* Γ.

As long as $\text{ind}(\Gamma) = 1$, Θ is termed the group inverse of Γ. For nonsingular Γ, $\text{ind}(\Gamma) = 0$, yielding $\Gamma^D = \Gamma^{-1}$.

The idempotent matrix $\Gamma\Gamma^D$ serves as a projector onto $\mathcal{R}(\Gamma^\iota)$ along $\mathcal{N}(\Gamma^\iota)$, where $\mathcal{R}(\Gamma^\iota)$ is the range of Γ^ι and $\mathcal{N}(\Gamma^\iota)$ its null space. For nilpotent Γ, $\Gamma^D = 0$; see [14] for further details.

Matrix iteration schemes are sensitive to the selection of the starting value Θ_0 for convergence towards Γ^D. Iteration solvers such as Schulz-like schemes are especially efficient for sparse matrices with sparse inverses, though often hampered by the need for an appropriate initial guess. The literature provides numerous approaches to this initial selection, as discussed comprehensively in [15].

To highlight key innovations of the proposed method compared to existing methods, in this article, we provide the following:

- Introduction of an iterative approach for computing the Drazin inverse.
- Improvement in CPU time compared to well-known existing methods.
- Analytical investigation of the method's behavior.
- Superior computational efficiency due to reduced computational complexity.

Following this introduction in this section, the rest of the work is structured as follows:

- Section 2 reviews key iteration solvers for the inverse of Drazin.
- In Section 3, we present our novel high-order scheme. Section 4 examines its sixth-order convergence characteristics.
- Section 5 addresses the computational complexity of iterative schemes, identifying the optimal choice.
- Section 6 applies our new scheme to illustrate reduced CPU time.
- Section 7 presents the final observations and insights.

2. Associated Studies

A classic approach for computing the inverse of an invertible Γ is the Schulz scheme, presented in [16], as comes next:

$$\Theta_{\varpi+1} = \Theta_\varpi(2I - \Gamma\Theta_\varpi), \quad \varpi = 0, 1, 2, \ldots, \tag{5}$$

where I denotes the unit matrix with identical dimensions to Γ.

The authors of [17] extended the applicability of the Schulz method (5) by proving its effectiveness to calculate the Drazin inverse for square matrices. They introduced the starting value below:

$$\Theta_0 = \alpha\Gamma^l, \quad l \geq \text{ind}(\Gamma) = \iota, \tag{6}$$

wherein α is selected such that we have

$$\|I - \Gamma\Theta_0\| < 1. \tag{7}$$

Utilizing an initial guess as (6) in conjunction with (5) yields a quadratically convergent iteration process for computing the inverse of Drazin.

Next, we review several higher-order iterative methods for this purpose, recognizing that efficiency gains are essential since the Schulz method (5) converges slowly in the early iteration stages, thereby increasing the overall computational effort required for matrix inversion.

The authors of [18] proposed an iteration scheme with a cubic convergence rate, formulated as

$$\Theta_{\varpi+1} = \Theta_\varpi(3I - \Gamma\Theta_\varpi(3I - \Gamma\Theta_\varpi)), \quad \varpi = 0, 1, 2, \ldots, \tag{8}$$

alongside an alternative scheme of the same order for approximating Γ^{-1} (or Γ^D with a suitable initial choice), defined by

$$\Theta_{\varpi+1} = \Theta_\varpi \left[\frac{1}{2}(I - \Gamma\Theta_\varpi)(I + (2I - \Gamma\Theta_\varpi)^2) + I\right], \quad \varpi = 0, 1, 2, \ldots. \tag{9}$$

Additionally, a generalized approach to derive similar iteration sequences is outlined in [19] (Chapter 5). The authors provided a 4th-order solver as follows:

$$\Theta_{\varpi+1} = \Theta_\varpi(I + \Xi_\varpi(I + \Xi_\varpi(I + \Xi_\varpi))), \quad \varpi = 0, 1, 2, \ldots, \tag{10}$$

where $\Xi_\varpi = I - \Gamma\Theta_\varpi$. More broadly, by applying Schröder's generalized iterative method [20] to the nonlinear problem

$$\Gamma\Theta = I, \tag{11}$$

we can derive the following solver [21]:

$$\begin{aligned} \Theta_{\varpi+1} &= \Theta_\varpi(I + \Xi_\varpi + \Xi_\varpi^2 + \cdots + \Xi_\varpi^{m-1}) \\ &= \Theta_\varpi(I + \Xi_\varpi(I + \Xi_\varpi(\cdots + \Xi_\varpi)\cdots)), \quad \varpi = 0, 1, 2, \ldots, \end{aligned} \tag{12}$$

with convergence order m, which requires m Horner-like matrix multiplications, where $\Xi_\varpi = I - \Gamma\Theta_\varpi$.

Recently, the authors of [5], through additional factorization and simplification steps, proposed the following iterative scheme:

$$\Theta_{\varpi+1} = \Theta_\varpi(I + \Xi_\varpi)\Big[(I + \beta_1\Xi_\varpi^2 + \Xi_\varpi^4)(I + \beta_2\Xi_\varpi^2 + \Xi_\varpi^4)\Big], \tag{13}$$

which reduces the computational load to only six matrix–matrix multiplications per cycle. Here, the constants β_1 and β_2 are given by

$$\beta_1 = \frac{1}{2}\left(1 - \sqrt{5}\right), \qquad \beta_2 = \frac{1}{2}\left(1 + \sqrt{5}\right). \tag{14}$$

3. Development of a Novel Iterative Approach

The impetus for this manuscript is to develop a multi-step rapid iterative solver that enhances both accuracy and efficiency in addressing nonlinear equations; see the pioneer discussions in the works [22,23]. By avoiding the necessity for second Fréchet derivatives, our approach seeks to mitigate the complexities and computational overhead associated with existing methodologies.

An iterative family of Chebyshev–Halley methods was first introduced and studied by [24,25], designed to locate simple roots of the following nonlinear problem:

$$g(x) = 0,$$

which can be presented as follows:

$$x_{\varpi+1} = x_\varpi - \left(1 + \frac{1}{2}\frac{L(x_\varpi)}{1 - aL(x_\varpi)}\right)\frac{g(x_\varpi)}{g'(x_\varpi)}, \tag{15}$$

wherein $a \in \mathbb{R}$,

$$L(x_\varpi) = \frac{g''(x_\varpi)g(x_\varpi)}{g'(x_\varpi)^2},$$

and the convergence order is cubic; for recent discussions about the solutions of nonlinear equations, see [26–28]. This scheme is an extension of the famous Newton's solver [29], which is given by

$$x_{\varpi+1} = x_\varpi - \frac{g(x_\varpi)}{g'(x_\varpi)}, \tag{16}$$

Here, we need to resolve the nonlinear problem below:

$$X^{-1} = A. \tag{17}$$

In the scalar version of (17), we obtain Schulz and Chebyshev's methods as discussed in Section 2. To propose a two-step method, we combine these two solvers by using

$$\begin{cases} y_{\varpi} = x_{\varpi} - \left(1 + \frac{1}{2}\frac{g''(x_{\varpi})g(x_{\varpi})}{g'(x_{\varpi})^2}\right)\dfrac{g(x_{\varpi})}{g'(x_{\varpi})}, \\ x_{\varpi+1} = y_{\varpi} - \dfrac{g(y_{\varpi})}{g'(y_{\varpi})}. \end{cases} \tag{18}$$

Note that for Chebyshev's method, involved in the first step of (18), its convergence for nonlinear equations was studied in [30]. To enhance the efficiency of this approach, we apply a series of factorization steps to streamline the expression in (18) to solve (17), thereby decreasing the matrix–matrix products involved. This yields

$$\begin{cases} \Lambda_{\varpi} = \Theta_{\varpi}(3I - \Gamma\Theta_{\varpi}(3I - \Gamma\Theta_{\varpi})), \\ \Theta_{\varpi+1} = \Lambda_{\varpi}(2I - \Gamma\Lambda_{\varpi}), \end{cases} \tag{19}$$

which requires five matrix–matrix products per iteration.

Schulz-type iterations, as exemplified in (19), are inherently numerically stable, exhibiting a self-correcting property and based primarily on efficient matrix multiplications per cycle as long as a proper initial guess is used. This framework is well suited to parallel processing, particularly with sparse matrices. Integrating (19) with sparse-saving techniques can further alleviate the computational demands of matrix–matrix products within each cycle.

The scheme in (19) for calculating the Drazin inverse converges, provided that the initial approximation is selected as [31]

$$\Theta_0 = \frac{2}{\mathrm{Tr}(\Gamma^{\iota+1})}\Gamma^{\iota}, \tag{20}$$

or equivalently,

$$\Theta_0 = \frac{1}{2\|\Gamma\|_2^{\iota+1}}\Gamma^{\iota}, \tag{21}$$

where $\mathrm{Tr}(\cdot)$ denotes the trace of a matrix under ι.

An examination of the convergence behavior of this solver is provided in the next section, and we offer detailed insights into the selection of an initial approximation that maintains the iteration convergence rate. Additionally, we outline conditions under which this novel approach may be effectively applied to compute the Drazin inverse of square matrices.

Before presenting the primary theorems concerning the convergence analysis and convergence speed of the furnished solver, we first outline several key lemmas.

Proposition 1 ([31]). *Consider $\Gamma \in \mathbb{C}^{N\times N}$ and a given $\varepsilon > 0$. A norm $\|\cdot\|$ is identified for which*

$$\rho(\Gamma) + \epsilon \geq \|\Gamma\| \geq \rho(\Gamma), \tag{22}$$

where $\rho(\Gamma)$ represents the spectral radius of Γ, defined as the maximum absolute value of its eigenvalues.

Proposition 2 ([31]). *Let $P_{L,M}$ denote the projection onto a subspace L along a subspace M. Next,*
(i) $P_{L,M}Q = Q$ iff $\mathcal{R}(Q) \subseteq L$;
(ii) $QP_{L,M} = Q$ iff $\mathcal{N}(Q) \supseteq M$.

4. Theoretical Parts

Theorem A0. *Suppose that $\Gamma \in \mathbb{C}^{N\times N}$ is an invertible matrix. Additionally, suppose the starting matrix Θ_0 is chosen according to either* (6) *or (20) and (21). Consequently, the sequence of matrices $\{\Theta_\varpi\}_{\varpi=0}^{\infty}$ generated by* (19) *adheres to the following error bound for approximating the Drazin inverse:*

$$\frac{\|\Gamma^D - \Theta_\varpi\|}{\|\Gamma^D\|} \leq \|I - \Gamma\Theta_0\|^{6^\varpi}. \tag{23}$$

Moreover, the convergence rate of the method is six.

Proof. We proceed by considering

$$\begin{aligned} \Xi_{\varpi+1} &= I - \Gamma\Theta_{\varpi+1} \\ &= I - \Gamma(\Lambda_\varpi(2I - \Gamma\Lambda_\varpi)) \\ &= I - \Gamma((\Theta_\varpi(3I - \Gamma\Theta_\varpi(3I - \Gamma\Theta_\varpi)))(2I \\ &\quad - \Gamma(\Theta_\varpi(3I - \Gamma\Theta_\varpi(3I - \Gamma\Theta_\varpi))))) \\ &= (I - \Gamma\Theta_\varpi)^6 \\ &= \Xi_\varpi^6. \end{aligned} \tag{24}$$

By applying an arbitrary matrix norm to the expression in (24), one can rewrite it as follows:

$$\|\Xi_{\varpi+1}\| \leq \|\Xi_\varpi\|^6. \tag{25}$$

Given that Θ_0 is selected according to either (6) or (20) and (21), it subsequently follows that

$$\Xi(\Theta_0) \subseteq \Xi(\Gamma^\iota). \tag{26}$$

This can now be expressed as

$$\Xi(\Theta_\varpi) \subseteq \Xi(\Theta_{\varpi-1}). \tag{27}$$

It is now concluded that

$$\Xi(\Theta_\varpi) \subseteq \Xi(\Gamma^\iota),\ \varpi \geq 0. \tag{28}$$

In a similar fashion, if the proposed solver for computing the Drazin inverse is formulated by performing left multiplication on Θ_ϖ, it can be concluded that

$$\mathcal{N}(\Theta_\varpi) \supseteq \mathcal{N}(\Gamma^\iota),\ \varpi \geq 0. \tag{29}$$

At this point, by applying the definition of the Drazin inverse, one obtains

$$\Gamma\Gamma^D = \Gamma^D\Gamma = P_{\mathcal{R}(\Gamma^\iota),\mathcal{N}(\Gamma^\iota)}. \tag{30}$$

By combining Proposition 2 with the expressions in (28)–(30), it follows that

$$\Theta_\varpi\Gamma\Gamma^D = \Theta_\varpi = \Gamma^D\Gamma\Theta_\varpi,\ \varpi \geq 0. \tag{31}$$

In order to finalize the proof, we continue as outlined below. The matrix representing the error is given by $\delta_\varpi = \Gamma^D - \Theta_\varpi$ satisfies the following

$$\begin{aligned} \delta_\varpi &= \Gamma^D - \Theta_\varpi \\ &= \Gamma^D - \Gamma^D\Gamma\Theta_\varpi \\ &= \Gamma^D(I - \Gamma\Theta_\varpi) \\ &= \Gamma^D\Xi_\varpi. \end{aligned}$$

Utilizing (25), one attains

$$\|\delta_{\varpi}\| = \|\Gamma^D\|\|\Xi_{\varpi}\| \leq \|\Gamma^D\|\|\Xi_0\|^{6^{\varpi}}. \tag{32}$$

This serves as a verification of the result in (23). As an immediate consequence of (32) and Proposition 2, it follows that we can derive

$$\begin{aligned} \Gamma\delta_{\varpi+1} &= \Gamma\Gamma^D - \Gamma\Theta_{\varpi+1} \\ &= \Gamma\Gamma^D - I + I - \Gamma\Theta_{\varpi+1} \\ &= \Gamma\Gamma^D - I + \Xi_{\varpi+1}. \end{aligned} \tag{33}$$

By examining (24) and performing a series of simplifications, we arrive at the conclusion that

$$\Gamma\delta_{\varpi+1} = \Gamma\Gamma^D - I + \Xi_{\varpi}^6. \tag{34}$$

Utilizing the idempotent characteristic $(I - \Gamma\Gamma^D)^t = (I - \Gamma\Gamma^D)$, where $t \geq 1$ denotes a natural number, along with the subsequent result derived from (31), we obtain the following:

$$\begin{aligned} (I - \Gamma\Gamma^D)\Gamma\delta_{\varpi} &= (I - \Gamma\Gamma^D)\Gamma(\Gamma^D - \Theta_{\varpi}) \\ &= \Theta_{\varpi} - \Gamma\Gamma^D\Theta_{\varpi} \\ &= 0. \end{aligned} \tag{35}$$

As a result, for every $t \geq 1$, we arrive at the following expression (where we apply (35) during the simplification process):

$$\begin{aligned} (\Xi_{\varpi})^t + \Gamma\Gamma^D - I &= (I - \Gamma\Theta_{\varpi})^t + \Gamma\Gamma^D - I \\ &= (I - \Gamma\Gamma^D + \Gamma\Gamma^D - \Gamma\Theta_{\varpi})^t + \Gamma\Gamma^D - I \\ &= \left((I - \Gamma\Gamma^D) + \Gamma\delta_{\varpi}\right)^t + \Gamma\Gamma^D - I \\ &= I - \Gamma\Gamma^D + (\Gamma\delta_{\varpi})^t + \Gamma\Gamma^D - I \\ &= (\Gamma\delta_{\varpi})^t. \end{aligned} \tag{36}$$

By combining (34) and (36), it follows that

$$\Gamma\delta_{\varpi+1} = (\Gamma\delta_{\varpi})^6. \tag{37}$$

Finally, one obtains

$$\|\Gamma\delta_{\varpi+1}\| \leq \|\Gamma\delta_{\varpi}\|^6. \tag{38}$$

At this point, it becomes evident how to determine the error bound for the proposed iterative scheme (19), by taking into account (38) along with the second criterion outlined in (4), which pertains to the computation of the Drazin inverse, as demonstrated below:

$$\begin{aligned} \|\delta_{\varpi+1}\| &= \|\Theta_{\varpi+1} - \Gamma^D\| \\ &= \|\Gamma^D AV_{\varpi+1} - \Gamma^D\Gamma\Gamma^D\| \\ &= \|\Gamma^D(\Gamma\Theta_{\varpi+1} - \Gamma\Gamma^D)\| \\ &\leq \|\Gamma^D\|\|\Gamma\delta_{\varpi+1}\| \\ &\leq \|\Gamma^D\|\|\delta_{\varpi}\|^6. \end{aligned} \tag{39}$$

The inequalities presented in (39) lead to the conclusion that Θ_{ϖ} converges to Γ^D as $\varpi \to +\infty$, with a convergence rate of the sixth order. We consider summarizing key points for readers unfamiliar with iterative methods as follows:

- The convergence proof demonstrates that the error decreases exponentially, with a sixth-order convergence rate, ensuring rapid approximation of the Drazin inverse.
- A key feature is the reduction in computational effort due to fewer matrix–matrix multiplications while maintaining high accuracy.
- The choice of an appropriate initial value plays a crucial role in ensuring the method's reliability.
- These insights provide a clear understanding of why the proposed method outperforms existing iterative schemes in both speed and efficiency, especially when the matrix norm-2 is required for each computing step.

This completes the proof. □

5. Efficiency Comparison

As discussed earlier, an effective iterative method is distinguished by its high convergence rate paired with minimal computational cost. When finding the Drazin inverse, a significant portion of computational resources is often consumed by matrix products.

Assuming unit cost for each matrix–matrix product, as is typical in floating-point calculations, we recall the inverse-finder informational efficiency index (IEI). It utilizes ρ and κ, representing the convergence rate and the quantity of matrix–matrix multiplications, in the respective order, and is defined as follows [20]:

$$IEI = \frac{\rho}{\kappa}. \tag{40}$$

On the other hand, the efficiency index (EI) for iterative solvers is defined as follows [20]:

$$EI = \sqrt[\kappa]{\rho}, \tag{41}$$

where κ represents the total computational cost. Thus, we undertake a theoretical analysis to compare the computational efficiency of various iterative schemes—namely, (5), (8), (9), (10), and (19)—as each of these approaches can converge to Γ^D provided a suitable initial guess is selected (6). An analytically favorable scheme should, therefore, aim to achieve a high convergence speed ρ with a minimal quantity of matrix–matrix products κ relative to competing methods, ideally satisfying $\kappa \leq \rho$.

The results summarized in Table 1 demonstrate that, for various values of v, the EIs of PM1 and PM2 outperform those of their competitors. The results confirm the almost equal or superior performance and enhanced efficiency of PM methods when compared to the main competing methods.

Table 1. A comparative analysis of the computational load associated with various methods, each evaluated across various indices.

Solvers	(5)	(8)	(9)	(10)	(19)
ρ	2	3	3	4	6
κ	2	3	4	4	5
IEI	$\frac{2}{2} = 1$	$\frac{3}{3} = 1$	$\frac{3}{4} = 0.75$	$\frac{4}{4} = 1$	$\frac{6}{5} \approx 1.2$
EI	$2^{\frac{1}{2}} \simeq 1.41$	$3^{\frac{1}{3}} \simeq 1.44$	$3^{\frac{1}{4}} \simeq 1.31$	$4^{\frac{1}{4}} \simeq 1.41$	$6^{\frac{1}{5}} \simeq 1.43$

6. Experiments

This section examines the computational precision and efficiency in calculating the Drazin inverse. The proposed iterative scheme (19) is notable for its implementation without requiring matrix exponentiation, facilitating its straightforward application in computing generalized inverses. For comparative computational analysis, we employ the schemes (5), (8), (9), and (19), referenced as SM2, CM3, LM3, and PM, in the respective order.

Several points merit attention:

- Simulations are conducted using Mathematica 13.0 [32,33].

- Computation times for obtaining approximate inverses are measured in seconds.
- When reporting elapsed times, all methods under comparison are executed within an identical computational environment.

Experiment 1. *This test is conducted to compute the Drazin inverse, given that the matrix is specified as in [17]:*

$$\Gamma = \begin{bmatrix} 2 & 4/10 & 0 & 0 & 0 & 0 & 0 & 0 & 0 & 0 & 0 & 0 \\ -2 & 4/10 & 0 & 0 & 0 & 0 & 0 & 0 & 0 & 0 & 0 & 0 \\ -1 & -1 & 1 & -1 & 0 & 0 & 0 & 0 & -1 & 0 & 0 & 0 \\ -1 & -1 & -1 & 1 & 0 & 0 & 0 & 0 & 0 & 0 & 0 & 0 \\ 0 & 0 & 0 & 0 & 1 & 1 & -1 & -1 & 0 & 0 & -1 & 0 \\ 0 & 0 & 0 & 0 & 1 & 1 & -1 & -1 & 0 & 0 & 0 & 0 \\ 0 & 0 & 0 & -1 & -2 & 4/10 & 0 & 0 & 0 & 0 & 0 & 0 \\ 0 & 0 & 0 & 0 & 2 & 4/10 & 0 & 0 & 0 & 0 & 0 & 0 \\ 0 & -1 & 0 & 0 & 0 & 0 & 0 & 0 & 1 & -1 & -1 & -1 \\ 0 & 0 & 0 & 0 & 0 & 0 & 0 & 0 & -1 & 1 & -1 & -1 \\ 0 & 0 & 0 & 0 & 0 & 0 & 0 & 0 & 0 & 0 & 4/10 & -2 \\ 0 & 0 & 0 & 0 & 0 & 0 & 0 & 0 & 0 & 0 & 4/10 & 2 \end{bmatrix},$$

with $\iota = \mathrm{ind}(\Gamma) = 3$. *The Drazin inverse in its exact form can be expressed as*

$$\Gamma^D = \begin{bmatrix} 0.25 & -0.25 & 0. & 0. & 0. & 0. & 0. & 0. & 0. & 0. & 0. & 0. \\ 1.25 & 1.25 & 0. & 0. & 0. & 0. & 0. & 0. & 0. & 0. & 0. & 0. \\ -1.66 & -0.99 & 0.25 & -0.25 & 0. & 0. & 0. & 0. & -0.06 & -0.06 & 0. & 0.15 \\ -1.19 & -0.67 & -0.25 & 0.25 & 0. & 0. & 0. & 0. & -0.06 & 0.18 & 0.68 & 1.34 \\ -2.76 & -1.04 & -1.87 & -1.25 & -1.25 & 1.25 & 1.25 & 1.25 & 1.48 & 2.57 & 3.32 & 6.64 \\ -2.76 & -1.04 & -1.87 & -1.25 & -1.25 & 1.25 & 1.25 & 1.25 & 1.48 & 2.57 & 4.57 & 8.51 \\ 14.10 & 6.30 & 6.62 & 3.37 & 5. & -3. & -5. & -5. & -4.18 & -8.5 & -10.50 & -22.46 \\ -19.32 & -8.50 & -9.75 & -5.25 & -7.5 & 4.5 & 7.5 & 7.5 & 6.37 & 12.56 & 15.97 & 33.78 \\ -0.62 & -0.31 & 0. & 0. & 0. & 0. & 0. & 0. & 0.25 & -0.25 & -0.87 & -1.62 \\ -1.25 & -0.93 & 0. & 0. & 0. & 0. & 0. & 0. & -0.25 & 0.25 & -0.87 & -1.62 \\ 0. & 0. & 0. & 0. & 0. & 0. & 0. & 0. & 0. & 0. & 1.25 & 1.25 \\ 0. & 0. & 0. & 0. & 0. & 0. & 0. & 0. & 0. & 0. & -0.25 & 0.25 \end{bmatrix}.$$

The termination criterion is defined as $||\Theta_{\iota+1} - \Theta_\iota||_\infty \leq 10^{-6}$. Verifying the requirements outlined in Definition 2 for the proposed iterative method PM leads to

$$\begin{aligned} ||\Gamma^{\iota+1}\Gamma^D - \Gamma^\iota||_\infty &= 2.58 \times 10^{-11}, \\ ||\Gamma^D\Gamma\Gamma^D - \Gamma^D||_\infty &= 4.87 \times 10^{-11}, \\ ||\Gamma\Gamma^D - \Gamma^D\Gamma||_\infty &= 7.64 \times 10^{-9}, \end{aligned} \tag{42}$$

which provides validation for the theoretical analysis.

Experiment 2. *The purpose of this test is to evaluate and compare the CPU times taken by various solvers when applied to ten randomly generated square matrices (denoted here by A for simplicity in coding) using the following piece of code:*

```
ClearAll["Global'*"]
SeedRandom[12];
n1 = 500; n2 = n1; number = 10; max1 = 75;
Table[A[j] = RandomReal[{0, 1}, {n1, n2}], {j, number}];
```

In this test, convergence is determined by the stopping criterion $||\Theta_{\varpi+1} - \Theta_\varpi||_2 \leq 10^{-6}$. *Additionally, the initial value is generated by means of*

$$\Theta_0 = \frac{\Gamma^T}{||\Gamma||_2^2}.$$

The outcomes of the comparative analysis for this test are displayed in Figures 1 and 2 (for two different choices of input size), where computations for regular inverses were carried out with a standard precision of 15 digits. Evidently, higher-order methods necessitate fewer iterations for convergence; hence, the primary emphasis is placed on the computational time required to achieve the specified tolerance. It can be observed that our proposed scheme (19) outperforms its competitors, further validating the theoretical discussions in Section 3.

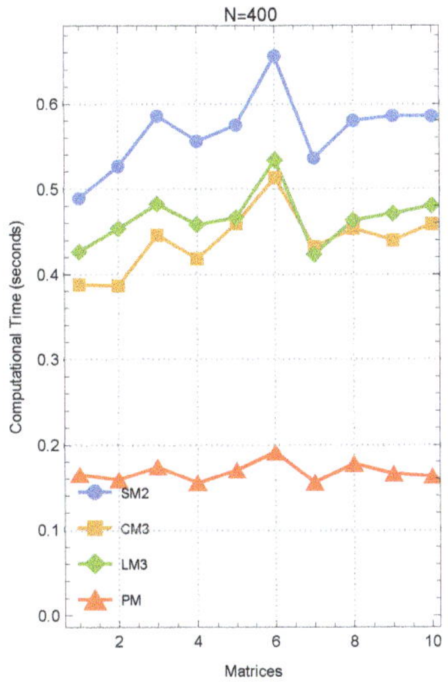

Figure 1. A comparative analysis of CPU times for different solvers, as conducted for Experiment 2, is presented for matrices of size 400×400.

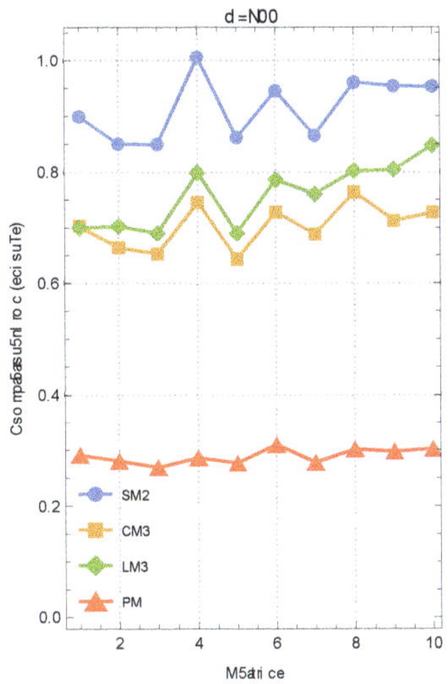

Figure 2. A comparison of the CPU times for different solvers for Experiment 2 for matrices of size 500×500.

Experiment 3. *The objective of this test is to evaluate and compare the CPU times required by various solvers under the conditions of Experiment 2, modifying only the stopping criteria:* $\|\Theta_{\varpi+1} - \Theta_{\varpi}\|_2 \leq 10^{-4}$ *and* $\|\Theta_{\varpi+1} - \Theta_{\varpi}\|_2 \leq 10^{-8}$.

The results of the comparative analysis are illustrated in Figures 3–6, and they provide evidence supporting the effectiveness and robustness of the proposed two-step solver for computing (generalized) inverses. The numerical experiments demonstrate that the sixth-order convergence of our method outperforms traditional iterative approaches, particularly in terms of computational efficiency and in norm 2. Across all test cases, our method requires fewer iterations and exhibits faster computational times, even when subjected to diverse stopping criteria. Furthermore, the method demonstrates exceptional scalability, effectively handling matrices of varying dimensions, including those with randomly generated entries.

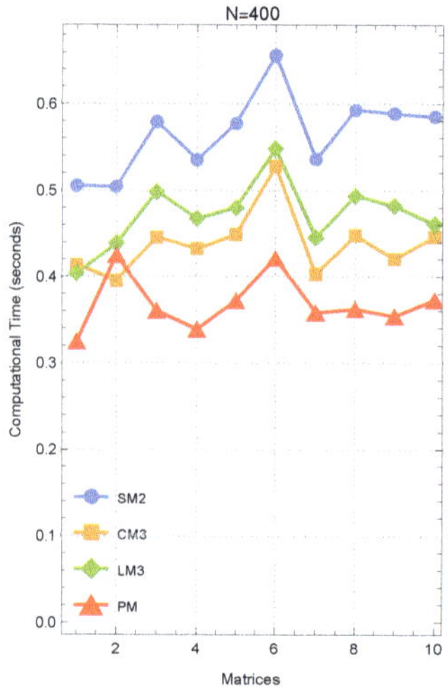

Figure 3. A comparison of the CPU times for different solvers for Experiment 3 for matrices of size 400×400 when $\|\Theta_{\varpi+1} - \Theta_{\varpi}\|_2 \leq 10^{-4}$.

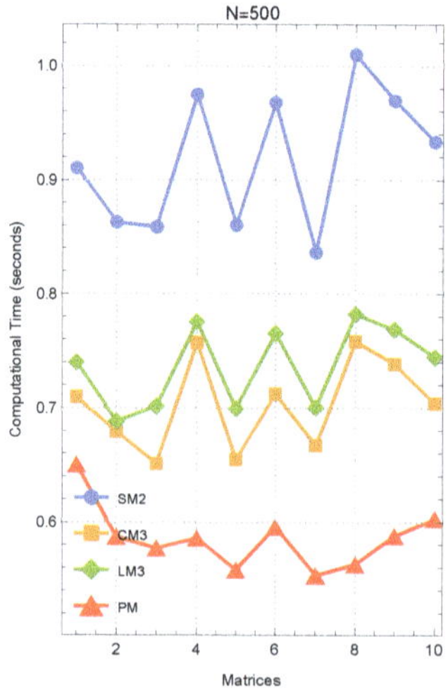

Figure 4. A comparison of the CPU times for different solvers for Experiment 3 for matrices of size 500×500 when $\|\Theta_{\varpi+1} - \Theta_{\varpi}\|_2 \leq 10^{-4}$.

Additionally, the two-step iterative framework ensures that the solver remains computationally efficient under varying input configurations, which is critical for applications involving high-dimensional datasets. Moreover, the high order of convergence directly translates into reduced computational complexity, making the method particularly advantageous for resource-intensive scenarios. Unlike lower-order methods, which may struggle to balance speed and accuracy, our solver achieves a trade-off between these two metrics. This makes it an ideal choice for real-world applications requiring rapid solutions to generalized inverse problems.

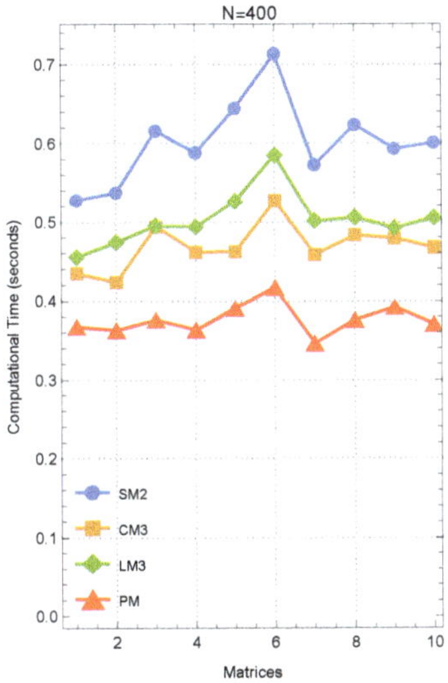

Figure 5. A comparison of the CPU times for different solvers for Experiment 3 for matrices of size 400×400 when $\|\Theta_{\varpi+1} - \Theta_{\varpi}\|_2 \leq 10^{-8}$.

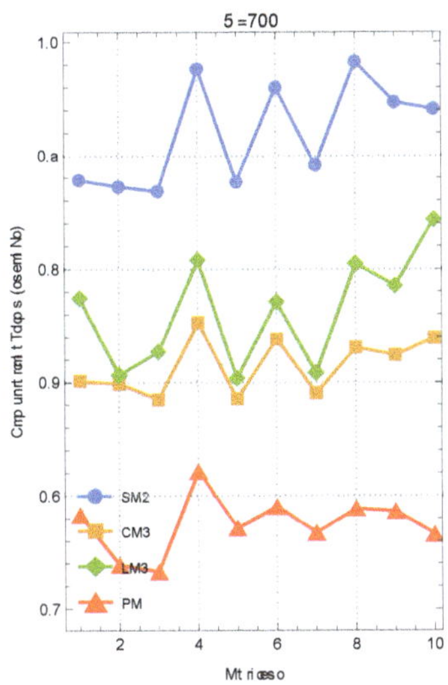

Figure 6. A comparison of the CPU times for different solvers for Experiment 3 for matrices of size 500×500 when $\|\Theta_{\varpi+1} - \Theta_{\varpi}\|_2 \leq 10^{-8}$.

7. Conclusions

The Drazin inverse is a fundamental concept in matrix theory, with its calculation being both challenging and highly applicable in practice. In conclusion, this study has presented a numerically efficient two-step iterative solver designed for calculating the Drazin generalized inverse with a sixth-order convergence rate, which qualifies it as a higher-order solver. We have rigorously analyzed the convergence properties of the proposed scheme, particularly emphasizing the importance of selecting an appropriate initial value, Θ_0, to ensure convergence towards Γ^D.

Our findings have demonstrated that matrix iteration schemes are highly sensitive to this initial value selection, especially for sparse matrices. The proposed method builds upon traditional Schulz-like iteration schemes, addressing the challenges associated with requiring an optimal initial guess while providing enhanced computational efficiency.

Extensive numerical tests have confirmed the theoretical results, showcasing both the speed and effectiveness of the proposed solver. Moreover, our analysis has revealed that this novel iterative approach achieves substantial improvements in CPU time over existing methods by reducing the quantity of matrix–matrix products. The obtained results further validate the effectiveness of the proposed iterative method (19), demonstrated by a notable decrease in the elapsed CPU times. This efficiency makes our solver particularly suitable for applications requiring the Drazin inverse, contributing a significant advancement to iteration solvers in numerical linear algebra.

Author Contributions: Conceptualization, K.Z. and F.S.; methodology, K.Z. and F.S.; software, K.Z. and F.S.; validation, K.Z., F.S. and S.S.; investigation, K.Z., F.S. and S.S.; data curation, K.Z., F.S. and S.S.; writing—original draft, K.Z., F.S. and S.S.; writing—review and editing, K.Z., F.S. and S.S.; visualization, K.Z., F.S. and S.S.; supervision, F.S.; project administration, K.Z., F.S. and S.S.; funding acquisition, S.S. Equal contributions were made by all authors in the development of this paper. All authors have read and agreed to the published version of the manuscript.

Funding: This research received no external funding.

Data Availability Statement: The original contributions presented in this study are included in the article. Further inquiries can be directed to the corresponding author.

Conflicts of Interest: The authors declare no conflicts of interest .

References

1. Ghorbanzadeh, M.; Mahdiani, K.; Soleymani, F.; Lotfi, T. A class of Kung-Traub-Type iterative algorithms for matrix inversion. *Int. J. Appl. Comput. Math.* **2016**, *2*, 641–648. [CrossRef]
2. Zehra, A.; Younus, A.; Tunç, C. Controllability and observability of linear impulsive differential algebraic system with Caputo fractional derivative. *Comput. Methods Differ. Equ.* **2022**, 10, 200–214.
3. Ben-Israel, A.; Greville, T.N.E. *Generalized Inverses: Theory and Applications*, 2nd ed.; Springer: New York, NY, USA, 2003.
4. Ma, X.; Kumar Nashine, H.; Shil, S.; Soleymani, F. Exploiting higher computational efficiency index for computing outer generalized inverses. *Appl. Numer. Math.* **2022**, *175*, 18–28. [CrossRef]
5. Jebreen, H.B.; Chalco-Cano, Y. An improved computationally efficient method for finding the Drazin inverse. *Discrete Dyn. Nat. Soc.* **2018**, *2018*, 6758302. [CrossRef]
6. Guo, L.; Hu, G.; Yu, D.; Luan, T. A representation of the Drazin inverse for the sum of two matrices and the anti-triangular block matrices. *Mathematics* **2023**, *11*, 3661. [CrossRef]
7. Sayevand, K.; Pourdarvish, A.; Machado, J.A.T.; Erfanifar, R. On the calculation of the Moore-Penrose and Drazin inverses: Application to fractional calculus. *Mathematics* **2021**, *9*, 2501. [CrossRef]
8. Shil, S.; Kumar Nashine, H.; Soleymani, F. On an inversion-free algorithm for the nonlinear matrix problem $\mathcal{X}^{\alpha} + \mathcal{A}^* \mathcal{X}^{-\beta} \mathcal{A} + \mathcal{B}^* \mathcal{X}^{-\gamma} \mathcal{B} = \mathcal{I}$. *Int. J. Comput. Math.* **2022**, *99*, 2555–2567. [CrossRef]
9. Wei, Y. Index splitting for the Drazin inverse and the singular linear system. *Appl. Math. Comput.* **1998**, *95*, 115–124. [CrossRef]
10. Drazin, M.P. Pseudoinverses in associative rings and semigroups. *Amer. Math. Monthly* **1958**, *65*, 506–514. [CrossRef]
11. Wilkinson, J.H. Note on the practical significance of the Drazin inverse. In *Recent Applications of Generalized Inverses, Pitman Advanced Publishing Program*; Campbell, S.L., Ed.; Research Notes in Mathematics No. 66, Boston; Pitman: London, UK, 1982; pp. 82–99.
12. Kaczorek, T.; Ruszewski, A. Application of the Drazin inverse to the analysis of pointwise completeness and pointwise degeneracy of descriptor fractional linear continuous-time systems. *Int. J. Appl. Math. Comput. Sci.* **2020**, *30*, 219–223. [CrossRef]

13. Romo, F.P. On G-Drazin inverses of finite potent endomorphisms and arbitrary square matrices. *Linear and Multilinear Algebra* **2022**, *70*, 2227–2247. [CrossRef]
14. Kyrchei, I. Explicit formulas for determinantal representations of the Drazin inverse solutions of some matrix and differential matrix equations. *Appl. Math. Comput.* **2013**, *219*, 7632–7644. [CrossRef]
15. Pan, V.Y. *Structured Matrices and Polynomials: Unified Superfast Algorithms*; BirkhWauser: Boston, FL, USA; Springer: New York, NY, USA, 2001.
16. Schulz, G. Iterative Berechnung der Reziproken matrix. *Z. Angew. Math. Mech.***1933**, *13*, 57–59. [CrossRef]
17. Li, X.; Wei, Y. Iterative methods for the Drazin inverse of a matrix with a complex spectrum. *Appl. Math. Comput.* **2004**, *147*, 855–862. [CrossRef]
18. Li, H.-B.; Huang, T.-Z.; Zhang, Y.; Liu, X.-P.; Gu, T.-X. Chebyshev-type methods and preconditioning techniques. *Appl. Math. Comput.* **2011**, *218*, 260–270. [CrossRef]
19. Krishnamurthy, E.V.; Sen, S.K. *Numerical Algorithms—Computations in Science and Engineering*; Affiliated East-West Press: New Delhi, India, 1986.
20. Traub, J.F. *Iterative Methods for Solution of Equations*; Prentice-Hall: Englewood Cliffs, NJ, USA, 1964.
21. Sen, S.K.; Prabhu, S.S. Optimal iterative schemes for computing Moore-Penrose matrix inverse. *Int. J. Sys. Sci.* **1976**, *8*, 748–753. [CrossRef]
22. Bini, D.A. Numerical computation of the roots of Mandelbrot polynomials: An experimental analysis. *Electron. Trans. Numer. Anal.* **2024**, *61*, 1–27. [CrossRef]
23. Ogbereyivwe, O.; Atajeromavwo, E.J.; Umar, S.S. Jarratt and Jarratt-variant families of iterative schemes for scalar and system of nonlinear equations. *Iran. J. Numer. Anal. Optim.* **2024**, *14*, 391–416.
24. Hernández, M.; Salanova, M. A family of Chebyshev-Halley type methods. *Int. J. Comput. Math.* **1993**, *47*, 59–63. [CrossRef]
25. Ivanov, S.I. Unified convergence analysis of Chebyshev-Halley methods for multiple polynomial zeros. *Mathematics* **2022**, *10*, 135. [CrossRef]
26. Amat, S.; Busquier, S. After notes on Chebyshev's iterative method. *Appl. Math. Nonlinear Sci.* **2017**, *2*, 1–12.
27. Artidiello, S.; Cordero, A.; Torregrosa, J.R.P.; Vassileva, M. Generalized inverses estimations by means of iterative methods with memory. *Mathematics* **2020**, *8*, 2. [CrossRef]
28. Torkashvand, V.; Kazemi, M.; Azimi, M. Efficient family of three-step with-memory methods and their dynamics. *Comput. Methods Differ. Equ.* **2024**, *12*, 599–609.
29. Canela, J.; Evdoridou, V.; Garijo, A.; Jarque, X. On the basins of attraction of a one-dimensional family of root finding algorithms: From Newton to Traub. *Math. Z.* **2023**, *303*, 55. [CrossRef]
30. Kostadinova, S.G.; Ivanov, S.I. Chebyshev's method for multiple zeros of analytic functions: Convergence, dynamics and real-world applications. *Mathematics* **2024**, *12*, 3043. [CrossRef]
31. Soleymani, F.; Stanimirović, P.S. A higher order iterative method for computing the Drazin inverse. *Sci. World J.* **2013**, *2013*, 708647. [CrossRef]
32. Sánchez León, J.G. *Mathematica Beyond Mathematics: The Wolfram Language in the Real World*; Taylor & Francis Group: Boca Raton, FL, USA, 2017.
33. Trott, M. *The Mathematica Guide-Book for Numerics*; Springer: New York, NY, USA, 2006.

axiom

MDPI

Article

Cantelli's Bounds for Generalized Tail Inequalities

Nicola Apollonio [1,2]

[1] Istituto per le Applicazioni del Calcolo, C.N.R.,Via dei Taurini 19, 00185 Roma, Italy; nicola.apollonio@cnr.it
[2] Istituto Nazionale di Alta Matematica Francesco Severi, Piazzale Aldo Moro 5, 00185 Roma, Italy

Abstract: Let X be a centered random vector in a finite-dimensional real inner product space $\mathcal{E}$. For a subset C of the ambient vector space V of $\mathcal{E}$ and $x, y \in V$, write $x \preceq_C y$ if $y - x \in C$. If C is a closed convex cone in $\mathcal{E}$, then $\preceq_C$ is a preorder on V, whereas if C is a proper cone in $\mathcal{E}$, then $\preceq_C$ is actually a partial order on V. In this paper, we give sharp Cantelli-type inequalities for generalized tail probabilities such as $\Pr\{X \succeq_C b\}$ for $b \in V$. These inequalities are obtained by "scalarizing" $X \succeq_C b$ via cone duality and then by minimizing the classical univariate Cantelli's bound over the scalarized inequalities. Three diverse applications to random matrices, tails of linear images of random vectors, and network homophily are also given.

Keywords: tail inequalities; cone duality; Wigner matrix; network homophily

MSC: 62G32; 52A07

1. Introduction

Let Y be a random variable with finite mean μ and variance σ^2. Thus, the random variable $X = Y - \mu$ is centered and has the same variance as Y. For a positive real number b, the celebrated Cantelli inequality—also known as the *one-sided Chebyshev's inequality*—reads as follows

$$\Pr\{X \geq b\} \leq \frac{\sigma^2}{b^2 + \sigma^2}. \tag{1}$$

Both Cantelli's inequality and the classical Chebyshev's inequality can be (and have been) extended in several ways [1,2] to a random vector $X = (X_1, \dots, X_n)'$ in $\mathbb{R}^n$—here and throughout the rest of the paper, u' denotes the transpose of the column vector $u \in \mathbb{R}^n$. As shown in [1,2], there is a standard recipe that yields such extensions: Let X be a random vector supported by a subset S of $\mathbb{R}^n$ and let Σ be the covariance matrix of X. Let T be a Borel subset of S and $f : S \to \mathbb{R}$ such that $f(x) \geq 0$ for all $x \in S$ and $f(x) \geq 1$ for all $x \in T$. Then, with $\mathbf{1}_T(\cdot)$ denoting the indicator of the set T over S, one has $f \geq \mathbf{1}_T$ and

$$\mathbb{E}(f(X)) \geq \mathbb{E}(f(X)\mathbf{1}_T(X)) \geq \mathbb{E}(\mathbf{1}_T(X)) = \Pr\{X \in T\}.$$

This technique is essentially a "Markov inequality". By taking f in the family $\{f_u \mid f_u : \mathbb{R}^n \to \mathbb{R}^n_+,\ u \in \mathbb{R}^n\}$, where $f_u(x) = \frac{(u'x + u'\Sigma u)^2}{1 + u'\Sigma u}$, and minimizing for u under the constraint $f \geq \mathbf{1}_T$, Marshall and Olkin obtained the following strong and general result.

Theorem 1 (Marshall and Olkin [1]). *Let T be a closed convex set in $\mathbb{R}^n$ not containing the origin. If X is a centered random vector of $\mathbb{R}^n$ with a positive-definite covariance matrix Σ, then*

$$\Pr\{X \in T\} \leq \inf_{\substack{u \in \mathbb{R}^n \\ u'x \geq 1,\, \forall x \in T}} \frac{u'\Sigma u}{1 + u'\Sigma u}. \tag{2}$$

Furthermore, the inequality is sharp, in the sense that there exists a centered random vector X_0 whose support contains T and whose covariance matrix is Σ, such that the inequality is attained as an equality.

Note that Cantelli's inequality (1) follows from inequality (2) after dividing the univariate random variable X by the positive threshold b and observing that the variance of X/b is σ^2/b^2. The minimization problem on the right-hand side of (2) is solved by minimizing the quadratic form $u'\Sigma u$ over the same set. This is a convex minimization problem that can be solved using the techniques described in [3]. As proved in [1], the infimum in (2) is attained. The function $f_{\hat{u}}$ corresponding to the vector $\hat{u}$, which attains the infimum in inequality (2), can be seen as a kind of envelope of a given shape (in this case quadratic) for the probability on the right-hand side. The same inequality can be interpreted in the following way: First, we linearly approximate T inside the probability. This approximation yields a family of linear inequalities, each of which is the tail of a scalar random variable. We then use Cantelli's inequality (1) to bound each of these tails, and finally, we choose the tightest one. Let us describe this process for a non-empty arbitrary Borel subset T of $\mathbb{R}^n$: Let $\mathfrak{b}(T) = \{u \in \mathbb{R}^n \mid u'x \geq 1, \quad \forall x \in T\}$—note that $\mathfrak{b}(T)$ is always a closed convex set regardless of the argument T (see Section 2 for more details) and hence a Borel set—since, by definition, $T \subseteq \mathfrak{b}(\mathfrak{b}(T))$ and $x \in \mathfrak{b}(\mathfrak{b}(T)) \Leftrightarrow u'x \geq 1, \forall u \in \mathfrak{b}(T)$, it follows that

$$\Pr\{X \in T\} \leq \Pr\{X \in \mathfrak{b}(\mathfrak{b}(T))\} = \Pr\{u'X \geq 1, \forall u \in \mathfrak{b}(T)\},$$

where X is a centered random vector with a positive-definite covariance matrix Σ. Here, for all $u \in \mathfrak{b}(T)$, the random variable $u'X$ is a centered random variable with variance $u'\Sigma u$. Thus, by Cantelli's inequality, for all $u \in \mathfrak{b}(T)$, it holds that

$$\Pr\{X \in T\} \leq \frac{u'\Sigma u}{1 + u'\Sigma u}.$$

Thus, if T is a non-empty convex set, after taking the infimum over $\mathfrak{b}(T)$, we recover (2) from another perspective. It is easy to see that the same result holds in any finite-dimensional Euclidean space $\mathcal{E}$. If T is of the form $b + C$, where C is a convex cone in $\mathcal{E}$, then we provide a specialized Cantelli bound that is sharp. Furthermore, if C has a non-empty interior, then C induces a preorder $\succeq_C$ on the ambient space of $\mathcal{E}$ such that the event $(X \in T)$ can be written as $(X \succeq_C b)$ and can be interpreted as a generalized tail inequality (we recover classical tail inequalities when C is the non-negative orthant). Thus, Cantelli's inequality naturally extends to generalized tail inequalities in finite-dimensional Euclidean spaces. While such an extension is not really genuine since, in the finite-dimensional case, it can be derived by standard arguments from the special case of the standard real n-dimensional Euclidean space (see Lemma 7), on the other hand, it allows a tight sharpening of the general case (Corollary 1) and also allows to cast seemingly more complicated events into the framework of tail inequalities, as they occur, for example, in random matrix theory. Consider the case where X is a random matrix sampled from a symmetric real ensemble (see Section 4.1 for precise definitions). A fundamental problem in this context is to understand, at least asymptotically, when the order of the matrix goes to ∞, the probability that the smallest eigenvalue of X is positive. This problem is completely and precisely solved for Gaussian matrices (see [4–6]): the probability of sampling a positive-definite matrix from a symmetric Gaussian ensemble goes to zero exponentially fast. In this paper, using Corollary 1 in Section 3, we prove that the same result holds more generally for the *Wigner* matrices of the form $\frac{M+M'}{2}$, where M is a random matrix whose entries are i.i.d. centered random variables, although the rate we can provide is much weaker. The result follows by looking at the random matrix X as a random vector in the Euclidean space

$\mathcal{E} = (S^n, \langle\cdot,\cdot\rangle_F)$, where S^n is the real vector space of real symmetric matrices and $\langle\cdot,\cdot\rangle_F$ is the Frobenius inner product. If S^n_+ denotes the cone of positive semi-definite matrices lying in $\mathcal{E}$ and $\succeq$ is the partial order induced by S^n_+, then, for a real number ϵ, with I being the identity matrix of order n, the generalized tail $(X \succeq_{S^n_+} \epsilon I)$ is the event that occurs when the least eigenvalue of X is at least ϵ. Another similar motivation for studying generalized tails comes from the need to compute the probability of the feasibility of systems of linear inequalities whose unknowns are real random variables and the coefficients of the system are deterministic (see Section 4.2). This problem can be cast in the context of concentration and tail inequalities for linear, possibly random images of random vectors [7,8]: Ref. [8] studies the related problem of determining general concentration inequalities, while [7] actually investigates the more general case of tails of random linear images of random vectors, which, in our interpretation, corresponds to the case where both the coefficients and the unknowns of the system are random variables. In this paper, we give a Cantelli-type bound on the feasibility of a system of linear inequalities with random unknowns and show that the "ordinary tails" of the linear image $f(X)$ of a random vector X under a surjective map f are just generalized tails for the random vector X itself taken with respect to a polyhedral cone. Equivalently, by pursuing the interpretation of tails of linear images as solution sets of a linear system of inequalities in the random vector X, we show that if the system has a right-invertible coefficient matrix, then its solution set is a generalized tail for X taken with respect to a polyhedral cone: the rows of the coefficient matrix are the normal vectors of the proper maximal faces of the cone.

It is clear from the discussion above that tail inequalities for random vectors depend crucially on their covariance functions Σ. When Σ has some additional structure, for special choices of the threshold b, Cantelli's inequality for generalized tails reads as a very simple expression in terms of certain norms of b. For instance (see Section 3 for details), for $b \geq 0$, if Σ^{-1} is a non-negative matrix, then

$$\Pr\{X \geq b\} \leq (1 + \|b\|_M^2)^{-1},$$

where $\|b\|_M = \sqrt{b'\Sigma^{-1}b}$ is the *Mahalanobis norm* of b. Note that inequality (1) specializes to the inequality above after dividing the numerator and denominator by σ^2. The assumption $\Sigma^{-1} \geq 0$ is only seemingly artificial. It is often satisfied by finitely supported random vectors that occur in network science. In Section 4.3, we will give one such important case. In light of Theorem 7, which rests on observations from [9], having easily computable bounds on tail probabilities, like the one above, is generally the best we can hope for, even if we have no control over the quality of the approximation.

The rest of the paper is organized as follows: In Section 2, we develop the machinery to state and prove the main results provided in Section 3, while in Section 4, we apply our results to the probability of sampling a positive-definite Wigner matrix, to the probability of feasibility of a system of linear inequalities, and to testing homophily in networks.

2. Preparatory Results

Finite-dimensional Euclidean spaces, namely, finite-dimensional real vector spaces V equipped with an inner product $\langle\cdot,\cdot\rangle$, are denoted by calligraphic letters such as $\mathcal{E}$. The symbol $\mathcal{R}^n$ stands for the Euclidean space $(\mathbb{R}^n, \langle\cdot,\cdot\rangle)$, where $\langle\cdot,\cdot\rangle$ is the standard dot product in $\mathbb{R}^n$. In the following, when we talk about Euclidean spaces, we mean finite-dimensional Euclidean spaces over reals.

When dealing with random vectors, the Borel sets we are interested in have the form $b + C$, where $b \in V$ and $C \subseteq V$ is a non-empty Borel set, often a *cone*. A *cone* in $\mathcal{E}$ is a subset C of V that is closed under taking positive scalar multiples, i.e., $\lambda C \subseteq C$ for every $\lambda > 0$, while a *convex cone* C is a cone that is closed under taking sum, i.e., $C + C \subseteq C$. The empty set, the set consisting only of the zero vector of V, and V itself are the *trivial cones*. In the following, when we speak of cones, we mean non-trivial cones. Crucial to the definition of *generalized inequality* is the following notion of duality of subsets of Euclidean spaces. First, identify the algebraic dual V^* of V with V by the inner product in $\mathcal{E}$ via the isomorphism $V \ni v \mapsto \langle v, \cdot \rangle \in V^*$. Let C be a non-empty subset of V. The *dual* C^* of C in $\mathcal{E}$ is the set

$$C^* = \{u \in V \mid \langle u, v \rangle \geq 0, \quad \forall v \in C\}.$$

Write C^{**} for the double dual of C, namely, $(C^*)^*$. The following facts, the first three of which are simple consequences of the definition, are known about the dual of a non-empty set C (see [10,11]).

Lemma 1. *Let $C \subseteq V$. Then,*

(a) C^* *is always a closed convex cone;*
(b) $C_1 \subseteq C_2 \Rightarrow C_1^* \supseteq C_2^*$*, i.e., duality is inclusion reversing;*
(c) $C \subseteq C^{**}$*;*
(d) $C = C^{**}$ *if and only if C is a closed convex cone.*

Proof. See [10,11]. □

The last property in the lemma implies that $C^* = C^{***}$ because C^* is a closed convex cone by (a). A cone C is *proper* whenever C is a closed convex cone that is also *pointed*, i.e., $C \cap -C = \{0\}$, where 0 is the zero vector of V, and has non-empty interior. A cone C is *self-dual in $\mathcal{E}$* if $C = C^*$.

For a random vector $X = (X_1, \ldots, X_n)' \in \mathbb{R}^n$ and $b = (b_1, \ldots, b_n)' \in \mathbb{R}^n$, the event $(X \geq b)$ is said to be a *tail* of X. Such an event reads as $(X_1 \geq b_1, \ldots, X_n \geq b_n)$ and is the same event as $X - b \in \mathbb{R}^n_+$. The non-negative orthant $\mathbb{R}^n_+$ is a self-dual cone in $\mathcal{R}^n$. Clearly, $X - b$ is non-negative if and only if $u'(X - b)$ is non-negative for all vectors $u \in \mathbb{R}^n_+$, i.e., for all u in the dual cone of $\mathbb{R}^n_+$. This fact can be generalized as follows. Let the ambient space of $\mathcal{E}$ be V and let C be a non-empty subset of V. For $x, y \in V$, write $y \succeq_C x$ if $y - x \in C$. If C is a convex cone, then $\succeq_C$ is a pre-order on V, while if C is a proper cone, then $\succeq_C$ is a partial order on V. In any case, even when C is arbitrary, by duality, one has

$$y \succeq_C x \Longrightarrow y \succeq_{C^{**}} x \Longleftrightarrow \langle u, y - x \rangle \geq 0, \forall u \in C^* \tag{3}$$

which reduces to

$$y \succeq_C x \Longleftrightarrow \langle u, y - x \rangle \geq 0, \forall u \in C^*$$

when C is a closed convex cone. Generalized inequalities, and hence generalized tails, are well behaved with respect to linear transformations of random vectors because cones are preserved by such maps. In fact, if the latter are invertible, closedness is preserved as well.

We also need a lesser-known duality device, which we borrow from the theory of *blocking pairs of polyhedra* [12]. Let V be the ambient space of $\mathcal{E}$. For $T \subseteq V$, the *blocker of T in $\mathcal{E}$* is the set

$$\mathfrak{b}(T) = \{u \in V \mid \langle u, x \rangle \geq 1, \quad \forall x \in T\}.$$

Analogous to the dual of T, the blocker of T has the following properties, the first three of which are straightforward.

Lemma 2. *In the Euclidean space* $\mathcal{E} = (V, \langle\cdot,\cdot\rangle)$, *let* $T \subseteq V$. *It holds that*

(i) *if* $T \neq \emptyset$, *then* $\mathfrak{b}(T)$ *is a non-empty closed convex set;*

(ii) *if* $T \subseteq T'$, *then* $\mathfrak{b}(T) \supseteq \mathfrak{b}(T')$;

(iii) $T \subseteq \mathfrak{b}(\mathfrak{b}(T))$;

(iv) *if* $T = b + C$ *where* $b \in V$ *and* C *is such that* $\emptyset \neq C \subseteq V$, *then*

$$\mathfrak{b}(b + C) \supseteq \mathfrak{b}(b + C^{**}) \supseteq C^* \cap \{u \in V \mid \langle u, b\rangle \geq 1\}; \tag{4}$$

moreover, if C *is a nontrivial cone, then*

$$C^* \cap \{u \in V \mid \langle u, b\rangle > 0\} \supseteq \mathfrak{b}(b + C) = C^* \cap \{u \in V \mid \langle u, b\rangle \geq 1\}. \tag{5}$$

Proof. If $T \neq \emptyset$, then $x/\sqrt{\langle x, x\rangle} \in \mathfrak{b}(T)$ for all $x \in T$. Hence, if T is non-empty, then so is $\mathfrak{b}(T)$. Moreover, since $\mathfrak{b}(T)$ is the intersection of closed half-spaces, then $\mathfrak{b}(T)$ is a closed convex set. This establishes (i). Statements (ii) and (iii) are straightforward. Let us prove (iv). To prove (4), first observe that if $u \in C^* \cap \{u \in V \mid \langle u, b\rangle \geq 1\}$, then $\langle u, b + y\rangle \geq 1$, $\forall y \in C^{**}$. Hence, $u \in \mathfrak{b}(b + C^{**})$ and $u \in \mathfrak{b}(b + C)$ because $\mathfrak{b}(b + C) \supseteq \mathfrak{b}(b + C^{**})$ by (ii). Let us prove (5). Since $C^* \cap \{u \in V \mid \langle u, b\rangle \geq 1\} \subseteq C^* \cap \{u \in V \mid \langle u, b\rangle > 0\}$, it follows that to prove (5) it suffices to prove that $\mathfrak{b}(b + C) = C^* \cap \{u \in V \mid \langle u, b\rangle \geq 1\}$, which follows by $\mathfrak{b}(b + C) \subseteq C^* \cap \{u \in V \mid \langle u, b\rangle \geq 1\}$ after (4). Let us prove the latter inclusion. Note that if $u \in \mathfrak{b}(b + C)$ and C is a cone, then necessarily $\langle u, y\rangle \geq 0$ for all $y \in C$ for, if not, there exists $y_0 \in C$ such that $\langle u, y_0\rangle < 0$ and $b + \lambda y_0 \in T$ for all $\lambda > 0$. Hence, $\langle u, b + \lambda y_0\rangle < 1$ for sufficiently large λ, which contradicts $u \in \mathfrak{b}(b + C)$. We conclude that $\langle u, y\rangle \geq 0$ for all $y \in C$, and thus, $\mathfrak{b}(b + C) \subseteq C^*$. By the same reasoning, it holds that $u \in \mathfrak{b}(b + C) \Rightarrow \langle u, b\rangle \geq 1$. To see this, assume by contradiction that $\langle u_0, b\rangle < 1$ for some $u_0 \in \mathfrak{b}(b + C)$. Since $u_0 \in \mathfrak{b}(b + C)$, there exists $y_0 \in C$, $y_0 \neq 0$, such that $\langle u_0, b + \lambda y_0\rangle \geq 1$ for all $\lambda > 0$. However, the latter inequality cannot be satisfied for a small enough λ. We conclude that the desired inclusion is true. □

Remark 1. *Usually the blocker of a polyhedron* T *of the form* $P + \mathbb{R}^n_+$ *is defined as the set* $B(T) = \{u \in \mathbb{R}^n_+ \mid u'x \geq 1, \forall x \in T\}$. *Hence,* $B(T) = \mathfrak{b}(T) \cap \mathbb{R}^n_+$ *in* $\mathcal{R}^n$. *However, the two definitions coincide in this case because, reasoning as in the proof of* (5), $\mathfrak{b}(T) \subseteq (\mathbb{R}^n_+)^* = \mathbb{R}^n_+$. *Therefore,* $\mathfrak{b}(T) = B(T)$.

In the Euclidean space $\mathcal{E} = (V, \langle\cdot,\cdot\rangle)$, for a set C and a vector b in V the set

$$\mathfrak{a}(b, C) = C^* \cap \{u \in V \mid \langle u, b\rangle > 0\}$$

plays an essential role in the following intermediate results.

Lemma 3. *Let* C *be a set in the Euclidean space* $\mathcal{E} = (V, \langle\cdot,\cdot\rangle)$. *One has* $\mathfrak{a}(b, C) \neq \emptyset$ *if and only if* $0 \notin b + C^{**}$. *Moreover, if* C *is a cone, then one has* $\mathfrak{a}(b, C) \neq \emptyset$ *if and only if* $\mathfrak{b}(b + C) \neq \emptyset$.

Proof. To prove the first assertion, note that

$$\mathfrak{a}(b, C) = \emptyset \Longleftrightarrow \langle u, b\rangle \leq 0\, \forall u \in C^* \Longleftrightarrow -b \in C^{**} \Longleftrightarrow 0 \in b + C^{**}.$$

For the second assertion observe that $\mathfrak{b}(b + C) \neq \emptyset \Rightarrow \mathfrak{a}(b, C) \neq \emptyset$ by (iv) in Lemma 2. Conversely, if $u \in \mathfrak{a}(b, C)$, then $\frac{u}{\langle u, b\rangle} \in \mathfrak{b}(b + C)$ by definition. □

Note that the condition $0 \notin b + C^{**}$ in Lemma 3 can be written as $b \in V \setminus -C^{**}$.

Lemma 4. *In the Euclidean space* $\mathcal{E} = (V, \langle \cdot, \cdot \rangle)$, *let* C *be a non-trivial cone, and* $b \in V \setminus -C^{**}$. *If* $f, g : V \to \mathbb{R}$ *are defined by*

$$f(u) = \frac{q(u)}{\langle u, b \rangle^2 + q(u)} \quad \text{and} \quad g(u) = \frac{q(u)}{1 + q(u)},$$

where $q : V \to \mathbb{R}$ *is a positive-definite quadratic form, then*

$$\inf_{\mathfrak{a}(b,C)} f(u) = \inf_{\mathfrak{b}(b+C)} g(u).$$

Proof. The assumption on b guarantees that $\mathfrak{a}(b, C)$ and $\mathfrak{b}(b + C)$ are both non-empty by Lemma 3. Since q is a quadratic form, it is homogeneous of degree 2. Hence, f is homogeneous of degree 0, namely, $f(\lambda u) = f(u)$. Observe that $f(u) \leq 1$ for all $u \in V$ and that $f(u) = 1$ over the hyperplane $\{u \in V \mid u'b = 0\}$. Thus, by homogeneity, for every $u \in C^*$, f is constant on the rays λu, $\lambda > 0$. In particular,

$$f(u) = f\left(\frac{u}{\langle u, b \rangle}\right) = g\left(\frac{u}{\langle u, b \rangle}\right), \quad \forall u \in C^* \cap \{u \in V \mid \langle u, b \rangle > 0\}. \tag{6}$$

Since, by (5), it holds that $\mathfrak{b}(b + C) = C^* \cap \{u \in V \mid \langle u, b \rangle \geq 1\}$, it follows that

$$f(u) = \frac{q(u)}{\langle u, b \rangle^2 + q(u)} \leq \frac{q(u)}{1 + q(u)} = g(u) \quad \forall u \in \mathfrak{b}(b + C). \tag{7}$$

Let $H = \{u \in V \mid \langle u, b \rangle = 1\}$ and observe that

$$\begin{aligned}
\inf_{\mathfrak{a}(b,C)} f(u) &= \inf_{\mathfrak{a}(b,C) \cap H} g(u) \quad \text{(by(6))} \\
&\geq \inf_{\mathfrak{b}(b+C)} g(u) \quad \text{(because } \mathfrak{a}(b, C) \cap H \subseteq \mathfrak{b}(b + C) \text{ by (5))} \\
&\geq \inf_{\mathfrak{b}(b+C)} f(u) \quad \text{(by (7))} \\
&\geq \inf_{\mathfrak{a}(b,C)} f(u) \quad \text{(because } \mathfrak{a}(b, C) \supseteq \mathfrak{b}(b + C) \text{ by (5))}
\end{aligned}$$

Therefore, equality must hold throughout, yielding the desired equality. □

Recall that given a self-adjoint positive-definite endomorphism of V in $\mathcal{E} = (V, \langle \cdot, \cdot \rangle)$, the bilinear form $\langle u, A(v) \rangle$ induces a norm p on V by $p(v) = \sqrt{\langle v, A(v) \rangle}$. The *dual norm* of p (see [13], Section 5.4) is the norm p^* such that

$$p^*(v) = \sup_{u \neq 0} \frac{|\langle u, v \rangle|}{\sqrt{\langle u, A(u) \rangle}}.$$

Lemma 5. *Let* A *be a self-adjoint positive-definite endomorphism of* V *in* $\mathcal{E} = (V, \langle \cdot, \cdot \rangle)$. *If* p *is the norm on* V *defined by* $p(v) = \sqrt{\langle v, A(v) \rangle}$, *then* $p^*(v) = \sqrt{\langle v, A^{-1}(v) \rangle}$.

Proof. Although this is actually a "folklore" fact, we were unable to locate a reference. Therefore, we provide a proof here.

Since A is a self-adjoint positive-definite endomorphism, $A = B^2$ for some self-adjoint positive-definite endomorphism B (B is a *square-root* of A). Hence, by the Cauchy–Schwarz inequality and because B is self-adjoint,

$$\begin{aligned} |\langle u, v\rangle| = |\langle u, BB^{-1}(v)\rangle| &= |\langle B(u), B^{-1}(v)\rangle| \\ &\leq \sqrt{\langle B(u), B(u)\rangle}\sqrt{\langle B^{-1}(v), B^{-1}(v)\rangle} \\ &= \sqrt{\langle u, A(u)\rangle}\sqrt{\langle v, A^{-1}(v)\rangle}. \end{aligned}$$

Therefore, $p^*(v) \leq \sqrt{\langle v, A^{-1}(v)\rangle}$ with equality for $v = 0$. On the other hand, if $v \neq 0$, then the vector $\overline{v}$ defined by

$$\overline{v} = \frac{A^{-1}(v)}{\sqrt{\langle v, A^{-1}(v)\rangle}}$$

is such that

$$p^*(v) \geq \frac{|\langle \overline{v}, v\rangle|}{\sqrt{\langle \overline{v}, A(\overline{v})\rangle}} = \sqrt{\langle v, A^{-1}(v)\rangle}.$$

Hence, p^* has the stated expression. □

Lemma 6. *In the Euclidean space $\mathcal{E} = (V, \langle\cdot,\cdot\rangle)$, let C be a closed convex cone, $b \in V \setminus -C$, and p the norm $p(v) = \sqrt{\langle v, A(v)\rangle}$ on V, where A is a self-adjoint positive-definite endomorphism of V. If $b \in A(C^*)$, then, with $q = p^2$, in the notation of Lemma 4,*

$$\inf_{\mathfrak{a}(b,C)} f(u) = \frac{1}{(p^*(b))^2 + 1}$$

where p^* is the dual norm of p, namely,

$$p^*(b) = \sup_{u\neq 0} \frac{\langle u, b\rangle}{p(u)} = \sqrt{\langle b, A^{-1}(b)\rangle}.$$

Proof. Since C is a closed convex cone, then $C = C^{**}$ by (d). Hence, the assumption on b guarantees that $\mathfrak{a}(b, C)$ is non-empty by Lemma 3. Therefore, we can divide the numerator and the denominator of $f(u)$ by $q(v)$. This yields

$$\inf_{\mathfrak{a}(b,C)} f(u) = \left(\sup_{\mathfrak{a}(b,C)} \left\{\frac{|\langle u, b\rangle|}{p(u)}\right\}^2 + 1\right)^{-1}.$$

Here, if $b \in A(C^*)$, then $A^{-1}(b) \in C^*$. Hence, $\hat{b} = \frac{A^{-1}(b)}{\sqrt{\langle b, A^{-1}(b)\rangle}}$ belongs to $\mathfrak{a}(C, b)$ because $\hat{b} \in C^*$, with $\hat{b}$ being a positive scalar multiple of $A^{-1}(b)$, and $\langle \hat{b}, b\rangle = \sqrt{\langle b, A^{-1}(b)\rangle} > 0$. By Lemma 5, after plugging $\hat{b}$ into $\frac{\langle u, b\rangle}{p(u)}$, we conclude that the supremum $p^*(b)$ of $\frac{|\langle u, b\rangle|}{p(u)}$ is attained over $\mathfrak{a}(b, C)$, and this concludes the proof. □

3. Results

Let $(\Omega, \mathcal{F}, \mathbb{P})$ be a probability space, where Ω is a set, $\mathcal{F}$ is a σ-algebra on Ω, and $\mathbb{P}$ is a probability measure on $\mathcal{F}$. Also, let $\mathcal{E} = (V, \langle \cdot, \cdot \rangle)$ be a Euclidean space and $\mathcal{B}$ the smallest σ-algebra containing all the open balls of V taken with respect to the norm induced by $\langle \cdot, \cdot \rangle$—this σ-algebra does not depend on the particular inner product chosen on V. A *random vector X in $\mathcal{E}$* is a $(\mathcal{F}, \mathcal{B})$-measurable map $X : \Omega \to V$. The algebra $\mathcal{B}$ is the *algebra of Borel sets of $\mathcal{E}$*. To prove our results, we first need the following lemma.

Lemma 7. *Let X be a centered random vector in $\mathcal{E} = (V, \langle \cdot, \cdot \rangle)$ with a positive-definite covariance function Σ. Let T be a non-empty Borel subset of V and $b \in V$, $b \neq 0$. Then, for all $u \in \mathfrak{b}(T)$, it holds that*

$$\Pr\{X \in T\} \leq \frac{\langle u, \Sigma(u) \rangle}{1 + \langle u, \Sigma(u) \rangle}.$$

Therefore, if $\mathfrak{b}(T)$ is non-empty, then

$$\Pr\{X \in T\} \leq \inf_{u \in \mathfrak{b}(T)} \frac{\langle u, \Sigma(u) \rangle}{1 + \langle u, \Sigma(u) \rangle}.$$

If T is a closed convex set such that $0 \notin T$, then the above bound is sharp.

Proof. The second inequality follows from the first provided that $\mathfrak{b}(T)$ is non-empty. The proof of the first inequality is formally identical to the proof of the same inequality in $\mathcal{R}^n$ given in Section 1 and is a direct consequence of (ii) and Cantelli's inequality (1) after noticing that, for a random vector X in $\mathcal{E}$, the variance of the random variable $\langle u, X \rangle$ is $\langle u, \Sigma u \rangle$. It remains to be shown that if T is closed and convex in $\mathcal{E}$ and $0 \notin T$, then the bound is sharp. We deduce this result from Theorem 1 after reducing the general case to $\mathcal{R}^n$ by the following argument. Every Euclidean space is a topological vector space with respect to the standard topology induced by the inner product (recall that, in our terminology, Euclidean spaces are finite-dimensional and, hence, Hilbert spaces). Euclidean spaces of the same dimension are pairwise homeomorphic, and all are homeomorphic to $\mathcal{R}^n$ under the coordinate map isomorphism f (with respect to a fixed orthonormal basis). Thus, if X is a centered random vector in $\mathcal{E}$, then $f(X)$ is a centered random vector in $\mathcal{R}^n$, and conversely. Moreover, if the covariance function Σ of X is positive-definite, then the covariance matrix $\widetilde{\Sigma}$ of $f(X)$ is positive-definite, and conversely. Furthermore, T is a convex closed set in $\mathcal{E}$ if and only if $f(T)$ is a closed set in $\mathcal{R}^n$ (with the standard Euclidean topology): linear images of convex sets are convex, and homeomorphic linear images of closed convex sets are closed and convex. Finally, since f maps the zero vector 0_V of $\mathcal{E}$ to the zero vector 0 of $\mathcal{R}^n$, it follows that $0_V \notin T$ if and only if $0 \notin f(T)$. Here,

$$\Pr\{X \in T\} = \Pr\{f(X) \in f(T)\}.$$

Therefore, if $\widetilde{X}_0$ is a random vector in $\mathcal{R}^n$ with a positive-definite matrix $\widetilde{\Sigma}$ that attains the bound in Theorem 1 as equality, which exists because the hypotheses on $f(T)$ are satisfied, then $f^{-1}(\widetilde{X}_0)$ is a random vector in $\mathcal{E}$ that attains the bound in this lemma. □

Theorem 2. *Let X be a centered random vector of $\mathcal{E} = (V, \langle \cdot, \cdot \rangle)$ with positive-definite covariance Σ. Let C be a non-empty Borel subset of V and $b \in V$, $b \neq 0$. Then, for all $u \in C^*$ such that $\langle u, b \rangle > 0$, it holds that*

$$\Pr\{X \succeq_C b\} \leq \frac{\langle u, \Sigma(u) \rangle}{\langle u, b \rangle^2 + \langle u, \Sigma(u) \rangle}.$$

If C is a closed convex cone in $\mathcal{E}$ and $b \in V \setminus -C$, then $\mathfrak{a}(b, C)$ is non-empty and

$$\Pr\{X \succeq_C b\} \leq \inf_{u \in \mathfrak{a}(b,C)} \frac{\langle u, \Sigma(u) \rangle}{\langle u, b \rangle^2 + \langle u, \Sigma(u) \rangle} = \inf_{u \in \mathfrak{b}(b+C)} \frac{\langle u, \Sigma(u) \rangle}{1 + \langle u, \Sigma(u) \rangle}.$$

Moreover, the above bound is sharp.

Proof. Since $\Pr\{X \succeq_C b\} \leq \Pr\{X \succeq_{C^{**}} b\}$, the first inequality follows from (3) (with X instead of y and b instead of x) by applying Cantelli's inequality (1) to the random variable $\langle u, X \rangle$. If C is a closed convex cone and $b \in V \setminus -C$, then $\mathfrak{a}(b, C)$ is non-empty because the hypotheses of Lemma 3 are satisfied (recall that since C is a closed convex cone, one has $C = C^{**}$ by (c) in Lemma 1). Moreover, still by Lemma 3, $\mathfrak{b}(b + C)$ is non-empty as well. Hence, the second inequality follows from the first by Lemma 4 with $q(u) = \langle u, \Sigma(u) \rangle$. It remains to be proven that the bound is sharp. Let $T = b + C$. Since C is closed and convex, then so is T. Moreover, the hypotheses on b and C implies $0 \notin T$. Therefore, Lemma 7 applies, and we conclude that the bound is sharp. □

Although the previous theorem deals with the special case of $T = b + C$ of Lemma 7, which, in turn, up to technicalities, follows by Theorems 1 and 2 provides a useful sharpening of the extended Cantelli's inequality given in Theorem 1, which is further exploited in the next corollary.

Corollary 1. *Let X be a centered random vector of $\mathcal{E} = (V, \langle \cdot, \cdot \rangle)$ with positive-definite covariance Σ. Let C be a closed convex cone in $\mathcal{E}$. If $b \in \Sigma(C^*) \setminus -C$, where $\Sigma(C^*)$ denotes the linear image of C^* under Σ, then*

$$\Pr\{X \succeq_C b\} \leq \frac{1}{1 + ||b||^2_{\Sigma^{-1}}}, \tag{8}$$

where $||b||_{\Sigma^{-1}} = \langle b, \Sigma^{-1}(b) \rangle$. Moreover, the bound is sharp.

Proof. Directly from Lemmas 4 and 6, with $p^* = \sqrt{\langle b, \Sigma^{-1}(b) \rangle}$. □

The previous corollary can be further (and straightforwardly) specialized in $\mathcal{R}^n$ if X has a *monotone* covariance matrix. Recall that an invertible real matrix A is monotone if A^{-1} has nonnegative entries (see [14], Chapter 6). Random vectors whose covariance matrix has this property are common in Network Science. See Section 4.3 for such an example.

Corollary 2. *Let X be a centered random vector in $\mathcal{R}^n$ with a positive monotone covariance matrix Σ. Let C be a closed convex cone in $\mathcal{R}^n$ contained in the orthant $\mathbb{R}^n_+$. If $b \in \mathbb{R}^n_+$, then the hypotheses of Corollary 1 are satisfied, and hence,* (5) *holds.*

Proof. We only need to show that the hypotheses of the present corollary guarantee that the hypotheses of Corollary 1 are met, namely,

$$\begin{cases} C = \mathbb{R}^n_+ \\ \quad b \geq 0 \\ \Sigma^{-1} \geq 0 \end{cases} \Longrightarrow b \in \Sigma(C^*) \setminus -C.$$

Clearly, $(\Sigma^{-1} \geq 0 \wedge b \geq 0) \Rightarrow \Sigma^{-1}b \geq 0$. Hence, just as clearly, $\Sigma^{-1}b \notin -C$. Since $\mathbb{R}^n_+$ is a self-dual closed convex cone, one has $C^* = \mathbb{R}^n_+$ and, thus, $\Sigma^{-1}b \in C^*$. Since $\Sigma^{-1}b \in C^* \Rightarrow b \in \Sigma(C^*)$, we conclude that $b \in \Sigma(C^*) \setminus -C$ as required. □

4. Some Applications

In this section, we discuss some applications of Theorem 2 and its corollary as well as of Theorem 1 in the perspective of the duality of cones and polyhedra. Indeed, we have already noticed that the minimization problem associated with the bounds given in the previous section reduces to minimizing the positive-definite quadratic form $q(u) = \langle u, \Sigma(u) \rangle$ over $\mathfrak{a}(b, C)$ or over $\mathfrak{b}(T)$. Even if $T = b + C$ and C is a closed convex cone, this minimization problem is a non-trivial convex programming problem [15]. However, knowing the structure of $\mathfrak{b}(T)$ allows us to easily compute upper bounds on the probability of certain interesting tail events.

4.1. Sampling Positive-Definite Matrices from a Random Ensemble

A random vector X in the Euclidean space $\mathcal{E} = (V, \langle \cdot, \cdot \rangle)$ with a covariance function Σ has a *weakly spherical distribution* if the distribution of X is such that $\Sigma = \sigma^2 \mathrm{id}_V$, where id_V is the identity endomorphism of V and σ^2 is a positive real number [16]. A square *random matrix* is a just a random vector in $(\mathbb{R}^{n \times n}, \langle \cdot, \cdot \rangle_F)$, where $\langle X, Y \rangle_F = \mathrm{Tr}(X'Y)$ is the Frobenius inner product. A symmetric random matrix is, thus, a random vector in $(S^n, \langle \cdot, \cdot \rangle_F)$, where S^n is the real vector space of real symmetric matrices. Several models (i.e., probability measures) of symmetric random matrices are known and well understood [17]. Probably the best-known example of such models is the *Symmetric Wigner Ensemble*, which includes the *Gaussian Orthogonal Ensemble*. A random matrix is a *symmetric Wigner matrix* (or *sampled from a symmetric Wigner ensemble*) if its diagonal entries are independently and identically distributed (i.i.d.) according to a given distribution and the off-diagonal elements in the upper triangular part are i.i.d. according to a given distribution that may differ from the former. A *symmetric real ensemble* is, thus, completely specified by the distribution of the entries of the matrix and, thus, does not depend on the order of the matrix. If the diagonal elements of a symmetric Wigner matrix W follow a standard normal distribution, while the off-diagonal elements follow a normal distribution with zero mean and variance $1/2$, then W is a matrix from the *Gaussian Orthogonal Ensemble*. Here is one of the simplest mechanisms that, given a random matrix ensemble, yields a symmetric random matrix ensemble: if M is a random matrix whose entries are i.i.d. random variables distributed according to the law P, then $S = \frac{M+M'}{2}$ is a symmetric Wigner matrix—taking $M'M$ for S instead yields the *symmetric Wishart ensemble*. If the first two moments of P are 0 and σ^2, respectively, for some positive real number σ, then we denote the resulting ensemble by $\mathcal{W}(\sigma)$. By construction, any matrix S sampled from $\mathcal{W}(\sigma)$ has a weakly spherical distribution. To see this, note that the variance of each diagonal entry of S is σ^2, while the variance of each off-diagonal entry of S is $\sigma^2/2$, since $S = (M + M')/2$ by construction.

Next, if $(E_{i,j} \mid i \leq j)$ is the standard basis of S^n, then, by the definition of the covariance function of random vectors in Euclidean spaces (see the previous section), one has

$$\mathbb{E}(\langle E_{i,j}, S\rangle_F \langle E_{h,k}, S\rangle_F) = \mathbb{E}(\mathrm{Tr}(E_{i,j}S)\mathrm{Tr}(E_{h,k}S)) = \begin{cases} \mathbb{E}\left(S_{i,i}^2\right) & \text{if } i = j = h = k \\ 4\mathbb{E}\left(S_{i,j}^2\right) & \text{if } \{i,j\} = \{h,k\},\ i \neq j \\ 0 & \text{otherwise.} \end{cases}$$

Therefore, since $\mathbb{E}\left(S_{i,i}^2\right) = \sigma^2$ and $\mathbb{E}\left(S_{i,j}^2\right) = \sigma^2/2$, it follows that

$$\mathbb{E}(\langle E_{i,j}, S\rangle_F \langle E_{h,k}, S\rangle_F) = \sigma^2 \langle E_{i,j}, E_{h,k}\rangle_F = \langle E_{i,j}, \sigma^2 \mathrm{id}_{S^n}(E_{h,k})\rangle_F.$$

One of the most fundamental problems in random matrix theory is to understand the spectrum of a random matrix from a given ensemble, at least asymptotically, namely, when the order of the matrix goes to ∞. Even more fundamental is to compute the probability that a random matrix X is positive-definite (or negative-definite), i.e., that its smallest eigenvalue $\lambda_n(X)$ is positive. This problem is completely and precisely solved for Gaussian matrices (see [4–6]): the probability of the event $\lambda_n(X) > 0$ when X is sampled from a symmetric Gaussian ensemble goes to zero as e^{-cn^2}, where $c = \ln 3/4$. Using corollary 1, we prove here that the same is true in general, although the rate we can provide is much weaker than e^{-cn^2}.

Lemma 8. *Let σ be a positive real number and $\lambda_n(X)$ be the least eigenvalue of the random matrix X sampled from $\mathcal{W}(\sigma)$. For any positive real number α and any positive number ξ, if $n \geq \sigma^2/\xi^{2+\alpha}$, then $\Pr\{\lambda_n(X) \geq \xi\} \leq \xi^\alpha$.*

Proof. Since the statement trivially holds when $\xi \geq 1$, we may assume that $\xi < 1$. The event $\lambda_n(X) \geq \xi$ is the same as the event $X \succeq_{S_+^n} \xi I_n$, where I_n is the identity matrix of order n and S_+^n denotes the cone of positive semi-definite matrices lying in $\mathcal{E} = (S^n, \langle\cdot,\cdot\rangle_F)$. As observed above, X has a weakly spherical distribution with a covariance function Σ of the form $\sigma^2 \mathrm{id}_{S^n}$. It is well known that S_n^+ is a self-dual closed convex cone [10]. Hence, $(S_n^+)^* = S_n^+$ and

$$\Sigma((S_n^+)^*) = \Sigma(S_n^+) = \sigma^2 \mathrm{id}_{S^n}(S_n^+) = S_n^+.$$

Since $\xi I_n \in S_+^n$, it follows that the hypotheses of Corollary 1 are satisfied by X with $b = \xi I_n$ and $C = S_+^n$. Therefore, after observing that $\|\xi I_n\|_{\Sigma^{-1}}^2 = \frac{n\xi^2}{\sigma^2}$, it follows by (8) that

$$\Pr\{\lambda_n(X) \geq \xi\} = \Pr\left\{X \succeq_{S_+^n} \xi I_n\right\} \leq \frac{1}{1 + \|\xi I_n\|_{\Sigma^{-1}}^2} = \frac{\sigma^2}{\sigma^2 + n\xi^2} \leq \xi^\alpha,$$

where the last inequality is implied by $n \geq \sigma^2/\xi^{2+\alpha}$. □

Theorem 3. *Let σ be a positive real number and $\lambda_n(X)$ be the least eigenvalue of the random matrix X sampled from $\mathcal{W}(\sigma)$. It holds that $\lim_{n\to\infty} \Pr\{\lambda_n(X) > 0\} = 0$.*

Proof. For any non-negative real number y, let $\ell_n(y) = \Pr\{\lambda_n(X) \geq y\}$. If $\Pr\{\lambda_n(X) > 0\}$ does not converge to zero, then there is a real number ξ and a sub-sequence $\{\ell_{n_\nu}(\xi)\}_{\nu\in\mathbb{N}}$ such that $0 < \xi < 1$ and $\lim_{\nu\to\infty} \ell_{n_\nu}(\xi) = \beta$ for some β such that $0 < \beta < 1$. Hence, for any $\epsilon \in \mathbb{R}$ such that $0 < \epsilon < \beta$, there is a $\nu_0 \in \mathbb{N}$ such that

$$\ell_{n_\nu}(\xi) \geq \beta - \epsilon \quad \forall \nu \geq \nu_0.$$

On the other hand, by Lemma 8, for every positive real number α, it holds that

$$\ell_n(\xi) \leq \xi^\alpha \quad \forall n \geq \frac{\sigma^2}{\xi^{2+\alpha}}.$$

Let

$$\alpha_0 = \frac{\ln(\beta - \epsilon)}{\ln(\xi)},$$

where ln is the natural logarithm. Since ξ and $\beta - \epsilon$ are both positive and strictly smaller than 1, it holds that $\alpha_0 > 0$. Hence, if $\alpha > \alpha_0$, then $\xi^\alpha < \beta - \epsilon$. If ν_1 is such that $n_{\nu_1} > \frac{\sigma^2}{\xi^{2+\alpha}}$, then for $\nu \geq \max\{\nu_0, \nu_1\}$, it holds that

$$\beta - \epsilon < \ell_{n_\nu}(\xi) \leq \xi^\alpha$$

But this contradicts $\xi^\alpha < \beta - \epsilon$, which holds by the choice of α. This contradiction proves the theorem. □

4.2. Tails of Linear Images of Random Vectors and Asymptotic Feasibility of Systems of Linear Inequalities

Concentration and tail inequalities for linear, possibly random images of random vectors are a challenging topic in probability and statistics [7,8]. Let X be a random vector in $\mathcal{R}^n$ and f be the linear map $X \mapsto AX$, where $A \in \mathbb{R}^{m \times n}$ is a given matrix. According to [7], a typical tail inequality is an inequality of the form

$$\Pr\{f(X) \succeq_{\mathbb{R}^m} sb\} \leq g(s)$$

for some function $g : \mathbb{R}_+ \to [0,1]$. See [8] for the related problem of determining general concentration inequalities. Notably, Ref. [7] investigates the more general case of the map $\mathcal{A}X$, where $\mathcal{A}$ is a random matrix and X is a random vector, under certain hypotheses on the distribution of $\mathcal{A}$, assuming that $\mathcal{A}$ and X are independent. If the matrix f is a deterministic linear map and X has a positive-definite covariance function Σ, then, as we will show in the next theorem, there always exists a rather general and easy-to-compute upper bound $g(s)$ on the probability measure of the tails of $f(X)$. In Theorem 5, on the other hand, we will exhibit a transparent relation between the ordinary tails of the linear images of a random vector X and the generalized tails of X.

Theorem 4. *Let $A \in \mathbb{R}^{m \times n}$ be a real matrix, $b = (b_1, \ldots, b_m)'$ be a real vector, and $b^+ \in \mathbb{R}^m$ be defined component-wise by $b_i^+ = \max(0, b_i)$, $i = 1\ldots, m$. If X is a centered random vector with a covariance matrix $\sigma^2 I_n$ and $b^+ \neq 0$, then*

$$\Pr\{AX \geq sb\} \leq \frac{\|A\|_{\text{op}}^2}{\|\frac{s}{\sigma}b^+\|^2 + \|A\|_{\text{op}}^2}, \tag{9}$$

where $s \geq 0$ is a real number and $\|\cdot\|$ and $\|\cdot\|_{\text{op}}$ are the Euclidean and the operator norm—induced by Euclidean norms—respectively.

Proof. Let $T(s) = \{x \in \mathbb{R}^n \mid Ax \geq sb\}$, and note that $T(s)$ is a possibly empty polyhedron. If $s = 0$, the result is trivial because the right side of (9) is 1 in this case. If $T(s)$ is empty, the result is also trivial because the left-hand side of (9) is zero. So, we assume that $s > 0$ and

$T(s)$ is not empty. Obviously, $T(s) = \{x \in \mathbb{R}^n \mid A(s)x \geq b\}$, where $A(s) = s^{-1}A$ for $s > 0$. Since $b^+ \neq 0$, it follows that $T(s)$ does not contain the origin of $\mathcal{R}^n$. Hence,

$$\Pr\{AX \geq sb\} = \Pr\{X \in T(s)\} \leq \inf_{u \in \mathfrak{b}(T(s))} \frac{\|\sigma u\|^2}{1 + \|\sigma u\|^2}$$

by Theorem 1 with $\Sigma = \sigma^2 I_n$. Let us compute the blocker $\mathfrak{b}(T(s))$ of $T(s)$. Let $c : \mathbb{R}^n \to \mathbb{R}$ be defined by

$$u \mapsto c(u) = \min\{u'x \mid x \in T(s)\};$$

that is, $c(u)$ is the minimum of a linear program over the non-empty polyhedron $T(s)$ and the minimum might be $-\infty$. By linear programming duality, it holds that $c(u) = \max\{v'b \mid A'(s)v = u,\ v \in \mathbb{R}^m_+\}$. Since, by definition,

$$u \in \mathfrak{b}(T(s)) \iff u'x \geq 1\ \forall x \in T(s) \iff c(u) \geq 1,$$

it follows that

$$\mathfrak{b}(T(s)) = \{A'(s)v \mid v'b \geq 1, v \in \mathbb{R}^m_+\}.$$

Therefore, if $\bar{v}$ is any vector in $\mathbb{R}^m_+$ such that $\bar{v}'b \geq 1$, then

$$\inf_{u \in \mathfrak{b}(T(s))} \frac{\|\sigma u\|^2}{1 + \|\sigma u\|^2} = \inf_{\substack{v \in \mathbb{R}^m_+ \\ v'b \geq 1}} \frac{\|\sigma A(s)'v\|^2}{1 + \|\sigma A(s)'v\|^2} \leq \frac{\|\sigma A(s)'\bar{v}\|^2}{1 + \|\sigma A(s)'\bar{v}\|^2}.$$

Since the map $\xi \mapsto \frac{\xi}{1+\xi}$ defines a strictly increasing function over $\mathbb{R}^+$ and since

$$\|\sigma A(s)'\bar{v}\|^2 = \left(\frac{\sigma}{s}\right)^2 \|A'\bar{v}\|^2 \leq \left(\frac{\sigma}{s}\right)^2 \|A'\|^2_{\text{op}} \|\bar{v}\|^2,$$

it follows that

$$\inf_{u \in \mathfrak{b}(T(s))} \frac{\|\sigma u\|^2}{1 + \|\sigma u\|^2} \leq \frac{\|A\|^2_{\text{op}} \|\bar{v}\|^2}{(\frac{s}{\sigma})^2 + \|A\|^2_{\text{op}} \|\bar{v}\|^2}.$$

To complete the proof, choose $\frac{b^+}{\|b^+\|^2}$ for $\bar{v}$ and check that $\frac{b^+}{\|b^+\|^2} \geq 0$ and that $b' \frac{b^+}{\|b^+\|^2} = 1$. □

Some remarks are in order.

Remark 2. *If X has a positive covariance matrix Σ, then the theorem is easily extended: just replace $\|A\|_{\text{op}}$ with $\|A\Sigma^{1/2}\|_{\text{op}}$ and set $\sigma = 1$.*

Remark 3. *If $T(s)$ is not full-dimensional and X has an absolutely continuous distribution with respect to the Lebesgue measure, then the result is useless because $T(s)$ is a null set; however, the result becomes interesting if either $T(s)$ has positive Lebesgue measure or X has a singular distribution with respect to the Lebesgue measure.*

Remark 4. *If $b \geq 0$, so $b = b^+$, then $T(s) \supseteq T(s')$ for $s \leq s'$. Thus, if $(a_n)_{n \in \mathbb{N}}$ is any strictly positive strictly increasing sequence, then $(T(a_n))_{n \in \mathbb{N}}$ is an (inclusion-wise) decreasing sequence of polyhedra; the theorem says no more than we expect in this case. However, this is no longer true if $b \neq b^+$. Indeed, let A and b be as follows*

$$A = \begin{pmatrix} -1 & 1 \\ -1 & -1 \\ 1 & 0 \end{pmatrix}, \quad b = \begin{pmatrix} 1 \\ -2 \\ -1 \end{pmatrix}.$$

With this choice of A and b, $T(s)$ is the triangle in $\mathcal{R}^2$ whose vertices are

$$\alpha(s) = \begin{pmatrix} -s \\ 0 \end{pmatrix}, \quad \beta(s) = \begin{pmatrix} -s \\ 3s \end{pmatrix}, \quad \gamma(s) = \begin{pmatrix} s/2 \\ 3s/2 \end{pmatrix},$$

and we see that $\{\alpha(s), \gamma(s)\} \subseteq T(s) \setminus T(s')$ for all $s' > s$, while the area of $T(s)$ is $\left(\frac{3s}{2}\right)^2$, which is clearly increasing in s.

Remark 5. *Theorem 4 can be used to study the asymptotic probability of feasibility of the system $T = \{x \in \mathbb{R}^n \mid Ax \geq b\}$ when A and b grow in some sense. More precisely, identify T with the pair (A, b) and consider the sequence $\{(A_\nu, b_\nu)\}_{\nu \in \mathbb{N}}$ of linear systems T_ν with $A_\nu \in \mathbb{R}^{m(\nu) \times n(\nu)}$ and $b_\nu \in \mathbb{R}^{m(\nu)}$, where the number of inequalities and the number of unknowns are both integer (possibly constant) functions of the index ν; also, let X_ν be a sequence of random vectors such that X_ν is in $\mathcal{R}^{n(\nu)}$ and X_ν has a covariance matrix $\Sigma_\nu = \sigma^2 I_{n(\nu)}$. Finally, let $p_\nu = \Pr\{A_\nu X_\nu \geq b_\nu\}$ be the probability that the system T_ν is feasible under the probability measure induced by X_ν. A straightforward consequence of Theorem 4 is that if $\|A_\nu\|_{\text{op}} = o(\|b_\nu^+\|)$, then $p_\nu = o(1)$. The condition $\|A_\nu\|_{\text{op}} = o(\|b_\nu^+\|)$ can be realized in several ways, either by keeping $m(\nu)$ and $n(\nu)$ constant or by letting them grow. Let us give a theoretical graph example in the latter case. Let G be a simple undirected graph with n vertices $\{v_1, \ldots, v_n\}$. For two vertices v_i, $v_j \in V(G)$, $i \neq j$, write $v_i \sim v_j$ whenever v_i ad v_j are adjacent in G. If $v_i \sim v_j$, then we say that v_i ad v_j are* neighbors. *Let d_i denote the* degree *of vertex v_i, namely, the number of neighbors of v_i in G. Also, denote, by $\Delta(G)$, the maximum of the degrees of G. The* Laplacian *matrix $L(G)$ of G is the order n matrix defined by*

$$(L(G))_{i,j} = \begin{cases} d_i & \text{if } i = j \\ -1 & \text{if } i \neq j \text{ and } v_i \sim v_j. \end{cases}$$

Recall that for functions $h, k : \mathbb{N} \to \mathbb{N}$, $k(n) = \Omega(h(n))$ means that $h(n) = O(k(n))$. Let $(G_\nu)_\nu$ be a sequence of graphs on $n(\nu)$ vertices, and let $(L_\nu)_\nu$ be the corresponding sequences of Laplacians. Also, let $\Delta_\nu := \Delta(G_\nu)$. It is a classical result of Fiedler [18] that the spectral radius of L_ν is, at most, $2\Delta_\nu$, so $\|A_\nu\|_{\text{op}} \leq 2\Delta_\nu = O(\Delta_\nu)$. Hence, if $\Delta_\nu = o(\sqrt{n})$ and b_ν is a dense $\{-1, 0, 1\}$ vector, say with $\Omega(n(\nu))$ non-zero entries, such that $\|b_\nu^+\| = \Omega(\|b_\nu\|)$, then the condition $\|A_\nu\|_{\text{op}} = o(\|b_\nu^+\|)$ is satisfied when $n(\nu)$ grows with ν.

The following result relates more transparently the ordinary tails of the linear image of a random vector X in $\mathcal{R}^n$ to the generalized tails of the same vector. Recall that a matrix $A \in \mathbb{R}^{m \times n}$ is *right-invertible* if there exists a matrix $A^\ddagger \in \mathbb{R}^{n \times m}$ such that $AA^\ddagger = I_m$ with I being the identity matrix of order m. If A has full row rank, then the Moore–Penroose pseudo-inverse $A^\dagger$ can be taken for $A^\ddagger$, where $A^\dagger = A'(AA')^{-1}$. A linear map $f : \mathbb{R}^n \to \mathbb{R}^m$ is right-invertible if the matrix representing f with respect to the canonical basis of $\mathbb{R}^n$ and $\mathbb{R}^m$ is such. Note that a right-invertible map is surjective.

Theorem 5. *Let $A \in \mathbb{R}^{m \times n}$ be a real matrix and $b \in \mathbb{R}^m$ be a real vector. Let $f : \mathbb{R}^n \to \mathbb{R}^m$ be the linear map $u \mapsto Au$ and let $C_A = \{u \in \mathbb{R}^n \mid Au \geq 0\}$. If X is a random vector in $\mathcal{R}^n$ and f is right-invertible, then*

$$\Pr\{f(X) \geq b\} = \Pr\Big\{X \succeq_{C_A} f^\ddagger(b)\Big\},$$

where $f^\ddagger$ is the linear map induced by $A^\ddagger$.

Proof. First of all, note that C_A is a polyhedral cone. So, C_A is a closed convex cone. However, unless f is injective, C_A is not a proper cone. Indeed, if f is not injective, then its kernel is a non-trivial subspace of $\mathcal{R}^n$ contained in C_A. However, C_A induces a pre-order, and so, $X \succeq_{C_A} f^{\ddagger}(b)$ is a well-defined generalized tail. It remains to be proven that the stated equality holds. This fact follows easily since $f(X - f^{\ddagger}(b)) = f(X) - b$. So, $f(X) - b \in \mathbb{R}^m_+ \Leftrightarrow (X - f^{\ddagger}(b)) \in C_A$. □

4.3. Testing Homophily in Randomly Colored Networks

Tail inequalities, albeit in a different guise, have been successfully used in [9] to evaluate what is called *network homophily*. Suppose we have a simple undirected graph on the vertex set V, a surjective map $f : V \to \{1, \ldots, s\}$, which can be thought of as coloring of the vertices, and a *coloring profile* $\mathbf{c} = (c_1 \cdots, c_s)$, where c_i is the number of vertices in $f^{-1}(i)$, $i = 1 \ldots, s$, i.e., c_i is the number of vertices of color i. With these data, we want to evaluate whether the graph is *homophilic*, i.e., whether it is true that the s-tuple $m = (m_1, \ldots, m_s)$, where m_i is the number of edges of the subgraph induced by the vertices of color i, is, in some sense, larger than what we would expect if the colors did not correlate with the adjacency of vertices—recall that an edge e of a graph G is induced by a subset U of the set of vertices $V(G)$ if both the end vertices of e are in U. The approach taken in [9] is to define the simple probability space $(\Phi_{\mathbf{c}}, \mathbb{P}_{\mathbf{c}})$—called the *random coloring model*—where $\Phi_{\mathbf{c}}$ is the set of all surjective maps $g : V \to \{1, \ldots, s\}$ such that $g^{-1}(i) = c_i$, $i = 1 \ldots, s$, and $\mathbb{P}_{\mathbf{c}}$ is the uniform measure $c_1! \ldots c_s!/n!$ on $\Phi_{\mathbf{c}}$. In the random coloring model, m is just the observed value of the random vector $M = (M_1 \ldots, M_s)'$, where M_i is the number of edges induced by the vertices of color i in a random coloring of V of G. Moreover, both the mean vector $\mu_{\mathbf{c}}$ and the covariance matrix $\Sigma_{\mathbf{c}}$ of M can be given in closed form under the random coloring model. Thus, if $\phi : \mathbb{R}^s \to \mathbb{R}_+$ is a linear function—e.g., the arithmetic mean—one can evaluate the homophily of the input graph by considering the one-sided tail probability $\Pr\{\phi(M - \mu) \geq \phi(m - \mu)\}$: any good upper bound on this tail probability can quantify the homophily of the given network by measuring, at least approximately, in terms of ϕ how significant the deviation of m from μ is. In particular, if $\phi(m - \mu) > 0$—otherwise, the network is declared not homophilic at all—one can apply the classical one-dimensional Cantelli inequality (1) to estimate the approximate significance of the deviation of the observed value from the expected one. Note that the linear map ϕ, say the arithmetic mean, acts as a global synthesis of network homophily but cannot identify hypodense or poorly significant color classes. We show here, as a consequence of Corollary 2, that generalized tails do not suffer from these limitations. To see this, for a set $R \subseteq \{1, \ldots, s\}$, let $\overline{R} = \{1, \ldots, s\} - R$ and $W_{\overline{R}} = \bigoplus_{\overline{R}} \mathbb{R}e_i$, where e_i is the i-th fundamental vector of $\mathbb{R}^s$, $i = 1 \ldots, s$. Thus, $W_{\overline{R}}$ is the subspace spanned by the coordinates whose index is in $\overline{R}$. The projection $\pi_R : \mathbb{R}^s \to W_{\overline{R}}$ of $\mathbb{R}^s$ onto $\mathbb{R}^s / W_{\overline{R}}$ takes the vector u to the vector u_R, suppressing the coordinates whose index is not in R—if $s = 4$ and $R = \{1, 3\}$, then $u_R = (u_1, u_3)'$. Also, recall that a graph G is said to be *over-dispersed* if the ratio of the variance to the mean of its degree distribution is greater than 1. Most protein–protein interaction networks are over-dispersed.

Theorem 6. *Let (G, f) be an over-dispersed colored graph where the coloring $f : V \to \{1, \ldots, s\}$ has the profile $\mathbf{c} = (c_1, \ldots, c_s)$, $c_i \geq 2$, $i = 1, \ldots, s$. Let m, M, $\mu_{\mathbf{c}}$ and $\Sigma_{\mathbf{c}}$ be defined as above, and let $x = m - \mu$, $X = M - \mu$, and*

$$S(m) = \left\{ i \in \{1, \ldots, s\}\} \mid \mu_i < m_i < \binom{c_i}{2} \right\}.$$

Also, for any $R \subseteq S(m)$, let μ_R and Σ_R be the mean vector and the covariance matrix of the random vector X_R image of the projection of X onto $W_{\overline{R}}$. If $S(m) \neq \emptyset$, then for any $R \subseteq S(m)$, it holds that

$$\Pr\{M_R \geq m_R\} \leq \frac{1}{1 + \|m_R - \mu_R\|^2_{\Sigma_R^{-1}}}, \tag{10}$$

where M_R and m_r are the projection of M and m onto $W_{\overline{R}}$, respectively.

Proof. Let σ_i^2 denote the variance of M_i, the i-th coordinate of M, where $i = 1 \ldots, s$. Fix $R \subseteq S(m)$ and observe that $M_R \geq m_R \Leftrightarrow X_R - x_R \in \mathbb{R}^r$, where r is the cardinality of R. Furthermore, it can be shown that $\mu_R = \mathbb{E}(\pi_R(X)) = \pi_R(\mathbb{E}(X))$ and that Σ_R is the submatrix of $\Sigma_\mathbf{c}$ obtained by suppressing the rows and the columns whose index is not in R. Since $x_R \gneqq 0$ and X_R is a centered random vector, it follows that the hypotheses of Corollary 2 are met if Σ_R is a monotone matrix. If Σ_R is monotone, then, by the corollary, $\Pr\{X_R \geq x_R\} \leq (1 + \|x_R\|^2_M)^{-1}$, where $\|x_R\|_M = \|x_R\|_{\Sigma_R^{-1}}$ is the so-called *Mahalanobis norm of* x_R. It remains to be shown that if G is an over-dispersed graph, then, for every $R \subseteq S(m)$, Σ_R is a monotone matrix, which means showing that Σ_R is invertible (hence, positive-definite) and $\Sigma_R^{-1} \geq 0$. According to the results in [9], the covariance matrix $\Sigma_\mathbf{c}$ is of the form $\Sigma_\mathbf{c} = D + \lambda(G)uu'$, where $u = (u_1, \ldots, u_s)'$ is such that $u_i > 0$ for $i = 1, \ldots, s$, D is a diagonal matrix whose i-th diagonal entry is $\sigma_i^2 - \lambda(G)u_i^2$, and $\lambda(G) \leq 0$ (because G is over-dispersed). Clearly, $\Sigma_R = D_R + \lambda(G)u_R u_R'$, where D_R is the sub-matrix of D obtained by suppressing the rows and the columns whose index is not in R. Since the off-diagonal elements of Σ_R are non-positive, Σ_R is a *Z-matrix*, and it is known (see [14] Chapter 6) that if a Z-matrix is positive-definite, then it is monotone. On the other hand, since Σ_R is a covariance matrix, it follows that Σ_R is positive semidefinite. Thus, to show that Σ_R is monotone, it is sufficient to show that Σ_R is non-singular. By the Sherman–Morrison formula, if D_R is non-singular, then Σ_R is also non-singular. Therefore, to prove that Σ_R is monotone, we simply check that $\sigma_i^2 - \lambda(G)u_i^2 \neq 0$ for $i \in S(m)$. Note that if $\lambda(G) \neq 0$, then $\sigma_i^2 - \lambda(G)u_i^2 > 0$ because $u_i^2 > 0$ and $\lambda(G) < 0$. So, the only possibility is that $\lambda(G) = 0$ and $\sigma_i^2 = 0$. However, by Theorem 1 in [19], $\sigma_i^2 = 0$ if and only if $m_i \in \{0, \binom{c_i}{2}\}$, which cannot happen because of the definition of $S(m)$, using the fact that $\mu_i \geq 0$, being that μ_i is the expected value of the non-negative random variable M_i. So, we conclude that $\Sigma_R^{-1} \geq 0$ for all $R \subseteq S(m)$, and this completes the proof. □

We conclude that under the random coloring model, the Mahalanobis norm of $m - \mu$ is a directed measure of the statistical significance of the deviation of m from μ, and thus, it can be taken as a measure of the joint homophily of the vertices whose color is in $S(m)$.

After an observation in [9], the random coloring model allows us to give a precise formalization of how difficult it can be to provide bounds on tail probabilities. First, recall that a subset I of vertices of a graph H is an *independent set of* H if I induces no edges. Also, recall that the *Independent Set Problem*, `INDEPENDENT SET`, is the problem of deciding whether, given a graph H and a non-negative integer k, $V(H)$ contains an independent set of at least k vertices. If H has an independent set of at least k vertices, we say that (H, k) is a `YES` instance of `INDEPENDENT SET`. `INDEPENDENT SET` is an archetypal hard problem, which means that it is in the NP-complete class (see [20], Section 3.1.3). It is widely believed that it cannot be decided in polynomial time whether instances of problems in such a class are `YES` instances. Next, let $X = M_i$ be the i-th coordinate of M and $\kappa = c_i$ be the i-th coordinate of the coloring profile $\mathbf{c}$. Without the loss of generality, $i = 1$ (the argument we will use is independent of i by symmetry). With this notation, $\Pr\{X \geq 1\}$ is the marginal tail probability $\Pr\{M_1 \geq 1\}$. By definition, X is the number of edges induced by a set of κ vertices sampled without repetition from the vertex set of the input graph G.

Theorem 7. *Let X and κ be as above. If G is the input graph in the random coloring model, then* $\Pr\{X \geq 1\} < 1$ *if and only if* (G, κ) *is a* `YES` *instance of* `INDEPENDENT SET`.

Proof. If (G, κ) is a `YES` instance of `INDEPENDENT SET`, then G has an independent set of at least κ vertices. Hence, $\Pr\{X = 0\} > 0$ because such a set is sampled with positive probability. Since $\Pr\{X = 0\} > 0 \Leftrightarrow \Pr\{X \geq 1\} < 1$, the only if part follows. Conversely, if $\Pr\{X \geq 1\} < 1$, then $\Pr\{X = 0\} > 0$. Therefore, the event $X = 0$ occurs with positive probability (i.e., 0 is in support of X). Since $X = 0$ occurs if and only if (G, κ) is a `YES` instance of `INDEPENDENT SET`, the if part follows as well. □

In other words, in general, even deciding the sign of $1 - \Pr\{X \geq 1\}$ for a finitely supported random variable X is a computationally hard problem.

5. Concluding Remarks

Tail inequalities are a challenging problem in probability and statistics. According to Theorem 7, we can expect no more than easily computable bounds for dealing with tail probabilities, even if we have no control over the quality of the approximation. One such bound is given by Cantelli's inequality (1). This bound was significantly extended by Marshall and Olkin (see Theorem 1) from random variables taking values on the real line to random vectors taking values in standard real n-dimensional Euclidean spaces. By looking at the inequality from the perspective of convex cone duality, as shown in Section 3, this paper naturally extends the inequality to any finite-dimensional Euclidean space. The new perspective allows us to cast (and bound) the probability of certain interesting events arising in random matrix theory, the theory of tail and concentration inequalities for linear images of random vectors, and network homophily as the probability of generalized tails, namely, inequalities induced by the pre-order (or the partial order) defined by convex cones. Besides Cantelli inequalities, there are several other tail inequalities. It would certainly be worthwhile to check whether some of these one-dimensional inequalities have a corresponding generalized version.

Funding: This research received no external funding.

Data Availability Statement: Data are contained within the article.

Acknowledgments: We are grateful to the reviewers for their careful reading and valuable comments, which have certainly contributed to the improvement of this article.

Conflicts of Interest: The author declares no conflict of interest.

References

1. Marshall, A.W.; Olkin, I. Multivariate Chebyshev Inequalities. *Ann. Math. Stat.* **1960**, *31*, 1001–1014. [CrossRef]
2. Vandenberghe, L.; Boyd, S.; Comanor, K. Generalized Chebyshev Bounds via Semidefinite Programming. *SIAM Rev.* **2007**, *49*, 52–64. [CrossRef]
3. Boyd, S.; Vandenberghe, L. *Convex Optimization*; Cambridge University Press: Cambridge, UK, 2004.
4. Arous, G.; Guionnet, A. Large deviations for Wigner's law and Voiculescu's non-commutative entropy. *Probab. Theory Relat. Fields* **1997**, *108*, 517–542. [CrossRef]
5. Bhargava, M.; Cremona, J.E.; Fisher, T.; Jones, N.G.; Keating, J.P. What is the probability that a random integral quadratic form in n variables has an integral zero? *Int. Math. Res. Not.* **2016**, *12*, 3828–3848. [CrossRef]
6. Dean, D.S.; Majumdar, S.N. Large deviations of extreme eigenvalues of random matrices. *Phys. Rev. Lett.* **2006**, *97*, 160201. [CrossRef] [PubMed]
7. Das, B.; Fasen-Hartmann, V.; Klüppelberg, C. Tail probabilities of random linear functions of regularly varying random vectors. *Extremes* **2022**, *25*, 721–758. [CrossRef]
8. Rudelson, M.; Vershynin, R. Small Ball Probabilities for Linear Images of High-Dimensional Distributions. *Int. Math. Res. Not.* **2015**, *19*, 9594–9617. [CrossRef]

9. Apollonio, N.; Franciosa, P.G.; Santoni, D. Network homophily via tail inequalities. *Phys. Rev. E* **2023**, *108*, 054130. [CrossRef] [PubMed]
10. Shaked-Monderer, N.; Berman, A. *Copositive and Completely Positive Matrices*; World Scientific Publishing: Hackensack, NJ, USA, 2021.
11. Schneider, R. *Convex Bodies: The Brunn–Minkowski Theory*; Encyclopedia of Mathematics and its Applications; Cambridge University Press: Cambridge, UK, 2013.
12. Schrijver, A. *Theory of Linear and Integer Programming*; Wiley: Chichester, UK, 1986.
13. Horn, R.; Johnson, C. *Matrix Analysis*, 2nd ed.; Cambridge University Press: Cambridge, UK, 2013.
14. Berman, A.; Plemmons, R.J. *Nonnegative Matrices in the Mathematical Sciences*; SIAM Press: Philadelphia, PA, USA, 1994.
15. Nemirovski, A. Advances in convex optimization: Conic programming. In Proceedings of the International Congress of Mathematicians, Madrid, Spain, 22–30 August 2006; Sanz-Sol, M., Soria, J., Varona, J.L., Verdera, J., Eds.; European Mathematical Society Publishing House: Berlin, Germany, 2007; Volume 1.
16. Eaton, M.L. *Multivariate Statistics: A Vector Space Approach*; Wiley: New York, NY, USA, 1983.
17. Edelman, A.; Rao, N.R. Random matrix theory. *Acta Numer.* **2005**, *14*, 233–297. [CrossRef]
18. Fiedler, M. Algebraic connectivity of graphs. *Czechoslov. Math. J.* **1973**, *23*, 298–305. [CrossRef]
19. Apollonio, N. Second-order moments of the size of randomly induced subgraphs of given order. *Discret. Appl. Math.* **2024**, *355*, 46–56. [CrossRef]
20. Garey, M.R.; Johnson, D.S. *Computers and Intractability: A Guide to the Theory of NP-Completeness*; Mathematical Sciences Series; Freeman and Company: San Francisco, CA, USA, 1979.

axioms

MDPI

Article

Round-Off Error Suppression by Statistical Averaging

Andrej Liptaj

Institute of Physics, Slovak Academy of Sciences, 845 11 Bratislava, Slovakia; andrej.liptaj@savba.sk

Abstract: Regarding round-off errors as random is often a necessary simplification to describe their behavior. Assuming, in addition, the symmetry of their distributions, we show that one can, in unstable (ill-conditioned) computer calculations, suppress their effect by statistical averaging. For this, one slightly perturbs the argument of $f(x_0)$ many times and averages the resulting function values. In this text, we forward arguments to support the assumed properties of round-off errors and critically evaluate the validity of the averaging approach in several numerical experiments.

Keywords: statistical averaging; round-off errors; numerical analysis; accuracy

MSC: 65G50; 65Y04; 65F22

1. Introduction

If a measurement can be regarded as an unbiased estimation of some observable, then, by definition, one can expect (in terms of probability) the mean of several measurements to be closer to the true value than what is given by a single measurement. This simple idea has many practical applications, but, surprisingly, no such idea can be found in the literature with respect to round-off errors (often thought of as random). Here, we elaborate on this idea, although the main concept is elementary and may intuitively be seen as valid. Therefore, we focus mostly on technical aspects and arguments to show its mechanism in more detail. The commonly used normal distribution, where individual measurements are assumed to have uncorrelated errors, leads to

$$\sigma_N(\mu) = \frac{\sigma_{\rm rf}}{\sqrt{N}}, \tag{1}$$

where $\sigma_N(\mu)$ is the error with which we estimate the mean, $\sigma_{\rm rf}$ is the standard deviation of the probability distribution with the mean μ from which the sample originates and N is the number of measurements. As can be readily seen, the precision increases with repeated measurements as $1/\sqrt{N}$.

We have already covered many aspects of this method in [1]; however, the primary focus there was on numerical differentiation. Here, we aim to adopt a more general approach whose scope is numerically unstable problems in general, which are usually (but not necessarily) ill conditioned (the instability of a numerical computation can result not only from the underlying ill-conditioned mathematical problem but also from an inappropriate implementation of the solution (see Section 3.1)) in the mathematical sense, too. Also, we want to examine new possible dependencies not covered until now, namely, the dependence of the results on the programming language, processor architecture and operating system.

One needs to understand what the method is suited for and what it is not. First of all, we regard our result primarily as a theoretical message, which was not so clearly stated until now: namely, one can, routinely and without some specific requirements, go beyond the usual round-off error precision. From the practical point of view, this, however, applies mostly to situations where no other means (such as arbitrary-precision software) for increasing the precision are available in circumstances where the increase in the precision is of uttermost importance. This may correspond to the evaluation of a black-box function in a fixed number format environment, like when using compiled libraries or when obtaining function values from a server where the function-evaluation process is hidden from the client. It may also possibly apply to situations where re-programming (let us say in arbitrary-precision software) is possible but very costly. The obvious disadvantage is the time consumption (see Equation (6)), together with the fact that a precision increase is typically limited to a few orders of magnitude (in absolute errors).

The extent of numerical problems we are aiming at is very broad: basically any unstable numerical computation. What generally applies to this domain is that round-off errors are considered random. This point of view is very common and found in many texts; see, e.g., [2–5]. What distinguishes us from these authors is the way we use the randomness assumption: the cited texts apply it to stable numerical problems, in which the control of the error is important, and theoretically derive confidence intervals for the results. We, on the contrary, analyze unstable computations, where we let the computer actually perform error propagation in the perturbed-argument scenario with subsequent outcome averaging. Our theoretical concern is only to show that the averaging is justified, our aim being less ambitious: support the claim that the error is generally reduced without precisely quantifying by how much (as numerical experiments show, this does depend on the problem and cannot be reliably quantified in the "black-box" scenario).

In Section 2, we carry out a theoretical analysis of the approach that we propose, and in Section 3, numerical experiments are presented.

2. Theoretical Analysis

2.1. Method Principle

The methods that implement the statistical averaging-out of round-off errors in the evaluation of $f(x_0)$ may differ in their details; here, we adopt a simple linear first-order estimator in a symmetric setting, as is explained below. In what follows, α_{fl} indicates the floating-point representation of the number α, and x_i is assumed to be a machine number. We also assume that round-off errors induce important fluctuations in the function value $f_{\mathrm{fl}}(x)$ for small perturbations of its argument x_0 and that these fluctuations are symmetrical and significantly greater (this requirement determines our scope to be unstable numerical computations) than the function value changes. We proceed as follows:

- We generate N random numbers $\{x_i\}_{i=1}^{N}$ in a small interval around x_0, $x_i \in I \equiv (x_0 - h, x_0 + h)$, $h \ll 1$, and we assume that, in this small interval, f can be very well approximated by a linear function. Numbers x_i are generated from a distribution that is symmetric with respect to x_0; in our case, we use a uniform distribution on the interval I.
- We evaluate computer-estimated function values $\{f_{\mathrm{fl}}^i\}_{i=1}^{N}$, $f_{\mathrm{fl}}^i \equiv f_{\mathrm{fl}}(x_i)$, which differ from the true function values by round-off errors, $f_{\mathrm{fl}}^i = f^i + \delta_i$.
- We estimate the value of $f(x_0)$ by computing the average:

$$f(x_0) \approx \frac{1}{N}\sum_{i=1}^{N} f_{\mathrm{fl}}^i \equiv f_{\mathrm{AV}}(x_0).$$

This can be interpreted as a linear regression $R(x)$ of the set $\{(x_i, f_{\mathrm{fl}}^i)\}_{i=1}^{N}$, which we understand as a simple estimator of the first order (first meaning linear). Because of the assumptions (linearity, symmetry), one arrives, in the large-N limit, at $R(x_0) = \overline{f_{\mathrm{fl}}^i}$; i.e., one can estimate $f(x_0) \approx R(x_0)$ just by averaging the function values.

To unravel the method principle, one simply writes down the expression with error terms:

$$\frac{1}{N}\sum_{i=1}^{N} f_{\text{fl}}^{i} = \frac{1}{N}\sum_{i=1}^{N}\left(f^{i}+\delta_i\right) = \frac{1}{N}\sum_{i=1}^{N}\left(f^{0}+\Delta_i f+\delta_i\right)$$
$$= f(x_0) + \frac{1}{N}\sum_{i=1}^{N}\Delta_i f + \frac{1}{N}\sum_{i=1}^{N}\delta_i,$$

where $\Delta_i f$ denotes the change in the (true) function value, and $\Delta_i f = f^i - f^0$. If the round-off errors δ_i have a symmetric distribution (we address this question later), then the error estimate for $N \to \infty$ becomes

$$E_A = \left| f(x_0) - \frac{1}{N}\sum_{i=1}^{N} f_{\text{fl}}^{i} \right|_{N\to\infty} = \left| \frac{1}{N}\sum_{i=1}^{N}\Delta_i f + \frac{1}{N}\sum_{i=1}^{N}\delta_i \right|_{N\to\infty}$$
$$= \left| \frac{1}{N}\sum_{i=1}^{N}\Delta_i f \right|_{N\to\infty},$$

which is to be compared with a single estimation of the function value

$$E_S = \left| f^0 - f_{\text{fl}}^0 \right| = |\delta_0|.$$

If f was exactly linear, then in the $N \to \infty$ limit for a symmetric x_i distribution, one has $\left(\sum_{i=1}^{N}\Delta_i f\right)/N = 0$; i.e., the average-based estimate is better than the single estimation $E_A < E_S$. For a realistic scenario where f is not exactly linear, one could make additional estimates, quantify the deviation and see how it propagates. We propose a simple one, with a bounded quadratic term and assuming, without loss of generality, $x_0 = 0$. One has

$$f(x) = a + bx + cx^2, \quad c \ll \frac{1}{h}. \tag{2}$$

Keeping all of the above-mentioned assumptions, averaging leads to

$$\left(\frac{1}{N}\sum_{i=1}^{N}\Delta_i f\right)_{N\to\infty} = \left(\frac{b}{N}\sum_{i=1}^{N}x_i\right)_{N\to\infty} + \left(\frac{c}{N}\sum_{i=1}^{N}x_i^2\right)_{N\to\infty}$$
$$\ll 0 + \left(\frac{1}{hN}Nh^2\right)_{N\to\infty} = h.$$

If the total variation Δf in f on I does not exceed h by orders of magnitude, $\Delta f \sim h$, then $E_A < E_S$, because the variation Δf is supposed to be significantly smaller than a typical δ_i (of which δ_0 is a representative):

$$E_A = \left| \frac{1}{N}\sum_{i=1}^{N}\Delta_i f \right|_{N\to\infty} < h \sim \Delta f < \overline{|\delta_i|} \sim |\delta_0| = E_S.$$

As is clear from this last example, even if the round-off errors were fully symmetric, systematic shifts (which do not average) are present in our method. There are, however, reasons to believe that these shifts are, for well-behaved functions, small with respect to round-off errors.

One can think of many alternatives for round-off error averaging. One could, for example, use a quadratic or even a higher-order regression. Alternatively, one could randomly generate m points in I, with m being a small integer, and then construct a polynomial $P_{m-1}(x)$ that interpolates them. Repeating this many times, one could average the values of these polynomials at x_0: $f(x_0) \approx \frac{1}{N}\sum_{i=1}^{N} P_{m-1}^{i}(x_0)$. We have tried this approach, and it did not improve our results. In fact, all of these higher-order methods are computationally more complicated, which can further increase round-off errors.

Finally, one may ask about the implications of the method for the backward error (BE) analysis. The method as constructed deals with the forward error (FE) $|f_{\mathrm{fl}}(x_0) - f(x_0)|$ and shows that it can be improved by replacing $f_{\mathrm{fl}}(x_0) \to f_{\mathrm{AV}}(x_0)$. It is a constructive approach that has a straightforward interpretation in terms of an increase in precision. The approach itself departs from simple definitions of forward/backward errors because it uses the propagation of modified arguments by the approximation f_{fl} of the true function f. A strict analogy applied to BE analysis would consist of perturbing the output $f_{\mathrm{fl}}(x_0)$ and studying the set of values $x^i \equiv f^{-1}(y^i)$, $y^i = f_{\mathrm{fl}}(x_0) + \epsilon_i$ as mapped by the inverse of the exact function. The interpretation of such a procedure is unclear, and therefore, we do not see a direct connection between our approach and the BE analysis.

2.2. *Symmetry Properties of Error Propagation*

For the method to work, it is important that round-off errors, if interpreted as random, have a distribution with some degree of symmetry.

2.2.1. Round-Off Error Models

Simple Model

Starting with a simple unrealistic model, we assume that the computations are not deterministic, but, when repeatedly executed with the same arguments, they gain random errors and lead to different results. We also assume that the errors are not generated during elementary processor operations (which are exact), but between them: an output of the nth operation $o^{[n]} = i_1^{[n]} \star i_2^{[n]}$, $\star \in \{+, -, \times, \div\}$ acquires, before becoming the input of the following operation, a random error $i^{[n+1]} = o^{[n]} + \delta^{[n]}$. Denoting a machine number as a true value with error, $x = \mu_x + \delta_x$, we have

$$x \pm y = (\mu_x \pm \mu_y) + [\delta_x \pm \delta_y], \tag{3}$$

$$xy = \mu_x\mu_y + [\mu_x\delta_y + \mu_y\delta_x + \delta_x\delta_y]. \tag{4}$$

If δ_x and δ_y originate from symmetric probability distributions, $\varrho(\delta) = \varrho(-\delta)$, and are uncorrelated, then the error distribution of the result (square brackets) is also symmetric. This follows from the fact that addition, mutual multiplication and multiplication by a constant preserve the symmetry.

This is no longer the case for division (an incorrect statement was for the division, in this regard, given in [1]; understood as a fraction $\frac{a}{b} = a \times \frac{1}{b}$, one sees that the asymmetry is generated by the second term (denominator)) and possibly other floating-point instructions that some processor architectures implement (such as the square-root "FSQRT" or sine "FSIN"). As is clear from our approach, we focus on the impact of a small perturbation of arguments on the round-off error of the result. If the perturbation ε is small, we can assume that, on the interval $(x_0 - \varepsilon, x_0 + \varepsilon)$, a linear approximation of the instruction $\star$ is valid. Since a random variable with a distribution symmetric around the mean transformed by a linear function yields a variable with a mean-symmetric distribution too, we achieve the propagation of the error symmetry, at least in this approximation.

As a consequence, symmetric error distributions are propagated, keeping the symmetry up to the final result. Generating many results and averaging them makes errors statistically cancel. In addition to the fact that the symmetry conservation is, for some operations, only approximate, other pitfalls are present, too. For example, one can mention large (round-off) errors in the input (so that the straight-line approximation is not valid) or correlated numbers, e.g., the evaluation of $f(x) = x^2$ in the proximity of zero, which leads to asymmetric errors in the result since the latter cannot reach negative values.

More Realistic Model

Still keeping the assumption about the randomness of round-off errors, in a more realistic approach, we need to take into account that their sources are the elementary processor operations. Since error averaging is of interest to us, we are concerned, as before, with the behavior regarding error-symmetry propagation. This is a known and non-trivial issue referred to as "bias" and does depend on the rounding strategy. Clearly, simple rounding (the rounding of the last mantissa digit is meant here) rules, such as "rounding half up", are biased for all positional numeral systems with an even base, where the bias increases for a decreasing radix (in this sense, the binary system is the worst [3]). The argument here is a deliberate human effort in designing the processor architecture: the rounding rules on all modern computers are purposely made such that they have zero bias (e.g., "round to nearest, ties to even"; see Section 4.3 of [6]), which, by definition, means that the "error production" toward higher and smaller numbers is symmetrical.

In summary, an (approximate) error-symmetry conservation of (ideal) mathematical operations, together with symmetric error production in non-ideal processor instructions, is a combination that (approximately) conserves the symmetry of the error distributions and propagates it until the final result. An (approximately) symmetric error distribution of the result errors implies that its mean value is (close to) zero; i.e., averaging is an effective tool for removing round-off errors.

Realistic Model

Computer calculations are deterministic, and therefore, we need to perturb the argument of the function to mimic the above-assumed random character of round-off errors. This raises questions about the proper size ε of the perturbation. A very small (a few last mantissa bits) ε is not suitable because it might lead to important precision losses in the computation of $R(x_0)$. An optimal step (i.e., ε) is expected to be significantly bigger than $\epsilon_M \times 2^E$, where ϵ_M is the machine epsilon and E the exponent, yet significantly smaller than the typical length by which the function varies (or better, strongly deviates from its linear approximation). A numerical test for the differentiation of common elementary functions performed with *double-precision* variables indeed indicates [1] a typical optimal value of $\varepsilon \approx 10^{-6} \gg 10^{-16} \approx \epsilon_M|_{E=0}$. For such functions (constant function excluded), it is reasonable to assume that, for evaluations at points far away from each other (measured in units $\epsilon_M \times 2^E$), the round-off errors are uncorrelated. The use of function values with arguments different from x_0 certainly introduces some bias, i.e., a discretization error, which cannot be removed by averaging, but we have forwarded arguments as to why we expect this effect to be small.

Let us summarize the main assumptions that we use in our argumentation:

- The local absolute errors σ_i can be thought of as random, described by symmetric probability distributions with a zero mean.
- The round-off errors are uncorrelated for evaluations of the function value at two different points.

2.2.2. Additional Arguments

A fully rigorous argument in favor of the averaging method can be made using only one simple assumption. Let us consider a set of function value estimates $f^i_{\rm fl}$ and assume that they are fully dominated by round-off errors (and not function value changes) so that we have no a priori way to assess which estimate is more precise than others (i.e., the information content is considered equal for all estimates). If we interpret $f^i_{\rm fl}$ as measurements with random errors described by a probability distribution, then, in terms of probability, it is always (non-strictly) better to estimate the true value of f^0 by taking the average of the numbers, $\bar{f} = \left(\sum_{i=1}^N f^i_{\rm fl}\right)/N$, than to estimate it by picking one $f^0_{\rm fl}$ (a single evaluation of the function value directly at x_0). In other words, the mean (squared) distance $\Delta(x_1, x_2) \in \left\{|x_1 - x_2|, (x_1 - x_2)^2\right\}$ of a single estimation of the true value f^0 is always (non-strictly) greater than that of the mean $\bar{f}$:

$$\Delta(\bar{f}, f_0) \leq \int_{-\infty}^{\infty} \Delta(f, f_0)\varrho(f)df = E[\Delta(f, f_0)], \tag{5}$$

where E represents the expected value, and $\varrho(f)$ is an (arbitrary) probability distribution that describes f^i values. This follows from the non-specific, purely mathematical properties of probability distributions; more details can be found in Appendix A (or Section 3.2 of [1]).

Except for the statement in the previous paragraph, our arguments are heuristic. Yet, any honest consideration of the problem of the round-off error propagation in realistic computer computations (that go beyond a single matrix inversion or a small number of processor instructions, or possibly some very specific calculation) has to come to the conclusion that the strict mathematical treatment (strict error bounds can be derived (very easily, if they are allowed to be arbitrarily large), and here, we mean equalities; we, of course, do not imply that the search for the best bounds is not valuable) of this topic from first principles (the arithmetic of computer registers) is, without additional assumptions, far too complex. Authors, with the aim of providing some rigorous mathematical statements, often introduce various strong assumptions (usually about the randomness and its type or the existence of derivatives), which are nothing else but heuristic, too. We prefer not to play this game, since it adds nothing to the exactness of results with respect to the first principles (but it makes the paper look more serious). Yet, we might provide some additional heuristic arguments in favor of our approach.

One of them is the central limit theorem, often mentioned in texts related to round-off errors if they are treated in a probabilistic manner. Computations typically contain many additions and, supposing that the errors related to the added values can be considered uncorrelated, the probability distribution of the result tends to the Gaussian distribution, whatever the distributions of the individual summands. The Gaussian distribution is, of course, symmetric with respect to its mean, and averaging the error annihilates it.

In a realistic computation, the perfect symmetry of the numerical error distribution cannot be expected. Yet, even for distorted, non-symmetric distributions, the estimation of the true value from the average is a better option compared to what provides a single evaluation (see the "rigorous argument" paragraph). A numerical test was also performed in Section 4.1 of [1] with respect to this issue. There, the central difference formula was used to estimate the derivatives of $\sin(x)$, $\exp(x)$ and $\ln(x)$ at $x = 1$, π and $1/2$, respectively. The mean discretization parameter h was chosen to be large, $h_0 = 10^{-5}$, and the produced distributions were asymmetric and, as expected for large h, shifted (not centered around the true value of the derivative). Nevertheless, the mean of each distribution was close to the true value of the central difference, which means that, even for such distorted distributions, the round-off errors average to a large extent.

2.2.3. Previous Tests and Performance

In previous numerical tests (Section 4.1 of [1]), it has been demonstrated that the expected features of our approach are manifested and that we are right in understanding how the method works. The studied distributions were highly symmetrical (the asymmetry of the charts in Figure 2 of [1] is expected due to the large bias originating from the discretization error (made large by purpose); for the highest precision, the discretization parameter needs to be small (Figure 1 of [1])), and the shrinking of the error with increasing statistics (or time t, Figure 3 of [1]) is as expected from (1):

$$\sigma(t) = \sigma_0 + \sigma_1/\sqrt{N} = \sigma_0 + \sigma_1/\sqrt{\alpha t}. \tag{6}$$

Here, σ_0 is the highest possible precision, which cannot be improved by averaging (a systematic bias such as an asymmetry of the distribution or a discretization error); σ_1 is the typical precision provided by a single estimation; and α is some proportionality constant.

3. Numerical Experiments

The numerical investigation of the averaging approach can be performed in a large number of directions. One could study the dependence of the results on the size of the perturbation h, on the precision order k of the estimator, on the function f and its test point x_0, on the statistics N or on the processor architecture and the programming language (and others). We applied our approach to the numerical differentiation in [1], where the dependencies on $\varepsilon, k, f(x_0)$ and N were studied, and we consider them covered. We, therefore, study the two remaining; plus, we test the behavior of the approach for functions with more parameters (which can be perturbed independently). In what follows, we investigate the following:

- The evaluation of a function of a single variable;
- A matrix inversion in the context of trigonometric interpolation;
- The evaluation of higher derivatives of a function.

In all cases, the numerical evaluation is (purposely made) unstable so as to make sense of the averaging procedure. The argument perturbations x_i are generated as random numbers with a uniform distribution from the interval $(x_0 - h, x_0 + h)$, where h is chosen in the form $h(n) = 10^{-n}$, $n \in \mathbb{N}$, such that it gives the best results. This means that we evaluate $f(x_0)$ using the averaging procedure for various $h(n)$, $n = 1, \ldots, 16$, and choose the best, which we then compare to the outcome of the single evaluation of $f(x_0)$. All variables are *double precision*.

The tested architectures are as follows:

- x86:
  - Linux: 8xIntel Core i7-4770 3.40 GHz;
  - Windows: Intel(R) Core(TM) i7-6700HQ CPU @ 2.60 GHz 2.60 GHz;
- ARM: Octa-core: 2×2.2 GHz Cortex-A78 and 6×2.0 GHz Cortex-A55.

The tested programming languages are as follows:

- Java (openjdk 11.0.9);
- C/C++
  - Linux: gcc 7.5.0;
  - Windows: g++ (MinGW.org GCC-6.3.0-1) 6.3.0;
- Python (2.7.17);
- JavaScript (1.5);
- MATLAB (online, version R2024a, August 2024).

Three operating systems were used:

- Linux Open SUSE Leap 15.1, kernel 4.12.14-lp151.28.91-default;
- Android 13, 5.10.186-android12, Motorola Moto G54 Power;
- Windows 10 Pro.

From these, the tested combinations (Cx) are shown in Table 1. When running JavaScript, the Chrome web browser was used in all cases.

Table 1. Tested environments.

Combination	Processor	Programming Language	Operating System
C1	x86	Java	Linux
C2	x86	C/C++	Linux
C3	x86	Python	Linux
C4	x86	JavaScript	Linux
C5	ARM	JavaScript	Android
C6	x86	C/C++	Windows
C7	x86	JavaScript	Windows
C8	(online)	MATLAB	(online)

For the averaging procedure, we used the Kahan summation algorithm [7] to have a numerically stable computation of arithmetic means.

3.1. *Simple Function*

We present two examples of the averaging method applied to the evaluation of a real function of one real variable.

3.1.1. First Example

Inspired by [8], we investigate the function

$$f(x) = r_{13}(x), \quad r_n(x) = x r_{n-1}(x) - \frac{1}{n}, \quad r_0 = \ln(x) - \ln(x-1) \tag{7}$$

at $x_0 = 10$. The implemented recurrent definition (7) is numerically unstable, although the alternative expression

$$r_n(x) = \int_0^1 \frac{t^n}{x-t} dt$$

implies that the mathematical dependence is not ill conditioned. Actually, a stable evaluation on a computer is also possible, e.g., using a numerical integration method. For averaging, we use $N = 10^6$ and determine the optimal step to be $h = 10^{-4}$. The results are shown in Table 2. We see an enhancement of the precision by orders of magnitude. Although the numbers differ in various rows, the difference seems to be mainly due to statistical fluctuations (random x_i generation). This can be seen by looking at the value from the single evaluation (at $x_0 = 10$) where differences are small: all Linux and ARM calculations agree that $f_{\text{fl}}^{\text{L}}(x_0) = 0.008235200679887617$, although Windows scenarios C6 and C7 give a quite different value: $f_{\text{fl}}^{\text{W}}(x_0) = 0.008235016561770745$8. Still, the difference $|f_{\text{fl}}^{\text{L}}(x_0) - f_{\text{fl}}^{\text{W}}(x_0)| \approx 1.8 \times 10^{-7}$ is significantly smaller than the error produced by the single evaluation, $\approx 3.6 \times 10^{-4}$. These large fluctuations at such large statistics are somewhat surprising; nevertheless, in any scenario, the precision increase is significant and exceeds one order of magnitude.

Table 2. The precision of the evaluation of $r_{13}(10)$, Equation (7), by the averaging method compared to the direct evaluation for different computing environments (Table 1). Despite the large statistics for randomly generated $\{x_i\}$, the results have large fluctuations and cannot be reproduced exactly.

	$f(x) = r_{13}(x), x_0 = 10, f(x_0) = 0.0078785198760532617\ldots, h = 10^{-4}$		
	$\triangle_{\text{AV}} = \lvert f_{\text{AV}}(x_0) - f(x_0)\rvert$	$\triangle_{\text{fl}} = \lvert f_{\text{fl}}(x_0) - f(x_0)\rvert$	$\triangle_{\text{fl}}/\triangle_{\text{AV}}$
C1	$\approx 9.2 \times 10^{-7}$	$\approx 3.6 \times 10^{-4}$	≈ 390
C2	$\approx 2.8 \times 10^{-6}$	$\approx 3.6 \times 10^{-4}$	≈ 130
C3	$\approx 3.5 \times 10^{-6}$	$\approx 3.6 \times 10^{-4}$	≈ 100
C4	$\approx 3.6 \times 10^{-6}$	$\approx 3.6 \times 10^{-4}$	≈ 100
C5	$\approx 6.3 \times 10^{-6}$	$\approx 3.6 \times 10^{-4}$	≈ 60
C6	$\approx 7.6 \times 10^{-6}$	$\approx 3.6 \times 10^{-4}$	≈ 50
C7	$\approx 1.1 \times 10^{-6}$	$\approx 3.6 \times 10^{-4}$	≈ 330
C8	$\approx 1.6 \times 10^{-6}$	$\approx 3.6 \times 10^{-4}$	≈ 220

It may be interesting to examine the statistical distribution of $\{f^i\}$. Because all computing environments give similar results, we show only scenario C1 in Figure 1. One sees that the distribution is very symmetric but quite broad, meaning that the single evaluation (blue triangle) is close to its peak when compared to the distribution spread. Yet, in sub-figure (b), one observes that the peak of the distribution is significantly closer to the true value (green diamond) than the single evaluation result.

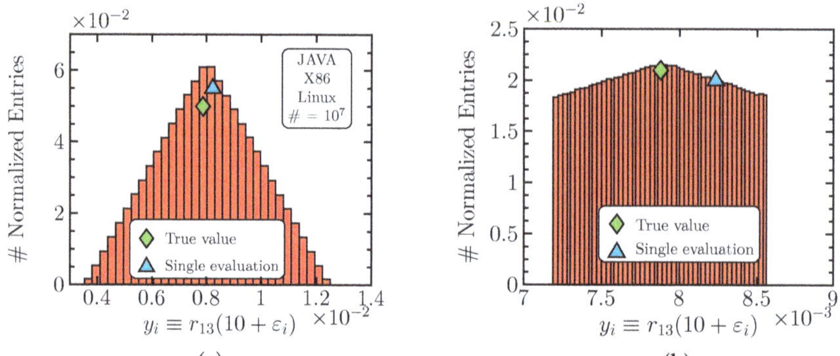

(a) (b)

Figure 1. Area-normalized statistical distribution of $r_{13}(10+\delta_i)$ for random δ_i uniformly distributed over $(-10^{-4}, 10^{-4})$, sub-figure (**a**). The peak area is enlarged in sub-figure (**b**).

3.1.2. Second Example

We investigate a simple exponentiation implemented in an unstable manner:

$$x^n = (2x)x^{n-2} + (x-2)x^{n-1}.$$

Choosing $x = 1/3$ and $n = 15$, we compute $a_{15} = 1/3^{15}$ using the recurrent relation

$$a_n = \frac{2}{3}a_{n-2} - \frac{5}{3}a_{n-1}, \quad a_1 = \frac{1}{3}, \quad a_2 = a_1^2, \tag{8}$$

where we perturb the value of a_1. We use $N = 10^6$ and $h = 10^{-7}$. The outcomes are shown in Table 3, and, again, the validity of the averaging approach is demonstrated despite important fluctuations in the entries in the table (observed when attempting to reproduce them). The effect is, however, smaller than in the previous case.

Table 3. The precision of the evaluation of $a_{15}(1/3)$, Equation (8), by the averaging method compared to the direct evaluation for different computing environments (Table 1). Despite the large statistics for randomly generated $\{x_i\}$, the results have large fluctuations and cannot be reproduced exactly.

	$f(x) = a_{15}(x)$, $x_0 = 1/3$, $f(x_0) = 0.00000006969171\ldots$, $h = 10^{-7}$		
	$\triangle_{AV} = \lvert f_{AV}(x_0) - f(x_0)\rvert$	$\triangle_{fl} = \lvert f_{fl}(x_0) - f(x_0)\rvert$	$\triangle_{fl}/\triangle_{AV}$
C1	$\approx 2.4 \times 10^{-16}$	$\approx 7.3 \times 10^{-16}$	≈ 3
C2	$\approx 8.2 \times 10^{-17}$	$\approx 7.3 \times 10^{-16}$	≈ 8
C3	$\approx 9.9 \times 10^{-17}$	$\approx 7.3 \times 10^{-16}$	≈ 7
C4	$\approx 1.1 \times 10^{-16}$	$\approx 7.3 \times 10^{-16}$	≈ 7
C5	$\approx 8.0 \times 10^{-17}$	$\approx 7.6 \times 10^{-16}$	≈ 9
C6	$\approx 3.2 \times 10^{-16}$	$\approx 3.5 \times 10^{-14}$	≈ 110
C7	$\approx 2.4 \times 10^{-16}$	$\approx 7.3 \times 10^{-16}$	≈ 3
C8	$\approx 1.7 \times 10^{-16}$	$\approx 7.3 \times 10^{-16}$	≈ 4

The error distribution for this computation in scenario C8 is shown in Figure 2.

The "simple function" examples fulfill the expectations that we have with respect to the method: we obtain a symmetric error distribution that provides, by averaging, a significant improvement in precision.

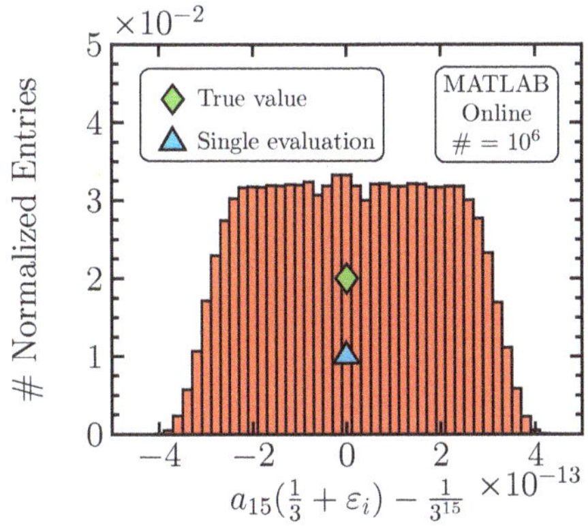

Figure 2. Area-normalized statistical distribution of $a_{15}(1/3+\delta_i) - 1/3^{15}$ for random δ_i uniformly distributed over $(-10^{-7}, 10^{-7})$ for the C8 scenario.

3.2. Matrix Inversion in Trigonometric Interpolation

In this section, we search for coefficients $c_{0,1,2,3}$ such that the trigonometric polynomial

$$f(x) = \sum_{n=0}^{3} c_n \cos(nx) \tag{9}$$

interpolates $\{(x_i, y_i)\}_{i=0}^{3}$, with $x_i = 1 + i \times \Delta$, $\Delta = 10^{-4}$ and $y_i = g(x_i)$, with

$$g(x) = -1 - \frac{1}{3}\cos(x) + \frac{1}{7}\cos(2x) - \frac{1}{11}\cos(3x).$$

Obviously, the correct values are $c_0 = -1$, $c_1 = -1/3$, $c_2 = 1/7$ and $c_3 = -1/11$. The problem is written in a matrix form, $\overrightarrow{y} = M\vec{c}$, where

$$M_{ij} = \cos(jx_i).$$

The task is to invert the matrix and find $\overrightarrow{c}$:

$$\vec{c} = M^{-1}\overrightarrow{y}.$$

As a matter of fact, the problem is ill conditioned because Δ is small, and rows of M are very similar. Various strategies can be adopted when implementing perturbations: e.g., perturb the elements of M, those of y, or both. Every option can be studied, but here, we have chosen the first one, because the problem is often stated as "matrix inversion" alone, not necessarily related to some specific vector y. In each studied case, we independently perturb every element of M by a random amount, with all perturbations being from the same interval I. We observe that a typical perturbation (to obtain the best results) is significantly smaller than in the previous case (the r_{13} function). The size of the statistical sample is $N = 10^5$. The code for matrix inversion differs considerably, depending on the programming language. For Java, we used the *Jama* "Matrix" library (https://math.nist.gov/javanumerics/jama/, accessed on 27 June 2024); for C(++), we borrowed a code published online (https://github.com/altafahmad623/Operation-Research/blob/master/inverse.c, accessed on 27 June 2024); for Python, the *linalg* library from the *numpy* package was called; and for JavaScript, we again referred to an implementation found online (https://web.archive.org/web/20210406035905/http://blog.acipo.com/matrix-inversion-in-javascript/, accessed on 27 June 2024). It turns out that the matrix inversion implementation is the most significant source of differences between various scenarios and, for the C(++) implementation, is unsatisfactory in the current setting due to producing nonsense numbers. For this reason, we make an exception and decrease, in this case, the condition number by setting $\Delta = 10^{-3}$. Each result is represented by a set of four numbers, and the outcomes produced under various conditions are summarized in Table 4. Illustrative error-distribution histograms for the c_0 coefficient are shown for the C1 and C3 scenarios in Figure 3. This time, the shape is Gaussian, and, surprisingly, the Python implementation manifests regular oscillatory structures, certainly a numerical effect, which is missing for Java. Still, both results are comparable since oscillations are also averaged.

Table 4. The precision of the evaluation of four trigonometric coefficients, Equation (9), by the averaging method, compared to the direct evaluation for different computing environments (Table 1). Despite the large statistics for randomly generated elements of M, the results have fluctuations and cannot be reproduced exactly.

	$c_i \equiv \left[\vec{f}(M)\right]_i = [M^{-1}\vec{y}]_i$			
	$f_0 = -1, f_1 = -1/3, f_2 = 1/7, f_3 = -1/11$			
	$\triangle^i_{\mathrm{AV}} =$	$\triangle^i_{\mathrm{fl}} =$	$R^i =$	h
	$\lvert f_{\mathrm{AV}}(M)_i - f(M)_i \rvert$	$\lvert f_{\mathrm{fl}}(M)_i - f(M)_i \rvert$	$\triangle^i_{\mathrm{fl}}/\triangle^i_{\mathrm{AV}}$	
C1	$\triangle^0 \approx 2.3 \times 10^{-5}$	$\triangle^0 \approx 1.8 \times 10^{-4}$	$R^0 \approx 8$	10^{-14}
	$\triangle^1 \approx 3.9 \times 10^{-5}$	$\triangle^1 \approx 2.0 \times 10^{-4}$	$R^1 \approx 5$	
	$\triangle^2 \approx 1.9 \times 10^{-5}$	$\triangle^2 \approx 1.6 \times 10^{-4}$	$R^2 \approx 8$	
	$\triangle^3 \approx 6.0 \times 10^{-6}$	$\triangle^3 \approx 2.8 \times 10^{-5}$	$R^3 \approx 5$	
C2	$\triangle^0 \approx 5.2 \times 10^{-3}$	$\triangle^0 \approx 1.0 \times 10^{-1}$	$R^0 \approx 20$	10^{-12}
$\Delta = 10^{-3}$	$\triangle^1 \approx 6.4 \times 10^{-3}$	$\triangle^1 \approx 6.3 \times 10^{-1}$	$R^1 \approx 100$	
	$\triangle^2 \approx 3.8 \times 10^{-3}$	$\triangle^2 \approx 1.3$	$R^2 \approx 340$	
	$\triangle^3 \approx 3.4 \times 10^{-3}$	$\triangle^3 \approx 9.8 \times 10^{-2}$	$R^3 \approx 30$	
C3	$\triangle^0 \approx 1.4 \times 10^{-5}$	$\triangle^0 \approx 1.2 \times 10^{-4}$	$R^0 \approx 8$	10^{-14}
	$\triangle^1 \approx 2.4 \times 10^{-5}$	$\triangle^1 \approx 1.6 \times 10^{-4}$	$R^1 \approx 7$	
	$\triangle^2 \approx 1.3 \times 10^{-5}$	$\triangle^2 \approx 3.5 \times 10^{-5}$	$R^2 \approx 3$	
	$\triangle^3 \approx 4.1 \times 10^{-6}$	$\triangle^3 \approx 3.3 \times 10^{-5}$	$R^3 \approx 8$	
C4	$\triangle^0 \approx 3.3 \times 10^{-6}$	$\triangle^0 \approx 3.1 \times 10^{-5}$	$R^0 \approx 9$	10^{-14}
	$\triangle^1 \approx 5.5 \times 10^{-6}$	$\triangle^1 \approx 8.1 \times 10^{-5}$	$R^1 \approx 14$	
	$\triangle^2 \approx 2.9 \times 10^{-6}$	$\triangle^2 \approx 6.5 \times 10^{-5}$	$R^2 \approx 22$	
	$\triangle^3 \approx 8.5 \times 10^{-7}$	$\triangle^3 \approx 3.5 \times 10^{-5}$	$R^3 \approx 41$	
C5	$\triangle^0 \approx 2.6 \times 10^{-5}$	$\triangle^0 \approx 3.1 \times 10^{-5}$	$R^0 \approx 1$	10^{-14}
	$\triangle^1 \approx 4.3 \times 10^{-5}$	$\triangle^1 \approx 8.1 \times 10^{-5}$	$R^1 \approx 2$	
	$\triangle^2 \approx 2.2 \times 10^{-5}$	$\triangle^2 \approx 6.5 \times 10^{-5}$	$R^2 \approx 3$	
	$\triangle^3 \approx 6.8 \times 10^{-6}$	$\triangle^3 \approx 3.5 \times 10^{-5}$	$R^3 \approx 5$	
C6	$\triangle^0 \approx 2.9 \times 10^{-4}$	$\triangle^0 \approx 2.6 \times 10^{-1}$	$R^0 \approx 890$	10^{-12}
$\Delta = 10^{-3}$	$\triangle^1 \approx 2.3 \times 10^{-3}$	$\triangle^1 \approx 1.9 \times 10^{-1}$	$R^1 \approx 80$	
	$\triangle^2 \approx 1.9 \times 10^{-3}$	$\triangle^2 \approx 3.5 \times 10^{-1}$	$R^2 \approx 190$	
	$\triangle^3 \approx 1.9 \times 10^{-4}$	$\triangle^3 \approx 6.5 \times 10^{-3}$	$R^3 \approx 34$	
C7	$\triangle^0 \approx 3.2 \times 10^{-5}$	$\triangle^0 \approx 3.1 \times 10^{-5}$	$R^0 \approx 1$	10^{-14}
	$\triangle^1 \approx 5.4 \times 10^{-5}$	$\triangle^1 \approx 8.1 \times 10^{-5}$	$R^1 \approx 2$	
	$\triangle^2 \approx 2.7 \times 10^{-5}$	$\triangle^2 \approx 6.5 \times 10^{-5}$	$R^2 \approx 2$	
	$\triangle^3 \approx 8.3 \times 10^{-6}$	$\triangle^3 \approx 3.5 \times 10^{-5}$	$R^3 \approx 4$	
C8	$\triangle^0 \approx 5.1 \times 10^{-6}$	$\triangle^0 \approx 6.1 \times 10^{-5}$	$R^0 \approx 12$	10^{-15}
	$\triangle^1 \approx 8.3 \times 10^{-6}$	$\triangle^1 \approx 2.0 \times 10^{-5}$	$R^1 \approx 2$	
	$\triangle^2 \approx 4.1 \times 10^{-6}$	$\triangle^2 \approx 1.6 \times 10^{-4}$	$R^2 \approx 39$	
	$\triangle^3 \approx 1.2 \times 10^{-6}$	$\triangle^3 \approx 1.8 \times 10^{-5}$	$R^3 \approx 15$	

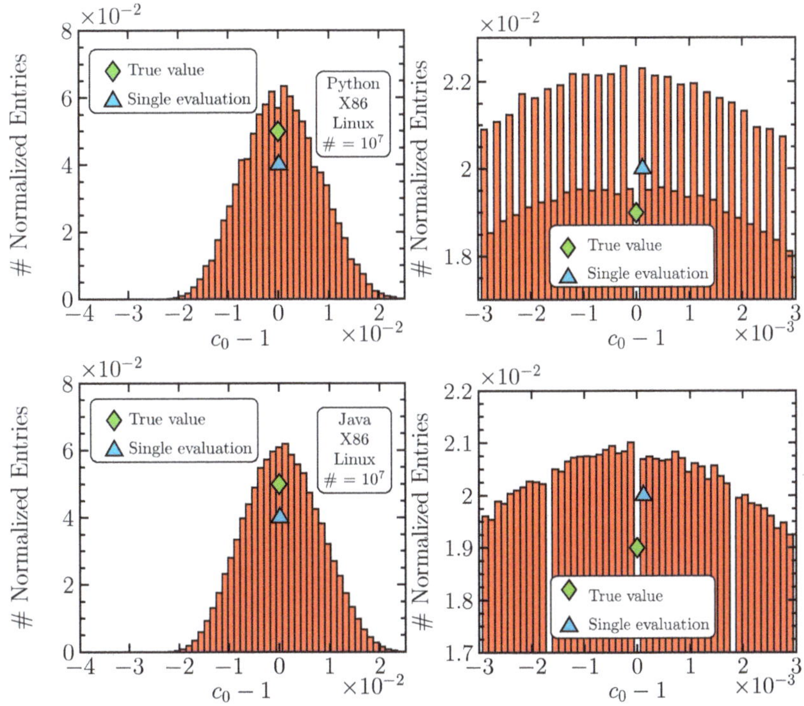

Figure 3. Area-normalized distributions of errors of the c_0 coefficient (9) around the true value with the averaging method, as observed for Python (**first row**, C3 setting) and Java (**second row**, C1 setting). In both cases, some numerical issues are observed. In the second column, the peak region is magnified.

The main conclusion that one can draw is that an increase in precision is observed with a significance of around one order of magnitude. Beyond doubt, this cannot be explained by statistical fluctuations, and the averaging method has an effect. The most important factor that determines the outcome is the implementation of the specific mathematical operation (matrix inversion, in our case), and, for an altered scenario with the C(++) code, the increase in precision is much more important (although the code's performance is much lower because it cannot deal with $\Delta = 10^{-4}$).

3.3. Higher-Order Derivatives

The numerical instability increases with the increasing derivative order, and at some point, any method of computation fails. It is interesting to see how various approaches behave in this respect. We obtain inspiration from [9] and differentiate

$$f(x) = \frac{e^x}{(\sin x)^3 + (\cos x)^3} \tag{10}$$

at $x = 0$. All derivatives are integers, and we focus on the few first of them:

$$\left\{ f^{(i)}(x)|_{x=0} \right\}_{i=1,2,3,4} = \{1, 4, 4, 28\}.$$

We use central difference formulas to obtain estimates; see Table 5. The formulas depend on two parameters, x_0 and ε, and we perturb both of them, one at a time, thus producing two result tables, Tables 6 and 7. Perturbing $x_0 = 0$ is straightforward, and ε is perturbed around the optimal value $\varepsilon_0 = 10^{-k}$, which we find by applying the averaging method for an integer k. Similarly, we compute derivatives (single estimations) at zero, testing different integers k, and, by comparing them to the true values, we choose the best. The values in the averaging approach are perturbed randomly in the interval $\varepsilon_i \in (\varepsilon_0/2, 3 \times \varepsilon_0/2)$. We set the statistics to $N = 10^5$. As illustrative examples, we provide histograms for error distributions of the second derivative for the C5 and C6 scenarios in Figures 4 and 5.

Table 5. Implemented central difference formulas with $y_n \equiv f(x_0 + n\varepsilon)$.

Deriv. Order	Formula
1	$(y_{-2}/12 - 2y_{-1}/3 + 2y_1/3 - y_2/12)/\varepsilon$
2	$(-y_{-2}/12 + 4y_{-1}/3 - 5y_0/2 + 4y_1/3 - y_2/12)/\varepsilon^2$
3	$(y_{-3}/8 - y_{-2} + 13y_{-1}/8 - 13y_1/8 + y_2 - y_3/8)/\varepsilon^3$
4	$(-y_{-3}/6 + 2y_2 - 13y_{-1}/2 + 28y_0/3 - 13y_1/2 + 2y_2 - y_3/6)/\varepsilon^4$

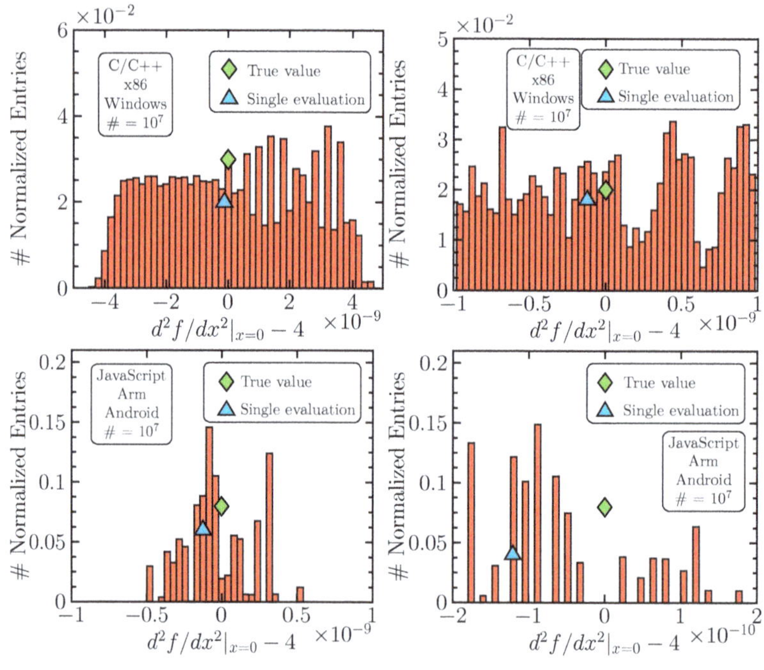

Figure 4. Area-normalized error distributions of the second-derivative estimates of (10) in the C5 (**lower row**) and C6 (**upper row**) scenarios perturbing x. In the pictures on the right, the peak area is enlarged.

One sees that the averaging method provides an improvement in precision for the first two derivatives, which is generally lost for the third and fourth derivatives. Also, the perturbation in ε gives more important improvements. It is necessary to understand why the method fails above the second derivative, and we provide, in what follows, a dedicated section to this issue.

Table 6. Compared precision of averaging and single estimation for various derivative orders D. The argument x is perturbed randomly with the amplitude h_x. The finite-difference step is fixed to $\varepsilon_0 = 10^{-4}$ for $D = 1$, $\varepsilon_0 = 10^{-3}$ for $D = 2, 3$ and $\varepsilon_0 = 10^{-2}$ for $D = 4$. Despite the large statistics, the results fluctuate significantly and cannot be reproduced exactly.

		$f^D(x) = \frac{d^D}{dx^D}\left[e^x/\left((\sin x)^3 + (\cos x)^3\right)\right]$			
		$f^1(0) = 1, f^2(0) = 4, f^3(0) = 4, f^4(0) = 28$			
		x Is Perturbed			
	D	$\triangle_{AV} =$ $\left\|f^D_{AV}(x_0) - f^D(x_0)\right\|$	$\triangle_{fl} =$ $\left\|f^D_{fl}(x_0) - f^D(x_0)\right\|$	$\triangle_{fl}/\triangle_{AV}$	h_x
C1	1	$\approx 1.2 \times 10^{-13}$	$\approx 8.6 \times 10^{-13}$	≈ 7	10^{-14}
	2	$\approx 4.8 \times 10^{-11}$	$\approx 1.2 \times 10^{-10}$	≈ 3	10^{-15}
	3	$\approx 2.0 \times 10^{-8}$	$\approx 2.1 \times 10^{-9}$	≈ 1	10^{-8}
	4	$\approx 1.2 \times 10^{-5}$	$\approx 1.4 \times 10^{-5}$	≈ 1	10^{-6}
C2	1	$\approx 1.2 \times 10^{-13}$	$\approx 8.6 \times 10^{-13}$	≈ 7	10^{-14}
	2	$\approx 4.8 \times 10^{-11}$	$\approx 1.2 \times 10^{-10}$	≈ 3	10^{-15}
	3	$\approx 8.2 \times 10^{-10}$	$\approx 2.1 \times 10^{-9}$	≈ 3	10^{-8}
	4	$\approx 1.4 \times 10^{-5}$	$\approx 1.4 \times 10^{-5}$	≈ 1	10^{-6}
C3	1	$\approx 1.2 \times 10^{-13}$	$\approx 8.6 \times 10^{-13}$	≈ 7	10^{-14}
	2	$\approx 4.8 \times 10^{-11}$	$\approx 1.2 \times 10^{-10}$	≈ 3	10^{-15}
	3	$\approx 3.7 \times 10^{-10}$	$\approx 2.1 \times 10^{-9}$	≈ 6	10^{-8}
	4	$\approx 1.3 \times 10^{-5}$	$\approx 1.4 \times 10^{-5}$	≈ 1	10^{-6}
C4	1	$\approx 1.2 \times 10^{-13}$	$\approx 8.6 \times 10^{-13}$	≈ 7	10^{-14}
	2	$\approx 4.8 \times 10^{-11}$	$\approx 1.2 \times 10^{-10}$	≈ 3	10^{-15}
	3	$\approx 5.9 \times 10^{-10}$	$\approx 2.1 \times 10^{-9}$	≈ 4	10^{-8}
	4	$\approx 1.4 \times 10^{-5}$	$\approx 1.4 \times 10^{-5}$	≈ 1	10^{-6}
C5	1	$\approx 1.2 \times 10^{-13}$	$\approx 8.6 \times 10^{-13}$	≈ 7	10^{-14}
	2	$\approx 4.7 \times 10^{-11}$	$\approx 1.2 \times 10^{-10}$	≈ 3	10^{-15}
	3	$\approx 1.7 \times 10^{-9}$	$\approx 2.1 \times 10^{-9}$	≈ 1	10^{-8}
	4	$\approx 1.4 \times 10^{-5}$	$\approx 1.4 \times 10^{-5}$	≈ 1	10^{-6}
C6	1	$\approx 4.5 \times 10^{-13}$	$\approx 5.7 \times 10^{-13}$	≈ 1	10^{-11}
	2	$\approx 2.6 \times 10^{-12}$	$\approx 1.3 \times 10^{-11}$	≈ 5	10^{-9}
	3	$\approx 9.1 \times 10^{-10}$	$\approx 1.6 \times 10^{-7}$	≈ 180	10^{-8}
	4	$\approx 1.4 \times 10^{-5}$	$\approx 1.4 \times 10^{-5}$	≈ 1	10^{-7}
C7	1	$\approx 1.2 \times 10^{-13}$	$\approx 8.6 \times 10^{-13}$	≈ 7	10^{-14}
	2	$\approx 4.7 \times 10^{-11}$	$\approx 1.2 \times 10^{-10}$	≈ 3	10^{-15}
	3	$\approx 2.7 \times 10^{-9}$	$\approx 2.1 \times 10^{-9}$	≈ 1	10^{-8}
	4	$\approx 1.4 \times 10^{-5}$	$\approx 1.4 \times 10^{-5}$	≈ 1	10^{-6}
C8	1	$\approx 1.2 \times 10^{-13}$	$\approx 8.6 \times 10^{-13}$	≈ 7	10^{-14}
	2	$\approx 4.7 \times 10^{-11}$	$\approx 1.2 \times 10^{-10}$	≈ 3	10^{-15}
	3	$\approx 1.6 \times 10^{-9}$	$\approx 2.1 \times 10^{-9}$	≈ 1	10^{-8}
	4	$\approx 1.4 \times 10^{-5}$	$\approx 1.4 \times 10^{-5}$	≈ 1	10^{-6}

Table 7. The precision of the averaging and the single estimation compared for various derivative orders D. The argument $x = 0$ is fixed. The finite-difference steps are perturbed around their central values ε_0 using $h_\varepsilon = \varepsilon_0/2$, and the displayed ε_0 values are those used in the averaging method. Despite the large statistics, the results fluctuate significantly and cannot be reproduced exactly.

$f^D(x) = \frac{d^D}{dx^D}\left[e^x/\left((\sin x)^3 + (\cos x)^3\right)\right]$					
$f^1(0) = 1, f^2(0) = 4, f^3(0) = 4, f^4(0) = 28$					
ε **Is Perturbed**					
	D	$\triangle_{AV} = \lvert f^D_{AV}(x_0) - f^D(x_0)\rvert$	$\triangle_{fl} = \lvert f^D_{fl}(x_0) - f^D(x_0)\rvert$	$\triangle_{fl}/\triangle_{AV}$	ε_0
C1	1	$\approx 3.8 \times 10^{-15}$	$\approx 8.6 \times 10^{-13}$	≈ 230	10^{-4}
	2	$\approx 2.3 \times 10^{-12}$	$\approx 1.2 \times 10^{-10}$	≈ 52	10^{-3}
	3	$\approx 8.1 \times 10^{-10}$	$\approx 2.1 \times 10^{-9}$	≈ 3	10^{-3}
	4	$\approx 2.1 \times 10^{-5}$	$\approx 1.4 \times 10^{-5}$	≈ 0.7	10^{-2}
C2	1	$\approx 3.5 \times 10^{-15}$	$\approx 8.6 \times 10^{-13}$	≈ 240	10^{-4}
	2	$\approx 2.2 \times 10^{-12}$	$\approx 1.2 \times 10^{-10}$	≈ 55	10^{-3}
	3	$\approx 2.6 \times 10^{-9}$	$\approx 2.1 \times 10^{-9}$	≈ 0.8	10^{-3}
	4	$\approx 2.1 \times 10^{-5}$	$\approx 1.4 \times 10^{-5}$	≈ 0.7	10^{-2}
C3	1	$\approx 1.8 \times 10^{-15}$	$\approx 8.6 \times 10^{-13}$	≈ 484	10^{-4}
	2	$\approx 4.1 \times 10^{-13}$	$\approx 1.2 \times 10^{-10}$	≈ 300	10^{-3}
	3	$\approx 2.6 \times 10^{-9}$	$\approx 2.1 \times 10^{-9}$	≈ 0.8	10^{-3}
	4	$\approx 2.1 \times 10^{-5}$	$\approx 1.4 \times 10^{-5}$	≈ 0.7	10^{-2}
C4	1	$\approx 2.2 \times 10^{-15}$	$\approx 8.6 \times 10^{-13}$	≈ 390	10^{-4}
	2	$\approx 9.4 \times 10^{-13}$	$\approx 1.2 \times 10^{-10}$	≈ 130	10^{-3}
	3	$\approx 5.4 \times 10^{-10}$	$\approx 2.1 \times 10^{-9}$	≈ 4	10^{-3}
	4	$\approx 2.1 \times 10^{-5}$	$\approx 1.4 \times 10^{-5}$	≈ 0.7	10^{-2}
C5	1	$\approx 2.0 \times 10^{-15}$	$\approx 8.6 \times 10^{-13}$	≈ 431	10^{-4}
	2	$\approx 1.9 \times 10^{-12}$	$\approx 1.2 \times 10^{-10}$	≈ 64	10^{-3}
	3	$\approx 1.9 \times 10^{-9}$	$\approx 2.1 \times 10^{-9}$	≈ 1	10^{-3}
	4	$\approx 2.1 \times 10^{-5}$	$\approx 1.4 \times 10^{-5}$	≈ 0.7	10^{-2}
C6	1	$\approx 3.5 \times 10^{-15}$	$\approx 5.7 \times 10^{-13}$	≈ 160	10^{-4}
	2	$\approx 3.4 \times 10^{-12}$	$\approx 1.3 \times 10^{-11}$	≈ 4	10^{-3}
	3	$\approx 1.6 \times 10^{-9}$	$\approx 1.6 \times 10^{-7}$	≈ 100	10^{-3}
	4	$\approx 1.7 \times 10^{-5}$	$\approx 1.4 \times 10^{-5}$	≈ 0.8	10^{-2}
C7	1	$\approx 3.1 \times 10^{-15}$	$\approx 8.6 \times 10^{-13}$	≈ 280	10^{-4}
	2	$\approx 2.2 \times 10^{-12}$	$\approx 1.2 \times 10^{-10}$	≈ 55	10^{-3}
	3	$\approx 2.1 \times 10^{-9}$	$\approx 2.1 \times 10^{-9}$	≈ 1	10^{-3}
	4	$\approx 2.1 \times 10^{-5}$	$\approx 1.4 \times 10^{-5}$	≈ 0.7	10^{-2}
C8	1	$\approx 2.7 \times 10^{-15}$	$\approx 8.6 \times 10^{-13}$	≈ 320	10^{-4}
	2	$\approx 3.6 \times 10^{-12}$	$\approx 1.2 \times 10^{-10}$	≈ 33	10^{-3}
	3	$\approx 9.9 \times 10^{-10}$	$\approx 2.1 \times 10^{-9}$	≈ 2	10^{-3}
	4	$\approx 2.1 \times 10^{-5}$	$\approx 1.4 \times 10^{-5}$	≈ 0.7	10^{-2}

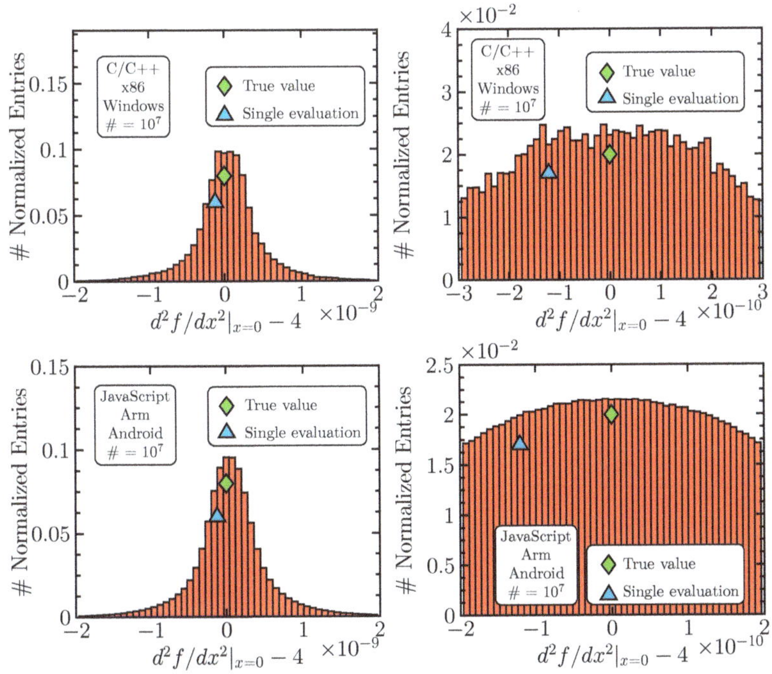

Figure 5. Area-normalized error distributions of the second-derivative estimates of (10) in the C5 (**lower row**) and C6 (**upper row**) scenarios perturbing the discretization parameter ε. In the pictures on the right, the peak area is enlarged.

The better performance of the ε-based approach may be qualitatively understood, since the smallness of the ε parameter causes *catastrophic cancellation*; i.e., if ε is big, then no instability will be present, even for small x-perturbations. Thus, by varying ε_0 in the finite difference $[f(x_0+\varepsilon_0)-f(x_0)]/\varepsilon_0$ (as an example), a large number of *various* values are created, forming an approximate Gaussian, and can be averaged (Figure 5). Performing a shift in x, i.e., varying δ_x in $[f(x_0+\delta_x+\varepsilon_0)-f(x_0+\delta_x)]/\varepsilon_0$ with ε_0 fixed, computes function values at two points, which always have the same distance, ε_0. The function value differences then tend to be strongly correlated, and a linear function gives a constant. At the scale $10^{-15} \lesssim h_x \lesssim 10^{-6}$ (see Table 6), the function (10) is well described by its linear approximation; the small deviation from linearity (and possibly rounding effects) leads to a limited number of floating-point values that the finite difference can take and that are, in addition, unevenly distributed (Figure 4). Nevertheless, one also observes some differences between the upper and lower pictures in Figure 5, which indicates that the computing environment also plays a role, because the program codes are more or less equivalent in all scenarios. Another interesting observation is the third derivative in the C6 scenario in both Tables 6 and 7; the precision is significantly increased (unlike in all other scenarios) and is even greater than for the second derivative in the same case. We do not have an understanding of this effect but see it as a further confirmation of the fact that the computing environment may induce important and unpredictable changes in results.

4. Fourth Derivative

For space and brevity reasons, we do not perform an exhaustive search including all scenarios and analyze the problem only in the C1 case (Java, Linux, x86) by perturbing ε. We believe that the generalization of our findings is valid, yet, for further confirmation, this issue may be subject to additional studies in the future.

We learn the most by looking at the error histograms. We produced a few of them using $\varepsilon_0^{\text{new}} = \varepsilon_0/100, \varepsilon_0/10, \varepsilon_0$ and $10 \times \varepsilon_0$ with $\varepsilon_0 = 10^{-2}$ (see Table 7); a larger variation, $100 \times \varepsilon_0$, already hits the closest singularity of (10) at $x = -\pi/4$ and leads to strongly disturbed results. The histograms are shown in Figure 6 and their zoomed-in versions in Figure 7. The impact of round-off errors is most easily assessed by (practically) removing them using arbitrary-precision software. In our case, we benefited from the *Apfloat* library (http://www.apfloat.org/, accessed on 27 June 2024) using 300 valid decimal digits and $N = 1000$ (and higher). Also, we did not use a random generation of $\varepsilon_i \in (\varepsilon_0/2, 3 \times \varepsilon_0/2)$ but regularly divided the interval and performed calculation scanning with the step ε_0/N. This was carried out with the aim of removing the possible bias from a non-ideal random number generator. This may introduce another bias, which would be, however, uncorrelated. The round-off-error-free histograms are presented in Figure 8.

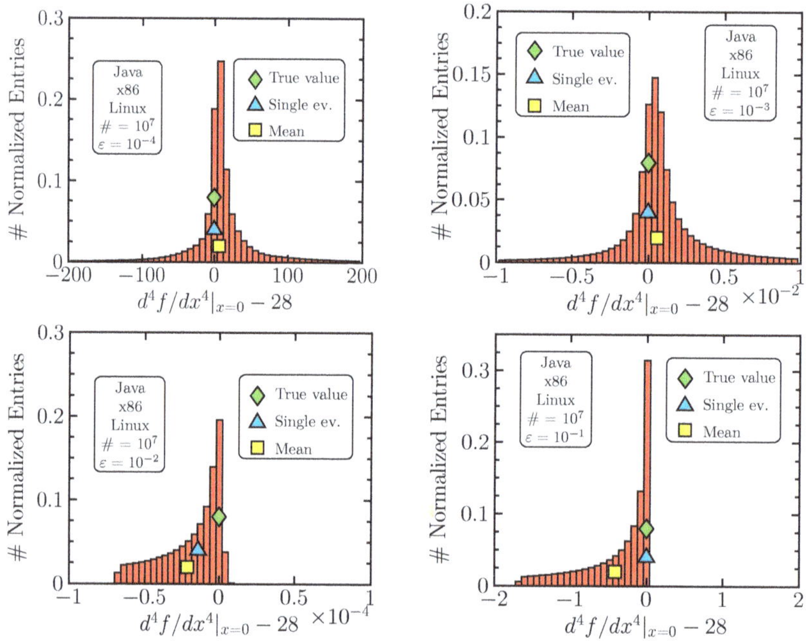

Figure 6. Area-normalized distributions of errors on the fourth derivative of (10) at zero in the C1 setting for various sizes of the mean value of the discretization parameter ε_0 (around which perturbations are randomly produced). One can note large changes in scale on the x-axis.

The mere description of what one sees in Figures 6 and 7 is that the distributions are shifted (the mean of the histogram is represented by the yellow square) and sometimes highly asymmetric. One also observes that the spread of the distribution changes dramatically when changing the discretization parameter ε_0. When compared to Figure 8, it becomes clear what is going on. For small $\varepsilon_0 = 10^{-3}, 10^{-4}$, round-off errors appear and make the distribution more symmetric (as we argued), with, however, a (very) large spread. All distributions have some systematic shift, as seen from plots in Figure 8, which, however, decreases (as expected) with decreasing ε_0. Despite the true value lying in the most probable bin, it is positioned at the edge of the distribution, which makes averaging ineffective. Nevertheless, it is still competitive in precision for $\varepsilon_0 = 10^{-2}$: the fact that the averaging method "loses" can be interpreted as random bad luck; the single-evaluation value (blue triangle, bottom-left graphics in Figure 6) could have been (if interpreted as random, with the histogram representing the probability distribution function) situated left to the mean. Nevertheless, it is clear that averaging is unable to provide any substantial improvement. For both values $\varepsilon_0 = 10^{-2},\ 10^{-1}$, the round-off effects lose significance, yet a notable rise in bias and spread appears.

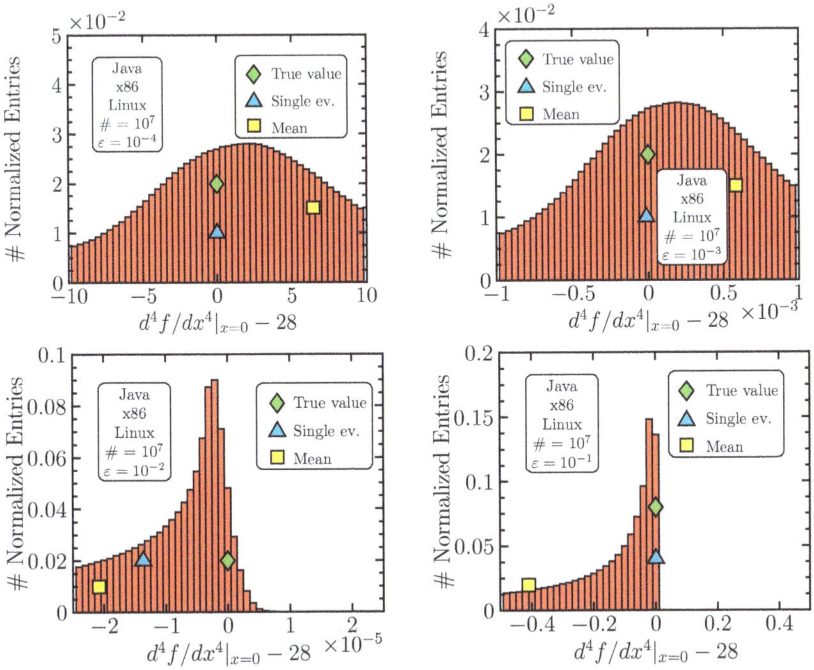

Figure 7. Distributions identical to those in Figure 6 but enlarged in the central area.

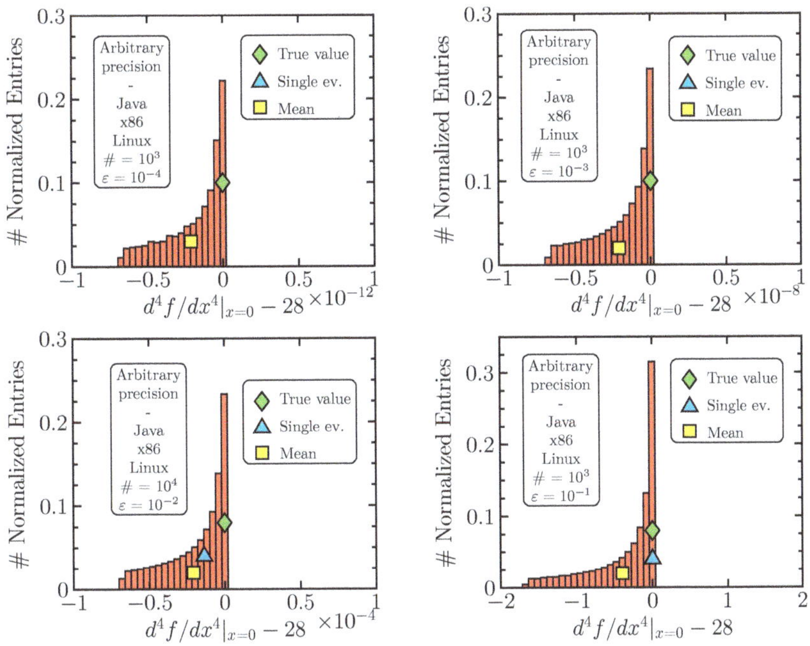

Figure 8. Modifications of distributions from Figure 6 with round-off errors (practically) removed.

As a general assertion, one may say that for very unstable computations, changes in the tested sizes of perturbations (we used a discrete set of the form 10^{-n}) may lead to a steep rise in the systematic bias (which cannot be averaged) and distribution widths. Here, one should distinguish between two cases:

1. The perturbation can be zero, i.e., the true value can be reached, such as in Section 3.1.
2. The perturbation cannot reach zero, such as the discretization parameter in derivative estimates.

In the second situation, the choice of some perturbation (e.g., $\varepsilon_0 = 10^{-n}$, $h_\varepsilon = \varepsilon_0/2$) may be too small, so the round-off effects dominate. The next, larger choice (e.g., $\varepsilon_0 = 10^{-n+1}$, $h_\varepsilon = \varepsilon_0/2$) may already be too big, so a significant bias is induced, implying that the region (interval) where the values of the parameter give reasonable results is very small. The first situation is similar: the interval that provides reasonable estimates may be very small around the true value, and going beyond it means a steep rise in the bias and distribution widths. In both scenarios, one can try to make the averaging approach work in this small interval.

In conclusion, we presume that the failure of the averaging approach is generally related to strong variations in the bias and width of the error distribution when perturbing the argument. This causes the interval of possible values of perturbations δ_i to be very small, conflicting with the fact that the machine numbers have non-zero spacing. The distributions to be averaged are then unevenly populated and strongly impaired by numerical effects, sometimes containing only a limited number of discrete values. If a perturbation from outside this interval is used, then other effects that are not round-off-error-related may appear and cause a systematic shift. Further interesting questions related to this topic are discussed in Appendix B.

At last, let us perform a simple test: if we change the mean size of the discretization parameter ε_0, we also change, by our convention, the amplitude of its perturbations $h_\varepsilon = \varepsilon_0/2$, i.e., $\varepsilon_i \in (\varepsilon_0 - h_\varepsilon, \varepsilon_0 + h_\varepsilon) = (\varepsilon_0/2, 3 \times \varepsilon_0/2)$. The average size of the perturbation and, consequently, the length of the interval from which ε_i values are taken are thus adjusted automatically once the choice of ε_0 is made. The latter takes the form $\varepsilon_0 = 10^{-n}$, which was chosen for a reason: in a black-box scenario, without the knowledge of the true values, one might only guess which ε_0 is desirable and cannot fine-tune. Keeping this in mind, we do not want our results to appear fine-tuned, so the step between the consecutive sizes that we tested is rather big. Let us now allow for some fine-tuning and see what happens for $\varepsilon_0 = 10^{-2}/2$. The results are $(N = 10^7)$

$$\triangle_{\text{AV}} \approx 1.12 \times 10^{-6}, \quad \triangle_{\text{fl}} \approx 13.7 \times 10^{-6}, \quad \triangle_{\text{fl}}/\triangle_{\text{AV}} \approx 12.19\,.$$

The effect is there: averaging "wins", and only the appropriate averaging interval went unnoticed by our $\varepsilon_0 = 10^{-n}$ scanning radar. The error histogram is shown in Figure 9—left.

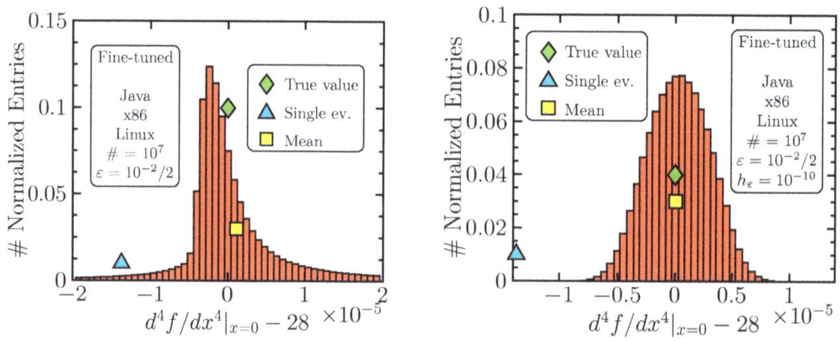

Figure 9. Area-normalized distributions of the fourth-derivative error for function (10) produced with $\varepsilon_0 = 10^{-2}/2$ and with $h_\varepsilon = 10^{-2}/4$ (**left**) and $h_\varepsilon = 10^{-10}$ (**right**).

The effect can be strongly amplified if we break our convention: by choosing a smaller value for $h_\varepsilon = 10^{-10}$, we significantly shorten the interval of the used perturbations $\varepsilon_i \in (10^{-2}/2 - 10^{-10}, 10^{-2}/2 + 10^{-10})$. One notices that the length of this interval is still much greater than computer precision. We obtain

$$\triangle_{\mathrm{AV}} \approx 4.7 \times 10^{-8}, \quad \triangle_{\mathrm{fl}} \approx 1.4 \times 10^{-5}, \quad \triangle_{\mathrm{fl}}/\triangle_{\mathrm{AV}} \approx 290\,.$$

See Figure 9—right.

5. Summary, Discussion, Conclusions and Outlook

As shown throughout this work, averaging, meant as a tool for suppressing round-off errors in unstable calculations, is effective. For this, we have provided theoretical support and several numerical experiments. If we have the means to fine-tune the size of perturbations and possibly other parameters (the step in differentiation), then in almost every numerical problem, one can choose such values as to outperform the single evaluation in precision. It may happen that the length of the interval around the true (or optimal) value, where the bias and width of the error distributions remain small, is very short and can be compared to the spacing of the floating-point numbers. Then, the averaging approach may suffer from severe numerical effects and may not provide an improvement (but remains competitive).

Averaging can be used in a scenario where any prior information (about the function or numerical effects) is poor, and the question about the optimal size of perturbations is difficult to answer. It seems safe to use perturbations that are small but greater (by an order of magnitude) than the smallest possible one (for a given floating-point arithmetic). With such a choice, an improvement is expected, yet it may be far from the optimal choice. One may also attempt to derive theoretical estimates if at least some constraints are available (bounds on the function and its derivatives); this is our outlook. Still, the safest approach for a given computation is probably to study special cases of this computation or problems that are computationally very similar and have known answers so that the amplitude of perturbations can be tuned.

Nevertheless, our goal is mainly to give a theoretical message, which, despite its simple underlying idea, is not found in the literature. Even so, this does not exclude practical applications of the method in some rare situations. This depends on the circumstances rather than on the method itself. It may happen that a numerical model that one uses and relies on is available only as an executable, without the source code and without the knowledge of its theoretical background. Then, averaging based on perturbing its input parameters may be the only way to increase the precision, if necessary. This could possibly also apply to situations where knowledge is available, but re-programming (let us say in an arbitrary-precision language) is costly. Some quantities (such as the first derivative) are improved significantly by the averaging method (Table 7), which may improve the practical application potential of averaging for such cases.

In this text, we have put the emphasis on the computing environment, and it indeed has an impact. These effects, complemented by other numerical effects, lead to various observations:

- Many numbers in the result tables have substantial fluctuations, as observed when reproducing them. This is in spite of the large statistic that is used.
- Distribution shapes vary: sometimes triangular (Figure 1) and sometimes Gaussian (Figure 5) or other.
- Changing the computational environment may make numerical disturbances (dis)appear. An example is the regular peaky structure seen in the upper-right picture in Figure 3.
- The third derivative is, for some reason, surprisingly precise for the C6 case (C++, Windows).

We do not have an understanding of these effects. Acquiring it would entail tedious work studying low-level computer arithmetic. But, this is not necessary for our purposes:

these effects exist, and the averaging approach is cross-platform valid thanks to its robust, statistical character.

Being persuaded that averaging is an existing numerical phenomenon that one can possibly profit from, there are many different directions in which one could investigate it further. One could, for example, search for rules to properly set the averaging parameters for higher-order derivatives, since somewhat disappointing numbers for $D = 3, 4$ in Table 7 can certainly be improved, as demonstrated in Section 4.

Funding: This work was supported by VEGA Grant No. 2/0105/21.

Data Availability Statement: The presented study uses no external data and all produced data are contained within the article. The source codes of programs used for the analysis are available at http://147.213.122.82/~andrej/2024_StatAvg/, accessed on 27 June 2024 or can be requested from the author.

Conflicts of Interest: The author has no conflicts of interest to declare.

Appendix A. Rigorous Argument

Our aim is to compare $f_{\text{fl}}^0 \equiv f_{\text{fl}}(x_0)$ and $\bar{f} \equiv \left(\sum_{i=1}^N f_{\text{fl}}^i\right)/N$ when estimating $f^0 \equiv f(x_0)$. For this, it is important to make an assumption about the set $\{f_{\text{fl}}^i\}_{i=1}^N \equiv \{f_{\text{fl}}(x_0 + \varepsilon_i)\}_{i=1}^N$ and correctly interpret it. What we assume is that the numbers $\{f_{\text{fl}}^i\}$ originate from *some* (fixed) probability distribution and are all, in this sense, equivalent. In other words, given two random values f_{fl}^m and f_{fl}^n, one is unable (by assumption) to say which one has a higher probability of better approximating f^0. This is not completely true in reality: f_{fl}^0 is affected only by round-off errors but has no discretization error (bias) and thus has a higher probability of being closer to the true value f^0 than an estimate f_{fl}^i that is affected by both discretization and round-off errors. Therefore, if given f_{fl}^0 and $f_{\text{fl}}^{i \neq 0}$, one is right to choose f_{fl}^0 as the estimate that has a higher probability of better approximating f^0. Since we are working with a scenario where we presume that the round-off errors are dominant, we consider the above-mentioned assumption as a good approximation. In consequence, we regard $\{f_{\text{fl}}^i\}_{i=1}^N$ as a sequence of random numbers that all approximate f^0, but index i no longer carries information about the size of ε_i. Let us note the probability distribution that describes $\{f_{\text{fl}}^i\}$ as $\varrho(f)$; i.e., the probability density that f_{fl}^i takes the value f is $\varrho(f)$. Let us recall that the randomness of the whole procedure originates in the random choices of ε_i.

We work in the large-N limit $N \to \infty$, and the question that we ask is the following: which of the two estimates, random f_{fl}^i (of which f_{fl}^0 is a representative) or $\bar{f}$, has a higher *probability* of lying closer to the true value f^0?

Being *close* assumes that there is some way of measuring the distance. We consider the two most common expressions, $\Delta(x_1, x_2) \in \left\{(x_1 - x_2)^2, |x_1 - x_2|\right\}$, i.e., the "squared" distance and the usual absolute-value distance. The mean distance from the true value f^0 is simply the expected value of this distance, i.e., the distance at f multiplied by the probability (density) $\varrho(f)$ of f being realized.

For the mean squared distance msd^2, one has

$$\begin{aligned} msd^2 &= \int_{-\infty}^{+\infty} \left(f - f^0\right)^2 \varrho(f) df, \quad t = f - f^0 \\ &= \int_{-\infty}^{+\infty} t^2 \varrho\left(t + f^0\right) dt, \quad \varrho\left(t + f^0\right) \equiv r(t) \\ &= \int_{-\infty}^{+\infty} t^2 r(t) dt. \end{aligned}$$

The well-known formula for the variance σ_r^2 of a distribution

$$\sigma_r^2 = \left(\int_{-\infty}^{+\infty} t^2 r(t) dt \right) - \bar{t}^2$$

gives

$$msd^2 = \bar{t}^2 + \sigma_r^2, \quad \sigma_r^2 \geq 0,$$

which implies that the mean squared distance from the true value f^0 is *always* (non-strictly) greater than the squared distance of the mean $\bar{f}$ from f^0. Indeed,

$$\bar{t}^2 = \overline{(f - f^0)}^2 = \left(\bar{f} - f^0 \right)^2.$$

The computations for the mean absolute distance *mad* are similar. We first assume $\bar{f} \geq f^0$, and one has

$$\begin{aligned} mad &= \int_{-\infty}^{+\infty} \left| f - f^0 \right| \varrho(f) df \\ &= \int_{-\infty}^{+\infty} |t| r(t) dt \\ &= \int_0^{+\infty} t\, r(t) dt + \int_{-\infty}^{0} t\, r(t) dt - 2 \int_{-\infty}^{0} t\, r(t) dt \\ &= \bar{t} - 2 \int_{-\infty}^{0} t r(t) dt \\ &= \bar{t} + R, \quad R = -2 \int_{-\infty}^{0} t r(t) dt \geq 0. \end{aligned}$$

The conclusion is similar: the mean absolute distance from the true value is *always* (non-strictly) greater than the absolute distance of the mean $\bar{f}$ from f^0

$$\bar{t} = \bar{f} - f^0 \geq 0,$$

the last inequality assumed. If $\bar{f} < f^0$, then $\bar{t}$ is negative and cannot be interpreted as an absolute distance. In this case, we introduce an f^0-reflected distribution $\tilde{\varrho}$:

$$\tilde{\varrho}(f^0 + f) = \varrho\left(f^0 - f \right),$$

which has, because of the symmetry, the same absolute distance from the mean to the true value. One then performs all of the above *mad* computations for $\tilde{\varrho}$ and arrives at the same conclusion, with $\bar{t}$ being positive (i.e., interpretable as a distance).

Both results imply that the mean distance (to the true value), i.e., the distance that one obtains *on average* when randomly picking f_{fl}^i, is greater than the distance of the mean (average). If one accepts the assumption, this represents a fully rigorous proof that shows that averaging f_{fl}^i is (on average) a better strategy when estimating f^0 than randomly picking one f_{fl}^i (such as f_{fl}^0).

Appendix B. Remarks on the Fourth Derivative

To keep the main text of Section 4 concise, we add a few remarks here. The remarks concern the topic studied in Section 4.

Appendix B.1. Systematic Bias

From what was carried out, it becomes clear that the systematic bias of distributions in Figure 8 is caused neither by round-off errors (which are missing) nor by a (possibly defective) random number generator (not used). It is therefore presumably due to the behavior of the function with respect to the finite-difference estimator (Table 5, last line);

i.e., it corresponds to the discretization error. We do not have an understanding of the low-level underlying mechanisms, but it has to be similar to what would be observed for a simple forward-difference estimator $E_{D=1}(x,\varepsilon) = [f(x+\varepsilon) - f(x)]/\varepsilon$ of the first derivative for a function which behaves similarly to $y = x^3$ at $x_0 = 0$. Such an estimator would systematically overestimate the derivative since any value of ε leads to a non-negative number, with the true value being approached only by the $\varepsilon \to 0$ edge of the distribution. In our [(10), $x_0 = 0$, $D = 4$] case, the derivative is systematically underestimated.

Appendix B.2. Averaging Distributions with Small Bias and Large Spread

To complete our arguments, one should also comment on the situation where the perturbation cannot reach zero (the "first" situation) and ε_0 chosen to be small. Here, one may argue that the spread is large, but we do not care about it because it averages. What counts is the bias, and this becomes small. So, why do we not obtain more precise results for such situations, as is shown, for example, in the upper-left picture in Figure 6? The answer lies in considering additional effects: a symmetric spread may be compensated by the averaging procedure in a strict mathematical sense, yet this is not true in practice. In addition to requiring larger statistics, the numerical error when averaging large numbers is larger than when averaging small numbers (the effect of the last mantissa digit for a larger exponent is, in the absolute value, greater than for a smaller exponent); i.e., the precision limitations from averaging large numbers may cause the result to be non-competitive with the single-evaluation value. In addition, round-off errors may have some bias, which may grow when errors grow. Indeed, the tails of the distributions in the upper row of Figure 6 are not symmetric (if investigated in detail).

Appendix B.3. Practical Limitations of Small Averaging Intervals

If an interval suitable for averaging (acceptable bias and spread) is very small, then the averaging method may be negatively affected. Two issues can be mentioned:

- If we are in a situation where the perturbation cannot reach zero, then, in a black-box function scenario, it is unrealistic to expect to find this small interval. One may only theorize about its existence.
- In any scenario (perturbing the true or the optimal value), one might adopt the smallest numbers that the number format allows, e.g., $\delta_i \sim 10^{-16}$ for *double*, assuming that the exponent is zero. Nevertheless, the spacing between machine numbers is non-zero; thus, the interval contains only a limited number of different floating-point values that show up in the error distribution, and it may suffer from strong numerical effects. Presumably, this effect is visible in the sub-figures of Figure 4, where the perturbation is small: see column h in Table 6. Averaging in this situation may be strongly impaired, providing small or no advantage over a single evaluation of the function.

Appendix B.4. Origins of Systematic Shifts

The distributions in Figure 8 show considerable bias and asymmetry. As already commented on above, this is understood as the actual mathematical dependence of these figures on the flat, uniform distribution of the generated perturbations. We have argued in this text (and this is confirmed by comparing Figures 6 and 8) that rounding effects are not the dominant source of bias or asymmetry. The latter is expected to be more noticeable for larger perturbations, where round-off errors play a less significant role. There, their appearance is natural; they stem from the discretization error, which we understand, in a very broad sense, as an error intentionally introduced into the calculations for practical reasons. This encompasses such effects as the deviation of the function from linearity (i.e., the error lies in assuming linearity), a non-infinitesimal differentiation step (for which the estimator systematically over/undershoots the true value) and so on. The various types of discretization error need not produce symmetric distributions (as a matter of fact, Figure 8), and a more complex analysis going beyond a simple quadratic Equation (eq:kvadratic) may be useful in this regard. To summarize, the systematic shift may be related to the following:

- Discretization errors;
- Non-ideal random number generators;
- (Remaining) rounding biases;
- Some other effects.

References

1. Liptaj, A. Statistical approach for highest precision numerical differentiation. *Math. Comput. Simul.* **2023**, *203*, 92–111. [CrossRef]
2. Hull, T.E.; Swenson, J.R. Tests of probabilistic models for propagation of roundoff errors. *Commun. ACM* **1966**, *9*, 108–113. [CrossRef]
3. Linnainmaa, S. Towards accurate statistical estimation of rounding errors in floating-point computations. *BIT* **1975**, *15*, 165–173. [CrossRef]
4. Brunet, M.C.; Chatelin, F. A probabilistic round-off error propagation model, application to the eigenvalue problem. In *Reliable Numerical Commputation*; Oxford Academic: Oxford, UK, 1990; pp. 139–160.
5. Higham, N.J.; Mary, T. A new approach to probabilistic rounding error analysis. *SIAM J. Sci. Comput.* **2019**, *41*, A2815–A2835. [CrossRef]
6. *IEEE Std 754-2019 (Revision of IEEE 754-2008)*; IEEE Standard for Floating-Point Arithmetic. IEEE: New York, NY, USA, 2019.
7. Kahan, W. Pracniques: Further remarks on reducing truncation errors. *Commun. ACM* **1965**, *8*, 40. [CrossRef]
8. Miel, G. Calculator calculus and roundoff errors. *Am. Math. Mon.* **1980**, *87*, 243–252. [CrossRef]
9. Fornberg, B. Numerical differentiation of analytic functions. *ACM Trans. Math. Softw.* **1981**, *7*, 512–526. [CrossRef]

axioms

MDPI

Article

Enhanced Fast Fractional Fourier Transform (FRFT) Scheme Based on Closed Newton-Cotes Rules

Aubain Nzokem [1,*,†], Daniel Maposa [2,†] and Anna M. Seimela [2,†]

[1] Department of Mathematics & Statistics, York University, Toronto, ON M3J 1P3, Canada
[2] Department of Statistics and Operations Research, University of Limpopo, Sovenga 0727, South Africa; daniel.maposa@ul.ac.za (D.M.); anna.seimela@ul.ac.za (A.M.S.)
* Correspondence: hilaire77@gmail.com
† These authors contributed equally to this work.

Abstract

The paper presents an enhanced numerical framework for computing the one-dimensional *fast Fractional Fourier Transform (FRFT)* by integrating *closed-form Composite Newton-Cotes quadrature rules*. We show that a FRFT of a QN-length weighted sequence can be decomposed analytically into two mathematically commutative compositions: one involving the composition of a FRFT of an N-length sequence and a FRFT of a Q-length weighted sequence, and the other in reverse order. The composite FRFT approach is applied to the inversion of Fourier and Laplace transforms, with a focus on estimating probability densities for distributions with *complex-valued characteristic functions*. Numerical experiments on the *Variance-Gamma (VG)* and *Generalized Tempered Stable (GTS)* models show that the proposed scheme significantly improves accuracy over *standard (non-weighted) fast FRFT* and *classical Newton-Cotes quadrature*, while preserving computational efficiency. The findings suggest that the composite FRFT framework offers a robust and mathematically sound tool for *transform-based numerical approximations*, particularly in applications involving *oscillatory integrals* and *complex-valued characteristic functions*.

Keywords: Composite Fast Fractional Fourier Transform (FRFT); Newton-Cotes quadrature; numerical inversion of transforms; oscillatory integrals; characteristic functions; Variance-Gamma (VG) distribution; Generalized Tempered Stable (GTS) distribution

MSC: 65D30; 65T50; 41A55; 42A38

1. Introduction

The *Fractional Fourier Transform (FRFT)* is a generalization of the classical Fourier Transform (FT), characterized by a fractional order parameter that allows for continuous interpolation between the time and frequency domains [1–5]. Since its introduction, the FRFT has proven to be a versatile tool in applied mathematics, with significant applications in signal processing, optics, quantum mechanics, and financial modeling [6–8]. The increasing relevance of the FRFT is primarily attributed to its ability to represent non-stationary signals and analyze problems where phase and frequency information evolve continuously.

In recent years, applications in *high-resolution radar imaging* [6], *quantum information systems* [9], and *fractional signal processing* [10] have underscored the demand for FRFT algorithms that are not only *computationally efficient* but also *numerically stable*. However, current fast FRFT algorithms often suffer from precision limitations due to step-function

https://doi.org/10.3390/axioms14070543

approximations or fail to provide robust numerical integration schemes when applied to *oscillatory integrals* and *complex-valued characteristic functions* [2,11,12].

Conversely, *Newton-Cotes quadrature rules*, especially in their composite form, have long been recognized as effective and robust numerical integration methods. These rules approximate definite integrals by interpolating the integrand with polynomials evaluated at equally spaced points [13–17]. In particular, closed Newton-Cotes formulas, such as *Simpson's rule* and the *3/8 rule*, have been extended to higher-order schemes that provide accurate results for smooth integrands [18,19].

The motivation for the present work stems from the structural similarity between FRFT algorithms and numerical quadrature techniques. Both rely on integral approximations based on polynomial interpolation and discretization of function samples. In particular, classical fast FRFT algorithms approximate oscillatory integrals in a manner reminiscent of step-wise Filon-type quadrature methods [20–23]. This similarity suggests that incorporating *high-order Newton-Cotes quadrature rules* into the FRFT could yield a more accurate and mathematically tractable framework for evaluating fractional transforms.

This paper presents a *composite FRFT scheme* that integrates *closed Newton-Cotes quadrature rules* of degree Q for improved numerical integration. The proposed framework offers both *computational efficiency* and *theoretical rigor*, surpassing conventional FRFT algorithms in terms of both *accuracy* and *numerical stability*. To demonstrate the efficacy of the proposed method, we empirically validate it using probability models [24–29] commonly employed in *financial mathematics*, including the *Variance-Gamma (VG)* and *Generalized Tempered Stable (GTS)* distributions. Our results reveal significant improvements in both accuracy and stability compared to standard FRFT and classical quadrature methods.

The remainder of the paper is organized as follows: Section 2 provides a detailed discussion on the construction and properties of closed Newton-Cotes rules. Section 3 introduces the composite FRFT framework and its two commutative decompositions. Section 4 presents numerical experiments and performance comparisons using the VG and GTS models to validate the proposed method.

2. Composite Newton-Cotes Quadrature Formulas

The Newton-Cotes rules value the integrand f at equally spaced points x_i over the interval $[a, b]$, where $x_i = a + i\frac{b-a}{M} = a + ih$ with $h = \frac{b-a}{M}$; $M = QN$ and $x_{Qp+Q} = x_{Q(p+1)}$, where Q is the number of h within the subinterval $[x_{Qp}, x_{Qp+Q}]$ of interval $[a, b]$.

2.1. Composite Rules

To have greater accuracy, the idea of the composite rule is to subdivide the interval [a, b] into smaller intervals such as $[x_{Qp}, x_{Qp+Q}]$, applying the quadrature formula in each of these smaller intervals and adding up the results to obtain more accurate approximations (1):

$$\int_a^b f(x)dx = \sum_{p=0}^{N-1} \int_{x_{Qp}}^{x_{Qp+Q}} f(x)\, dx. \tag{1}$$

We define the Lagrange basis polynomials over the sub-interval $[x_{Qp}, x_{Qp+Q}]$ (2):

$$l_{Qp+j}(x) = \prod_{\substack{i \neq j \\ i=0}}^{Q} \frac{x - x_{Qp+i}}{x_{Qp+j} - x_{Qp+i}}, \quad l_j(x_i) = \delta_{ij} = \begin{cases} 0 & : i \neq j \\ 1 & : i = j. \end{cases} \tag{2}$$

The Lagrange interpolating polynomial and the integration can be derived (3):

$$\tilde{f}(x) = \textstyle\sum_{j=0}^{Q} f(x_{Qp+j}) l_{Qp+j}(x), \quad \int_{x_{Qp}}^{x_{Qp+Q}} \tilde{f}(x)dx = \sum_{j=0}^{Q} f(x_{Qp+j}) \int_{x_{Qp}}^{x_{Qp+Q}} l_{Qp+j}(x)\, dx. \tag{3}$$

The integration of Lagrange basis polynomials (4):

$$\int_{x_{Qp}}^{x_{Qp+Q}} l_{Qp+j}(x)dx = \frac{b-a}{M}\frac{(-1)^{(Q-j)}}{j!(Q-j)!}\int_0^Q \prod_{\substack{i\neq j\\ i=0}}^{Q}(y-i)dy. \tag{4}$$

We have the Lagrange Interpolating integration over $[x_{Qp}, x_{Qp+Q}]$ (5)

$$\int_{x_{Qp}}^{x_{Qp+Q}} \tilde{f}(x)dx = \frac{b-a}{M}\sum_{j=0}^{Q}{}' W_j f(x_{Qp+j}) \qquad W_j = \frac{(-1)^{(Q-j)}}{j!(Q-j)!}\int_0^Q \prod_{\substack{i\neq j\\ i=0}}^{Q}(y-i)dy. \tag{5}$$

For theoretical and applied perspectives on Composite Newton-Cotes quadrature methods, see [30–34] and [35–38], respectively.

Proposition 1. *For Q even, $M = QN$ integer, and $f \in \mathcal{C}^{Q+2}([a,b])$, there exists $\eta \in]a,b[$ such that*

$$\int_a^b f(x)\,dx = \tfrac{b-a}{M}\sum_{p=0}^{\frac{M}{Q}-1}\sum_{j=0}^{Q} W_j f(x_{Qp+j}) + h^{Q+3}\tfrac{Nf^{(Q+2)}(\eta)}{(Q+2)!}\int_0^Q\int_0^y \prod_{i=0}^{Q}(a-i)\,da\,dy, \tag{6}$$

with

$$W_j = \frac{(-1)^{(Q-j)}}{j!(Q-j)!}\int_0^Q \prod_{\substack{i\neq j\\ i=0}}^{Q}(y-i)dy.$$

For Proposition 1 proof, see [39,40]

The error analysis of the Newton-Cotes formulas of degree Q in [39–42] shows that the level of accuracy is greater when Q is even. In fact, we have $O(h^{Q+3})$ for Q even, against $O(h^{Q+2})$ for Q odd.

2.2. Weights Computation

Before using the formula in (6), the expression of $\{W_j\}_{0\leq j\leq Q}$ can be simplified as follows:

Proposition 2. *For Q even and $M = QN$ integer, $j \in \{0,1,2,\ldots,Q\}$*

$$W_j = \sum_{i=0}^{Q} C_i^j \frac{Q^{i+1}}{i+1}\frac{(-1)^{(Q-j)}}{j!(Q-j)!}. \tag{7}$$

For Proposition 2 proof, see [39,40].

The coefficient values $(C_i^j)_{\substack{0\leq i\leq Q\\ 0\leq j\leq Q}}$ of the polynomial function are obtained by solving the following Equation (8) with a Vandermonde matrix [43].

$$\prod_{\substack{i\neq j\\ i=0}}^{Q}(y-i) = \sum_{i=0}^{Q} C_i^j y^i. \tag{8}$$

For $Q \leq 12$, Table 1 provides the values of weights $\{W_j\}_{0\leq j\leq Q}$ in (7)

Remark 1. *For $Q > 12$, the weights $\{W_j\}_{0\leq j\leq Q}$ can be computed using the MATLAB R2023b scripts provided in Appendix A. Notably:*

- *The return distribution and risk profile analysis in [44] utilized the weights with parameter values $Q = 12$ and $Q = 13$.*
- *The methodology for modeling financial return data in [45] adopted $Q = 15$.*

Table 1. Weight values $\{W_j\}_{0 \le j \le Q}$.

Q	W_0	W_1	W_2	W_3	W_4	W_5	W_6	W_7	W_8	W_9	W_{10}	W_{11}	W_{12}
1	$\frac{1}{2}$	$\frac{1}{2}$	0	0	0	0	0	0	0	0	0	0	0
2	$\frac{1}{3}$	$\frac{4}{3}$	$\frac{1}{3}$	0	0	0	0	0	0	0	0	0	0
3	$\frac{3}{8}$	$\frac{9}{8}$	$\frac{9}{8}$	$\frac{3}{8}$	0	0	0	0	0	0	0	0	0
4	$\frac{14}{45}$	$\frac{64}{45}$	$\frac{8}{15}$	$\frac{64}{45}$	$\frac{14}{45}$	0	0	0	0	0	0	0	0
5	$\frac{95}{288}$	$\frac{125}{96}$	$\frac{125}{144}$	$\frac{125}{144}$	$\frac{125}{96}$	$\frac{95}{288}$	0	0	0	0	0	0	0
6	$\frac{41}{140}$	$\frac{54}{35}$	$\frac{27}{140}$	$\frac{68}{35}$	$\frac{27}{140}$	$\frac{54}{35}$	$\frac{41}{140}$	0	0	0	0	0	0
7	$\frac{108}{355}$	$\frac{810}{559}$	$\frac{343}{640}$	$\frac{649}{536}$	$\frac{649}{536}$	$\frac{343}{640}$	$\frac{810}{559}$	$\frac{108}{355}$	0	0	0	0	0
8	$\frac{499}{1788}$	$\frac{1183}{712}$	$\frac{-182}{695}$	$\frac{388}{131}$	$\frac{-319}{249}$	$\frac{388}{131}$	$\frac{-182}{695}$	$\frac{1183}{712}$	$\frac{499}{1788}$	0	0	0	0
9	$\frac{130}{453}$	$\frac{419}{265}$	$\frac{23}{212}$	$\frac{307}{158}$	$\frac{213}{367}$	$\frac{213}{367}$	$\frac{307}{158}$	$\frac{23}{212}$	$\frac{419}{265}$	$\frac{130}{453}$	0	0	0
10	$\frac{139}{518}$	$\frac{245}{138}$	$\frac{-171}{211}$	$\frac{414}{91}$	$\frac{-557}{128}$	$\frac{1763}{247}$	$\frac{-557}{128}$	$\frac{414}{91}$	$\frac{-171}{211}$	$\frac{245}{138}$	$\frac{139}{518}$	0	0
11	$\frac{65}{237}$	$\frac{850}{499}$	$\frac{-83}{203}$	$\frac{787}{247}$	$\frac{-223}{184}$	$\frac{227}{116}$	$\frac{227}{116}$	$\frac{-223}{184}$	$\frac{787}{247}$	$\frac{-83}{203}$	$\frac{850}{499}$	$\frac{65}{237}$	0
12	$\frac{20}{77}$	$\frac{375}{199}$	$\frac{-270}{187}$	$\frac{673}{99}$	$\frac{-1019}{104}$	$\frac{816}{49}$	$\frac{-1537}{92}$	$\frac{816}{49}$	$\frac{-1019}{104}$	$\frac{673}{99}$	$\frac{-270}{187}$	$\frac{375}{199}$	$\frac{20}{77}$

Figure 1 compares the performance of the standard non-weighted fast FRFT and the Composite Newton-Cotes integration scheme defined in Equation (6), using the approximation error $(\check{f} - f)$ and $(\overline{f} - f)$ as evaluation metrics. The Variance-Gamma (VG*) distribution corresponds to the risk-neutral Probability Density Function (PDF) of the Variance-Gamma $(\mu, \delta, \alpha, \theta, \sigma)$ model, as detailed in [46,47] and further elaborated in Section 4. The resulting error profiles reveal distinct behaviors for the two methods. The Composite Newton-Cotes approach, depicted by the blue curve, yields consistently lower approximation errors and thus demonstrates enhanced numerical accuracy.

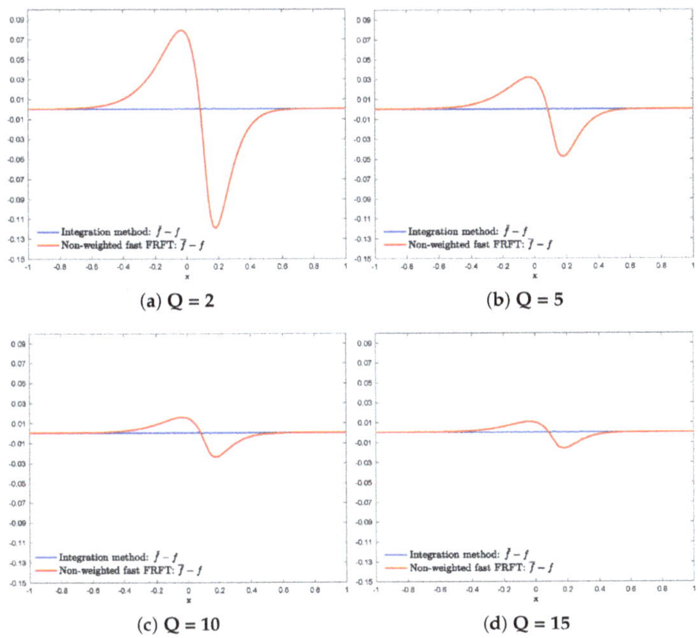

(a) Q = 2 (b) Q = 5 (c) Q = 10 (d) Q = 15

Figure 1. Variance-Gamma (VG*) PDF Error: $(\check{f} - f)$ versus $(\overline{f} - f)$, **N = 6000, b − a = 100.**

3. Fast Fractional Fourier Transform (FRFT) and Composite Newton-Cotes Quadrature Rules

3.1. Fast Fourier Transform and Fractional Fourier Transform

The conventional fast Fourier transform (FFT) algorithm is widely used to compute discrete convolutions, discrete Fourier transforms (DFT) of sparse sequences, and perform high-resolution trigonometric interpolation [2,48]. The discrete Fourier transforms (DFT) are based on N^{th} roots of unity $e^{-\frac{2\pi i}{N}}$. The generalization of DFT is the FRFT, which is based on fractional roots of unity $e^{-2\pi i\alpha}$, where α is an arbitrary complex number.
The FRFT is defined on M-long sequence $(x_1, x_2, \ldots, x_M)$ as follows:

$$G_{k+s}(x,\delta) = \sum_{j=0}^{M-1} x_j e^{-2\pi i j(k+s)\delta}, \qquad 0 \le k < M, \quad 0 \le s \le 1. \tag{9}$$

Let us have $2j(k+s) = j^2 + (k+s)^2 - (k-j+s)^2$; Equation (9) becomes (10)

$$\begin{aligned} G_{k+s}(x,\delta) &= \sum_{j=0}^{M-1} x_j e^{-\pi i(j^2+(k+s)^2-(k-j+s)^2)\delta} \\ &= e^{-\pi i(k+s)^2\delta} \sum_{j=0}^{M-1} x_j e^{-\pi i j^2\delta} e^{\pi i(k-j+s)^2\delta} = e^{-\pi i(k+s)^2} \sum_{j=0}^{M-1} y_j z_{k-j}. \end{aligned} \tag{10}$$

The expression $\sum_{j=0}^{M-1} y_j z_{k-j}$ is a discrete convolution. Still, we need a circular convolution (i.e., $z_{k-j} = z_{k-j+M}$) to evaluate $G_{k+s}(x,\delta)$. The conversion from discrete convolution to discrete circular convolution is possible by extending the sequences y and z to length $2M$, as defined below:

$$\begin{aligned} &y_j = x_j e^{-\pi i j^2\delta}, && z_j = e^{\pi i(j+s)^2\delta}, && 0 \le j < M. \\ &y_j = 0, && z_j = e^{\pi i(j+s-2M)^2\delta}, && M \le j < 2M. \end{aligned}$$

Taking into account the $2M$-long sequence, the previous FRFT becomes

$$G_{k+s}(x,\delta) = e^{-\pi i(k+s)^2\delta} \sum_{j=0}^{2M-1} y_j z_{k-j} = e^{-\pi i(k+s)^2\delta} DFT_k^{-1}[DFT(y)DFT(z)], \tag{11}$$

where DFT is the Discrete Fourier Transform, and DFT^{-1} is the inverse of DFT. For an M-long sequence z, we have

$$DFT_k(z) = \sum_{j=0}^{M-1} z_j e^{-\frac{2\pi}{M} jk}, \qquad DFT_k^{-1}(z) = \frac{1}{M-1} \sum_{j=0}^{M-1} z_j e^{\frac{2\pi}{M} jk}. \tag{12}$$

This procedure is referred to in the literature as the fast FRFT Algorithm, with a total computational cost of $20M\log_2 M + 44M$ operations [48].

We assume that $\mathscr{F}[f](y)$ is zero outside the interval $[-\frac{a}{2}, \frac{a}{2}]$; and $\beta = \frac{a}{M}$ is the step size of the M input values of $\mathscr{F}[f](y)$, defined by $y_j = (j - \frac{M}{2})\beta$ for $0 \le j < M$. Similarly, γ is the step size of the M output values of $f(x)$, defined by $x_k = (k - \frac{M}{2})\gamma$ for $0 \le k < M$.

By choosing the step size β on the input side and the step size γ in the output side, we fix the FRFT parameter $\delta = \frac{\beta\gamma}{2\pi}$ and yield [49] the density function f at x_{k+s} (13).

$$\begin{aligned} f(x_{k+s}) &= \frac{1}{2\pi} \int_{-\infty}^{+\infty} \mathscr{F}[f](y) e^{ix_{k+s}y} dy \approx \frac{1}{2\pi} \int_{-a/2}^{a/2} \mathscr{F}[f](y) e^{ix_{k+s}y} dy \\ &\approx \frac{\gamma}{2\pi} \sum_{j=0}^{M-1} \mathscr{F}[f](y_j) e^{2\pi i(k+s-\frac{M}{2})(j-\frac{M}{2})\delta} = \frac{\gamma}{2\pi} e^{-\pi i(k+s-\frac{M}{2})M\delta} G_{k+s}(\mathscr{F}[f](y_j)e^{-\pi i j M\delta}, -\delta). \end{aligned}$$

We have:

$$\tilde{f}(x_{k+s}) = \frac{\gamma}{2\pi} e^{-\pi i(k+s-\frac{M}{2})M\delta} G_{k+s}(\mathscr{F}[f](y_j)e^{-\pi ijM\delta}, -\delta), \qquad 0 \le s < 1. \tag{13}$$

3.2. FRFT of QN-Long Weighted Sequence

The Q-point rule Composite Newton-Cotes Quadrature (6) is integrated into the Fractional Fourier (FRFT) algorithm (13) to produce a FRFT of QN-long weighted sequence.

We assume that $\mathscr{F}[f](x)$ is zero outside the interval $[-\frac{a}{2}, \frac{a}{2}]$, $M = QN$, and $\beta = \frac{a}{M}$ is the step size of the M input values $\mathscr{F}[f](y)$, defined by $y_{j+Qp} = (Qp + j - \frac{M}{2})\beta$ for $0 \le p < N$ and $0 \le j < Q$. Similarly, the output values of $f(x)$ are defined by $x_{Ql+f+s} = (Ql + f + s - \frac{M}{2})\gamma$ for $0 \le l < N, 0 \le f < Q$ and $0 \le s \le 1$.

$$\begin{aligned} f(x_{Ql+f+s}) &= \frac{1}{2\pi}\int_{\infty}^{+\infty} e^{iyx_{Ql+f+s}} F[f](y)dy = \frac{1}{2\pi}\int_{-a/2}^{a/2} e^{iyx_{Ql+f+s}} F[f](y)dy \\ &= \frac{1}{2\pi}\sum_{p=0}^{N-1}\int_{y_{Qp}}^{y_{Qp+Q}} e^{iyx_{Ql+f+s}} F[f](y)dy \quad \text{(composite rule)}. \end{aligned} \tag{14}$$

Based on the Lagrange interpolating integration over $[y_{Qp}, y_{Qp+Q}]$ [39,40], we have (15):

$$\int_{y_{Qp}}^{y_{Qp+Q}} e^{iyx_{Ql+f+s}} F[f](y)dy \approx \beta \sum_{j=0}^{Q} w_j e^{iy_{j+Qp}x_{Ql+f+s}} F[f](y_{j+Qp}). \tag{15}$$

$\tilde{f}(x_{Ql+f+s})$ is the approximation of $f(x_{Ql+f+s})$, and (14) becomes (16):

$$\begin{aligned} \tilde{f}(x_{Ql+f+s}) &= \frac{\beta}{2\pi}\sum_{p=0}^{N-1}\sum_{j=0}^{Q} w_j F[f](y_{j+Qp})e^{ix_{Ql+f+s}y_{j+Qp}}, \quad 0 \le s < 1; \\ &= \frac{\beta}{2\pi}\sum_{j=0}^{Q}\sum_{p=0}^{N-1} w_j F[f](y_{j+Qp})e^{2\pi i\delta(Ql+f+s-\frac{M}{2})(Qp+j-\frac{M}{2})}, \quad \beta\gamma = 2\pi\delta; \\ &= \frac{\beta}{2\pi} e^{-\pi i\delta M(Ql+f+s-\frac{M}{2})} G_{Ql+f+s}(w_j \mathscr{F}[f](y_{j+Qp})e^{-\pi i(j+Qp)M\delta}, -\delta). \end{aligned} \tag{16}$$

We have the following inverse Fourier transform function (17):

$$\tilde{f}(x_{Ql+f+s}) = \frac{\beta}{2\pi} e^{-\pi i\delta M(Ql+f+s-\frac{M}{2})} G_{Ql+f+s}(w_j \mathscr{F}[f](y_{j+Qp})e^{-\pi i(j+Qp)M\delta}, -\delta). \tag{17}$$

FRFT is applied on the QN-long weighted sequence $\left\{w_j \mathscr{F}[f](y_{j+Qp})e^{-\pi i(j+Qp)M\delta}\right\}_{\substack{0\le j<Q \\ 0\le p<N}}$.

3.3. Composite of FRFTs: FRFT of Q-Long Weighted Sequence and FRFT of N-Long Sequence

We consider $\tilde{f}_{QN}(x_{Ql+f+s})$ to be the approximation of $f(x_{Ql+f+s})$. We have the following development:

$$\begin{aligned} \tilde{f}_{QN}(x_{Ql+f+s}) &= \frac{\beta}{2\pi}\sum_{p=0}^{N-1}\sum_{j=0}^{Q} w_j F[f](y_{j+Qp})e^{ix_{Ql+f+s}y_{j+Qp}} \\ &= \frac{\beta}{2\pi}\sum_{j=0}^{Q} w_j \sum_{p=0}^{N-1} F[f](y_{j+Qp})e^{2\pi i\delta(Ql+f+s-\frac{M}{2})(Qp+j-\frac{M}{2})}, \qquad \beta\gamma = 2\pi\delta \\ &= \frac{\beta}{2\pi} e^{-\pi i\delta M(Ql+f+s-\frac{M}{2})} \sum_{j=0}^{Q} w_j e^{2\pi i\delta(Ql+f+s-\frac{M}{2})j} \sum_{p=0}^{N-1} F[f](y_{j+Qp})e^{2\pi i\delta(Ql+f+s-\frac{M}{2})Qp} \\ &= \frac{\beta}{2\pi} e^{-\pi i\delta M(Ql+f+s-\frac{M}{2})} \sum_{j=0}^{Q} w_j G_{l+\frac{f+s}{Q}}(\xi_p, -\delta Q^2)e^{2\pi i\delta(Ql-\frac{M}{2})j} e^{2\pi i\delta(f+s)j}, \end{aligned}$$

where $G_{l+\frac{f+s}{Q}}$ is a FRFT on N-long complex sequence $\{\xi_p\}_{0\le p<N}$. Let us have $\alpha_1 = -\delta Q^2$; then,

$$G_{l+\frac{f+s}{Q}}(\xi_p,\alpha_1) = \sum_{p=0}^{N-1} \xi_p e^{-2\pi i(l+\frac{f+s}{Q})p\alpha_1}, \quad \xi_p = e^{-\pi i M p Q\delta} F[f](y_{j+Qp}) \tag{18}$$

and $\tilde{f}_{QN}(x_{Ql+f+s})$ becomes (19)

$$\tilde{f}_{QN}(x_{Ql+f+s}) = \frac{\beta}{2\pi} e^{-\pi i\delta M(Ql+f+s-\frac{M}{2})} G_{f+s}(z_j,-\delta), \tag{19}$$

where G_{f+s} is a FRFT on Q-long complex sequence $\{z_j\}_{0\le j\le Q}$. Let us have $\alpha_2 = -\delta$; then,

$$G_{f+s}(z_j,\alpha_2) = \sum_{j=0}^{Q} z_j e^{-2\pi i(f+s)j\alpha_2}, \qquad z_j = w_j G_{l+\frac{f+s}{Q}}(\xi_p,\alpha_1) e^{2\pi i\delta(Ql-\frac{M}{2})j}.$$

To sum up, we have the following expression for $\tilde{f}_{QN}(x_{Ql+f+s})$:

$$\tilde{f}_{QN}(x_{Ql+f+s}) = \frac{\beta}{2\pi} e^{-\pi i\delta M(Ql+f+s-\frac{M}{2})} G_{f+s}(G_{l+\frac{f+s}{Q}}(\xi_p,\alpha_1) w_j e^{2\pi i\delta(Ql-\frac{M}{2})j},\alpha_2). \tag{20}$$

It can be observed from (17) and (20) that the FRFT (G_{Ql+f}) is equivalent to the composition of G_{f+s} and $G_{l+\frac{f+s}{Q}}$, which means that

$$G_{Ql+f+s}(w_j \mathscr{F}[f](y_{j+Qp}) e^{-\pi i(j+Qp)N\delta},\alpha_2) = G_{f+s}\left(G_{l+\frac{f+s}{Q}}(\xi_p,\alpha_1) w_j e^{2\pi i\delta(Ql-\frac{M}{2})j},\alpha_2\right). \tag{21}$$

Figure 2 displays the approximation errors, $(\bar{f}-f)$ and $(\hat{f}-f)$, corresponding to the non-weighted fast FRFT (Equation (13)) and the composite FRFT method (Equation (20)), respectively. The observed error profiles are consistent with those in Figure 1, reinforcing the robustness of the results across different numerical schemes. The underlying Variance-Gamma (VG*) Probability Density Function (PDF) is derived from the risk-neutral distribution of the Variance-Gamma model, parameterized by $(\mu,\delta,\alpha,\theta,\sigma)$, as detailed in Section 4.

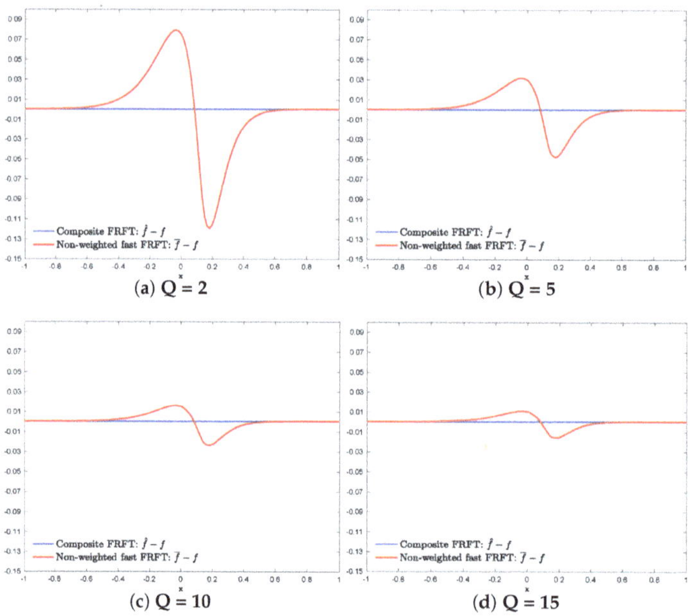

Figure 2. Variance-Gamma (VG*) PDF Error: $(\hat{f}-f)$ versus $(\bar{f}-f)$, **N = 6000, b − a = 100.**

3.4. Composite of FRFTs: FRFT of N-Long Sequence and FRFT of Q-Long Weighted Sequence

The expression in (16) is recalled for further development:

$$\tilde{f}_{NQ}(x_{Ql+f+s}) = \frac{\beta}{2\pi}\sum_{p=0}^{N-1}\sum_{j=0}^{Q} w_j F[f](y_{j+Qp}) e^{ix_{Ql+f+s}y_{j+Qp}}, \qquad \beta\gamma = 2\pi\delta$$

$$= \frac{\beta}{2\pi} e^{-\pi i\delta M(Ql+f+s-\frac{M}{2})} \sum_{p=0}^{N-1} e^{2\pi i\delta(Ql+f+s-\frac{M}{2})Qp} \sum_{j=0}^{Q} w_j F[f](y_{j+Qp}) e^{2\pi i\delta(Ql-\frac{M}{2})j} e^{2\pi i\delta(f+s)j}$$

$$= \frac{\beta}{2\pi} e^{-\pi i\delta M(Ql+f+s-\frac{M}{2})} \sum_{p=0}^{N-1} G_{f+s}(z_j,-\delta) e^{-\pi i\delta MQp} e^{2\pi i(l+\frac{f+s}{Q})\delta Q^2 p},$$

where G_{f+s} is a FRFT on Q-long complex sequence $\{z_j\}_{0\le j<Q}$

$$G_{f+s}(z_j,\alpha_2) = \sum_{j=0}^{Q} z_j e^{-2\pi i(f+s)j\alpha_2}, \qquad z_j = w_j F[f](y_{j+Qp}) e^{2\pi i\delta(Ql-\frac{M}{2})j}, \tag{22}$$

and $\tilde{f}_{NQ}((x_{Ql+f+s})$ becomes

$$\tilde{f}_{NQ}((x_{Ql+f+s}) = \frac{\beta}{2\pi} e^{-\pi i\delta M(Ql+f+s-\frac{M}{2})} G_{l+\frac{f+s}{Q}}(\xi_p,\alpha_1), \tag{23}$$

where $G_{l+\frac{f+s}{Q}}$ is a FRFT on N-long complex sequence $\{\xi_p\}_{0\le p<N}$

$$G_{l+\frac{f+s}{Q}}(\xi_p,\alpha_1) = \sum_{p=0}^{N-1} \xi_p e^{-2\pi i(l+\frac{f+s}{Q})p\alpha_1}, \qquad \xi_p = G_{f+s}(z_j,\alpha_2) e^{-\pi i\delta MQp}. \tag{24}$$

As a result, we have the following expression for $\tilde{f}_{NQ}(x_{Ql+f+s})$:

$$\tilde{f}_{NQ}(x_{Ql+f+s}) = \frac{\beta}{2\pi} e^{-\pi i\delta M(Ql+f+s-\frac{M}{2})} G_{l+\frac{f+s}{Q}}(G_{f+s}(z_j,-\delta) e^{-\pi i\delta MQp}, -\delta Q^2). \tag{25}$$

By comparing the inverse Fourier transform in (17) and (25), we deduce that the FRFT (G_{Ql+f+s}) is a composition of two FRFTs ($G_{l+\frac{f+s}{Q}}$ and G_{f+s}). The result (26) is similar to the result (21).

$$G_{Ql+f+s}(w_j \mathscr{F}[f](y_{j+Qp}) e^{-\pi i(j+Qp)N\delta},\alpha_2) = G_{l+\frac{f+s}{Q}}\left(G_{f+s}(z_j,\alpha_2) e^{-\pi i\delta MQp},\alpha_1\right). \tag{26}$$

Based on the numerical results obtained from Equations (20) and (25), the estimated error is between $\tilde{f}NQ$ and $\tilde{f}QN$ is shown in Figure 3.

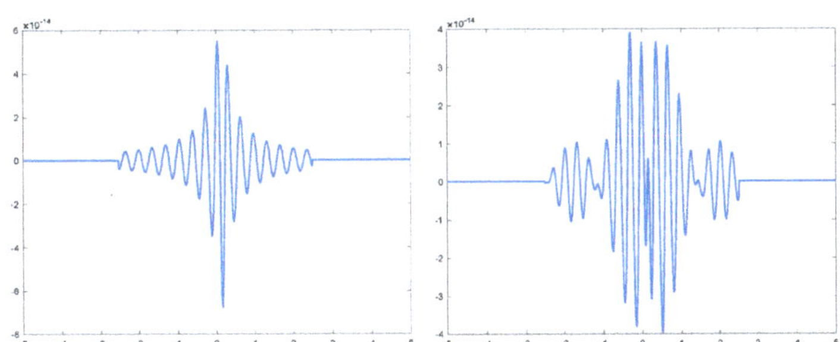

(a) Q = 2 (b) Q = 5

Figure 3. *Cont.*

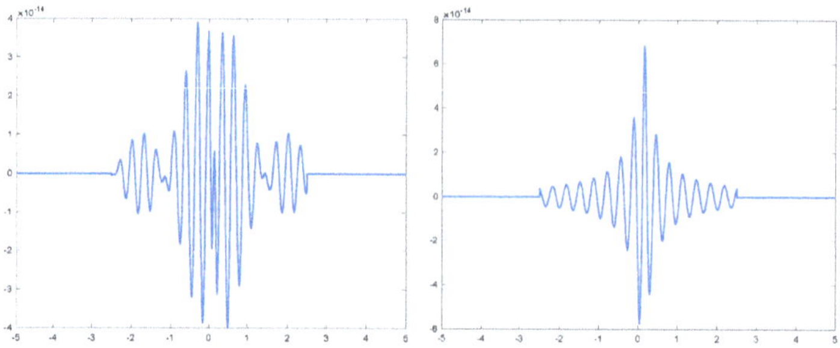

(c) Q = 10 (d) Q = 15

Figure 3. Variance-Gamma (VG*) PDF Error ($\tilde{f}_{NQ}(x_k) - \tilde{f}_{QN}(x_k)$): **N = 6000, b − a = 100.**

Figure 3 indicates that the composite FRFT formulations in Equations (21) and (26) are equivalent not only algebraically, but also numerically.

4. Illustration Examples

4.1. Variance-Gamma (VG) Distribution

In the study, the VG model has five parameters: parameters of location (μ), symmetry (δ), volatility (σ), and the Gamma parameters of shape (α) and scale (θ). The VG model density function can be proven to be (27):

$$f(y) = \frac{1}{\sigma\Gamma(\alpha)\theta^{\alpha}} \int_0^{+\infty} \frac{1}{\sqrt{2\pi v}} e^{-\frac{(y-\mu-\delta v)^2}{2v\sigma^2}} v^{\alpha-1} e^{-\frac{v}{\theta}}\, dv. \tag{27}$$

The VG model density function (27) has an analytical expression with a modified Bessel function of the second kind. The expression can be obtained by making some transformations and changing variables as follows:

$$-\frac{(y-\mu-\delta v)^2}{2v\sigma^2} - \frac{v}{\theta} = \delta(\frac{y-\mu}{\sigma^2}) - \frac{1}{2\sigma^2}(\delta^2 + \frac{2\sigma^2}{\theta})v - (\frac{y-\mu}{\sigma})^2 \frac{1}{2v}, \tag{28}$$

and (27) becomes

$$f(y) = \frac{e^{\delta(\frac{y-\mu}{\sigma^2})}}{\sqrt{2\pi}\sigma\Gamma(\alpha)\theta^{\alpha}} \int_0^{+\infty} e^{-\frac{1}{2\sigma^2}(\delta^2 + \frac{2\sigma^2}{\theta})v - (\frac{y-\mu}{\sigma})^2 \frac{1}{2v}} v^{\alpha-\frac{3}{2}}\, dv. \tag{29}$$

By considering the modified Bessel function of the second kind ($k_{\alpha}(z)$) [50], we have

$$k_{\alpha}(z) = \frac{1}{2}(\frac{1}{2}z)^{\alpha} \int_0^{+\infty} e^{(-t-\frac{z^2}{4t})} \frac{1}{t^{\alpha+1}}\, dt, \qquad |arg(z)| \leq \frac{\pi}{4}, \tag{30}$$

where $k_{\alpha}(z)$ is the second kind of solution for the modified Bessel's equation:

$$z^2\frac{d^2w}{dz^2} + z\frac{dw}{dz} - (z^2 + \alpha^2)w = 0. \tag{31}$$

By changing variable, $u = \frac{1}{2\sigma^2}(\delta^2 + \frac{2\sigma^2}{\theta})v$, (29) becomes

$$f(y) = \frac{2e^{\delta(\frac{y-\mu}{\sigma^2})}}{\sqrt{2\pi}\sigma\Gamma(\alpha)\theta^{\alpha}} \left(\frac{|y-\mu|}{\sqrt{\delta^2 + \frac{2\sigma^2}{\theta}}}\right)^{\alpha-\frac{1}{2}} k_{-\alpha+\frac{1}{2}}\left(\frac{\sqrt{\delta^2 + \frac{2\sigma^2}{\theta}}|y-\mu|}{\sigma^2}\right). \tag{32}$$

By choosing $\theta = 2$, one recovers the four-parameter Variance–Gamma (VG) distribution as highlighted in recent reviews and foundational work [51,52]. Equivalently, setting $\alpha = \frac{1}{\theta}$ yields a form often referred to as the generalized Laplace or Bessel-function distribution, which includes the symmetric Laplace distribution as a special case [53,54].

A special case $f(\mu)$ provides a simplified expression

$$f(\mu) = \frac{1}{\sqrt{2\pi}\sigma\Gamma(\alpha)\theta^{\alpha}} \int_0^{+\infty} e^{-\frac{1}{2\sigma^2}(\delta^2+\frac{2\sigma^2}{\theta})\nu} \nu^{\alpha-\frac{3}{2}}\, d\nu = \frac{\Gamma(\alpha-\frac{1}{2})}{\sqrt{2\pi\theta}\sigma\Gamma(\alpha)(1+\frac{\theta}{2}\frac{\delta^2}{\sigma^2})^{\alpha-\frac{1}{2}}}. \quad (33)$$

Table 2 provides estimation results of the five parameters $(\mu, \delta, \alpha, \theta, \sigma)$ of the Variance-Gamma variable. VG model estimation in the first row of Table 2 was obtained by the maximum likelihood method [46,55,56]. The VG(*) model estimation in the second row of Table 2 is the Equivalent Martingale Measure (EMM) [57] and generates a risk-neutral probability density function for a 0.8-year period.

Table 2. Estimated parameters for the Variance-Gamma (VG) distribution.

Model	μ	δ	σ	α	θ
VG	0.08476896	−0.0577418	1.02948292	0.88450029	0.93779517
VG(*)	0.11998901	−0.0343164	0.10294829	2.54736083	0.98780338

Figure 4a provides a graphical representation of the risk-neutral probability associated with the Variance Gamma (VG*) model for a 0.8-year period. In this case, the probability density at u satisfies $f(\hat{\mu}) \approx 0.8552$ for the Variance-Gamma (VG) model and $f(\hat{\mu}) \approx 2.5949$ for the Variance-Gamma (VG*) model.

The Fourier transform function of the Variance Gamma distribution has an explicit closed form, and the inverse function is summarized as follows:

$$\mathscr{F}[f](x) = \frac{e^{-i\mu x}}{\left(1 + \frac{1}{2}\theta\sigma^2 x^2 + i\delta\theta x\right)^{\alpha}}, \qquad f(y) = \frac{1}{2\pi}\int_{-\infty}^{+\infty} e^{iyx+\Psi(-x)}dx. \quad (34)$$

Based on the integral method in Proposition 1 (6), the non-weighted fast FRFT, and the composite FRFTs developed in (13) and (20), respectively, we have the following numerical estimation methods of the inverse function (34).

$$\hat{f}(x_{Ql+f}) = \frac{\beta}{2\pi} e^{-\pi i\delta M(Ql+f-\frac{M}{2})} G_f(G_{l+\frac{f}{Q}}(\xi, \alpha_1) w_j e^{2\pi i\delta(Ql-\frac{M}{2})j}, \alpha_2) \text{ (Composite FRFT).} \quad (35)$$

$$\overline{f}(x_k) = \frac{\gamma}{2\pi} e^{-\pi i(k-\frac{N}{2})N\delta} G_k(\mathscr{F}[f](y_j) e^{-\pi ijN\delta}, -\delta) \quad \text{(Non-weighted fast FRFT).} \quad (36)$$

$$\check{f}(x_k) = \frac{\beta}{2\pi} \sum_{p=0}^{N-1} \sum_{j=0}^{Q} W_j e^{(iy_{j+Qp}x_k)} F[f](y_{j+Qp}) \quad \text{(Integral approximation).} \quad (37)$$

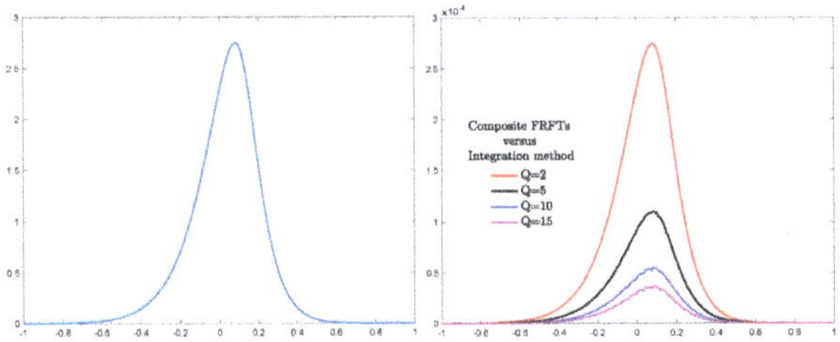

(**a**) VG* Risk Neutral PDF. (**b**) VG* PDF Error $(\hat{f} - \check{f})$.

Figure 4. VG* probability density estimation error.

The error in the VG* probability density ($\hat{f} - \check{f}$), shown in Figure 4b, indicates that the composite FRFTs (35) perform better than the Newton-Cotes integration (37). However, as the values of Q increase, the improvement in accuracy becomes marginal.

4.2. Generalized Tempered Stable (GTS) Distribution

We consider a GTS variable $Y = \mu + X = \mu + X_+ - X_- \sim GTS(\mu, \beta_+, \beta_-, \alpha_+, \alpha_-, \lambda_+, \lambda_-)$ with $X_+ \sim TS(\beta_+, \alpha_+, \lambda_+, \lambda_-)$ and $X_- \sim TS(\beta_-, \alpha_-, \lambda_-, \lambda_-)$. The characteristic exponent can be written [44]

$$\Psi(\xi) = \mu\xi i + \alpha_+\Gamma(-\beta_+)\Big((\lambda_+ - i\xi)^{\beta_+} - \lambda_+{}^{\beta_+}\Big) + \alpha_-\Gamma(-\beta_-)\Big((\lambda_- + \xi)^{\beta_-} - \lambda_-{}^{\beta_-}\Big). \quad (38)$$

Table 3 presents the estimation results of the seven-parameter $(\beta_+, \beta_-, \alpha_+, \alpha_-, \lambda_+, \lambda_-)$ Generalized Tempered Stable (GTS) Distribution. The GTS model estimations presented in the first row of Table 3 were obtained using the Maximum Likelihood method, as described in [45,47].

Table 3. Estimated parameters for the Generalized Tempered Stable (GTS) distribution.

Model	μ	β_+	β_-	α_+	α_-	λ_+	λ_-
GTS	−0.693477	0.682290	0.242579	0.458582	0.414443	0.822222	0.727607
GTS*	−0.208043	0.682290	0.242579	0.594234	4.068436	84.667097	70.31591

The GTS(*) model estimations in the second row of Table 2 are the Equivalent Martingale Measure (EMM) [58] and generate a risk-neutral probability density function for a month period. Figure 5a provides a graphical representation of risk-neutral probability associated with the GTS Distribution for a month period. The characteristic function of the GTS variable, the Fourier Transform ($F(f)$), and the corresponding density function f are given by the following expressions:

$$\vartheta(\xi) = E\Big[e^{iY\xi}\Big] = e^{\Psi(\xi)} \qquad F[f](\xi) = \vartheta(-\xi) \quad f(y) = \frac{1}{2\pi}\int_{-\infty}^{+\infty} e^{iyx+\Psi(-x)}dx. \quad (39)$$

The GTS probability density function does not have a closed-form expression. Figure 5 provides an estimation of the GTS* risk neutral probability density error using three methods: the integration method ($\check{f}$) in Equation (37), the non-weighted fast FRFT ($\overline{f}$) in Equation (36), and the composite FRFTs ($\hat{f}$) in Equation (35). As shown in Figure 5c,d, the composite FRFTs and the integration method outperform the non-weighted fast FRFT. Figure 5b produces the same results as Figure 4b.

Refer to Appendices A–D for the Matlab scripts supporting the empirical results.

To complement the graphical evaluation with a quantitative assessment, we introduce the following error metrics, which serve to measure the magnitude of discrepancy between the proposed and reference methods.

$$R(\hat{f}, \overline{f}) = \int_{-\infty}^{+\infty} \Big|\hat{f}(x) - \overline{f}(x)\Big|\,dx \quad (40)$$

$$R(\hat{f}, \check{f}) = \int_{-\infty}^{+\infty} \Big|\hat{f}(x) - \check{f}(x)\Big|\,dx \quad (41)$$

$R(\hat{f}, \overline{f})$ quantifies the absolute error between the composite FRFT method (Equation (35)) and the standard non-weighted fast FRFT (Equation (36)), without considering the direction of the error. Similarly, $R(\hat{f}, \check{f})$ measures the absolute discrepancy between the composite FRFT method (Equation (35)) and the integral approximation approach (Equation (37)).

Table 4 reports the numerical estimates of $R(\check{f}, \overline{f})$ and $R(\hat{f}, \check{f})$ for both the Variance-Gamma (VG) and the Generalized Tempered Stable (GTS) distributions.

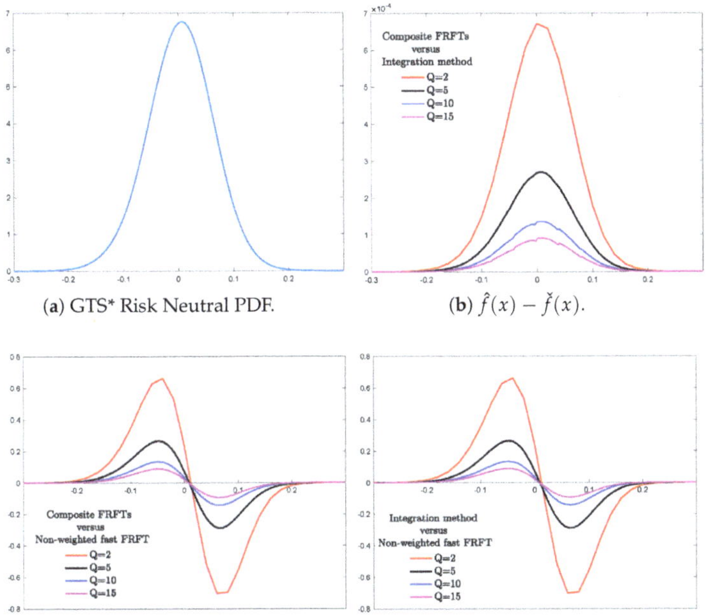

(**a**) GTS* Risk Neutral PDF. (**b**) $\hat{f}(x) - \check{f}(x)$. (**c**) $\hat{f}(x) - \overline{f}(x)$. (**d**) $\check{f}(x) - \overline{f}(x)$.

Figure 5. GTS* probability density estimation error.

Table 4. Absolute Error Metrics between approximation methods for the VG and GTS distributions at various levels Q.

	$R(\hat{f}, \overline{f})$		$R(\hat{f}, \check{f})$	
Q	**VG**	**GTS**	**VG**	**GTS**
2	0.0550	0.1350	9.975×10^{-05}	9.975×10^{-05}
5	0.0220	0.0538	3.983×10^{-05}	3.983×10^{-05}
10	0.0110	0.0270	1.947×10^{-05}	1.947×10^{-05}
15	0.0073	0.0181	1.307×10^{-05}	1.307×10^{-05}

Remark 2. *The risk-neutral Probability Density Function (PDF) and its estimation play a vital role in option pricing as they provide insight into market expectations about future asset prices [59–62]. However, their significance extends beyond pricing, with several important applications in other areas of finance including:*

- ***Risk Management:*** *Assesses the potential for losses or gains in derivative portfolios.*
- ***Investment Strategy:*** *Informs investment decisions by revealing market expectations about future asset prices.*
- ***Financial Analysis:*** *Aids in analyzing the prices of financial instruments and evaluating their relative value.*

5. Conclusions

This study presents an enhanced computational framework for the *fast Fractional Fourier Transform (FRFT)* by integrating *closed-form Composite Newton-Cotes quadrature rules*. The key theoretical contribution is the demonstration that the FRFT of a QN-length weighted sequence can be decomposed into two commutative compositions: (1) a composition of an N-length FRFT and a Q-length weighted FRFT, and (2) the reverse composition.

The proposed composite FRFT scheme significantly improves numerical accuracy compared to *standard fast FRFT* and *classical Newton-Cotes quadrature* while preserving computational efficiency. Comprehensive error analysis and numerical experiments, particularly on *Variance-Gamma (VG)* and *Generalized Tempered Stable (GTS)* distributions, validate the scheme's accuracy and stability.

The composite FRFT's ability to handle *oscillatory integrals* and *complex-valued characteristic functions* makes it particularly valuable for applications in signal processing, financial mathematics, and scientific computing, where *high-precision transform inversion* is critical.

Future research directions include extending the framework to multidimensional cases, exploring adaptive quadrature rules for further optimization, and investigating potential applications in machine learning for spectral and frequency-domain analysis. The paper establishes a robust and efficient alternative to existing FRFT methods, offering both theoretical rigor and practical utility in numerical analysis and applied mathematics.

Author Contributions: Conceptualization, A.N., D.M. and A.M.S.; methodology, A.N., D.M. and A.M.S.; visualization, A.N., D.M. and A.M.S.; resources, A.N., D.M. and A.M.S.; and writing—original draft and Editing, A.N., D.M. and A.M.S. All authors have read and agreed to the published version of the manuscript.

Funding: This research received no external funding.

Data Availability Statement: The data supporting the findings of this study are available in Table 1 of the following sources: for the Variance-Gamma (VG) distribution, refer to [57] ; for the Generalized Tempered Stable (GTS) distribution, see Table 1 in [44].

Acknowledgments: The authors would like to thank the University of Limpopo for supporting the publication of this study.

Conflicts of Interest: The authors declare no conflicts of interest.

Appendix A. Weight Vector Computation: weig(q)

$$W_j = \sum_{i=0}^{Q} C_i^j \frac{Q^{i+1}}{i+1} \frac{(-1)^{(Q-j)}}{j!(Q-j)!}$$

```
function result=weig(q);
% input: q
% initialisation
res=zeros(q+1,q+1); x=zeros(q+1,1); y=ones(q+1,1);
z=ones(q+1,1); w=zeros(q+1,1); u1=ones(1);
% Compute the coefficients(res(i,k)) for a polynomial p(x) of
    degree q that is the best fit (in a least-squares sense)
    for the data in y
for k=1:(q+1)
x(k)=k-1;
end;
% solving the following equations with a Vandermonde matrix
for k=1:(q+1)
y=ones(q+1,1);
for j=1:(q+1)
for i=1:(q+1)
if x(k)==(i-1)  u1=u1;  else u1=u1*(x(j)-(i-1)); end;
```

```
end;
y(j)=u1;  u1=1;
end;
z=polyfit(x,y,q);
for i=1:(q+1)
res(i,k)=z(q+1-(i-1));
end;
end;
res=transpose(res);
% compute the weight vector (output) : w(k) k=1,...,q,q+1
for k=1:(q+1)
for j=1:(q+1)
w(k)= w(k) + res(k,j)*(q^(j))*((-1)^(q-(k-1)))/(j*factorial(k
    -1)*factorial(q-(k-1)));
end;
end;
result=w;
```

Appendix B. Standard fast FRFT Algorithm: GFR(f,k,s,alpha)

$$G_{k+s}(x,\delta) = e^{-\pi i(k+s)^2\delta} \sum_{j=0}^{2M-1} y_j z_{k-j} = e^{-\pi i(k+s)^2\delta} DFT_k^{-1}[DFT(y)DFT(z)]$$

```
function result=weig(q);
% input: q
% initialisation
res=zeros(q+1,q+1); x=zeros(q+1,1); y=ones(q+1,1);
z=ones(q+1,1); w=zeros(q+1,1); u1=ones(1);
% Compute the coefficients(res(i,k)) for a polynomial p(x) of
    degree q that is the best fit (in a least-squares sense)
    for the data in y
for k=1:(q+1)
x(k)=k-1;
end;
% solving the following equations with a Vandermonde matrix
for k=1:(q+1)
y=ones(q+1,1);
for j=1:(q+1)
for i=1:(q+1)
if x(k)==(i-1)  u1=u1;  else u1=u1*(x(j)-(i-1)); end;
end;
y(j)=u1;  u1=1;
end;
z=polyfit(x,y,q);
for i=1:(q+1)
res(i,k)=z(q+1-(i-1));
end;
end;
res=transpose(res);
% compute the weight vector (output) : w(k) k=1,...,q,q+1
```

```
for k=1:(q+1)
for j=1:(q+1)
w(k)= w(k) + res(k,j)*(q^(j))*((-1)^(q-(k-1)))/(j*factorial(k
   -1)*factorial(q-(k-1)));
end;
end;
result=w;
```

Appendix C. Composite of FRFTs: FRFT of N-Long Sequence and FRFT of Q-Long Weighted Sequence

$$\tilde{f}_{NQ}(x_{Ql+f+s}) = \frac{\beta}{2\pi} e^{-\pi i\delta M(Ql+f+s-\frac{M}{2})} G_{l+\frac{f+s}{Q}}(G_{f+s}(z_j, -\delta) e^{-\pi i\delta MQp}, -\delta Q^2)$$

```
function zxf=CompositeFRNQ(f,zx,q,alpha,beta,limit);

% compute the weight vector of size q
w=zeros(q,1); w=weig(q); pd=size(w,2);
if size(w,2)==1. pd=size(w,1); end;  pd=pd-1;

% compute sizes: m, datm of the input vectors f and zx
m=size(f,2)-1; if size(f,2)==1  m=size(f,1)-1; end; n=m/pd;
datm=size(zx,2); if size(zx,2)==1 datm=size(zx,1);  end;

% compute the lower (u1) and upper (u1) boundaries
u1=0; u2=0; i=1;
if min(zx(:)) < -limit   while zx(i)< -limit i=i+1; end;
u1=i; else u1=i; end;
i=1; if limit<max(zx(:)) while zx(i)<limit i=i+1; end;
u2=i; else u2=datm; end;

% adjusting, creating and initializing variables
zx=scalev(zx,m,beta); alpha1=alpha*pd; alpha2=alpha*pd*pd;
s=zeros(1,datm); zxf=zeros(1,datm); res=zeros(1,datm);
quot=zeros(1,datm); quotq=zeros(1,datm); uyz=zeros(1,2*m);
vyz=zeros(1,2*m); wyz=zeros(1,2*m); fp=zeros(n,pd+1);
comp=zeros(n,datm); gp=zeros(n,datm);
if m==(datm-1)  zx=round(zx); end;

% data zx decomposition: Dividend( zx(P), Divisor (pd),
   Quotient (quot(p)), Remainder(res(p))
for p=1:datm
s(p)=(zx(p)-fix(zx(p))); res(p)=mod(fix(zx(p)),pd);
quot(p)=(fix(zx(p))-res(p))/pd; quotq(p)=(res(p)+ s(p))/pd;
end;

for p=u1:u2
for k=1:n

% adjusting the data f
```

```
for j=1:(pd+1)
fp(k,j)=w(j)*f(j+pd*(k-1))*exp(-2*pi*alpha*(pd*quot(p)-(m/2))
    *(j-1)*(1i));
end;
end;

%  Computation of the FRFT compositions
for k=1:n
comp(k,p)=GFR(fp(k,:),res(p),s(p),alpha);
gp(k,p)=comp(k,p)*exp(pi*alpha*m*pd*(k-1)*(1i));
end;

% output
zxf(p)=GFR(gp(:,p),quot(p),quotq(p),alpha2);
zxf(p)=beta*zxf(p)*exp(pi*alpha*m*(zx(p)-(m/2))*(1i));
if alpha<0  zxf(p)=zxf(p)/(2*pi); end;
end;
```

Appendix D. Composite of FRFTs: FRFT of Q-Long Weighted Sequence and FRFT of N-Long Sequence

$$\tilde{f}_{QN}(x_{Ql+f+s}) = \frac{\beta}{2\pi}e^{-\pi i\delta M(Ql+f+s-\frac{M}{2})}G_{f+s}(G_{l+\frac{f+s}{Q}}(\xi_p,\alpha_1)w_j e^{2\pi i\delta(Ql-\frac{M}{2})j},\alpha_2)$$

```
function zxf=CompositeFRQN(f,zx,q,alpha,beta,limit);

% compute the weight vector of size q
w=zeros(q,1);w=weig(q); pd=size(w,2);
if size(w,2)==1 pd=size(w,1); end; pd=pd-1;

% compute sizes: m, datm of the input vectors f and zx
m=size(f,2)-1; if size(f,2)==1 m=size(f,1)-1; end;  n=m/pd;
datm=size(zx,2); if size(zx,2)==1 datm=size(zx,1); end;

% compute the lower (u1) and upper (u1) boundaries
u1=0; u2=0; i=1;
if min(zx(:)) < -limit  while zx(i)< -limit  i=i+1;end;
u1=i;else u1=i; end;
i=1; if limit<max(zx(:))  while zx(i)<limit i=i+1; end;
u2=i; else u2=datm; end;

% adjusting, creating and initializing variables
zx=scalev(zx,m,beta); alpha1=alpha*pd; alpha2=alpha*pd*pd;
s=zeros(1,datm); zxf=zeros(1,datm); res=zeros(1,datm);
quot=zeros(1,datm); quotq=zeros(1,datm); uyz=zeros(1,2*m);
vyz=zeros(1,2*m); wyz=zeros(1,2*m); fp=zeros(n,pd+1);
comp=zeros(pd+1,datm); gp=zeros(pd+1,datm);
if m==(datm-1) zx=round(zx); end

% adjusting the data f
```

```
for k=1:n
for j=1:(pd+1)
fp(k,j)=f(j+pd*(k-1))*exp(m*pi*alpha1*(k-1)*(1i));
end;
end;

% data zx decomposition: Dividend( zx(P), Divisor (pd),
   Quotient (quot(p)), Remainder(res(p))
for p=1:datm
s(p)=(zx(p)-fix(zx(p))); res(p)=mod(fix(zx(p)),pd);
quot(p)=(fix(zx(p))-res(p))/pd; quotq(p)=(res(p)+ s(p))/pd;
end;

%  FRFT composition computation
for p=u1:u2
for k=1:(pd+1)
comp(k,p)=GFR(fp(:,k),quot(p),quotq(p),alpha2);
gp(k,p)=w(k)*comp(k,p)*exp(-2*((pd*quot(p))-(m/2))*pi*alpha*(k
   -1)*(1i));
end;
% output

zxf(p)=GFR(gp(:,p),res(p),s(p),alpha); zxf(p)=beta*zxf(p)*exp(
   pi*alpha*m*(zx(p)-(m/2))*(1i));
if alpha<0  zxf(p)=zxf(p)/(2*pi); end;
end;
```

References

1. Zhang, Y.; Wang, S.; Yang, J.F.; Zhang, Z.; Phillips, P.; Sun, P.; Yan, J. Comprehensive Survey on Fractional Fourier Transform. *Fundam. Informaticae* **2017**, *151*, 48. [CrossRef]
2. Bailey, D.H.; Swarztrauber, P.N. A Fast Method for the Numerical Evaluation of Continuous Fourier and Laplace Transforms. *SIAM J. Sci. Comput.* **1994**, *15*, 1105–1110. [CrossRef]
3. Mei, L.; Sha, X.; Ran, Q.; Zhang, N. Research on the Application of 4-Weighted Fractional Fourier Transform in Communication System. *Sci. China Inf. Sci.* **2010**, *53*, 1251–1260. [CrossRef]
4. Creutzburg, R.; Rundblad, E.; Labunets, V.G. Fast Algorithms for Fractional Fourier Transforms. In Proceedings of the NSIP, Chicago, IL, USA, 5–7 November 1999 ; pp. 383–387.
5. Wang, Y. Fractional Fourier Transform and Its Application. *Theor. Nat. Sci.* **2024**, *42*, 8–12. [CrossRef]
6. Singh, U.; Singh, S.N. Application of Fractional Fourier Transform for Classification of Power Quality Disturbances. *IET Sci. Meas. Technol.* **2017**, *11*, 67–76. [CrossRef]
7. Sejdić, E.; Djurović, I.; Stanković, L. Fractional Fourier Transform as a Signal Processing Tool: An Overview of Recent Developments. *Signal Process.* **2011**, *91*, 1351–1369. [CrossRef]
8. Ma, J.; Miao, H.; Su, X.; Gao, C.; Kang, X.; Tao, R. Research Progress in Theories and Applications of the Fractional Fourier Transform. *Opto-Electron. Eng.* **2018**, *45*, 170747. [CrossRef]
9. Zhao, T.; Chi, Y. Circuit of Quantum Fractional Fourier Transform. *Fractal Fract.* **2024**, *8*, 464. [CrossRef]
10. Gupta, P.; Verma, A. Recent trends in Fourier-type transforms: A survey. *arXiv* **2024**, arXiv:2402.06645.
11. Pavlíček, V.; Bhandari, A. Sparse Sampling in Fractional Fourier Domain: Recovery Guarantees and Cramér–Rao Bounds. *IEEE Signal Process. Lett.* **2024**, *31*, 1665–1669. [CrossRef]
12. Li, B.; Zhang, Z. Synchroextracting Transform Based on the Novel Short-Time Fractional Fourier Transform. *Fractal Fract.* **2024**, *8*. [CrossRef]
13. Press, W.H.; Teukolsky, S.A.; Vetterling, W.T.; Flannery, B.P. *Numerical Recipes 3rd Edition: The Art of Scientific Computing*; Cambridge University Press: Cambridge, UK, 2007.
14. Chapra, S.C.; Canale, R.P. *Numerical Methods for Engineers*, 6th ed.; McGraw-Hill: New York, NY, USA, 2010.

15. Guicciardini, N. Newton on Quadratures: A Brief Outline. In *Theory, Evidence, Data: Themes from George E. Smith*; Springer: Berlin/Heidelberg, Germany, 2023; pp. 197–222. [CrossRef]
16. Iserles, A. On the numerical quadrature of highly-oscillating integrals I: Fourier transforms. *IMA J. Numer. Anal.* **2004**, *24*, 365–391. [CrossRef]
17. Júnior, P.A.A.M.; Magalhães, C.A. Higher-Order Newton–Cotes Formulas. *J. Math. Stat.* **2010**, *6*, 193–204. [CrossRef]
18. Shampine, L.F.; Allen, R.C.; Pruess, S. *Fundamentals of Numerical Computing*; John Wiley & Sons: New York, NY, USA, 1997.
19. Rangel-Kuoppa, V.T. Newton–Cotes Quadrature Formula, 3/8 Rule, and Boole's Rule Integration. *Discov. Electron.* **2024**, *1*, 31. [CrossRef]
20. Tuck, E.O. A Simple "Filon-Trapezoidal" Rule. *Math. Comput.* **1967**, *21*, 239–241. [CrossRef]
21. Milovanović, G.V.; Stanić, M.P. Numerical Integration of Highly Oscillating Functions. In *Analytic Number Theory, Approximation Theory, and Special Functions*; Springer: Heidelberg, Germany, 2014; pp. 613–649. [CrossRef]
22. Barakat, R.; Sandler, B.H. Filon Trapezoidal Schemes for Hankel Transforms of Orders Zero and One. *Comput. Math. Appl.* **2000**, *40*, 1037–1041. [CrossRef]
23. Majidian, H. A Comparative Study of Filon-Type Rules for Oscillatory Integrals. *J. Numer. Anal. Approx. Theory* **2024**, *53*, 130–143. [CrossRef]
24. Rachev, S.T.; Kim, Y.S.; Bianchi, M.L.; Fabozzi, F.J. Stable and Tempered Stable Distributions. In *Financial Models with Lévy Processes and Volatility Clustering*; The Frank J. Fabozzi Series; Rachev, S.T., Kim, Y.S., Bianchi, M.L., Fabozzi, F.J., Eds.; John Wiley & Sons, Ltd.: Hoboken, NJ, USA, 2011; Volume 187, Chapter 3, pp. 57–85. [CrossRef]
25. Boyarchenko, S.I.; Levendorskiĭ, S.Z. *Non-Gaussian Merton-Black-Scholes Theory*; Advanced Series on Statistical Science & Applied Probability; World Scientific: Singapore; River Edge, NJ, USA, 2002; Volume 9. [CrossRef]
26. Küchler, U.; Tappe, S. Bilateral Gamma distributions and processes in financial mathematics. *Stoch. Process. Their Appl.* **2008**, *118*, 261–283. [CrossRef]
27. Küchler, U.; Tappe, S. Tempered stable distributions and processes. *Stoch. Process. Their Appl.* **2013**, *123*, 4256–4293. [CrossRef]
28. Carr, P.; Geman, H.; Madan, D.B.; Yor, M. Stochastic volatility for Lévy processes. *Math. Financ.* **2003**, *13*, 345–382. [CrossRef]
29. Nzokem, A.H. Self-Decomposable Laws Associated with General Tempered Stable (GTS) Distribution and their Simulation Applications. *arXiv* **2024**, arXiv:2405.16614. [CrossRef]
30. Sermutlu, E. A close look at Newton–Cotes integration rules. *Results Nonlinear Anal.* **2022**, *2*, 48–60.
31. Trefethen, L.N. Exactness of Quadrature Formulas. *SIAM Rev.* **2022**, *64*, 132–150. [CrossRef]
32. Abramowitz, M.; Stegun, I.A. *Handbook of Mathematical Functions with Formulas, Graphs, and Mathematical Tables*; Dover: New York, NY, USA, 1972.
33. Huybrechs, D. Stable high-order quadrature rules with equidistant points. *J. Comput. Appl. Math.* **2009**, *231*, 933–947. [CrossRef]
34. Aguilar, J.C. Higher-order Newton–Cotes rules with end corrections. *Appl. Numer. Math.* **2015**, *88*, 66–77. [CrossRef]
35. Wiersma, M. Quadrature Rules with (Not Too Many) Derivatives. *Atl. Electron. J. Math.* **2012**, *5*, 60–67.
36. Graça, M.M. A Simple Derivation of Newton-Cotes Formulas with Realistic Errors. *J. Math. Res.* **2012**, *4*, 34–47. [CrossRef]
37. Moheuddin, M.M.; Uddin, M.J.; Kowsher, M. A New Study of Trapezoidal, Simpson's 1/3 and Simpson's 3/8 Rules of Numerical Integral Problems. *Appl. Math. Sci. Int. J. (MathSJ)* **2019**, *6*, 1–12. [CrossRef]
38. Catapang, L.A.; Mendaje, J.R.; Siong, V.D. Convergence Analysis of Newton–Cotes Methods: Optimizing Sub-Intervals Selection for Precise Integral Approximation. *Appl. Math. Sci. Int. J. (MathSJ)* **2024**, *11*, 1–21. [CrossRef]
39. Nzokem, A.H. Numerical Solution of a Gamma-Integral Equation Using a Higher Order Composite Newton-Cotes Formulas. *J. Phys. Conf. Ser.* **2021**, *2084*, 012019. [CrossRef]
40. Nzokem, A.H. Stochastic and Renewal Methods Applied to Epidemic Models. Ph.D. Thesis, York University, North York, ON, Canada, 2020.
41. Krylov, V.I.; Stroud, A.H. *Approximate Calculation of Integrals*, 6th ed.; Dover Books on Mathematics; Dover Publications: Mineola, NY, USA, 2006.
42. AL-Sammarraie, O.A.; Bashir, M.A. Error Analysis of the High Order Newton-Cotes Formulas. *Int. J. Sci. Res. Publ.* **2015**, *5*, 1–6.
43. Kalman, D. The Generalized Vandermonde Matrix. *Math. Mag.* **1984**, *57*, 15–21. [CrossRef]
44. Nzokem, A.H.; Maposa, D. Bitcoin versus S&P 500 Index: Return and Risk Analysis. *Math. Comput. Appl.* **2024**, *29*, 44. [CrossRef]
45. Nzokem, A.; Maposa, D. Fitting the Seven-Parameter Generalized Tempered Stable Distribution to Financial Data. *J. Risk Financ. Manag.* **2024**, *17*, 531. [CrossRef]
46. Nzokem, A.H. Gamma Variance Model: Fractional Fourier Transform (FRFT). *J. Phys. Conf. Ser.* **2021**, *2090*, 012094. [CrossRef]
47. Nzokem, A.H.; Montshiwa, V.T. Fitting Generalized Tempered Stable Distribution: Fractional Fourier Transform (FRFT) Approach. *arXiv* **2022**, arXiv:2205.00586. [CrossRef]
48. Bailey, D.H.; Swarztrauber, P.N. The Fractional Fourier Transform and Applications. *SIAM Rev.* **1991**, *33*, 389–404. [CrossRef]
49. Nzokem, A.H. Fitting Infinitely Divisible Distribution: Case of Gamma-Variance Model. *arXiv* **2021**, arXiv:2104.07580. [CrossRef]

50. Olver, F.W.J.; Olde Daalhuis, A.B.; Lozier, D.W.; Schneider, B.I.; Boisvert, R.F.; Clark, C.W.; Miller, B.R.; Saunders, B.V.; Cohl, H.S.; McClain, M.A. *NIST Digital Library of Mathematical Functions*; Release 1.1.11; NIST: Gaithersburg, MD, USA , 2023.
51. Fischer, A.; Gaunt, R.E.; Sarantsev, A. The Variance–Gamma Distribution: A Review. *Statist. Sci.* **2024**, *40*, 235–258. [CrossRef]
52. Gaunt, R.E. Variance–Gamma approximation via Stein's method. *Electron. J. Probab.* **2014**, *19*, 1–33. [CrossRef]
53. Nestler, S.; Hall, A. The variance gamma distribution. *Significance* **2019**, *16*, 10–11. [CrossRef]
54. Kotz, S.; Kozubowski, T.J.; Podgórski, K. *The Laplace Distribution and Generalizations: A Revisit with Applications to Communications, Economics, Engineering, and Finance*, 1st ed.; Birkhäuser: Boston, MA, USA, 2001. [CrossRef]
55. Nzokem, A.H.; Montshiwa, V.T. The Ornstein-Uhlenbeck Process and Variance Gamma Process: Parameter Estimation and Simulations. *Thai J. Math.* **2023**, *21*, 160–168.
56. Nzokem, A.H. Five-Parameter Variance-Gamma Process: Lévy versus Probability Density. *AIP Conf. Proc.* **2024**, *3005*, 020030. [CrossRef]
57. Nzokem, A.H. Pricing European Options under Stochastic Volatility Models: Case of Five-Parameter Variance-Gamma Process. *J. Risk Financ. Manag.* **2023**, *16*, 55. [CrossRef]
58. Nzokem, A.H. European Option Pricing Under Generalized Tempered Stable Process: Empirical Analysis. *arXiv* **2023**, arXiv:2304.06060. [CrossRef]
59. Figlewski, S. Risk-Neutral Densities: A Review. *Annu. Rev. Financ. Econ.* **2018**, *10*, 329–359. [CrossRef]
60. Ivanov, R.V. On the Stochastic Volatility in the Generalized Black-Scholes-Merton Model. *Risks* **2023**, *11*, 111. [CrossRef]
61. Qayyum, M.; Ahmad, E. New Solutions of Time-and Space-Fractional Black–Scholes European Option Pricing Model via Fractional Extension of He-Aboodh Algorithm. *J. Math.* **2024**, *2024*, 6623636. [CrossRef]
62. Malz, A.M. A Simple and Reliable Way to Compute Option-Based Risk-Neutral Distributions. In *FRB of New York Staff Report*; Federal Reserve Bank of New York: New York, NY, USA, 2014.

axioms

MDPI

Article

The Numerical Solution of Volterra Integral Equations

Peter Junghanns

Faculty of Mathematics, Chemnitz University of Technology, 09107 Chemnitz, Germany;
peter.junghanns@mathematik.tu-chemnitz.de

Abstract

Recently we studied a collocation–quadrature method in weighted $\mathbf{L}^2$ spaces as well as in the space of continuous functions for a Volterra-like integral equation of the form $u(x) - \int_{\alpha x}^{1} h(x - \alpha y)u(y)\, dy = f(x)$, $0 < x < 1$, where $h(x)$ (with a possible singularity at $x = 0$) and $f(x)$ are given (in general complex-valued) functions, and $\alpha \in (0,1)$ is a fixed parameter. Here, we want to investigate the same method for the case when $\alpha = 1$. More precisely, we consider (in general weakly singular) Volterra integral equations of the form $u(x) - \int_0^x h(x,y)(x-y)^\kappa u(y)\, dy = f(x)$, $0 < x < 1$, where $\kappa > -1$, and $h : D \longrightarrow \mathbb{C}$ is a continuous function, $D = \{(x,y) \in \mathbb{R}^2 : 0 < y < x < 1\}$. The passage from $0 < \alpha < 1$ to $\alpha = 1$ and the consideration of more general kernel functions $h(x,y)$ make the studies more involved. Moreover, we enhance the family of interpolation operators defining the approximating operators, and, finally, we ask if, in comparison to collocation–quadrature methods, the application of the Nyström method together with the theory of collectively compact operator sequences is possible.

Keywords: Volterra integral equations; collocation-quadrature method; Nyström method

MSC: 65R20; 45D05; 46N40

1. Introduction

In [1], a collocation–quadrature method is studied in weighted $\mathbf{L}^2$ spaces as well as in the space of continuous functions for a Volterra-like integral equation of the form

$$u(x) - \int_{\alpha x}^{1} h(x - \alpha y)u(y)\, dy = f(x),\ 0 < x < 1,$$

where $h(x)$ (with a possible singularity at $x = 0$) and $f(x)$ are given (in general complex-valued) functions, and $\alpha \in (0,1)$ is a fixed parameter (see [1], Section 3.2). Here, we are interested in the numerical solution of Volterra integral equations of the second kind,

$$u(x) - \int_0^x g(x,y)u(y)\, dy = f(x), \quad 0 < x < 1, \tag{1}$$

where the functions $f : (0,1) \longrightarrow \mathbb{C}$ and $g : D \longrightarrow \mathbb{C}$ with $D = \{(x,y) \in \mathbb{R}^2 : 0 < y < x < 1\}$ are given. In particular, we prefer global polynomials as ansatz functions for the approximating solution $u_n(x)$ and the application of Gaussian rules for the approximation of the integral operator. We do this with the aim not to restrict the convergence rate of the method by taking piecewise polynomials of fixed degree. As a consequence, the convergence rate of the method is only bounded by the smoothness of the given data $g(x,y)$ and $f(x)$.

The following result (see Lemma 1) on the solvability of (1) is well known and very special for Volterra integral equations of the above type. The space of continuous functions $f : [0,1] \longrightarrow \mathbb{C}$ is denoted by $\mathbf{C} = \mathbf{C}[0,1]$ and equipped with the infinity norm $\|f\|_\infty = \max\{|f(x)| : x \in [0,1]\}$, making $(\mathbf{C}[0,1], \|.\|_\infty)$ a Banach space.

Equation (1) is written in operator form as

$$(\mathcal{I} - \mathcal{K})u = f, \tag{2}$$

where $\mathcal{I} : \mathbf{C} \longrightarrow \mathbf{C}$ and $\mathcal{K} : \mathbf{C} \longrightarrow \mathbf{C}$ denote the identity and the integral operator

$$(\mathcal{K}u)(x) = \int_0^x g(x,y)u(y)\,dy, \quad 0 < x < 1, \tag{3}$$

respectively. In particular, the special case of Volterra convolution equations is of interest, where the kernel function of the integral operator is of the form $g(x-y)$ with a given continuous function $g : (0,1) \longrightarrow \mathbb{C}$,

$$u(x) - \int_0^x g(x-y)u(y)\,dy = f(x), \quad 0 < x < 1. \tag{4}$$

Often the kernel function of the integral operator is not continuous but weakly singular along the line $\{(x,y) \in D : x = y\}$ of triangle D. That is why, in what follows, we consider a kernel function of the form $g_\kappa(x,y) = h(x,y)(x-y)^\kappa$ with a continuous function $h : D \longrightarrow \mathbb{C}$ or, in case of the convolution equation, of the form $g_\kappa(x,y) = h_0(x-y)(x-y)^\kappa$ (i.e., $h(x,y) = h_0(x-y)$) with a continuous function $h_0 : (0,1) \longrightarrow \mathbb{C}$, where $\kappa > -1$ is a given real number. The respective integral operator is denoted by $\mathcal{K}_\kappa$, i.e.,

$$(\mathcal{K}_\kappa u)(x) = \int_0^x g_\kappa(x,y)u(y)\,dy, \quad -1 < x < 1. \tag{5}$$

The corresponding integral Equations (1) and (4) are written as

$$(\mathcal{I} - \mathcal{K}_\kappa)u = f. \tag{6}$$

The remainder of this paper is organized as follows: In Section 2 we collect a series of mapping properties of the above-mentioned integral operators in weighted $\mathbf{L}^2$ spaces as well as in the space of continuous functions. In Section 3 we describe the collocation–quadrature method, study its stability and convergence, and prove convergence rates for the approximate solutions. In Section 4 we answer the question under which conditions it is possible to apply the famous Nyström method (see, for example, [2], Chapter 4, and [3], Section 12.2) together with the theory of collectively compact operator sequences to the Volterra integral equations under consideration. We will see that from a theoretical point of view (concerning stability and convergence rates) the collocation–quadrature method outperforms the Nyström method. The present paper concentrates on these theoretical issues. The discussion of computational aspects of the proposed collocation–quadrature method is reserved for forthcoming studies.

2. Mapping Properties of the Involved Integral Operators

From ([3], Theorems 3.10 and 10.17), we infer the following Lemma. $\overline{D}$ denotes the closure of the set D, $\overline{D} = \{(x,y) \in \mathbb{R}^2 : 0 \le y \le x \le 1\}$.

Lemma 1. *If $h : \overline{D} \longrightarrow \mathbb{C}$ is continuous, then the linear operator $\mathcal{I} - \mathcal{K}_\kappa : \mathbf{C} \longrightarrow \mathbf{C}$ is invertible, i.e., for every $f \in \mathbf{C}$ there exists a unique solution $u = u^* \in \mathbf{C}$ of (6).*

In the following we try to extend this result to weighted spaces of continuous functions as well as weighted spaces of square integrable functions. First, we weaken the assumption on the kernel function $h(x,y)$ in Lemma 3. Let $v^{\gamma,\delta}$ denote the Jacobi weight function $v^{\gamma,\delta}(x) = (1-x)^\gamma x^\delta$, $-1 < x < 1$. For $\gamma, \delta \geq 0$, we define the space $\widetilde{\mathbf{C}}_{\gamma,\delta} = \widetilde{\mathbf{C}}_{\gamma,\delta}(0,1)$ as the set of all continuous functions $f : (0,1) \longrightarrow \mathbb{C}$, such that $v^{\gamma,\delta} f$ belongs to $\mathbf{C}$, i.e., for which the finite limits $\lim_{x\to 1-0} v^{\gamma,\delta}(x) f(x)$ and $\lim_{x\to+0} v^{\gamma,\delta}(x) f(x)$ exist. Equipped with the norm

$$\|f\|_{\gamma,\delta,\infty} = \sup\left\{v^{\gamma,\delta}(x)|f(x)| : 0 < x < 1\right\},$$

$\widetilde{\mathbf{C}}_{\gamma,\delta}$ becomes a Banach space. $\mathbf{C}_{\gamma,\delta} = \mathbf{C}_{\gamma,\delta}(0,1)$ refers to the closed subspace of $\widetilde{\mathbf{C}}_{\gamma,\delta}$ of all functions $f \in \widetilde{\mathbf{C}}_{\gamma,\delta}$, for which

$$\lim_{x\to 1-0} v^{\gamma,\delta}(x) f(x) = 0 \text{ if } \gamma > 0 \quad \text{and} \quad \lim_{x\to+0} v^{\gamma,\delta}(x) f(x) = 0 \text{ if } \delta > 0.$$

Obviously, the map $\mathcal{T} : \widetilde{\mathbf{C}}_{\gamma,\delta} \longrightarrow \mathbf{C}$, $f \mapsto v^{\gamma,\delta} f$ is an isometric isomorphism. Thus, the operator $\mathcal{I} - \mathcal{K}_\kappa : \widetilde{\mathbf{C}}_{\gamma,\delta} \longrightarrow \widetilde{\mathbf{C}}_{\gamma,\delta}$ is invertible if and only if the operator $\mathcal{I} - \mathcal{T}\mathcal{K}_\kappa\mathcal{T}^{-1} : \mathbf{C} \longrightarrow \mathbf{C}$ is invertible. Note that

$$\left(\mathcal{T}\mathcal{K}_\kappa\mathcal{T}^{-1} f\right)(x) = \int_0^x v^{\gamma,\delta}(x) h(x,y)(x-y)^\kappa v^{-\gamma,-\delta}(y) f(y)\, dy. \tag{7}$$

Consequently, a simple conclusion of Lemma 1 is the following corollary:

Corollary 1. *If $\gamma, \delta \geq 0$ and the function $\overline{D} \longrightarrow \mathbb{C}$, $(x,y) \mapsto v^{\gamma,\delta}(x) h(x,y) v^{-\gamma,-\delta}(y)$ is continuous, then for every $f \in \widetilde{\mathbf{C}}_{\gamma,\delta}$, Equation (6) has a unique solution $u \in \widetilde{\mathbf{C}}_{\gamma,\delta}$.*

We continue to discuss the unique solvability in $\widetilde{\mathbf{C}}_{\gamma,\delta}$. In comparison to the previous corollary, in the following lemma we weaken the condition on the kernel function part $h(x,y)$. In what follows we assume that there are non-negative numbers $\gamma_0, \delta_0, \gamma_1, \delta_1$ such that the following condition (A) is fulfilled:

(A) The function $\overline{D} \longrightarrow \mathbb{C}$, $(x,y) \mapsto v^{\gamma_1,\delta_1}(x) h(x,y) v^{\gamma_0,\delta_0}(y)$ is continuous.

Lemma 2. *Let condition (A) be satisfied, and take $\gamma, \delta \geq 0$ such that $\gamma_1 \leq \gamma$, $\delta_1 \leq \delta$, and $\delta_0 + \delta < 1$. Moreover, assume that*

$$1 + \kappa - \gamma_* - \delta_* > 0, \text{ where } \gamma_* = \gamma_0 + \gamma_1,\ \delta_* = \delta_0 + \delta_1.$$

Then, for $f \equiv 0$, (6) has only the trivial solution in $\widetilde{\mathbf{C}}_{\gamma,\delta}$.

Proof. With $M := \sup\{v^{\gamma_1,\delta_1}(x)|h(x,y)|v^{\gamma_0,\delta_0}(y) : x,y \in D\}$ we have, for $u \in \widetilde{\mathbf{C}}_{\gamma,\delta}$,

$$\begin{aligned} |(\mathcal{K}_\kappa u)(x)| &= \left|\int_0^x h(x,y)(x-y)^\kappa u(y)\, dy\right| \\ &\leq M v^{-\gamma_1,-\delta_1}(x) \int_0^x (x-y)^\kappa v^{-\gamma_0,-\delta_0}(y)|u(y)|\, dy, \quad 0 < x < 1. \end{aligned} \tag{8}$$

By induction we prove that, for $m \in \mathbb{N}$,

$$|(\mathcal{K}_\kappa^m u)(x)| \leq C_m v^{-\gamma_1,-\delta_1}(x) \int_0^x (x-y)^{\kappa+(m-1)(1+\kappa-\gamma_*-\delta_*)} v^{-\gamma_0,-\delta_0}(y)|u(y)|\, dy, \tag{9}$$

where the constant C_m does not depend on $x \in (0,1)$ and $u \in \mathbf{C}(0,1)$. Of course, this is true for $m = 1$ with $C_1 = M$ due to (8). Let (9) be true for some $m \in \mathbb{N}$. Then, using (8) again, we get

$$
\begin{aligned}
&\left|\left(\mathcal{K}_\kappa^{m+1}u\right)(x)\right| \\
&\le M v^{-\gamma_1,-\delta_1}(x)\int_0^x (x-y)^\kappa v^{-\gamma_0,-\delta_0}(y)|(\mathcal{K}_\kappa^m u)(y)|\,dy \\
&\le M\mathcal{C}_m v^{-\gamma_1,-\delta_1}(x)\cdot \\
&\qquad \cdot\int_0^x (x-y)^\kappa v^{-\gamma_*,-\delta_*}(y)\int_0^y (y-z)^{\kappa+(m-1)(1+\kappa-\gamma_*-\delta_*)}v^{-\gamma_0,-\delta_0}(z)|u(z)|\,dz\,dy \\
&= M\mathcal{C}_m v^{-\gamma_1,-\delta_1}(x)\cdot \\
&\qquad \cdot\int_0^x\int_z^x (x-y)^\kappa (y-z)^{\kappa+(m-1)(1+\kappa-\gamma_*-\delta_*)}v^{-\gamma_*,-\delta_*}(y)\,dy\,v^{-\gamma_0,-\delta_0}(z)|u(z)|\,dz\,,
\end{aligned}
$$

where, using the substitution $y = z + s(x-z), 0 \le s \le 1$,

$$
\begin{aligned}
&\int_z^x (x-y)^\kappa (y-z)^{\kappa+(m-1)(1+\kappa-\gamma_*-\delta_*)}v^{-\gamma_*,-\delta_*}(y)\,dy \\
&\quad = (x-z)^{\kappa+\kappa+(m-1)(1+\kappa-\gamma_*-\delta_*)+1}\cdot \\
&\qquad\quad \cdot\int_0^1 (1-s)^\kappa s^{\kappa+(m-1)(1+\kappa-\gamma_*-\delta_*)}[1-z-s(x-z)]^{-\gamma_*}[z+s(x-z)]^{-\delta_*}\,ds \\
&\quad \le (x-z)^{\kappa+\kappa+(m-1)(1+\kappa-\gamma_*-\delta_*)+1-\gamma_*-\delta_*}\int_0^1 (1-s)^{\kappa-\gamma_*}s^{\kappa+(m-1)(1+\kappa-\gamma_*-\delta_*)-\delta_*}\,ds \\
&\quad = \widetilde{\mathcal{C}}_m (x-z)^{\kappa+m(1+\kappa-\gamma_*-\delta_*)}.
\end{aligned}
$$

Thus, we obtain (9) for $m := m+1$ and $\mathcal{C}_{m+1} := M\mathcal{C}_m\widetilde{\mathcal{C}}_m$. Now, we choose $m_0 \in \mathbb{N}$ such that $\kappa + (m_0-1)(1+\kappa-\gamma_*-\delta_*) - \gamma_0 - \gamma \ge 0$. Then, due to (9),

$$
\begin{aligned}
\left|(\mathcal{K}_\kappa^{m_0}u)(x)\right| &\le \mathcal{C}_{m_0}v^{-\gamma_1,-\delta_1}(x)\int_0^x (1-y)^\gamma y^{-\delta_0}|u(y)|\,dy \\
&\le \mathcal{C}_{m_0}v^{-\gamma_1,-\delta_1}(x)\int_0^x y^{-\delta_0-\delta}\,dy\|u\|_{\gamma,\delta,\infty}, \quad 0<x<1.
\end{aligned} \tag{10}
$$

Let $u \in \widetilde{\mathbf{C}}_{\gamma,\delta}$ be a solution of the homogeneous equation $u = \mathcal{K}_\kappa u$. Then, u is also a solution of $u = \mathcal{K}_\kappa^{m_0}u$, and, again by induction, we can prove

$$
|u(x)| \le v^{-\gamma_1,-\delta_1}(x)\left(\frac{\mathcal{C}_{m_0}}{1-\delta_0-\delta}\right)^n \|u\|_{\gamma,\delta,\infty}\frac{x^{n(1-\delta_0-\delta)}}{n!}, \quad n\in\mathbb{N}, 0<x<1. \tag{11}
$$

Indeed, from $u(x) = (\mathcal{K}_\kappa^{m_0}u)(x)$ and (10) we see that (11) is true for $n=1$. If we assume that (11) is true for some $n \in \mathbb{N}$, then

$$
\begin{aligned}
|u(x)| &\overset{(10)}{\le} \mathcal{C}_{m_0}v^{-\gamma_1,-\delta_1}(x)\int_0^x (1-y)^\gamma y^{-\delta_0}|u(y)|\,dy \\
&\overset{(11)}{\le} \frac{v^{-\gamma_1,-\delta_1}(x)\mathcal{C}_{m_0}^{n+1}\|u\|_{\gamma,\delta,\infty}}{(1-\delta_0-\delta)^n n!}\int_0^x (1-y)^{\gamma-\gamma_1}y^{-\delta_0-\delta_1+n(1-\delta_0-\delta)}\,dy \\
&\le \frac{v^{-\gamma_1,-\delta_1}(x)\mathcal{C}_{m_0}^{n+1}\|u\|_{\gamma,\delta,\infty}}{(1-\delta_0-\delta)^n n!}\int_0^x y^{-\delta_0-\delta+n(1-\delta_0-\delta)}\,dy \\
&= v^{-\gamma_1,-\delta_1}(x)\left(\frac{\mathcal{C}_{m_0}}{1-\delta_0-\delta}\right)^{n+1}\|u\|_{\gamma,\delta,\infty}\frac{x^{(n+1)(1-\delta_0-\delta)}}{(n+1)!}.
\end{aligned}
$$

We send n to infinity in (11) and conclude that $u(x) = 0$ for all $x \in (0,1)$. □

For $\gamma, \delta > -1$, $\mathbf{L}^2_{\gamma,\delta}$ refers to the Hilbert space of all with respect to the Jacobi weight $v^{\gamma,\delta}$ square integrable functions on the interval $(0,1)$ equipped with the inner product

$$\langle u, v \rangle_{\gamma,\delta} = \int_0^1 u(x)\overline{v(x)} v^{\gamma,\delta}(x)\, dx$$

and the norm $\|u\|_{\gamma,\delta} = \sqrt{\langle u, u \rangle_{\gamma,\delta}}$.

In what follows, C denotes a generic positive constant, which can assume different values in different places. Moreover, $C \neq C(n, x, \ldots)$ indicates that C does not depend on $n, x, \ldots$ Let $\|h\|_\infty$ denote the value $\sup\{h(x,y) : x, y \in D\}$.

Lemma 3. *Assume that $h : \overline{D} \longrightarrow \mathbb{C}$ is continuous. Then, for $\kappa > -\frac{1}{2}$, $-1 < \gamma, \delta < 1$, and $\max\{0,\gamma\} + \max\{0,\delta\} < 1 + 2\kappa$, the operator $\mathcal{K}_\kappa : \mathbf{L}^2_{\gamma,\delta} \longrightarrow \mathbf{C}$ is compact.*

Proof. Let $u \in \mathbf{L}^2_{\gamma,\delta}$ and $x \in [-1,1]$. Then, using the substitution $x - y = xz$,

$$\begin{aligned}
|(\mathcal{K}_\kappa u)(x)| &\leq \|h\|_\infty \sqrt{\int_0^x |u(y)|^2 v^{\gamma,\delta}(y)\, dy} \sqrt{\int_0^x (x-y)^{2\kappa} v^{-\gamma,-\delta}(y)\, dy} \\
&\leq \|h\|_\infty \|u\|_{\gamma,\delta} \sqrt{x^{1+2\kappa-\delta} \int_0^1 z^{2\kappa}(1 - x + xz)^{-\gamma}(1-z)^{-\delta}\, dz} \\
&\leq \|h\|_\infty \|u\|_{\gamma,\delta} \sqrt{x^{1+2\kappa-\delta-\max\{0,\gamma\}} \int_0^1 z^{2\kappa-\max\{0,\gamma\}}(1-z)^{-\delta}\, dz} \\
&\leq \|h\|_\infty \|u\|_{\gamma,\delta} \sqrt{\int_0^1 (1-z)^{-\delta} z^{2\kappa-\max\{0,\gamma\}}\, dz} = C\|u\|_{\gamma,\delta},
\end{aligned} \tag{12}$$

where the constant C does not depend on $u \in \mathbf{L}^2_{\gamma,\delta}$. Now, for $0 \leq x_1 < x_2 \leq 1$, we can estimate

$$\begin{aligned}
&|(\mathcal{K}_\kappa u)(x_2) - (\mathcal{K}_\kappa u)(x_1)| \\
&\quad = \left| \int_0^{x_2} h(x_2, y)(x_2 - y)^\kappa u(y)\, dy - \int_0^{x_1} h(x_1, y)(x_1 - y)^\kappa u(y)\, dy \right| \\
&\quad \leq \left| \int_{x_1}^{x_2} h(x_2, y)(x_2 - y)^\kappa u(y)\, dy \right| \\
&\qquad + \left| \int_0^{x_1} [h(x_2, y) - h(x_1, y)](x_2 - y)^\kappa u(y)\, dy \right| \\
&\qquad + \left| \int_0^{x_1} h(x_1, y)[(x_2 - y)^\kappa - (x_1 - y)^\kappa] u(y)\, dy \right| \\
&\quad =: I_1 + I_2 + I_3.
\end{aligned}$$

We estimate these three terms separately. Firstly, we have

$$I_1 \leq \|h\|_\infty \sqrt{\int_{x_1}^{x_2} |u(y)|^2 v^{\gamma,\delta}(y)\, dy} \sqrt{\int_{x_1}^{x_2} (x_2 - y)^{2\kappa} v^{-\gamma,-\delta}(y)\, dy} \leq \|h\|_\infty \|u\|_{\gamma,\delta} \sqrt{A},$$

where, taking into account $2\kappa - \max\{0,\gamma\} - \max\{0,\delta\} > -1$,

$$
\begin{aligned}
A &= (x_2 - x_1) \int_0^1 [(x_2 - x_1)(1-z)]^{2\kappa} [1 - x_1 - (x_2 - x_1)z]^{-\gamma} [(x_2 - x_1)z + x_1]^{-\delta}\, dz \\
&\le (x_2 - x_1)^{1+2\kappa} \int_0^1 (1-z)^{2\kappa} \cdot \\
&\quad \cdot \left\{ \begin{array}{ccc} 1 & : & \gamma \le 0 \\ (x_2 - x_1)^{-\gamma}(1-z)^{-\gamma} & : & \gamma > 0 \end{array} \right\} \left\{ \begin{array}{ccc} 1 & : & \delta \le 0 \\ (x_2 - x_1)^{-\delta} z^{-\delta} & : & \delta > 0 \end{array} \right\} dz \\
&\le (x_2 - x_1)^{1+2\kappa - \max\{0,\gamma\} - \max\{0,\delta\}} \int_0^1 (1-z)^{2\kappa - \max\{0,\gamma\}} z^{-\max\{0,\delta\}}\, dz \\
&= C (x_2 - x_1)^{1+2\kappa - \max\{0,\gamma\} - \max\{0,\delta\}}.
\end{aligned}
$$

Hence,

$$
I_1 \le C \|u\|_{\gamma,\delta} (x_2 - x_1)^{\frac{1}{2}(1+2\kappa - \max\{0,\gamma\} - \max\{0,\delta\})}, \quad C \ne C(x_1, x_2, u). \tag{13}
$$

Secondly, let $\varepsilon > 0$. Then, there is an $\eta > 0$ such that $|h(x_1, y) - h(x_2, y)| < \varepsilon$ for all $x_1, x_2, y \in [-1, 1]$ with $0 \le y \le x_1 \le x_2 \le x_1 + \eta$. Thus, for $0 \le x_1 \le x_2 \le x_1 + \eta$,

$$
\begin{aligned}
I_2 &\le \varepsilon \|u\|_{\gamma,\delta} \sqrt{\int_0^{x_1} (x_2 - y)^{2\kappa} v^{-\gamma,-\delta}(y)\, dy} \\
&\le \varepsilon \|u\|_{\gamma,\delta} \left\{ \begin{array}{ccc} \sqrt{\int_0^1 v^{-\gamma,-\delta}(y)\, dy} & : & \kappa \ge 0, \\ \sqrt{\int_0^{x_1} (x_1 - y)^{2\kappa} (x_1 - y)^{-\max\{0,\gamma\}} y^{-\max\{0,\delta\}}\, dy} & : & \kappa < 0, \end{array} \right. \\
&= \varepsilon \|u\|_{\gamma,\delta} \left\{ \begin{array}{ccc} \sqrt{\int_0^1 v^{-\gamma,-\delta}(y)\, dy} & : & \kappa \ge 0, \\ \sqrt{x_1^{1+2\kappa - \max\{0,\gamma\} - \max\{0,\delta\}} \int_0^1 (1-y)^{2\kappa - \max\{0,\gamma\}} y^{-\max\{0,\delta\}}\, dy} & : & \kappa < 0. \end{array} \right.
\end{aligned}
$$

Consequently,

$$
I_2 \le C\varepsilon \|u\|_{\gamma,\delta}, \quad C \ne C(x_1, x_2, u). \tag{14}
$$

Finally, we refer to the inequality (see [4], Chapter 1 (5.2))

$$
\left| \xi_1^{\mu} - \xi_2^{\mu} \right| \le |\xi_1 - \xi_2|^{\mu}, \quad 0 \le \mu \le 1, \ \xi_1, \xi_2 \ge 0, \tag{15}
$$

and obtain

$$
I_3 \le \|h\|_\infty \|u\|_{\gamma,\delta} \sqrt{\int_0^{x_1} [(x_2 - y)^{\kappa} - (x_1 - y)^{\kappa}]^2 v^{-\gamma,-\delta}(y)\, dy} =: \|h\|_\infty \|u\|_{\gamma,\delta} \sqrt{B}
$$

with $B \le C(x_2 - x_1)^{2\min\{\kappa,1\}}$ if $\kappa > 0$. In case of $-\frac{1}{2} < \kappa < 0$, we choose $\chi > 0$ such that $\kappa + \chi < 0$ and $\max\{0, \gamma\} + \max\{0, \delta\} < 1 + 2(\kappa - \chi)$. Then, using the equality

$$
|(x_2 - y)^{\kappa} - (x_1 - y)^{\kappa}| = (x_2 - y)^{\kappa} \left[(x_2 - y)^{-\kappa} - (x_1 - y)^{-\kappa} \right] (x_1 - y)^{\kappa},
$$

we get

$$\begin{aligned} B &\leq (x_2-x_1)^{-2\kappa}\int_0^{x_1}(x_2-y)^{2\kappa}(x_1-y)^{2\kappa}v^{-\gamma,-\delta}(y)\,dy \\ &= (x_2-x_1)^{-2\kappa}\int_0^{x_1}(x_2-y)^{2(\kappa+\chi)}(x_2-y)^{-2\chi}(x_1-y)^{2\kappa}v^{-\gamma,-\delta}(y)\,dy \\ &\leq (x_2-x_1)^{2\chi}\int_0^{x_1}(x_1-y)^{2(\kappa-\chi)}v^{-\gamma,-\delta}(y)\,dy \\ &\leq C(x_2-x_1)^{2\chi}x_1^{1+2(\kappa-\chi)-\delta}\int_0^1(1-z)^{2(\kappa-\chi)-\max\{0,\gamma\}}z^{-\delta}\,dz \\ &\leq C(x_2-x_1)^{2\chi}. \end{aligned}$$

Hence,

$$I_3 \leq C\|u\|_{\gamma,\delta}(x_2-x_1)^{\chi_0}, \quad \chi_0 = \begin{cases} \min\{\kappa,1\} & : \ \kappa>0, \\ \chi & : \ \kappa<0, \end{cases} \qquad C \neq C(x_1,x_2,u). \tag{16}$$

As a conclusion of the relations (12), (13), (14), and (16), the set $\left\{\mathcal{K}_\kappa u : u \in \mathbf{L}^2_{\gamma,\delta},\ \|u\|_{\gamma,\delta} \leq 1\right\}$ is uniformly bounded and equicontinuous. It remains to refer to the Arzela–Ascoli theorem (see [2], Section 1.2.1). □

Corollary 2. *If condition* (A) *is valid, then the operator* $\mathcal{K}_\kappa : \mathbf{L}^2_{\gamma,\delta} \longrightarrow \widetilde{\mathbf{C}}_{\gamma_1,\delta_1}$ *is compact if*

$$\kappa > -\frac{1}{2}, \ -1 < 2\gamma_0+\gamma, 2\delta_0+\delta < 1, \ \textit{and} \ \max\{0,2\gamma_0+\gamma\}+\max\{0,2\delta_0+\delta\} < 1+2\kappa.$$

Proof. We can write $\mathcal{K}_\kappa = \mathcal{J}_1^{-1}\mathcal{K}_\kappa^{0,1}\mathcal{J}_0^{-1}$, where

$$\left(\mathcal{K}_\kappa^{0,1}f\right)(x) = \int_0^x v^{\gamma_1,\delta_1}h(x,y)v^{\gamma_0,\delta_0}(y)(x-y)^\kappa f(y)\,dy,$$

and $\mathcal{J}_0 f = v^{\gamma_0,\delta_0}f$, $\mathcal{J}_1 f = v^{\gamma_1,\delta_1}f$. The mappings $\mathcal{J}_0 : \mathbf{L}^2_{2\gamma_0+\gamma,2\delta_0+\delta} \longrightarrow \mathbf{L}^2_{\gamma,\delta}$ and $\mathcal{J}_1 : \widetilde{\mathbf{C}}_{\gamma_1,\delta_1} \longrightarrow \mathbf{C}$ are isometrical isomorphisms, and from Lemma 3, the operator $\mathcal{K}_\kappa^{0,1} : \mathbf{L}^2_{2\gamma_0+\gamma,2\delta_0+\delta} \longrightarrow \mathbf{C}$ is compact. Hence,

$$\mathcal{K}_\kappa : \mathbf{L}^2_{\gamma,\delta} \xrightarrow{\mathcal{J}_0^{-1}} \mathbf{L}^2_{2\gamma_0+\gamma,2\delta_0+\delta} \xrightarrow{\mathcal{K}_\kappa^{0,1}} \mathbf{C} \xrightarrow{\mathcal{J}_1^{-1}} \widetilde{\mathbf{C}}_{\gamma_1,\delta_1}$$

is compact. □

3. A Collocation–Quadrature Method for Equation (6)

3.1. The Method

We proceed with proposing a collocation–quadrature method for the numerical solution of the integral Equation (6). Note that the integral operator in this equation can be written in the form

$$(\mathcal{K}_\kappa u)(x) = x^{1+\kappa}\int_0^1 h(x,xz)(1-z)^\kappa u(xz)\,dz, \quad 0<x<1. \tag{17}$$

To define an approximation of this operator, we use the Gaussian rule

$$\int_0^1 f(x)v^{\alpha,\beta}(x)\,dx = \sum_{k=1}^n \lambda_{nk}^{\alpha,\beta}f(x_{nk}^{\alpha,\beta}) + e_n^{\alpha,\beta}(f) \tag{18}$$

with the error term $e_n^{\alpha,\beta}(f)$, where $x_{nk}^{\alpha,\beta}$ denotes the kth zero of the nth orthonormal polynomial $p_n^{\alpha,\beta}(x)$ with respect to the weight function $v^{\alpha,\beta}(x)$, $0 < x_{nn}^{\alpha,\beta} < \ldots < x_{n1}^{\alpha,\beta} < 1$, and $\lambda_{nk}^{\alpha,\beta}$ is the respective Christoffel number

$$\lambda_{nk}^{\alpha,\beta} = \int_0^1 \ell_{nk}^{\alpha,\beta}(x)v^{\alpha,\beta}(x)\,dx, \quad \ell_{nk}^{\alpha,\beta}(x) = \prod_{j=1,j\neq k}^{n} \frac{x - x_{nk}^{\alpha,\beta}}{x_{nj}^{\alpha,\beta} - x_{nk}^{\alpha,\beta}} = \frac{p_n^{\alpha,\beta}(x)}{\left(p_n^{\alpha,\beta}\right)'(x_{nk}^{\alpha,\beta})\,(x - x_{nk}^{\alpha,\beta})}.$$

$\mathcal{L}_n^{\alpha,\beta}$ refers to the polynomial interpolation operator associated with the nodes $x_{nk}^{\alpha,\beta}$, i.e.,

$$(\mathcal{L}_n^{\alpha,\beta} f)(x) = \sum_{k=1}^{n} f(x_{nk}^{\alpha,\beta})\ell_{nk}^{\alpha,\beta}(x) \tag{19}$$

for every function $f : (-1,1) \longrightarrow \mathbb{C}$. Let $\mathbf{C}(0,1)$ refer to the set of continuous functions $f : (0,1) \longrightarrow \mathbb{C}$. Writing $(1-z)^\kappa = v^{\kappa-\alpha,-\beta}(z)v^{\alpha,\beta}(z)$ and applying the quadrature rule (18) to (17), we define the quadrature operator $\mathcal{K}_{\kappa,n}^{\alpha,\beta} : \mathbf{C}(0,1) \longrightarrow \mathbf{C}(0,1)$ as

$$(\mathcal{K}_{\kappa,n}^{\alpha,\beta} f)(x) = x^{1+\kappa} \sum_{k=1}^{n} \lambda_{nk}^{\alpha,\beta} h(x, x\,x_{nk}^{\alpha,\beta})v^{\kappa-\alpha,-\beta}(x_{nk}^{\alpha,\beta})f(x\,x_{nk}^{\alpha,\beta}). \tag{20}$$

As a possible approximation of the operator $\mathcal{K}_\kappa : \mathbf{L}^2_{\gamma,\delta} \longrightarrow \mathbf{L}^2_{\gamma,\delta}$, we take the composed operator $\mathcal{L}_n^{\alpha,\beta}\mathcal{K}_{\kappa,n}^{\alpha,\beta}\mathcal{P}_n^{\gamma,\delta}$, where $\mathcal{P}_n^{\gamma,\delta} : \mathbf{L}^2_{\gamma,\delta} \longrightarrow \mathbf{P}_n$ denotes the orthonormal projector

$$(\mathcal{P}_n^{\gamma,\delta} f)(x) = \sum_{j=0}^{n-1} \langle f, p_j^{\gamma,\delta}\rangle_{\gamma,\delta} p_j^{\gamma,\delta}(x),$$

and $\mathbf{P}_n$ refers to the linear space of all algebraic polynomials of degree less than n. In other words, we are looking for an approximate solution $u_n \in \mathbf{P}_n$ of (6) by trying to solve the following equation:

$$u_n - \mathcal{L}_n^{\alpha,\beta}\mathcal{K}_{\kappa,n}^{\alpha,\beta} u_n = f_n, \tag{21}$$

where $f_n \in \mathbf{P}_n$ is an approximation of f satisfying $\lim_{n\to\infty}\|f_n - f\|_{\gamma,\delta} = 0$. For example, if $f \in \mathbf{C}(0,1)$, then we can choose (under certain conditions, see [5] Lemma 15 as well as the beginning of Section 3.2) $f_n = \mathcal{L}_n^{\alpha,\beta} f$. In that case, (21) is equivalent to

$$u_n(x_{nj}^{\alpha,\beta}) - (\mathcal{K}_{\kappa,n}^{\alpha,\beta} u_n)(x_{nj}^{\alpha,\beta}) = f(x_{nj}^{\alpha,\beta}), \quad j = 1, \ldots, n.$$

From the definition (20) of the operator $\mathcal{K}_{\kappa,n}^{\alpha,\beta} : \mathbf{C}(0,1) \longrightarrow \mathbf{C}(0,1)$, we have

$$(\mathcal{K}_{\kappa,n}^{\alpha,\beta} f)(x) = x^{1+\kappa} \int_0^1 \mathcal{L}_n^{\alpha,\beta}\left[h(x, x\cdot)v^{\kappa-\alpha,-\beta} f(x\cdot)\right](y)v^{\alpha,\beta}(y)\,dy.$$

Due to the algebraic accuracy of the Gaussian rule (18), for $p_n \in \mathbf{P}_n$, we get

$$(\mathcal{K}_{\kappa,n}^{\alpha,\beta} p_n)(x) = x^{1+\kappa} \int_0^1 \mathcal{L}_n^{\alpha,\beta}\left[h(x, x\cdot)v^{\kappa-\alpha,-\beta}\right](y)p_n(xy)v^{\alpha,\beta}(y)\,dy.$$

Using this relation, we can try to extend the operator $\mathcal{K}_{\kappa,n}^{\alpha,\beta} : \mathbf{P}_n \longrightarrow \mathbf{L}^2_{\gamma,\delta}$ using linearity to a linear and bounded operator $\mathcal{K}_{\kappa,n}^{\alpha,\beta} : \mathbf{L}^2_{\gamma,\delta} \longrightarrow \mathbf{L}^2_{\gamma,\delta}$,

$$(\mathcal{K}_{\kappa,n}^{\alpha,\beta} f)(x) = x^{1+\kappa} \int_0^1 \mathcal{L}_n^{\alpha,\beta}\left[h(x, x\cdot)v^{\kappa-\alpha,-\beta}\right](y)f(xy)v^{\alpha,\beta}(y)\,dy. \tag{22}$$

For this we need the boundedness of the operator $\mathcal{K}^{\alpha,\beta}_{\kappa,n} : \mathbf{P}_n \longrightarrow \mathbf{L}^2_{\gamma,\delta}$, i.e., the existence of a constant $\rho_n \in \mathbb{R}$ such that

$$\left\| \mathcal{K}^{\alpha,\beta}_{\kappa,n} p_n \right\|_{\gamma,\delta} \le \rho_n \| p_n \|_{\gamma,\delta} \quad \forall\, p_n \in \mathbf{P}_n.$$

To find out under which conditions of the involved parameters we can guarantee the existence of such a constant, we assume that $h(x,y)$ satisfies condition (A) and estimate for $p_n \in \mathbf{P}_n$, $q_n(x,y) := v^{\gamma_1,\delta_1}(x)\mathcal{L}^{\alpha,\beta}_n\left[h(x,\cdot)v^{\kappa-\alpha,-\beta}\right](y)$, and $C_n := \sup\{|q_n(x,y)| : x,y \in [0,1]\}$,

$$\begin{aligned}
&\left\| \mathcal{K}^{\alpha,\beta}_{\kappa,n} p_n \right\|^2_{\gamma,\delta} \\
&= \int_0^1 x^{2(1+\kappa)} v^{-2\gamma_1,-2\delta_1}(x) \left| \int_0^1 q_n(x,y) p_n(xy) v^{\alpha,\beta}(y)\, dy \right|^2 v^{\gamma,\delta}(x)\, dx \\
&\le C_n^2 \int_0^1 x^{2(1+\kappa)} v^{-2\gamma_1,-2\delta_1}(x) \cdot \\
&\qquad \cdot \int_0^1 |p_n(xy)|^2 v^{\gamma,\delta}(xy)\, dy \int_0^1 (1-xy)^{-\gamma}(xy)^{-\delta}(1-y)^{2\alpha} y^{2\beta}\, dy\, v^{\gamma,\delta}(x)\, dx \\
&= C_n^2 \int_0^1 x^{1+2\kappa} v^{-2\gamma_1,-2\delta_1}(x) \int_0^x |p_n(z)|^2 v^{\gamma,\delta}(z)\, dz \cdot \\
&\qquad \cdot \int_0^1 (1-xy)^{-\gamma}(1-y)^{2\alpha} y^{2\beta-\delta}\, dy\, (1-x)^{\gamma}\, dx \\
&\le C_n^2 \|p_n\|^2_{\gamma,\delta} \int_0^1 (1-x)^{\gamma-\max\{0,\gamma\}-2\gamma_1} x^{1+2\kappa-2\delta_1}\, dx \int_0^1 (1-y)^{2\alpha} y^{2\beta-\delta}\, dy.
\end{aligned}$$

Thus, we can choose

$$\rho_n = C_n \sqrt{\int_0^1 (1-x)^{\gamma-\max\{0,\gamma\}-2\gamma_1} x^{1+2\kappa-2\delta_1}\, dx \int_0^1 (1-y)^{2\alpha} y^{2\beta-\delta}\, dy}$$

if

$$\frac{1+\gamma-\max\{0,\gamma\}}{2} > \gamma_1, \quad 1+\kappa > \delta_1, \quad \alpha > -\frac{1}{2} \quad \text{and} \quad \beta > \frac{\delta-1}{2}. \tag{23}$$

With definition (22) of $\mathcal{K}^{\alpha,\beta}_{\kappa,n} : \mathbf{L}^2_{\gamma,\delta} \longrightarrow \mathbf{L}^2_{\gamma,\delta}$, every solution $u_n \in \mathbf{L}^2_{\gamma,\delta}$ of Equation (21) belongs automatically to $\mathbf{P}_n$ if $f_n \in \mathbf{P}_n$.

3.2. Stability and Convergence

Analogously to $\widetilde{\mathbf{C}}_{\gamma,\delta} = \widetilde{\mathbf{C}}_{\gamma,\delta}(0,1)$ and $\mathbf{C}_{\gamma,\delta} = \mathbf{C}_{\gamma,\delta}(0,1)$, we define the sets $\widetilde{\mathbf{R}}_{\gamma,\delta} = \widetilde{\mathbf{R}}_{\gamma,\delta}(0,1)$ and $\mathbf{R}_{\gamma,\delta} = \mathbf{R}_{\gamma,\delta}(0,1)$ by replacing the space $\mathbf{C}(0,1)$ of continuous functions $f : (0,1) \longrightarrow \mathbb{C}$ with the set $\mathbf{R} = \mathbf{R}(0,1)$ of all functions $f : (0,1) \longrightarrow \mathbb{C}$ being bounded and Riemann-integrable on each closed subinterval of the interval $(0,1)$. Moreover, for $\gamma_0, \delta_0 > 0$, we set

$$\mathbf{R}^0_{\gamma_0,\delta_0} = \bigcup_{0 \le \gamma < \gamma_0, 0 \le \delta < \delta_0} \mathbf{R}_{\gamma,\delta}.$$

Note that

$$\begin{aligned}\mathbf{R}^0_{\gamma_0,\delta_0} &= \bigcup_{0\le\gamma<\gamma_0, 0\le\delta<\delta_0} \widetilde{\mathbf{R}}_{\gamma,\delta} \\ &= \Big\{ f\in \mathbf{R}(0,1) : \exists C>0,\ \exists \varepsilon>0 \text{ with } |f(x)| \le C v^{\varepsilon-\gamma_0,\varepsilon-\delta_0}(x)\ \forall x\in(0,1)\Big\}.\end{aligned}$$

Let us recall the following lemma ([5], Lemma 15):

Lemma 4. *Let $\psi,\chi\in\mathbb{R}$, $\alpha,\beta,\gamma,\delta>-1$, and $f\in \mathbf{R}^0_{\frac{1+\gamma}{2},\frac{1+\delta}{2}}$. Then we have, for $n\longrightarrow\infty$,*

$$v^{\psi,\chi}\mathcal{L}_n^{\alpha,\beta}v^{-\psi,-\chi}f \longrightarrow f \quad in \quad \mathbf{L}^2_{\gamma,\delta}$$

if

$$-\frac{1}{2} < \gamma+2\psi-\alpha < \frac{3}{2} \quad and \quad \gamma+2\psi > -1,$$

and if

$$-\frac{1}{2} < \delta+2\chi-\beta < \frac{3}{2} \quad and \quad \delta+2\chi > -1.$$

From Lemma 4 we infer that

$$\lim_{n\to\infty}\Big\| \mathcal{L}_n^{\alpha,\beta}f - f\Big\|_{\gamma,\delta} = 0 \quad \forall f\in \widetilde{\mathbf{R}}_{\gamma^*,\delta^*} \tag{24}$$

if

$$0\le\gamma^* < \frac{1+\gamma}{2},\quad 0\le\delta^*<\frac{1+\delta}{2},\quad \text{and} \quad -\frac{1}{2}<\gamma-\alpha,\delta-\beta<\frac{3}{2}. \tag{25}$$

Since pointwise convergence becomes uniform on each compact subset, the compactness of the operator $\mathcal{K}_\kappa : \mathbf{L}^2_{\gamma,\delta} \longrightarrow \widetilde{\mathbf{C}}_{\gamma_1,\delta_1}$ (see Corollary 2) implies the norm convergence

$$\lim_{n\to\infty}\Big\| \mathcal{L}_n^{\alpha,\beta}\mathcal{K}_\kappa - \mathcal{K}_\kappa\Big\|_{\mathbf{L}^2_{\gamma,\delta}\to\mathbf{L}^2_{\gamma,\delta}} = 0 \tag{26}$$

if condition (25) is fulfilled for $\gamma^*=\gamma_1$ and $\delta^*=\delta_1$. For the proof of the next proposition, we need the following lemma (see [5], Lemma 16).

Lemma 5. *Let $-1<\alpha,\beta,\gamma,\delta$, $0\le\tau<\frac{1+\alpha}{2}$, $0\le\chi<\frac{1+\beta}{2}$, and $-\frac{1}{2}<\gamma-\alpha,\delta-\beta<\frac{3}{2}$ be satisfied. If the function*

$$[-1,1]\times[-1,1]\longrightarrow\mathbb{C},\quad (x,y)\mapsto g(x,y)(1-y)^\tau y^\chi$$

is continuous, then

$$\lim_{n\to\infty}\sup\Big\{ \|\mathcal{L}_n^{\alpha,\beta}g(x,\cdot)-g(x,\cdot)\|_{\gamma,\delta} : 0\le x\le 1\Big\} = 0.$$

Now, let us prove a first result on the stability and the convergence of the collocation–quadrature method (21). We have the following proposition:

Proposition 1. *Assume that the function $h(x,y)$ satisfies condition* (A) *with $\gamma_0=\delta_0=0$,*

$$\delta_1<1,\quad 1+\kappa-\gamma_1-\delta_1>0,\quad and \quad \gamma_1<\frac{1+\gamma-\max\{0,\gamma\}}{2},\ \delta_1<\frac{1+\delta}{2}. \tag{27}$$

Let $f \in \mathbf{L}^2_{\gamma,\delta}$, and $f_n \in \mathbf{P}_n$, $n \in \mathbb{N}$, with $\lim_{n\to\infty}\|f_n - f\|_{\gamma,\delta} = 0$. Furthermore, assume that

$$\kappa > -\frac{1}{2}, \quad 0 \le \gamma < 1, \quad -1 < \delta < 1, \quad \gamma + \max\{0,\delta\} < 1 + 2\kappa, \tag{28}$$

$$-\frac{1}{2} < \alpha, \quad \textit{and} \quad \frac{\delta-1}{2} < \beta, \tag{29}$$

and

$$-\frac{1}{2} < \gamma - \alpha, \delta - \beta \le 0, \tag{30}$$

$$0 \le 1 + 2\kappa + \gamma - 2\alpha + \delta - 2\beta, \quad \alpha - \kappa < \frac{1+\alpha}{2}, \quad \textit{and} \quad \beta < \frac{1+\beta}{2}, \ \textit{i.e.,}\ \beta < 1. \tag{31}$$

Then, for all sufficiently large n, the collocation–quadrature Equation (21) *has a unique solution $u_n^* \in \mathbf{P}_n$ tending to the unique solution $u^* \in \mathbf{L}^2_{\gamma,\delta}$ of Equation* (6) *in the norm of the space $\mathbf{L}^2_{\gamma,\delta}$ if n tends to infinity.*

Proof. Due to the last two inequalities in (27), the space $\widetilde{\mathbf{C}}_{\gamma_1,\delta_1}$ is continuously embedded in $\mathbf{L}^2_{\gamma,\delta}$. Hence, from Corollary 2 (see the conditions in (28)), we infer that the operator $\mathcal{I} - \mathcal{K}_\kappa : \mathbf{L}^2_{\gamma,\delta} \longrightarrow \mathbf{L}^2_{\gamma,\delta}$ is compact.

Let $u_H \in \mathbf{L}^2_{\gamma,\delta}$ be a solution of the homogeneous equation $(\mathcal{I} - \mathcal{K}_\kappa)u = 0$. Then, due to Corollary 2, u_H belongs to $\widetilde{\mathbf{C}}_{\gamma_1,\delta_1}$ and is identically zero due to Lemma 2 (see the first two conditions in (27)). Thus, the operator $\mathcal{I} - \mathcal{K}_\kappa : \mathbf{L}^2_{\gamma,\delta} \longrightarrow \mathbf{L}^2_{\gamma,\delta}$ has a trivial null space. This, together with the compactness of $\mathcal{K}_\kappa : \mathbf{L}^2_{\gamma,\delta} \longrightarrow \mathbf{L}^2_{\gamma,\delta}$ and the Fredholm alternative, leads to the invertibility of the operator $\mathcal{I} - \mathcal{K}_\kappa : \mathbf{L}^2_{\gamma,\delta} \longrightarrow \mathbf{L}^2_{\gamma,\delta}$. Thus, Equation (6) has a unique solution $u^* \in \mathbf{L}^2_{\gamma,\delta}$.

Due to our assumptions we can use definition (22) of the operator $\mathcal{K}^{\alpha,\beta}_{\kappa,n}$ (see (23) with (29) as well as the second and third inequalities in (27)). For every $u \in \mathbf{L}^2_{\gamma,\delta}$, we have

$$\begin{aligned}\left\|(\mathcal{K}_\kappa - \mathcal{L}^{\alpha,\beta}_n \mathcal{K}^{\alpha,\beta}_{\kappa,n})u\right\|_{\gamma,\delta} &\le \left\|(\mathcal{K}_\kappa - \mathcal{L}^{\alpha,\beta}_n \mathcal{K}_\kappa)u\right\|_{\gamma,\delta} + \left\|\mathcal{L}^{\alpha,\beta}_n(\mathcal{K}_\kappa - \mathcal{K}^{\alpha,\beta}_{\kappa,n})u\right\|_{\gamma,\delta} \\ &\le \left\|\mathcal{K}_\kappa - \mathcal{L}^{\alpha,\beta}_n \mathcal{K}_\kappa\right\|_{\mathbf{L}^2_{\gamma,\delta}\to\mathbf{L}^2_{\gamma,\delta}} \|u\|_{\gamma,\delta} + C\left\|(\mathcal{K}_\kappa - \mathcal{K}^{\alpha,\beta}_{\kappa,n})u\right\|_{\gamma_1,\delta_1,\infty},\end{aligned}$$

where $C = \sup\left\{\|\mathcal{L}^{\alpha,\beta}_n\|_{\widetilde{\mathbf{C}}_{\gamma_1,\delta_1}\to\mathbf{L}^2_{\gamma,\delta}} : n \in \mathbb{N}\right\} < \infty$ due to (24) (see (25) with (27), (30)), and the Banach–Steinhaus theorem. Now, we are going to prove that, for all $u \in \mathbf{L}^2_{\gamma,\delta}$,

$$\left\|(\mathcal{K}_\kappa - \mathcal{K}^{\alpha,\beta}_{\kappa,n})u\right\|_{\gamma_1,\delta_1,\infty} \le \gamma_n \|u\|_{\gamma,\delta} \quad \text{with} \quad \gamma_n \longrightarrow 0 \quad \text{if} \quad n \longrightarrow \infty. \tag{32}$$

For this, we again use the definition (22) of the operator $\mathcal{K}^{\alpha,\beta}_{\kappa,n}$ and obtain, for every $u \in \mathbf{L}^2_{\gamma,\delta}$,

$$\begin{aligned}&\left\|(\mathcal{K}_\kappa - \mathcal{K}^{\alpha,\beta}_{\kappa,n})u\right\|_{\gamma_1,\delta_1,\infty} \\ &\le \max_{0\le x\le 1} x^{1+\kappa}\int_0^1 \Big|v^{\gamma_1,\delta_1}(x)h(x,xy)v^{\kappa-\alpha,-\beta}(y) \\ &\qquad - \mathcal{L}^{\alpha,\beta}_n\big[v^{\gamma_1,\delta_1}(x)h(x,x\cdot)v^{\kappa-\alpha,-\beta}\big](y)\Big| \cdot |u(xy)| v^{\alpha,\beta}(y)\,dy \\ &\le \max_{0\le x\le 1} x^{1+\kappa}\left\|v^{\gamma_1,\delta_1}(x)h(x,x\cdot)v^{\kappa-\alpha,-\beta} - \mathcal{L}^{\alpha,\beta}_n v^{\gamma_1,\delta_1}(x)h(x,x\cdot)v^{\kappa-\alpha,-\beta}\right\|_{\gamma,\delta} \cdot \\ &\qquad \cdot \left\|u(x\cdot)v^{\alpha-\gamma,\beta-\delta}\right\|_{\gamma,\delta} \\ &\le \max_{0\le x\le 1} x^{\frac{1}{2}(1+2\kappa-2\alpha+\gamma-2\beta+\delta)} \cdot \\ &\qquad \cdot \left\|v^{\gamma_1,\delta_1}(x)h(x,x\cdot)v^{\kappa-\alpha,-\beta} - \mathcal{L}^{\alpha,\beta}_n v^{\gamma_1,\delta_1}(x)h(x,x\cdot)v^{\kappa-\alpha,-\beta}\right\|_{\gamma,\delta}\|u\|_{\gamma,\delta},\end{aligned} \tag{33}$$

where we have taken into account the estimate (note that $\gamma, \alpha-\gamma, \beta-\delta \geq 0$ due to (28) and (30))

$$\begin{aligned} & \left\| u(x\cdot)v^{\alpha-\gamma,\beta-\delta} \right\|_{\gamma,\delta}^2 \\ & = \int_0^1 |u(xy)|^2 v^{2\alpha-\gamma,2\beta-\delta}(y)\,dy \\ & = x^{-1-2\alpha+\gamma-2\beta+\delta} \int_0^x |u(z)|^2 (x-z)^{2(\alpha-\gamma)} z^{2(\beta-\delta)} (x-z)^\gamma z^\delta\,dz \\ & \leq x^{-1-2\alpha+\gamma-2\beta+\delta} \int_0^x |u(z)|^2 (1-z)^\gamma z^\delta\,dz = x^{-1-2\alpha+\gamma-2\beta+\delta} \|u\|_{\gamma,\delta}^2. \end{aligned} \tag{34}$$

Applying Lemma 5 for $g(x,y) = v^{\gamma_1,\delta_1}(x)h(x,xy)v^{\kappa-\alpha,-\beta}(y)$, $\tau = \max\{0, \alpha-\kappa\}$, and $\chi = \max\{0,\beta\}$, we get (32) with (see (31))

$$\gamma_n = \sup\left\{ \|v^{\gamma_1,\delta_1}(x)h(x,x\cdot)v^{\kappa-\alpha,-\beta} - \mathcal{L}_n^{\alpha,\beta} v^{\gamma_1,\delta_1}(x)h(x,x\cdot)v^{\kappa-\alpha,-\beta}\|_{\gamma,\delta} : 0 \leq x \leq 1 \right\}.$$

Together with (26) we obtain

$$\lim_{n\to\infty} \left\| \mathcal{L}_n^{\alpha,\beta} \mathcal{K}_{\kappa,n}^{\alpha,\beta} - \mathcal{K}_\kappa \right\|_{\mathbf{L}^2_{\gamma,\delta} \to \mathbf{L}^2_{\gamma,\delta}} = 0.$$

(Here and in what follows, $\|\mathcal{A}\|_{\mathbf{X}\to\mathbf{Y}}$ denotes the norm of the linear and bounded operator $\mathcal{A} : \mathbf{X} \longrightarrow \mathbf{Y}$ defined on the Banach space $\mathbf{X}$ and mapping into the Banach space $\mathbf{Y}$.) Now, a Neumann series argument shows that, for all sufficiently large n (say $n \geq n_0$), the operators $\mathcal{I} - \mathcal{L}_n^{\alpha,\beta}\mathcal{K}_{\kappa,n}^{\alpha,\beta} : \mathbf{L}^2_{\gamma,\delta} \longrightarrow \mathbf{L}^2_{\gamma,\delta}$ are invertible and their inverses are uniformly bounded, i.e.,

$$C^* := \sup\left\{ \left\| \left(\mathcal{I} - \mathcal{L}_n^{\alpha,\beta}\mathcal{K}_{\kappa,n}^{\alpha,\beta}\right)^{-1} \right\|_{\mathbf{L}^2_{\gamma,\delta} \to \mathbf{L}^2_{\gamma,\delta}} : n \geq n_0 \right\} < \infty, \tag{35}$$

which means that the method is stable.

Let u^* and u_n^*, $n \geq n_0$ be the unique solutions of Equations (6) and (21), respectively. Then,

$$\begin{aligned} u_n^* - u^* &= \left(\mathcal{I} - \mathcal{L}_n^{\alpha,\beta}\mathcal{K}_{\kappa,n}^{\alpha,\beta}\right)^{-1} \left[f_n - \left(\mathcal{I} - \mathcal{L}_n^{\alpha,\beta}\mathcal{K}_{\kappa,n}^{\alpha,\beta}\right) u^* \right] \\ &= \left(\mathcal{I} - \mathcal{L}_n^{\alpha,\beta}\mathcal{K}_{\kappa,n}^{\alpha,\beta}\right)^{-1} \left[f_n - f + \left(\mathcal{L}_n^{\alpha,\beta}\mathcal{K}_{\kappa,n}^{\alpha,\beta} - \mathcal{K}_\kappa\right) u^* \right]. \end{aligned} \tag{36}$$

Consequently,

$$\|u_n^* - u^*\|_{\gamma,\delta} \leq C^* \left(\|f_n - f\|_{\gamma,\delta} + \left\| \mathcal{L}_n^{\alpha,\beta}\mathcal{K}_{\kappa,n}^{\alpha,\beta} - \mathcal{K}_\kappa \right\|_{\mathbf{L}^2_{\gamma,\delta} \to \mathbf{L}^2_{\gamma,\delta}} \|u^*\|_{\gamma,\delta} \right),$$

and the proof is finished. □

In the following corollary we reformulate Proposition 1 for the case of $\alpha = \gamma$, $\beta = \delta$, and $\gamma_0 = \gamma_1 = \delta_0 = \delta_1 = 0$.

Corollary 3. *Assume that the function $h : \overline{D} \longrightarrow \mathbb{C}$ is continuous. Let $f \in \mathbf{L}^2_{\gamma,\delta}$ and $f_n \in \mathbf{P}_n$, $n \in \mathbb{N}$, with $\lim_{n\to\infty} \|f_n - f\|_{\gamma,\delta} = 0$. Assume that $\kappa > -\frac{1}{2}$, $0 \leq \gamma < 1$, $-1 < \delta < 1$, $\gamma + \max\{0,\delta\} < 1 + 2\kappa$, and $\gamma - \kappa < \frac{1+\gamma}{2}$. Then, for all sufficiently large n, the collocation–quadrature equation*

$$u_n - \mathcal{L}_n^{\gamma,\delta}\mathcal{K}_{\kappa,n}^{\gamma,\delta} u_n = f_n \tag{37}$$

has a unique solution $u_n^* \in \mathbf{P}_n$ tending to the unique solution $u^* \in \mathbf{L}^2_{\gamma,\delta}$ of Equation (6) in the norm of the space $\mathbf{L}^2_{\gamma,\delta}$ if n tends to infinity.

3.3. Convergence Rates

To prove convergence rates we recall some estimates for the interpolation error. For this, we define the space $\mathbf{W}^r$, $r \in \mathbb{N}$, of all functions $f : (0,1) \longrightarrow \mathbb{C}$, which are $r-1$ times differentiable, and the $(r-1)$-th derivative is absolutely continuous on $(0,1)$. $\mathbf{L}^p(a,b)$, $p \in (1,\infty)$ denotes the usual $\mathbf{L}^p$ space on the interval (a,b), $\mathbf{L}^p := \mathbf{L}^p(0,1)$. For $1 < p < \infty$ and all $f \in \mathbf{W}^r$, we have (see [6] (3.2.63))

$$\left\| \left(f - \mathcal{L}_n^{\alpha,\beta} f \right) v^{\frac{\gamma}{p},\frac{\delta}{p}} \right\|_{\mathbf{L}^p} \le \frac{\mathcal{C}}{n^r} \left\| f^{(r)} \varphi^r v^{\frac{\gamma}{p},\frac{\delta}{p}} \right\|_{\mathbf{L}^p}, \quad \mathcal{C} \ne \mathcal{C}(n,f), \tag{38}$$

if and only if

$$\frac{\alpha}{2} + \frac{1}{4} - \frac{1}{p} < \frac{\gamma}{p} < \frac{\alpha}{2} + \frac{5}{4} - \frac{1}{p} \quad \text{and} \quad \frac{\beta}{2} + \frac{1}{4} - \frac{1}{p} < \frac{\delta}{p} < \frac{\beta}{2} + \frac{5}{4} - \frac{1}{p},$$

where $\varphi(x) = \sqrt{(1-x)x}$. For $r \in \mathbb{N}$, we define the space

$$\mathbf{W}^r_{\gamma,\delta} = \left\{ f \in \mathbf{L}^2_{\gamma,\delta} : f^{(r-1)} \in \mathbf{AC}(0,1),\ f^{(r)} \varphi^r \in \mathbf{L}^2_{\gamma,\delta} \right\},$$

where $\mathbf{AC}(0,1)$ is the set of all absolutely continuous functions $f : (0,1) \longrightarrow \mathbb{C}$. In the case $p = 2$ and for $r \in \mathbb{N}$ and all $f \in \mathbf{W}^r_{\gamma,\delta}$, we get

$$\| f - \mathcal{L}_n^{\alpha,\beta} f \|_{\gamma,\delta} \le \frac{\mathcal{C}}{n^r} \| f^{(r)} \varphi^r \|_{\gamma,\delta}, \quad \mathcal{C} \ne \mathcal{C}(n,f), \tag{39}$$

if and only if

$$\gamma - \alpha, \delta - \beta \in \left(-\frac{1}{2}, \frac{3}{2} \right). \tag{40}$$

We will restrict ourselves to the case $\alpha = \gamma$ and $\beta = \delta$, such that condition (40) is satisfied. Nevertheless, with the help of (39), analogous but more involved considerations are possible if $\alpha \ne \gamma$ and/or $\beta \ne \delta$. Thus, we assume that the conditions of Corollary 3 are in force. Then, due to (35) and (36),

$$\|u_n^* - u^*\|_{\gamma,\delta} \le C^* \left(\|f_n - f\|_{\gamma,\delta} + C \| (\mathcal{K}^{\gamma,\delta}_{\kappa,n} - \mathcal{K}_\kappa) u^* \|_\infty + \| (\mathcal{L}_n^{\gamma,\delta} - \mathcal{I}) \mathcal{K}_\kappa u^* \|_{\gamma,\delta} \right). \tag{41}$$

Let us check which further conditions on the given data $f(x)$ and $h(x,y)$ are suitable to obtain convergence rates from estimate (41).

1. Of course, the first addend in the brackets on the right-hand side in (41) can be estimated with the help of (39) by $\mathcal{C} n^{-r} \left\| f^{(r)} \varphi^r \right\|_{\gamma,\delta}$ if we choose $f_n = \mathcal{L}_n^{\gamma,\delta} f$ and assume that $f \in \mathbf{W}^r_{\gamma,\delta}$, $r \in \mathbb{N}$.
2. Let us consider the second addend. Due to (22), we can estimate $\| (\mathcal{K}^{\gamma,\delta}_{\kappa,n} - \mathcal{K}_\kappa) u^* \|_\infty$ by

$$\sup_{0 \le x \le 1} \left| x^{1+\kappa} \int_0^1 \left[\mathcal{L}_n^{\gamma,\delta} \left[h(x, x\cdot) v^{\kappa-\gamma,-\delta} \right](y) - h(x, xy) v^{\kappa-\gamma,-\delta}(y) \right] u^*(xy) v^{\gamma,\delta}(y)\, dy \right|$$

$$\le \sup_{0 \le x \le 1} x^{1+\kappa} \| \mathcal{L}_n^{\gamma,\delta} \left[h(x, x\cdot) v^{\kappa-\gamma,-\delta} \right] - h(x, x\cdot) v^{\kappa-\gamma,-\delta} \|_{\gamma,\delta} \| u^*(x\cdot) \|_{\gamma,\delta},$$

where

$$\|u(x\cdot)\|_{\gamma,\delta}^2 = \int_0^1 |u(xy)|^2(1-y)^\gamma y^\delta\, dy = x^{-1-\gamma-\delta}\int_0^x |u(z)|^2(x-z)^\gamma z^\delta\, dz$$
$$\overset{\gamma\geq 0}{\leq} x^{-1-\gamma-\delta}\int_0^x |u(z)|^2(1-z)^\gamma z^\delta = x^{-1-\gamma-\delta}\|u\|_{\gamma,\delta}^2$$

(see (34)). Hence, since $1+2\kappa-\gamma-\delta\geq 0$ (due to the assumptions in Corollary 3),

$$\left\|(\mathcal{K}_{\kappa,n}^{\gamma,\delta}-\mathcal{K}_\kappa)u^*\right\|_\infty \leq \sup_{0\leq x\leq 1}\left\|\mathcal{L}_n^{\gamma,\delta}\left[h(x,x\cdot)v^{\kappa-\gamma,-\delta}\right]-h(x,x\cdot)v^{\kappa-\gamma,-\delta}\right\|_{\gamma,\delta}\|u^*\|_{\gamma,\delta}$$
$$\leq Cn^{-r}\|u^*\|_{\gamma,\delta}\,,$$

if

$$h(x,x\cdot)v^{\kappa-\gamma,-\delta}\in \mathbf{W}_{\gamma,\delta}^r \quad \text{uniformly with respect to} \quad x\in[0,1]\,. \tag{42}$$

This can be guaranteed if, for example, the function

$$\overline{D}\longrightarrow\mathbb{C}\,,\ (x,y)\mapsto \frac{\partial^r h(x,y)}{\partial y^r} \tag{43}$$

is continuous, and

(a) $\gamma=\kappa$, $\delta=0$.

Since $\frac{d^r}{dy^r}\left[(1-y)^\alpha y^\beta\right]=(1-y)^{\alpha-r}y^{\beta-r}g_{\alpha,\beta,r}(y)$ with $g_{\alpha,\beta,r}\in\mathbf{C}[0,1]$, we have (42) if (43) is satisfied together with

(b) $1+2\kappa-\gamma-r>0$, and $1-\delta-r>0$ (i.e. $-1<\delta<0$, and $r=1$),

or

(c) $\gamma=\kappa$, $-1<\delta<0$, and $r=1$,

or

(d) $1+2\kappa-\gamma-r>0$, and $\delta=0$.

3. For the last addend on the right-hand side of (41), we can again use (39) if we know that $\mathcal{K}_\kappa u^*\in\mathbf{W}_{\gamma,\delta}^r$. Assume that the functions

$$\overline{D}\longrightarrow\mathbb{C}\,,\ (x,y)\mapsto \frac{\partial^k}{\partial x^k}h(x,y)\,,\ k=0,1,\ldots,r, \tag{44}$$

are continuous.

(a) If $f\in\mathbf{C}[0,1]$, then, due to Lemma 3, the solution u^* also belongs to $\mathbf{C}[0,1]$. Consequently, in view of

$$(\mathcal{K}_\kappa u^*)(x)=\int_0^x h(x,y)(x-y)^\kappa u^*(x)\,dx,$$

we have $\mathcal{K}_\kappa u^*\in\mathbf{W}_{\gamma,\delta}^r$ if $\kappa\in\mathbb{N}_0$ (a non-negative integer) and $r\leq 1+\kappa$ (see (54)).

(b) If $f\in\mathbf{C}[0,1]$, $r\in\mathbb{N}$ (a positive integer), and $r-1<\kappa<r$, then we can also conclude $\mathcal{K}_\kappa u^*\in\mathbf{W}_{\gamma,\delta}^r$, since the operator $\mathcal{K}_\beta$ for $\beta>-1$ maps $\mathbf{C}$ into $\mathbf{C}$ (see Lemma 1 and (54)).

Let us summarize the considerations in items 1 to 3 in the following proposition.

Proposition 2. *Assume that the conditions of Corollary 3 are valid. Let* $u^* \in \mathbf{L}^2_{\gamma,\delta}$ *and* $u_n^* \in \mathbf{L}^2_{\gamma,\delta}$ *denote the solutions of* (6) *and* (37), *respectively. Moreover, let* $r \in \mathbb{N}$, $f \in \mathbf{W}^r_{\gamma,\delta}$, *and* $f_n = \mathcal{L}_n^{\gamma,\delta} f$, *and let the conditions* (43) *and* (44) *be fulfilled. Then, there is a constant* $C \neq C(n)$ *such that*

$$\|u_n^* - u^*\|_{\gamma,\delta} \le C n^{-r},$$

if one of conditions 2.(a)–2.(d) *and one of conditions* 3.(a)–3.(b) *are additionally satisfied by the given data.*

We see that the case where $-\frac{1}{2} < \kappa < 0$ (not prohibited in Corollary 3) does not fit the conditions of Proposition 2. That is why we consider that case separately. We assume $f \in \mathbf{C}[0,1]$, which implies $u^* \in \mathbf{C}[0,1]$ (see Lemma 1). Let $0 \le x_1 < x_2 \le 1$ and estimate

$$\begin{aligned}
|(\mathcal{K}_\kappa u^*)(x_2) - (\mathcal{K}_\kappa u^*)(x_1)| \le{}& \left| \int_{x_1}^{x_2} h(x_2,y)(x_2-y)^\kappa u^*(y)\,dy \right| \\
&+ \left| \int_0^{x-1} [h(x_2,y) - h(x_1,y)](x_2-y)^\kappa u^*(y)\,dy \right| \\
&+ \left| \int_0^{x_1} h(x_1,y)[(x_2-y)^\kappa - (x_1-y)^\kappa] u^*(y)\,dy \right| \\
=:{}& J_1 + J_2 + J_3,
\end{aligned}$$

where, with the notation $\|u^*\|_\infty = \|u^*\|_{0,0,\infty}$,

$$J_1 \le \|h\|_\infty \|u^*\|_\infty \int_{x_1}^{x_2} (x_2-y)^\kappa\,dy = \|h\|_\infty \|u^*\|_\infty \frac{1}{1+\kappa}(x_2-x_1)^{1+\kappa},$$

$$J_2 \le \|u^*\|_\infty \sup_{0\le y\le x_1} |h(x_2,y) - h(x_1,y)| \frac{1}{1+\kappa}\left[x_2^{1+\kappa} - (x_2-x_1)^{1+\kappa}\right],$$

$$J_3 \le \|h\|_\infty \|u^*\|_\infty \frac{1}{1+\kappa}\left[x_2^{1+\kappa} - x_1^{1+\kappa} + (x_2-x_1)^{1+\kappa}\right] \le \frac{2\|h\|_\infty \|u^*\|_\infty}{1+\kappa}(x_2-x_1)^{1+\kappa}.$$

Hence, if we assume that the function $h(x,y)$ is uniformly Hölder-continuous in x with exponent $1+\kappa$ with respect to y, i.e.,

$$\sup_{0\le y\le x_1} |h(x_2,y) - h(x_1,y)| \le C(x_2-x_1)^{1+\kappa} \tag{45}$$

$\forall\, x_1, x_2,\ 0 \le x_1 < x_2 \le 1,\ C \neq C(x_1,x_2)$, then we have

$$\mathcal{K}_\kappa u^* \in \mathbf{C}^{1+\kappa}[0,1], \tag{46}$$

where $\mathbf{C}^\chi[0,1]$ denotes the space of Hölder-continuous functions on $[0,1]$ (with Hölder exponent $\chi \in (0,1]$).

For a function g satisfying $gu \in \mathbf{L}^p(0,1)$ for a Jacobi weight function $w \in \mathbf{L}^p(0,1)$ and some $p \in (1,\infty)$, we introduce the main part of the weighted modulus of smoothness:

$$\Omega^r_\varphi(g,t)_{w,p} = \sup_{0<h\le t} \left\| \left(\Delta^r_{h\varphi} g\right) w \right\|_{\mathbf{L}^p(4h^2,1-4h^2)},$$

where, for $r \in \mathbb{N}$,

$$\left(\Delta^r_{h\varphi} g\right)(x) = \sum_{k=0}^r (-1)^k \binom{r}{k} g\left(x + \left(\frac{r}{2} - k\right) h\varphi(x)\right).$$

Let us recall the relation (see [7], Theorem 3.1)

$$\left\|\left(g-\mathcal{L}_n^{\gamma,\delta}g\right)w\right\|_{\mathbf{L}^p}\le Cn^{-\frac{1}{p}}\int_0^{\frac{1}{n}}\frac{\Omega_\varphi^r(g,t)_{w,p}\,dt}{t^{1+\frac{1}{p}}},\quad C\neq C(n,g), \tag{47}$$

which is true if and only if

$$\frac{w}{\sqrt{v^{\gamma,\delta}\varphi}}\in\mathbf{L}^p(0,1)\quad\text{and}\quad\frac{\sqrt{v^{\gamma,\delta}\varphi}}{w}\in\mathbf{L}^q(0,1),\quad\frac{1}{p}+\frac{1}{q}=1. \tag{48}$$

Note that, when $w=v^{\gamma_1,\delta_1}$, condition (48) is equivalent to

$$\frac{\gamma}{2}+\frac{1}{4}-\frac{1}{p}<\gamma_1<\frac{\gamma}{2}+\frac{5}{4}-\frac{1}{p}\quad\text{and}\quad\frac{\delta}{2}+\frac{1}{4}-\frac{1}{p}<\delta_1<\frac{\delta}{2}+\frac{5}{4}-\frac{1}{p}. \tag{49}$$

Corollary 4. *Let $-\frac{1}{2}<\kappa<0$ and $-\frac{1}{2}\le\delta<1$. In additional to the conditions of Corollary 3, assume that $h(\cdot,y)\in\mathbf{C}^{1+\kappa}[0,1]$ holds uniformly with respect to $y\in[0,1]$ (see (45)), the function $\overline{D}\longrightarrow\mathbb{C}$, $(x,y)\mapsto\frac{\partial}{\partial y}h(x,y)$ is continuous, $f\in\mathbf{C}^{1+\kappa}[0,1]$, and $f_n=\mathcal{L}_n^{\gamma,\delta}f$. Then, there is a constant $C\neq C(n)$ such that, for all sufficiently large n,*

$$\|u_n^*-u^*\|_{\gamma,\delta}\le Cn^{-(1+\kappa)},$$

where u_n^* and u^* are the unique solutions in $\mathbf{L}^2_{\gamma,\delta}$ of (37) and (6), respectively.

Proof. Due to the above considerations and our assumptions, we have $\mathcal{K}_\kappa u^*\in\mathbf{C}^{1+\kappa}[0,1]$. Consequently, $\Omega_\varphi^1(\mathcal{K}_\kappa u^*,t)_{u,2}\le Ct^{1+\kappa}$, which follows directly from the definition of $\Omega_\varphi^1(g,t)_{u,p}$ using $\left|(\mathcal{K}_\kappa u^*)(x+\frac{h}{2})-(\mathcal{K}_\kappa u^*)(x-\frac{h}{2})\right|\le Ch^{1+\kappa}$. When $u=v^{\frac{\gamma}{2},\frac{\delta}{2}}$ and $p=q=2$, condition (49) is satisfied, so that from (47) we can infer

$$\left\|(\mathcal{L}_n^{\gamma,\delta}-\mathcal{I})\mathcal{K}_\kappa u^*\right\|_{\gamma,\delta}\le Cn^{-(1+\kappa)}.$$

The same convergence rate is obtained for the first addend on the right-hand side of (41) since $f\in\mathbf{C}^{1+\kappa}[0,1]$ and $f_n=\mathcal{L}_n^{\gamma,\delta}f$ are assumed.

It remains to estimate the second addend. For this, set $g_x(y)=h(x,xy)v^{\kappa-\gamma,-\delta}(y)$. Moreover, let $\gamma_0+\gamma_1=\gamma$ and $\delta_0+\delta_1=\delta$. Then, from (22),

$$\begin{aligned}\left\|(\mathcal{K}_{\kappa,n}^{\gamma,\delta}-\mathcal{K}_\kappa)u^*\right\|_\infty&=\sup_{0\le x\le1}\left|x^{1+\kappa}\int_0^1\left[(\mathcal{L}_n^{\gamma,\delta}g_x)(y)-g_x(y)\right]u^*(xy)v^{\gamma,\delta}(y)\,dy\right|\\&\le\sup_{0\le x\le1}\|(\mathcal{L}_n^{\gamma,\delta}g_x-g_x)v^{\gamma_0,\delta_0}\|_{\mathbf{L}^2}\|u^*(x\cdot)v^{\gamma_1,\delta_1}\|_{\mathbf{L}^2}.\end{aligned} \tag{50}$$

Since the solution u^* is a continuous function, we have

$$\|u(x\cdot)v^{\gamma_1,\delta_1}\|_{\mathbf{L}^2}^2=\int_0^1|u^*(xy)|^2v^{2\gamma_1,2\delta_1}(y)\,dy\le C\neq C(x)<\infty,$$

if $\gamma_1,\delta_1>-\frac{1}{2}$. From (38) we conclude

$$\|(\mathcal{L}_n^{\gamma,\delta}g_x-g_x)v^{\gamma_0,\delta_0}\|_{\mathbf{L}^2}\le Cn^{-1}\|g_x'\varphi v^{\gamma_0,\delta_0}\|_{\mathbf{L}^2}$$

if $\frac{\gamma}{2}-\frac{1}{4}<\gamma_0<\frac{\gamma}{2}-\frac{3}{4}$ and $\frac{\delta}{2}-\frac{1}{4}<\delta_0<\frac{\delta}{2}-\frac{3}{4}$. Thus, we have to show that γ_0,δ_0 and γ_1,δ_1 can be chosen in such a way that the norm $\|g_x'\varphi v^{\gamma_0,\delta_0}\|_{\mathbf{L}^2}$ can be bounded by a constant $C\neq C(x)$.

We choose γ_0, δ_0 and γ_1, δ_1 so that $\gamma_0 + \gamma_1 = \gamma$, $\delta_0 + \delta_1 = \delta$, $\gamma_0 > \gamma - \kappa$, $\delta_0 > \delta$, and $\gamma_1, \delta_1 > -\frac{1}{2}$. This is possible, since $\kappa > -\frac{1}{2}$ and $\delta - \frac{1}{2} < \delta$. The inequalities $\gamma < 1 + 2\kappa$ and $\delta < 1$ ensure that γ_0 and δ_0 can be chosen in such a way that $\gamma_0 < \frac{\gamma}{2} + \frac{3}{4}$ and $\delta_0 < \frac{\delta}{2} + \frac{3}{4}$. Furthermore, we have

$$\frac{\gamma}{2} - \frac{1}{4} < \frac{1}{2}\left(\gamma + \frac{1}{2}\right) - \kappa - \frac{1}{2} < \gamma + \frac{1}{2} - \kappa - \frac{1}{2} = \gamma - \kappa < \gamma_0$$

and

$$\frac{\delta}{2} - \frac{1}{4} = \frac{1}{2}\left(\delta + \frac{1}{2}\right) - \frac{1}{2} < \delta < \delta_0.$$

Finally, since

$$|g_x'(y)|\varphi(y)v^{\gamma_0,\delta_0}(y) \leq C(1-y)^{\gamma_0+\kappa-\gamma-\frac{1}{2}}y^{\delta_0-\delta-\frac{1}{2}}, \quad C \neq C(x,y),$$

and $\gamma_0 + \kappa - \gamma > 0$, $\delta_0 - \delta > 0$, we have $\|g_x'\varphi v^{\gamma_0,\delta_0}\|_{\mathbf{L}^2} \leq C \neq C(x)$, which finishes the proof of the corollary. □

3.4. *Uniform Convergence*

In the previous sections, the studies were restricted to the case where $\kappa > -\frac{1}{2}$. The reason for this is the respective condition in Lemma 3, which is important for the proof of the stability of the collocation–quadrature method in the $\mathbf{L}^2_{\gamma,\delta}$ space (see the proof of Proposition 1). As one can see from Corollary 5, under certain conditions the operator $\mathcal{K}_\kappa : \mathbf{C} \longrightarrow \mathbf{C}$ is compact for $\kappa > -1$. That is why we studied the collocation–quadrature method (37) in the $\mathbf{C}$ space, which allowed us to prove convergence rates in the infinity norm.

If $A = A(x,n,\ldots)$ and $B = B(x,n,\ldots)$ are two positive functions depending on certain parameters $n, x, \ldots$, then we use the notion $A \sim_{x,n,\ldots} B$ if there is a positive constant $C \neq C(x,n,\ldots)$ such that $C^{-1}B \leq A \leq CB$. Let us recall the following classical result on the Lebesgue constant $\|\mathcal{L}_n^{\gamma,\delta}\|_{\mathbf{C}\to\mathbf{C}}$, being the norm of the interpolation operator $\mathcal{L}_n^{\gamma,\delta}$ in the $\mathbf{C}$ space.

Lemma 6 ([8], Theorem 14.4, p. 335). *For all $n \in \mathbb{N}$, we have*

$$\|\mathcal{L}_n^{\gamma,\delta}\|_{\mathbf{C}\to\mathbf{C}} \sim_n \begin{cases} 1 + \log n & : \quad -1 < \gamma, \delta \leq -\frac{1}{2}, \\ n^{\max\{\gamma,\delta\}+\frac{1}{2}} & : \quad \text{otherwise.} \end{cases}$$

Note that, for $f \in \mathbf{C}$ and every $p \in \mathbf{P}_n$,

$$\|f - \mathcal{L}_n^{\gamma,\delta} f\|_\infty = \|f - p + \mathcal{L}_n^{\gamma,\delta}(p - f)\|_\infty \leq (1 + \|\mathcal{L}_n^{\gamma,\delta}\|_{\mathbf{C}\to\mathbf{C}})\|p - f\|_\infty.$$

Hence,

$$\|f - \mathcal{L}_n^{\gamma,\delta} f\|_\infty \leq (1 + \|\mathcal{L}_n^{\gamma,\delta}\|_{\mathbf{C}\to\mathbf{C}})E_n(f)_\infty, \tag{51}$$

where $E_n(f)_\infty$ denotes the best approximation of f by polynomials $p \in \mathbf{P}_n$ in the infinity norm,

$$E_n(f)_\infty = \inf_{p\in\mathbf{P}_n} \|p - f\|_\infty.$$

We remember the following inequality (see [9], (2.5.22)):

$$E_n(f)_\infty \leq \frac{C}{n^r}\|f^{(r)}\varphi^r\|_\infty, \quad N, r \in \mathbb{N}, \quad C \neq C(n,f), \tag{52}$$

which is true for all $f \in \mathbf{C}$ satisfying $f^{(r)}\varphi^r \in \mathbf{C}$ and is a consequence of the iterated Favard inequality

$$E_n(f)_\infty \le \frac{C}{n^r} E_{N-r}\left(f^{(r)}\right)_{\varphi^r,\infty}, \quad f^{(r)}\varphi^r \in C,\ n > r \in \mathbb{N},\ C \ne C(n,f), \tag{53}$$

with $E_n(f)_{\varphi^r,\infty} = \inf_{p\in\mathbf{P}_n} \left\|(p-\psi)\varphi^r\right\|_\infty$. In what follows we will assume that, for some $r \in \mathbb{N}_0$,

(D) the functions $\overline{D} \longrightarrow \mathbb{C}, \quad (x,y) \mapsto \dfrac{\partial^k h(x,y)}{\partial x^k}, k = 0,1,\dots,r,$ are continuous.

If $\kappa \ge 0$ and $u \in \mathbf{C}$, then one can see by induction and

$$(\mathcal{K}_\kappa u)'(x) = \begin{cases} \displaystyle\int_0^x \left[\frac{\partial h(x,y)}{\partial x}(x-y)^\kappa + \kappa\, h(x,y)(x-y)^{\kappa-1}\right] u(y)\,dy & : \ \kappa > 0, \\ \displaystyle\int_0^x \frac{\partial h(x,y)}{\partial x} u(y)\,dy + h(x,x)u(x) & : \ \kappa = 0, \end{cases} \tag{54}$$

that $\mathcal{K}_\kappa u$ belongs to $\mathbf{C}^{(r)}$ if $r \le 1+\kappa$. Moreover, there is a constant $C \ne C(x,u)$ such that, for all $u \in \mathbf{C}$ and all $x \in [0,1]$,

$$\left|(\mathcal{K}_\kappa u)^{(r)}(x)\right| \le C\|u\|_\infty. \tag{55}$$

For example, for $r = 1$ and $\kappa > 0$ we can take

$$C = \sup_{0\le x\le 1} \int_0^x \left[\left|\frac{\partial h(x,y)}{\partial x}\right|(x-y)^\kappa + \kappa\,|h(x,y)|(x-y)^{\kappa-1}\right] dy.$$

If we define the weighted modulus of smoothness $\omega_\varphi(f,t)_\infty$ as

$$\omega_\varphi(f,t)_\infty = \sup_{0<h\le t} \left\| f\left(\cdot + \frac{h\varphi}{2}\right) - f\left(\cdot - \frac{h\varphi}{2}\right)\right\|_\infty,$$

where $f\left(x \pm \frac{h\varphi(x)}{2}\right) := 0$ if $x \pm \frac{h\varphi(x)}{2} \notin [0,1]$, then the following Lemma is true (see [10], Theorem 7.2.19):

Lemma 7. *For $f \in \mathbf{C}$ and $n \in \mathbb{N}$,*

$$E_n(f)_\infty \le C\omega_\varphi(f,n^{-1})_\infty, \quad C \ne C(n,f).$$

In the following lemma we estimate the norm of the linear operator $\mathcal{K}_\kappa - \mathcal{K}_{\kappa,n}^{\gamma,\delta} : \mathbf{C} \longrightarrow \mathbf{C}$ for certain constellations of the parameters γ, δ and κ.

Lemma 8. *Let $h(x,y)$ satisfy condition* (D) *and $\gamma,\delta,\kappa > -1$. Then, for all $n \in \mathbb{N}$ and $f \in \mathbf{C}$,*

$$\left\|(\mathcal{K}_\kappa - \mathcal{K}_{\kappa,n}^{\gamma,\delta})f\right\|_\infty \le Cn^{-\rho}\|f\|_\infty, \quad C \ne C(n,f)),$$

where

(a) $\rho = r$, if $\kappa - \gamma \in \mathbb{N}_0$, $\delta = 0$, and $r \in \mathbb{N}$;
(b) $\rho = 1$, if $\kappa - \gamma \in \mathbb{N}_0$, $-\frac{1}{2} \le \delta < 0$ or $0 < \delta < \frac{3}{2}$, and $r = 1$;
(c) $\rho = \kappa - \gamma$, if $r - 1 < \kappa - \gamma < r$, $\delta = 0$, and $r \in \mathbb{N}$;
(d) $\rho = \min\{\kappa - \delta, -\delta\}$, if $0 < \kappa - \gamma < 1$, $-1 < \delta < 0$, and $r = 1$.

Proof. Note that we can use definition (22) for the operator $\mathcal{K}_{\kappa,n}^{\gamma,\delta} : \mathbf{C} \longrightarrow \mathbf{C}$ without further conditions like (23) in case of the $\mathbf{L}^2_{\gamma,\delta}$ space. As in (50) we have, for $1 < p < \infty$ and $f \in \mathbf{C}$,

$$\begin{aligned} \left\|(\mathcal{K}_\kappa - \mathcal{K}_{\kappa,n}^{\gamma,\delta})f\right\|_\infty &\le \sup_{0\le x\le 1} \left\|(g_x - \mathcal{L}_n^{\gamma,\delta} g_x)v^{\gamma_0,\delta_0}\right\|_{\mathbf{L}^p} \left\|f(x\cdot)v^{\gamma_1,\delta_1}\right\|_{\mathbf{L}^q} \\ &\le \sup_{0\le x\le 1} \left\|(g_x - \mathcal{L}_n^{\gamma,\delta} g_x)v^{\gamma_0,\delta_0}\right\|_{\mathbf{L}^p} \left\|v^{\gamma_1,\delta_1}\right\|_{\mathbf{L}^q} \|f\|_\infty , \end{aligned} \tag{56}$$

where $g_x(y) = h(x,xy)v^{\kappa-\gamma,-\delta}(y)$, $\frac{1}{p}+\frac{1}{q} = 1$, $\gamma_1, \delta_1 > -\frac{1}{q} = \frac{1}{p} - 1$, and $\gamma_0 + \gamma_1 = \gamma$, $\delta_0 + \delta_1 = \delta$.

If $\kappa - \gamma \in \mathbb{N}_0$ and $\delta = 0$, then $g_x \in \mathbf{C}^{(r)}[0,1]$ holds uniformly with respect to $x \in [0,1]$. With $\gamma_0 = \gamma_1 = \frac{\gamma}{2}$ and $\delta_0 = \delta_1 = \frac{\delta}{2}$ in (56), we obtain, due to (39),

$$\sup_{0\le x\le 1} \left\|(g_x - \mathcal{L}_n^{\gamma,\delta} g_x)v^{\gamma_0,\delta_0}\right\|_{\mathbf{L}^2} = \sup_{0\le x\le 1} \left\|g_x - \mathcal{L}_n^{\gamma,\delta} g_x\right\|_{\gamma,\delta} \le Cn^{-r},$$

and (a) is proven.

If $\kappa - \gamma$ is a non-negative integer, $-\frac{1}{2} \le \delta < \frac{3}{2}$, and $r = 1$, then $g_x'(y) = g_1(x,y)y^{-\delta-1}$ with a continuous function $g_1 : [0,1]^2 \longrightarrow \mathbb{C}$. We choose γ_0, γ_1 such that $\frac{\gamma}{2} + \frac{1}{4} - \frac{1}{p} < \gamma_0 < \frac{\gamma}{2} + \frac{5}{4} - \frac{1}{p}$ and $\delta_1 > \frac{1}{p} - 1$, which is possible because of $\left(\frac{\gamma}{2} + \frac{1}{4} - \frac{1}{p}\right) + \left(\frac{1}{p} - 1\right) = \frac{\gamma}{2} - \frac{3}{4} < \gamma$. Furthermore, we can choose δ_0, δ_1 such that $\frac{\delta}{2} + \frac{5}{4} - \frac{1}{p} > \delta_0 > \delta + \frac{1}{2} - \frac{1}{p}$ (i.e., $g_x'\varphi v^{\gamma_0,\delta_0} \in \mathbf{L}^p$) and $\delta_1 > \frac{1}{p} - 1$, which is possible since $\left(\delta + \frac{1}{2} - \frac{1}{p}\right) + \left(\frac{1}{p} - 1\right) = \delta - \frac{1}{2} < \delta$. Finally, we have $\frac{\delta}{2} + \frac{1}{4} - \frac{1}{p} \le \delta + \frac{1}{2} - \frac{1}{p} < \frac{\delta}{2} + \frac{5}{4} - \frac{1}{p}$ due to $-\frac{1}{2} \le \delta < \frac{3}{2}$. Consequently, from (38) we can infer

$$\left\|(g_x - \mathcal{L}_n^{\gamma,\delta} g_x)v^{\gamma_0,\delta_0}\right\|_{\mathbf{L}^p} \le Cn^{-1}\left\|g_x'\varphi v^{\gamma_0,\delta_0}\right\|_{\mathbf{L}^p} \le Cn^{-1}, \quad C \ne C(x)$$

to obtain assertion (b).

If $r - 1 < \kappa - \gamma < r$ for some $r \in \mathbb{N}$ and $\delta = 0$, then $g_x^{(r-1)} \in \mathbf{C}^{\kappa-\gamma-r+1}[0,1]$, where

$$\left|g_x^{(r-1)}(y_1) - g_x^{(r-1)}(y_2)\right| \le C|y_1 - y_2|^{\kappa-\gamma-r+1}, \quad y_1, y_2 \in [0,1],\ C \ne C(x).$$

From this we obtain

$$\Omega_\varphi^r(g_x, t)_{v^{\gamma_0,\delta_0}} \le Ct^{\kappa-\gamma}. \tag{57}$$

Indeed, from the mean value theorem, we have

$$\begin{aligned} \left(\Delta_{h\varphi}^2 f\right)(x) &= f(x + h\varphi(x)) - 2f(x) + f(x - h\varphi(x)) \\ &= [f(x + h\varphi(x)) - f(x)] - [f(x) - f(x - h\varphi(x))] \\ &= [f'(\xi_2) - f'(\xi_1)]h\varphi(x), \end{aligned}$$

where $x - h\varphi(x) \le \xi_1 \le x \le \xi_2 \le x + h\varphi(x)$. Hence,

$$\begin{aligned} \left(\Delta_{h\varphi}^3 f\right)(x) &= \left(\Delta_{h\varphi}^1\left(\Delta_{h\varphi}^2 f\right)\right)(x) = \left(\Delta_{h\varphi}^2 f\right)\left(x + \frac{h}{2}\varphi(x)\right) - \left(\Delta_{h\varphi}^2 f\right)\left(x - \frac{h}{2}\varphi(x)\right) \\ &= [f'(\eta_4) - f'(\eta_3)]h\varphi(x) - [f'(\eta_2) - f'(\eta_1)]h\varphi(x) \\ &= [f''(\zeta_2)(\eta_4 - \eta_3) - f''(\zeta_1)(\eta_2 - \eta_1)]h\varphi(x) \end{aligned}$$

with $x - \frac{3}{2}h\varphi(x) \le \eta_1 \le x - \frac{h}{2}\varphi(x) \le \eta_2, \eta_3 \le x + \frac{h}{2}\varphi(x) \le \eta_4 \le x + \frac{3}{2}h\varphi(x)$ as well as $x - \frac{3}{2}h\varphi(x) \le \zeta_1, \zeta_2 \le x + \frac{3}{2}h\varphi(x)$. Consequently, $\left|\left(\Delta^3_{h\varphi}f\right)(x)\right| \le C|f''(\zeta_2) - f''(\zeta_1)|[h\varphi(x)]^2$. Since $\left(\Delta^r_{h\varphi}f\right)(x) = \left(\Delta^1_{h\varphi}\left(\Delta^{r-1}_{h\varphi}f\right)\right)(x)$ we obtain by induction

$$\left(\Delta^r_{h\varphi}f\right)(x) \le C\left|f^{(r-1)}(\omega_2) - f^{(r-1)}(\omega_1)\right|[h\varphi(x)]^{r-1}$$

for some $\omega_1, \omega_2 \in \left[x - \frac{r}{2}h\varphi(x), x + \frac{r}{2}h\varphi(x)\right]$. This leads to

$$\begin{aligned}\left|\left(\Delta^r_{h\varphi}g_x\right)(x)\right| &\le C\left|g_x^{(r-1)}(\omega_2) - g_x^{(r-1)}(\omega_1)\right|[h\varphi(x)]^{r-1} \\ &\le C|\omega_2 - \omega_1|^{\kappa-\gamma-r+1}[h\varphi(x)]^{r-1} \le Ch^{\kappa-\gamma},\end{aligned}$$

from which (57) follows.

Now, choose a large enough $p \in (1, \infty)$ such that $\kappa - \gamma > \frac{1}{p}$, $\gamma_1, \delta_1 > \frac{1}{p} - 1$, $\frac{\gamma}{2} + \frac{1}{4} - \frac{1}{p} < \gamma_0 < \frac{\gamma}{2} + \frac{5}{4} - \frac{1}{p}$, $\gamma_0 + \gamma_1 = \gamma$, $\delta_0 = -\delta_1$, and $\frac{1}{4} - \frac{1}{p} < \delta_0 < \frac{5}{4} - \frac{1}{p}$. This is possible, since $\left(\frac{\gamma}{2} + \frac{1}{4} - \frac{1}{p}\right) + \left(\frac{1}{p} - 1\right) = \frac{\gamma}{2} - \frac{3}{4} < \gamma$ and $\left(\frac{1}{4} - \frac{1}{p}\right) + \left(\frac{1}{p} - 1\right) = -\frac{3}{4} < 0 = \delta_0 + \delta_1 < \frac{9}{4} - \frac{2}{p} = \left(\frac{5}{4} - \frac{1}{p}\right) + \left(1 - \frac{1}{p}\right)$. Applying (47) yields

$$\left\|(g_x - \mathcal{L}_n^{\gamma,\delta}g_x)v^{\gamma_0,\delta_0}\right\|_{\mathbf{L}^p} \le Cn^{-\frac{1}{p}}\int_0^{\frac{1}{n}} t^{\kappa-\gamma-1-\frac{1}{p}}\,dt = Cn^{-(\kappa-\gamma)},$$

and the proof of (c) is finished.

Assertion (d) can be proved analogously to (c). □

Proposition 3. *Assume that $\kappa \in \mathbb{N}_0$ and that, for some $r \in \mathbb{N}$, the kernel function $h(x,y)$ fulfills condition* (D). *Furthermore, assume that the right-hand side of* (6) *belongs to $\mathbf{C}^{(r)}$. Moreover, let $\gamma, \delta > -1$ be chosen in such a way that one of the conditions* (a)–(d) *of Lemma 8 and the condition*

$$\max\{\gamma,\delta\} + \frac{1}{2} < \min\{1+\kappa, \rho\} \tag{58}$$

with ρ defined in Lemma 8 are satisfied. Then, for all sufficiently large n, the collocation–quadrature Equation (37) *has a unique solution $u_n^* \in \mathbf{C}$, which converges in the infinity norm to the unique solution $u^* \in \mathbf{C}$ of* (6), *where, for $f_n = \mathcal{L}_n^{\gamma,\delta}f$,*

$$\|u_n^* - u^*\|_\infty \le Cn^{-\rho}\left\|\mathcal{L}_n^{\gamma,\delta}\right\|_{\mathbf{C}\to\mathbf{C}} \tag{59}$$

with a constant $C \ne C(n)$.

Proof. The unique solvability of (6) in $\mathbf{C}$ is guaranteed by Lemma 1. Now, our aim is to estimate

$$\left\|\mathcal{K}_\kappa - \mathcal{L}_n^{\gamma,\delta}\mathcal{K}_{\kappa,n}^{\gamma,\delta}\right\|_{\mathbf{C}\to\mathbf{C}} \le \left\|\mathcal{K}_\kappa - \mathcal{L}_n^{\gamma,\delta}\mathcal{K}_\kappa\right\|_{\mathbf{C}\to\mathbf{C}} + \left\|\mathcal{L}_n^{\gamma,\delta}\right\|_{\mathbf{C}\to\mathbf{C}}\left\|\mathcal{K}_\kappa - \mathcal{K}_{\kappa,n}^{\gamma,\delta}\right\|_{\mathbf{C}\to\mathbf{C}}. \tag{60}$$

For the second addend on the right-hand side, we can use Lemma 6 and Lemma 8, while for the first addend we take into account $\mathcal{K}_\kappa g \in \mathbf{C}^{(s)}$ and $\left|(\mathcal{K}_\kappa g)^{(s)}(x)\right| \le C\|g\|_\infty$ for all $g \in \mathbf{C}$ and $s = 1 + \kappa$ (see (55)). Hence, due to (51) and (52),

$$\left\|\mathcal{K}_\kappa g - \mathcal{L}_n^{\gamma,\delta}\mathcal{K}_\kappa g\right\|_\infty \le Cn^{-(1+\kappa)}\left\{\begin{array}{ccc} 1 + \log n & : & -1 < \gamma,\delta \le -\frac{1}{2} \\ n^{\max\{\gamma,\delta\}+\frac{1}{2}} & : & \text{otherwise} \end{array}\right\}\|g\|_\infty.$$

Thus, from (59) together with (58), we infer

$$\|\mathcal{K}_\kappa - \mathcal{L}_n^{\gamma,\delta}\mathcal{K}_{\kappa,n}^{\gamma,\delta}\|_{\mathbf{C}\to\mathbf{C}} \le \mathcal{C}\left(n^{-(1+\kappa)} + n^{-\rho}\right)\left\{\begin{array}{ccc} 1+\log n & : & -1<\gamma,\delta\le -\frac{1}{2} \\ n^{\max\{\gamma,\delta\}+\frac{1}{2}} & : & \text{otherwise} \end{array}\right\} \longrightarrow 0,$$

which, in view of the invertibility of the operator $\mathcal{I}-\mathcal{K}_\kappa : \mathbf{C} \longrightarrow \mathbf{C}$ and a standard Neumann series argument, implies the invertibility of $\mathcal{I}-\mathcal{L}_n^{\gamma,\delta}\mathcal{K}_{\kappa,n}^{\gamma,\delta} : \mathbf{C} \longrightarrow \mathbf{C}$ for all sufficiently large n, say $n > n_0$, and

$$\mathcal{C}_* := \sup\left\{\left\|\left(\mathcal{I}-\mathcal{L}_n^{\gamma,\delta}\mathcal{K}_{\kappa,n}^{\gamma,\delta}\right)^{-1}\right\|_{\mathbf{C}\to\mathbf{C}}\right\} < \infty.$$

Since $\kappa \ge 0$, from (54) and $u^* = f + \mathcal{K}_\kappa u^*$, we conclude $u^* \in \mathbf{C}^{(1)}$. By induction we obtain $\mathcal{K}_\kappa u^* \in \mathbf{C}^{(r)}$ and, for $f_n = \mathcal{L}_n^{\gamma,\delta} f$,

$$\begin{aligned}
&\|u_n^* - u^*\|_\infty \\
&\quad\le \mathcal{C}_*\left\|\left(\mathcal{I}-\mathcal{K}_{\kappa,n}^{\gamma,\delta}\right)(u_n^*-u^*)\right\|_\infty \\
&\quad\le \mathcal{C}_*\left(\left\|\mathcal{L}_n^{\gamma,\delta}f - f\right\|_\infty + \left\|\mathcal{K}_\kappa u^* - \mathcal{L}_n^{\gamma,\delta}\mathcal{K}_\kappa u^*\right\|_\infty + \left\|\mathcal{L}_n^{\gamma,\delta}\right\|_{\mathbf{C}\to\mathbf{C}}\left\|\mathcal{K}_\kappa - \mathcal{K}_{\kappa,n}^{\gamma,\delta}\right\|_{\mathbf{C}\to\mathbf{C}}\|u^*\|_\infty\right) \\
&\quad\le \mathcal{C}\left\|\mathcal{L}_n^{\gamma,\delta}\right\|_{\mathbf{C}\to\mathbf{C}} n^{-\rho},
\end{aligned}$$

taking into account (51) and (52) as well as Lemma 8, together with $\rho \le r$. This completes the proof. □

Proposition 4. *Let $r \in \mathbb{N}_0$, $r-1<\kappa<r$, and condition* (D) *be satisfied, where*

$$\sup_{0\le y\le x_1}\left|\frac{\partial^r h(x_2,y)}{\partial y^r} - \frac{\partial^r h(x_1,y)}{\partial y^r}\right| \le \mathcal{C}(x_2-x_1)^{\chi_0} \quad \forall\, x_1,x_2,\ 0\le x_1<x_2\le 1,\ \mathcal{C}\ne\mathcal{C}(x_1,x_2),$$

for a certain number $\chi_0 \in (0,1]$. Moreover, let $f \in \mathbf{C}^{(r)}$ with $f^{(r)} \in \mathbf{C}^{\min\{\chi_0,1+\kappa-r\}}[0,1]$. Assume that the parameters $\gamma,\delta > -1$ fulfill one of the conditions (a)–(d) *as well as condition* (58)*. Then, for all sufficiently large n, the collocation–quadrature Equation* (37) *has a unique solution $u_n^* \in \mathbf{C}$, which converges in the infinity norm to the unique solution $u^* \in \mathbf{C}$ of* (6)*, where, for $f_n = \mathcal{L}_n^{\gamma,\delta} f$,*

$$\|u_n^* - u^*\|_\infty \le \mathcal{C} n^{-\chi}\left\|\mathcal{L}_n^{\gamma,\delta}\right\|_{\mathbf{C}\to\mathbf{C}} \tag{61}$$

with $\chi = \min\{\chi_0 + r, 1+\kappa, \rho\}$ and a constant $\mathcal{C} \ne \mathcal{C}(n)$.

Proof. We can proceed as in the proof for the previous proposition. We only have to check the estimate of $\left\|\mathcal{K}_\kappa u^* - \mathcal{L}_n^{\gamma,\delta}\mathcal{K}_\kappa u^*\right\|_\infty$. Since $r-1<\kappa<r$, from the proof of (46), we can infer $\left(\mathcal{K}_\kappa u\right)^{(r)} \in \mathbf{C}^{\min\{\chi_0,1+\kappa\}-r}[0,1]$, where

$$\left|\left(\mathcal{K}_\kappa u\right)^{(r)}(x_1) - \left(\mathcal{K}_\kappa u\right)^{(r)}(x_2)\right| \le \mathcal{C}\|u\|_\infty |x_1-x_2|^{\min\{\chi_0,1+\kappa-r\}}, \tag{62}$$

$x_1,x_2 \in [0,1]$, $u \in \mathbf{C}$, $\mathcal{C} \ne \mathcal{C}(u,x_1,x_2)$. This leads to

$$\begin{aligned}\|\mathcal{K}_\kappa u^* - \mathcal{L}_n^{\gamma,\delta}\mathcal{K}_\kappa u^*\|_\infty &\overset{(51)}{\leq} (1+\|\mathcal{L}_n^{\gamma,\delta}\|_{\mathbf{C}\to\mathbf{C}})E_n(\mathcal{K}_\kappa u^*)_\infty \\ &\overset{(53)}{\leq} \mathcal{C}n^{-r}(1+\|\mathcal{L}_n^{\gamma,\delta}\|_{\mathbf{C}\to\mathbf{C}})E_{n-r}((\mathcal{K}_\kappa u^*)^{(r)})_\infty \\ &\overset{\text{Lemma 7}}{\leq} \mathcal{C}n^{-r}(1+\|\mathcal{L}_n^{\gamma,\delta}\|_{\mathbf{C}\to\mathbf{C}})\omega_\varphi((\mathcal{K}_\kappa u^*)^{(r)}, n^{-1})_\infty \\ &\overset{(62)}{\leq} \mathcal{C}(1+\|\mathcal{L}_n^{\gamma,\delta}\|_{\mathbf{C}\to\mathbf{C}})n^{-r-\min\{\chi_0,1+\kappa-r\}},\end{aligned}$$

where we took into account that, for $g \in \mathbf{C}^\psi[0,1]$,

$$\omega_\varphi(g,t)_\infty \leq \mathcal{C} \sup_{0<h\leq t}\ \sup_{0\leq x\leq 1} h^\psi[\varphi(x)]^\psi = \mathcal{C}t^\psi.$$

Analogously, we get $\|\mathcal{L}_n^{\gamma,\delta}f - f\|_\infty \leq \mathcal{C}n^{-r-\chi_0}$. Thus, as at the end of the proof of Proposition 3,

$$\begin{aligned}\|u_n^* - u^*\|_\infty &\leq \mathcal{C}\|\mathcal{L}_n^{\gamma,\delta}\|_{\mathbf{C}\to\mathbf{C}}(n^{-r-\chi_0} + n^{-r-\min\{\chi_0,1+\kappa-r\}} + n^{-\rho}) \\ &\leq \mathcal{C}\|\mathcal{L}_n^{\gamma,\delta}\|_{\mathbf{C}\to\mathbf{C}}n^{-\min\{\chi_0+r,1+\kappa,\rho\}},\end{aligned}$$

and the proposition is proved. □

4. What About the Nyström Method?

In different papers the Nyström method was studied for Volterra integral equations (see, for example, [11–16] for linear equations and [17,18] for nonlinear equations).

Let us use the interpolation operator $\mathcal{L}_n^{\alpha,\beta}$, $\alpha,\beta > -1$ to construct a Nyström approximation for the solution of (6) based on a product integration rule, namely, (cf. [13], (6),(7))

$$\begin{aligned}\left(\mathcal{K}_{\kappa,n}^{N,\alpha,\beta}u\right)(x) &= \int_0^x (x-y)^\kappa \mathcal{L}_n^{\alpha,\beta}\left[h(x,\cdot)v^{-\alpha,-\beta}u\right](y)v^{\alpha,\beta}(y)\,dy \\ &= \sum_{k=1}^n q_{nk}^{\alpha,\beta}(x)h(x,x_{nk}^{\alpha,\beta})v^{-\alpha,-\beta}(x_{nk}^{\alpha,\beta})u(x_{nk}^{\alpha,\beta}) =: \sum_{k=1}^n \Lambda_{nk}^{\alpha,\beta}(x)u(x_{nk}^{\alpha,\beta})\end{aligned} \tag{63}$$

with

$$q_{nk}^{\alpha,\beta}(x) = \int_0^x (x-y)^\kappa v^{\alpha,\beta}(y)\ell_{nk}^{\alpha,\beta}(y)\,dy = \lambda_{nk}^{\alpha,\beta}\sum_{j=0}^{n-1} p_j^{\alpha,\beta}(x_{nk}^{\alpha,\beta})\int_0^x p_j^{\alpha,\beta}(y)(x-y)^\kappa v^{\alpha,\beta}(y)\,dy.$$

With the aim of studying the Nyström method for Equation (6) in the weighted space $\widetilde{\mathbf{C}}_{\gamma,\delta}$ of continuous functions, we multiply equation

$$\left(\mathcal{I} + \mathcal{K}_{\kappa,n}^{N,\alpha,\beta}\right)u_n = f \tag{64}$$

by $v^{\gamma,\delta}(x)$, collocate at the points $x_{nj}^{\alpha,\beta}$, $j = 1,\ldots,n$, and take $a_k := v^{\gamma,\delta}(x_{nk}^{\alpha,\beta})u(x_{nk}^{\alpha,\beta})$, $k = 1,\ldots,n$, as the unknowns. This results in the following system:

$$\sum_{k=1}^n \left[\delta_{jk} + q_k(x_{nj}^{\alpha,\beta})v^{\gamma,\delta}(x_{nj}^{\alpha,\beta})h(x_{nj}^{\alpha,\beta},x_{nk}^{\alpha,\beta})v^{-\alpha-\gamma,-\beta-\delta}(x_{nk}^{\alpha,\beta})\right]a_k = \widetilde{f}(x_{nj}^{\alpha,\beta}), \tag{65}$$

$j = 1, \ldots, n$, where $\widetilde{f}(x) := v^{\gamma,\delta}(x) f(x)$. Note that we obtain the same system (65) if we consider equation

$$\left(\mathcal{I} - \widetilde{\mathcal{K}}_\kappa\right)\widetilde{u} := \left(\mathcal{I} - \mathcal{T}\mathcal{K}_\kappa\mathcal{T}^{-1}\right)\widetilde{u} = \widetilde{f} := \mathcal{T} f \tag{66}$$

(see (7)) in the **C** space of continuous functions on $[0,1]$ and approximate the operator $\widetilde{\mathcal{K}}_\kappa$,

$$\left(\widetilde{\mathcal{K}}_\kappa \widetilde{u}\right)(x) = \int_0^x (x-y)^\kappa \widetilde{h}(x,y)\widetilde{u}(y)\, dy, \quad \widetilde{h}(x,y) = v^{\gamma,\delta}(x) h(x,y) v^{-\gamma,-\delta}(y),$$

by

$$\begin{aligned} \left(\widetilde{\mathcal{K}}_{\kappa,n}^{N,\alpha,\beta}\widetilde{u}\right)(x) &= \int_0^x (x-y)^\kappa \mathcal{L}_n^{\alpha,\beta}\left[\widetilde{h}(x,\cdot) v^{-\alpha,-\beta}\widetilde{u}\right](y) v^{\alpha,\beta}(y)\, dy \\ &= \sum_{k=1}^n q_k(x) \widetilde{h}(x, x_{nk}^{\alpha,\beta}) v^{-\alpha,-\beta}(x_{nk}^{\alpha,\beta}) \widetilde{u}(x_{nk}^{\alpha,\beta}). \end{aligned}$$

That is why we will study (63) in the **C** space assuming that $h : D \longrightarrow \mathbb{C}$ is a continuous function.

We refer to the notation in ([6], Chapter 6) and consider an operator

$$\mathcal{K}_\kappa : \mathbf{C}[0,1] \longrightarrow \mathbf{C}[0,1], \quad (\mathcal{K}_\kappa f)(x) = \int_0^1 K(x,y) f(y)\, dy$$

with

$$K(x,y) = \begin{cases} h(x,y)(x-y)^\kappa & : \; 0 \le y \le x, \\ 0 & : \; x < y \le 1, \end{cases}$$

where $\kappa > -1$ is a fixed real number. For a function $f : [0,1] \longrightarrow \mathbb{C}$, $\gamma, \delta \in \mathbb{R}$, and $0 \le a \le b \le 1$, we use the following notations (cf. the beginning of Section 2):

- $\|f\|_{\gamma,\delta,\infty,[a,b]} = \sup\{|f(y)|v^{\gamma,\delta}(y) : a \le y \le b\}$, $\|f\|_{\gamma,\delta,\infty} = \|f\|_{\mathbf{C}_{\gamma,\delta}} = \|f\|_{\gamma,\delta,\infty,[0,1]}$,
- $\|f\|_{\gamma,\delta,p,[a,b]} = \left(\int_a^b |f(y)|v^{\gamma,\delta}(y)\, dy\right)^{\frac{1}{p}}$, $\|f\|_{\gamma,\delta,p} = \|f\|_{\mathbf{L}^p_{\gamma,\delta}} = \|f\|_{\gamma,\delta,p,[0,1]}$.

Let us consider conditions (K1)–(K4) in ([6], p. 356) (cf. also [19]). The first condition is

$$(\mathrm{K1}) : \quad \int_0^1 |K(x,y)|\, dy < \infty \quad \forall\, x \in [0,1]. \tag{67}$$

We estimate

$$\int_0^x |h(x,y)|(x-y)^\kappa\, dy \le \begin{cases} \|h(x,\cdot)\|_{\gamma,\delta,\infty,[0,x]} \int_0^x (x-y)^\kappa v^{-\gamma,-\delta}(y)\, dy, \\ \|h(x,\cdot)\|_{\gamma,\delta,p,[0,x]} \left(\int_0^x (x-y)^{\kappa q} v^{-\gamma,-\delta}(y)\, dy\right)^{\frac{1}{q}}, \end{cases} \tag{68}$$

where (also hereafter) $1 < p < \infty$ and $\frac{1}{p} + \frac{1}{q} = 1$. Note that, for $q \in [1,\infty)$ and all $x \in [0,1]$, the integral

$$\int_0^x (x-y)^{\kappa q} v^{-\gamma,-\delta}(y)\, dy = x^{1+\kappa q-\delta} \int_0^1 (1-z)^{\kappa q}(1-xz)^{-\gamma} z^{-\delta}\, dz$$

is finite if and only if

$$1 + \kappa q - \delta \ge 0,\; 1 + \kappa q - \gamma > 0,\; 1 + \kappa q > 0, \quad \text{and} \quad 1 > \delta. \tag{69}$$

Let us turn to the second condition:

$$\text{(K2)}: \quad \lim_{x \to x_0} \int_0^1 |K(x,y) - K(x_0,y)|\, dy = 0 \quad \forall\, x_0 \in [0,1]. \tag{70}$$

Let $0 \le x_1 < x_2 \le 1$. Then,

$$\begin{aligned}
&\int_0^1 |K(x_2,y) - K(x_1,y)|\, dy \\
&= \int_{x_1}^{x_2} |h(x_2,y)|(x_2-y)^\kappa\, dy + \int_0^{x_1} |h(x_2,y)(x_2-y)^\kappa - h(x_1,y)(x_1-y)^\kappa|\, dy \\
&\le \int_{x_1}^{x_2} |h(x_2,y)|(x_2-y)^\kappa\, dy + \int_0^{x_1} |h(x_2,y) - h(x_1,y)|(x_2-y)^\kappa\, dy \\
&\qquad + \int_0^{x_1} |h(x_1,y)|\,|(x_2-y)^\kappa - (x_1-y)^\kappa|\, dy \\
&=: I_1 + I_2 + I_3\,.
\end{aligned}$$

Let us estimate these three terms separately. Analogously to (68) we get

$$I_1 \le \begin{cases} \|h(x_2,\cdot)\|_{\gamma,\delta,\infty,[x_1,x_2]} \displaystyle\int_{x_1}^{x_2} (x_2-y)^\kappa v^{-\gamma,-\delta}(y)\, dy, \\ \|h(x_2,\cdot)\|_{\gamma,\delta,p,[x_1,x_2]} \left(\displaystyle\int_{x_1}^{x_2} (x_2-y)^{\kappa q} v^{-\gamma,-\delta}(y)\, dy\right)^{\frac{1}{q}}, \end{cases}$$

where, for $q \in [1,\infty)$,

$$\begin{aligned}
&\int_{x_1}^{x_2} (x_2-y)^{\kappa q} v^{-\gamma,-\delta}(y)\, dy \\
&\quad = (x_2-x_1)^{1+\kappa q} \int_0^1 (1-z)^{\kappa q} [1 - x_1 - (x_2-x_1)z]^{-\gamma} [(x_2-x_1)z + x_1]^{-\delta}\, dz \\
&\quad \le \mathcal{C}(x_2-x_1)^{1+\kappa q - \max\{0,\gamma\} - \max\{0,\delta\}} \int_0^1 (1-z)^{\kappa q - \max\{0,\gamma\}} z^{-\max\{0,\delta\}}\, dz \\
&\quad \le \mathcal{C}(x_2-x_1)^{1+\kappa q - \max\{0,\gamma\} - \max\{0,\delta\}} \longrightarrow 0 \quad \text{if} \quad x_2 - x_1 \longrightarrow 0,
\end{aligned}$$

if

$$1 + \kappa q - \max\{0,\gamma\} - \max\{0,\delta\} > 0 \quad \text{and} \quad 1 > \delta. \tag{71}$$

For the second term we get

$$I_2 \le \begin{cases} \|h(x_2,\cdot) - h(x_1,\cdot)\|_{\gamma,\delta,\infty,[0,x_1]} \displaystyle\int_0^{x_1} (x_2-y)^\kappa v^{-\gamma,-\delta}(y)\, dy \\ \|h(x_2,\cdot) - h(x_1,\cdot)\|_{\gamma,\delta,p,[0,x_1]} \left(\displaystyle\int_0^{x_1} (x_2-y)^{\kappa q} v^{-\gamma,-\delta}(y)\, dy\right)^{\frac{1}{q}}, \end{cases}$$

where, for $q \in [1,\infty)$,

$$\begin{aligned}
\int_0^{x_1} (x_2-y)^{\kappa q} v^{-\gamma,-\delta}(y)\, dy &\le \int_0^{x_1} (x_2-y)^{\kappa q - \max\{0,\gamma\}} y^{-\delta}\, dy \\
&\le \mathcal{C} x_2^{1+\kappa q - \max\{0,\gamma\} - \delta} \int_0^1 (1-z)^{\kappa q - \max\{0,\gamma\}} z^{-\delta}\, dz \\
&\le \mathcal{C} \ne \mathcal{C}(x_2),
\end{aligned}$$

if and only if

$$1+\kappa q-\max\{0,\gamma\}-\delta\geq 0\,,\ 1+\kappa q-\max\{0,\gamma\}>0\,,\quad\text{and}\quad 1>\delta. \tag{72}$$

Finally, we estimate the third term and obtain

$$I_3\leq\begin{cases}\|h(x_1,\cdot)\|_{\gamma,\delta,\infty,[0,x_1]}\displaystyle\int_0^{x_1}|(x_2-y)^\kappa-(x_1-y)^\kappa|v^{-\gamma,-\delta}(y)\,dy,\\ \|h(x_1,\cdot)\|_{\gamma,\delta,p,[0,x_1]}\left(\displaystyle\int_0^{x_1}|(x_2-y)^\kappa-(x_1-y)^\kappa|^q v^{-\gamma,-\delta}(y)\,dy\right)^{\frac{1}{q}},\end{cases}$$

where, for $q\in[1,\infty)$ and $\kappa>0$,

$$\int_0^{x_1}|(x_2-y)^\kappa-(x_1-y)^\kappa|^q v^{-\gamma,-\delta}(y)\,dy\leq C(x_2-x_1)^{q\min\{1,\kappa\}}\int_0^1 v^{-\gamma,-\delta}(y)\,dy\longrightarrow 0$$

(see also (15)) for $x_2-x_1\longrightarrow 0$, if $1>\gamma,\delta$. For $-1<\kappa<0$, we choose $\chi>0$ such that $\kappa+\chi<0$ and again use the relation (15) to obtain

$$\begin{aligned}&\int_0^{x_1}|(x_2-y)^\kappa-(x_1-y)^\kappa|^q v^{-\gamma,-\delta}(y)\,dy\\ &=\int_0^{x_1}(x_1-y)^{\kappa q}\left[(x_2-y)^{-\kappa}-(x_1-y)^{-\kappa}\right]^q(x_2-y)^{\kappa q}v^{-\gamma,-\delta}(y)\,dy\\ &\leq(x_2-x_1)^{-\kappa q}\int_0^{x_1}(x_1-y)^{\kappa q}(x_2-y)^{\kappa q}v^{-\gamma,-\delta}(y)\,dy\\ &=(x_2-x_1)^{-\kappa q}\int_0^{x_1}(x_2-y)^{\kappa q}(x_2-y)^{(\kappa+\chi)q}(x_2-y)^{-\chi q}v^{-\gamma,-\delta}(y)\,dy\\ &\leq(x_2-x_1)^{\chi q}x_1^{1+(\kappa-\chi)q-\delta}\int_0^1(1-z)^{(\kappa-\chi)q-\max\{0,\gamma\}}z^{-\delta}\,dz\\ &\leq C(x_2-x_1)^{\chi q},\end{aligned}$$

if

$$1+\kappa q-\max\{0,\gamma\}>0\,,\ 1+\kappa q-\delta>0\,,\quad\text{and}\quad 1>\delta, \tag{73}$$

and $\chi>0$ is small enough.

Note that (K1) and (K2) are necessary and sufficient for $\mathcal{K}_\kappa:\mathbf{C}\longrightarrow\mathbf{C}$ to be a compact operator (see [6], Proposition 5.3.2). Thus, by using (69), (71), (72), and (73), we obtain the following corollary:

Corollary 5. *The operator $\mathcal{K}_\kappa:\mathbf{C}\longrightarrow\mathbf{C}$ is compact if one of the following conditions is satisfied:*

(A) *There exist numbers $\gamma,\delta\in(-1,1)$, such that*

$$1+\kappa-\max\{0,\gamma\}-\max\{0,\delta\}>0,$$

$$\sup\left\{\|h(x,\cdot)\|_{\gamma,\delta,\infty,[0,x]}:x\in[0,1]\right\}<\infty$$

and, for all $x_0\in[0,1)$,

$$\lim_{x\to x_0+0}\|h(x,\cdot)-h(x_0,\cdot)\|_{\gamma,\delta,\infty,[0,x_0]}=0.$$

(B) *There exist numbers $\gamma,\delta\in(-1,1)$ and $p>1$, such that, for $\frac{1}{p}+\frac{1}{q}=1$,*

$$1+\kappa q-\max\{0,\gamma\}-\max\{0,\delta\}>0,$$

$$\sup\Big\{ \|h(x,\cdot)\|_{\gamma,\delta,p,[0,x]} : x \in [0,1] \Big\} < \infty$$

and, for all $x_0 \in [0,1)$,

$$\lim_{x\to x_0+0} \|h(x,\cdot) - h(x_0,\cdot)\|_{\gamma,\delta,p,[0,x_0]} = 0.$$

The following two conditions (K3) and (K4) concern the question as to whether the operators $\mathcal{K}_{\kappa,n}^{N,\alpha,\beta} : \mathbf{C} \longrightarrow \mathbf{C}$ form a collectively compact and strongly converging operator sequence. In particular, the following lemma is true (see [6], Lemma 6.1.1, cf. also [19], Section 2, Lemma and [20], Section 3, Theorem 1).

Lemma 9. *Suppose that the conditions* (K1) *and* (K2) *are in force. Then, the operators* $\mathcal{K}_{\kappa,n}^{N,\alpha,\beta}$: $\mathbf{C} \longrightarrow \mathbf{C}$, $n \in \mathbb{N}$, *are collectively compact and strongly convergent to* $\mathcal{K}_\kappa : \mathbf{C} \longrightarrow \mathbf{C}$ *if and only if the conditions* (K3) *and* (K4) *below are satisfied.*

Remembering the definition of $\mathcal{K}_{\kappa,n}^{N,\alpha,\beta}$ (see (63)), we consider the third condition:

$$\text{(K3)}: \quad \lim_{n\to\infty} \sum_{k=1}^{n} \Lambda_{nk}^{\alpha,\beta}(x) f(x_{nk}^{\alpha,\beta}) = \int_0^1 K(x,y) f(y)\, dy \quad \forall\, x \in [0,1]\,,\ \forall\, f \in \mathbf{C}[0,1]\,. \tag{74}$$

To obtain conditions under which (74) is fulfilled, we estimate

$$\int_0^x (x-y)^\kappa \left| \mathcal{L}_n^{\alpha,\beta}\big[h(x,\cdot)v^{-\alpha,-\beta}f\big](y) - h(x,y)v^{-\alpha,-\beta}(y)f \right| v^{\alpha,\beta}(y)\, dy$$
$$\leq \begin{cases} \left\| \mathcal{L}_n^{\alpha,\beta}\big[h(x,\cdot)v^{-\alpha,-\beta}f\big] - h(x,\cdot)v^{-\alpha,-\beta}f \right\|_{\gamma,\delta,\infty,[0,x]} \displaystyle\int_0^x (x-y)^\kappa v^{-\alpha-\gamma,-\beta-\delta}(y)\, dy, \\ \left\| \mathcal{L}_n^{\alpha,\beta}\big[h(x,\cdot)v^{-\alpha,-\beta}f\big] - h(x,\cdot)v^{-\alpha,-\beta}f \right\|_{\gamma,\delta,p,[0,x]} \displaystyle\int_0^x (x-y)^{\kappa q} v^{-\alpha q-\gamma,-\beta q-\delta}(y)\, dy, \end{cases}$$

where, for some $q \in [1,\infty)$ and all $x \in [0,1]$, the integral

$$\int_0^x (x-y)^{\kappa q} v^{-\alpha q-\gamma,-\beta q-\delta}(y)\, dy$$

is finite if and only if (compare with (69))

$$1+\kappa q-\beta q-\delta \geq 0,\ 1+\kappa q-\alpha q-\gamma > 0,\ 1+\kappa q > 0, \quad \text{and} \quad 1 > \beta q+\delta. \tag{75}$$

Moreover, we have to find conditions under which

$$\lim_{n\to\infty} \left\| \mathcal{L}_n^{\alpha,\beta}\big[h(x,\cdot)v^{-\alpha,-\beta}f\big] - h(x,\cdot)v^{-\alpha,-\beta} \right\|_{\gamma,\delta,p,[0,x]} = 0 \tag{76}$$

is true for all $x \in [0,1]$ and for some $p \in (1,\infty]$. Let us restrict to $p=2$ and try to apply Lemma 4. If we set

$$g_x(y) = \begin{cases} h(x,y)v^{-\alpha,-\beta}(y)f(y) & : \ 0 \leq y \leq x, \\ 0 & : \ x < y \leq 1, \end{cases}$$

we can replace condition (76) with

$$\lim_{n\to\infty} \left\| \mathcal{L}_n^{\alpha,\beta} g_x - g_x \right\|_{\gamma,\delta} = 0 \quad \forall\, x \in [0,1]. \tag{77}$$

Applying Lemma 4 when $\psi = \chi = 0$, we obtain the conditions

$$-\frac{1}{2} < \gamma - \alpha, \delta - \beta < \frac{3}{2} \tag{78}$$

and, for some $\varepsilon > 0$ and all $x \in [0,1]$,

$$h_x \in \mathbf{R}(0,x), \quad |h(x,y)| \le C(1-y)^{\varepsilon+\alpha-\frac{1+\gamma}{2}} y^{\varepsilon+\beta-\frac{1+\delta}{2}} \; \forall y \in (0,x). \tag{79}$$

Let us turn to the last condition:

$$(\text{K4}): \quad \lim_{x \to x_0} \sup \left\{ \sum_{k=1}^{n} \left| \Lambda_{nk}^{\alpha,\beta}(x) - \Lambda_{nk}^{\alpha,\beta}(x_0) \right| : n \in \mathbb{N} \right\} = 0 \quad \forall x_0 \in [0,1]. \tag{80}$$

We represent $\Lambda_{nk}^{\alpha,\beta}(x)$ in the form

$$\Lambda_{nk}^{\alpha,\beta}(x) = \lambda_{nk}^{F}(H(x,\cdot))S(x, x_{nk}^{\alpha,\beta}),$$

where $K(x,y) = H(x,y)S(x,y)$ with

$$H(x,y) = \begin{cases} (x-y)^{\kappa} v^{\alpha,\beta}(y) & : \; 0 \le y \le x, \\ 0 & : \; x < y \le 1, \end{cases}$$

and

$$S(x,y) = \begin{cases} h(x,y) v^{-\alpha,-\beta}(y) & : \; 0 \le y \le x, \\ 0 & : \; x < y \le 1, \end{cases}$$

as well as

$$\lambda_{nk}^{F} f = \int_0^1 f(y) \ell_{nk}^{\alpha,\beta}(y)\, dy.$$

Let $\alpha, \beta > -1$, $1 > \gamma, \delta > -1$, and $-\frac{1}{2} < \gamma - \alpha, \delta - \beta < \frac{3}{2}$. With the help of Lemma 4, we have

$$\begin{aligned} \left| \sum_{k=1}^{n} \lambda_{nk}^{F}(f) g(x_{nk}^{\alpha,\beta}) - \int_0^1 f(y) g(y)\, dy \right| &= \left| \int_0^1 f(y) \left[\left(\mathcal{L}_n^{\alpha,\beta} g \right)(y) - g(y) \right] dy \right| \\ &\le \|f\|_{-\gamma,-\delta} \left\| \mathcal{L}_n^{\alpha,\beta} g - g \right\|_{\gamma,\delta} \longrightarrow 0 \end{aligned} \tag{81}$$

for all $f \in \mathbf{L}^2_{-\gamma,-\delta}$ and $g \in \mathbf{R}^0_{\frac{1+\gamma}{2},\frac{1+\delta}{2}}$. For fixed γ_0, δ_0 with $0 \le \gamma_0 < \frac{1+\gamma}{2}$ and $0 \le \delta_0 < \frac{1+\delta}{2}$, define

$$\mathcal{G}_n f : \widetilde{\mathbf{R}}_{\gamma_0,\delta_0} \longrightarrow \mathbb{C}, \quad g \mapsto \sum_{k=1}^{n} \lambda_{nk}^{F}(f) g(x_{nk}^{\alpha,\beta}),$$

and equip the space $\widetilde{\mathbf{R}}_{\gamma_0,\delta_0}$ with the norm $\|.\|_{\gamma_0,\delta_0,\infty}$. It is easy to see that

$$\|\mathcal{G}_n f\|_{\widetilde{\mathbf{R}}_{\gamma_0,\delta_0} \to \mathbb{C}} = \sum_{k=1}^{n} \frac{|\lambda_{nk}^{F}(f)|}{v^{\gamma_0,\delta_0}(x_{nk}^{\alpha,\beta})}$$

such that the Banach–Steinhaus theorem (principle of uniform boundedness), together with (81) implies, for all $f \in \mathbf{L}^2_{-\gamma,-\delta}$,

$$\|\mathcal{G}_n f\|_{\widetilde{\mathbf{R}}_{\gamma_0,\delta_0}\to\mathbb{C}} = \sum_{k=1}^{n} \frac{|\lambda^F_{nk}(f)|}{v^{\gamma_0,\delta_0}(x^{\alpha,\beta}_{nk})} \leq \mathcal{C}_1 = \mathcal{C}_1(f) < \infty \quad \forall\, n \in \mathbb{N}. \tag{82}$$

Considering $\mathcal{G}_n$ as a linear map from $\mathbf{L}^2_{-\gamma,-\delta}$ into the dual space of $\widetilde{\mathbf{R}}_{\gamma_0,\delta_0}$ and again applying the principle of uniform boundedness to (82), we get

$$\mathcal{C}_2 := \sup\left\{ \|\mathcal{G}_n\|_{\mathbf{L}^2_{-\gamma,-\delta}\to(\widetilde{\mathbf{R}}_{\gamma_0,\delta_0})^*} : n \in \mathbb{N} \right\} < \infty.$$

Together with (82), this implies

$$\sum_{k=1}^{n} \frac{|\lambda^F_{nk}(f)|}{v^{\gamma_0,\delta_0}(x^{\alpha,\beta}_{nk})} \leq \mathcal{C}_2 \|f\|_{-\gamma,-\delta} \quad \forall\, f \in \mathbf{L}^2_{-\gamma,-\delta}. \tag{83}$$

We conclude

$$\begin{aligned}
&\sum_{k=1}^{n} \left| \Lambda^{\alpha,\beta}_{nk}(x) - \Lambda^{\alpha,\beta}_{nk}(x_0) \right| \\
&= \sum_{k=1}^{n} \left| \left[\lambda^F_{nk}(H(x,\cdot) - H(x_0,\cdot)) \right] S(x, x^{\alpha,\beta}_{nk}) + \lambda^F_{nk}(H(x_0,\cdot)) \left[S(x, x^{\alpha,\beta}_{nk}) - S(x_0, x^{\alpha,\beta}_{nk}) \right] \right| \\
&\leq \sum_{k=1}^{n} \frac{|\lambda^F_{nk}(H(x,\cdot) - H(x_0,\cdot))|}{v^{\gamma_0,\delta_0}(x^{\alpha,\beta}_{nk})} \|S(x,\cdot)\|_{\gamma_0,\delta_0,\infty} \\
&\qquad + \sum_{k=1}^{n} \frac{|\lambda^F_{nk}(H(x_0,\cdot)|}{v^{\gamma_0,\delta_0}(x^{\alpha,\beta}_{nk})} \|S(x,\cdot) - S(x_0,\cdot)\|_{\gamma_0,\delta_0,\infty} \\
&\leq \mathcal{C}_2 \big[\|H(x,\cdot) - H(x_0,\cdot)\|_{-\gamma,-\delta} \|S(x,\cdot)\|_{\gamma_0,\delta_0,\infty} \\
&\qquad + \|H(x_0,\cdot)\|_{-\gamma,-\delta} \|S(x,\cdot) - S(x_0,\cdot)\|_{\gamma_0,\delta_0,\infty} \big].
\end{aligned}$$

From the estimate of the terms I_1 and I_3 above (cf. (71) and (73)), we infer that, for $0 \leq x_1 < x_2 \leq 1$,

$$\begin{aligned}
&\|H(x_2,\cdot) - H(x_1,\cdot)\|^2_{-\gamma,-\delta} \\
&\quad = \int_{x_1}^{x_2} (x_2 - y)^{2\kappa} v^{2\alpha-\gamma,2\beta-\delta}(y)\, dy \\
&\qquad + \int_0^{x_1} |(x_2 - y)^{\kappa} - (x_1 - y)^{\kappa}|^2 v^{2\alpha-\gamma,2\beta-\delta}(y)\, dy \\
&\quad \leq C(x_2 - x_1)^{\eta},
\end{aligned} \tag{84}$$

where $\eta = 2\min\{1,\kappa\}$ if $\kappa > 0$ and $\eta = 2\chi$ (with some sufficiently small $\chi > 0$) if $\kappa < 0$, supposing that $1 + 2\kappa - \max\{0, \gamma - 2\alpha\} - \max\{0, \delta - 2\beta\} \geq 0$ and $2\alpha - \gamma, 2\beta - \delta > -1$. (Note that it is possible to weaken the conditions on the parameters if we use a respective weighted $\mathbf{L}^p$-space, $1 < p < 2$, instead of the space $\mathbf{L}^2_{-\gamma,-\delta}$.) Relation (84) implies

$$\lim_{x\to x_0} \|H(x,\cdot) - H(x_0,\cdot)\|^2_{-\gamma,-\delta} = 0 \tag{85}$$

if the conditions on the parameters $\kappa, \alpha, \beta, \gamma, \delta$ are fulfilled. The most critical question is under which conditions the limit relation

$$\lim_{x \to x_0} \|S(x, \cdot) - S(x_0, \cdot)\|_{\gamma_0, \delta_0, \infty} = 0 \tag{86}$$

is true. Let us assume that the function

$$\left\{(x, y) \in \mathbb{R}^2 : 0 \le y \le x \le 1\right\} \longrightarrow \mathbb{C}, \quad (x, y) \mapsto h(x, y) v^{\gamma_0 - \alpha, \delta_0 - \beta}(y)$$

is continuous. Since, for $0 \le x_1 < x_2 \le 1$,

$$\begin{aligned} \|S(x_2, \cdot) - S(x_1, \cdot)\|_{\gamma_0, \delta_0, \infty} &= \sup\left\{|h(x_2, y) - h(x_1, y)| v^{\gamma_0 - \alpha, \delta_0 - \beta}(y) : 0 \le y \le x_1\right\} \\ &\quad + \sup\left\{|h(x_2, y)| v^{\gamma_0 - \alpha, \delta_0 - \beta}(y) : x_1 < y \le x_2\right\}, \end{aligned}$$

we get

$$\lim_{x \to x_0} \|S(x, \cdot) - S(x_0, \cdot)\|_{\gamma_0, \delta_0, \infty} = h(x_0, x_0) v^{\gamma_0 - \alpha, \delta_0 - \beta}(x_0),$$

i.e., we can obtain (86) only if

$$h(x, x) v^{\gamma_0 - \alpha, \delta_0 - \beta}(x) = 0, \quad \forall\, x \in [0, 1]. \tag{87}$$

As an example, let us consider the situation where the function $h : \overline{D} \longrightarrow \mathbb{C}$ is continuous, and we choose $\alpha = \beta = \gamma = \delta = 0$. Then condition (A) of Corollary 5 is satisfied for $\kappa > -1$. Also, (76) and (85) hold true. Note that (85) was above proven for $\kappa > -\frac{1}{2}$. But, as already mentioned in the brackets after (85), this condition can be weakened to $\kappa > -1$ in the present situation. Thus, to be able to apply the theory of collectively compact operator sequences, due to (87), we have to assume that $h(x, x) = 0$ for all $x \in [0, 1]$.

If $\left(a_k^*\right)_{k=1}^n$ is the solution of (65) (when $\alpha = \beta = 0$) and

$$u_n^{N,*}(x) = f(x) + \sum_{k=1}^{n} q_{nk}^{0,0}(x) h(x, x_{nk}^{0,0}) a_k^*$$

is the respective Nyström interpolant, then we have the error estimate (see [3], Theorem 10.9)

$$\begin{aligned} \left\|u_n^{N,*} - u^*\right\|_\infty &\le C \left\|\mathcal{K}_{\kappa,n}^{N,0,0} u^* - \mathcal{K}_\kappa u^*\right\|_\infty \\ &\le \sup_{0 \le x \le 1} \int_0^x (x - y)^\kappa \left|\mathcal{L}_n^{0,0}[h(x, \cdot) u^*](y) - h(x, y) u^*(y)\right| dy. \end{aligned}$$

In order to obtain the convergence rates from this estimate, it is necessary to assume smoothness properties of the function

$$[0, 1]^2 \longrightarrow \mathbb{C}, \quad (x, y) \mapsto \begin{cases} h(x, y) & : \ 0 \le y \le x, \\ 0 & : \ x < y \le 1, \end{cases}$$

while for the collocation–quadrature method studied in Section 3, only smoothness properties of the function

$$\overline{D} \longrightarrow \mathbb{C}, \quad (x, y) \mapsto h(x, y)$$

are needed (see condition (D)).

5. Conclusions

From a theoretical point of view, concerning stability and convergence, the collocation–quadrature method is better than the Nyström method, since the latter requires additional conditions on the kernel function (see (87)). But, at first glance the collocation–quadrature method is more expensive (i.e., has a higher computational complexity) than the Nyström method. The speed (and cost) of the collocation–quadrature method must be examined in future studies.

Funding: This research received no external funding.

Data Availability Statement: The original contributions presented in this study are included in this article. Further inquiries can be directed to the author.

Conflicts of Interest: The author declares no conflict of interest.

References

1. Junghanns, P.; Knoth, S. On Volterra like integral equations coming from statistical process monitoring. *Math. Control Related Fields* 2025, *in print*. [CrossRef]
2. Atkinson, K.E. *The Numerical Solution of Integral Equations of the Second Kind*; Cambridge Monographs on Applied and Computational Mathematics; Cambridge University Press: Cambridge, UK, 1997; Volume 4.
3. Kress, R. Linear integral equations. In *Applied Mathematical Sciences*, 3rd ed.; Springer: New York, NY, USA, 2014; Volume 82.
4. Muskhelishvili, N.I. *Singular Integral Equations. Boundary Problems of Function Theory and Their Application to Mathematical Physics*; Radok, J.R.M., Translator; Wolters-Noordhoff Publishing: Groningen, The Netherlands, 1953.
5. Junghanns, P.; Kaiser, R. Quadrature methods for singular integral equations of Mellin type based on the zeros of classical Jacobi polynomials. *Axioms* **2023**, *12*, 55. [CrossRef]
6. Junghanns, P.; Mastroianni, G.; Notarangelo, I. *Weighted Polynomial Approximation and Numerical Methods for Integral Equations*; Pathways in Mathematics; Birkhäuser: Basel, Switzerland; Springer: Cham, Switzerland, 2021.
7. Mastroianni, G.; Russo, M.G. Lagrange interpolation in weighted Besov spaces. *Constr. Approx.* **1999**, *15*, 257–289. [CrossRef]
8. Szegő, G. *Orthogonal Polynomials*, 4th ed.; Colloquium Publications; American Mathematical Society: Providence, RI, USA, 1975; Volume XXIII.
9. Mastroianni, G.; Milovanović, G.V. *Interpolation Processes: Basic Theory and Applications*; Springer Monographs in Mathematics; Springer: Berlin/Heidelberg, Germany, 2008.
10. Ditzian, Z.; Totik, V. *Moduli of Smoothness*; Springer Series in Computational Mathematics; Springer: New York, NY, USA, 1987; Volume 9.
11. Baratella, P. A Nyström interpolant for some weakly singular linear Volterra integral equations. *J. Comput. Appl. Math.* **2009**, *231*, 725–734. [CrossRef]
12. Fermo, L.; Mezzanotte, D.; Occorsio, D. On the numerical solution of Volterra integral equations on equispaced nodes. *Electron. Trans. Numer. Anal.* **2023**, *59*, 9–23. [CrossRef]
13. Fermo, L.; Occorsio, D. Weakly singular linear Volterra integral equations: A Nyström method in weighted spaces of continuous functions. *J. Comput. Appl. Math.* **2022**, *406*, 114001. [CrossRef]
14. Han, G.Q. Asymptotic error expansion for the Nyström method of nonlinear Volterra integral equation of the second kind. *J. Comput. Math.* **1994**, *12*, 31–35.
15. Ma, Z.; Stynes, M. A Nyström method based on product integration for weakly singular Volterra integral equations with variable exponent. *J. Comput. Appl. Math.* **2025**, *454*, 116164. [CrossRef]
16. Okayama, T.; Matsuo, T.; Sugihara, M. Theoretical analysis of sinc-Nyström methods for Volterra integral equations. *Math. Comp.* **2015**, *84*, 1189–1215. [CrossRef]
17. Baratella, P. A Nyström interpolant for some weakly singular nonlinear Volterra integral equations. *J. Comput. Appl. Math.* **2013**, *23*, 542–555. [CrossRef]
18. Han, G.Q. Asymptotic error expansion for the Nyström method for a nonlinear Volterra-Fredholm integral equation. *J. Comput. Appl. Math.* **1995**, *59*, 49–59. [CrossRef]
19. Sloan, I.H. Analysis of general quadrature methods for integral equations of the second kind. *Numer. Math.* **1981**, *38*, 263–278. [CrossRef]
20. Sloan, I.H. Quadrature methods for integral equations of the second kind over infinite intervals. *Math. Comp.* **1981**, *36*, 511–523. [CrossRef]

axioms

MDPI

Article

On the Derivation of a Fast Solver for Nonlinear Systems of Equations Utilizing Frozen Substeps with Applications

Mingming Liu [1] **and Stanford Shateyi** [2,*]

[1] School of Statistics and Big Data, Zhengzhou College of Finance and Economics, Zhengzhou 450000, China; liumingming@zzife.edu.cn
[2] Department of Mathematics and Applied Mathematics, School of Mathematical and Natural Sciences, University of Venda, P. Bag X5050, Thohoyandou 0950, South Africa
* Correspondence: stanford.shateyi@univen.ac.za

Abstract: In this manuscript, we propose a multi-step framework for solving nonlinear systems of algebraic equations. To improve the solver's efficiency, the Jacobian matrix is held constant during the second sub-step, while a specialized strategy is applied in the third sub-step to maximize convergence speed without necessitating additional Jacobian evaluations. The proposed method achieves fifth-order convergence for simple roots, with its theoretical convergence established. Finally, computational experiments are conducted to illustrate the performance of the proposed solver in addressing nonlinear equation systems.

Keywords: three-step method; fifth rate of convergence; Jacobian; Newton's method; Fréchet derivative

MSC: 41A25; 65H10

1. Preliminary Discussion

1.1. Nonlinear Equations

Nonlinear sets of equations are integral to numerous scientific and engineering applications, serving as fundamental tools in modeling and analysis [1–4]. These equations, due to their complexity, often defy exact analytical solutions (denoted by r), making their resolution an active area of research in applied mathematics. As a result, numerical iterative methods have become essential in approximating their solutions [5,6]. Iterative numerical methods play a vital role in resolving nonlinear sets of algebraic equations due to the inherent complexity and computational demands associated with such systems. The challenge becomes even more pronounced when dealing with high-dimensional systems where the number of equations and variables is substantial. Iterative methods provide a systematic approach to approximate the solution of nonlinear systems through successive refinements, enabling the computation of accurate results with manageable computational resources. Their ability to converge towards a solution makes iterative techniques indispensable in numerical analysis [7–9].

1.2. The Need in Differential Equations

Nonlinear partial differential equations (PDEs) [10,11] frequently arise in diverse scientific and engineering fields, such as fluid mechanics. These equations are generally challenging to solve analytically due to the lack of closed-form solutions, requiring the development and application of numerical solvers. One common approach involves discretizing the continuous problem using methods like finite difference (FD), which reformulates the PDE into a set of nonlinear algebraic equations. To tackle such resulting systems efficiently, advanced iterative solvers, such as the higher-order methods furnished in this study, can be employed. These solvers utilize higher-order procedures and exploit enhanced convergence features to provide fast and efficient solutions while substantially reducing calculational effort compared to conventional approaches.

Higher-order iterative solvers for solving nonlinear PDEs consist of several crucial stages. The process begins with discretizing the PDE, converting it into a large and often sparse nonlinear algebraic system. Subsequently, an initial approximation for the solution is provided, serving as a starting point for the iterative refinement.

Another advantage of iterative methods is their scalability to large-dimensional problems [12]. Consider, for instance, a system of nonlinear equations arising from modeling a three-dimensional fluid dynamics problem, such as simulating airflow over an aircraft. Such systems can involve millions of variables and equations derived from discretizing PDEs governing fluid flow. Iterative methods, on the other hand, decompose the problem into smaller, more manageable steps. By iteratively improving the solution starting from an initial guess, these methods can efficiently handle large systems while taking advantage of sparsity and other problem-specific structures to reduce computational overhead (see [13] for more).

1.3. Our Aim and Contribution

This study is driven by the necessity to develop a robust iterative framework that emphasizes computational efficiency and precision. By drawing on foundational ideas from prior research [14,15], our approach introduces a strategy that circumvents the need for second-order Fréchet derivative calculations. This not only simplifies the computational process but also contributes to advancing numerical methodologies in the field. The core aim is to design a solver capable of handling both real and complex roots, achieving high convergence rates while minimizing computational demands such as matrix inversions and function evaluations. To enhance the solver's efficiency, the Jacobian matrix is frozen during the second sub-step, while a strategy is employed in the third sub-step to maximize convergence speed without requiring additional Jacobian computations. This approach achieves a fifth-order convergence rate for simple roots, and its theoretical convergence has been rigorously analyzed.

1.4. Existing Approaches

The problem under consideration is formulated as follows [16,17]:

$$H(s) = 0, \tag{1}$$

where

$$H(s) = (f_1(s), f_2(s), \ldots, f_N(s))^T,$$

and $f_i(s)$, $1 \leq i \leq N$ are component functions defined over a convex domain $D \subset \mathbb{R}^N$. To build on the current state of knowledge, we revisit and assess several classical iterative methods for solving (1).

One widely studied technique is Newton's method (NM), which operates as follows [18,19]:

$$\begin{aligned} H'(w^{(\alpha)})\delta^{(\alpha)} &= -H(w^{(\alpha)}), \quad \alpha = 0, 1, 2, \ldots, \\ w^{(\alpha+1)} &= w^{(\alpha)} + \delta^{(\alpha)}. \end{aligned} \tag{2}$$

NM is well known for its quadratic convergence rate, provided the initial vector $w^{(0)}$ lies sufficiently near to the simple zero. Nevertheless, its reliance on Jacobian computations can pose challenges, leading to the development of alternative methods.

It is noted that iterative methods provide flexibility in handling systems with nonlinearity and lack of symmetry, which are common in practical applications. For example, nonlinear systems often arise in optimization, structural engineering, and machine learning, where the governing equations are complex and highly sensitive to initial conditions. Iterative approaches, such as Newton's solver and its other alternatives, can adapt to these challenges. This adaptability ensures that iterative methods remain effective across a wide spectrum of applications, making them an essential tool in computational mathematics.

Derivative-free techniques such as Steffensen's method (SM) have been proposed as follows [20]:

$$\begin{aligned} \lambda^{(\alpha)} &= H(w^{(\alpha)}) + w^{(\alpha)}, \\ w^{(\alpha+1)} &= w^{(\alpha)} - [w^{(\alpha)}, \lambda^{(\alpha)}, H]^{-1} H(w^{(\alpha)}), \quad \alpha = 0,1,2,\ldots, \end{aligned} \tag{3}$$

where the divided difference operator (DDO) is central to its implementation. For vectors θ and z, the DDO is defined as:

$$[\theta, z; H]_{i,j} = \frac{-H_i(\theta_1, \ldots, \theta_{j-1}, z_j, \ldots, z_m) + H_i(\theta_1, \ldots, \theta_j, z_{j+1}, \ldots, z_m)}{-z_j + \theta_j}. \tag{4}$$

The author in [6] furnished an improvement to the NM that reaches local third order (here abbreviated as TM) as follows:

$$\begin{cases} \gamma^{(\alpha)} = w^{(\alpha)} - H'(w^{(\alpha)})^{-1} H(w^{(\alpha)}), \\ w^{(\alpha+1)} = \gamma^{(\alpha)} - H'(w^{(\alpha)})^{-1} H(\gamma^{(\alpha)}). \end{cases} \tag{5}$$

Despite the utility of the above methods, certain drawbacks persist, such as the formation of dense matrices during DDO computations, which limit their scalability to large systems.

1.5. Outlines

Motivated by these challenges, this manuscript proposes an innovative multistep solver with fifth-order convergence rates. The solver is particularly designed to eliminate the need for second-order Fréchet derivatives. The structure of the manuscript is given as follows. Section 2 introduces the design of a proposed multistep solver, highlighting its computational efficiency through reduced LU decompositions. Section 3 presents a detailed theoretical error analysis to confirm the convergence properties. Section 4 applies the presented solver to benchmark test cases. Section 5 concludes with a summary of observations and suggests potential directions for future investigations.

2. A Novel Iterative Framework

This section introduces a refined iterative methodology derived from the foundational techniques outlined in Section 1. The proposed scheme utilizes multiple steps while maintaining a fixed Jacobian matrix to achieve improved computational performance. We first consider the the following three-step strategy:

$$\begin{cases} y^{(\alpha)} = w^{(\alpha)} - H'(w^{(\alpha)})^{-1} H(w^{(\alpha)}), \\ \mu^{(\alpha)} = y^{(\alpha)} - H'(y^{(\alpha)})^{-1} H(y^{(\alpha)}), \\ w^{(\alpha+1)} = \mu^{(\alpha)} - H'(\mu^{(\alpha)})^{-1} H(\mu^{(\alpha)}). \end{cases} \tag{6}$$

Evidently, (6) is a three-step structure of (2) and reaches the eighth order of convergence, but requires Jacobian computation three times and makes no meaningful advance in contrast to (2). To improve this, we follow the Traub's idea in (5) and consider a frozen structure as follows:

$$\begin{cases} y^{(\alpha)} = w^{(\alpha)} - H'(w^{(\alpha)})^{-1}H(w^{(\alpha)}), \\ \mu^{(\alpha)} = y^{(\alpha)} - H'(w^{(\alpha)})^{-1}H(y^{(\alpha)}), \\ w^{(\alpha+1)} = \mu^{(\alpha)} - H'(w^{(\alpha)})^{-1}H(\mu^{(\alpha)}). \end{cases} \tag{7}$$

The scheme (8) is not that useful since it follows (5) and reaches only the fourth convergence speed. To furnish a useful technique, a DDO is designed carefully in the third substep. For such a target, we first consider:

$$\begin{cases} y^{(\alpha)} = w^{(\alpha)} - H'(w^{(\alpha)})^{-1}H(w^{(\alpha)}), \\ \mu^{(\alpha)} = y^{(\alpha)} - H'(w^{(\alpha)})^{-1}H(y^{(\alpha)}), \\ w^{(\alpha+1)} = \mu^{(\alpha)} - DDO1^{-1}H'(w^{(\alpha)})^{-1}H(\mu^{(\alpha)}), \end{cases} \tag{8}$$

where for the sake of simplicity in the scalar case, the DDO1 is given by:

$$DDO1 = \frac{A_1H(\mu^{(\alpha)}) - A_2H(y^{(\alpha)})}{\mu^{(\alpha)} - y^{(\alpha)}}. \tag{9}$$

Here, A_1 and A_2 are two appropriate parameters that must be set using the knowledge of the previous substeps to gain as must possible of convergence order. We choose:

$$A_1 = A_2 = H'(w^{(\alpha)})^{-1}. \tag{10}$$

Since the Jacobian $H'(w^{(\alpha)})$ has already been computed in the first substep, it does not add extra new functional or derivative evaluations to the structure of the proposed method. Hence, the final formulation is expressed as follows (CS5):

$$\begin{cases} y^{(\alpha)} = w^{(\alpha)} - H'(w^{(\alpha)})^{-1}H(w^{(\alpha)}), \\ \mu^{(\alpha)} = y^{(\alpha)} - H'(w^{(\alpha)})^{-1}H(y^{(\alpha)}), \\ w^{(\alpha+1)} = \mu^{(\alpha)} - [\frac{H'(w^{(\alpha)})^{-1}H(\mu^{(\alpha)}) - H'(w^{(\alpha)})^{-1}H(y^{(\alpha)})}{\mu^{(\alpha)} - y^{(\alpha)}}]^{-1}H'(w^{(\alpha)})^{-1}H(\mu^{(\alpha)}). \end{cases} \tag{11}$$

In practical computations, direct matrix inversion is computationally expensive and should be avoided. Instead, LU decomposition is employed to solve the associated linear systems. Consequently, during the implementation of CS5, several distinct linear systems are solved at each iteration to estimate the resolution of the nonlinear problem (1):

$$\begin{cases} H'(w^{(\alpha)})C_1^{(\alpha)} = H(w^{(\alpha)}), \\ H'(w^{(\alpha)})C_2^{(\alpha)} = H(y^{(\alpha)}), \\ H'(w^{(\alpha)})C_3^{(\alpha)} = H(\mu^{(\alpha)}), \\ [y^{(\alpha)}, \mu^{(\alpha)}, H]C_4^{(\alpha)} = H(\mu^{(\alpha)}), \end{cases} \tag{12}$$

Rewriting the iterative schemes for practical implementation, CS5 is reformulated as:

$$\begin{cases} y^{(\alpha)} = w^{(\alpha)} - C_1^{(\alpha)}, \\ \mu^{(\alpha)} = y^{(\alpha)} - C_2^{(\alpha)}, \\ w^{(\alpha+1)} = \mu^{(\alpha)} - C_4^{(\alpha)}. \end{cases} \tag{13}$$

This acceleration improves computational efficiency, particularly for complex and high-dimensional problems. The efficiency of a numerical algorithm is a cornerstone of computational mathematics, dictated by its convergence rate and structural design relative to computational costs. The quality of a solver is evaluated based on these factors, considering the number of function evaluations, Jacobian computations, and LU decompositions. This will be discussed later at the beginning of Section 4.

3. Investigating the Convergence Rate

Here, we conduct a convergence analysis to determine the convergence rates of the solver (13), or equivalently (11). Before presenting the main analytical order, the N-D Taylor series is furnished. The convergence rate for the solver CS5 is derived using the N-dimensional Taylor series. Let $\mathrm{err}^{(\alpha)} = w^{(\alpha)} - r$ show the error at the α-th loop. As detailed in [21], the following relationship holds:

$$\mathrm{err}^{(\alpha+1)} = (F)\mathrm{err}^{(\alpha)^p} + O(\mathrm{err}^{(\alpha)^{p+1}}), \tag{14}$$

where F exhibits the properties of a p-linear map, and $F \in \mathcal{H}(\mathbb{R}^N, \mathbb{R}^N, \ldots, \mathbb{R}^N)$. Additionally, the following holds:

$$\mathrm{err}^{(\alpha)^p} = (\underbrace{\mathrm{err}^{(\alpha)}, \mathrm{err}^{(\alpha)}, \ldots, \mathrm{err}^{(\alpha)}}_{p \text{ terms}}). \tag{15}$$

Assuming that $H : D \subseteq \mathbb{R}^N \to \mathbb{R}^N$ is Fréchet differentiable over D [22], the m-th derivative of H at $u \in \mathbb{R}^N$ for $m \geq 1$ can be expressed as an m-linear map, i.e.,

$$H^{(m)}(u) : \mathbb{R}^N \times \cdots \times \mathbb{R}^N \to \mathbb{R}^N, \tag{16}$$

such that $H^{(m)}(u)(v_1, \ldots, v_m) \in \mathbb{R}^N$. For $r + h \in \mathbb{R}^N$ near r, the Taylor series expansion is given by [22]:

$$H(r+h) = H'(r)\left[h + \sum_{m=2}^{p-1} \Xi_m h^m\right] + O(h^p), \tag{17}$$

wherein

$$\Xi_m = \frac{1}{m!}[H'(r)]^{-1} H^{(m)}(r), \quad m \geq 2. \tag{18}$$

It follows that $\Xi_m h^m \in \mathbb{R}^N$ and $[H'(r)]^{-1} \in \mathcal{H}(\mathbb{R}^N)$. Moreover, for $H'(\cdot)$, the following expansion holds:

$$H'(r+h) = H'(r)\left[I + \sum_{m=2}^{p-1} m\Xi_m h^{m-1}\right] + O(h^p), \tag{19}$$

whereas I is the unit matrix, and $m\Xi_m h^{m-1} \in \mathcal{H}(\mathbb{R}^N)$.

Theorem 1. *Let $H : D \subseteq \mathbb{R}^N \to \mathbb{R}^N$ be suitably smooth in the Fréchet sense at each node in D, and suppose $H(r) = 0$ at some $r \in \mathbb{R}^N$. Furthermore, assume that $H'(s)$ is smooth and invertible at r. Then, the sequence $\{w^{(\alpha)}\}_{\alpha \geq 0}$ via CS5 locally tends to r with 5th-rate.*

Proof. To establish the convergence rate, we use the expansions from (17) and (19) to obtain the following expressions:

$$H(w^{(\alpha)}) = H'(r)\Big[\mathrm{err}^{(\alpha)} + \Xi_2 \mathrm{err}^{(\alpha)^2} + \Xi_3 \mathrm{err}^{(\alpha)^3} + \Xi_4 \mathrm{err}^{(\alpha)^4} + \Xi_5 \mathrm{err}^{(\alpha)^5}\Big] + O(\mathrm{err}^{(\alpha)^6}), \tag{20}$$

and

$$H'(w^{(\alpha)}) = H'(r)\Big[I + 2\Xi_2 \mathrm{err}^{(\alpha)} + 3\Xi_3 \mathrm{err}^{(\alpha)^2} + 4\Xi_4 \mathrm{err}^{(\alpha)^3} + 5\Xi_5 \mathrm{err}^{(\alpha)^4}\Big] + O(\mathrm{err}^{(\alpha)^5}), \tag{21}$$

where $\Xi_i = \frac{1}{i!}[H'(r)]^{-1} H^{(i)}(r)$ for $i \geq 2$, and $\mathrm{err}^{(\alpha)} = w^{(\alpha)} - r$. Using these expansions, we derive:

$$y^{(\alpha)} = r + \frac{1}{3}\mathrm{err}^{(\alpha)} + \frac{2}{3}\Xi_2 \mathrm{err}^{(\alpha)^2} + O(\mathrm{err}^{(\alpha)^3}). \tag{22}$$

A similar Taylor expansion using (20)–(22) gives the error at the end of the second sub-step of CS5 as follows:

$$\mu^{(\alpha)} - r = \left(\Xi_2^2\right)\mathrm{err}^{(\alpha)^3} + \left(-3\Xi_2^3 + 3\Xi_3\Xi_2\right)\mathrm{err}^{(\alpha)^4} + \cdots + O(\mathrm{err}^{(\alpha)^6}). \tag{23}$$

Subsequently, we obtain:

$$H(\mu^{(\alpha)}) = H'(r)\Big[\Xi_3 \mathrm{err}^{(\alpha)^3} + \Xi_4 \mathrm{err}^{(\alpha)^4} + \cdots\Big] + O(\mathrm{err}^{(\alpha)^6}). \tag{24}$$

By employing these expressions in the 3rd sub-step of CS5, we obtain:

$$\mathrm{err}^{(\alpha+1)} = 2\Xi_2^4 \mathrm{err}^{(\alpha)^5} + O(\mathrm{err}^{(\alpha)^6}), \tag{25}$$

which demonstrates that the method achieves a fifth-order, requiring only two LU decompositions for every iterates. This completes the proof. □

4. Numerical Tests

The primary objective here is to demonstrate the applicability and efficacy of the proposed CS5 scheme. Some remarks are given as:

- Computational experiments were performed using Wolfram software 13.3 [23,24], with all programming conducted in a multiple-precision arithmetic framework using 2500-digit precision except the last test. This setup allowed us to rigorously observe and verify the higher speeds reflected in the computational pieces of evidence.
- Linear systems arising during the process were efficiently solved through LU factorization using `LinearSolver[]`.
- All numerical tests were carried out in a consistent computational environment to ensure reliability and reproducibility.
- For comparative analysis, the proposed higher-order method was benchmarked against existing approaches, including NM and SM, for resolving nonlinear collections of equations.

Prior to presenting the numerical results, we highlight the efficiency indices (EI) of the solvers under comparison. Attaining fifth-order convergence with the CS5 scheme requires solving three linear systems per iteration cycle. However, computational efficiency is enhanced by requiring only two LU factorizations per cycle, followed by matrix-vector multiplications, thereby eliminating the need for repeated matrix inversions within each iteration. The efficiency index, as defined in [20], is calculated as:

$$EI = \sqrt[\mathfrak{C}]{\mathfrak{p}}, \tag{26}$$

whereas

- C shows the cost, and
- $\mathfrak{p}$ shows the rate in terms of function evaluations.

For evaluating the EI of the CS5 scheme, we detail the required functional evaluation costs in ν-dimensional functions and their Jacobians as follows: For $H(w), H(w), H(w)$, ν evaluations are required for each. For $H'(w)$, ν^2 evaluations are needed. Similarly, for the divided difference operator (DDO1), ν^2 evaluations are also involved.

The results summarized in Table 1 clearly show that when changing ν, the EI of the proposed solver surpasses that of its competitors. A comparative analysis of different solvers, visualized in Figure 1, underscores the superiority of the CS5 scheme.

Table 1. Comparison of various techniques based on their efficiency indices.

Techniques	NM	SM	PM
$\mathfrak{p}$	2	2	5
Functional evaluations	$\nu+\nu^2$	$\nu+\nu^2$	$3\nu+2\nu^2$
No. of LU factorization	1	1	2
The classic EI	$2^{\frac{1}{\nu+\nu^2}}$	$2^{\frac{1}{\nu+\nu^2}}$	$5^{\frac{1}{3\nu+2\nu^2}}$

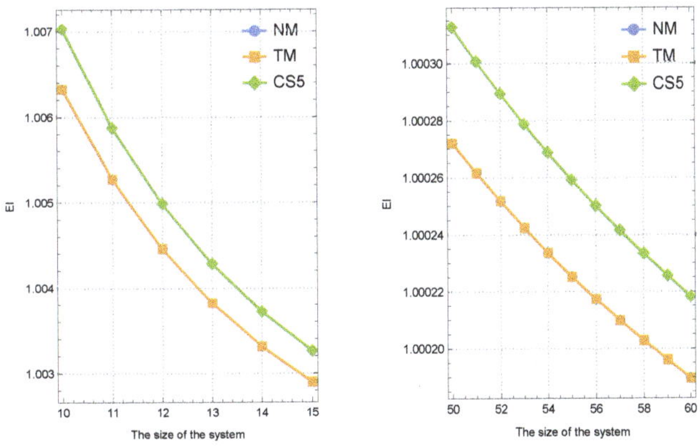

Figure 1. Evaluation of EIs for different values of ν.

Example 1. *The nonlinear set $H(s) = 0$, which encompasses a real root, is analyzed in detail as described in the following*

$$H(s) = \begin{cases} \sin(s_1 + s_2 - s_3), \\ \cos(s_1 - s_2), \\ s_1^2 + s_2^2 - s_3, \end{cases} \tag{27}$$

where its simple root is:

$$r \simeq (3.7177, 2.1470, 18.431)^*. \tag{28}$$

The computational results are presented in Figures 2–4. Here, different starting points have been compared for any of the figures to reveal the usefulness of the new method. Furthermore, the norm of residual is expressed through the use of the $\|\cdot\|_2$ notation, providing a concise representation of the error magnitude.

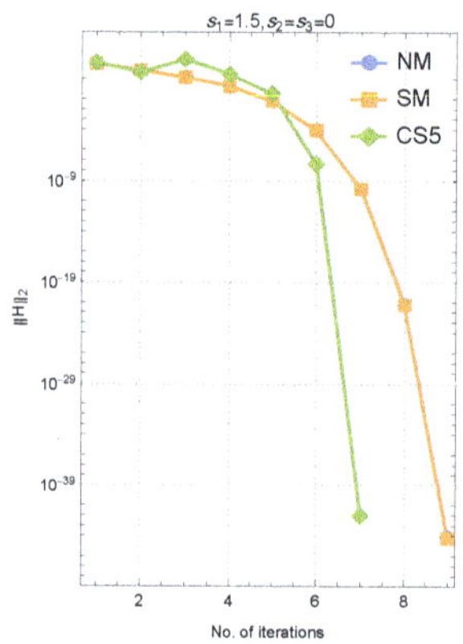

Figure 2. Results of comparions for different solvers under $w^{(0)} = (1.5, 0, 0)$. Here, NM and SM coincide very much with each other.

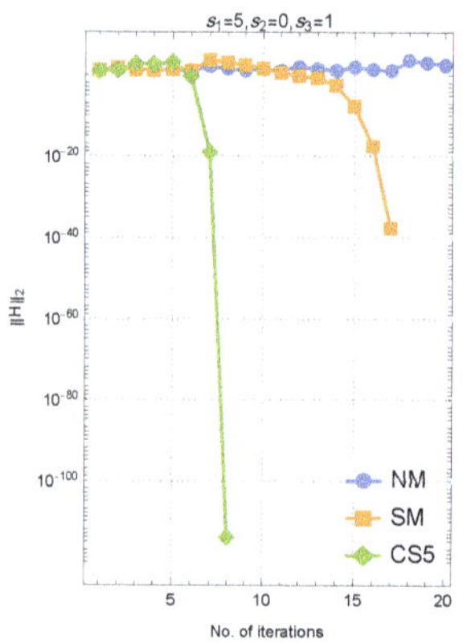

Figure 3. Results of comparisons for different solvers under $w^{(0)} = (5, 0, 1)$.

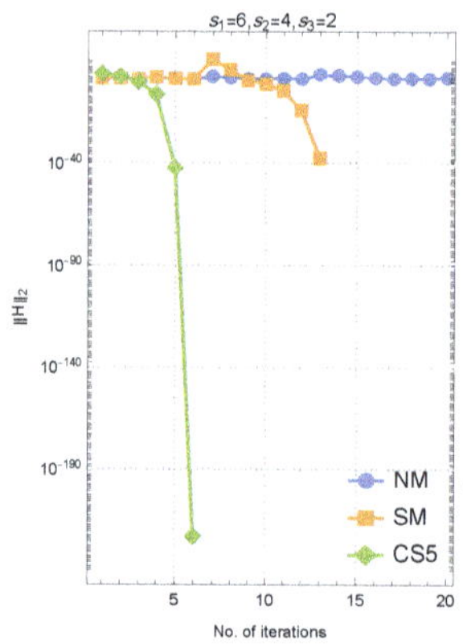

Figure 4. Results of comparisons for different solvers under $w^{(0)} = (6, 4, 2)$.

A simple yet effective implementation for CS5 in Example 1 has now been provided in the Mathematica environment to make the process easier for readers as follows (noting that the notations may not be necessarily the same as the mathematical notations in the derivation of the method):

```
ClearAll["Global`*"];
digits = 2500; size = 3;
f[{x1_, x2_, x3_}] :=
  {
   Sin[x1 + x2 - x3],
   Cos[x1 - x2],
   x1^2 + x2^2 - x3
   };
J[{x1_, x2_, x3_}] = D[f[{x1, x2, x3}], {{x1, x2, x3}}];
x = SetAccuracy[{6, 4, 2}, digits];

max = 6; fx = f[x];

point1[j_] := Join[x1[[;; j]], w[[j + 1 ;;]]];
point2[j_] := Join[x1[[;; j - 1]], w[[j ;;]]];

Do[{
    f1x = J[x];
    yy = LinearSolve[f1x];
    w = x - yy[fx];
    fw = f[w];
    x1 = w - yy[fw];
    fx1 = f[x1];
    T = Transpose@
      SparseArray@
       Table[(f[point1[j]] - f[point2[j]])/(x1[[j]] - w[[j]]), {j,
         size}];
    fun = LinearSolve[T];
    x = x1 - fun[(fx1)];
    fx = f[x];
    L[i] = Norm[fx, 2];
    }, {i, 1, max}
   ]; // AbsoluteTiming

s3 = Table[N[L[k], 5], {k, 1, max}]

N[x, 5]
```

Example 2. *The performance and accuracy of the presented scheme is validated by solving the following nonlinear test problem:* $H(s_1, s_2) = 0$*, where* $H : (0, 30) \times (0, 30) \to \mathbb{R}^2$*. The function* H *is defined as:*

$$H(s) = H(s_1, s_2) = \left(s_1^2 - s_2 - 19, \frac{s_2^3}{6} - s_1^2 + s_2 - 17 \right). \tag{29}$$

The iterative process begins with the initial vector $w^{(0)} = (40.5, -5.5)^*$*, with the objective of converging to the exact solution* $r = (5, 6)^*$.

Numerical experiments, presented in Table 2, highlight the robustness of the proposed scheme in solving a variety of nonlinear equations. These computational tests reveal that the CS5 scheme converges to the solutions in only a few iterations while delivering high accuracy at every iterate. Furthermore, the numerical rate consistently aligns with the analytically expected higher speeds, confirming the reliability and efficiency of the method.

Table 2. A presentation of the numerical outcomes obtained from the application of various methods in Example 2.

Methods	$\|\|H(w^{(6)})\|\|$	$\|\|H(w^{(7)})\|\|$	$\|\|H(w^{(8)})\|\|$	$\|\|H(w^{(9)})\|\|$
NM	8.69×10^1	1.88×10^1	2.08	3.78×10^{-2}
SM	2.04×10^6	1.93×10^6	1.82×10^6	1.70×10^6
CS5	7.11×10^{-6}	2.72×10^{-34}	2.24×10^{-176}	

Example 3. *To have a test problem of higher dimensions, we take into account*

$$\begin{cases} s_i s_{i+1} - 1 = 0, \quad i = 1, 2, \ldots, N-1, \\ s_N s_1 - 1 = 0, \end{cases} \tag{30}$$

in which the simple root is $r = (1, \ldots, 1)^T$ *for odd N. Here we test the performance of CS5 for* $N = 199$ *in three different initial guesses.*

The results for this problem are illustrated in Figure 5, re-verifying the effectiveness of the proposed procedure for higher dimensional test problems. The fast convergence for CS5 in machine precision can be observed for all the considered initial guesses.

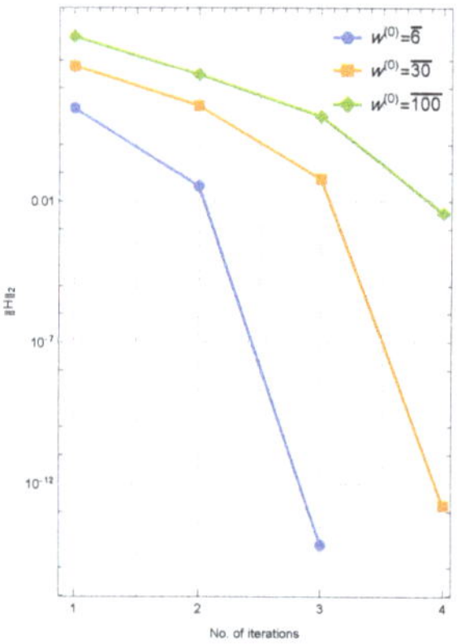

Figure 5. Results of comparisons for different initial approximations using CS5 in Example 3.

Discussion

In this section, we illustrate the performance of the proposed solver, CS5, in solving systems of nonlinear equations. Our observations indicate that the CS5 scheme demonstrates rapid convergence for both low-dimensional and high-dimensional systems. Moreover, in several cases, it exhibits a superior convergence radius compared to classical methods such as the NM and the SM. The proposed scheme comprises three steps, utilizing a single Jacobian matrix for the first two steps and a DDO in the final sub-step to achieve local fifth-order convergence.

5. Summary

In this work, we have introduced and analyzed a novel iteration solver aimed at resolving collections of nonlinear equations efficiently and accurately. Building upon existing techniques, we have furnished an enhanced multi-step scheme, denoted as CS5, that incorporates fixed Jacobian approximations to balance computational cost and convergence performance. Through careful design and theoretical underpinnings, these method has demonstrated fifth-order convergence, achieving higher efficiency while requiring fewer computations per iteration compared to traditional approaches. The analysis has relied on the Taylor series expansion and Frèchet differentiability, which have provided the foundation for establishing convergence rates.

Throughout this study, we have emphasized the balance between computational efficiency and accuracy, showcasing that our methods align well with the principles of numerical optimization. The proposed iterative schemes not only reduce the need for matrix inversion by adopting LU decomposition techniques but also maintain a high degree of flexibility in practical implementation. This balance ensures their suitability for a wide range of nonlinear problems, making them valuable tools in computational mathematics. We have demonstrated the capacity of a fifth-order iterative method to offer competitive solutions despite the existence of higher-order methods. By strategically freezing or updating the derivative operator at critical stages, our method has exhibited the ability to expand the convergence domain while maintaining simplicity and practical relevance. Future directions might be focused on several aspects. First, it is of theoretical interest to investigate how freezing the DDO at the third substep for CS5 can impact the convergence order when it is frozen an arbitrary multi-step format. Additionally, studying the semi local convergence of the scheme in order to relax the assumption of the smoothness of the function can be investigated further.

Author Contributions: Conceptualization, M.L.; Methodology, M.L.; Formal analysis, M.L.; Investigation, S.S.; Writing—original draft, M.L.; Writing—review & editing, S.S.; Visualization, S.S.; Supervision, S.S.; Funding acquisition, S.S. All writers equally contributed to this paper. All authors have read and agreed to the published version of the manuscript.

Funding: This research received no external funding.

Data Availability Statement: The findings and contributions outlined in this research are documented within the manuscript. Any additional questions or requests for clarification may be addressed by reaching out to the corresponding author.

Conflicts of Interest: The writers state that they have no conflicts of interest.

References

1. Soheili, A.R.; Amini, M.; Soleymani, F. A family of Chaplygin–type solvers for Itô stochastic differential equations. *Appl. Math. Comput.* **2019**, *340*, 296–304. [CrossRef]
2. Behl, R. A derivative free fourth-order optimal scheme for applied science problems. *Mathematics* **2022**, *10*, 1372. [CrossRef]
3. Gdawiec, K.; Kotarski, W.; Lisowska, A. Visual analysis of the Newton's method with fractional order derivatives. *Symmetry* **2019**, *11*, 1143. [CrossRef]
4. Chanu, W.H.; Panday, S.; Thangkhenpau, G. Development of optimal iterative methods with their applications and basins of attraction. *Symmetry* **2022**, *14*, 2020. [CrossRef]
5. Ortega, J.M.; Rheinboldt, W.C. *Iterative Solutions of Nonlinear Equations in Several Variables*; Academic Press: New York, NY, USA, 1970.
6. Traub, J. *Iterative Methods for the Solution of Equations*, 2nd ed.; Chelsea Publishing Company: New York, NY, USA, 1982.
7. Wang, X.; Zhang, T.; Qin, Y. Efficient two-step derivative-free iterative methods with memory and their dynamics. *Int. J. Comput. Math.* **2016**, *93*, 1423–1446. [CrossRef]
8. Proinov, P.D. New general convergence theory for iterative processes and its applications to Newton-Kantorovich type theorems. *J. Complex.* **2010**, *26*, 3–42. [CrossRef]
9. Ivanov, S.I. A general approach to the study of the convergence of Picard iteration with an application to Halley's method for multiple zeros of analytic functions. *J. Math. Anal. Appl.* **2022**, *513*, 126238. [CrossRef]
10. Qasim, S.; Ali, S.; Ahmad, F.; Serra-Capizzano, S.; Ullah, M.Z.; Mahmood, A. Solving systems of nonlinear equations when the nonlinearity is expensive. *Comput. Math. Appl.* **2016**, *71*, 1464–1478. [CrossRef]

11. Soheili, A.R.; Soleymani, F. Iterative methods for nonlinear systems associated with finite difference approach in stochastic differential equations. *Numer. Algorithms* **2016**, *71*, 89–102. [CrossRef]
12. Cordero, A.; Jordán, C.; Sanabria-Codesal, E.; Torregrosa, J.R. Solving nonlinear vectorial problems with a stable class of Jacobian-free iterative processes. *J. Appl. Math. Comput.* **2024**, *70*, 5023–5048. [CrossRef]
13. Shil, S.; Nashine, H.K.; Soleymani, F. On an inversion-free algorithm for the nonlinear matrix problem $\mathcal{X}^{\alpha} + \mathcal{A}^*\mathcal{X}^{-\beta}\mathcal{A} + \mathcal{B}^*\mathcal{X}^{-\gamma}\mathcal{B} = \mathcal{I}$. *Int. J. Comput. Math.* **2022**, *99*, 2555–2567. [CrossRef]
14. Abdullah, S.; Choubey, N.; Dara, S. An efficient two-point iterative method with memory for solving non-linear equations and its dynamics. *J. Appl. Math. Comput.* **2023**, *70*, 285–315. [CrossRef]
15. Cordero, A.; Garrido, N.; Torregrosa, J.R.; Triguero-Navarro, P. Design of iterative methods with memory for solving nonlinear systems. *Math. Method. Appl. Sci.* **2023**, *46*, 12361–12377. [CrossRef]
16. Batra, P. Simultaneous point estimates for Newton's method. *BIT* **2002**, *42*, 467–476. [CrossRef]
17. McNamee, J.M.; Pan, V.Y. *Numerical Methods for Roots of Polynomials–Part I*; Elsevier: Amsterdam, The Netherlands, 2007.
18. Kyncheva, V.K.; Yotov, V.V.; Ivanov, S.I. Convergence of Newton, Halley and Chebyshev iterative methods as methods for simultaneous determination of multiple polynomial zeros. *Appl. Numer. Math.* **2017**, *112*, 146–154. [CrossRef]
19. McNamee, J.M.; Pan, V.Y. *Numerical Methods for Roots of Polynomials–Part II*; Elsevier: Amsterdam, The Netherlands, 2013.
20. Grau-Sánchez, M.; Grau, À.; Noguera, M. On the computational efficiency index and some iterative methods for solving systems of nonlinear equations. *J. Comput. Appl. Math.* **2011**, *236*, 1259–1266. [CrossRef]
21. Sharma, J.R.; Guha, R.K.; Sharma, R. An efficient fourth order weighted-Newton method for systems of nonlinear equations. *Numer. Algorithms* **2013**, *62*, 307–323. [CrossRef]
22. Cordero, A.; Hueso, J.L.; Martínez, E.; Torregrosa, J.R. A modified Newton-Jarratt's composition. *Numer. Algorithms* **2010**, *55*, 87–99. [CrossRef]
23. Dubin, D. *Numerical and Analytical Methods for Scientists and Engineers using Mathematica*; John Wiley & Sons: Hoboken, NJ, USA, 2003.
24. Clark, J.; Kapadia, D. *Introduction to Calculus: A Computational Approach*; Wolfram Media: Champaign, IL, USA, 2024.

axioms

MDPI

Article

An Enhanced Method with Memory Derived from Newton's Scheme in Solving Nonlinear Equations: Higher R-Order Convergence and Numerical Performance

Runqi Xue [1], Yalin Li [2], Enbin Song [1] and Tao Liu [2,*]

1 College of Mathematics, Sichuan University, Chengdu 610064, China
2 School of Mathematics and Statistics, Northeastern University at Qinhuangdao, Qinhuangdao 066004, China; 2372155@stu.neu.edu.cn
* Correspondence: liutao@neuq.edu.cn

Abstract: This article introduces a novel iterative solver with memory, derived from Newton's scheme, for nonlinear scalar equations. The key innovation lies in integrating memory into the iterative process, enhancing the convergence rate without increasing the quantity of functional evaluations compared to conventional two-point solvers. The proposed method achieves a superior R-order of convergence by adaptively utilizing past iterates to refine the current approximation. A rigorous theoretical analysis is presented to establish the convergence properties of the method. Extensive computational experiments demonstrate that the method with memory not only accelerates convergence but also enhances accuracy with fewer iterations. These findings suggest that the proposed solver has significant potential for applications in scientific computing and numerical optimization, where efficient and high-order iterative methods are crucial.

Keywords: nonlinear equations; root; iteration solvers; with memory; without memory; enhanced

MSC: 41A25; 65H05

1. Introductory Notes

Solving nonlinear scalar equations is fundamental in numerous scientific and engineering disciplines, as many real-world problems involve nonlinear behavior that cannot be accurately captured by linear models [1–3]. These equations frequently arise in physics, engineering, economics, and biology, where exact analytical solutions are often unavailable [4,5]. In physics and engineering, nonlinear equations govern the behavior of complex systems such as fluid dynamics, structural mechanics, and electrodynamics [6]. A notable example is the motion of a projectile under air resistance, modeled by the following equation:

$$\bar{m}\frac{dv}{dt} = \bar{m}g - \bar{k}v^2, \tag{1}$$

where $vs.$ represents velocity, $\bar{m}$ is the mass, g is gravitational acceleration, and $\bar{k}$ is the drag coefficient. Similarly, in financial mathematics [7], the valuation of options under transactions is determined by the nonlinear Black–Scholes equation, which is inherently nonlinear due to the presence of transactions. To enlighten the issue, when solving the nonlinear partial differential equation using the finite difference discretization, this process leads to a collection of nonlinear algebraic equations, mainly of a large sparse size, that needs to be tackled by iterative Newton-type methods. Biological and medical sciences also rely heavily on nonlinear models to describe population dynamics, such as the logistic growth model, as follows:

$$\frac{dP}{dt} = \bar{r}P\left(1 - \frac{P}{K}\right), \tag{2}$$

wherein $\bar{r}$ is the intrinsic growth rate, P is the population size, and K shows the carrying capacity of the environment.

Let us now introduce the fundamental concepts of solving nonlinear equations using iterative methods [1], with a particular focus on multipoint methods. These methods are known for their higher computational efficiency compared to classical one-point methods. We provide a classification of iteration solvers via the information needed from current and previous iterates, and we discuss key features such as the convergence order, computational efficiency, initial approximations, and stopping criteria.

1.1. Classification of Iterative Solvers

Iterative schemes for resolving

$$f(x) = 0,$$

can be classified based on the information they use [8,9]:

- One-point methods: These methods use only the current approximation x_k to calculate the subsequent approximation x_{k+1}. A classic example is Newton's scheme (NIM, second-order speed), expressed as follows:

$$x_{k+1} = x_k - \frac{f(x_k)}{f'(x_k)}. \tag{3}$$

- One-point methods with memory [8]: These methods reuse previous approximations $x_{k-1}, \ldots, x_{k-n}$ to compute x_{k+1}. The secant solver is a well-known instance expressed as follows:

$$x_{k+1} = x_k - \frac{x_k - x_{k-1}}{f(x_k) - f(x_{k-1})} f(x_k).$$

- Multipoint methods without memory: These methods use the current approximation x_k and additional expressions $w_1(x_k), w_2(x_k), \ldots, w_n(x_k)$ to compute x_{k+1}; see [10,11] for more details.
- Multipoint methods with memory: These methods use information from multiple previous iterates, including both approximations and additional expressions [12,13].

Despite the widespread use of Newton-type iterative methods, traditional solvers face several well-known limitations. One-point methods, like Newton's method, exhibit quadratic convergence but require the computation of derivatives, which can be computationally expensive or analytically intractable for complex functions. Additionally, these methods are highly sensitive to the choice of the initial approximation; poor initial guesses can lead to divergence or slow convergence. To address these issues, multipoint methods have been developed, improving convergence rates by incorporating additional function evaluations. However, these approaches often come at the cost of increased computational effort, as each iteration requires multiple function evaluations, reducing overall efficiency.

Multipoint methods without memory aim to balance accuracy and computational cost by evaluating the function at strategically chosen auxiliary points [14]. Nevertheless, their performance is still limited by the quantity of function evaluations required per cycle, which restricts their efficacy for large-scale problems. On the other hand, schemes with memory offer a promising alternative by utilizing past iterates to boost convergence without additional functional evaluations. This advantage allows them to achieve higher-order convergence while maintaining computational efficiency. However, existing memory-based approaches often lack a systematic framework for integrating historical information optimally, leading to suboptimal performance in certain cases. The present work aims to address these limitations by constructing a Newton-type iterative solver with memory that maximizes convergence efficiency while preserving the quantity of function evaluations per cycle.

1.2. One-Point Iteration Solvers

Several one-point iterative schemes for finding simple zeros are reviewed, including that in [15]; Halley's method (cubic convergence), expressed as follows [16]:

$$x_{k+1} = x_k - \frac{f(x_k)}{f'(x_k)} \frac{1}{1 - \frac{f''(x_k)f(x_k)}{2f'(x_k)^2}}. \tag{4}$$

And the Chebyshev's method (cubic convergence), expressed as follows [17]:

$$x_{k+1} = x_k - \frac{f(x_k)}{f'(x_k)} \left(1 + \frac{f''(x_k)f(x_k)}{2f'(x_k)^2}\right). \tag{5}$$

1.3. Methods for Multiple Zeros

For functions with multiple zeros, modified versions of one-point methods are introduced. For example, Schröder's method for multiple zeros of multiplicity m is given by the following [18,19]:

$$x_{k+1} = x_k - m\frac{f(x_k)}{f'(x_k)}.$$

1.4. Motivation and Organization

The development of methods with memory has been a research direction in recent years [20,21], as such methods offer the potential for higher convergence rates while preserving computational efficiency. By integrating memory into a Newton-type solver, it is possible to construct a more effective iterative scheme that reduces the number of required iterations and improves accuracy. Motivated by these considerations, this study aims to construct a higher-order iterative scheme with memory that outperforms traditional solvers in terms of convergence speed and computational cost. Our approach is designed to achieve a superior R-order of convergence while maintaining the identical quantity of function evaluations as existing two-point methods. Through rigorous analysis and extensive numerical tests, we show that the proposed scheme provides a practical and efficient alternative in resolving nonlinear equations.

The remainder of this investigation is structured as follows. Section 2 lays out the mathematical formulations for two-point solvers, providing the necessary theoretical background. Section 3 presents our main contribution–a two-step method with memory and a derivative-free approach–derived from a Newton-type solver. We provide a detailed derivation of the proposed method along with a mathematical analysis of its convergence order. Section 4 validates the efficacy of the proposed scheme through various numerical tests and test scenarios. Finally, Section 5 concludes the study with a discussion of the findings and several directions for forthcoming research.

2. Concerning Two-Point Methods

This section provides an overview of two-point methods, which give a significant role in the computational resolution of nonlinear equations; see, e.g., [22,23]. The development of such methods aims at enhancing convergence efficiency by utilizing function evaluations at multiple points within each iteration.

Two-point methods extend the classical one-point iterative schemes by incorporating an additional evaluation point, thus improving the order of convergence. The pioneering work of Traub (1964) [8] established the systematic study of these methods, although optimal schemes emerged later. Notably, Ostrowski's fourth-order method, developed in 1960, set a foundation for subsequent advancements.

2.1. Order of Convergence

The convergence speed r of an iterative scheme is defined as the rate at which the sequence of approximations $\{x_k\}$ tends to the root α. For an iteration function ϕ, the speed of convergence is provided by the following [8]:

$$\lim_{k\to\infty} \frac{|\phi(x_k) - \alpha|}{|x_k - \alpha|^r} = A_r,$$

where A_r is the asymptotic error constant.

In [1], the authors provided a generic definition of the convergence order, known as the R-order given as follows ($k = 0, 1, \ldots$)

$$R_r\{x_k\} = \begin{cases} \lim_{k\to\infty} \sup(e_k)^{\frac{1}{k}}, & \text{if} \quad r = 1, \\ \lim_{k\to\infty} \sup(e_k)^{\frac{1}{r^k}}, & \text{if} \quad r > 1, \end{cases} \tag{6}$$

wherein $e_k = x_k - \alpha$, and R_r is the R-factor. The R-order of convergence for an iteration process at the point α is

$$R - \text{order} = \begin{cases} \infty, & \text{if} \quad R_m = 0, \text{ for all } m \in [1, \infty), \\ \inf\{m \in [1, \infty) : R_m = 1\}, & \text{otherwise}. \end{cases} \tag{7}$$

2.2. Calculational Efficacy

The computational efficacy of an iteration solver is a measure of its performance, considering both the convergence speed and the cost per iterate. The efficiency index (TEI) is defined as [8]:

$$TEI = r^{1/\theta_f},$$

where θ_f is the quantity of functional evaluations per iterate. The conjecture of Kung–Traub [24] suggests that multipoint solvers without memory, needing $n + 1$ functional evaluations per iterate, can have maximum order 2^n. Only the optimal schemes reach this level, but they are few.

2.3. Composite Solvers

Composite multipoint schemes construct higher-order schemes by composing existing iterations. For example, combining Newton's scheme and Halley's method as follows:

$$\phi_2(x) = x - \frac{f(x)}{-\frac{f(x)f''(x)}{2f'(x)} + f'(x)}, \tag{8}$$

leads to a sixth-order iteration defined by the following:

$$\phi_3(x) = \phi_2(\phi_1(x)). \tag{9}$$

Although theoretically promising, the computational efficiency of such compositions must be carefully analyzed to justify their practical use.

2.4. Traub's Two-Point Methods

Traub introduced several third-order two-point methods based on interpolation. A representative iteration is provided by the following:

$$x_{k+1} = x_k - \frac{f(x_k)}{f'(x_k - \frac{1}{2}u(x_k))}, \tag{10}$$

wherein $u(x) = \frac{f(x)}{f'(x)}$ and the denominator estimates the derivative at an adjusted point to improve accuracy.

In the 1960s and 1970s, Traub [8] pioneered the study of multipoint schemes, systematically improving Newton-type and Steffensen-type solvers by incorporating interpolation and additional function evaluations to enhance convergence rates. His work laid the foundation for what are now known as optimal iterative methods, striking a balance between computational efficiency and convergence order. Traub's third-order two-point methods, such as the iteration scheme given above, exemplify this approach by refining derivative approximations through strategically chosen auxiliary points. These advancements influenced subsequent research on iterative schemes with/without memory, inspiring the development of more efficient solvers that exploit past iterates to further improve convergence without additional function evaluations. Today, Traub's framework remains fundamental in the design of high-order root-finding algorithms, particularly in contexts requiring rapid and accurate numerical solutions.

2.5. Ostrowski's Fourth-Order Method

Ostrowski's method (OSM) was one of the first two-point schemes achieving fourth-order convergence while maintaining only three functional evaluations per iteration; see for instance [25]. It is given as follows:

$$\begin{cases} y_k = x_k - \dfrac{f(x_k)}{f'(x_k)}, \\ x_{k+1} = y_k - \dfrac{f(y_k)}{f'(x_k)} \cdot \dfrac{f(x_k)}{f(x_k) - 2f(y_k)}. \end{cases} \tag{11}$$

This solver serves as a basis for many generalizations, including King's family of methods [26].

The method excels when applied to functions with well-behaved derivatives, where the denominator in (11) remains stable, ensuring numerical robustness. In cases where the function exhibits strong smoothness properties, OSM provides rapid convergence with fewer iterations compared to lower-order methods. However, its performance can degrade when applied to functions with multiple roots or near singularities, where derivative approximations may lead to numerical instability.

2.6. Derivative-Free Approximations and Generalizations

Several approaches avoid explicit second derivatives by using divided differences or numerical integration techniques [27]. A notable example is the Newton-secant two-point solver expressed as follows:

$$x_{k+1} = x_k - \frac{u(x_k)f(x_k)}{f(x_k) - f(x_k - u(x_k))}, \tag{12}$$

which approximates $f'(x)$ using secant-based estimations.

Optimal two-point methods achieve the best trade-off between convergence rate and computational cost, with Ostrowski's method and its variants reaching a TEI of approximately 1.587.

Two-point methods offer advantages in solving nonlinear equations, particularly when derivative evaluations are costly or unreliable. Their development continues to be an active area of research, with modern extensions incorporating adaptive strategies and hybrid approaches to further enhance robustness and performance.

Before ending this section, it is worth mentioning that the author in [28] proposed an effective one-step Steffensen-like solver with memory, achieving an R-order of convergence equal to $\frac{1}{2}(3+\sqrt{17})$, which is formulated as

$$\begin{cases} w_k = x_k + \beta_k f(x_k), \\ \beta_k = -\dfrac{1}{N_2'(x_k)}, \qquad p_k = -\dfrac{N_3''(w_k)}{2N_3'(w_k)}, \\ x_{k+1} = x_k - \dfrac{f(x_k)}{f[x_k, w_k] + p_k f(w_k)}, \end{cases} \tag{13}$$

where $N(\cdot)$ is an interpolatory polynomial of appropriate degree. Method (13) provides a family of methods with two parameters, which could be adapted in order to enhance the convergence order without any additional function evaluations. This motivates us to investigate a bi-parametric family of methods in the next section.

3. An Enhanced Iterative Scheme with Memory

Let us initially consider the following structure:

$$\begin{cases} z_k = x_k - \dfrac{f(x_k)}{f'(x_k)}, \qquad k \geq 0, \\ x_{k+1} = z_k - \dfrac{f(z_k)}{f'(x_k)} \dfrac{f(x_k) - (1/2)f(z_k)}{f(x_k) - (5/2)f(z_k)}. \end{cases} \tag{14}$$

Now we propose a Newton-type iteration method by modifying Newton's scheme in the first substep and introducing a free parameter a. This modification preserves the convergence order while incorporating a into the error equation, allowing for enhanced solver speed. So first we consider

$$\begin{cases} z_k = x_k - \dfrac{f(x_k)}{f'(x_k)} \left(1 + \dfrac{a}{2}\left(\dfrac{f(x_k)}{f'(x_k)}\right)^2\right), \qquad k \geq 0, \\ x_{k+1} = z_k - \dfrac{f(z_k)}{f'(x_k)} \dfrac{f(x_k) - (1/2)f(z_k)}{f(x_k) - (5/2)f(z_k)}, \end{cases} \tag{15}$$

and then, we replace the first derivative of this Newton-type method (15) as follows:

$$\begin{cases} z_k = x_k - \dfrac{f(x_k)}{\text{Appr}} \left(1 + \dfrac{a}{2}\left(\dfrac{f(x_k)}{\text{Appr}}\right)^2\right), \qquad k \geq 0, \\ x_{k+1} = z_k - \dfrac{f(z_k)}{\text{Appr}} \dfrac{f(x_k) - (1/2)f(z_k)}{f(x_k) - (5/2)f(z_k)}, \end{cases} \tag{16}$$

where

$$\text{Appr} = \frac{f(x_k) - f(h_k)}{x_k - h_k} = f[x_k, h_k], \quad h_k = x_k + \beta f(x_k)^3, \quad \beta \in \mathbb{R}\backslash\{0\}. \tag{17}$$

On the one hand, this iteration scheme is based on the Newton-type solver (15), while on the other hand, it can lead to a Steffensen-type method (16) and could also be called a Steffensen-type method. Writing Taylor series up to appropriate orders and making several simplification, it is possible to derive the theorem below.

Theorem 1. *Suppose that $\alpha \in D$ is a simple zero of the sufficiently differentiable smooth function $f : D \subseteq \mathbb{C} \to \mathbb{C}$. As long as the initial guess x_0 is selected close enough to α, then (16) converges to α with fourth-order accuracy.*

Proof. The proof is straightforward (and is similar to [27,29]). Let α be the simple root of the function f. Assuming that f is adequately smooth, we expand $f(x_k)$ and its derivative $f'(x_k)$ in a Taylor series over α, leading to the following expressions:

$$f(x_k) = f'(\alpha)\left[err_k + l_2 err_k^2 + l_3 err_k^3 + l_4 err_k^4 + O(err_k^5)\right], \tag{18}$$

and

$$\text{Appr} = f'(\alpha)\left[1 + 2l_2 err_k + 3l_3 err_k^2 + 4l_4 err_k^3 + O(err_k^4)\right]. \tag{19}$$

In this context, the error term is represented as $err_k = x_k - \alpha$, while the coefficients l_k are defined as

$$l_k = \frac{1}{k!}\frac{f^{(k)}(\alpha)}{f'(\alpha)}, \quad k \geq 2.$$

Inserting Equations (18) and (19) into (16), we arrive at the following:

$$z_k = \alpha + l_2 err_k^2 + \left(-\frac{\text{a}}{2} - 2l_2^2 + 2l_3\right)err_k^3 - \left(l_2\left(\frac{3\text{a}}{2} + \beta f'(\alpha)^3 - 7l_3\right) + 4l_2^3 + 3l_4\right)err_k^4 + O(err_k^5). \tag{20}$$

Utilizing Equations (18)–(20), the corresponding error equation associated with (16) is given by the following:

$$\text{err}_{k+1} = l_2(a + l_3)\text{err}_k^4 + O(\text{err}_k^5). \tag{21}$$

This concludes the proof by illustrating the fourth convergence order. □

Our objective is to eliminate the asymptotic error constant, expressed as $\eta = l_2(a + l_3)$. To achieve this, the R-order can be enhanced by implementing the following transformation:

$$a = -l_3. \tag{22}$$

Since the exact location of the root is unknown, the direct application of relation (22) is not feasible in its precise form. Therefore, an iterative approximation must be employed. This gives the improvement of a memory-enhanced variant of Newton's scheme, constructed using the following:

$$a_k \approx -\bar{l}_3, \tag{23}$$

where $\bar{l}_j \approx l_j$. Consider the case where $N_3(t)$ represents the Newton interpolatory polynomial of degree three, constructed from the four available approximates of the root x_k, x_{k-1}, z_{k-1}, h_{k-1} at the conclusion of every cycle. In this context, we introduce a novel method with memory, as follows (PM1):

$$\begin{cases} z_k = x_k - \dfrac{f(x_k)}{\text{Appr}}\left(1 + \dfrac{a_k}{2}\left(\dfrac{f(x_k)}{\text{Appr}}\right)^2\right), & k \geq 0, \\ x_{k+1} = z_k - \dfrac{f(z_k)}{\text{Appr}}\dfrac{f(x_k) - 1/2f(z_k)}{f(x_k) - 5/2f(z_k)}, \\ a_k = -((1/6)N_3'''(x_k)/N_3'(x_k)), & k \geq 1. \end{cases} \tag{24}$$

It is important to note that the interpolating polynomial can be expressed in the following form in the Wolfram Mathematica environment [30]:

```
data = {{x, fx}, {W, fW}, {Y, fY}, {X, fX}};
L[t_] := InterpolatingPolynomial[data, t] // Simplify;
a1[k] = (1/6) (L'''[X]/L'[X]);
```

The speed enhancement for (24) relies on the introduction of a free nonzero parameter, which is varied at each iteration. This parameter is computed via information from both the current and previous iterations. Therefore, the method can be classified as one with memory, as per Traub's classification [8].

We now proceed to discuss the analytical aspects underlying our presented scheme, defined in (24).

Theorem 2. *Consider a function $f(x)$ that is adequately smooth in the vicinity of its simple zero, denoted by α. If an initial estimate x_0 is chosen such that it lies adequately close to α, then the iterative scheme (24) incorporating memory exhibits an R-order of convergence of no less than 4.23607.*

Proof. Suppose $\{x_k\}$ denotes the sequence of approximated roots obtained via (24). The error equations for (24), with the self-accelerator $a = a_k$, are given by the following:

$$\hat{\mathrm{err}}_k = h_k - \alpha \sim l_{k,1}\mathrm{err}_k. \tag{25}$$

$$\tilde{\mathrm{err}}_k = z_k - \alpha \sim l_{k,2}\mathrm{err}_k^2. \tag{26}$$

$$\mathrm{err}_{k+1} = x_{k+1} - \alpha \sim l_{k,4}\mathrm{err}_k^4. \tag{27}$$

A key distinction between our approach and previous methodologies, such as the one presented in [28], lies in the treatment of the acceleration parameter. In prior works, the acceleration was primarily implemented through modifications to the parameter β. In contrast, our approach retains β as a fixed nonzero parameter while incorporating a novel memorization mechanism applied to the new parameter a at the conclusion of the first substep. This modification introduces an alternative acceleration strategy that differs fundamentally from the conventional adjustments made solely to β. We derive the following result:

$$l_2(a + l_3) \sim \mathrm{err}_{k-1}. \tag{28}$$

By substituting the expression for $l_2(a + l_3)$ from (28) into (27), the following formulation can be obtained:

$$\mathrm{err}_{k+1} \sim l_{k,4}\mathrm{err}_{k-1}\mathrm{err}_k^4. \tag{29}$$

It is possible to notice that, in general, the error equation takes the form $\mathrm{err}_{k+1} \sim A\mathrm{err}_k^r$, where the parameters A and r must be determined. Consequently, it follows that $\mathrm{err}_k \sim A\mathrm{err}_{k-1}^r$, leading to the subsequent derivation:

$$\mathrm{err}_{k-1} \sim A^{-1/r}\mathrm{err}_k^{1/r}. \tag{30}$$

From this, it is straightforward to obtain

$$\mathrm{err}_k^r \sim A^{-1/r}C\,\mathrm{err}_k^{4+1/r}, \tag{31}$$

where C is a constant. This formulation ultimately leads to the equation

$$r = 4 + \frac{1}{r}, \tag{32}$$

which admits the following two possible solutions: $\{2 - \sqrt{5}, \sqrt{5} + 2\}$. Evidently, the value $r = \sqrt{5} + 2$ is the appropriate choice, establishing the R-order of convergence for the memory-based method (24). This concludes the proof. □

The enhancement of the R-order is attained without introducing any additional functional evaluations, ensuring that the newly developed memory-based method maintains a high TEI. This approach extends the existing scheme (16), effectively increasing the R-order from 4 to $\sqrt{5} + 2$. The procedure of the proposed solver is provided in the Flowchart Figure 1.

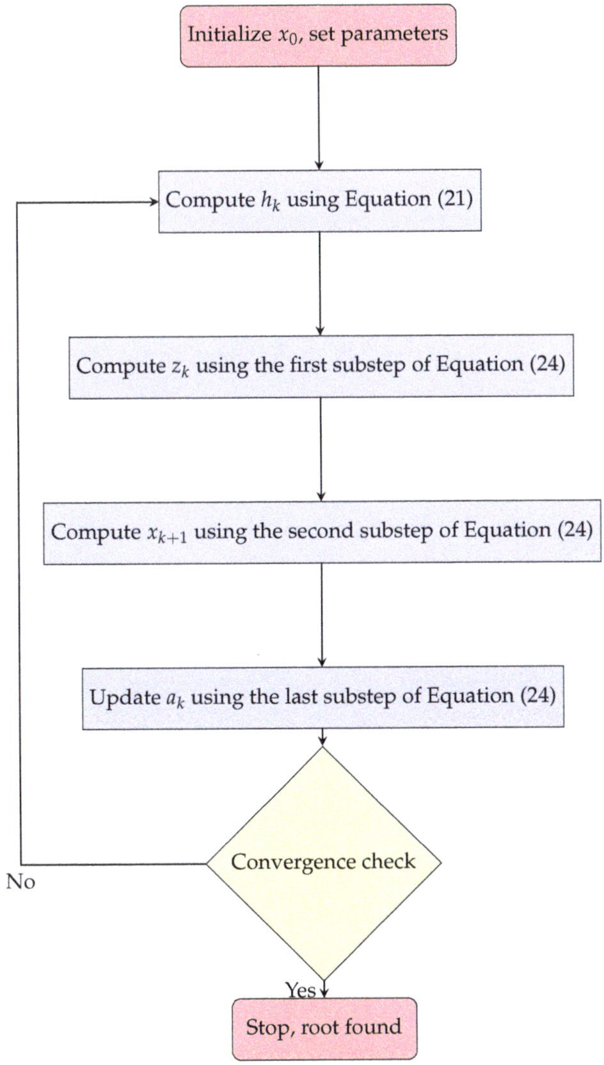

Figure 1. Flowchart of the proposed memory-based solver.

The proposed acceleration scheme (24) is novel and effective, offering an improvement in the speed, while requiring no further functional evaluations. This advantage sets it apart from optimal two-step methods that lack memory.

Furthermore, it is worth mentioning that another formulation of the presented memory-based scheme can be derived by employing a backward finite difference approximation at the initial stage of the first substep, coupled with a slight modification in the acceleration parameters. In other words, we introduce an alternative memory-based approach (PM2) that preserves the R-order of $r = \sqrt{5} + 2$, which is formulated as follows (only h_k differs and Appr will not be changed compared to PM1):

$$\begin{cases} h_k = x_k - \beta f(x_k)^3, \\ z_k = x_k - \dfrac{f(x_k)}{\text{Appr}}\left(1 + \dfrac{a_k}{2}\left(\dfrac{f(x_k)}{\text{Appr}}\right)^2\right), \qquad k \geq 0, \\ x_{k+1} = z_k - \dfrac{f(z_k)}{\text{Appr}}\dfrac{f(x_k) - 1/2f(z_k)}{f(x_k) - 5/2f(z_k)}, \\ a_k = -((1/6)N_3'''(x_k)/N_3'(x_k)), \qquad k \geq 1. \end{cases} \tag{33}$$

Theorem 3. *Consider a function $f(x)$ that is adequately smooth in the vicinity of its simple zero, denoted by α. If a starting estimate x_0 is chosen such that it lies close enough to α, then the solver (33) incorporating memory exhibits an R-order of convergence of no less than 4.23607.*

Proof. Since the proof follows the same reasoning as Theorem 2, it is omitted for brevity. □

From one perspective, since β is a parameter that can assume either a positive or negative sign, the order of convergence and the conditions required to achieve it remain identical, as established in Theorems 2 and 3. However, in practical computations, the choice of sign influences the magnitude of posterior error as well as round-off errors, which, in turn, may lead to variations in the final numerical results. These differences will be analyzed in Section 4.

The extension of the proposed techniques to the broader context of solving nonlinear systems of equations $F(x) = 0$ may be systematically achieved by incorporating the formal definition of divided difference operators (DDOs), thereby enabling the effective treatment of these operators in the following manner. Specifically, the first-order DDO of the vector-valued function F, evaluated at the pair of points x and y, can be formulated in a component-wise fashion, described as follows:

$$[x, y; F]_{i,j} = \frac{F_i(x_1, \ldots, x_j, y_{j+1}, \ldots, y_n) - F_i(x_1, \ldots, x_{j-1}, y_j, \ldots, y_n)}{x_j - y_j}, \quad 1 \leq i, j \leq n. \tag{34}$$

The expression under consideration represents a bounded linear operator that fulfills the identity $[y, x; F](y - x) = F(y) - F(x)$. According to the result established by Potra [31], a necessary and sufficient criterion exists for characterizing the divided difference operator through the framework of the Riemann integral; more specifically, if function F adheres to the Lipschitz-type continuity condition

$$\|[x, y; F] - [u, v; F]\| \leq H(\|x - u\| + \|y - v\|).$$

It is worth mentioning that the work in [32] proposed a symmetric operator for the second-order DDO, albeit at a higher computational expense compared to the first-order DDO. Accordingly, it must be stated that the extension of the proposed solvers for a nonlinear system is inefficient due to the load of computing DDO matrices. Because of this, we restrict our investigation to the scalar case in which the proposed methods are efficient.

4. Computational Aspects

The computational efficacy of various iteration solvers, both with and without memory, could be systematically assessed by employing the definition of the TEI given in Section 1. Based on this criterion, we obtain

$$TEI(3) \approx 1.4142 < TEI(4) = TEI(5) \approx 1.4422$$
$$< TEI(11) = TEI(16) \approx 1.5874 < TEI(24) = TEI(33) \approx 1.6180. \quad (35)$$

We perform an evaluation and comparative analysis of different iterative schemes for determining the simple roots of several nonlinear test functions. These experiments are implemented in the Mathematica programming environment [33], utilizing multiple-precision arithmetic with 5000-digit precision to accurately illustrate the high R-order exhibited by both PM1 and PM2. The comparison is conducted among methods that require the same number of functional evaluations per iterate.

In this section, the computational order of convergence is determined utilizing the following relation [29,34,35]:

$$\zeta = \frac{\ln |\frac{f(x_k)}{f(x_{k-1})}|}{\ln |\frac{f(x_{k-1})}{f(x_{k-2})}|}. \quad (36)$$

The obtained ζ value provides a reliable estimation of the theoretical order of convergence, provided that the iterative method does not exhibit pathological behavior, such as slow convergence in the initial iterations or oscillatory behavior of approximations.

Finally, the pieces of evidence of numerical comparisons for the selected experiments are presented. These experiments were conducted using the stopping criterion set as $\delta = 10^{-500}$. Additionally, a parameter $\beta = a_0 = 0.0001$ was used when necessary to fine-tune the iterative process, especially in cases where small initial approximations were employed.

The selection of starting approximations is crucial for the convergence of iteration solvers. A non-iterative method via numerical integration, known as the numerical integration method, was introduced for finding initial approximations [36]. This method uses sigmoid-like functions such as tanh and arctan to approximate the root without requiring derivative information.

Common criteria include checking the difference between successive approximations as follows:

$$|x_k - x_{k-1}| < \tau,$$

or evaluating the function value at the following approximation:

$$|f(x_k)| < \delta.$$

These criteria ensure that the iterative process terminates when the desired accuracy is achieved or when further iterations are unlikely to improve the result.

Example 1 ([37]). *We examine the nonlinear test within the domain $D = [1.5, 2.5]$ below*

$$f_1(x) = (x^3 - 8)(x - 2\tan(x)), \quad (37)$$

utilizing an initial estimate of $x_0 = 1.9$ and $\alpha = 2$. The associated observations are provided in Table 1.

Table 1. Detailed comparative analysis of the results obtained for Example 1.

Solvers	$f(x_1)$	$f(x_2)$	$f(x_3)$	$f(x_4)$	$f(x_5)$	ζ
NIM	1.20	2.22×10^{-2}	7.48×10^{-6}	8.46×10^{-13}	1.08×10^{-26}	2.00
OSM	2.64×10^{-2}	2.39×10^{-12}	1.60×10^{-52}	3.22×10^{-213}	5.26×10^{-856}	4.00
PM1	5.49×10^{-2}	4.22×10^{-11}	8.76×10^{-50}	1.25×10^{-213}	1.09×10^{-907}	4.23
PM2	3.33×10^{-2}	4.28×10^{-12}	5.66×10^{-54}	2.21×10^{-231}	6.85×10^{-983}	4.23

It is crucial to emphasize that when applying any root-finding algorithm exhibiting local convergence, the careful selection of starting approximations is of paramount significance. If the starting values lie sufficiently near to the desired zeros, the anticipated (analytical) convergence order is observed in practice. Conversely, when the starting approximations are distant from the actual roots, iterative methods tend to exhibit slower convergence, particularly in the early stages of the iterative process.

Example 2. *Next, we analyze the performance of different iterative methods in determining the complex root of the nonlinear problem*

$$f_2(x) = \sin(x) + \frac{1}{x} + x + (-1 + 2I), \tag{38}$$

by initializing the procedure with $x_0 = 1.3 - 2.3I$, where the exact root is given by $\alpha \simeq 0.2886 - 1.2422I$. The results for this scenario are presented in Table 2.

Table 2. Detailed comparative analysis of the results obtained for Example 2.

Solvers	$f(x_1)$	$f(x_2)$	$f(x_3)$	$f(x_4)$	$f(x_5)$	ζ
NIM	2.13	0.93	0.04	1.20×10^{-4}	8.93×10^{-10}	2.00
OSM	0.76	1.98×10^{-4}	1.71×10^{-18}	9.53×10^{-75}	9.12×10^{-300}	4.00
PM1	1.03	7.86×10^{-4}	8.13×10^{-17}	9.95×10^{-72}	2.30×10^{-304}	4.23
PM2	0.95	5.63×10^{-4}	2.02×10^{-17}	2.72×10^{-74}	3.23×10^{-315}	4.23

A close inspection of Tables 1 and 2 clearly demonstrates that the root approximations exhibit remarkable accuracy when the proposed memory-based method is employed. Furthermore, the values from the fourth and fifth iterations, as reported in Tables 1 and 2, are included solely to illustrate the convergence speed of the evaluated solvers. In most practical applications, such additional iterations are generally unnecessary.

The numerical observations presented in Tables 1 and 2 illustrate the convergence behavior of various iterative methods applied to solve nonlinear scalar equations. In Example 1, the methods were tested on the function $f_1(x)$ within the domain $D = [1.5, 2.5]$, with a starting guess $x_0 = 1.9$. The obtained results demonstrate that the OSM, the PM1, and the PM2 exhibit significantly faster convergence rates compared to the NIM. Specifically, OSM, PM1, and PM2 attain highly accurate solutions within just five iterations, with residual function values decreasing to approximately 10^{-856}, 10^{-907}, and 10^{-983}, respectively. Additionally, the convergence factor ζ confirms the expected order of convergence, where NIM converges quadratically ($\zeta = 2.00$), while OSM, PM1, and PM2 attain higher convergence rates. The higher accuracy of PM1 and PM2 compared to OSM suggests the effectiveness of approximations in accelerating convergence.

For the complex-valued nonlinear Equation $f_2(x)$ analyzed in Example 2, a similar pattern emerges. The iterative methods were initialized at $x_0 = 1.3 - 2.3I$, targeting the exact complex root $\alpha \simeq 0.2886 - 1.2422I$. The numerical findings in Table 2 further confirm the superiority of higher-order methods over NIM. OSM, PM1, and PM2 exhibit remarkably small residual function values in just five iterations, dropping to approximately 10^{-300}, 10^{-304}, and 10^{-315}, respectively. Again, the order of convergence values, $\zeta \approx 4.00$ for OSM and $\zeta \approx 4.23$ for PM1 and PM2, validate the high efficiency of these methods. Notably, while NIM requires more iterations to reach a reasonable accuracy, the new approaches maintain their superior convergence behavior, reinforcing their practical utility in solving nonlinear problems with complex roots. For Example 2, we provide Figure 2, which shows the history of convergence for another initial approximation through the comparison of different methods.

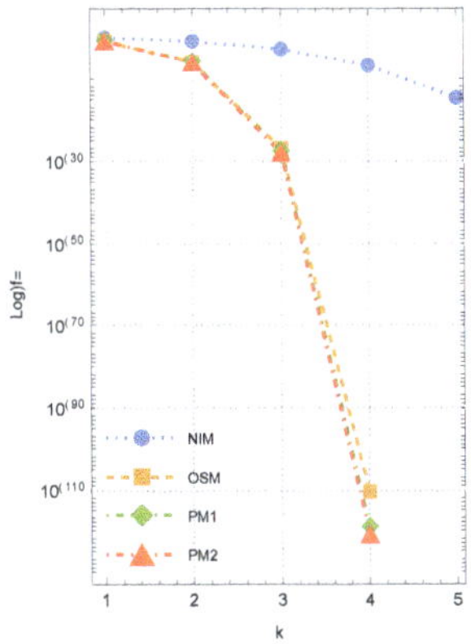

Figure 2. Convergence histories for different methods under $x_0 = 1 - 2I$.

A value for parameter beta has been selected for numerical testing and it is better to choose a small value in order to lead to larger attraction basins. However, based on the structure of either PM1 or PM2, memorization has been done only on a_k, which means that there is no adaptation or acceleration based on β. This is because in $h_k = x_k - \beta f(x_k)^3$, there is a power of three for $f(x_k)$.

Moreover, the developed memory-based approaches (24) and (33) have been applied to a range of test problems, consistently yielding results that align with the aforementioned observations. Consequently, we can assert that the theoretical findings are well supported by numerical tests, thereby affirming the robustness and high computational efficiency of the proposed method.

5. Conclusions

Classical iteration solvers, such as Newton's scheme, are widely employed due to their quadratic convergence properties; however, their efficiency can be further enhanced by incorporating memory, which exploits previously computed information to accelerate convergence without increasing the number of function evaluations. In this article, we have introduced a scheme with memory. The construction of this method leverages the existing framework of Newton's method while incorporating memory to improve the convergence properties. Theoretical analysis confirms that the presented scheme achieves a higher R-order of convergence compared to the original two-point solver, without increasing the computational cost in terms of functional evaluations. Numerical experiments further validate the efficiency and robustness of the method, demonstrating its superiority in terms of convergence speed and accuracy.

The success of the proposed solver with memory provides some avenues for future works. Firstly, the extension of this approach to other families of iteration solvers, such as Halley's or Chebyshev's schemes, could be explored to further enhance their convergence properties. Secondly, the application of the method with memory to systems of nonlinear equations is a promising direction. Additionally, the development of hybrid methods that combine memory-based techniques with other acceleration strategies, such as weight functions or parameter optimization, could lead to even more efficient algorithms.

Author Contributions: All authors contributed equally. All authors have read and agreed to the published version of the manuscript.

Funding: This research was funded by the Scientific Research Project of Jilin Provincial Department of Education (JJKH20251638KJ), the Open Fund Project of Marine Ecological Restoration and Smart Ocean Engineering Research Center of Hebei Province (HBMESO2321), the Technical Service Project of Eighth Geological Brigade of Hebei Bureau of Geology and Mineral Resources Exploration (KJ2022-021), the Technical Service Project of Hebei Baodi Construction Engineering Co., Ltd. (KJ2024-012) and the Sichuan Science and Technology Program (2025ZNSFSC0073).

Institutional Review Board Statement: Not applicable.

Informed Consent Statement: Not applicable.

Data Availability Statement: It is important to highlight that data sharing does not apply to this manuscript, as no novel datasets were produced during the course of this study.

Conflicts of Interest: The authors declare no conflicts of interest.

References

1. Ortega, J.M.; Rheinboldt, W.C. *Iterative Solutions of Nonlinear Equations in Several Variables*; Academic Press: New York, NY, USA, 1970.
2. Soheili, A.R.; Amini, M.; Soleymani, F. A family of Chaplygin–type solvers for Itô stochastic differential equations. *Appl. Math. Comput.* **2019**, *340*, 296–304. [CrossRef]
3. Adullah, S.; Choubey, N.; Dara, S. A new three-step optimal without memory iterative scheme for solving non-linear equations with basins of attraction. *Comput. Methods Differ. Equ.* **2024**, *in press* . [CrossRef]
4. Algehyne, E.A.; Ebaid, A.; El-Zahar, E.R.; Aldhabani, M.S.; Areshi, M.; Al-Jeaid, H.K. Projectile Motion in Special Theory of Relativity: Re-Investigation and New Dynamical Properties in Vacuum. *Mathematics* **2023**, *11*, 3890. [CrossRef]
5. Shil, S.; Kumar Nashine, H.; Soleymani, F. On an inversion-free algorithm for the nonlinear matrix problem $X\alpha+A*X-\beta A+B*X-\gamma B=I$. *Int. J. Comput. Math.* **2022**, *99*, 2555–2567. [CrossRef]
6. Ahmad, F.; ur Réhman, S.; Zaka Ullah, M.; Moaiteq Aljahdali, H.; Ahmad, S.; Alshomrani, A.S.; Carrasco, J.A.; Ahmad, S.; Sivasankaran, S. Frozen Jacobian multistep iterative method for solving nonlinear IVPs and BVPs. *Complexity* **2017**, *2017*, 9407656. [CrossRef]
7. Al-Zhour, Z.; Barfeie, M.; Soleymani, F.; Tohidi, E. A computational method to price with transaction costs under the nonlinear Black-Scholes model. *Chaos Solitons Fractals* **2019**, *127*, 291–301. [CrossRef]
8. Traub, J. *Iterative Methods for the Solution of Equations*, 2nd ed.; Chelsea Publishing Company: New York, NY, USA, 1982.
9. McNamee, J.M.; Pan, V.Y. *Numerical Methods for Roots of Polynomials–Part II*; Elsevier: Amsterdam, The Netherlands, 2013.
10. Bahi, M.; Beggas, M.; Nesba, N.; Imtiaz, A. A numerical solution of parabolic quasi-variational inequality nonlinear using Newton-multigrid method. *Iran. J. Numer. Anal. Optim.* **2024**, *14*, 991–1015.
11. Torkashv, V.; Kazemi, M.; Azimi, M. Efficient family of three-step with-memory methods and their dynamics. *Comput. Methods Differ. Equ.* **2024**, *12*, 599–609.
12. Wang, X.; Tao, Y. A new Newton method with memory for solving nonlinear equations. *Mathematics* **2020**, *8*, 108. [CrossRef]
13. Torkashvand, V.; Lotfi, T.; Fariborzi Araghi, M.A. A new family of adaptive methods with memory for solving nonlinear equations. *Math. Sci.* **2019**, *13*, 1–20. [CrossRef]
14. Ma, X.; Nashine, H.K.; Shil, S.; Soleymani, F. Exploiting higher computational efficiency index for computing outer generalized inverses. *Appl. Numer. Math.* **2022**, *175*, 18–28. [CrossRef]
15. Kyncheva, V.K.; Yotov, V.V.; Ivanov, S.I. Convergence of Newton, Halley and Chebyshev iterative methods as methods for simultaneous determination of multiple polynomial zeros. *Appl. Numer. Math.* **2017**, *112*, 146–154. [CrossRef]
16. Halley, E. A new, exact, and easy method of finding the roots of any equations generally, and that without any previous reduction. *Philos. Trans. R. Soc.* **1694**, *18*, 136–148. (In Latin) [CrossRef]
17. Chebyshev, P. *Complete Works of P.L. Chebishev*; USSR Academy of Sciences: Moscow, Russia, 1973; pp. 7–25. (In Russian)
18. Ivanov, S.I. A general approach to the study of the convergence of Picard iteration with an application to Halley's method for multiple zeros of analytic functions. *J. Math. Anal. Appl.* **2022**, *513*, 126238. [CrossRef]

19. Ivanov, S.I. Unified Convergence Analysis of Chebyshev-Halley Methods for Multiple Polynomial Zeros. *Mathematics* **2022**, *10*, 135. [CrossRef]
20. Cordero, A.; Torregrosa, J.R. Low-complexity root-finding iteration functions with no derivatives of any order of convergence. *J. Comput. Appl. Math.* **2014**, *275*, 502–515. . [CrossRef]
21. Liu, C.-S.; Chang, C.-W. Updating to optimal parametric values by memory-dependent methods: Iterative schemes of fractional type for solving nonlinear equations. *Mathematics* **2024**, *12*, 1032. [CrossRef]
22. Abdullah, S.; Choubey, N.; Dara, S. An efficient two-point iterative method with memory for solving non-linear equations and its dynamics. *J. Appl. Math. Comput.* **2023**, *70*, 285–315. [CrossRef]
23. Džunić, J.; Petković, M.S. On generalized biparametric multipoint root finding methods with memory. *J. Comput. Appl. Math.* **2014**, *255*, 362–375. [CrossRef]
24. Kung, H.T.; Traub, J.F. Optimal order of one-point and multi-point iteration. *J. ACM* **1974**, *21*, 643–651. [CrossRef]
25. Ostrowski, A.M. *Solution of Equations and Systems of Equations*; Academic Press: New York, NY, USA, 1966.
26. King, R. A family of fourth order methods for nonlinear equations. *SIAM J. Numer. Anal.* **1973**, *10*, 876–879. [CrossRef]
27. Kiyoumarsi, F. On the construction of fast Steffensen–type iterative methods for nonlinear equations. *Int. J. Comput. Meth.* **2018**, *15*, 1850002. [CrossRef]
28. Džunić, J. On efficient two-parameter methods for solving nonlinear equations. *Numer. Algor.* **2013**, *63*, 549–569. [CrossRef]
29. Cordero, A.; Lotfi, T.; Bakhtiari, P.; Torregrosa, J.R. An efficient two-parametric family with memory for nonlinear equations. *Numer. Algor.* **2015**, *68*, 323–335. [CrossRef]
30. Kumar, N.; Cordero, A.; Jaiswal, J.P.; Torregrosa, J.R. An efficient extension of three-step optimal iterative scheme into with memory and its stability. *J. Anal.* **2025**, *33*, 267–290. [CrossRef]
31. Potra, F.-A. A characterisation of the divided differences of an operator which can be represented by Riemann integrals. *Revu. Anal. Numér. Théor. Approx.* **1980**, *2*, 251–253.
32. Grau-Sánchez, M.; Noguera, M.; Amat, S. On the approximation of derivatives using divided difference operators preserving the local convergence order of iterative methods. *J. Comput. Appl. Math.* **2013**, *237*, 363–372. [CrossRef]
33. Wagon, S. *Mathematica in Action*, 3rd ed.; Springer: New York, NY, USA, 2010.
34. Wang, X.; Zhang, T. A new family of Newton-type iterative methods with and without memory for solving nonlinear equations. *Calcolo* **2014**, *51*, 1–15. [CrossRef]
35. Kumar Mittal, S.; Panday, S.; Jäntschi, L. Enhanced ninth-order memory-based iterative technique for efficiently solving nonlinear equations. *Mathematics* **2024**, *12*, 3490. [CrossRef]
36. Yun, B.I. A non-iterative method for solving non-linear equations. *Appl. Math. Comput.* **2008**, *198*, 691–699. [CrossRef]
37. Sharifi, M.; Karimi Vanani, S.; Khaksar Haghani, F.; Arab, M.; Shateyi, S. On a derivative-free variant of King's family with memory. *Sci. World J.* **2014**, *2014*, 514075. [CrossRef] [PubMed]

axioms

Article

Superconvergence of Mixed Finite Element Method with Bernstein Polynomials for Stokes Problem

Lanyin Sun *, Siya Wen and Ziwei Dong

School of Mathematics and Statistics, Xinyang Normal University, Xinyang 464000, China;
siya@xynu.edu.cn (S.W.); ziweidong@xynu.edu.cn (Z.D.)
* Correspondence: lysun@xynu.edu.cn

Abstract: In this paper, we employ interpolation and projection methodologies to establish a superconvergence outcome for the Stokes problem, as approximated by the mixed finite element method (FEM) utilizing Bernstein polynomial basis functions. It is widely recognized that the convergence rate of the FEM in the L^2-norm is $\mathcal{O}(h^{m+1})$. However, this paper presents an innovative superconvergence result: specifically, in terms of the L^2-norm, the error convergence rate between the mixed finite element approximate solution and the local projection is $\mathcal{O}(h^{m+2})$, with m denoting the order of the Bernstein polynomial basis function.

Keywords: superconvergence; mixed finite element method; Stokes problem; error estimate; Bernstein polynomials

MSC: 65D17; 65M60

1. Introduction

With the development of engineering mechanics and computers, FEM [1–3] has become an important tool to solve partial differential equations (PDEs) [4–6], and the accuracy requirement of finite element numerical solutions is also increasing. So, how to further improve the accuracy of finite element solutions has become an increasingly significant research topic. The following are some commonly used methods, including increasing the number of calculation iterations, selecting an appropriate mesh size, determining suitable basis functions, and using the superconvergence of finite element solutions. Additionally, the meshless method [7,8] has been proposed as an effective approach to mitigate issues related to meshing. Now, the superconvergence of finite element solutions has become an important study area [9–11]. Superconvergence is the use of simple post-processing techniques such as interpolation and weighted averaging to significantly improve the approximation accuracy of finite element solutions without increasing the amount of calculation. In this paper, our main purpose is to verify the superconvergence result of a Stokes problem by using an interpolation method.

Superconvergence analysis offers significant advantages in enhancing computational accuracy, streamlining the calculation process, and bolstering flexibility and adaptability, providing it important application value for solving a wide range of complex problems. In practical application, the study of superconvergence can help us to improve the accuracy of finite element solutions, thereby more accurately simulating the behavior of complex systems, which has important research value in Structural Mechanics [12,13], Telecommunication Technology [14–16], Physics [17,18], and other fields [19–21].

Since the 1970s, many experts have conducted extensive research on the phenomenon of superconvergence analysis [22–25]. In 1973, Douglas and Dupont [26] proved the superconvergence of finite element solutions of two-point boundary value problems by local projection. In 1985, Douglas and Robert [27] proved the superconvergence of linear elliptic boundary value problems by using the kernel average method. In 1999, Ewing et al. [28] established the superconvergence results of approximate solutions of second-order elliptic equations by using the mixed FEM on quadrilateral elements. In 2002, Ewing et al. [29] obtained the superconvergence of numerical solutions of elliptic problems by using a Raviart–Thomas mixed FEM on rectangular elements. In 2009, Chen and Dai [30] proved the superconvergence of the optimal control problem for semilinear elliptic equations. In 2012, Shi et al. [31] used interpolation post-processing technology to derive the convergence and superconvergence results of a Signorini problem. In 2024, Shi and Zhang [32] obtained superconvergence results of nonlinear parabolic integro-differential equations via interpolation post-processing technology.

The Bernstein polynomial basis function was put forward by Sergei Natanovich Bernstein [33] in 1912, which was used to study the properties of piecewise curves. In recent years, the research on Bernstein polynomials has achieved remarkable progress, and many scholars have strongly promoted it. For example, the introduction of new forms such as the λ-Bernstein polynomial and α-Bernstein polynomial not only enriches the theoretical framework of the Bernstein polynomial but also greatly expands its application scope in practical problems.

In 2010, Ye et al. [34] proposed a set of new Bézier basis functions with shape parameter λ, which provided a flexible framework for curve and surface modeling. In 2018, Cai et al. [35] popularized the Bernstein operator, which enhanced the flexibility of the λ-Bézier basis function in approximation problems and provided better tools for various approximation tasks. In the same year, Hu et al. [36] constructed a generalized developable Bézier surface whose shape parameters can be adjusted and realized various geometric configurations, which further verified the practical application value of the λ-Bézier basis function. In the field of approximation theory, in 1965, Schurer [37] introduced a non-negative integer into the classical Bernstein basis and put forward the Schurer operator, which laid the foundation for subsequent research. In 2018, Yilmaz et al. [38] introduced the generalized Baskakov–Schurer–Szász operator, which significantly improved the approximation performance by retaining the exponential function characteristics. In 2023, Ayman-Mursaleen et al. [39] incorporated the shape parameter α into the Bernstein–Schurer operator, which further improved its uniform approximation ability. In this paper, our objective is to establish the superconvergence results of finite element solutions for Stokes equations by utilizing interpolation and post-processing techniques with Bernstein tensor product polynomials on rectangular domains.

This paper is organized as follows. In Section 2, we review the content of the Stokes equation and mixed FEM. In Section 3, we establish a basic framework of superconvergence analysis. In Section 4, we demonstrate some superconvergence results for mixed finite elements. In Section 5, we use a numerical example to verify the correctness and feasibility of the theory. In Section 6, we formulate the conclusion and consider prospects for future work.

2. Review the Stokes Problem and Mixed FEM

Now we consider the Stokes equation with homogeneous Dirichlet boundary conditions. Let Ω be an open bounded set on $\mathbb{R}^d (d = 2, 3)$ with Lipschitz continuous boundary.

$$\begin{cases} -\nabla\cdot\mathbb{T}(\mathbf{u},p)=\mathbf{f}, & in \quad \Omega, \\ \nabla\cdot\mathbf{u}=0, & in \quad \Omega, \\ \mathbf{u}=\mathbf{0}, & in \quad \partial\Omega, \end{cases} \tag{1}$$

where $\mathbf{f} \in L^2(\Omega)^d$ represents the unit external volumetric force acting on the fluid, $\mathbf{u} \in H^1(\Omega)^d$ is the velocity vector, $p \in L^2(\Omega)$ refers to fluid pressure, $\mathbb{T}(\mathbf{u},p) = 2\nu\mathbb{D}(u) - p\mathbb{I}$ is stress tensor, and $\nu > 0$ is a given constant representing the viscosity coefficient of the fluid; in more detail, the symmetric velocity gradient can be written as

$$\mathbb{D}(\mathbf{u}) = \begin{pmatrix} \frac{\partial u_1}{\partial x} & \frac{1}{2}\left(\frac{\partial u_1}{\partial y}+\frac{\partial u_2}{\partial x}\right) \\ \frac{1}{2}\left(\frac{\partial u_1}{\partial y}+\frac{\partial u_2}{\partial x}\right) & \frac{\partial u_2}{\partial y} \end{pmatrix}. \tag{2}$$

In this paper, we assume $d = 2, \nu = 1$. We set $\nu = 1$ merely for the convenience of the proof, which does not affect the generality and validity of the final results.

Define a Sobolev space as follows $\mathbf{U} = H^1(\Omega) \times H^1(\Omega)$ with the norm

$$\|\mathbf{u}\|_U = \left(\|\mathbf{u}\|_0^2 + \|\nabla\cdot\mathbf{u}\|_0^2\right)^{\frac{1}{2}}. \tag{3}$$

Let $W = L_0^2(\Omega)$ be the space of functions in $L^2(\Omega)$ with mean value zero.

The variational form of Equation (1) finds $(\mathbf{u};p) \in (H^1)^2 \times W$, satisfying

$$\begin{aligned} a(\mathbf{u},\mathbf{v}) - b(\mathbf{v},p) &= (\mathbf{f},\mathbf{v}), \quad \forall\, \mathbf{v} \in (H_0^1)^2, \\ b(\mathbf{u},q) &= 0, \qquad\quad \forall\, q \in W, \end{aligned} \tag{4}$$

where

$$\begin{aligned} a(\mathbf{u},\mathbf{v}) &= \int_\Omega 2\mathbb{D}(\mathbf{u}) : \mathbb{D}(\mathbf{v})\, dxdy, \\ b(\mathbf{u},q) &= (\nabla\cdot\mathbf{u},\, q) = \int_\Omega \nabla\cdot\mathbf{u}\, q dxdy, \end{aligned} \tag{5}$$

here,

$$\begin{aligned} &\mathbb{D}(\mathbf{u}) : \mathbb{D}(\mathbf{v}) \\ =&\frac{\partial u_1}{\partial x}\frac{\partial v_1}{\partial x} + \frac{\partial u_2}{\partial y}\frac{\partial v_2}{\partial y} + \frac{1}{2}\frac{\partial u_1}{\partial y}\frac{\partial v_1}{\partial y} + \frac{1}{2}\frac{\partial u_1}{\partial y}\frac{\partial v_2}{\partial x} + \frac{1}{2}\frac{\partial u_2}{\partial x}\frac{\partial v_1}{\partial y} + \frac{1}{2}\frac{\partial u_2}{\partial x}\frac{\partial v_2}{\partial x}. \end{aligned} \tag{6}$$

and fulfills the following continuity conditions on page 57 of [40]

$$\begin{aligned} a(\mathbf{u},\mathbf{v}) &\le \|\mathbf{u}\|_U\|\mathbf{v}\|_U, \qquad \forall \mathbf{u},\mathbf{v} \in \mathbf{U}, \\ b(\mathbf{v},q) &\le \|\mathbf{v}\|_U\|q\|_0, \qquad \forall \mathbf{v} \in \mathbf{U}, \forall q \in W. \end{aligned} \tag{7}$$

Let $\mathbf{U}_h \subset \mathbf{U}$ and $W_h \subset W$ be any two finite element spaces for velocity $\mathbf{u}$ and pressure p, respectively. In order to generate a locally finite-dimensional space $\mathbf{U}_h$ and W_h, we first introduce the one-dimensional Bernstein polynomial basis functions.

Definition 1. *Bernstein polynomial basis of degree n is defined by*

$$B_i^n(x) = \binom{n}{i} x^i(1-x)^{n-i}, i = 1, 2, \cdots, n, \tag{8}$$

where $\binom{n}{i} = \frac{n!}{i!(n-i)!}, i = 0, 1, \cdots, n$. *For simplicity, when* $i < 0$ *or* $i > n$, *let* $B_i^n(x) = 0$, $x \in [0, 1]$.

Then, we divide the bounded region Ω into finite uniform rectangles e and remember the division as $\mathcal{T}_h = \{e\}$. Later, in order to construct the shape function on the local element, we take any element e on $\mathcal{T}_h$ and set its vertexes as $P_{i,j}(x_i, y_j), P_{i+1,j}(x_{i+1}, y_j), P_{i,j+1}(x_i, y_{j+1}), P_{i+1,j+1}(x_{i+1}, y_{j+1})$, as shown in Figure 1.

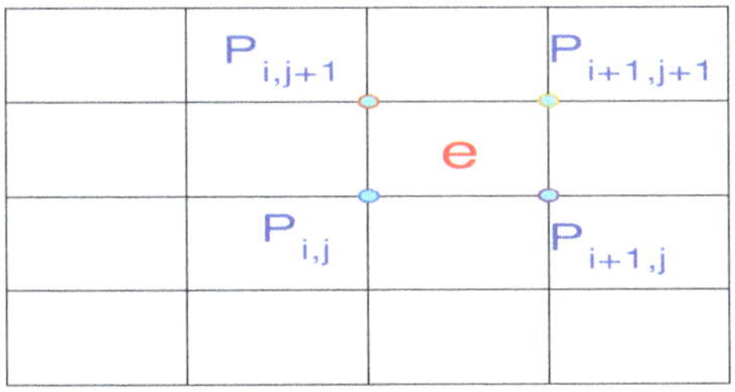

Figure 1. Element mesh on subdivision $\mathcal{T}_h$.

In this paper, we choose $m \times n$ tensor product Bernstein polynomial function $\mathcal{B}_{i,j}^{m,n}$ as basis function for the finite element space; here, m and n are both positive integers. Bernstein polynomial basis functions of tensor-product type are generated from Equation (8) by making a tensor.

Definition 2. *A tensor-product-type Bernstein polynomial basis of $m \times n$ degree is in the reference element $[0,1] \times [0,1]$ defined by*

$$\mathcal{B}_{i,j}^{m,n}(s,\tau) = B_i^m(s)B_j^n(\tau), i = 0,1,\ldots,m, j = 0,1,\ldots,n. \tag{9}$$

Let $\bar{s} = (\mathbf{b} - \mathbf{a})s + \mathbf{a}, \bar{\tau} = (\mathbf{d} - \mathbf{c})\tau + \mathbf{c}$, where $\bar{s} \in [\mathbf{a}, \mathbf{b}], \bar{\tau} \in [\mathbf{c}, \mathbf{d}]$ and where $[\mathbf{a}, \mathbf{b}]$ and $[\mathbf{c}, \mathbf{d}]$, respectively, refer to any closed interval. We obtain the Bernstein polynomial basis function of tensor product type on any element

$$\overline{\mathcal{B}}_{i,j}^{m,n}(\bar{s},\bar{\tau}) = B_i^m(\frac{\bar{s} - \mathbf{a}}{\mathbf{b} - \mathbf{a}})B_j^n(\frac{\bar{\tau} - \mathbf{c}}{\mathbf{d} - \mathbf{c}}), i = 0,1,\ldots,m, j = 0,1,\ldots,n. \tag{10}$$

Subsequently, complete affine transformation; let $s = \frac{x - x_i}{h_1}, \tau = \frac{y - y_j}{h_2}$, where h_1 and h_2 refer to the grid size in the x direction and the y direction respectively. So, we obtain the shape function on the local element e

$$\mathcal{B}_{i,j}^{m,n}(x,y) = B_i^m(\frac{x - x_i}{h_1})B_j^n(\frac{y - y_j}{h_2}), i = 0,1,\ldots,m, j = 0,1,\ldots,n. \tag{11}$$

It should be noted that, in order to satisfy the inf-sup condition on page 342 of [40], the polynomial degree in W_h must be at least one order lower than that in $\mathbf{U}_h$. Assume that the polynomial space $\mathbf{U}_h$ consists of P_k for $k \geq 2$, which contains polynomials of degree no more than k, and W_h is composed of P_{k-1}.

From Equation (11), the following finite-dimensional space can be obtained:

$$\begin{aligned} \mathbf{U}_h &= \{\mathbf{u} \in \mathbf{U}, \mathbf{u}|_e \in span\{\{\mathcal{B}_{i,j}^{m,m}\} \times \{\mathcal{B}_{i,j}^{m,m}\}\}, e \in \mathcal{T}_h\}, \\ W_h &= \{w \in W, w|_e \in span\{\mathcal{B}_{i,j}^{m-1,m-1}\}, e \in \mathcal{T}_h\}. \end{aligned} \tag{12}$$

where e is any rectangle element in $\mathcal{T}_h$; h and l represent the degree of x and y in W_h, respectively. Define $\mathbf{U}_{h0} = \{\mathbf{u} \in \mathbf{U}_h, \mathbf{u} = \mathbf{0} \; on \; \partial\Omega\}$.

Then, the discrete scheme of Equation (4) is provided by $\mathbf{u}_h \in \mathbf{U}_h$ and $p_h \in W_h$, satisfying

$$\begin{aligned} a(\mathbf{u}_h, \mathbf{v}) - b(\mathbf{v}, p_h) &= (\mathbf{f}, \mathbf{v}), \quad \forall\, \mathbf{v} \in \mathbf{U}_{h0}, \\ b(\mathbf{u}_h, q) &= 0, \qquad\quad \forall\, q \in W_h. \end{aligned} \tag{13}$$

It is known that Equation (13) satisfies the inf-sup condition, which can be verified by using a projection operator $\pi_h : \mathbf{U} \to \mathbf{U}_h$ that satisfies

$$(\nabla \cdot (\mathbf{u} - \pi_h \mathbf{u}), q) = 0, \qquad \forall\, q \in W_h. \tag{14}$$

For any sufficiently smooth vector-valued function $\mathbf{u} \in \mathbf{U}$, $e \in \mathcal{T}_h$, we define its local projection $\pi_e \mathbf{u} \in \mathbf{U}_h$, which satisfies the following equations:

$$\begin{aligned} &\int_{\ell_i} (\mathbf{u} - \pi_e \mathbf{u}) \cdot \mathbf{n}_i \phi ds = 0, \phi \in P_{m-2}(\ell_i), \; i = 1,2,3,4, \\ &\int_e (\mathbf{u} - \pi_e \mathbf{u}) \cdot \boldsymbol{\psi} dxdy = 0, \boldsymbol{\psi} \in \mathcal{B}_{i,j}^{m-2,m-2} \times \mathcal{B}_{i,j}^{m-2,m-2}, \end{aligned} \tag{15}$$

where $\ell_i, (i = 1,2,3,4)$ represents the edges of the element e.

Next, we use local projection operator π_e to define global projection operator π_h : $\mathbf{U} \to \mathbf{U}_h$

$$(\pi_h \mathbf{u})\,(x,y) = \pi_e \mathbf{u}(x,y) \quad \forall (x,y) \in e,\, e \in \mathcal{T}_h, \tag{16}$$

which satisfies Formula (14). Furthermore, π_h can be written in the form of two components as follows:

$$\pi_h \mathbf{u} = (\pi_1 u_1, \pi_2 u_2), \tag{17}$$

among them, π_1 and π_2 are independent of each other.

Lastly, define the L^2 projection $\mathcal{P}_h : W \to W_h$.

3. A General Framework for Superconvergence

In order to prove superconvergence analysis, we first provide a theorem to describe the error estimation between projection and approximate solution.

Theorem 1. *Assume $(\mathbf{u}; p) \in (H^1)^2 \times L_0^2$ is the solution of Equation (4). Let $(\mathbf{u}_h; p_h) \in \mathbf{U}_h \times W_h$ solve Equation (13). Let*

$$\mathbf{e}_h = \mathbf{u}_h - \pi_h \mathbf{u}; \quad \xi_h = p_h - \mathcal{P}_h p. \tag{18}$$

If there exists a constant $M = M(\mathbf{u}, p)$ and parameter s satisfying

$$\sup_{\mathbf{v} \in \mathbf{U}_{h0}} \frac{a((\mathbf{u} - \pi_h \mathbf{u}), \mathbf{v})}{\|\mathbf{v}\|_{\mathbf{U}}} \le M(\mathbf{u}, p) h^{m+s}, \tag{19}$$

then there will be a constant C that is independent of h such that

$$\|\mathbf{e}_h\|_0 + \|\xi_h\|_0 \le CM(\mathbf{u}, p) h^{m+s}. \tag{20}$$

Proof. Subtract Equation (13) from Equation (4) and we obtain the error equation

$$\begin{aligned} a(\mathbf{u} - \mathbf{u}_h, \mathbf{v}) - b(\mathbf{v}, p - p_h) &= 0, \quad \forall\, \mathbf{v} \in \mathbf{U}_{h0}, \\ b(\mathbf{u} - \mathbf{u}_h, q) &= 0, \quad \forall\, q \in W_h. \end{aligned} \tag{21}$$

So, we have

$$\begin{aligned} &a(\mathbf{u}_h - \pi_h \mathbf{u}, \mathbf{v}) - b(\mathbf{v}, p_h - \mathcal{P}_h p) = a(\mathbf{u} - \pi_h \mathbf{u}, \mathbf{v}) - b(\mathbf{v}, p - \mathcal{P}_h p), \quad \forall\, \mathbf{v} \in \mathbf{U}_{h0}, \\ &b(\mathbf{u} - \pi_h \mathbf{u}, q) + b(\pi_h \mathbf{u} - \mathbf{u}_h, q) = 0, \quad \forall\, q \in W_h. \end{aligned} \tag{22}$$

Based on the definition of L^2 projection and Equation (14), substituting Equation (18) into the above equation yields

$$\begin{aligned} a(\mathbf{e}_h, \mathbf{v}) - b(\mathbf{v}, \xi_h) &= a(\mathbf{u} - \pi_h \mathbf{u}, \mathbf{v}), && \forall\, \mathbf{v} \in \mathbf{U}_{h0}, \\ b(\mathbf{e}_h, q) &= 0, && \forall\, q \in W_h. \end{aligned} \tag{23}$$

From the second equation of Equation (23), we find that $\nabla \cdot \mathbf{e}_h = 0$. In the first equation of Equation (23), by taking $\mathbf{v} = \mathbf{e}_h$, and, in the second equation, taking $q = \xi_h$, then we have

$$a(\mathbf{e}_h, \mathbf{e}_h) = a(\mathbf{u} - \pi_h \mathbf{u}, \mathbf{e}_h). \tag{24}$$

From condition (19) and $\nabla \cdot \mathbf{e}_h = 0$, it can be inferred that

$$a(\mathbf{e}_h, \mathbf{e}_h) \le CM(\mathbf{u}, p) h^{m+s} \|\mathbf{e}_h\|_0, \tag{25}$$

so,

$$\|\mathbf{e}_h\|_0 \le C h^{m+s} M(\mathbf{u}, p). \tag{26}$$

Then, now we estimate the L^2-norm of ξ_h. From the inf-sup condition and continuity condition, we arrive at

$$\begin{aligned} \|\xi_h\|_0 &\le C \sup_{\mathbf{v} \in \mathbf{U}_{h0}} \frac{b(\mathbf{v}, \xi_h)}{\|\mathbf{v}\|_U} \\ &= C \sup_{\mathbf{v} \in \mathbf{U}_{h0}} \frac{b(\mathbf{v}, p_h - p)}{\|\mathbf{v}\|_U} \\ &= C \sup_{\mathbf{v} \in \mathbf{U}_{h0}} \frac{a(\mathbf{v}, \mathbf{u}_h - \mathbf{u})}{\|\mathbf{v}\|_U} \\ &= C \sup_{\mathbf{v} \in \mathbf{U}_{h0}} \frac{a(\mathbf{v}, \mathbf{u}_h - \pi_h \mathbf{u}) + a(\mathbf{v}, \pi_h \mathbf{u} - \mathbf{u})}{\|\mathbf{v}\|_U} \\ &\le C \sup_{\mathbf{v} \in \mathbf{U}_{h0}} \frac{a(\mathbf{v}, \mathbf{u} - \pi_h \mathbf{u})}{\|\mathbf{v}\|_U} + C\|\mathbf{u}_h - \pi_h \mathbf{u}\|_0 \\ &\le C h^{m+s} M(\mathbf{u}, p). \end{aligned} \tag{27}$$

This completes the proof. □

4. Main Results of Superconvergence

Theorem 1 shows that, if a corresponding estimate in bilinear form $\mathcal{A}(\mathbf{v}) = a((\mathbf{u} - \pi_h \mathbf{u}), \mathbf{v})$ is established in a mixed finite element space $\mathbf{U}_{h0}$, superconvergence will be guaranteed. In this section, we divide $\mathcal{A}(\mathbf{v})$ into six parts and verify error estimates separately, ultimately achieving the desired superconvergence result.

Let us introduce some short-hand notation for partial derivatives, the multi-index notation. A multi-index, α, is an n-tuple of non-negative integers, α_i. The length of α is provided by

$$|\alpha| := \sum_{i=1}^{n} \alpha_i. \tag{28}$$

For $\phi \in \mathbb{C}^{\infty}$, denote by

$$D^{\alpha}\phi = (\frac{\partial}{\partial x_1})^{\alpha_1} \cdots (\frac{\partial}{\partial x_n})^{\alpha_n}\phi. \tag{29}$$

First, let us review the definition of the norm in Sobolev spaces. Denote the seminorm and the norm in the Sobolev space $W^{k,r}(\Omega)$ with integer $k \geq 0$ and real number $r \geq 1$ by

$$|\mathbf{u}|_{k,r;\Omega} = \sum_{|\alpha|=k} \|D^{\alpha}\mathbf{u}\|_{L^r}, \|\mathbf{u}\|_{k,r;\Omega} = \sum_{j=0}^{k} |\mathbf{u}|_{j,r;\Omega}.$$

And, define the seminorm of any piecewise polynomial q with

$$|q|_{k,r,h} = \sum_{|\alpha|=k} \left(\sum_{e \in \mathcal{T}_h} \|D^{\alpha}q\|^r_{L^r(e)} \right)^{1/r}.$$

Let σ be any smooth vector-valued function on a rectangular element e and satisfy the following system:

$$\begin{aligned} \int_{\ell_i} \sigma dy &= 0, \qquad i = 1,2,3,4, \\ \int_e x^j \sigma dxdy &= 0, \qquad 0 \leq j \leq \lambda - 1. \end{aligned} \tag{30}$$

We introduce σ to facilitate the estimation of the following components. Therefore, the following lemma holds.

Lemma 1 ([29]). *Let ℓ_1, ℓ_3 be two vertical sides of element $e = [x_i, x_{i+1}] \times [y_j, y_{j+1}]$, $2h_e = x_{i+1} - x_i$ is the length of ℓ_2, and ℓ_4, (x_e, y_e) is the center of e, $E(x) = (x - x_e)^2 - h_e^2$. Then, for any integer $k \leq \lambda + 1$, we have*

$$\int_e (x - x_e)^k \sigma dxdy = \frac{(-1)^k k!}{(2k+2)!} \int_e E^{k+1}(x) \partial_x^{k+2} \sigma dxdy. \tag{31}$$

For the bilinear form $\mathcal{A}(\mathbf{v}) = a((\mathbf{u} - \pi_h \mathbf{u}), \mathbf{v})$, where $\mathbf{v} = (v_1, v_2)$, we can write the bilinear form $\mathcal{A}(\mathbf{v})$ as six components

$$\begin{aligned} \mathcal{A}(\mathbf{v}) &= [2(\partial_x(u_1 - \pi_1 u_1), \partial_x v_1) + (\partial_y(u_1 - \pi_1 u_1), \partial_y v_1)] + [2(\partial_y(u_2 - \pi_2 u_2), \partial_y v_2) \\ &\quad + (\partial_x(u_2 - \pi_2 u_2), \partial_x v_2)] + (\partial_x(u_2 - \pi_2 u_2), \partial_y v_1) + (\partial_y(u_1 - \pi_1 u_1), \partial_x v_2) \\ &= \sum_{e \in \mathcal{T}_h} (2(\partial_x(u_1 - \pi_1 u_1), \partial_x v_1))_e + \sum_{e \in \mathcal{T}_h} ((\partial_y(u_1 - \pi_1 u_1), \partial_y v_1))_e \\ &\quad + \sum_{e \in \mathcal{T}_h} (2(\partial_y(u_2 - \pi_2 u_2), \partial_y v_2))_e + \sum_{e \in \mathcal{T}_h} ((\partial_x(u_2 - \pi_2 u_2), \partial_x v_2))_e \\ &\quad + \sum_{e \in \mathcal{T}_h} (\partial_x(u_2 - \pi_2 u_2), \partial_y v_1)_e + \sum_{e \in \mathcal{T}_h} (\partial_y(u_1 - \pi_1 u_1), \partial_x v_2)_e \\ &= \mathcal{A}_1 + \mathcal{A}_2 + \mathcal{A}_3 + \mathcal{A}_4 + \mathcal{A}_5 + \mathcal{A}_6. \end{aligned} \tag{32}$$

Next, we will begin to estimate the six components of the bilinear form.

Lemma 2. *For any integer $m \geq 1$ and a sufficiently smooth function u_1 on the rectangular element e, let v_1 be a polynomial with degree of x and y no more than m and v_2 be any sufficiently smooth function on e. Then, there will be an area integral $J_{1,e}$ on e, and $J_{1,e}$ satisfies*

$$\begin{aligned} &(2(\partial_x(u_1 - \pi_1 u_1), \partial_x v_1))_e \\ &= J_{1,e} - \frac{(-1)^m}{(2m)!} (\int_{\ell_2} - \int_{\ell_4}) F^m(y) \partial_x \partial_y^{m+1} u_1 \partial_y^{m-1} v_1(x, y_e) dy, \end{aligned} \tag{33}$$

and follows the estimate

$$|J_{1,e}| \leq \frac{2(-1)^m k_e^{2m}}{(2m)!}\left[|u_1|_{m+3,\alpha;e}|v_1|_{m-1,\beta;e} + k_e|u_1|_{m+3,\alpha;e}|v_1|_{2,\beta;e} + \frac{k_e^2}{(2m+1)(2m+2)}|u_1|_{m+3,\alpha;e}|v_1|_{2,\beta;e}\right], \tag{34}$$

where α *and* β *are a pair of conjugate numbers and satisfy* $\frac{1}{\alpha} + \frac{1}{\beta} = 1, \alpha, \beta \geq 1.$

Proof. Firstly, Taylor of v_1 at $y = y_e$ is expanded as follows

$$(v_1)_x = \sum_{i=0}^{m} \frac{1}{i!}(y - y_e)^i \partial_x \partial_y^i v_1(x, y_e), \tag{35}$$

we divide $(v_1)_x$ into two parts, $i \leq m-2$ and $i = m-1, m$, and then

$$\begin{aligned} 2(\partial_x(u_1 - \pi_1 u_1), \partial_x v_1)_e &= 2\int_e (u_1 - \pi_1 u_1)_x \sum_{i=0}^{m} \frac{1}{i!}(y - y_e)^i \partial_x \partial_y^i v_1(x, y_e) dxdy \\ &= 2\int_e (u_1 - \pi_1 u_1)_x \sum_{i=0}^{m-2} \frac{1}{i!}(y - y_e)^i \partial_x \partial_y^i v_1(x, y_e) dxdy \\ &+ 2\int_e (u_1 - \pi_1 u_1)_x \frac{1}{m-1!}(y - y_e)^{m-1} \partial_x \partial_y^{m-1} v_1(x, y_e) dxdy \\ &+ 2\int_e (u_1 - \pi_1 u_1)_x \frac{1}{m!}(y - y_e)^m \partial_x \partial_y^m v_1(x, y_e) dxdy. \end{aligned} \tag{36}$$

We first analyze the first one on the right side of the above formula. According to the definition of projection operator π_e, $u_1 - \pi_1 u_1$ is orthogonal to Bernstein polynomial space $U_h(m-2, m-2)$; therefore,

$$\begin{aligned} & 2\int_e (u_1 - \pi_1 u_1)_x \sum_{i=0}^{m-2} \frac{1}{i!}(y - y_e)^i \partial_x \partial_y^i v_1(x, y_e) dxdy \\ &= \left(\int_{\ell_2} - \int_{\ell_4}\right) 2(u_1 - \pi_1 u_1) \sum_{i=0}^{m-2} \frac{1}{i!}(y - y_e)^i \partial_x \partial_y^i v_1(x, y_e) dy \\ &- 2\int_e (u_1 - \pi_1 u_1) \sum_{i=0}^{m-2} \frac{1}{i!}(y - y_e)^i \partial_x^2 \partial_y^i v_1(x, y_e) dxdy \\ &= 0. \end{aligned} \tag{37}$$

When $i = m-1, m$,

$$\begin{aligned} \frac{1}{m-1!}(y - y_e)^{m-1} &= \frac{1}{2m!}(F^m(y))^{(m+1)} + H_1(y), \quad H_1(y) \in P_{m-3}(y), \\ \frac{1}{m!}(y - y_e)^m &= \frac{1}{(2m+2)!}(F^{m+1}(y))^{(m+2)} + H_2(y), \quad H_2(y) \in P_{m-2}(y), \end{aligned} \tag{38}$$

then, by the definition of interpolation function and the above formula, we have

$$\begin{aligned} & 2\int_e (u_1 - \pi_1 u_1)_x \frac{1}{m-1!}(y - y_e)^{m-1} \partial_x \partial_y^{m-1} v_1(x, y_e) dxdy \\ &+ 2\int_e (u_1 - \pi_1 u_1)_x \frac{1}{m!}(y - y_e)^m \partial_x \partial_y^m v_1(x, y_e) dxdy \\ &= \frac{2}{2m!}\int_e ((F^m(y))^{(m+1)} + H_1(y))(u_1 - \pi_1 u_1)_x \partial_x \partial_y^{m-1} v_1(x, y_e) dxdy \\ &+ \frac{2}{(2m+2)!}\int_e ((F^{m+1}(y))^{(m+2)} + H_2(y))(u_1 - \pi_1 u_1)_x \partial_x \partial_y^m v_1(x, y_e) dxdy \end{aligned} \tag{39}$$

$$
\begin{aligned}
&= \frac{2}{2m!}\Big(\int_{\ell_1} - \int_{\ell_3}\Big)(u_1 - \pi_1 u_1)_x (F^m(y))^{(m)} \partial_x \partial_y^{m-1} v_1(x, y_e) dx \\
&- \frac{2}{2m!}\int_e (u_1 - \pi_1 u_1)_{xy} (F^m(y))^{(m)} \partial_x \partial_y^{m-1} v_1(x, y_e) dxdy \\
&+ \frac{2}{(2m+2)!}\Big(\int_{\ell_1} - \int_{\ell_3}\Big)(u_1 - \pi_1 u_1)_x (F^{m+1}(y))^{(m+1)} \partial_x \partial_y^{m} v_1(x, y_e) dx \\
&- \frac{2}{(2m+2)!}\int_e (u_1 - \pi_1 u_1)_{xy} (F^{m+1}(y))^{(m+1)} \partial_x \partial_y^{m} v_1(x, y_e) dxdy.
\end{aligned} \tag{40}
$$

Because $(F^m(y))^{(k_1)} = 0, k_1 \le m-1$ and $(F^{m+1}(y))^{(k_2)} = 0, k_2 \le m$, from the definition of interpolation function and partial integration,

$$
\begin{aligned}
&2\int_e (u_1 - \pi_1 u_1)_x \frac{1}{m-1!}(y - y_e)^{m-1} \partial_x \partial_y^{m-1} v_1(x, y_e) dxdy \\
&+ 2\int_e (u_1 - \pi_1 u_1)_x \frac{1}{m!}(y - y_e)^{m} \partial_x \partial_y^{m} v_1(x, y_e) dxdy \\
&= \frac{2(-1)^{m+1}}{(2m)!}\int F^m(y) \partial_x \partial_y^{m+1} u_1 \partial_x \partial_y^{m-1} v_1(x, y_e) dxdy \\
&+ \frac{2(-1)^{m+1}}{(2m+2)!}\int (F^{m+1})'(y) \partial_x \partial_y^{m+1} u_1 \partial_x \partial_y^{m} v_1(x, y_e) dxdy \\
&= -\frac{2(-1)^{m}}{(2m)!}\Big(\int_{\ell_2} - \int_{\ell_4}\Big) F^m(y) \partial_x \partial_y^{m+1} u_1 \partial_y^{m-1} v_1(x, y_e) dy \\
&+ \frac{2(-1)^{m}}{(2m)!}\int_e F^m(y) \partial_x^2 \partial_y^{m+1} u_1 \partial_y^{m-1} v_1(x, y_e) dxdy \\
&- \frac{2(-1)^{m+1}}{(2m+2)!}\int F^{m+1}(y) \partial_x \partial_y^{m+2} u_1 \partial_x \partial_y^{m} v_1 dxdy \\
&= I_1 + I_2 + I_3.
\end{aligned} \tag{41}
$$

Since $\partial_y^{m-1} v_1(x, y)$ is linear with respect to y, $\partial_y^{m-1} v_1(x, y_e) = \partial_y^{m-1} v_1(x, y) + (y_e - y)\partial_y^m v_1(x, y)$,

$$
\begin{aligned}
I_2 &= \frac{2(-1)^{m}}{(2m)!}\int_e F^m(y) \partial_x^2 \partial_y^{m+1} u_1 \big(\partial_y^{m-1} v_1(x, y) + (y_e - y)\partial_y^m v_1(x, y)\big) dxdy \\
&= \frac{2(-1)^{m}}{(2m)!}\int_e F^m(y) \partial_x^2 \partial_y^{m+1} u_1 \partial_y^{m-1} v_1 dxdy + \frac{2(-1)^{m}}{(2m)!}\int_e F^m(y) \partial_x^2 \partial_y^{m+1} u_1 (y_e - y)\partial_y^m v_1 dxdy
\end{aligned} \tag{42}
$$

Let $J_{1,e}$ represent the sum of the above area integrals, i.e.,

$$
\begin{aligned}
J_{1,e} &= \frac{2(-1)^{m}}{(2m)!}\int_e F^m(y) \partial_x^2 \partial_y^{m+1} u_1 \partial_y^{m-1} v_1 dxdy + \frac{2(-1)^{m}}{(2m)!}\int_e F^m(y) \partial_x^2 \partial_y^{m+1} u_1 (y_e - y)\partial_y^m v_1 dxdy \\
&+ \frac{2(-1)^{m}}{(2m+2)!}\int_e F^{m+1}(y) \partial_x \partial_y^{m+2} u_1 \partial_x \partial_y^{m} v_1 dxdy,
\end{aligned} \tag{43}
$$

so, we yield

$$
\begin{aligned}
&\big(2(\partial_x(u_1 - \pi_1 u_1), \partial_x v_1)\big)_e \\
&= J_{1,e} - \frac{2(-1)^{m}}{(2m)!}\Big(\int_{\ell_2} - \int_{\ell_4}\Big) F^m(y) \partial_x \partial_y^{m+1} u_1 \partial_y^{m-1} v_1(x, y_e) dy.
\end{aligned} \tag{44}
$$

Then, we estimate the sum $J_{1,e}$ of the area integrals. Because (x_e, y_e) is the center of the rectangle element e, there is $|y - y_e| \le k_e, \Rightarrow |F(y)| = |(y - y_e)^2 - k_e^2| \le k_e^2$. Subsequently, we use the Hölder inequality, yielding

$$|J_{1,e}| \le \frac{2(-1)^m k_e^{2m}}{(2m)!}\Big[|u_1|_{m+3,\alpha;e}|v_1|_{m-1,\beta;e} + k_e|u_1|_{m+3,\alpha;e}|v_1|_{2,\beta;e} + \frac{k_e^2}{(2m+1)(2m+2)}|u_1|_{m+3,\alpha;e}|v_1|_{2,\beta;e}\Big]. \tag{45}$$

Thus, we have completed the derivation of Lemma 2. □

Lemma 3. *For any integer $m \ge 1$ and a sufficiently smooth function u_2 on the rectangular element e, let v_2 be a polynomial with degree of x and y no more than m on e. Then, there will be an area integral $J_{2,e}$ on e that satisfies*

$$\begin{aligned}&((\partial_x(u_2 - \pi_2 u_2), \partial_x v_1))_e\\ &= J_{2,e} - \frac{(-1)^m}{(2m)!}\Big(\int_{\ell_2} - \int_{\ell_4}\Big)F^m(y)\partial_x\partial_y^{m+1}u_2\partial_y^{m-1}v_2(x,y_e)dy,\end{aligned} \tag{46}$$

and follows the estimate

$$|J_{2,e}| \le \frac{(-1)^m k_e^{2m}}{(2m)!}\Big[|u_2|_{m+3,\alpha;e}|v_2|_{m-1,\beta;e} + k_e|u_2|_{m+3,\alpha;e}|v_2|_{2,\beta;e} + \frac{k_e^2}{(2m+1)(2m+2)}|u_2|_{m+3,\alpha;e}|v_2|_{2,\beta;e}\Big]. \tag{47}$$

where α and β are a pair of conjugate numbers and satisfy $\frac{1}{\alpha} + \frac{1}{\beta} = 1, \alpha, \beta \ge 1$.

The proof of Lemma 3 is similar to Lemma 2, so we omit the detailed proof here.

Lemma 4. *For any integer $n \ge 1$ and a sufficiently smooth function u_1 on the rectangular element e, let v_1 be a polynomial with degree of x and y no more than m on e. Then, there will be an area integral $J_{3,e}$ on e, and $J_{3,e}$ satisfies*

$$\begin{aligned}&((\partial_y(u_1 - \pi_1 u_1), \partial_y v_1))_e\\ &= J_{3,e} + \frac{(-1)^m}{2m!}\Big(\int_{\ell_1} - \int_{\ell_3}\Big)E^m(x)\partial_x^{m+1}u_1\partial_y^2\partial_x^m v_1 dx\\ &+ \frac{(-1)^m}{2m!(2m+2)}\Big(\int_{\ell_1} - \int_{\ell_3}\Big)E^{m+1}(x)\partial_x^{m+2}u_1\partial_y\partial_x^m v_1 dx\\ &- \frac{(-1)^m}{2m!(2m+2)}\Big(\int_{\ell_2} - \int_{\ell_4}\Big)E^{m+1}(x)\partial_x^{m+1}u_1\partial_y^2\partial_x^m v_1 dy\\ &+ \frac{(-1)^m}{(2m+2)!}\Big(\int_{\ell_1} - \int_{\ell_3}\Big)E^{m+1}(x)\partial_x^{m+2}u_1\partial_y\partial_x^m v_1 dx,\end{aligned} \tag{48}$$

and follows the estimate

$$|J_{3,e}| \le \frac{(-1)^m h_e^{2m}}{(2m)!}\Big[|u_1|_{m+2,\alpha;e}|v_1|_{m,\beta;e} + \frac{1}{2m+2}|u_1|_{m+3,\alpha;e}|v_1|_{2,\beta;e} + \frac{h_e^2}{(2m+2)(2m+1)}|u_1|_{m+3,\alpha;e}|v_1|_{2,\beta;e}\Big], \tag{49}$$

Proof. Expand v_1 in a Taylor series at $x = x_e$,

$$v_1 = \sum_{i=0}^{m}\frac{1}{i!}(x - x_e)^i\partial_x^i v_1(x_e, y). \tag{50}$$

Therefore,

$$
\begin{aligned}
&((\partial_y(u_1-\pi_1 u_1),\partial_y v_1))_e \\
&=\int_e (u_1-\pi_1 u_1)_y \sum_{i=0}^{m}\frac{1}{i!}(x-x_e)^i\partial_y\partial_x^i v_1(x_e,y)dxdy \\
&=(\int_{\ell_1}-\int_{\ell_3})(u_1-\pi_1 u_1)\sum_{i=0}^{m}\frac{1}{i!}(x-x_e)^i\partial_y\partial_x^i v_1(x_e,y)dx \\
&-\int_e (u_1-\pi_1 u_1)\sum_{i=0}^{m}\frac{1}{i!}(x-x_e)^i\partial_y^2\partial_x^i v_1(x_e,y)dxdy \\
&=-\int_e (u_1-\pi_1 u_1)\sum_{i=0}^{m}\frac{1}{i!}(x-x_e)\partial_y^2\partial_x^i v_1(x_e,y)dxdy,
\end{aligned}
\tag{51}
$$

By the definition of interpolation functions, we can obtain

$$
\begin{aligned}
&((\partial_y(u_1-\pi_1 u_1),\partial_y v_1))_e \\
&=-\int_e (u_1-\pi_1 u_1)\frac{1}{(m-1)!}(x-x_e)^{m-1}\partial_y^2\partial_x^{m-1}v_1(x_e,y)dxdy \\
&-\int_e (u_1-\pi_1 u_1)\frac{1}{m!}(x-x_e)^m\partial_y^2\partial_x^m v_1(x_e,y)dxdy \\
&=I_4+I_5.
\end{aligned}
\tag{52}
$$

We first discuss I_4. Let $\sigma_1=(u_1-\pi_1 u_1)\partial_y^2\partial_x^{m-1}v_1(x_e,y)$, and then we use Lemma 1 to obtain

$$
\begin{aligned}
I_4&=\frac{(-1)^m}{(2m)!}\int_e E^m(x)\partial_x^{m+1}u_1\partial_y^2\partial_x^{m-1}v_1(x_e,y)dxdy \\
&=\frac{(-1)^m}{(2m)!}\int_e E^m(x)\partial_x^{m+1}u_1\partial_y^2(\partial_x^{m-1}v_1+(x_e-x)\partial_x^m v_1)dxdy \\
&=\frac{(-1)^m}{(2m)!}\int_e E^m(x)\partial_x^{m+1}u_1\partial_y^2\partial_x^{m-1}v_1dxdy+\frac{(-1)^m}{(2m)!}\int_e(x_e-x)E^m(x)\partial_x^{m+1}u_1\partial_y^2\partial_x^m v_1dxdy \\
&=\frac{(-1)^m}{(2m)!}(\int_{\ell_1}-\int_{\ell_3})E^m(x)\partial_x^{m+1}u_1\partial_y\partial_x^{m-1}v_1dx-\frac{(-1)^m}{(2m)!}(\int_{\ell_1}-\int_{\ell_3})E^m(x)\partial_y\partial_x^{m+1}u_1\partial_x^{m-1}v_1dx \\
&-\frac{(-1)^m}{(2m)!}\int_e E^m(x)\partial_y\partial_x^{m+1}u_1\partial_y\partial_x^{m-1}v_1dxdy+\frac{(-1)^m}{(2m)!}\int_e(x_e-x)E^m(x)\partial_x^{m+1}u_1\partial_y^2\partial_x^m v_1dxdy,
\end{aligned}
\tag{53}
$$

due to $(x-x_e)E^m(x)=\frac{1}{2m+2}\partial_x E^{m+1}(x)$,

$$
\begin{aligned}
I_4&=\frac{(-1)^m}{(2m)!}(\int_{\ell_1}-\int_{\ell_3})E^m(x)\partial_x^{m+1}u_1\partial_y\partial_x^{m-1}v_1dx-\frac{(-1)^m}{(2m)!}\int_e E^m(x)\partial_y\partial_x^{m+1}u_1\partial_y\partial_x^{m-1}v_1dxdy \\
&-\frac{(-1)^m}{(2m)!(2m+2)}(\int_{\ell_2}-\int_{\ell_4})E^{m+1}(x)\partial_x^{m+1}u_1\partial_y^2\partial_x^m v_1dy-\frac{(-1)^m}{(2m)!(2m+2)}\int_e E^{m+1}(x)\partial_x^{m+2}\partial_y u_1\partial_x^m v_1dxdy \\
&+\frac{(-1)^m}{(2m)!(2m+2)}(\int_{\ell_1}-\int_{\ell_3})E^{m+1}(x)\partial_x^{m+2}u_1\partial_y\partial_x^m v_1dx.
\end{aligned}
\tag{54}
$$

Next, we analyze I_5 in a similar way.

$$
I_5=\frac{(-1)^m}{(2m+2)!}(\int_{\ell_1}-\int_{\ell_3})E^{m+1}(x)\partial_x^{m+2}u_1\partial_y\partial_x^m v_1dx-\frac{(-1)^m}{(2m+2)!}\int_e E^{m+1}(x)\partial_y\partial_x^{m+2}u_1\partial_y\partial_x^m v_1dxdy.
\tag{55}
$$

And let $J_{3,e}$ represent the sum of all the above areas.

$$\begin{aligned} J_{3,e} = & -\frac{(-1)^m}{(2m)!}\int_e E^m(x)\partial_y\partial_x^{m+1}u_1\partial_y\partial_x^{m-1}v_1dxdy \\ & -\frac{(-1)^m}{(2m)!(2m+2)}\int_e E^{m+1}(x)\partial_x^{m+2}\partial_y u_1\partial_x^m v_1dxdy \\ & -\frac{(-1)^m}{(2m+2)!}\int_e E^{m+1}(x)\partial_y\partial_x^{m+2}u_1\partial_y\partial_x^m v_1dxdy. \end{aligned} \tag{56}$$

So, from the above deduction, we can see that

$$\begin{aligned} & ((\partial_y(u_1-\pi_1u_1),\partial_y v_1))_e \\ & = J_{3,e}+\frac{(-1)^m}{2m!}(\int_{\ell_1}-\int_{\ell_3})E^m(x)\partial_x^{m+1}u_1\partial_y^2\partial_x^m v_1dx \\ & +\frac{(-1)^m}{2m!(2m+2)}(\int_{\ell_1}-\int_{\ell_3})E^{m+1}(x)\partial_x^{m+2}u_1\partial_y\partial_x^m v_1dx \\ & -\frac{(-1)^m}{2m!(2m+2)}(\int_{\ell_2}-\int_{\ell_4})E^{m+1}(x)\partial_x^{m+1}u_1\partial_y^2\partial_x^m v_1dy \\ & +\frac{(-1)^m}{(2m+2)!}(\int_{\ell_1}-\int_{\ell_3})E^{m+1}(x)\partial_x^{m+2}u_1\partial_y\partial_x^m v_1dx. \end{aligned} \tag{57}$$

Next, we estimate the sum $J_{3,e}$ of all surface integrals. Considering that (x_e, y_e) serves as the center of the rectangular element e, there is $|x-x_e|\le h_e, \Rightarrow |E(x)| = |(x-x_e)^2 - h_e^2| \le h_e^2$. Following this, by invoking the Hölder inequality,

$$\begin{aligned} |J_{3,e}| \le & \frac{(-1)^m h_e^{2m}}{(2m)!}\Big[|u_1|_{m+2,\alpha;e}|v_1|_{m,\beta;e}+\frac{1}{2m+2}|u_1|_{m+3,\alpha;e}|v_1|_{2,\beta;e} \\ & +\frac{h_e^2}{(2m+2)(2m+1)}|u_1|_{m+3,\alpha;e}|v_1|_{2,\beta;e}\Big]. \end{aligned} \tag{58}$$

So far, we have completed the proof of Lemma 4. □

Lemma 5. *For any integer $m \ge 1$ and a sufficiently smooth function u_2 on the rectangular element e, let v_2 be a polynomial with degree of x and y no more than m on e. Then, there will be an area integral $J_{4,e}$ on e that satisfies*

$$\begin{aligned} & (2(\partial_y(u_2-\pi_2u_2),\partial_y v_2))_e \\ & = J_{4,e}+\frac{2(-1)^m}{2m!}(\int_{\ell_1}-\int_{\ell_3})E^m(x)\partial_x^{m+1}u_2\partial_y^2\partial_x^m v_2dx \\ & +\frac{(-1)^m}{2m!(m+1)}(\int_{\ell_1}-\int_{\ell_3})E^{m+1}(x)\partial_x^{m+2}u_2\partial_y\partial_x^m v_2dx \\ & -\frac{(-1)^m}{2m!(m+1)}(\int_{\ell_2}-\int_{\ell_4})E^{m+1}(x)\partial_x^{m+1}u_2\partial_y^2\partial_x^m v_2dy \\ & +\frac{2(-1)^m}{(2m+2)!}(\int_{\ell_1}-\int_{\ell_3})E^{m+1}(x)\partial_x^{m+2}u_2\partial_y\partial_x^m v_2dx, \end{aligned} \tag{59}$$

and follows the estimate

$$\begin{aligned} |J_{4,e}| \le & \frac{2(-1)^m h_e^{2m}}{(2m)!}\Big[|u_2|_{m+2,\alpha;e}|v_2|_{m,\beta;e}+\frac{1}{2m+2}|u_2|_{m+3,\alpha;e}|v_2|_{2,\beta;e} \\ & +\frac{h_e^2}{(2m+2)(2m+1)}|u_2|_{m+3,\alpha;e}|v_2|_{2,\beta;e}\Big], \end{aligned} \tag{60}$$

where α and β are a pair of conjugate numbers and satisfy $\frac{1}{\alpha}+\frac{1}{\beta}=1, \alpha, \beta \geq 1$.

The proof of Lemma 5 follows a parallel structure to that of Lemma 4 and thus is not provided here.

Lemma 6. *For any integer $m \geq 1$ and a sufficiently smooth function u_2 on the rectangular element e, let v_1 be a polynomial with degree of x and y no more than m. Then, there will be an area integral $J_{5,e}$ on e, and $J_{5,e}$ satisfies*

$$(\partial_x(u_2-\pi_2 u_2), \partial_y v_1)_e = J_{5,e} + \frac{(-1)^m}{2m!}\Big(\int_{\ell_1} - \int_{\ell_3}\Big)\partial_x^{m+1} u_2 E^m(x) \partial_x^m v_1 dx, \tag{61}$$

and follows the estimate

$$\begin{aligned} |J_{5,e}| \leq \frac{(-1)^m}{(2m)!}\Big[& k_e^{2m}|u_2|_{m+2,\alpha;e}|v_1|_{2,\beta;e} + h_e^{2m}|u_2|_{m+2,\alpha;e}|v_1|_{m,\beta;e} \\ &+ Ck_e^{2m}|u_2|_{m+3,\alpha;e}|v_1|_{2,\beta;e}\Big], \end{aligned} \tag{62}$$

where α and β are a pair of conjugate numbers and satisfy $\frac{1}{\alpha}+\frac{1}{\beta}=1, \alpha, \beta \geq 1$.

Proof. Perform a Taylor expansion of v_1 about x and y,

$$\begin{aligned} \partial_y v_1 &= \sum_{i=0}^{m-1} \frac{1}{i!}(x-x_e)^i \partial_x^i \partial_y v_1(x_e, y) + \frac{1}{m!}(x-x_e)^m \partial_x^m \partial_y v_1 \\ &= \sum_{j=0}^{m-2}\sum_{i=0}^{m-1} \frac{1}{j!}\frac{1}{i!}(x-x_e)^i (y-y_e)^j \partial_x^i \partial_y^{j+1} v_1(x_e, y_e) \\ &+ \frac{1}{(m-1)!}\sum_{i=0}^{m-1}\frac{1}{i!}(x-x_e)^i(y-y_e)^{m-1}\partial_x^i\partial_y^m v_1(x_e,y) + \frac{1}{m!}(x-x_e)^m\partial_x^m\partial_y v_1. \end{aligned} \tag{63}$$

Let

$$H(x,y) = \sum_{j=0}^{m-2}\sum_{i=0}^{m-1} \frac{1}{j!}\frac{1}{i!}(x-x_e)^i (y-y_e)^j \partial_x^i \partial_y^{j+1} v_1(x_e, y_e), \tag{64}$$

when x is fixed, $H(x,y) \in P_{m-2}$, $(H(x,y))_x \in span\{\{\mathcal{B}_{i,j}^{m-2,m-2}\}\}$. As can be seen from the definition of interpolation function,

$$\int_e (u_2-\pi_2 u_2)_x H(x,y) = \Big(\int_{\ell_2} - \int_{\ell_4}\Big)(u_2-\pi_2 u_2)H(x,y)dy - \int_e (u_2-\pi_2 u_2)H(x,y)_x dxdy = 0. \tag{65}$$

So, we have

$$\begin{aligned} &(\partial_x(u_2-\pi_2 u_2), \partial_y v_1)_e \\ &= \int_e (u_2-\pi_2 u_2)_x \frac{1}{(m-1)!}\sum_{i=0}^{m-1}\frac{1}{i!}(x-x_e)^i(y-y_e)^{m-1}\partial_x^i\partial_y^m v_1(x_e,y)dxdy \\ &+ \int_e (u_2-\pi_2 u_2)_x \frac{1}{m!}(x-x_e)^m \partial_x^m \partial_y v_1 dxdy \\ &= I_6 + I_7. \end{aligned} \tag{66}$$

It is similar to the proof of Lemma 3, so there is

$$I_6 = -\frac{(-1)^m}{2m!}\int_e F^m(y)\partial_x \partial_y^{m+1} u_2 \sum_{i=0}^{m-1}\frac{1}{i!}(x-x_e)^i \partial_x^i \partial_y^m v_1(x_e, y). \tag{67}$$

We continue to analyze I_7, owing to $\frac{1}{m!}(x-x_e)^m = \frac{1}{2m!}(E^m(x))^{(m)} + \widehat{H}(x), \widehat{H}(x) \in P_{m-2}(x)$, so

$$\begin{aligned}
I_7 &= \int_e (u_2-\pi_2u_2)_x[\frac{1}{2m!}(E^m(x))^{(m)} + \widehat{H}(x)]\partial_x^m\partial_y v_1(x,y)dxdy \\
&= \frac{1}{2m!}\int_e (u_2-\pi_2u_2)_x(E^m(x))^{(m)}\partial_x^m\partial_y v_1(x,y)dxdy \\
&+ \int_e (u_2-\pi_2u_2)_x\widehat{H}(x)(\sum_{i=0}^{m-2}\frac{1}{i!}(y-y_e)^i\partial_x^m\partial_y^{i+1}v_1(x,y_e))dxdy \\
&+ \int_e (u_2-\pi_2u_2)_x\widehat{H}(x)\frac{1}{(m-1)!}(y-y_e)^{m-1}\partial_x^m\partial_y^m v_1dxdy \\
&= \frac{(-1)^m}{2m!}\int_e \partial_x^{m+1}u_2E^m(x)\partial_x^m\partial_y v_1dxdy + 0 \\
&- \frac{(-1)^m}{2m!}\int_e F^m(y)\partial_x\partial_y^{m+1}u_2\widehat{H}(x)\partial_x^m\partial_y^m v_1dxdy \\
&= \frac{(-1)^m}{2m!}(\int_{\ell_1} - \int_{\ell_3})\partial_x^{m+1}u_2E^m(x)\partial_x^m v_1dx - \frac{(-1)^m}{2m!}\int_e \partial_x^{m+1}\partial_y u_2E^m(x)\partial_x^m v_1dxdy \\
&- \frac{(-1)^m}{2m!}\int_e F^m(y)\partial_x\partial_y^{m+1}u_2\widehat{H}(x)\partial_x^m\partial_y^m v_1dxdy.
\end{aligned} \tag{68}$$

And let $J_{5,e}$ represent the sum of all area integrals in the mixed term $(\partial_x(u_2-\pi_2u_2), \partial_y v_1)_e$,

$$\begin{aligned}
J_{5,e} = &-\frac{(-1)^m}{2m!}\int_e F^m(y)\partial_x\partial_y^{m+1}u_2\sum_{i=0}^{m-1}\frac{1}{i!}(x-x_e)^i\partial_x^i\partial_y^m v_1(x_e,y) \\
&-\frac{(-1)^m}{2m!}\int_e \partial_x^{m+1}\partial_y u_2E^m(x)\partial_x^m v_1dxdy \\
&-\frac{(-1)^m}{2m!}\int_e F^m(y)\partial_x\partial_y^{m+1}u_2\widehat{H}(x)\partial_x^m\partial_y^m v_1dxdy,
\end{aligned} \tag{69}$$

therefore,

$$(\partial_x(u_2-\pi_2u_2), \partial_y v_1)_e = J_{5,e} + \frac{(-1)^m}{2m!}(\int_{\ell_1} - \int_{\ell_3})\partial_x^{m+1}u_2E^m(x)\partial_x^m v_1dx. \tag{70}$$

Now, we use the Hölder inequality to estimate the $J_{5,e}$, obtaining

$$\begin{aligned}
|J_{5,e}| \le \frac{(-1)^m}{(2m)!}&\Big[k_e^{2m}|u_2|_{m+2,\alpha;e}|v_1|_{2,\beta;e} + h_e^{2m}|u_2|_{m+2,\alpha;e}|v_1|_{m,\beta;e} \\
&+ Ck_e^{2m}|u_2|_{m+3,\alpha;e}|v_1|_{2,\beta;e}\Big],
\end{aligned} \tag{71}$$

here, α and β are a pair of conjugate numbers and satisfy $\frac{1}{\alpha}+\frac{1}{\beta}=1, \alpha, \beta \ge 1$.

So far, we have completed the proof of Lemma 6. □

Lemma 7. *For any integer $n \ge 1$ and a sufficiently smooth function u_1 on the rectangular element e, let v_2 be a polynomial with degree of x and y no more than m on e. Then, there will be an area integral $J_{6,e}$ on e, and $J_{6,e}$ satisfies*

$$(\partial_y(u_1-\pi_1u_1), \partial_x v_2)_e = J_{6,e} + \frac{(-1)^m}{2m!}(\int_{\ell_2} - \int_{\ell_4})\partial_y^{m+1}u_1F^m(y)\partial_y^m v_2dy, \tag{72}$$

and follows the estimate

$$
\begin{aligned}
|J_{6,e}| \leq \frac{(-1)^m}{(2m)!}\Big[& h_e^{2m}|u_1|_{m+2,\alpha;e}|v_2|_{2,\beta;e} + k_e^{2m}|u_1|_{m+2,\alpha;e}|v_2|_{m,\beta;e} \\
& + Ch_e^{2m}|u_1|_{m+3,\alpha;e}|v_2|_{2,\beta;e}\Big],
\end{aligned} \tag{73}
$$

where α and β are a pair of conjugate numbers and satisfy $\frac{1}{\alpha}+\frac{1}{\beta}=1, \alpha, \beta \geq 1$.

The proof of Lemma 7 is similar to Lemma 6, so we skip proof here.

Based on the estimates of the components of $\mathcal{A}(\mathbf{v})$ provided above, we now begin to prove the main result of this paper, superconvergence analysis. According to Lemma 2,

$$
\mathcal{A}_1 = \sum_{e\in\mathcal{T}_h} J_{1,e} - \frac{(-1)^m}{(2m)!}\sum_{e\in\mathcal{T}_h}\Big(\int_{\ell_2} - \int_{\ell_4}\Big)F^m(y)\partial_x\partial_y^{m+1}u_1\partial_y^{m-1}v_1(x,y_e)dy. \tag{74}
$$

Observing the line integral term in $\mathcal{A}_1(\mathbf{v}_1)$, on the inner edge outside the boundary, the corresponding line integrals will cancel out each other due to adjacent elements, ensuring that the total is zero. This is because each inner edge is a shared boundary between two adjacent elements, and each of these two elements contributes a line integral with opposite signs to that edge. Therefore,

$$
\mathcal{A}_1 = \sum_{e\in\mathcal{T}_h} J_{1,e}.
$$

We estimate $\mathcal{A}_1$ by using Lemma 2, taking $\alpha=\beta=2$, and find that

$$
\begin{aligned}
|\mathcal{A}_1| &\leq \sum_{e\in\mathcal{T}_h}|J_{1,e}| \\
&\leq \sum_{e\in\mathcal{T}_h}\frac{2(-1)^m k_e^{2m}}{(2m)!}\Big[|u_1|_{m+3,\alpha;e}|v_1|_{m-1,\beta;e} + k_e|u_1|_{m+3,\alpha;e}|v_1|_{2,\beta;e} \\
&+ \frac{k_e^2}{(2m+1)(2m+2)}|u_1|_{m+3,\alpha;e}|v_1|_{2,\beta;e}\Big] \\
&\leq \sum_{e\in\mathcal{T}_h}\frac{2(-1)^m \rho^{2m}}{(2m)!}\Big[|u_1|_{m+3,\alpha;e}|v_1|_{m-1,\beta;e} + k_e|u_1|_{m+3,\alpha;e}|v_1|_{2,\beta;e} \\
&+ \frac{\rho^2}{(2m+1)(2m+2)}|u_1|_{m+3,\alpha;e}|v_1|_{2,\beta;e}\Big],
\end{aligned} \tag{75}
$$

where $\rho = max_{e\in\mathcal{T}_h}(h_e,k_e)$. Then, we use the inverse inequality on various norms of $\mathbf{v}$ in above Equation (75), yielding

$$
\begin{aligned}
|\mathcal{A}_1| &\leq C\rho^{m+3}||u_1||_{m+3,2;\Omega}||v_1||_2 \\
&\leq C\rho^{m+2}||u_1||_{m+3,2;\Omega}||v_1||_1 \\
&\leq C\rho^{m+2}||u_1||_{m+3,2;\Omega}||\mathbf{v}||_{\mathbf{U}}.
\end{aligned} \tag{76}
$$

In like manner,

$$
\begin{aligned}
|\mathcal{A}_2| &\leq C\rho^{m+2}||u_2||_{m+3,2;\Omega}||\mathbf{v}||_{\mathbf{U}}, \\
|\mathcal{A}_3| &\leq C\rho^{m+2}||u_1||_{m+3,2;\Omega}||\mathbf{v}||_{\mathbf{U}}, \\
|\mathcal{A}_4| &\leq C\rho^{m+2}||u_2||_{m+3,2;\Omega}||\mathbf{v}||_{\mathbf{U}}, \\
|\mathcal{A}_5| &\leq C\rho^{m+2}||u_2||_{m+3,2;\Omega}||\mathbf{v}||_{\mathbf{U}}, \\
|\mathcal{A}_6| &\leq C\rho^{m+2}||u_1||_{m+3,2;\Omega}||\mathbf{v}||_{\mathbf{U}},
\end{aligned} \tag{77}
$$

Substituting Equation (32) with Equations (76) and (77), we arrive at

$$|\mathcal{A}(\mathbf{v})| \leq C\rho^{m+2}||\mathbf{u}||_{m+3,2;\Omega}||\mathbf{v}||_{\mathbf{U}}. \tag{78}$$

At this point, we have demonstrated that condition (19) stated in Theorem 1 is satisfied for $s = 2$. Consequently, by summarizing the above arguments, we have established a superconvergence result.

Theorem 2. *Assume $(\mathbf{u}; p) \in (H^1)^2 \times L_0^2$ is the solution of Equation (4) and $\mathbf{u} \in [H^{\widehat{m}+2}]^2$. Let $(\mathbf{u}_h; p_h) \in \mathbf{U}_h \times W_h$ solve Equation (13). Let $\mathcal{A}(\mathbf{v}) = a((\mathbf{u} - \pi_h \mathbf{u}), \mathbf{v})$ be the form defined in Equation (32). Then, there will be a constant C that is independent of h such that*

$$\|\mathbf{u}_h - \pi_h \mathbf{u}\|_0 + \|p_h - P_h p\|_0 \leq Ch^{\widehat{m}+2}\|\mathbf{u}\|_{\widehat{m}+2,2;\Omega}. \tag{79}$$

In this section, we have demonstrated the superconvergence in the L^2-norm between the locally defined projection $\pi_h \mathbf{u}$ and the approximate solution $\mathbf{u}_h$ of the velocity $\mathbf{u}$ through a series of estimation and analysis. Specifically, we showed that, within the given mixed finite element space, higher-than-expected convergence rates $\mathcal{O}(h^{m+2})$ can be achieved using appropriate estimates and interpolation techniques.

Even if there is a large interpolation error between the interpolation solution $\pi_h \mathbf{u}$ and the exact solution $\mathbf{u}$, we can construct a new approximate solution based on the existing finite element approximate solution $\mathbf{u}_h$ by using the local characteristics of $\pi_h \mathbf{u}$ and Theorem 2. The purpose of this process is to obtain a higher convergence order, thus significantly improving the accuracy of the solution. Specifically, this goal is achieved by introducing the post-processing operator Π_h, which is responsible for mapping the original finite element space to a higher-order new finite element space and satisfying $\Pi_h \pi_h \mathbf{u} = \Pi_h \mathbf{u}$ [23,41]. In this new space, the polynomial degree on each element is increased to $m + s$ to enhance the smoothness and accuracy of the solution. Therefore, by this progress, an approximate solution $\Pi_h \mathbf{u}$ with superconvergence can be obtained, which is closer to the real solution of actual physical phenomena.

Then, we can estimate the error of the $\Pi_h \mathbf{u}$ and $\mathbf{u}$ as follows:

$$\begin{aligned} \|\mathbf{u} - \Pi_h \mathbf{u}_h\|_0 &\leq \|\mathbf{u} - \Pi_h \mathbf{u}\|_0 + \|\Pi_h \mathbf{u} - \Pi_h \mathbf{u}_h\|_0 \\ &\leq \|\mathbf{u} - \Pi_h \mathbf{u}\|_0 + \|\Pi_h(\pi_h \mathbf{u} - \mathbf{u}_h)\|_0 \\ &\leq Ch^{\widehat{m}+s+1}\|\mathbf{u}\|_{\widehat{m}+s+1} + Ch^{\widehat{m}+2}\|\mathbf{u}\|_{\widehat{m}+2}. \end{aligned} \tag{80}$$

5. Numerical Example

In this section, to verify the effectiveness and correctness of the superconvergence result, we considered a specific numerical example.

Example 1. *Consider Stokes Equation (1) in rectangular domain $\Omega = [0,1] \times [0,1]$. We take the exact solution $\mathbf{u} = (u_1, u_2)^t$ and $p(x,y)$ as follows*

$$\begin{aligned} u_1(x,y) &= x^2(1-x)^2(2y - 6y^2 + 4y^3), \\ u_2(x,y) &= -y^2(1-y)^2(2x - 6x^2 + 4x^3), \\ p(x,y) &= x - x^2. \end{aligned} \tag{81}$$

The domain Ω is partitioned into uniform rectangles.

In this numerical example, we used a direct linear solver for the L^2-norm error at the Gaussian points. The results are shown in Tables 1 and 2 below. Additionally, the Actual CPU time (ACPU) *is included in this table. Since both* **u** *and* p *were computed simultaneously, we have listed the computation time only in Table 1 for simplicity.*

Table 1. The comparison of numerical errors and the convergence order of biquadratic basis for **u** in L^2-norm.

h	$\|\|\mathbf{u}-\mathbf{u}_h\|\|_{L^2}$	ACPU(s)	Order	$\|\|\Pi_h\mathbf{u}-\mathbf{u}_h\|\|_{L^2}$	ACPU(s)	Order
$[\frac{1}{4},\frac{1}{4}]$	2.2975×10^{-4}	0.5483	–	2.1856×10^{-5}	0.5310	–
$[\frac{1}{8},\frac{1}{8}]$	2.9674×10^{-5}	2.0413	2.9528	1.3619×10^{-6}	2.0157	4.0043
$[\frac{1}{16},\frac{1}{16}]$	3.7355×10^{-6}	8.1164	2.9898	8.5129×10^{-8}	8.1057	3.9998
$[\frac{1}{32},\frac{1}{32}]$	4.6772×10^{-7}	36.5913	2.9976	5.3207×10^{-9}	36.5823	4.0000

Table 2. The comparison of numerical errors and the convergence order of bilinear basis for p in L^2-norm.

h	$\|\|p-p_h\|\|_{L^2}$	Order	$\|\|\Pi_h p-p_h\|\|_{L^2}$	Order
$[\frac{1}{4},\frac{1}{4}]$	1.0400×10^{-2}	–	1.3793×10^{-4}	–
$[\frac{1}{8},\frac{1}{8}]$	2.6000×10^{-3}	2.0000	1.3793×10^{-4}	3.6748
$[\frac{1}{16},\frac{1}{16}]$	6.5301×10^{-4}	1.9977	1.0800×10^{-5}	3.9180
$[\frac{1}{32},\frac{1}{32}]$	1.6289×10^{-4}	2.0000	7.1446×10^{-7}	3.9796

It can be clearly observed from the data in Tables 1 and 2 that the convergence order of both velocity **u** *and pressure* p *tends to stabilize. Furthermore, when* $h\to0$*, the convergence order of* $||\mathbf{u}-\mathbf{u}_h||_{L^2}$ *is* $\mathcal{O}(h^{m+1})$ *and that of* $||\Pi_h\mathbf{u}-\mathbf{u}_h||_{L^2}$ *is* $\mathcal{O}(h^{m+2})$*. Moreover, when* $h\to0$*, the convergence order of* $||p-p_h||_{L^2}$ *is* $\mathcal{O}(h^{m+1})$ *and that of* $||\Pi_h p-p_h||_{L^2}$ *is* $\mathcal{O}(h^{m+3})$*. This is completely consistent with the results of theoretical analysis. At the same time, we find that, when the accuracy is improved, the time is basically unchanged. This means that the improvement in accuracy will not be at the expense of increasing running time, which makes this method very efficient and feasible for large-scale simulations.*

6. Conclusions and Further Work

In this paper, a mixed FEM is employed, and the superconvergence results of the Stokes problem are obtained by using interpolation and projection techniques, leveraging the high-precision characteristics of Bernstein elements.

However, the limitations of this method lie in its requirement for geometric shapes and computational complexity. Future work will aim to address these issues and extend the applicability of the method.

Author Contributions: Methodology, L.S.; Software, S.W.; Formal analysis, Z.D.; Writing—original draft, S.W.; Writing—review & editing, Z.D.; Visualization, S.W.; Supervision, L.S.; Project administration, L.S. All authors have read and agreed to the published version of the manuscript.

Funding: This research received no external funding.

Data Availability Statement: Data are contained within the article.

Conflicts of Interest: The authors declare no conflict of interest.

References

1. Zhao, M.; Shi, J.; Wang, L. A three-dimensional Petrov-Galerkin finite element interface method for solving inhomogeneous anisotropic Maxwell's equations in irregular regions. *Comput. Math. Appl.* **2023**, *152*, 364–377. [CrossRef]
2. Carrasco, S.; Caucao, S.; Gatica, G.N. New mixed finite element methods for the coupled convective Brinkman-Forchheimer and Double-Diffusion equations. *J. Sci. Comput.* **2023**, *97*, 1–81. [CrossRef]

3. Wu, C.T.; Wu, S.W.; Niu, R.P.; Jiang, C.; Liu, G. The polygonal finite element method for solving heat conduction problems. *Eng. Anal. Bound. Elem.* **2023**, *155*, 935–947. [CrossRef]
4. Zhao, W. Higher order weak Galerkin methods for the Navier–Stokes equations with large Reynolds number. *Numer. Methods Partial. Differ. Equ.* **2022**, *38*, 1967–1992. [CrossRef]
5. Bochev, P.B.; Dohrmann, C.R.; Gunzburger, M.D. Stabilization of low-order mixed finite elements for the Stokes equations. *SIAM J. Numer. Anal.* **2006**, *44*, 82–101. [CrossRef]
6. Gunzburger, M.D.; Zhao, W. Descriptions, Discretizations, and Comparisons of Time/Space Colored and White Noise Forcings of the Navier–Stokes Equations. *SIAM J. Sci. Comput.* **2019**, *41*, A2579–A2602. [CrossRef]
7. Li, X. Element-free Galerkin analysis of Stokes problems using the reproducing kernel gradient smoothing integration. *J. Sci. Comput.* **2023**, *96*, 1–38. [CrossRef]
8. Li, X. A weak Galerkin meshless method for incompressible Navier–Stokes equations. *J. Comput. Appl. Math.* **2024**, *445*, 1–21. [CrossRef]
9. Wang, J.; Li, Q. Superconvergence analysis of a linearized three-step backward differential formula finite element method for nonlinear Sobolev equation. *Math. Methods Appl. Sci.* **2019**, *42*, 3359–3376. [CrossRef]
10. Mandal, M.; Nelakanti, G. Superconvergence results of Legendre spectral projection methods for weakly singular Fredholm–Hammerstein integral equations. *J. Comput. Appl. Math.* **2019**, *349*, 114–131. [CrossRef]
11. Zhang, G.; Dai, X. Superconvergence of discontinuous Galerkin method for neutral delay differential equations. *Int. J. Comput. Math.* **2021**, *98*, 1648–1662. [CrossRef]
12. Guo, H.; Yang, X.; Zhang, Z. Superconvergence of partially penalized immersed finite element methods. *IMA J. Numer. Anal.* **2018**, *38*, 2123–2144. [CrossRef]
13. Zhang, S.; Sun, S.; Yang, H. Optimal convergence of discontinuous Galerkin methods for continuum modeling of supply chain networks. *Comput. Math. Appl.* **2014**, *68*, 681–691. [CrossRef]
14. Shi, D.; Wu, Y. Uniform superconvergent analysis of a new mixed finite element method for nonlinear Bi-wave singular perturbation problem. *Appl. Math. Lett.* **2019**, *93*, 131–138. [CrossRef]
15. Anshelevich, M.; Wang, J.C.; Zhong, P. Local limit theorems for multiplicative free convolutions. *J. Funct. Anal.* **2014**, *267*, 3469–3499. [CrossRef]
16. Zhang, T.; Zhang, S. Finite element derivative interpolation recovery technique and superconvergence. *Appl. Math.* **2011**, *56*, 513–531. [CrossRef]
17. Schneider, M.; Wicht, D. Superconvergence of the effective Cauchy stress in computational homogenization of inelastic materials. *Int. J. Numer. Methods Eng.* **2023**, *124*, 959–978. [CrossRef]
18. Huang, Y.; Li, J.; Wu, C. Averaging for superconvergence: Verification and application of 2D edge elements to Maxwell's equations in metamaterials. *Comput. Methods Appl. Mech. Eng.* **2013**, *255*, 121–132. [CrossRef]
19. Ren, J.; Long, X.; Mao, S.; Zhang, J. Superconvergence of finite element approximations for the fractional diffusion-wave equation. *J. Sci. Comput.* **2017**, *72*, 917–935. [CrossRef]
20. Danielson, K.T. Barlow's method of superconvergence for higher-order finite elements and for transverse stresses in structural elements. *Finite Elem. Anal. Des.* **2018**, *141*, 84–95. [CrossRef]
21. Kim, N.I.; Choi, D.H. Super convergent shear deformable finite elements for stability analysis of composite beams. *Compos. Part Eng.* **2013**, *44*, 100–111. [CrossRef]
22. Douglas, J.; Wang, J. Superconvergence of mixed finite element methods on rectangular domains. *Calcolo* **1989**, *26*, 121–133. [CrossRef]
23. Durán, R. Superconvergence for rectangular mixed finite elements. *Numer. Math.* **1990**, *58*, 287–298. [CrossRef]
24. Ewing, R.; Lazarov, R.; Wang, J. Superconvergence of the velocity along the Gauss lines in mixed finite element methods. *SIAM J. Numer. Anal.* **1991**, *28*, 1015–1029. [CrossRef]
25. Wang, J.P. Superconvergence and extrapolation for mixed finite element methods on rectangular domains. *Math. Comput.* **1991**, *56*, 477–503. [CrossRef]
26. Douglas, J.; Dupont, T. Superconvergence for Galerkin methods for the two point boundary problem via local projections. *Numer. Math.* **1973**, *21*, 270–278. [CrossRef]
27. Douglas, J.J.; Milner, F.A. Interior and superconvergence estimates for mixed methods for second order elliptic problems. *ESAIM Math. Model. Numer. Anal.* **1985**, *19*, 397–428. [CrossRef]
28. Ewing, R.E.; Liu, M.M.; Wang, J. Superconvergence of mixed finite element approximations over quadrilaterals. *SIAM J. Numer. Anal.* **1999**, *36*, 772–787. [CrossRef]
29. Ewing, R.E.; Liu, M.; Wang, J. A new superconvergence for mixed finite element approximations. *SIAM J. Numer. Anal.* **2002**, *40*, 2133–2150. [CrossRef]
30. Chen, Y.; Dai, Y. Superconvergence for optimal control problems governed by semi-linear elliptic equations. *J. Sci. Comput.* **2009**, *39*, 206–221. [CrossRef]

31. Shi, D.; Ren, J.; Gong, W. Convergence and superconvergence analysis of a nonconforming finite element method for solving the Signorini problem. *Nonlinear Anal. Theory, Methods Appl.* **2012**, *75*, 3493–3502. [CrossRef]
32. Shi, D.; Zhang, L. Superconvergence analysis of Galerkin finite element method for the nonlinear parabolic intergro-differential equation. *J. Xinyang Norm. Univ. Nat. Sci. Ed.* **2024**, *37*, 45–50.
33. Bernstein, S. Démonstration du Théoréme de Weierstrass fonde sur le calcul des Probabilités. *Commun. SociéTé MathéMatique Kharkov Ser. Xiii* **1912**, *13*, 1–2.
34. Ye, Z.; Long, X.; Zeng, X.M. Adjustment algorithms for Bézier curve and surface. In Proceedings of the 2010 5th International Conference on Computer Science & Education, Hefei, China, 24–27 August 2010; pp. 1712–1716.
35. Cai, Q.; Lian, B.; Zhou, G. Approximation properties of λ-Bernstein operators. *J. Inequalities Appl.* **2018**, *2018*, 61. [CrossRef] [PubMed]
36. Hu, G.; Cao, H.; Qin, X. Construction of generalized developable Bézier surfaces with shape parameters. *Math. Methods Appl. Sci.* **2018**, *41*, 7804–7829. [CrossRef]
37. Schurer, F. On Linear Positive Operators in Approximation Theory. Ph.D. Thesis, Eindhoven University of Technology, Eindhoven, The Netherlands, 1965.
38. Yilmaz, O.; Bodur, M.; Aral, A. On approximation properties of Baskakov-Schurer-Szász operators preserving exponential functions. *Filomat* **2018**, *32*, 5433–5440. [CrossRef]
39. Ayman-Mursaleen, M.; Rao, N.; Rani, M.; Kilicman, A.; Al-Abied, A.A.H.A.; Malik, P. A note on approximation of blending type Bernstein–Schurer–Kantorovich operators with shape parameter α. *J. Math.* **2023**, *2023*, 1–13. [CrossRef]
40. Brenner, S.C.; Scott, L. *The Mathematical Theory of Finite Element Methods*; Springer: Berlin/Heidelberg, Germany, 2008.
41. Duran, R.; Muschietti, M.A.; Rodriguez, R. Asymptotically exact error estimators for rectangular finite elements. *SIAM J. Numer. Anal.* **1992**, *29*, 78–88. [CrossRef]

axioms

MDPI

Article

Asymptotic Formulas for the Haezendonck–Goovaerts Risk Measure of Sums with Consistently Varying Increments

Jonas Šiaulys *, Mantas Dirma, Neda Nakliuda and Luca Zanardelli

Institute of Mathematics, Vilnius University, Naugarduko Str. 24, LT-03225 Vilnius, Lithuania; mantasdirma96@gmail.com (M.D.); neda.nakliuda@mif.vu.lt (N.N.); luca.zanardelli@mif.stud.vu.lt (L.Z.)

* Correspondence: jonas.siaulys@mif.vu.lt

Abstract

The Haezendonck–Goovaerts (HG) risk measure defined on Orlicz spaces via the so-called normalised Young function is a direct generalisation of the Expected Shortfall risk measure. The HG measure is known to be a coherent one, thus making it more robust than some of the alternatives, such as Value-at-Risk, for aggregating and comparing risks, and at the same time more flexible for capital allocation problems, risk premium estimation, solvency assessment, and stress testing in insurance and finance. As random risk in practical applications is often assessed in a portfolio setting—a collection of insurance policies or financial assets, like stocks or bonds—we examine the situation in which the total portfolio risk is expressed as the sum of individual random risks. For this, we consider the sum $S_n^{(\xi)} = \xi_1 + \ldots + \xi_n$ of possibly dependent and non-identically distributed real-valued random variables $\xi_1, \ldots, \xi_n$ with consistently varying distributions. Assuming that the collection $\{\xi_1, \ldots, \xi_n\}$ follows the dependence structure, similar to the asymptotic independence, we obtain the asymptotic estimations of the HG risk measure for the sum $S_n^{(\xi)}$ when the confidence level tends to 1. The formulas presented in our work show that in the case where a portfolio of random losses contains consistently varying losses and the others are asymptotically negligible, it is sufficient for risk assessment to consider only the tails of those dominant losses.

Keywords: sum of random variables; asymptotic independence; tail-moment; heavy tail; consistently varying distribution; Haezendonck–Goovaerts risk measure

MSC: 91B05; 60F10; 91G15

1. Introduction

Risk measurement plays a central role in modern actuarial science, financial regulation, and quantitative risk management. As markets become increasingly complex and uncertain, the limitations of classical risk measures, such as variance, Value-at-Risk (VaR), and Expected Shortfall (ES), have become more apparent. In particular, widely used regulatory metrics often fail to adequately capture tail risk, lack desirable coherence properties, or provide insufficient flexibility to model risk preferences. For instance, it is well known that the VaR measure in general does not satisfy the sub-additivity axiom, and, as a result, fails to obey the diversification principle. Additionally, as it is defined as a certain percentile of the loss distribution, it does not account for the severity of losses beyond that percentile [1]. Therefore, it may underestimate risk in market stress situations under extreme asset price fluctuations [2]. These challenges have motivated the search for more robust and theoretically sound alternatives. One such alternative is the so-called Haezendonck–Goovaerts (HG) risk measure, which is defined in Section 1.6. The HG risk measure, like other risk measures, is a method to assess the amount of capital we should hold to protect ourselves against impending losses, taking into account the level of risk aversion. The HG risk measure is actually a family of risk measures that depend on the so-called Young function φ. Choosing another Young function yields a different version of this risk measure. The HG risk measure derived from the principles of premium calculation in [3] unifies economic intuition with strong mathematical foundations. According to the results of [4,5], the HG risk measure has many properties necessary for risk measurements. In particular, this measure belongs to the class of coherent risk measures in the sense of Artzner et al. [1], as it is monotonic, translation-invariant, sub-additive, and homogeneous, and, as a result, is a monetary and convex risk measure as in [6,7]. It is well known that the simplest case of HG risk measure is the Expected Shortfall (ES) (or, synonymously, Conditional Value-at-Risk or Tail Value-at-Risk or Conditional Tail Expectation, considered in detail in [8]. The ES risk measure can be obtained from the HG risk measure using the Young function $\varphi(t) = t$. Therefore, the HG risk measure is a direct generalisation of the ES risk measure.

The HG risk measure is particularly useful in actuarial science and financial risk management, where capturing heavy-tailed and extreme losses is essential. Its foundation in Orlicz functions allows flexible modelling of risk aversion and tail behavior, making it well suited for premium calculation, solvency assessment, and capital allocation. In particular, the flexibility to select the Young function, which characterises the behaviour of the measure, gives more control over the degree to which extreme losses influence the risk assessment. It is important to note that, despite being more theoretically grounded than some of the alternatives, the HG risk measure might be more challenging to implement in practice.

Tang and Yang in [9] provided a formula for calculating the HG risk measure when the Young function is a power function, see Theorem 3 below. However, in the same article, the authors mention that in the general case, an analytical formula for calculating the HG risk measure does not exist, since the calculation of the values of this measure is related to finding quantiles. In this case, the authors of the article [9] suggest using asymptotic formulas by writing one of the formulas of this form for random risk with a regularly varying tail, see Theorem 4 below.

We observe that a random risk is often expressed as a sum of random variables when it represents the aggregate loss of multiple individual risks. This occurs, for example, when modelling total claims in an insurance portfolio, where each claim amount is a random variable. It also arises in finance when a portfolio's total loss is composed of the losses of individual assets. More generally, any situation involving accumulated, component-wise, or event-based contributions—such as operational losses, credit defaults, or catastrophe events—naturally leads to a representation as a sum of random variables. In this paper, we consider the case where the random risk is written as a sum of random variables that are somehow dependent. We consider the case where, among the summable random variables, there is a subset of variables with consistently varying tails, and the tails of the other random variables are vanishing with respect to the latter. The main results of the work are formulated in Theorems 6 and 7.

1.1. Preliminaries

Let $n \in \mathbb{N} = \{1,2,\ldots\}$, and let $\{\xi_1,\ldots,\xi_n\}$ be a collection of possibly dependent and non-identically distributed random variables (r.v.'s). Denote

$$S_n^{(\xi)} := \xi_1 + \ldots + \xi_n. \tag{1}$$

In the main results of the paper, we assume that random summands have consistently varying distributions. Before a more detailed discussion on heavy-tailed distributions, we first define the support of any distribution or distribution function (d.f.). For a d.f. $F : \mathbb{R} \to [0,1]$, the support of F is defined as

$$\begin{aligned}\operatorname{supp} F &= \{x : F(x+\delta) - F(x-\delta) > 0 \text{ for all } \delta > 0\} \\ &= \{x : \overline{F}(x-\delta) - \overline{F}(x+\delta) > 0 \text{ for all } \delta > 0\},\end{aligned}$$

where $\overline{F} = 1 - F$ denotes the tail function (t.f.). If $\operatorname{supp} F \subset [0,\infty)$, then we say that the distribution (or d.f.) F is supported on $\mathbb{R}^+$. If $\operatorname{supp} F \not\subset [0,\infty)$, then we say that the distribution (or d.f.) F is supported on $\mathbb{R}$.

1.2. Heavy-Tailed Distributions

In this subsection, we discuss the class of heavy-tailed distributions and the most popular and closest subclasses of this class of distributions.

- *A d.f. F supported on $\mathbb{R}$ is said to be heavy-tailed, written as $F \in \mathscr{H}$, if for all $\delta > 0$, we have*

$$\int_{-\infty}^{\infty} \mathrm{e}^{\delta x} \mathrm{d}F(x) = \infty.$$

Due to the alternative expectation formula (see, e.g., [10,11]), we have

$$\int_{[0,\infty)} \mathrm{e}^{\delta x} \mathrm{d}F(x) = 1 + \delta \int_0^{\infty} \mathrm{e}^{\delta x} \overline{F}(x)\,\mathrm{d}x$$

implying that

$$\begin{aligned}&F \in \mathscr{H} \;\Rightarrow\; \overline{F}(x) > 0,\ x \in \mathbb{R};\\ &F \in \mathscr{H} \;\Leftrightarrow\; \limsup_{x\to\infty} \mathrm{e}^{\delta x}\, \overline{F}(x) = \infty \ \text{ for each } \delta > 0.\end{aligned}$$

- *A d.f. F supported on $\mathbb{R}$ is said to be regularly varying with index $\alpha \geqslant 0$, written as $F \in \mathscr{R}_\alpha$, if for any $y > 0$, we have*

$$\lim_{x\to\infty} \frac{\overline{F}(xy)}{\overline{F}(x)} = y^{-\alpha}.$$

It is easy to verify that the Pareto law with d.f.

$$F(x) = \left(1 - \frac{1}{(x+1)^\alpha}\right) \mathbb{I}_{[0,\infty))}(x)$$

belongs to the class $\mathscr{R}_\alpha$ for any positive α.

- *A d.f. F supported on $\mathbb{R}$ is said to be extended regularly varying with indices $0 \leqslant \alpha \leqslant \beta$, written as $F \in \mathscr{ERV}_{\{\alpha,\beta\}}$, if for any $y > 1$, we have*

$$y^{-\beta} \leqslant \liminf_{x\to\infty} \frac{\overline{F}(xy)}{\overline{F}(x)} \leqslant \limsup_{x\to\infty} \frac{\overline{F}(xy)}{\overline{F}(x)} \leqslant y^{-\alpha}.$$

Due to the results of [12], the distribution with t.f.

$$\overline{F}(x) = \exp\{ -\lfloor \log x \rfloor - (\log x - \lfloor \log x \rfloor)^2 \},\ x \geqslant 1,$$

belongs to the class $\bigcup_{0 \leqslant \alpha \leqslant \beta} \mathscr{ERV}_{\{\alpha,\beta\}}$.

- *A d.f. F supported on* $\mathbb{R}$ *is said to be consistently varying, written as* $F \in \mathscr{C}$, *if*

$$\lim_{y \uparrow 1} \limsup_{x \to \infty} \frac{\overline{F}(xy)}{\overline{F}(x)} = 1.$$

It can be shown (see [13,14]) that the distribution with t.f.

$$\overline{F}(x) = p^{\lfloor \log_2 x \rfloor}\left(2 - p - (1-p)\frac{x}{2^{\lfloor \log_2 x \rfloor}}\right),\ x \geqslant 1,$$

belongs to the subclass $\mathscr{C} \setminus \bigcup_{\alpha \geqslant 0} \mathscr{R}_\alpha$ for any parameter $p \in (0,1)$.

- *A d.f. F supported on* $\mathbb{R}$ *is said to be dominatedly varying, written as* $F \in \mathscr{D}$, *if for any* $y \in (0,1)$, *we have*

$$\limsup_{x \to \infty} \frac{\overline{F}(xy)}{\overline{F}(x)} < \infty.$$

The presented definition implies that the generalized Peter–Paul distribution with d.f.

$$F(x) = 1 - b^{-a\lfloor \log_b x \rfloor},\ x \geqslant 1,$$

belongs to the subclass $\mathscr{D} \setminus \mathscr{C}$ for all possible parameters $a > 0, b > 1$, see [15].

It is well known (see, for instance, [13]) that

$$\mathscr{R} = \bigcup_{\alpha \geqslant 0} \mathscr{R}_\alpha \subset \bigcup_{0 \leqslant \alpha \leqslant \beta} \mathscr{ERV}_{\{\alpha,\beta\}} \subset \mathscr{C} \subset \mathscr{D} \subset \mathscr{H}.$$

The following two indices are important to determine whether the distribution F belongs to the aforementioned classes. The first index is the so-called upper Matuszewska index (see, e.g., [16] (Section 2), [12,17]), defined as

$$J_F^+ = \inf_{y > 1}\left\{ -\frac{1}{\log y} \log \liminf_{x \to \infty} \frac{\overline{F}(xy)}{\overline{F}(x)} \right\} = -\lim_{y \to \infty} \frac{1}{\log y} \log \liminf_{x \to \infty} \frac{\overline{F}(xy)}{\overline{F}(x)}.$$

The other index, the so-called L-index, is defined as

$$L_F = \lim_{y \downarrow 1} \liminf_{x \to \infty} \frac{\overline{F}(xy)}{\overline{F}(x)}.$$

For instance, this index is used in the main results of [18–20]. The definitions of the aforementioned heavy-tailed distribution classes imply that

$$F \in \mathscr{D} \Leftrightarrow J_F^+ < \infty \Leftrightarrow L_F > 0;$$
$$F \in \mathscr{C} \Leftrightarrow L_F = 1 \Rightarrow J_F^+ < \infty;$$
$$F \in \mathscr{R}_\alpha \Rightarrow L_F = 1,\ J_F^+ = \alpha.$$

The classes of distributions $\mathscr{R}$ and $\mathscr{D}$ have been extensively used in real analysis and various spheres of probability (see, e.g., [16,21–24]). The class of consistently varying distributions $\mathscr{C}$ was introduced as a generalization of the class $\mathscr{R}$ in [25] and was referred to as "intermediate regular variation". The concept of consistent variation has been applied in various studies within the context of applied probability, including queueing systems and ruin theory (see, e.g., [12,13,26–32]).

1.3. Asymptotic Relations

In this subsection, we introduce the notation used throughout the paper. For two positive functions f and g, we write the following:

$$\begin{aligned} f(x) \underset{x\to\infty}{\lesssim} g(x) &\quad \text{if} \quad \limsup_{x\to\infty} \frac{f(x)}{g(x)} \leqslant 1; \\ f(x) = O(g(x)) &\quad \text{if} \quad \limsup_{x\to\infty} \frac{f(x)}{g(x)} < \infty; \\ f(x) \asymp g(x) &\quad \text{if} \quad f(x) = O(g(x)) \text{ and } g(x) = O(f(x)); \\ f(x) \underset{x\to\infty}{\sim} g(x) &\quad \text{if} \quad \lim_{x\to\infty} \frac{f(x)}{g(x)} = 1. \end{aligned}$$

In addition, we use the standard notation for indicators:

$$\mathbb{I}_A(\omega) := \begin{cases} 1 & \text{if } \omega \in A, \\ 0 & \text{if } \omega \notin A; \end{cases}$$

and for positive and negative parts of any real x,

$$x^+ := \max\{0, x\}, \;\; x^- := \max\{0, -x\}.$$

1.4. Quasi-Asymptotic Independence

In this paper, we suppose that the collection $\{\xi_1, \ldots, \xi_n\}$ consists of pairwise quasi-asymptotically independent r.v.'s. This dependence structure, which is a direct generalization of independence, was introduced by Chen and Yuen [28] and has been considered in [33–39], among others.

- *Real-valued r.v.'s $\xi_1, \ldots, \xi_n$, $n \in \mathbb{N}$, with distributions supported on $\mathbb{R}$ are called pairwise quasi-asymptotically independent* (pQAI), *if for all pairs of indices $k, l \in \{1, \ldots, n\}$, $k \neq l$, it holds that*

$$\lim_{x\to\infty} \frac{\mathbb{P}(\xi_k^+ > x,\, \xi_l^+ > x)}{\mathbb{P}(\xi_k^+ > x) + \mathbb{P}(\xi_l^+ > x)} = \lim_{x\to\infty} \frac{\mathbb{P}(\xi_k^+ > x,\, \xi_l^- > x)}{\mathbb{P}(\xi_k^+ > x) + \mathbb{P}(\xi_l^+ > x)} = 0.$$

The following statement is Theorem 3.1 in [28]. It provides an asymptotic result for the tail probabilities of sums of pQAI r.v.'s with distributions from the class $\mathscr{C}$.

Theorem 1. *Let $\{\xi_1, \ldots, \xi_n\}$ be a collection of real-valued* pQAI *r.v.'s, such that $F_{\xi_k} \in \mathscr{C}$ for all $k \in \{1, \ldots, n\}$. Then, for the random sum defined in* (1), *we have*

$$\mathbb{P}(S_n^{(\xi)} > x) \underset{x\to\infty}{\sim} \sum_{k=1}^{n} \overline{F}_{\xi_k}(x).$$

The following statement directly generalises Theorem 1. The paper [40] (see Theorem 4 and the remark below the theorem) gives its detailed proof.

Theorem 2. *Let* $\{\xi_1, \dots, \xi_n\}$ *be a collection of real-valued* pQAI *r.v.'s, such that* $F_{\xi_L} \in \mathscr{C}$ *for some* $L \in \{1, \dots, n\}$, *and for other indices* $k \neq L$ *suppose* $F_{\xi_k} \in \mathscr{C}$ *or* $\mathbb{P}(|\xi_k| > x) = o(\overline{F}_{\xi_L}(x))$. *If* $\max\limits_{1 \leqslant k \leqslant n} \mathbb{E}(\xi_k^+)^\alpha < \infty$, *then for each* $\beta \in [0, \alpha]$,

$$\mathbb{E}\Big((S_n^{(\xi)})^\beta \mathbb{I}_{\{S_n^{(\xi)} > x\}}\Big) \underset{x\to\infty}{\sim} \sum_{k\in\mathcal{I}_n} \mathbb{E}\Big(\xi_k^\beta \, \mathbb{I}_{\{\xi_k > x\}}\Big), \tag{2}$$

and for each $\beta \in (0, \alpha]$,

$$\mathbb{E}\Big(\big((S_n^{(\xi)} - x)^+\big)^\beta\Big) \underset{x\to\infty}{\sim} \sum_{k\in\mathcal{I}_n} \mathbb{E}\big((\xi_k - x)^+\big)^\beta, \tag{3}$$

where $\mathcal{I}_n \subseteq \{1, \dots, n\}$ *is a subset of indices such that* $F_{\xi_k} \in \mathscr{C}$ *for* $k \in \mathcal{I}_n$.

1.5. Positively Decreasing Distribution

In this paper, we will use another concept to describe the monotonicity of a function. This concept can be applied to a fairly broad class of functions, see [41,42]. However, we will only consider the relevant subclass of d.f.'s considered in [16,43,44] among others.

- *A d.f. F supported on* $\mathbb{R}$ *is said to have a positively decreasing tail, written as* $F \in \mathcal{PD}$, *if for any fixed* $y \in (0, 1)$
$$\liminf_{x\to\infty} \frac{\overline{F}(yx)}{\overline{F}(x)} > 1,$$
or equivalently
$$\limsup_{x\to\infty} \frac{\overline{F}(yx)}{\overline{F}(x)} < 1$$
for any $y > 1$.

We observe that

$$\mathscr{R}_+ := \bigcup_{\alpha>0} \mathscr{R}_\alpha \subset \mathcal{PD}; \quad \mathscr{R}_0 \cap \mathcal{PD} = \varnothing; \quad \mathscr{C} \cap \mathcal{PD} \neq \varnothing.$$

Other properties of distributions from the class $\mathcal{PD}$ are presented in [43].

1.6. Haezendonck–Goovaerts Risk Measure

To give a precise definition of the HG risk measure, let us suppose that X is a real-valued r.v. with a d.f. F_X representing a random risk.

- *A function* φ *defined on* $\mathbb{R}$ *is said to be a normalised Young function if* φ *is nonnegative and convex on the interval* $[0, \infty)$ *and such that* $\varphi(0) = 0, \varphi(1) = 1, \varphi(\infty) = \infty$.

The Orlicz space $\mathbb{L}^\varphi$ and the Orlicz heart $\mathbb{L}_0^\varphi$ of real-valued r.v.'s X associated with the function φ are defined as

$$\mathbb{L}^\varphi = \Big\{X : \mathbb{E}(\varphi(cX)) < \infty \text{ for some } c > 0\Big\}, \quad \mathbb{L}_0^\varphi = \Big\{X : \mathbb{E}(\varphi(cX)) < \infty \text{ for all } c > 0\Big\}.$$

It is obvious that $\mathbb{L}^\varphi = \mathbb{L}_0^\varphi$ if

$$\limsup_{x\to\infty} \frac{\varphi(2x)}{\varphi(x)} < \infty.$$

- *Let* φ *be a Young function,* $q \in (0, 1)$, *and* $X \in \mathbb{L}_0^\varphi$. *The Haezendonck–Goovaerts (HG) risk measure for variable X is defined as*

$$HG_q(X) = \inf_{x\in\mathbb{R}} \big(x + h(x, q)\big), \tag{4}$$

where $h = h(x, q)$ is a solution of the equation

$$\mathbb{E}\varphi\left(\frac{(X - x)^+}{h}\right) = 1 - q \tag{5}$$

if $\overline{F}_X(x) > 0$, and $h(x, q) = 0$ if $\overline{F}_X(x) = 0$.

According to Proposition 3(b,d) from [5], the minimiser (x_*, h_*) to the Equation (4) exists for all $q \in (0,1)$, and it is unique if the function φ is strictly convex. The HG risk measure has received much attention in insurance and finance. The risk measure was first introduced by Haezendonck–Goovaerts in [3]. For more results on HG risk measures, see, e.g., [5,9,45,46] and references therein. As it is remarked in [9], an analytic expression for the risk measure $HG_q(X)$ is not possible in general because an explicit solution of Equation (5) is generally not available. However, in the case of the power function $\varphi(t) = t^\varkappa$, $\varkappa \geqslant 1$, the analytic expressions and asymptotic formulas can be derived for certain distributions. Below, we present two statements from the paper [9] (see Equality (1.3), Theorem 2.1, and Theorem 4.1).

Theorem 3. *Consider the power Young function $\varphi(t) = t^\varkappa$ with $\varkappa \geqslant 1$.*

(i) *If $q \in (0,1)$, $\varkappa = 1$, and $\mathbb{E}X^+ < \infty$, then*

$$HG_q(X) = \overleftarrow{F}_X(q) + \frac{\mathbb{E}\left(X - \overleftarrow{F}_X(q)\right)^+}{1-q}, \tag{6}$$

where $\overleftarrow{F}_X(q) = \inf\{x \in \mathbb{R} : F_X(x) \geqslant q\} = \inf\{x \in \mathbb{R} : \overline{F}_X(x) \leqslant 1 - q\}$ is the quantile function of r.v. X.

(ii) *If $q \in (0,1)$, $\varkappa > 1$, $\mathbb{P}(X = \overleftarrow{F}_X(1)) = 0$, and $\mathbb{E}(X^+)^\varkappa < \infty$, then*

$$HG_q(X) = x + \left(\frac{\mathbb{E}((X - x)^+)^\varkappa}{1-q}\right)^{1/\varkappa}, \tag{7}$$

where $x = x(q) \in \left(-\infty, \overleftarrow{F}_X(1)\right)$ is the unique solution of the equation

$$\frac{\left(\mathbb{E}((X - x)^+)^{\varkappa-1}\right)^\varkappa}{\left(\mathbb{E}((X - x)^+)^\varkappa\right)^{\varkappa-1}} = 1 - q. \tag{8}$$

Theorem 4. *Consider the power Young function $\varphi(t) = t^\varkappa$ with $\varkappa \geqslant 1$, and let X be the real-valued r.v. such that $F_X \in \mathscr{R}_\alpha$ for some $\alpha > \varkappa$. Then,*

$$HG_q(X) \underset{q\uparrow 1}{\sim} \frac{\alpha(\alpha - \varkappa)^{(\varkappa/\alpha)-1}}{\varkappa^{(\varkappa-1)/\alpha}} \left(B(\alpha - \varkappa, \varkappa)\right)^{1/\alpha} \overleftarrow{F}_X(q),$$

where

$$B(a, b) = \int_0^1 y^{a-1}(1-y)^{b-1} \mathrm{d}y, \; a > 0, b > 0,$$

is the beta function.

In this paper, we obtain asymptotic formulas similar to those in Theorem 4 of HG risk measure for distributions from the class $\mathscr{C}$. More precisely, we derive asymptotic formulas for the HG risk measure when the risk variable X represents a sum of consistently varying risks $S_n^{(\xi)}$. The main results of this paper are based on general Formulas (7), (8) and asymptotic relations (2), (3).

Note that the obtained asymptotic formulas can be applied to a special-form set of random variables $\{\theta_1 X_1, \ldots, \theta_n X_n\}$, where $\{X_1, \ldots, X_n\}$ are real-valued primary r.v.'s, and $\{\theta_1, \ldots, \theta_n\}$ are nonnegative random weights. In such a case, the sum (1) becomes the randomly weighted sum

$$S_n^{(\theta X)} = \sum_{k=1}^{n} \theta_k X_k.$$

In actuarial applications, this sum usually represents the present value of the total future net loss of the insurance company during the first n time periods. In this case, the real-valued r.v. X_k represents a net loss of an insurance company during the k-th time period, and the random weight θ_k is a stochastic discount factor from time k to time 0. A financial interpretation of the sum $S_n^{(\theta X)}$ is based on the construction of the portfolio. Each investment portfolio consists of n lines of risks with random losses X_k and random weights θ_k describing the investment environment. In such a case, the sum $S_n^{(\theta X)}$ represents the total amount of future losses potentially incurred by the investment portfolio. The problems related to the asymptotic behavior of the sum $S_n^{(\theta X)}$ were considered in [37,47–61], and asymptotic properties of distributions of sums $S_n^{(\theta X)}$ related to the asymptotic behavior of risk measures, similar to the ES risk measure, were considered in [62–67].

The transition from the asymptotic properties of the sum $S_n^{(\xi)}$ to the analogous properties of the sum $S_n^{(\theta X)}$ is ensured by the product-convolution properties reviewed in detail in Chapter 5 of [44]. We only recall that for two independent r.v.'s. X and Y, the distribution of the product XY is described by the product-convolution of the d.f.'s. $F_X \otimes F_Y$. Below, we formulate a particular statement on the product-convolution closure (see Proposition 5.2(iii), Proposition 5.3(iii), Proposition 5.4(i) in [44]).

Theorem 5. *Let F be a distribution on $\mathbb{R}$ and G be a distribution such that $G(0-) = 0$ and $G(0) < 1$.*

(i) *If $F \in \mathscr{R}_\alpha$ and $\overline{G}(yx) = o(\overline{F}(x))$ for some $y > 0$, then $F \otimes G \in \mathscr{R}_\alpha$;*
(ii) *If $F \in \mathscr{C}$ and $\overline{G}(yx) = o(\overline{F}(x))$ for some $y > 0$, then $F \otimes G \in \mathscr{C}$;*
(iii) *If $F \in \mathscr{D}$, then $F \otimes G \in \mathscr{D}$.*

The rest of the paper is organised as follows. In Section 2, we provide a formulation of the main results. Section 3 deals with the auxiliary results that are essentially related to the properties of quantile functions. Section 4 presents the proof of the asymptotic formulas for the HG risk measure. Section 5 deals with the analysis of the particular example illustrating the accuracy of the derived asymptotic formula. Finally, Section 6 concludes.

2. Main Results

In this section, we state two theorems on the asymptotic behavior of the HG risk measure in the case where that measure is determined for the sum of distributions from the class $\mathscr{C}$. The first theorem is derived for the sum of simple r.v.'s, and the second theorem is derived for the sum of weighted r.v.'s.

Theorem 6. *Consider the power Young function $\varphi(t) = t^{\varkappa}$ with $\varkappa \geqslant 1$, and let $\{\xi_1, \ldots, \xi_n\}$ be a collection of real-valued* pQAI *r.v.'s.*

(i) *Let* $\varkappa = 1$, $\max\limits_{1 \leqslant k \leqslant n} \mathbb{E}(\xi_k^+) < \infty$, $F_{\xi_L} \in \mathscr{C}$ *for some* $L \in \{1, \ldots, n\}$, *and for other indices* $k \neq L$ *let* $F_{\xi_k} \in \mathscr{C}$ *or* $\mathbb{P}(|\xi_k| > x) = o(\overline{F}_{\xi_L}(x))$. *If* $F_{\xi_k} \in \mathcal{PD}$ *for all* $k \in \mathcal{I}_n = \{k \in \{1, \ldots, n\} : F_{\xi_k} \in \mathscr{C}\}$, *then*

$$HG_q\left(S_n^{(\xi)}\right) \underset{q \uparrow 1}{\sim} \overleftarrow{H}_n(q) + \frac{1}{1-q} \sum_{k \in \mathcal{I}_n} \mathbb{E}\left(\xi_k - \overleftarrow{H}_n(q)\right)^+,$$

where $\overleftarrow{H}_n$ *is the quantile function of the d.f.*

$$H_n := \max\left\{0, 1 - \sum_{k \in \mathcal{I}_n} \overline{F}_{\xi_k}\right\}.$$

(ii) *Let* $\varkappa \geqslant 2$, $\max\limits_{1 \leqslant k \leqslant n} \mathbb{E}(\xi_k^+)^{\varkappa} < \infty$, $F_{\xi_L} \in \mathscr{C}$ *for some* $L \in \{1, \ldots, n\}$, *and for other indices* $k \neq L$ *let* $F_{\xi_k} \in \mathscr{C}$ *or* $\mathbb{P}(|\xi_k| > x) = o(\overline{F}_{\xi_L}(x))$. *Let, in addition,*

$$\left(\max_{k \in \mathcal{I}_n} \limsup_{x \to \infty} \frac{\overline{F}_{\xi_k}(yx)}{\overline{F}_{\xi_k}(x)}\right)^{\varkappa} \left(\max_{k \in \mathcal{I}_n} \limsup_{x \to \infty} \frac{\overline{F}_{\xi_k}(x)}{\overline{F}_{\xi_k}(yx)}\right)^{\varkappa - 1} < 1 \tag{9}$$

for some $y > 1$, *where* $\mathcal{I}_n = \{k \in \{1, \ldots, \} : F_{\xi_k} \in \mathscr{C}\}$. *Then,*

$$HG_q\left(S_n^{(\xi)}\right) \underset{q \uparrow 1}{\sim} \widehat{x}(q) + \left(\frac{1}{1-q} \sum_{k \in \mathcal{I}_n} \mathbb{E}\left((\xi_k - \widehat{x}(q))^+\right)^{\varkappa}\right)^{1/\varkappa},$$

where $\widehat{x} = \widehat{x}(q)$ *is the unique solution to the equation*

$$\frac{\left(\sum_{k \in \mathcal{I}_n} \mathbb{E}\left((\xi_k - \widehat{x})^+\right)^{\varkappa - 1}\right)^{\varkappa}}{\left(\sum_{k \in \mathcal{I}_n} \mathbb{E}\left((\xi_k - \widehat{x})^+\right)^{\varkappa}\right)^{\varkappa - 1}} = 1 - q.$$

As mentioned earlier, our second main theorem is on the asymptotics of the HG risk measure for a weighted sum. We remark only that in this theorem, we suppose that not some, but all distributions of primary r.v.'s belong to the class $\mathscr{C}$.

Theorem 7. *Consider the same power Young function as in Theorem 6. Let* $\{X_1, \ldots, X_n\}$ *be a collection of real-valued pQAI r.v.'s with corresponding d.f.'s* $\{F_{X_1}, \ldots, F_{X_n}\}$ *belonging to class* $\mathscr{C}$. *Let* $\{\theta_1, \ldots, \theta_n\}$ *be another collection of arbitrary dependent, nonnegative, and nondegenerate at zero r.v.'s. Suppose that collections* $\{X_1, \ldots, X_n\}$ *and* $\{\theta_1, \ldots, \theta_n\}$ *are independent and that* $\max\limits_{1 \leqslant k \leqslant n} \{\mathbb{E}\theta_k^p\}$ *is finite for some* $p > \max\limits_{1 \leqslant k \leqslant n} J_{F_{X_k}}^+$.

(i) *If* $\varkappa = 1$, $\max\limits_{1 \leqslant k \leqslant n} \mathbb{E}(X_k^+) < \infty$, *and* $F_{X_k} \in \mathcal{PD}$ *for all* $k \in \{1, \ldots, n\}$, *then,*

$$HG_q\left(S_n^{(\theta X)}\right) \underset{q \uparrow 1}{\sim} \overleftarrow{H}_n^*(q) + \frac{1}{1-q} \sum_{k=1}^{n} \mathbb{E}\left(\theta_k X_k - \overleftarrow{H}_n^*(q)\right)^+,$$

where $\overleftarrow{H}_n^*$ *is the quantile function of the d.f.*

$$H_n^* := \max\left\{0, 1 - \sum_{k=1}^{n} \overline{F}_{\theta_k X_k}\right\}.$$

(ii) *Let* $\varkappa \geqslant 2$ *and* $\max\limits_{1\leqslant k\leqslant n} \mathbb{E}(X_k^+)^{\varkappa} < \infty$. *Let, in addition,*

$$\left(\max_{1\leqslant k\leqslant n} \limsup_{x\to\infty} \frac{\overline{F}_{X_k}(yx)}{\overline{F}_{X_k}(x)}\right)^{\varkappa} \left(\max_{1\leqslant k\leqslant n} \limsup_{x\to\infty} \frac{\overline{F}_{X_k}(x)}{\overline{F}_{X_k}(yx)}\right)^{\varkappa-1} < 1$$

for some $y > 1$. *Then,*

$$HG_q\left(S_n^{(\theta X)}\right) \underset{q\uparrow 1}{\sim} x^*(q) + \left(\frac{1}{1-q}\sum_{k=1}^{n} \mathbb{E}\left(\left(\theta_k X_k - x^*(q)\right)^+\right)^{\varkappa}\right)^{1/\varkappa},$$

where $x^* = x^*(q)$ *is the unique solution to the equation*

$$\frac{\left(\sum_{k=1}^n \mathbb{E}\left(\left(\theta_k X_k - x^*\right)^+\right)^{\varkappa-1}\right)^{\varkappa}}{\left(\sum_{k=1}^n \mathbb{E}\left(\left(\theta_k X_k - x^*\right)^+\right)^{\varkappa}\right)^{\varkappa-1}} = 1-q.$$

3. Auxiliary Statements

3.1. Some Properties of Quantile Functions

In this subsection, we formulate and prove several auxiliary results on useful properties of the quantile functions. Analogs of many of the statements formulated below can be found in articles [41,42,68,69]. For completeness, we present their complete proofs.

Lemma 1. *Let F be a d.f. from the class* $\mathscr{C}$. *Then,*

$$F\left(\overleftarrow{F}(q)\right) \underset{q\uparrow 1}{\sim} q, \quad \text{and} \quad \overline{F}\left(\overleftarrow{\overline{F}}(p)\right) \underset{p\downarrow 0}{\sim} p$$

where

$$\overleftarrow{F}(q) = \inf\{x : F(x) \geqslant q\}, q \in (0,1),$$

is the quantile function for F, and

$$\overleftarrow{\overline{F}}(p) = \inf\{x : \overline{F}(x) \leqslant p\}, p \in (0,1),$$

is the quantile function for t.f. $\overline{F}$.

Proof. Let $q \in (0,1)$. Since d.f. is right-continuous, the set $\{x : F(x) \geqslant q\} := \mathcal{A}_q$ is closed. Hence, $\overleftarrow{F}(q) \in \mathcal{A}_q$, which implies that

$$F\left(\overleftarrow{F}(q)\right) \geqslant q \tag{10}$$

for any $q \in (0,1)$. Therefore,

$$F\left(\overleftarrow{F}(q)\right) \underset{q\uparrow 1}{\gtrsim} q. \tag{11}$$

For the first asymptotic relation of the lemma, it remains to prove that

$$\limsup_{q\uparrow 1} \frac{F\left(\overleftarrow{F}(q)\right)}{q} \leqslant 1. \tag{12}$$

Suppose, on the contrary, that

$$\limsup_{q\uparrow 1}\frac{F\Big(\overset{\leftarrow}{F}(q)\Big)}{q}>1.$$

Then, there exist $\Delta>0$ and the sequence $q_n\uparrow 1$ such that

$$\lim_{n\to\infty}\frac{F\Big(\overset{\leftarrow}{F}(q_n)\Big)}{q_n}=1+\Delta,$$

implying that $F\Big(\overset{\leftarrow}{F}(q_n)\Big)>(1+\Delta/2)q_n$ for large n. Since $F(x)\leqslant 1$ for all x, we have that

$$q_n<(1+\Delta/2)^{-1}$$

for large n. This is impossible because $q_n\uparrow 1$. The obtained contradiction proves estimate (12). Estimates (11) and (12) imply the first asymptotic relation of the lemma.

Now, consider the second relation of the lemma. Let $p>0$. Due to inequality (10), we have

$$\begin{aligned}\overline{F}\Big(\overset{\leftarrow}{\overline{F}}(p)\Big)&=1-F\big(\inf\{x:\overline{F}(x)\leqslant p\}\big)=1-F\big(\inf\{x:F(x)\geqslant 1-p\}\big)\\&=1-F\Big(\overset{\leftarrow}{F}(1-p)\Big)\leqslant p,\end{aligned}\tag{13}$$

implying that

$$\overline{F}\Big(\overset{\leftarrow}{\overline{F}}(p)\Big)\underset{p\downarrow 0}{\lesssim}p.\tag{14}$$

It remains to prove that

$$\liminf_{p\downarrow 0}\frac{\overline{F}\Big(\overset{\leftarrow}{\overline{F}}(p)\Big)}{p}\geqslant 1.\tag{15}$$

Suppose, on the contrary, that

$$\liminf_{p\downarrow 0}\frac{\overline{F}\Big(\overset{\leftarrow}{\overline{F}}(p)\Big)}{p}<1.$$

From this, it follows that there exist $\Delta\in(0,1)$ and a sequence $p_n\downarrow 0$ such that

$$\lim_{n\to\infty}\frac{\overline{F}\Big(\overset{\leftarrow}{\overline{F}}(p_n)\Big)}{p_n}=1-\Delta.$$

Hence,

$$\overline{F}\Big(\overset{\leftarrow}{\overline{F}}(p_n)\Big)=\overline{F}\big(\inf\{x:\overline{F}(x)\leqslant p_n\}\big)<(1-\Delta/2)p_n,$$

or, equivalently,

$$F\big(\inf\{x:\overline{F}(x)\leqslant p_n\}\big)=F\big(\inf\{x:F(x)\geqslant 1-p_n\big)>1-p_n+p_n(\Delta/2)$$

for large n.

Let us temporarily denote

$$x_n = \inf\{x : F(x) \geqslant 1 - p_n\}.$$

Since $\overline{F}(x) > 0$ for all x, the sequence x_n is nondecreasing, and $x_n \uparrow \infty$. In addition, the d.f. F is right-continuous so that $F(x_n) \geqslant 1 - p_n$. For fixed n, there are two possible cases: $F(x_n) = 1 - p_n$ or $F(x_n) > 1 - p_n$. In the first case, we get

$$1 - p_n > 1 - p_n + p_n(\Delta/2),$$

which is impossible due to the positivity of Δ. Consequently, the d.f. F has a jump at each point x_n, from which it follows that

$$F((1-\varepsilon_n)x_n) < 1 - p_n \text{ and } F(x_n) > (1-p_n) + p_n(\Delta/2),$$

or, equivalently,

$$\overline{F}((1-\varepsilon_n)x_n) > p_n \text{ and } \overline{F}(x_n) < p_n(1-\Delta/2)$$

for some sequence $\varepsilon_n \downarrow 0$. These estimates imply that

$$\lim_{n\to\infty} \frac{\overline{F}(((1-\varepsilon_n)x_n)}{\overline{F}(x_n)} \geqslant \frac{2}{2-\Delta} > 1$$

for some sequences $x_n \uparrow \infty$ and $\varepsilon_n \downarrow 0$. The derived relation contradicts the condition $F \in \mathscr{C}$, because it should be

$$\lim_{\varepsilon\downarrow 0} \limsup_{x\to\infty} \frac{\overline{F}((1-\varepsilon)x)}{\overline{F}(x)} \leqslant 1.$$

by the definition of the class $\mathscr{C}$ presented in Section 1.2.

The obtained contradiction proves the validity of inequality (15), which, together with estimate (14), proves the second asymptotic relation of the lemma. □

Lemma 2. *Let F be a d.f. from the class $\mathcal{PD}$. Then,*

$$\overleftarrow{\overline{F}}\,(\overline{F}(x)) \underset{x\to\infty}{\sim} x, \quad \text{and} \quad \overleftarrow{F}\,(F(x)) \underset{x\to\infty}{\sim} x,$$

where the quantile functions $\overleftarrow{\overline{F}}$ and $\overleftarrow{F}$ are defined in Lemma 1.

Proof. Consider the first relation. By the definition of the quantile function $\overleftarrow{\overline{F}}$, we have

$$\overleftarrow{\overline{F}}\,(\overline{F}(x)) = \inf\{y : \overline{F}(y) \leqslant \overline{F}(x)\}.$$

Since the function $\overline{F}$ is nonincreasing, that is $\overline{F}(y) \leqslant \overline{F}(x)$ for $y \geqslant x$, we have that $\overleftarrow{\overline{F}}\,(\overline{F}(x)) \leqslant x$, implying

$$\overleftarrow{\overline{F}}\,(\overline{F}(x)) \underset{x\to\infty}{\lesssim} x. \tag{16}$$

It remains to prove that

$$\overleftarrow{\overline{F}}\left(\overline{F}(x)\right) \underset{x\to\infty}{\gtrsim} x. \tag{17}$$

Suppose, on the contrary, that

$$\liminf_{x\to\infty} \frac{\overleftarrow{\overline{F}}\left(\overline{F}(x)\right)}{x} < 1.$$

In such a case, there exist $\Delta \in (0,1)$ and a sequence $x_n \uparrow \infty$ such that

$$\lim_{n\to\infty} \frac{\overleftarrow{\overline{F}}\left(\overline{F}(x_n)\right)}{x_n} = 1 - \Delta.$$

Hence,

$$\overleftarrow{\overline{F}}\left(\overline{F}(x_n)\right) = \inf\{y : \overline{F}(y) \leqslant \overline{F}(x_n)\} \leqslant (1 - 2\Delta/3)x_n$$

for sufficiently large n, say $n \geqslant N_\Delta$. This relation implies that

$$\overline{F}\Big(\Big(1 - \frac{\Delta}{2}\Big)x_n\Big) \leqslant \overline{F}(x_n)$$

Since the function $\overline{F}$ is nonincreasing, it must be

$$\overline{F}\Big(\Big(1 - \frac{\Delta}{2}\Big)x_n\Big) = \overline{F}(x_n)$$

for $n \geqslant N_\Delta$. Therefore,

$$\lim_{n\to\infty} \frac{\overline{F}\Big(\Big(1 - \frac{\Delta}{2}\Big)x_n\Big)}{\overline{F}(x_n)} = 1,$$

which contradicts the definition of $F \in \mathcal{PD}$ presented in Section 1.5. Consequently, the asymptotic Relation (17) holds. Relations (16) and (17) imply the first one of the lemma.

The second relation of the lemma follows from the equalities

$$\begin{aligned}
\lim_{x\to\infty} \frac{\overleftarrow{F}\left(F(x)\right)}{x} &= \lim_{x\to\infty} \frac{1}{x} \inf\{y : F(y) \geqslant F(x)\} \\
&= \lim_{x\to\infty} \frac{1}{x} \inf\{y : \overline{F}(y) \leqslant \overline{F}(x)\} \\
&= \lim_{x\to\infty} \frac{\overleftarrow{\overline{F}}\left(\overline{F}(x)\right)}{x} = 1.
\end{aligned}$$

The lemma is now proved. □

Lemma 3. *Let d.f.* $F \in \mathcal{PD}$. *Then, for any two positive functions* $a(x)$ *and* $b(x)$ *such that* $a(x) \underset{x\to\infty}{\sim} b(x)$ *and* $a(x) \underset{x\to\infty}{\to} 0$*, we have that*

$$\overleftarrow{\overline{F}}\left(a(x)\right) \underset{x\to\infty}{\sim} \overleftarrow{\overline{F}}\left(b(x)\right)$$

and for any positive functions $\hat{a}(p)$, $\hat{b}(p)$ *such that* $\hat{a}(p) \underset{p\downarrow 0}{\sim} \hat{b}(p)$ *and* $\hat{a}(p) \underset{p\downarrow 0}{\to} 0$*, we have*

$$\overleftarrow{\overline{F}}\left(\hat{a}(p)\right) \underset{p\downarrow 0}{\sim} \overleftarrow{\overline{F}}\left(\hat{b}(p)\right).$$

Proof. It suffices to prove the first equivalence relation because the second relation follows from the first one by noting that

$$\lim_{p\downarrow 0} \frac{\overleftarrow{\overline{F}}\,(\hat{a}(p))}{\overleftarrow{\overline{F}}\,(\hat{b}(p))} = \lim_{x\to\infty} \frac{\overleftarrow{\overline{F}}\left(\hat{a}\left(\frac{1}{x}\right)\right)}{\overleftarrow{\overline{F}}\left(\hat{b}\left(\frac{1}{x}\right)\right)}.$$

Consider the first relation. Firstly, we will show that

$$\liminf_{x\to\infty} \frac{\overleftarrow{\overline{F}}(a(x))}{\overleftarrow{\overline{F}}(b(x))} \geqslant 1. \tag{18}$$

We will proceed with the proof by contradiction again. Assume that

$$\liminf_{x\to\infty} \frac{\overleftarrow{\overline{F}}(a(x))}{\overleftarrow{\overline{F}}(b(x))} < 1.$$

This means that there exist $\Delta > 0$ and a sequence $x_n \uparrow \infty$ such that

$$\lim_{n\to\infty} \frac{\overleftarrow{\overline{F}}(a(x_n))}{\overleftarrow{\overline{F}}(b(x_n))} = 1 - \Delta.$$

It follows that

$$\frac{\overleftarrow{\overline{F}}(a(x_n))}{\left(1-\frac{\Delta}{2}\right)} < \overleftarrow{\overline{F}}(b(x_n))$$

for large enough n. By the definition of $\overleftarrow{\overline{F}}$, we have

$$\overline{F}\left(\frac{\overleftarrow{\overline{F}}(a(x_n))}{\left(1-\frac{\Delta}{2}\right)}\right) > b(x_n).$$

This relation, together with (13), implies

$$\frac{\overline{F}\left(\left(1-\frac{\Delta}{2}\right)\frac{\overleftarrow{\overline{F}}(a(x_n))}{(1-\frac{\Delta}{2})}\right)}{\overline{F}\left(\frac{\overleftarrow{\overline{F}}(a(x_n))}{(1-\frac{\Delta}{2})}\right)} = \frac{\overline{F}\left(\overleftarrow{\overline{F}}\,(a(x_n))\right)}{\overline{F}\left(\frac{\overleftarrow{\overline{F}}(a(x_n))}{(1-\frac{\Delta}{2})}\right)} \leqslant \frac{a(x_n)}{b(x_n)} \underset{n\to\infty}{\to} 1,$$

since $a(x) \underset{x\to\infty}{\sim} b(x)$. Thus,

$$\lim_{n\to\infty} \frac{\overline{F}\left(\left(1-\frac{\Delta}{2}\right)\frac{\overleftarrow{\overline{F}}(a(x_n))}{(1-\frac{\Delta}{2})}\right)}{\overline{F}\left(\frac{\overleftarrow{\overline{F}}(a(x_n))}{(1-\frac{\Delta}{2})}\right)} \leqslant 1$$

for some sequence $\overleftarrow{\overline{F}}(a(x_n))/(1-\Delta/2) \underset{n\to\infty}{\to} \infty$. This contradicts the definition of $F \in \mathcal{PD}$ in Section 1.2.

It remains to prove that

$$\limsup_{x\to\infty} \frac{\overleftarrow{\overline{F}}(a(x))}{\overleftarrow{\overline{F}}(b(x))} \leqslant 1.$$

Suppose, on the contrary, that

$$\limsup_{x\to\infty} \frac{\overleftarrow{\overline{F}}(a(x))}{\overleftarrow{\overline{F}}(b(x))} > 1.$$

It follows that there exist $\Delta > 0$ and a sequence $x_n \uparrow \infty$ such that

$$\lim_{n\to\infty} \frac{\overleftarrow{\overline{F}}(a(x_n))}{\overleftarrow{\overline{F}}(b(x_n))} = 1 + \Delta.$$

Consequently,

$$\overleftarrow{\overline{F}}(a(x_n)) > \left(1 + \frac{\Delta}{2}\right) \overleftarrow{\overline{F}}(b(x_n))$$

for large n. By the definition of $\overleftarrow{\overline{F}}$, it follows that

$$a(x_n) < \overline{F}\left(\left(1 + \frac{\Delta}{2}\right) \overleftarrow{\overline{F}}(b(x_n))\right).$$

This relation, together with (13), implies

$$\frac{\overline{F}\left(\left(1 + \frac{\Delta}{2}\right) \overleftarrow{\overline{F}}(b(x_n))\right)}{\overline{F}\left(\overleftarrow{\overline{F}}(b(x_n))\right)} \geqslant \frac{a(x_n)}{b(x_n)} \underset{n\to\infty}{\to} 1,$$

since $a(x) \underset{x\to\infty}{\sim} b(x)$. Thus,

$$\lim_{n\to\infty} \frac{\overline{F}\left(\left(1 + \frac{\Delta}{2}\right) \overleftarrow{\overline{F}}\,(b(x_n))\right)}{\overline{F}\left(\overleftarrow{\overline{F}}\,(b(x_n))\right)} \geqslant 1$$

for some sequence $\overleftarrow{\overline{F}}(b(x_n)) \underset{n\to\infty}{\to} \infty$. This contradicts the definition of $F \in \mathcal{PD}$ in Section 1.2. The lemma is now proved. □

Lemma 4. *Let F and G be two d.f.'s such that $F \in \mathscr{C} \cap \mathcal{PD}$, and $\overline{G}(x) \underset{x\to\infty}{\sim} c\overline{F}(x)$ for some constant $c > 0$. Then,*

$$\overleftarrow{G}(1-p) \underset{p\downarrow 0}{\sim} \overleftarrow{F}\left(1 - \frac{p}{c}\right).$$

Proof. The condition $F \in \mathcal{PD}$ and Lemmas 2 and 3 imply that

$$x \underset{x\to\infty}{\sim} \overleftarrow{\overline{F}}\left(\overline{F}(x)\right) \underset{x\to\infty}{\sim} \overleftarrow{\overline{F}}\left(\frac{\overline{G}(x)}{c}\right). \tag{19}$$

The conditions $F \in \mathscr{C} \cap \mathcal{PD}$ and $\overline{G}(x) \underset{x\to\infty}{\sim} c\overline{F}(x)$ imply that $G \in \mathscr{C} \cap \mathcal{PD}$. Hence, $\overline{G}(x) > 0$ for all $x \in \mathbb{R}$, and therefore, $\overleftarrow{\overline{G}}(p) \to \infty$ as $p \downarrow 0$. By taking $x = \overleftarrow{\overline{G}}(p)$ in (19), we get

$$\overleftarrow{\overline{G}}(p) \underset{p\downarrow 0}{\sim} \overleftarrow{\overline{F}}\left(\frac{1}{c}\overline{G}\left(\overleftarrow{\overline{G}}(p)\right)\right).$$

By Lemma 1, we have

$$\overline{G}\left(\overleftarrow{\overline{G}}(p)\right) \underset{p\downarrow 0}{\sim} p.$$

Hence, from Lemma 3, we derive that

$$\overleftarrow{\overline{G}}(p) \underset{p\downarrow 0}{\sim} \overleftarrow{\overline{F}}\left(\frac{p}{c}\right),$$

or, equivalently,

$$\overleftarrow{G}(1-p) \underset{p\downarrow 0}{\sim} \overleftarrow{F}\left(1-\frac{p}{c}\right).$$

The lemma is proved. □

3.2. Properties of the Special Function in Equation (8)

Let X be an r.v. such that $\mathbb{E}(X^+)^\varkappa < \infty$ and $\overline{F}_X(x) = \mathbb{P}(X > x) > 0$ for all $x \in \mathbb{R}$. Let

$$\gamma_X(x) = \frac{\left(\mathbb{E}((X-x)^+)^{\varkappa-1}\right)^\varkappa}{\left(\mathbb{E}((X-x)^+)^\varkappa\right)^{\varkappa-1}}, \quad x \in \mathbb{R}, \tag{20}$$

be a well-defined function from Equation (8). In this subsection, we consider properties of the function γ_X and its components. The first such statement is proved in [9] (Lemma 2.1).

Lemma 5. *Let X be an r.v. such that $\mathbb{E}(X^+)^\varkappa < \infty$ and $\overline{F}_X(x) > 0$ for all real x. If $\varkappa > 1$, then function $g(x) := \mathbb{E}((X-x)^+)^\varkappa$ is continuously differentiable with*

$$g'(x) = -\varkappa\mathbb{E}((X-x)^+)^{\varkappa-1}, \quad x \in \mathbb{R}.$$

If $\varkappa = 1$, then for each $x \in \mathbb{R}$, the derivative from the right $g'_+(x) = -\overline{F}(x)$ and the derivative from the left $g'_-(x) = -\overline{F}(x-0)$.

Other statements directly concern the properties of the function γ_X.

Lemma 6. *Let X be an r.v. such that $\mathbb{E}(X^+)^\varkappa < \infty$ and $\overline{F}_X(x) > 0$ for all $x \in \mathbb{R}$. Let γ_X be the function defined in Equation (20). If $\varkappa > 1$, then*

$$\lim_{x\to-\infty} \gamma_X(x) = 1 \quad \text{and} \quad \lim_{x\to\infty} \gamma_X(x) = 0.$$

Proof. While the main steps of the proof are outlined in [9] (see the proof of Theorem 2.1), we provide the complete proof here in more detail. Since $F_X(x) > 0$, we have that

$$\mathbb{E}((X-x)^+)^\varkappa = \varkappa\int_x^\infty (u-x)^{\varkappa-1}\overline{F}_X(u)\mathrm{d}u > 0$$

for any $x \in \mathbb{R}$. By using the classical Hölder's inequality, we get

$$\begin{aligned}\gamma_X(x) &= \frac{\left(\mathbb{E}\left(((X-x)^+)^{\varkappa-1}\mathbb{1}_{(x,\infty)}(X)\right)\right)^{\varkappa}}{\left(\mathbb{E}((X-x)^+)^{\varkappa}\right)^{\varkappa-1}} \\ &\leqslant \frac{1}{\left(\mathbb{E}((X-x)^+)^{\varkappa}\right)^{\varkappa-1}}\left\{\left(\mathbb{E}((X-x)^+)^{(\varkappa-1)\frac{\varkappa}{\varkappa-1}}\right)^{\frac{\varkappa-1}{\varkappa}}\left(\mathbb{E}\left(\mathbb{1}_{(x,\infty)}(X)\right)^{\varkappa}\right)^{\frac{1}{\varkappa}}\right\}^{\varkappa} \\ &= \overline{F}_X(x),\end{aligned}$$

which implies the second equality of the lemma.

Let us consider the first equality. It is obvious that

$$\lim_{x\to-\infty}\gamma_X(x) = \lim_{x\to\infty}\frac{\left(\mathbb{E}\left(\frac{(X+x)^+}{x}\right)^{\varkappa-1}\right)^{\varkappa}}{\left(\mathbb{E}\left(\frac{(X+x)^+}{x}\right)^{\varkappa}\right)^{\varkappa-1}}. \tag{21}$$

The classical c_r-inequality and inequality $(a+b)^+ \leqslant a^+ + b^+$ provided for any real numbers a, b imply that for positive x

$$\mathbb{E}\left(\frac{(X+x)^+}{x}\right)^{\varkappa-1} \leqslant \mathbb{E}\left(\frac{X^+ + x}{x}\right)^{\varkappa-1} \leqslant c_{\varkappa}\left(\frac{1}{x^{\varkappa-1}}\mathbb{E}(X^+)^{\varkappa-1} + 1\right) < \infty,$$

where

$$c_{\varkappa} = \begin{cases} 1 & \text{if} \quad 1 < \varkappa \leqslant 2, \\ 2^{\varkappa-2} & \text{if} \quad \varkappa > 2. \end{cases}$$

Hence,

$$\lim_{x\to\infty}\left(\mathbb{E}\left(\frac{(X+x)^+}{x}\right)^{\varkappa-1}\right)^{\varkappa} = \left(\mathbb{E}\lim_{x\to\infty}\left(\frac{(X+x)^+}{x}\right)^{\varkappa-1}\right)^{\varkappa} = 1$$

by the dominated convergence theorem.
Similarly,

$$\lim_{x\to\infty}\left(\mathbb{E}\left(\frac{(X+x)^+}{x}\right)^{\varkappa}\right)^{\varkappa-1} = 1.$$

Now, we can derive the first equality of the lemma by substituting the last two relations into equality (21). The lemma is proved. □

Lemma 7. *Let X be an r.v. such that $\mathbb{E}(X^+)^{\varkappa} < \infty$ and $\overline{F}_X(x) > 0$ for $x \in \mathbb{R}$. If $\varkappa \geqslant 2$, then the function γ_X is continuous and strongly decreasing on $\mathbb{R}$.*

Proof. At first, let us consider the case $\varkappa > 2$. By denoting $\eta_x = (X-x)^+$, we have

$$\gamma_X(x) = \frac{(\mathbb{E}\eta_x^{\varkappa-1})^{\varkappa}}{(\mathbb{E}\eta_x^{\varkappa})^{\varkappa-1}}.$$

Due to Lemma 5, we get

$$\gamma'_X(x) = -\varkappa(\varkappa-1)\,\frac{(\mathbb{E}\eta_x^{\varkappa-1})^{\varkappa-1}}{(\mathbb{E}\eta_x^{\varkappa})^{\varkappa}}\left(\mathbb{E}\eta_x^{\varkappa-2}\mathbb{E}\eta_x^{\varkappa} - (\mathbb{E}\eta_x^{\varkappa-1})^2\right),\ x \in \mathbb{R}.$$

The classical Cauchy–Schwarz inequality and condition $\overline{F}_X(x) > 0,\ x \in \mathbb{R}$, imply that

$$\mathbb{E}\eta_x^{\varkappa-1} = \mathbb{E}\eta_x^{\frac{\varkappa-2}{2}}\eta_x^{\frac{\varkappa}{2}} < \left(\mathbb{E}\eta_x^{\varkappa-2}\right)^{\frac{1}{2}}\left(\mathbb{E}\eta_x^{\varkappa}\right)^{\frac{1}{2}}.$$

Therefore, $\gamma_X'(x) < 0$ for $x \in \mathbb{R}$ implying the assertion of the lemma in the case $\varkappa > 2$.

Now, let us suppose that $\varkappa = 2$. In this case,

$$\gamma_X(x) = \frac{(\mathbb{E}\eta_x)^2}{\mathbb{E}\eta_x^2}.$$

Using Lemma 5, we obtain the derivative from the right

$$\{\gamma_X\}_+'(x) = -2\,\frac{\mathbb{E}\eta_x}{\left(\mathbb{E}\eta_x^2\right)^2}\left(\overline{F}(x)\mathbb{E}\eta_x^2 - (\mathbb{E}\eta_x)^2\right)$$

is negative for any $x \in \mathbb{R}$ due to the Hölder inequality

$$\mathbb{E}\eta_x = \mathbb{E}\,\eta_x \mathbb{1}_{(x,\infty)}(X) < \left(\mathbb{E}\,\eta_x^2\right)^{\frac{1}{2}}\left(\mathbb{E}\mathbb{1}_{(x,\infty)}(X)\right)^{\frac{1}{2}} = \left(\mathbb{E}\,\eta_x^2\right)^{\frac{1}{2}}\left(\overline{F}(x)\right)^{\frac{1}{2}},$$

where the strictness of the inequality follows from the condition $\overline{F}_X(x) > 0, x \in \mathbb{R}$. In the same way, we get that the derivative from the left $\{\gamma_X\}_-'(x)$ is also negative for any real x because

$$\mathbb{E}\eta_x \mathbb{1}_{(x,\infty)}(X) = \mathbb{E}\eta_x \mathbb{1}_{[x,\infty)}(X),\ x \in \mathbb{R}.$$

The derived properties of the function γ_X imply that this function is continuous and strongly decreasing on $\mathbb{R}$. The lemma is proved. □

Lemma 8. *Let X be an r.v. such that $\mathbb{E}(X^+)^{\varkappa} < \infty$ and $F_X \in \mathscr{C}$. If $\varkappa > 1$, then*

$$\lim_{y\uparrow 1}\limsup_{x\to\infty}\frac{\gamma_X(xy)}{\gamma_X(x)} \leqslant 1.$$

Proof. If $\mathbb{E}(X^+)^{\varkappa}$ is finite, then

$$\mathbb{E}((X-x)^+)^p = p\int_x^{\infty}(u-x)^{p-1}\mathbb{P}(X > u)\mathrm{d}u$$

for any $0 < p \leqslant \varkappa$. Therefore, for all positive x and y

$$\begin{aligned}
\frac{\gamma_X(xy)}{\gamma_X(x)} &= \left(\frac{\mathbb{E}((X-xy)^+)^{\varkappa-1}}{\mathbb{E}((X-x)^+)^{\varkappa-1}}\right)^{\varkappa}\left(\frac{\mathbb{E}((X-x)^+)^{\varkappa}}{\mathbb{E}((X-yx)^+)^{\varkappa}}\right)^{\varkappa-1}\\
&= \left(\frac{\int_{xy}^{\infty}(u-xy)^{\varkappa-2}\overline{F}_X(u)\mathrm{d}u}{\int_x^{\infty}(u-x)^{\varkappa-2}\overline{F}_X(u)\mathrm{d}u}\right)^{\varkappa}\left(\frac{\int_x^{\infty}(u-x)^{\varkappa-1}\overline{F}_X(u)\mathrm{d}u}{\int_{xy}^{\infty}(u-xy)^{\varkappa-1}\overline{F}_X(u)\mathrm{d}u}\right)^{\varkappa-1}\\
&= \left(\frac{\int_x^{\infty}(u-x)^{\varkappa-2}\overline{F}_X(uy)\mathrm{d}u}{\int_x^{\infty}(u-x)^{\varkappa-2}\overline{F}_X(u)\mathrm{d}u}\right)^{\varkappa}\left(\frac{\int_x^{\infty}(u-x)^{\varkappa-1}\overline{F}_X(u)\mathrm{d}u}{\int_x^{\infty}(u-x)^{\varkappa-1}\overline{F}_X(uy)\mathrm{d}u}\right)^{\varkappa-1}\\
&\leqslant \left(\sup_{u\geqslant x}\frac{\overline{F}_X(uy)}{\overline{F}_X(u)}\right)^{\varkappa}\left(\sup_{u\geqslant x}\frac{\overline{F}_X(u)}{\overline{F}_X(uy)}\right)^{\varkappa-1}.
\end{aligned} \tag{22}$$

If $y \in (0,1)$, then

$$\limsup_{x\to\infty}\frac{\gamma_X(xy)}{\gamma_X(x)} \leqslant \left(\limsup_{x\to\infty}\sup_{u\geqslant x}\frac{\overline{F}_X(uy)}{\overline{F}_X(u)}\right)^{\varkappa}.$$

Since d.f. $F_X \in \mathscr{C}$, the last inequality implies the statement of the lemma. □

Lemma 9. *Let X be an r.v. with d.f. F_X such that $\mathbb{E}(X^+)^{\varkappa} < \infty$ and*

$$\left(\limsup_{x\to\infty} \frac{\overline{F}_X(yx)}{\overline{F}_X(x)}\right)^{\varkappa} \left(\limsup_{x\to\infty} \frac{\overline{F}_X(x)}{\overline{F}_X(yx)}\right)^{\varkappa-1} < 1 \tag{23}$$

for some $\varkappa > 1$ and some $y > 1$. Then,

$$\limsup_{x\to\infty} \frac{\gamma_X(xy)}{\gamma_X(x)} < 1.$$

for some $y > 1$.

Remark 1. *Since $\overline{F}_X(x) \geqslant \overline{F}_X(vx)$ for any $v > 1$, condition (23) implies that $F_X \in \mathcal{PD}$. If $F_X \in \mathscr{R}_\alpha$ for some $\alpha > 0$, then the condition (23) holds for all $\varkappa > 1$. If $F_X \in \mathscr{ERV}_{\{\alpha,\beta\}} \subset \mathscr{C}$ with some $0 < \alpha < \beta < \infty$, then condition (23) holds in the case $1 < \varkappa < \frac{\beta}{\beta-\alpha}$.*

Proof of the lemma. Let $\varkappa > 1$ and $y > 1$ be such that condition (23) holds. By estimate (22), we obtain

$$\begin{aligned}\limsup_{x\to\infty} \frac{\gamma_X(xy)}{\gamma_X(x)} &\leqslant \limsup_{x\to\infty} \left(\sup_{u\geqslant x} \frac{\overline{F}_X(uy)}{\overline{F}_X(u)}\right)^{\varkappa} \left(\sup_{u\geqslant x} \frac{\overline{F}_X(u)}{\overline{F}_X(uy)}\right)^{\varkappa-1} \\ &= \left(\limsup_{x\to\infty} \frac{\overline{F}_X(xy)}{\overline{F}_X(x)}\right)^{\varkappa} \left(\limsup_{x\to\infty} \frac{\overline{F}_X(x)}{\overline{F}_X(xy)}\right)^{\varkappa-1}.\end{aligned}$$

Now, the lemma follows from condition (23). The lemma is proved. □

Corollary 1. *Let $\varkappa \geqslant 2$ and let X be an r.v. with d.f. F_X satisfying condition (23). Then, the function γ_X defined in equality (20) is the t.f. of d.f. $1-\gamma_X$ belonging to the class $\mathscr{C} \cap \mathcal{PD}$.*

The corollary immediately follows from Lemmas 6–9.

3.3. Some Closure Properties

In this subsection, we present some closure properties of d.f.'s with respect to the dependence structure and the product convolution. We use the results of this subsection to derive Theorem 7. The proof of the first such lemma can be found in [18] (Lemma 4).

Lemma 10. *Let X_1, X_2 be QAI r.v.'s with d.f. $F_{X_1} \in \mathscr{D}$, $F_{X_2} \in \mathscr{D}$. Let θ_1, θ_2 be two non-negative nondegenerate at zero r.v.'s such that vectors (X_1, X_2) and (θ_1, θ_2) are independent. If $\max\{\theta_1^p, \theta_2^p\} < \infty$ for some $p > \max\{J^+_{F_{X_1}}, J^+_{F_{X_2}}\}$ then the r.v.'s $\theta_1 X_1$ and $\theta_2 X_2$ are QAI.*

The second lemma on the closure of class $\mathscr{C}$ with respect to the product convolution is proved in [70] (Lemma 2.5).

Lemma 11. *Let X and θ be independent r.v.'s, and let d.f. F_X belong to the class $\mathscr{C}$. If θ is a nonnegative, nondegenerate at zero r.v. such that $\mathbb{E}\theta^p < \infty$ for some $p > J^+_{F_X}$, then d.f. $F_{\theta X}$ of the product θX also belongs to the class $\mathscr{C}$.*

The next lemma is on the closure of class $\mathcal{PD}$.

Lemma 12. *Let X be an r.v. with d.f.* $F_X \in \mathcal{PD} \cap \mathscr{D}$, *and let* θ *be an independent of X, nonnegative, and nondegenerate at zero r.v. such that* $\mathbb{E}\theta^p < \infty$ *for some* $p > J^+_{F_X}$. *Then, the product d.f.* $F_{\theta X}$ *belongs to the class* $\mathcal{PD}$.

Proof. Fix $y > 1$ such that

$$\limsup_{x\to\infty} \frac{\overline{F}_X(xy)}{\overline{F}_X(x)} < 1,$$

and let $a \in (0,1)$ and $b > 0$ be such that $\mathbb{P}(b > 0) > 0$. If x is sufficiently large, then

$$\begin{aligned}
\frac{\overline{F}_{\theta X}(xy)}{\overline{F}_{\theta X}(x)} &= \frac{\mathbb{P}(\theta X > xy, \theta \leqslant x^a)}{\mathbb{P}(\theta X > x)} + \frac{\mathbb{P}(\theta X > xy, \theta > x^a)}{\mathbb{P}(\theta X > x)} \\
&\leqslant \frac{\mathbb{P}(\theta X > xy, \theta \leqslant x^a)}{\mathbb{P}(\theta X > x, \theta \leqslant x^a)} + \frac{\mathbb{P}(\theta > x^a)}{\mathbb{P}(\theta X > x, \theta > b)} \\
&\leqslant \frac{\mathbb{P}(\theta X > xy, 0 < \theta \leqslant x^a)}{\mathbb{P}(\theta X > x, 0 < \theta \leqslant x^a)} + \frac{\mathbb{E}\theta^p}{x^{ap}\mathbb{P}(\theta > b)\mathbb{P}(X > x/b)} \\
&\leqslant \sup_{0<u\leqslant x^a} \frac{\overline{F}_X\left(\frac{yx}{u}\right)}{\overline{F}_X\left(\frac{x}{u}\right)} + \frac{\mathbb{E}\theta^p}{\mathbb{P}(\theta > b)} \frac{1}{x^{ap}\overline{F}_X(x)} \frac{\overline{F}_X(x)}{\overline{F}\left(\frac{x}{b}\right)} \\
&= \sup_{z\geqslant x^{1-a}} \frac{\overline{F}_X(zy)}{\overline{F}_X(z)} + \frac{\mathbb{E}\theta^p}{\mathbb{P}(\theta > b)} \frac{1}{x^{ap}\overline{F}_X(x)} \frac{\overline{F}_X(x)}{\overline{F}\left(\frac{x}{b}\right)}.
\end{aligned} \tag{24}$$

Since $F_X \in \mathscr{D}$, it is obvious that $\overline{F}_X = O(\overline{F}_X(x/b))$. Moreover, $\lim_{x\to\infty} x^q\overline{F}_X(x) = \infty$ for $q > J^+_{F_X}$; see, e.g., Lemma 3.5 in [54]. If $p > J^+_{F_X}$, then there exists $a \in (0,1)$ such that $ap > J^+_{F_X}$. For this particular a, the second term on the right side of (24) tends to zero as x tends to infinity. Consequently, for this particular $a \in (0,1)$

$$\limsup_{x\to\infty} \frac{\overline{F}_{\theta X}(xy)}{\overline{F}_{\theta X}(x)} \leqslant \limsup_{x\to\infty} \sup_{z\geqslant x^{1-a}} \frac{\overline{F}_X(zy)}{\overline{F}_X(z)} = \limsup_{x\to\infty} \frac{\overline{F}_X(xy)}{\overline{F}_X(x)} < 1. \tag{25}$$

The lemma is proved. We remark only that a similar statement, but for a positive random weight, is proved in Theorem 4.1 of [71]. □

Lemma 13. *Let X be an r.v. with d.f.* $F_X \in \mathscr{D}$, *and let* θ *be an independent of X, nonnegative, and nondegenerate at zero r.v. such that* $\mathbb{E}\theta^p < \infty$ *for some* $p > J^+_{F_X}$. *Then, for all* $y > 0$

$$\limsup_{x\to\infty} \frac{\overline{F}_{\theta X}(yx)}{\overline{F}_{\theta X}(x)} \leqslant \limsup_{x\to\infty} \frac{\overline{F}_X(yx)}{\overline{F}_X(x)} \quad \text{and} \quad \limsup_{x\to\infty} \frac{\overline{F}_{\theta X}(x)}{\overline{F}_{\theta X}(yx)} \leqslant \limsup_{x\to\infty} \frac{\overline{F}_X(x)}{\overline{F}_X(yx)}.$$

Proof. According to (25)

$$\limsup_{x\to\infty} \frac{\overline{F}_{\theta X}(yx)}{\overline{F}_{\theta X}(x)} \leqslant \limsup_{x\to\infty} \sup_{z\geqslant x^{1-a}} \frac{\overline{F}_X(yz)}{\overline{F}_X(z)} = \limsup_{x\to\infty} \frac{\overline{F}_X(yx)}{\overline{F}_X(x)}$$

with some special $a \in (0,1)$. Hence, the first inequality of the lemma holds. Similarly to (24), we obtain

$$\frac{\overline{F}_{\theta X}(x)}{\overline{F}_{\theta X}(yx)} \leqslant \sup_{z\geqslant x^{1-a}} \frac{\overline{F}(z)}{\overline{F}(yz)} + \frac{\mathbb{E}\theta^p}{\mathbb{P}(\theta > b)} \frac{1}{(yx)^{ap}\overline{F}_X(x)} \frac{\overline{F}_X(x)}{\overline{F}_X(yx/b)}$$

for large x, $b > 0$ such that $\mathbb{P}(\theta > b) > 0$, and for $a \in (0,1)$ such that $ap > J^{+}_{F_X}$. The same arguments as in the derivation of (25) imply the second inequality of the lemma. The lemma is proved. □

4. Proof of the Main Results

Proof of Theorem 6.

• Let us begin with part (i) of the theorem. By Relation (2) of Theorem 2, we have

$$\mathbb{E}\Big((S_n^{(\xi)})^{\beta} \mathbb{I}_{\{S_n^{(\xi)} > x\}} \Big) \underset{x\to\infty}{\sim} \sum_{k\in\mathcal{I}_n} \mathbb{E}\Big(\xi_k^{\beta}\, \mathbb{I}_{\{\xi_k > x\}} \Big), \tag{26}$$

for any $\beta \in [0,1]$. In the particular case, if $\beta = 0$, we get

$$\overline{F}_{S_n^{(\xi)}}(x) = \mathbb{P}(S_n^{(\xi)} > x) \underset{x\to\infty}{\sim} \sum_{k\in\mathcal{I}_n} \overline{F}_{\xi_k}(x) \underset{x\to\infty}{\sim} \overline{H}_n(x). \tag{27}$$

We observe that $\overline{F}_{\xi_k}(x) > 0$ for each $k \in \mathcal{I}_n$ if x is sufficiently large. Hence, according to the min-max inequality

$$\min\left\{ \frac{a_1}{b_1}, \ldots \frac{a_m}{b_m} \right\} \leqslant \frac{a_1 + \ldots + a_m}{b_1 + \ldots + b_m} \leqslant \left\{ \frac{a_1}{b_1}, \ldots \frac{a_m}{b_m} \right\}, \tag{28}$$

provided if $a_i \geqslant 0$, and $b_i > 0$ for $i \in \{1, \ldots, m\}$, we get that

$$\min_{k\in\mathcal{I}_n} \frac{\overline{F}_{\xi_k}(xy)}{\overline{F}_{\xi_k}(x)} \leqslant \frac{\overline{H}_n(yx)}{\overline{H}_n(x)} \leqslant \max_{k\in\mathcal{I}_n} \frac{\overline{F}_{\xi_k}(xy)}{\overline{F}_{\xi_k}(x)} \tag{29}$$

for each $y \in (0,1]$ and sufficiently large x. This double inequality shows that the d.f. H_n, together with the d.f. $F_{S_n^{(\xi)}}$, belongs to the class $\mathscr{C} \cap \mathcal{PD}$. Hence, by Lemma 4, we have

$$\overleftarrow{F}_{S_n^{(\xi)}}(q) \underset{q\uparrow 1}{\sim} \overleftarrow{H}_n(q). \tag{30}$$

For $q \in (0,1)$, by equality (6) and the min-max inequality (28), we derive that

$$\begin{aligned}
&\frac{HG_q\Big(S_n^{(\xi)}\Big)}{\overleftarrow{H}_n(q) + \frac{1}{1-q} \sum\limits_{k\in\mathcal{I}_n} \mathbb{E}\Big(\xi_k - \overleftarrow{H}_n(q)\Big)^{+}} \\
&\leqslant \max\left\{ \frac{\overleftarrow{F}_{S_n^{(\xi)}}(q)}{\overleftarrow{H}_n(q)}, \frac{\mathbb{E}\Big(S_n^{(\xi)} - \overleftarrow{F}_{S_n^{(\xi)}}(q)\Big)^{+}}{\mathbb{E}\Big(S_n^{(\xi)} - \overleftarrow{H}_n(q)\Big)^{+}} \frac{\mathbb{E}\Big(S_n^{(\xi)} - \overleftarrow{H}_n(q)\Big)^{+}}{\sum\limits_{k\in\mathcal{I}_n} \mathbb{E}\Big(\xi_k - \overleftarrow{H}_n(q)\Big)^{+}} \right\} \\
&\leqslant \frac{\overleftarrow{F}_{S_n^{(\xi)}}(q)}{\overleftarrow{H}_n(q)} \max\left\{ 1, \frac{\mathbb{E}\Big(S_n^{(\xi)} - \overleftarrow{H}_n(q)\Big)^{+}}{\sum\limits_{k\in\mathcal{I}_n} \mathbb{E}\Big(\xi_k - \overleftarrow{H}_n(q)\Big)^{+}} \sup_{u \geqslant \overleftarrow{H}_n(q)} \frac{\mathbb{P}\Big(S_n^{(\xi)} > u\, \overleftarrow{F}_{S_n^{(\xi)}}(q) / \overleftarrow{H}_n(q)\Big)}{\mathbb{P}(S_n^{(\xi)} > u)} \right\}
\end{aligned} \tag{31}$$

because, according to the alternative expectation formula,

$$\frac{\mathbb{E}(\eta - x_1)^{+}}{\mathbb{E}(\eta - x_2)^{+}} = \frac{\int\limits_{x_1}^{\infty} \mathbb{P}(\eta > u)\mathrm{d}u}{\int\limits_{x_2}^{\infty} \mathbb{P}(\eta > u)\mathrm{d}u} \leqslant \frac{x_1}{x_2} \sup_{u \geqslant x_2} \frac{\mathbb{P}(\eta > u x_1 / x_2)}{\mathbb{P}(\eta > u)}$$

for all positive x_1, x_2, and every r.v. η such that $\mathbb{P}(\eta > x) > 0$, $x \in \mathbb{R}$. Now, let $\varepsilon \in (0, 1/2)$. By Relations (30) and (31), we get that

$$\frac{HG_q\left(S_n^{(\xi)}\right)}{\overleftarrow{H}_n(q) + \frac{1}{1-q}\sum\limits_{k\in\mathcal{I}_n}\mathbb{E}\left(\xi_k - \overleftarrow{H}_n(q)\right)^+}$$
$$\leqslant (1+\varepsilon)\max\left\{1, \frac{\mathbb{E}\left(S_n^{(\xi)} - \overleftarrow{H}_n(q)\right)^+}{\sum\limits_{k\in\mathcal{I}_n}\mathbb{E}\left(\xi_k - \overleftarrow{H}_n(q)\right)^+}\sup_{u\geqslant\overleftarrow{H}_n(q)}\frac{\mathbb{P}(S_n^{(\xi)} > u(1-\varepsilon))}{\mathbb{P}(S_n^{(\xi)} > u)}\right\}$$

for all q sufficiently close to the unit from the left. Since $\overleftarrow{H}_n(q) \to \infty$ if $q \uparrow 1$, we get from the last estimate

$$\limsup_{q\uparrow 1}\frac{HG_q\left(S_n^{(\xi)}\right)}{\overleftarrow{H}_n(q) + \frac{1}{1-q}\sum\limits_{k\in\mathcal{I}_n}\mathbb{E}\left(\xi_k - \overleftarrow{H}_n(q)\right)^+}$$
$$\leqslant (1+\varepsilon)\max\left\{1, \limsup_{q\uparrow 1}\frac{\mathbb{E}\left(S_n^{(\xi)} - \overleftarrow{H}_n(q)\right)^+}{\sum\limits_{k\in\mathcal{I}_n}\mathbb{E}\left(\xi_k - \overleftarrow{H}_n(q)\right)^+}\limsup_{q\uparrow 1}\sup_{u\geqslant\overleftarrow{H}_n(q)}\frac{\mathbb{P}(S_n^{(\xi)} > u(1-\varepsilon))}{\mathbb{P}(S_n^{(\xi)} > u)}\right\}$$
$$= (1+\varepsilon)\max\left\{1, \limsup_{x\to\infty}\frac{\mathbb{E}(S_n^{(\xi)} - x)^+}{\sum\limits_{k\in\mathcal{I}_n}\mathbb{E}(\xi_k - x)^+}\limsup_{x\to\infty}\sup_{u\geqslant x}\frac{\mathbb{P}(S_n^{(\xi)} > u(1-\varepsilon))}{\mathbb{P}(S_n^{(\xi)} > u)}\right\}.$$

The fact that $F_{S_n^{(\xi)}} \in \mathscr{C}$, Relation (3) of Theorem 2, and the arbitrariness of $\varepsilon \in (0, 1/2)$ imply that

$$\limsup_{q\uparrow 1}\frac{HG_q\left(S_n^{(\xi)}\right)}{\overleftarrow{H}_n(q) + \frac{1}{1-q}\sum\limits_{k\in\mathcal{I}_n}\mathbb{E}\left(\xi_k - \overleftarrow{H}_n(q)\right)^+} \leqslant 1. \tag{32}$$

In a similar way, we can obtain

$$\liminf_{q\uparrow 1}\frac{HG_q\left(S_n^{(\xi)}\right)}{\overleftarrow{H}_n(q) + \frac{1}{1-q}\sum\limits_{k\in\mathcal{I}_n}\mathbb{E}\left(\xi_k - \overleftarrow{H}_n(q)\right)^+}$$
$$\geqslant (1-\varepsilon)\min\left\{1, \liminf_{x\to\infty}\frac{\mathbb{E}(S_n^{(\xi)} - x)^+}{\sum\limits_{k\in\mathcal{I}_n}\mathbb{E}(\xi_k - x)^+}\liminf_{x\to\infty}\inf_{u\geqslant x}\frac{\mathbb{P}(S_n^{(\xi)} > u(1+\varepsilon))}{\mathbb{P}(S_n^{(\xi)} > u)}\right\}$$

for all $\varepsilon \in (0, 1/2)$, and by similar arguments, we can derive that

$$\liminf_{q\uparrow 1}\frac{HG_q\left(S_n^{(\xi)}\right)}{\overleftarrow{H}_n(q) + \frac{1}{1-q}\sum\limits_{k\in\mathcal{I}_n}\mathbb{E}\left(\xi_k - \overleftarrow{H}_n(q)\right)^+} \geqslant 1.$$

The last estimate, jointly with inequality (32), finishes the proof of the first part of Theorem 6.

• Now, suppose $\varkappa \geqslant 2$, and all conditions of part (ii) of Theorem 6 are satisfied. Due to Theorem 3

$$HG_q(S_n^{(\xi)}) = \widetilde{x} + \left(\frac{\mathbb{E}\Big(\big((S_n^{(\xi)} - \widetilde{x})^+ \big)^{\varkappa} \Big)}{1-q} \right)^{1/\varkappa}, \tag{33}$$

where $\widetilde{x} = \widetilde{x}(q)$ is the unique solution of the equation

$$\frac{\Big(\mathbb{E}\Big(\big((S_n^{(\xi)} - \widetilde{x})^+ \big)^{\varkappa-1} \Big) \Big)^{\varkappa}}{\Big(\mathbb{E}\Big(\big((S_n^{(\xi)} - \widetilde{x})^+ \big)^{\varkappa} \Big) \Big)^{\varkappa-1}} = \gamma_{S_n^{(\xi)}}(\widetilde{x}) = 1 - q.$$

Let H_n be the d.f. defined in part (i) of Theorem 6. Due to the asymptotic Relation (27), the upper bound in (29), and the conditions of the theorem, we have that the d.f.'s $F_{S_n^{(\xi)}}$ and H_n both belong to the class $\mathscr{C}$. In addition, according to Relation (27), the min-max inequality (28), and condition (9), we get that

$$\begin{aligned}
&\left(\limsup_{x\to\infty} \frac{\overline{F}_{S_n^{(\xi)}}(yx)}{\overline{F}_{S_n^{(\xi)}}(x)} \right)^{\varkappa} \left(\limsup_{x\to\infty} \frac{\overline{F}_{S_n^{(\xi)}}(x)}{\overline{F}_{S_n^{(\xi)}}(yx)} \right)^{\varkappa-1} \\
&= \left(\limsup_{x\to\infty} \frac{\overline{H}_n(yx)}{\overline{H}_n(x)} \right)^{\varkappa} \left(\limsup_{x\to\infty} \frac{\overline{H}_n(x)}{\overline{H}_n(yx)} \right)^{\varkappa-1} \\
&\leqslant \left(\max_{k\in\mathcal{I}_n} \limsup_{x\to\infty} \frac{\overline{F}_{\xi_k}(yx)}{\overline{F}_{\xi_k}(x)} \right)^{\varkappa} \left(\max_{k\in\mathcal{I}_n} \limsup_{x\to\infty} \frac{\overline{F}_{\xi_k}(x)}{\overline{F}_{\xi_k}(yx)} \right)^{\varkappa-1} < 1
\end{aligned} \tag{34}$$

for some $y > 1$. Therefore, Corollary 1 implies that the d.f. $1 - \gamma_{S_n^{(\xi)}}$ belongs to the class $\mathscr{C} \cap \mathcal{PD}$.

For sufficiently large x, by the alternative expectation formula, we have that

$$\begin{aligned}
\frac{\left(\sum\limits_{k\in\mathcal{I}_n} \mathbb{E}\big((\xi_k - x)^+ \big)^{\varkappa-1} \right)^{\varkappa}}{\left(\sum\limits_{k\in\mathcal{I}_n} \mathbb{E}\big((\xi_k - x)^+ \big)^{\varkappa} \right)^{\varkappa-1}} &= \frac{\left((\varkappa-1) \int\limits_x^{\infty} (u-x)^{\varkappa-2} \overline{H}_n(u) \mathrm{d}u \right)^{\varkappa}}{\left(\varkappa \int\limits_x^{\infty} (u-x)^{\varkappa-1} \overline{H}_n(u) \mathrm{d}u \right)^{\varkappa-1}} \\
&= \frac{\Big(\mathbb{E}\big((\zeta_n - x)^+ \big)^{\varkappa-1} \Big)^{\varkappa}}{\Big(\mathbb{E}\big((\zeta_n - x)^+ \big)^{\varkappa} \Big)^{\varkappa-1}} := \gamma_{\zeta_n}(x),
\end{aligned}$$

where ζ_n is an r.v. with d.f. H_n. Due to the estimate (34) d.f. $F_{\zeta_n} = H_n$ satisfies condition (23) which, according to Corollary 1, implies that the d.f. $1 - \gamma_{\zeta_n}$ belongs to the class $\mathscr{C} \cap \mathcal{PD}$ together with the d.f. $1 - \gamma_{S_n^{(\xi)}}$.

On the other hand, Relation (3) of Theorem 2 implies that

$$\gamma_{S_n^{(\xi)}}(x) \underset{x\to\infty}{\sim} \gamma_{\zeta_n}(x).$$

Consequently, all conditions of Lemma 4 are satisfied with $c = 1$ and d.f.'s $1 - \gamma_{S_n^{(\xi)}}, 1 - \gamma_{\zeta_n}$. According to this lemma, we get that

$$\widetilde{x}(q) \underset{q\uparrow 1}{\sim} \widehat{x}(q). \tag{35}$$

Now, we continue the proof of this part in the same way as in the proof of part (i). For any $q \in (0,1)$, by Relation (33) and the min-max inequality (28), we get

$$\frac{HG_q\big(S_n^{(\xi)}\big)}{\widehat{x}(q) + \Big(\frac{1}{1-q}\sum\limits_{k\in\mathcal{I}_n}\mathbb{E}\Big(\big(\xi_k - \widehat{x}(q)\big)^+\Big)^{\varkappa}\Big)^{1/\varkappa}}$$
$$\leqslant \max\left\{\frac{\widetilde{x}(q)}{\widehat{x}(q)}, \left(\frac{\mathbb{E}\Big(\big(S_n^{(\xi)} - \widetilde{x}(q)\big)^+\Big)^{\varkappa}}{\sum\limits_{k\in\mathcal{I}_n}\mathbb{E}\Big(\big(\xi_k - \widehat{x}(q)\big)^+\Big)^{\varkappa}}\right)^{1/\varkappa}\right\}$$
$$= \max\left\{\frac{\widetilde{x}(q)}{\widehat{x}(q)}, \left(\frac{\mathbb{E}\Big(\big(S_n^{(\xi)} - \widetilde{x}(q)\big)^+\Big)^{\varkappa}}{\sum\limits_{k\in\mathcal{I}_n}\mathbb{E}\Big(\big(\xi_k - \widetilde{x}(q)\big)^+\Big)^{\varkappa}}\,\frac{\sum\limits_{k\in\mathcal{I}_n}\mathbb{E}\Big(\big(\xi_k - \widetilde{x}(q)\big)^+\Big)^{\varkappa}}{\sum\limits_{k\in\mathcal{I}_n}\mathbb{E}\Big(\big(\xi_k - \widehat{x}(q)\big)^+\Big)^{\varkappa}}\right)^{1/\varkappa}\right\}.$$

If q is sufficiently close to the unit from the left, then

$$\frac{\sum\limits_{k\in\mathcal{I}_n}\mathbb{E}\Big(\big(\xi_k - \widetilde{x}(q)\big)^+\Big)^{\varkappa}}{\sum\limits_{k\in\mathcal{I}_n}\mathbb{E}\Big(\big(\xi_k - \widehat{x}(q)\big)^+\Big)^{\varkappa}} = \frac{\int_{\widetilde{x}(q)}^{\infty}\big(u - \widetilde{x}(q)\big)^{\varkappa-1}\overline{H}_n(u)\mathrm{d}u}{\int_{\widehat{x}(q)}^{\infty}\big(u - \widehat{x}(q)\big)^{\varkappa-1}\overline{H}_n(u)\mathrm{d}u}$$
$$= \left(\frac{\widetilde{x}(q)}{\widehat{x}(q)}\right)^{\varkappa}\frac{\int_{\widehat{x}(q)}^{\infty}\big(u - \widehat{x}(q)\big)^{\varkappa-1}\overline{H}_n\Big(\frac{\widetilde{x}(q)}{\widehat{x}(q)}u\Big)\mathrm{d}u}{\int_{\widehat{x}(q)}^{\infty}\big(u - \widehat{x}(q)\big)^{\varkappa-1}\overline{H}_n(u)\mathrm{d}u}$$
$$\leqslant \left(\frac{\widetilde{x}(q)}{\widehat{x}(q)}\right)^{\varkappa}\sup_{u\geqslant\widehat{x}(q)}\frac{\overline{H}_n\Big(\frac{\widetilde{x}(q)}{\widehat{x}(q)}u\Big)}{\overline{H}_n(u)}.$$

Consequently, for q sufficiently close to the unit from the left, we have

$$\frac{HG_q\big(S_n^{(\xi)}\big)}{\widehat{x}(q) + \Big(\frac{1}{1-q}\sum\limits_{k\in\mathcal{I}_n}\mathbb{E}\Big(\big(\xi_k - \widehat{x}(q)\big)^+\Big)^{\varkappa}\Big)^{1/\varkappa}}$$
$$\leqslant \frac{\widetilde{x}(q)}{\widehat{x}(q)}\max\left\{1, \left(\frac{\mathbb{E}\Big(\big(S_n^{(\xi)} - \widetilde{x}(q)\big)^+\Big)^{\varkappa}}{\sum\limits_{k\in\mathcal{I}_n}\mathbb{E}\Big(\big(\xi_k - \widetilde{x}(q)\big)^+\Big)^{\varkappa}}\sup_{u\geqslant\widehat{x}(q)}\frac{\overline{H}_n\Big(\frac{\widetilde{x}(q)}{\widehat{x}(q)}u\Big)}{\overline{H}_n(u)}\right)^{1/\varkappa}\right\}.$$

Since $\widetilde{x}(q) \underset{q\uparrow 1}{\to} \infty$, $\widetilde{x}(q) \underset{q\uparrow 1}{\sim} \widehat{x}(q)$ and the d.f. H_n belongs to the class $\mathscr{C}$, the last estimate and the asymptotic Relation (3) of Theorem 2 imply that

$$\limsup_{q\uparrow 1}\frac{HG_q\big(S_n^{(\xi)}\big)}{\widehat{x}(q) + \Big(\frac{1}{1-q}\sum\limits_{k\in\mathcal{I}_n}\mathbb{E}\Big(\big(\xi_k - \widehat{x}(q)\big)^+\Big)^{\varkappa}\Big)^{1/\varkappa}} \leqslant 1.$$

Similarly, we can derive that

$$\liminf_{q\uparrow 1} \frac{HG_q\big(S_n^{(\xi)}\big)}{\widehat{x}(q) + \left(\frac{1}{1-q}\sum\limits_{k\in\mathcal{I}_n} \mathbb{E}\Big(\big(\xi_k - \widehat{x}(q)\big)^+\Big)^{\varkappa}\right)^{1/\varkappa}} \geqslant 1.$$

This finishes the proof of the second part of the theorem. □

Proof of Theorem 7.

• We begin with case $\varkappa = 1$. According to the conditions and Lemma 10, a collection of r.v.'s $\{\theta_1 X_1, \ldots, \theta_n X_n\}$ follows the pQAI dependence structure. By Lemma 11, we have that the d.f.'s $F_{\theta_k X_k}$ belong to the class $\mathscr{C}$ for all $k \in \{1,2,\ldots,n\}$. Since $\max\limits_{1\leqslant k\leqslant n} \mathbb{E}X_k^+ < \infty$ and $p > \max\limits_{1\leqslant k\leqslant n} J^+_{F_{X_k}}$, by Lemma 3.5 of [54], we get that $\mathbb{E}\,\theta_k X_x^+ < \infty$ for $k \in \{1,2,\ldots,n\}$, because

$$\sup\left\{v : \int\limits_{[0,\infty)} x^v \mathrm{d}F(x) < \infty\right\} \leqslant J_F^+$$

for every d.f. F from the class $\mathscr{D}$. Finally, by Lemma 12, we derive that $F_{\theta_k X_k} \in \mathcal{PD}$ for all $k \in \{1,2,\ldots,n\}$. Hence, the collection of r.v.'s $\{\theta_1 X_1, \ldots, \theta_n X_n\}$ satisfies all conditions of part (i) of Theorem 6. This implies the statement of Theorem 7(i).

• Now, let us consider part (ii) of the theorem. If $\varkappa \geqslant 2$, Theorem 7(ii) follows from Theorem 6(ii) by completely analogous reasoning as in the first part of the proof, only instead of Lemma 12, we need to use Lemma 13. □

5. Illustrative Example

In this section, we present an example showing how Theorem 6 can be applied to the evaluation of the HG risk measure when the risk level is close to unity and the leading risk has a consistently varying distribution.

Example 1. *Let us consider collection of independent r.v.'s $\{\xi_1, \xi_2, \xi_3, \xi_4\}$ with the following d.f.'s:*

$$F_1(x) = \left(1 - \frac{1}{(x+1)^3}\right)\mathbb{I}_{[0,\infty)}(x),\ \ F_2(x) = \left(1 - \frac{1}{2(x+1)^3}\right)\mathbb{I}_{[0,\infty)}(x),$$
$$F_3(x) = F_4(x) = (1 - \mathrm{e}^{-x})\mathbb{I}_{[0,\infty)}(x).$$

We derive asymptotic formulas for HG_q risk measures in the cases of the power Young functions $\varphi(t) = t^{\varkappa}$ with $\varkappa = 1$ and $\varkappa = 2$.

It is clear that the collection of r.v.'s satisfies the conditions of Theorem 6 with $\mathcal{I}_4 = \{1,2\}$. In the case $\varkappa = 1$, we have

$$HG_q\big(S_4^{(\xi)}\big) \underset{q\uparrow 1}{\sim} \overleftarrow{H_4}(q) + \frac{1}{1-q}\Big(\mathbb{E}\big(\xi_1 - \overleftarrow{H_4}(q)\big) + \mathbb{E}\big(\xi_2 - \overleftarrow{H_4}(q)\big)\Big),$$

where $\overleftarrow{H_4}$ is the quantile function of the d.f.

$$H_4 = \max\{0, 1 - \overline{F}_1 - \overline{F}_2\}.$$

For large x

$$H_4(x) = 1 - \frac{3}{2}\frac{1}{(1+x)^3}.$$

Therefore,

$$\overleftarrow{H}_4(q) = \frac{1}{\sqrt[3]{\frac{2}{3}(1-q)}} - 1$$

for q sufficiently close to unity. For any sufficiently large x,

$$\mathbb{E}(\xi_1 - x)^+ = \frac{1}{2(x+1)^2}, \ \mathbb{E}(\xi_2 - x)^+ = \frac{1}{4(x+1)^2}.$$

Therefore, in the case $\varkappa = 1$

$$\begin{aligned} HG_q\left(S_4^{(\xi)}\right) &\underset{q\uparrow 1}{\sim} \frac{1}{\sqrt[3]{\frac{2}{3}(1-q)}} - 1 + \frac{1}{1-q}\frac{3}{4}\left(\sqrt[3]{\frac{2}{3}(1-q)}\right)^2 \\ &= \frac{1}{\sqrt[3]{1-q}}\left(\frac{3}{2}\right)^{\frac{4}{3}} - 1. \end{aligned}$$

The graph of this function, together with the values of $HG_q\left(S_4^{(\xi)}\right)$ obtained using the Monte-Carlo (MC) method, can be seen in Figure 1. The Monte-Carlo simulations were performed using statistical software **R** (v4.0.3); the graphs provided in this section were generated in **R** using ggplot2 and tikzDevice libraries. .

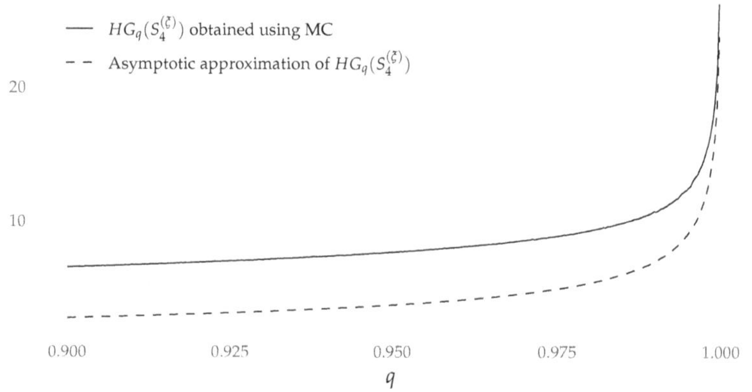

Figure 1. Simulated and asymptotically approximated values of $HG_q(S_4^{(\xi)})$ in the case $\varkappa = 1$.

If $\varkappa = 2$, then

$$HG_q\left(S_4^{(\xi)}\right) \underset{q\uparrow 1}{\sim} \widehat{x}(q) + \frac{1}{\sqrt{1-q}}\left(\mathbb{E}\left((\xi_1 - \widehat{x}(q))^+\right)^2 + \mathbb{E}\left((\xi_2 - \widehat{x}(q))^+\right)^2\right)^{1/2},$$

where $\widehat{x}(q)$ is the solution of the equation

$$\frac{\mathbb{E}(\xi_1 - x)^+ + \mathbb{E}(\xi_2 - x)^+}{\mathbb{E}\left((\xi_1 - x)^+\right)^2 + \mathbb{E}\left((\xi_2 - x)^+\right)^2} = 1 - q.$$

In the case under consideration,

$$\begin{aligned} \mathbb{E}(\xi_1 - x)^+ &= \frac{1}{2(x+1)^2}, \quad \mathbb{E}(\xi_2 - x)^+ = \frac{1}{4(x+1)^2}, \\ \mathbb{E}\left((\xi_1 - x^+\right)^2 &= \frac{1}{x+1}, \qquad \mathbb{E}\left((\xi_2 - x^+\right)^2 = \frac{1}{2(x+1)}. \end{aligned}$$

Hence,

$$\widehat{x}(q) = \sqrt[3]{\frac{3}{8(1-q)}} - 1$$

and

$$HG_q(S_4^{(\xi)}) \underset{q\uparrow 1}{\sim} \frac{3}{2}\sqrt[3]{\frac{3}{1-q}} - 1.$$

The graph of this function, together with the values of $HG_q(S_4^{(\xi)})$ obtained using the Monte-Carlo method, can be seen in Figure 2.

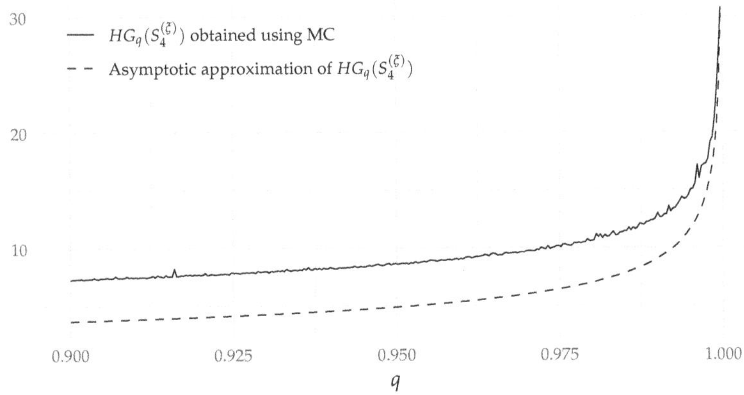

Figure 2. Simulated and asymptotically approximated values of $HG_q(S_4^{(\xi)})$ in the case $\varkappa = 2$.

6. Concluding Remarks

The study of risk measures is a relatively popular topic in probability theory, as risk measures are applied in numerous fields where uncertainty and potential losses must be quantified, including banking and finance, insurance, investment management, and energy markets. Acceptable properties of risk measures are listed, for example, in the work [1]. The book [72] discusses classical mathematical problems related to risk measures. The mathematical problems of risk measures are still being intensively studied today. Let us mention a few works. Distortion risk measures are considered, e.g., in [73,74]. The duality of risk measures is considered in [75]. Risk measures with special properties are analysed, e.g., in [76–78]. In addition, we note that our results complement those of the papers [79–82], which also utilise higher-order moments in the construction of risk measures.

As already mentioned, the HG risk measure is a direct generalisation of the ES risk measure by introducing a governing Young function. Other generalisations of the ES measure are obtained by replacing quantiles with generalised quantiles or expectiles. Such risk measures are described and studied in [83–85].

In our paper, we study the properties of the HG risk measure, which was first defined in [3]. The main result of our work is given in Theorem 6. It follows from this result that, to find the asymptotics of the HG risk measure for the sum of random risks, it is sufficient to determine the appropriate characteristics of the sum of dominant risks. From Theorem 6, we see that such a result holds when the distribution functions of the dominant risks are consistently varying and satisfy additional requirements related to having positively decreasing tails. In addition, Theorem 6 implies that in order to find the asymptotics of the HG risk measure for the sum of random risks, there is no need to calculate complex convolutions. It is enough to construct the distribution function from the sum of the distribution functions of the selected group. The next main theorem of the work, Theorem 7, is actually a consequence of Theorem 6. This theorem demonstrates that the procedure for determining the asymptotics of the HG risk measure also applies in cases where a set of random variables with random weights is considered.

Possibly similar results on the asymptotic behavior of the HG risk measure can be obtained for a wider class of distributions $\mathscr{D}$, i.e., for distributions with dominatedly varying d.f.'s. However, in this case, the asymptotic formulas should have additional constants resulting in less strict asymptotic bounds, or additional constraints should be imposed on the d.f.'s of random risks to preserve exact asymptotic relations. In the near future, we hope to determine how the asymptotic formulas of the HG risk measure change when the distribution class $\mathscr{C}$ is replaced by the wider distribution class $\mathscr{D}$.

Author Contributions: Conceptualisation, J.Š.; methodology, J.Š. and M.D.; software, M.D. and L.Z.; validation, M.D., N.N., and L.Z.; formal analysis, L.Z.; investigation, M.D. and N.N.; resources, J.Š.; data curation, M.D.; writing—original draft preparation, J.Š and M.D.; writing—review and editing, M.D. and N.N.; visualisation, M.D. and L.Z.; supervision, J.Š.; project administration, J.Š. and L.Z.; funding acquisition, J.Š. and N.N. All authors have read and agreed to the published version of the manuscript.

Funding: This research received no external funding.

Data Availability Statement: The original contributions presented in this study are included in the article. Further inquiries can be directed to the corresponding author.

Acknowledgments: The authors are very grateful to the editors and the anonymous referees for their constructive and valuable suggestions and comments, which have helped to improve the previous version of the paper.

Conflicts of Interest: The authors declare no conflicts of interest.

Abbreviations

The following abbreviations are used in this manuscript:

HG	Haezendonck–Goovaerts risk measure
HG_q	Haezendonck–Goovaerts risk measure with level q
ES	Expected Shortfall (particular case of HG risk measure)
r.v.	random variable
d.f.	distribution function
t.f.	tail function
pQAI	(pairwise) quasi-asymptotically independent (random variables)
$\mathcal{PD}$	positively decreasing (distribution function)
MC	Monte-Carlo (method)

References

1. Artzner, P.; Delbaen, F.; Eber, J.M.; Heath, D. Coherent measures of risks. *Math. Financ.* **1999**, *9*, 203–228. [CrossRef]
2. Yamai, Y.; Yoshiba, T. Value-at-risk versus expected shortfall: A practical perspective. *J. Bank. Financ.* **2005**, *29*, 997–1015. [CrossRef]
3. Haezendonck, J.; Goovaerts, M. A new premium calculation principle based on Orlitz norms. *Insur. Math. Econ.* **1982**, *1*, 41–53. [CrossRef]
4. Goovaerts, M.; Kaas, R.; Dhaene, J.; Tang, Q. Some new classes of consistent risk measures. *Insur. Math. Econ.* **2004**, *34*, 505–516. [CrossRef]
5. Bellini, F.; Rosazza Gianin, E. Haezendonck–Goovaerts risk measures and Orlicz quantiles. *Insur. Math. Econ.* **2012**, *51*, 107–114. [CrossRef]
6. Föllmer, H.; Schied, A. Convex measures of risk and trading constraints. *Financ. Stoch.* **2002**, *6*, 429–447. [CrossRef]

7. Frittelli, M.; Gianin, E.R. Putting order in risk measures. *J. Bank. Financ.* **2002**, *26*, 1473–1486. [CrossRef]
8. Rockafellar, R.; Uryasev, S. Optimization of conditional value-at-risk. *J. Risk* **2000**, *2*, 21–41. [CrossRef]
9. Tang, Q.; Yang, F. On the Haezendonck-Goovaerts risk measure for extreme risks. *Insur. Math. Econ.* **2012**, *50*, 217–227. [CrossRef]
10. Liu, Y. A general treatment of alternative expectation formula. *Statist. Probab. Lett.* **2020**, *166*, 108863. [CrossRef]
11. Song, P.; Wang, S. On the moment generating functions for integer valued random variables. *Commun. Statist. Theory Methods* **2019**, *48*, 5169–5174. [CrossRef]
12. Cline, D.; Samorodnitsky, G. Subexponentiality of the product of independent random variables. *Stoch. Process. Appl.* **1994**, *49*, 75–98. [CrossRef]
13. Cai, J.; Tang, Q. On max-sum equivalence and convolution closure of heavy-tailed distributions and their applications. *J. Appl. Probab.* **2004**, *41*, 117–130. [CrossRef]
14. Dirma, M.; Paukštys, S.; Šiaulys, J. Tails of the moments for sums with dominatedly varying random summands. *Mathematics* **2021**, *9*, 824. [CrossRef]
15. Berkes, I.; Györi, L.; Kevei, P. Tail probabilities of St. Peterburg sums, trimed sums, and their limit. *J. Theor. Probab.* **2017**, *30*, 1104–1129. [CrossRef]
16. Bingham, N.; Goldie, C.; Teugels, J. *Regular Variation*; Encyclopedia of Mathematics and its Applications; Cambridge University Press: Cambridge, UK, 1987; Volume 27.
17. Matuszewska, W. On generalization of regularly increasing functions. *Studia Math.* **1964**, *24*, 271–279. [CrossRef]
18. Jaunė, E.; Ragulina, O.; Šiaulys, J. Expectation of the truncated randomly weighted sums with dominatedly varying summands. *Lith. Math. J.* **2018**, *58*, 421–440. [CrossRef]
19. Leipus, R.; Šiaulys, J.; Vareikaitė, I. Tails of the higher-order moments with dominatedly varying summands. *Lith. Math. J.* **2019**, *59*, 389–407. [CrossRef]
20. Yang, Y.; Wang, Y.; Leipus, R.; Šiaulys, J. Asymptotics for tail probability of total claim amount with negatively dependent claim sizes and its applications. *Lith. Math. J.* **2009**, *49*, 337–352. [CrossRef]
21. Embrechts, P.; Klüppelberg, C.; Mikosch, T. *Modelling Extremal Events for Insurance and Finance*; Springer: New York, NY, USA, 1997.
22. Resnick, S. *Extreme Values, Regular Variation and Point Process*; Springer: New York, NY, USA, 1987.
23. Puišys, R.; Lewkiewicz, S.; Šiaulys, J. Properties of the random effect transformation. *Lith. Math. J.* **2024**, *64*, 177–189. [CrossRef]
24. Sprindys, J.; Šiaulys, J. Regularly distributed randomly stopped sum, minimum and maximum. *Nonlinear Anal. Model. Control* **2020**, *25*, 509–522. [CrossRef]
25. Cline, D. Intermediate regular and Π variation. *Proc. Lond. Math. Soc.* **1994**, *68*, 594–611. [CrossRef]
26. Andrulytė, I.; Manstavičius, M.; Šiaulys, J. Randomly stopped maximum and maximum of sums with consistently varying distributions. *Mod. Stoch. Theory Appl.* **2017**, *4*, 65–78. [CrossRef]
27. Buldygin, V.; Indlekofer, K.; Klesov, O.; Steinebach, J. *Pseudo-Regularly Varying Functions and Generalized Renewal Processes*; Springer: Cham, Switzerland, 2018.
28. Chen, Y.; Yuen, K. Sums of pairwise quasi-asymptotically independent random variables with consistent variation. *Stoch. Model.* **2009**, *25*, 76–89. [CrossRef]
29. Cuberos, A.; Masiello, E.; Maume-Deschamps, V. High level quantile estimation of sums of risks. *Depend. Model.* **2015**, *3*, 000010151520150010. [CrossRef]
30. Foss, S.; Korshunov, D.; Zachary, S. *An Introduction to Heavy-Tailed and Subexponential Distributions*, 2nd ed.; Springer: New York, NY, USA, 2013.
31. Kizinevič, E.; Sprindys, J.; Šiaulys, J. Randomly stopped sums with consistently varying distributions. *Mod. Stoch. Theory Appl.* **2016**, *3*, 165–179. [CrossRef]
32. Wang, S.; Guo, D.; Wang, W. Closure property of consistently varying random variables based on precise large deviation principles. *Commun. Stat. Theory Methods* **2019**, *48*, 2218–2228. [CrossRef]
33. Dirma, M.; Nakliuda, N.; Šiaulys, J. Generalized moments of sums with heavy-tailed random summands. *Lith. Math. J.* **2023**, *63*, 254–271. [CrossRef]
34. Geluk, J.; Tang, Q. Asymptotic tail probabilities of sums of dependent subexponential random variables. *J. Theoret. Probab.* **2009**, *22*, 871–882. [CrossRef]
35. Li, J. On pairwise quasi-asymptotically independent random variables and their applications. *Statist. Probab. Lett.* **2013**, *83*, 2081–2087. [CrossRef]
36. Liu, X.; Gao, Q.; Wang, Y. A note on a dependent risk model with constant interest rate. *Stat. Probab. Lett.* **2011**, *82*, 707–712. [CrossRef]
37. Wang, K. Randomly weighted sums of dependent subexponential random variables. *Lith. Math. J.* **2011**, *51*, 573–586. [CrossRef]
38. Wang, S.; Chen, C.; Wang, X. Some novel results on pairwise quasi-asymptotical independence with applications to risk theory. *Commun. Statist. Theory Methods* **2017**, *46*, 9075–9085. [CrossRef]

39. Xu, C.; Peng, J.; Zou, L. Asymptotic estimates for systemic risk with dependent heavy-tailed losses. *Lith. Math. J.* **2025**, *65*, 134–150. [CrossRef]
40. Sprindys, J.; Šiaulys, J. Asymptotic formulas for the left truncated moments of sums with consistently varying distributed increments. *Nonlinear Anal. Model. Control* **2021**, *26*, 1200–1212. [CrossRef]
41. Buldygin, V.; Klesov, O.; Steinebach, J.G. Properties of a subclass of Avakumović functions and their generalized inverse. *Ukr. Math. J.* **2002**, *54*, 149–169. [CrossRef]
42. Buldygin, V.; Klesov, O.; Steinebach, J.G. On some properties of asymptotic quasi-inverse functions. *Theory Probab. Math. Stat.* **2008**, *77*, 15–30. [CrossRef]
43. Konstantinides, D.; Passalidis, C. Positively decreasing and related distributions under dependence. *Teor. Veroyatnost. Primenen.* **2025**, *70*, 461–486. [CrossRef]
44. Leipus, R.; Šiaulys, J.; Konstantinides, D. *Closure Properties for Heavy-Tailed and Related Distributions*; Springer: Cham, Switzerland, 2023.
45. Tang, Q.; Yang, F. Extreme value analysis of the Haezendonck-Goovaerts risk measure with a general Young function. *Insur. Math. Econ.* **2014**, *59*, 311–320. [CrossRef]
46. Wang, X.; Liu, Q.; Hou, Y.; Peng, L. Nonparametric inference for sensitivity of Haezendonck-Goovaerts risk measure. *Scand. Actuar. J.* **2018**, *2018*, 661–680. [CrossRef]
47. Chen, Y.; Liu, J.; Liu, F. Ruin with insurance and financial risks following the least risky FGM dependence structure. *Insur. Math. Econ.* **2015**, *62*, 98–106. [CrossRef]
48. Cheng, F.; Cheng, D. Randomly weighted sums of dependent subexponential random variables with applications to risk theory. *Scand. Actuar. J.* **2018**, *2018*, 98–106. [CrossRef]
49. Gao, Q.; Wang, Y. Randomly weighted sums with dominated varying-tailed increments and applications to risk theory. *J. Korean Stat. Soc.* **2010**, *39*, 305–314. [CrossRef]
50. Hashorva, E.; Li, J. Asymptotics for a discrete-time risk model with the emphasis on financial risk. *Probab. Eng. Inf. Sci.* **2014**, *28*, 573–588. [CrossRef]
51. Huang, X.; Zhang, T.; Yang, Y.; Jiang, T. Ruin probabilities in a dependent discrete-time risk model with gamma-like tailed insurance risks. *Risks* **2017**, *5*, 14. [CrossRef]
52. Liu, R.; Wang, D. The ruin probabilities of a discrete-time risk model with dependent insurance and financial risks. *J. Math. Anal. Appl.* **2016**, *444*, 80–94. [CrossRef]
53. Nyrhinen, H. Finite and infinite time ruin probabilities in a stochastic economic environment. *Stoch. Process. Appl.* **2001**, *92*, 265–285. [CrossRef]
54. Tang, Q.; Tsitsiashvili, G. Precise estimates for the ruin probability in finite horizon in a discrete-time model with heavy-tailed insurance and financial risks. *Stoch. Process. Appl.* **2003**, *108*, 299–325. [CrossRef]
55. Tang, Q.; Tsitsiashvili, G. Finite and infinite time ruin probabilities in the presence of stochastic return on investments. *Adv. Appl. Probab.* **2004**, *36*, 1278–1299. [CrossRef]
56. Wang, K.; Gao, M.; Yang, Y.; Chen, Y. Asymptotics for the finite-time ruin probability in a discrete-time risk model with dependent insurance and financial risks. *Lith. Math. J.* **2018**, *58*, 113–125. [CrossRef]
57. Yang, Y.; Konstantinides, D. Asymptotics for ruin probabilities in a discrete-time risk model with dependent financial and insurance risks. *Scand. Actuar. J.* **2015**, *2015*, 641–659. [CrossRef]
58. Yang, Y.; Leipus, R.; Šiaulys, J. Asymptotics for randomly weighted and stopped dependent sums. *Stochastics* **2016**, *88*, 300–319. [CrossRef]
59. Yang, Y.; Yuen, K. Asymptotics for a discrete-time risk model with gamma-like insurance risks. *Scand. Actuar. J.* **2016**, *2016*, 565–579. [CrossRef]
60. Yi, L.; Chen, Y.; Su, C. Approximation of the tail probability of randomly weighted sums of dependent random variables with dominated variation. *J. Math. Anal. Appl.* **2011**, *376*, 365–372. [CrossRef]
61. Geng, B.; Liu, Z.; Wang, S. A Kesten-type inequality for randomly weighted sums of dependent subexponential random variables with applications to risk theory. *Lith. Math. J.* **2023**, *63*, 81–91. [CrossRef]
62. Asimit, A.; Furman, E.; Tang, Q.; Vernic, R. Asymptotics for risk capital allocations based on Conditional Tail Expectation. *Insur. Math. Econ.* **2011**, *49*, 310–324. [CrossRef]
63. Fougeres, A.; Mercadier, C. Risk measures and multivariate extensions of Breiman's theorem. *J. Appl. Probab.* **2012**, *49*, 364–384. [CrossRef]
64. Hua, L.; Joe, H. Second order regular variation and conditional tail expectation of multiple risks. *Insur. Math. Econ.* **2011**, *49*, 537–546. [CrossRef]
65. Tang, Q.; Yuen, Z. Randomly weighted sums of subexponential random variables with application to capital allocation. *Extremes* **2014**, *17*, 467–493. [CrossRef]

66. Wang, S.; Hu, Y.; Yang, L.; Wang, W. Randomly weighted sums under a wide type dependence structure with applications to conditional tail expectation. *Commun. Statist. Theory Methods* **2018**, *47*, 5054–5063. [CrossRef]
67. Zhu, L.; Li, H. Asymptotic analysis of multivariate tail conditional expectations. *N. Am. Actuar. J.* **2012**, *16*, 350–363. [CrossRef]
68. Buldygin, V.; Klesov, O.; Steinebach, J.G. Some properties of asymptotic quasi-inverse functions and their applications. I. *Theory Probab. Math. Stat.* **2005**, *70*, 11–28. [CrossRef]
69. Buldygin, V.; Klesov, O.; Steinebach, J.G. Some properties of asymptotic quasi-inverse functions and their applications. II. *Theory Probab. Math. Stat.* **2005**, *71*, 37–52. [CrossRef]
70. Wang, D.; Su, C.; Zeng, Y. Uniform estimate for maximum of randomly weighted sums with applications to insurance risk theory. *Sci. China Ser. A-Math.* **2018**, *48*, 1378–1394. [CrossRef]
71. Konstantinides, D.; Passalidis, G.; Porichis, N. Closure properties in positively decreasing and related distributions under dependence. *arXiv* **2024**, arXiv:2402.05936. [CrossRef]
72. Rüschendorf, L. *Mathematical Risk Analysis*; Springer: Berlin/Heidelberg, Germany, 2013.
73. Alkasasbeh, M.; Lee, C.; Famoge, F. Transmuted distortion functions for measuring risks. *Risks* **2024**, *12*, 153. [CrossRef]
74. Paulusch, J.; Moser, T.; Sulima, A. Distortion risks measures of increasing rearrangement. *J. Risk Financ. Manag.* **2024**, *17*, 461. [CrossRef]
75. Kountzakis, C.; Rassello, D. Risk measures' duality on ordered linear spaces. *Mathematics* **2024**, *12*, 1165. [CrossRef]
76. Wang, H.; Gong, S.; Hu, Y. Strong comonotonic additive systemic risk measures. *Axioms* **2024**, *13*, 347. [CrossRef]
77. Yan, T.; Lu, Y.; Jeang, H. Dependence modelling for heavy-tailed multi-peril insurance losses. *Risks* **2024**, *12*, 97. [CrossRef]
78. Jaworski, P.; Zalewska, A. Portfolio selection based on modified CoVaR in Gaussian framework. *Mathematics* **2024**, *12*, 3766. [CrossRef]
79. Gomez, F.; Tang, Q.; Tong, Z. The gradient allocation principle based on the higher moment risk measure. *J. Bank. Financ.* **2022**, *143*, 106544. [CrossRef]
80. Pichler, A. Connection between higher order measures of risk and stochastic dominance. *Comput. Manag. Sci.* **2024**, *21*, 41. [CrossRef]
81. Chen, Y.; Liu, J. Asymptotic capital allocation based on the higher moment risk measure. *Eur. Actuar. J.* **2024**, *14*, 657–684. [CrossRef]
82. Liu, J.; Yi, Q. Asymptotics for the conditional higher moment coherent risk measure with weak contagion. *ASTIN Bull.* **2025**, *55*, 121–143. [CrossRef]
83. Bellini, F.; Klar, B.; Müller, A.; Rosazza Gianin, E. Generalized quantiles as risk measures. *Insur. Math. Econ.* **2014**, *54*, 41–48. [CrossRef]
84. Bellini, F.; Di Bernardino, E. Risk management with expectiles. *Eur. J. Financ.* **2017**, *23*, 487–506. [CrossRef]
85. Zaevski, T.; Nedeltchev, D. From BASEL III to BASEL IV and beyond: Expected shortfall and expectile risk measures. *Int. Rev. Financ. Anal.* **2023**, *87*, 102645. [CrossRef]

axioms

MDPI

Article

Optimizing Textile Manufacturing with an $M^X/G/1$ Queueing Model: Two Heterogeneous Services, Bernoulli Vacations, and Disaster–Repair Interventions

Logapriya Balasubramaniam [1,*], Saeid Jafari [2,*], Vidhya Dhayalan [3] and Shobana Arunachalam [4]

[1] Department of Science and Humanities, Karpagam College of Engineering, Coimbatore 641032, India
[2] Department of Mathematics, College of Vestsjaelland South Herrestarede 11, DK 4200 Slagelse, Denmark
[3] Department of Science and Humanities, Karpagam Institute of Technology, Coimbatore 641021, India; vidhyanallamani@gmail.com
[4] Department of Science and Humanities, Nehru Institute of Technology, Coimbatore 641105, India; shobanaamaths@gmail.com
* Correspondence: priyaramesh24.kce@gmail.com (L.B.); jafaripersia@gmail.com (S.J.)

Abstract

This study investigates an $M^X/G/1$ queueing system tailored to the textile manufacturing industry, incorporating two heterogeneous service types, Bernoulli vacation schedules, and the effects of disasters and repairs. The system handles bulk fabric arrivals following a Poisson process, where customers can opt for either standard finishing or advanced finishing services. Disasters such as equipment malfunctions cause system interruptions, necessitating stochastic repair periods, while Bernoulli vacation schedules allow the machines to take probabilistic vacations based on operational conditions. By employing the supplementary variable technique, the probability generating function (PGF) for the number of customers in the system is obtained. Key performance metrics are derived alongside rate arguments to analyze system behavior comprehensively. Numerical techniques are utilized to explore and illustrate the influence of model parameters, providing practical insights for optimizing resource allocation, enhancing production efficiency, and maintaining system reliability in textile manufacturing operations.

Keywords: supplementary variable technique; heterogeneous service; disaster; Bernoulli vacation schedule

MSC: 90B22

1. Introduction

Queueing systems play a vital role in the analysis and optimization of service and manufacturing processes, especially during interruptions, service variability, and in crucial workload management. This study focuses on modeling an $M^X/G/1$ queueing system characterized by two heterogeneous services, Bernoulli vacation schedules, and the influence of disasters and repairs. The concept of heterogeneous services reflects real-world settings where a server offers two distinct types of service differing in complexity, resource requirements, or in time. Disasters represent system-wide failures that interrupt operations, necessitating repair periods to restore functionality. The inclusion of a Bernoulli vacation schedule adds flexibility by allowing the server to probabilistically decide on taking a vacation. In this study, these features are integrated into a unified framework to derive key system performance metrics, including the probability generating function (PGF) for the number of customers in the system, using the supplementary variable technique.

The present study contributes to the literature on bulk-arrival single-server systems by formulating an $M^X/G/1$ model that simultaneously incorporates heterogeneous service choice, Bernoulli-type vacations, and disaster–repair interruptions within a unified analytical framework. Earlier works of certain model addresses these mechanisms only in isolation or partial combinations, whereas the current model captures their joint influence through a coupled supplementary-variable structure and modified steady-state balance equations. This integrated formulation enables system descriptors that explicitly reflect the interaction among service heterogeneity, probabilistic vacations, and breakdown–repair cycles, yielding structural and parametric behaviors not observed in models with only one or two of these features. This establishes the technical novelty and broadens the applicability of $M^X/G/1$ queueing models to more realistic operational environments.

The development of this model is grounded upon significant prior work. The integration of disasters and repairs builds on the foundational work of Afanasyev [1], who examined the busy period in queueing systems with vacations, providing insights into the probabilistic structure of service interruptions. Afthab Begum et al. [2] extended disaster models by including working breakdowns. Arumuganathan and Jeyakumar [3] studied bulk queueing systems with service feedback and control policies. In a related context, Barron [4] developed a replenishment inventory model under random environments with stock- and age-dependent cost functions, bridging queueing theory and inventory control under stochastic conditions. Similarly, Choi and Lim [5] proposed a Markovian queueing model with an alternating server and queue-length-based threshold control, contributing to adaptive service mechanisms. Choudhury and Paul [6] examined two-phase queueing systems with feedback, while Choudhury and Deka [7] explored single-server systems operating under Bernoulli vacation schedules in disaster-prone environments. Fu et al. [8] analyzed optimization decisions in customer-intensive services under bounded rationality, incorporating behavioral uncertainty through Gumbel distributions. Guendouzi and Bouzebda [9] optimized a GI/M/2/N queue with heterogeneous servers, working vacations, and impatience using the Bat algorithm, demonstrating the potential of metaheuristic techniques in queue optimization. Jeyakumar and Logapriya [10–12] further explored non-terminating vacation policies, single vacation policies, and compulsory vacation policies in queueing systems under disaster and repair conditions. Jeyakumar and Senthilnathan [13] provided insights into the behavior of bulk queueing systems with multiple vacations and breakdowns, emphasizing their relevance to real-world operations. The role of Bernoulli vacation schedules is highlighted by Jingjing et al. [14]. Kadi et al. [15] analyzed an M/M/1/K queue with single working vacation, feedback, and impatience under an N-policy. Collectively, these studies form the foundation on which the present comprehensive queueing model is developed to address real-world challenges in manufacturing and service industries.

In addition to these foundational contributions, several recent studies have advanced the analysis and optimization of queueing systems under modern operational complexities. Ke and Pearn [16] discussed optimal management policies in vacation models, while Kim and Lee [17] analyzed working breakdowns in M/G/1 queues. Kumar and Arivudainambi [18] examined queueing systems with catastrophes. The inclusion of heterogeneous services is inspired by Madan [19] and Madan et al. [20], who studied two-stage and multi-type service models. Mahanta et al. [21] and Mytalas and Zazanis [22] extended disaster models by considering working breakdowns and MAV policies, respectively. Niranjan et al. [23] studied bulk queueing models with load balancing and vacation, relevant to distributed and industrial service systems. Palaniammal and Kumar [24] further investigated the implications of heterogeneity on queueing performance across various industries. Applications of similar models in manufacturing environments have been demonstrated by Park et al. [25] in stochastic disaster systems. Sasikala et al. [26] focused on Bernoulli vacation schedules in retrial queueing systems, while Singh C.J., Jain M., and Kumar B. [27] analyzed an $M^X/G/1$ unreliable retrial queue with the option of additional service and Bernoulli vacation. Xie et al. [28] investigated equilibrium and optimization in multi-server queues with heterogeneous information and reneging. Yechiali [29] examined queues with system disasters and impatient customers, contributing substantially to research on vacation policies. Zhu and Wang [30] explored strategic joining in single-server Markovian queues with Bernoulli working vacations, revealing the behavioral dynamics of customers in such systems. Collectively, these recent developments emphasize a growing research interest in queueing models with vacations, customer heterogeneity, and stochastic disruptions—providing strong motivation for the present study.

Accordingly, the current work proposes a queueing model featuring two heterogeneous services, Bernoulli vacation schedules, and disaster–repair interventions, which is formulated to optimize textile manufacturing operations. The model captures realistic production characteristics such as probabilistic breakdowns, rest periods, and service variability, offering a unified analytical framework for improving efficiency and reliability in manufacturing environments.

The comparison in Table 1 clearly highlights that most existing studies address only one or two aspects, such as vacations, breakdowns, or service heterogeneity, in isolation. The present work uniquely combines bulk arrivals, two heterogeneous services, Bernoulli vacation schedules, and disaster–repair mechanisms within a unified $M^X/G/1$ queueing framework. Furthermore, the model is applied to a real-world textile manufacturing scenario, providing both analytical insight and practical relevance. This integrated approach distinguishes the present study from earlier theoretical models and offers a novel contribution toward performance optimization and operational reliability in industrial systems.

Table 1. Comparison of the Present Study with Existing Related Works.

Year	Model	Heterogeneous Services	Bulk Arrivals	Bernoulli Vacation	Disaster/ Breakdown	Repair Mechanism	Application
2000	M/M/1 with Catastrophes	✗	✗	✗	✓	✓	Theoretical
2007	Queue with Disasters and Impatience	✗	✗	✗	✓	✓	Theoretical
2014	Single-Server with Bernoulli Vacation	✗	✗	✓	✓	✗	✗
2011	Two-Stage/Multi-Type Service Models	✓	✗	✗	✗	✗	✗
2018	Bulk Queue with Feedback	✗	✓	✗	✗	✗	✗
2020	Retrial Queue with Bernoulli Vacation	✗	✗	✓	✗	✗	✗
2024	Bulk Queue with Load Balancing and Vacation	✗	✓	✓	✗	✗	✗
2025	GI/M/2/N with Working Vacation, Feedback, and Impatience	✓	✗	✓	✗	✗	✗
Present Study	Two Heterogeneous Services, Bernoulli Vacation, and Disaster–Repair	✓	✓	✓	✓	✓	✓

The aim of this model is to analyze complex queueing scenarios that arise in industries where bulk arrivals, diverse service options, and system disruptions are common. In a textile manufacturing unit, fabric rolls (customers) arrive in bulk for processing. The server (machine) provides two types of finishing services that are Standard Finishing and Advanced Finishing. Finishing services play a crucial role in enhancing the properties and appearance of fabrics to meet specific customer demands. Finishing is often the final stage of production that adds value to the product, ensuring it meets both functional and aesthetic requirements. Customers may opt for standard fabric finishing (basic chemical treatments for durability) or advanced finishing (waterproofing, anti-bacterial coatings, or wrinkle resistance) based on their needs and budget. Occasionally, the machine (server) undergoes disasters like machine malfunctions due to wear and tear in standard finishing service (service 1) and high-tech failures due to issues in UV curing machines in advanced finishing services (service 2), requiring repair before resuming operations. During periods of low workload, the machine may enter a Bernoulli vacation state for maintenance or energy conservation. This model helps in evaluating the system performance, optimizing machine utilization, improve production efficiency, and in maintaining high customer satisfaction while managing the inherent uncertainties in manufacturing operations.

Beyond textile manufacturing, similar queueing dynamics are observed in other industrial and service sectors. For instance, in automobile assembly lines, robotic units often alternate between routine operations and calibration (vacation periods), while different service stations handle heterogeneous assembly or finishing tasks. In semiconductor fabrication plants, equipment frequently undergoes maintenance and repair cycles, and production batches (bulk arrivals) must queue for standard or specialized processing steps. Likewise, in healthcare service systems, diagnostic centers face bulk patient arrivals, where medical devices or testing units provide heterogeneous services (basic vs. advanced tests) and occasionally undergo service interruptions or recalibrations.

Thus, the proposed queueing model with heterogeneous services, Bernoulli vacations, and disaster–repair mechanisms capture a wide range of real-world operations, providing valuable insights for optimizing resource utilization, improving service efficiency, and maintaining customer satisfaction under uncertainty.

The present study can be extended in several meaningful directions to enhance its analytical scope and practical relevance. Future research may incorporate customer impatience, reneging, or feedback mechanisms to model situations where fabric batches or customers withdraw or rejoin the system depending on service delays. The framework can also be generalized to multi-server or parallel-machine environments, reflecting large-scale textile or manufacturing systems with coordinated operations and load balancing. Introducing finite buffer capacity and priority-based service rules would allow analysis of preferential treatment for high-value or urgent orders. Moreover, the development of data-driven or machine learning-based control policies could optimize vacation scheduling, repair decisions, and service switching in real time. Further, integrating the queueing framework with inventory or supply-chain models would provide a holistic view of production and material flow. Allowing general or state-dependent distributions for repair and vacation times could also capture practical uncertainties in maintenance processes. Finally, future studies may conduct simulation-based validation or empirical analysis using industrial data to evaluate economic and energy efficiency, thereby strengthening the real-world applicability of the proposed model.

The paper is organized as follows. Section 2 presents the mathematical model of the queueing system with two heterogeneous services, Bernoulli vacations, and disaster–repair mechanisms. Section 3 details the derivation of the steady-state equations using the supplementary variable approach and the probability generating function (PGF) methodology. Section 4 analyzes the queue size distribution and key performance measures, while Section 5 illustrates the numerical results and discusses the impact of various system parameters. Finally, Section 6 concludes the study and highlights potential directions for future research.

2. Model Formulation

The system considers a bulk-arrival process in which customer batches arrive according to a Poisson process with rate λ. The size of each arriving batch is modeled by the random variable C. A batch of customers i with the parameters λ , $\lambda > 0$ joins the system with a provided with two kinds of heterogeneous service under first come, first serve discipline. The mean batch size is denoted by $E(C)$. An arriving customer has the option to select either the first service with a probability 'p' or second service with a probability '$1-p$'. Let $\mu_1(x)$ and $\mu_2(x)$ be the hazard rate function of the of both the services, with the corresponding density functions $S_1{}'$ and $S_2{}'$ and with the mean service times $E(S_1)$ and $E(S_2)$. After completing service, the server may either take vacation with probability b or with probability $1-b$, where the server may wait in the system to serve the arriving customer. Let $v(x)$ be the hazard rate function of the vacation, with the mean vacation time being $E(L)$. All vacation periods are independent of each other. Finally, disaster is assumed to happen in the system during either the first or second kind of service. With the disaster rate δ, it removes all the customers, including the one being served by the system, and the system is immediately moved to a repair period. Let $r(x)$ be the hazard rate function of the repair period with density function R' and mean repair time $E(R)$. The customers who arrive during repair time may wait in the queue.

In this model, we aim to derive the KolmogorovChapman equations for a bulk arrival single-server queueing system with two different kinds of heterogeneous service, server vacations, and disasters requiring repairs. Let $S_{i,t}, \mathrm{i} = 1,2$ and L_t be introduced as supplementary variables to obtain a Markov Process as $\{N_t, \Omega(t), S_{i,t}, R_t, L_t, t \geq 0\}$.

Let N_t and $\Omega(t)$ be the system size and random variable corresponding to server's status at a time t. For the various server's states, the limiting probabilities are defined as follows:

Server's idle state: P_0 at $\Omega(t) = 0$ represents the probability that the system is empty and the server is idle. Server's busy state (first kind of service): $P_n^{(s1)}(x)$ at $\Omega(t) = 1$ represents the joint probability of having n customers in the system and the server busy with the first kind of service. Server's busy state (second kind of service): $P_n^{(s2)}(x)$ at $\Omega(t) = 2$ represents the joint probability of having n customers in the system and the server busy with the second kind of service. Server's repair state: $R_n(x)$ at $\Omega(t) = 3$ represents the probability of having n customers in the system and the server undergoing repairs. Server's vacation state: $L_n(x)$ at $\Omega(t) = 4$ represents the probability of having n customers in the system and the server is on vacation. Symbols and notations are listed in Appendix A.

3. Supplementary Variable Approach to Steady-State Differential Equations

The supplementary variable technique is a powerful tool in queueing theory for deriving steady-state differential equations and analyzing system performance. This method is particularly effective for systems with bulk arrivals, general service distributions, and stochastic disruptions like disasters and repairs. Building on our earlier studies on single vacation policies [5] and non-terminating vacation models in $M^X/G/1$ queues [6], this work extends the application of the supplementary variable technique to explore steady-state behaviors in two different heterogeneous services.

The governing equations for various states of the system are framed for $n > 0$ *as*

$$0 = -\lambda P_0 + \int_0^\infty L_0(x)v(x)dx + (1-b)\left(\int_0^\infty P_1^{(s2)}(x)\mu_2(x)dx + \int_0^\infty \begin{array}{c} P_1^{(s1)}(x)\mu_1(x)dx+ \\ \int_0^\infty R_0(x)r(x)dx \end{array}\right) \quad (1)$$

$$\left(\frac{d}{dx} + \lambda + \mu_1(x) + \delta\right)P_n^{(s1)}(x) = \lambda\sum_{i=1}^{n-1} C_i P_{n-i}^{(s1)}(x)\ , n \geq 1 \quad (2)$$

$$\left(\frac{d}{dx} + \lambda + \mu_2(x)\right)P_n^{(s2)}(x) = \lambda\sum_{i=1}^{n-1} C_i P_{n-i}^{(s2)}(x)\ , n \geq 1 \quad (3)$$

$$\left(\frac{d}{dx} + \lambda + r(x)\right)R_n(x) = \lambda\sum_{i=1}^{n-1} C_i R_{n-i}(x), n \geq 1 \quad (4)$$

$$\left(\frac{d}{dx} + \lambda + v(x)\right)L_n(x) = \lambda\sum_{i=1}^{n-1} C_i L_{n-i}(x), n \geq 1 \quad (5)$$

With the boundary conditions

$$P_n^{(s1)}(0) = p\left(\int_0^\infty L_n(x)v(x)dx + \int_0^\infty P_{n+1}^{(s2)}(x)\mu_2(x)dx + \int_0^\infty \begin{array}{c} P_{n+1}^{(s1)}(x)\mu_1(x)dx + \int_0^\infty R_n(x)r(x)dx+ \\ \lambda C_n P_0 \end{array}\right) \quad (6)$$

$$P_n^{(s2)}(0) = (1-p)\left(\int_0^\infty L_n(x)v(x)dx + \int_0^\infty P_{n+1}^{(s2)}(x)\mu_2(x)dx + \int_0^\infty \begin{array}{c} P_{n+1}^{(s1)}(x)\mu_1(x)dx + \int_0^\infty R_n(x)r(x)dx \\ +\lambda C_n P_0 \end{array}\right) \quad (7)$$

$$R_0(0) = \delta\left(\sum_{n=1}^{\infty}\int_0^\infty P_n^{(s1)}(x)dx + \sum_{n=1}^{\infty}\int_0^\infty P_n^{(s2)}(x)dx\right) \quad (8)$$

$$L_n(0) = b\left(\int_0^\infty P_n^{(s2)}(x)\mu_2(x)dx + \int_0^\infty P_{n+1}^{(s1)}(x)\mu_1(x)dx\right) \quad (9)$$

4. PGF-Based Steady-State Analysis

We derive the steady-state probability generating function (PGF) by systematically linking each balance equation to the corresponding operational condition of the system. Intermediate steps are outlined to clarify how the supplementary variables capture service heterogeneity, vacation decisions, and disaster–repair dynamics. By presenting the derivation in a stepwise manner, the structure of the PGF becomes transparent, showing how each component of the model contributes to the steady-state representation.

To obtain the PGF, we define the functions as

$$\begin{array}{l} P^{(s1)}(x,z) = \sum_{n=1}^{\infty} P_n^{(s1)}(x)z^n, P_n^{(s1)}(z) = \sum_{n=1}^{\infty} P_n^{(s1)}z^n \\ P^{(s2)}(x,z) = \sum_{n=1}^{\infty} P_n^{(s2)}(x)z^n, P_n^{(s2)}(z) = \sum_{n=1}^{\infty} P_n^{(s2)}z^n \\ L(x,z) = \sum_{n=0}^{\infty} L_n(x)z^n, R(x,z) = \sum_{n=0}^{\infty} R_n(x)z^n \end{array} \quad (10)$$

By multiplying Equations (2)–(9) with certain powers of z and summing it over n , we obtain the PDEs as

$$\begin{array}{l} \frac{d}{dx}P^{(s1)}(x,z) + (\lambda + \mu_1(x) + \delta - \lambda C(z))P^{(s1)}(x,z) = 0 \\ \frac{d}{dx}P^{(s2)}(x,z) + (\lambda + \mu_2(x) + \delta - \lambda C(z))P^{(s2)}(x,z) = 0 \\ \frac{d}{dx}R(x,z) + (\lambda + r(x) - \lambda C(z))R(x,z) = 0 \\ \frac{d}{dx}L(x,z) + (\lambda + v(x) - \lambda C(z))L(x,z) = 0 \end{array} \quad (11)$$

$$\begin{array}{l} P^{(s1)}(0,z) = (p)\Big(\int_0^\infty (L(x,z) - L_0(x))v(x)dx + \int_0^\infty \left(\frac{1}{z}P^{(s2)}(x,z) - P_1^{(s2)}(x)\right)\mu_2(x)dx + \\ \int_0^\infty \left(\frac{1}{z}P^{(s1)}(x,z) - P_1^{(s1)}(x)\right)\mu_1(x)dx + \int_0^\infty (R(x,z) - R_0(x))r(x)dx + \lambda C(z)P_0\Big) \end{array} \quad (12)$$

$$P^{(s2)}(0,z) = (1-p)\Big(\int_0^\infty (L(x,z) - L_0(x))v(x)dx + \int_0^\infty \left(\tfrac{1}{z} P^{(s2)}(x,z) - P_1^{(s2)}(x) \right) \mu_2(x)dx + \int_0^\infty \left(\tfrac{1}{z} P^{(s1)}(x,z) - P_1^{(s1)}(x) \right) \mu_1(x)dx + \int_0^\infty (R(x,z) - R_0(x))r(x)dx + \lambda C(z)P_0 \Big) \tag{13}$$

$$R(0,z) = \delta\left(\int_0^\infty P^{(s1)}(x,1)dx + \int_0^\infty P^{(s1)}(x,1)dx \right) \tag{14}$$

$$L(0,z) = b\left(\int_0^\infty P_n^{(s1)}(x,z)\mu_2(x)dx + \int_0^\infty P_n^{(s2)}(x,z)\mu_1(x)dx \right) \tag{15}$$

Upon solving Equation (11), we have

$$\begin{aligned} P^{(s1)}(x,z) &= P^{(s1)}(0,z)(1 - S_1(x))e^{-(\lambda+\delta-\lambda C(z))x} \\ P^{(s2)}(x,z) &= P^{(s2)}(0,z)(1 - S_2(x))e^{-(\lambda+\delta-\lambda C(z))x} \\ R(x,z) &= R(0,z)(1 - R(x))e^{-(\lambda-\lambda C(z))x} \\ L(x,z) &= L(0,z)(1 - L(x))e^{-(\lambda-\lambda C(z))x} \end{aligned} \tag{16}$$

By integrating the Equation (16) again, we have

$$\begin{aligned} P^{(s1)}(z) &= P^{(s1)}(0,z)\left(\frac{1-S_1^*(\lambda+\delta-\lambda C(z))}{\lambda+\delta-\lambda C(z)} \right) \\ P^{(s2)}(z) &= P^{(s2)}(0,z)\left(\frac{1-S_2^*(\lambda+\delta-\lambda C(z))}{\lambda-\lambda C(z)} \right) \\ R(z) &= R(0,z)\left(\frac{1-R^*(\lambda-\lambda C(z))}{\lambda-\lambda C(z)} \right) \\ L(z) &= L(0,z)\left(\frac{1-L^*(\lambda-\lambda C(z))}{\lambda-\lambda C(z)} \right) \end{aligned} \tag{17}$$

$S_1^*(\lambda+\delta-\lambda C(z))$ *and* $S_2^*(\lambda+\delta-\lambda C(z))$ represent the Laplace-Stieltjes transforms of the first and second types of service time distributions, respectively. Similarly, $R^*(\lambda-\lambda C(z))$ denotes the Laplace-Stieltjes transform of the repair time distributions, and $L^*(\lambda-\lambda C(z))$ corresponds to the Laplace-Stieltjes transform of the vacation time distribution. These transforms are essential in expressing the steady-state characteristics of the queueing system.

Equations (13)–(16) are evaluated to determine and obtain the integral equations as,

$$\int_0^\infty P^{(s1)}(x,z)\mu_1(x)dx = P^{(s1)}(0,z)S_1^*(\lambda+\delta-\lambda C(z)) \tag{18}$$

$$\int_0^\infty P^{(s2)}(x,z)\mu_2(x)dx = P^{(s2)}(0,z)S_2^*(\lambda+\delta-\lambda C(z)) \tag{19}$$

$$\int_0^\infty R(x,z)r(x)dx = R(0,z)R^*(\lambda-\lambda C(z)) \tag{20}$$

$$\int_0^\infty L(x,z)v(x)dx = L(0,z)L^*(\lambda-\lambda C(z)) \tag{21}$$

In the given queueing system, it is assumed that no customers are present immediately after the completion of a vacation period or a repair period that follows a disaster. This condition arises because the system state resets at the end of these events. Consequently, the joint probabilities associated with the number of customers in the system and the system's phase simplify PGFs $L(0,z)$ *as* $L_0(0)$ and $R(0,z)$ *as* $R_0(0)$.

5. Queue Size Distribution Under Different Operational States

The analysis of the queue size distribution proceeds by decomposing the overall PGF into parts associated with the key operational states of the system—busy operation, vacation periods, disaster epochs, and repair phases. Each resulting expression is accompanied by brief interpretative remarks illustrating how the model parameters influence the distribution under these conditions. This separation of structural components provides clearer insight into how the combined effects of bulk arrivals, service heterogeneity, vacations, and breakdown–repair cycles shape the system's queue length behavior.

Queueing systems are subjected to disruptions like vacations, repairs, and varying server availability, and the queue size distribution depends significantly on the operational state of the server. By deriving the PGFs for different states, such as when the server is busy, under repair, or on vacation, this enables us to compute key performance metrics like mean queue length and waiting time.

$$P^{(s1)}(0,z) = \frac{zp\left(\delta\left(P^{(s1)}(1) + P^{(s2)}(1)\right)R^*(A_z) - \lambda P_0 H_z\right)}{z - (pS_1^*(A_z+\delta) + (1-p).S_2^*(A_z+\delta))(zbL^*(A_z)+1)} \tag{22}$$

where $A_z = \lambda - \lambda C(z)$, and $H_z = \frac{1}{1-b} - C(z)$.

Therefore Equation (17) becomes

$$P^{(s1)}(z) = \frac{zp\left(\delta\left(P^{(s1)}(1) + P^{(s2)}(1)\right)R^*(A_z) - \lambda P_0 H_z\right)}{z - (pS_1^*(A_z+\delta) + (1-p).S_2^*(A_z+\delta))(zbL^*(A_z)+1)}\left(\frac{1-S_1^*(A_z+\delta)}{A_z+\delta}\right) \tag{23}$$

To establish the existence of a unique root inside the unit disk, we apply Rouche's theorem. If possible, let $z = z_\theta$ be the unique solution of $z = (pS_1^*(A_z+\delta) + (1-p).S_2^*(A_z+\delta))$ $(zbL^*(A_z)+1)$. In that case, equality becomes $\lambda P_0 H_{z_\theta} = \delta\left(P^{(s1)}(1) + P^{(s2)}(1)\right)R^*(A_{z_\theta})$. Let us set $\pi = \frac{H_{z_\theta}}{R^*(A_{z_\theta})}$.

Results:

The probability generating functions (PGFs) for the size of the system at different epochs—corresponding to the first kind of service, second kind of service, repair phase, and vacation phase—are derived as follows:

The PGF at the epoch of the first kind of service is given as

$$P^{(s1)}(z) = \frac{zp(\pi\lambda P_0 R^*(A_z) - \lambda P_0 H_z)}{z - (pS_1^*(A_z+\delta) + (1-p).S_2^*(A_z+\delta))(zbL^*(A_z)+1)}\left(\frac{1-S_1^*(A_z+\delta)}{A_z+\delta}\right) \tag{24}$$

The PGF at the epoch of the second kind of service is given as

$$P^{(s2)}(z) = \frac{z(1-p)(\pi\lambda P_0 R^*(A_z) - \lambda P_0 H_z)}{z - (pS_1^*(A_z+\delta) + (1-p).S_2^*(A_z+\delta))(zbL^*(A_z)+1)}\left(\frac{1-S_2^*(A_z+\delta)}{A_z+\delta}\right) \tag{25}$$

The PGF at the epoch under repair is given as

$$R(z) = \frac{\lambda P_0\left(\pi - \frac{b}{1-b}\right)(P(1-S_1^*(\delta)) + (1-P)(1-S_2^*(\delta)))(1-R^*(A_z))}{(1-(b+1)(p(S_1^*(\delta)) + (1-p)(S_2^*(\delta)))A_z} \tag{26}$$

The PGF at the epoch of under vacation is given as

$$L(z) = \frac{zb(\pi\lambda P_0 R^*(A_z) - \lambda P_0 H_z)(pS_1^*(A_z+\delta) + ((1-p).S_2^*(A_z+\delta)))(1-L^*(A_z))}{(z - (pS_1^*(A_z+\delta) + (1-p).S_2^*(A_z+\delta))(zbL^*(A_z)+1)A_z} \tag{27}$$

Using the normalizing condition *at* $z = 1$, the probability P_0 is obtained when the server being idle as

$$P_0 = \left(1 + \frac{\lambda\left(\pi - \frac{b}{1-b}\right)\{(p(1-S_1^*(\delta)) + (1-p)(1-S_2^*(\delta)))(1+\delta E(R)) + \delta(p(S_1^*(\delta)) + (1-p)(S_2^*(\delta)))\}}{\delta(1-(b+1)(p(S_1^*(\delta)) + (1-p)(S_2^*(\delta))))}\right)^{-1} \tag{28}$$

Finally, the total PGF of queue size $X(z)$ is obtained as

$$X(z) = \left(1 + \frac{\lambda\left(\pi - \frac{b}{1-b}\right)\left\{\left(p\left(1-S_1^*(\delta)\right)+(1-p)\left(1-S_2^*(\delta)\right)\right)(1+\delta E(R))+\delta\left(p\left(S_1^*(\delta)\right)+(1-p)\left(S_2^*(\delta)\right)\right)\right\}}{\delta\left(1-(b+1)\left(p\left(S_1^*(\delta)\right)+(1-p)\left(S_2^*(\delta)\right)\right)\right)}\right)^{-1}\Bigg[1+ \frac{z(\pi\lambda P_0 R^*(A_z)-\lambda P_0 H_z)}{z-\left(pS_1^*(A_z+\delta)+(1-p).S_2^*(A_z+\delta)\right)(zbL^*(A_z)+1)}\left(\frac{p\left(1-S_1^*(A_z+\delta)\right)+(1-p)\left(1-S_2^*(A_z+\delta)\right)}{A_z+\delta}+ \frac{b\left(pS_1^*(A_z+\delta)+\left((1-p).S_2^*(A_z+\delta)\right)\right)(1-L^*(A_z))}{A_z}\right)+\frac{\lambda P_0\left(\pi-\frac{b}{1-b}\right)\left(P\left(1-S_1^*(\delta)\right)+(1-P)\left(1-S_2^*(\delta)\right)\right)(1-R^*(A_z))}{\left(1-(b+1)\left(p\left(S_1^*(\delta)\right)+(1-p)\left(S_2^*(\delta)\right)\right)A_z\right.}\Bigg] \quad (29)$$

Also, due to disaster, the PGF of the total number of customers removed from the queueing system is given as

$$X_d(z) = \frac{z\delta(\pi R^*(A_z) - H_z)(1-(b+1)(p(S_1^*(\delta)) + (1-p)(S_2^*(\delta))))}{(z-(pS_1^*(A_z+\delta) + (1-p).S_2^*(A_z+\delta))(zbL^*(A_z)+1))\left(\pi - \frac{b}{1-b}\right)}\left(\frac{1-S_1^*(A_z+\delta)}{(1-S_1^*(\delta))\,(A_z+\delta)} + \frac{1-S_2^*(A_z+\delta)}{(1-S_2^*(\delta))\,(A_z+\delta)}\right) \quad (30)$$

6. Performance Measures

The expected queue length $(E(Q_L))$ and waiting time $(E(W_T))$ of the customer in the system are derived using L' Hospital's rule. By applying this rule to the PGF obtained from the Equation (29), the mean queue length of the customer in the queue and mean waiting time of the customer are calculated. It produces valuable insights into the performance of the queueing system.

$$E(Q_L) = \frac{\begin{array}{c}\lambda E(c)\left(\frac{(\delta(1-(b+1)S_a))}{\delta(1-(b+1)S_a)+\lambda\lambda_c(\,S_c(1+\delta E(R))+\delta\,S_a E(L))}\right)\\ \left(\begin{array}{c}S_d\,\lambda_c\left(\frac{\lambda}{\delta}-\frac{b\lambda}{2}E(L)\right)+S_c\left(S_e+\lambda_c\left(S_f-\frac{\lambda}{\delta}(b+1)S_d\right)-S_a\left((b+1)S_e-\lambda_c\left((b+1)S_f+\frac{1}{\delta E(c)}-\frac{\lambda}{\delta}E(L)\right)\right)\right)\\ +S_a\left(S_g+\lambda_c\left(S_h-S_d\left(\frac{b(b+1)}{2}\lambda E(L)-\frac{\lambda}{\delta}(1+b)\right)\right)-S_a(\,S_g-\lambda_c(1+b))\right)\end{array}\right)\end{array}}{(1-(b+1)S_a)^2} \quad (31)$$

$$E(W_T) = \frac{\begin{array}{c}\left(\frac{(\delta(1-(b+1)S_a))}{\delta(1-(b+1)S_a)+\lambda\lambda_c(\,S_c(1+\delta E(R))+\delta\,S_a E(L))}\right)\\ \left(\begin{array}{c}S_d\,\lambda_c\left(\frac{\lambda}{\delta}-\frac{b\lambda}{2}E(L)\right)+S_c\left(S_e+\lambda_c\left(S_f-\frac{\lambda}{\delta}(b+1)S_d\right)-S_a\left((b+1)S_e-\lambda_c\left((b+1)S_f+\frac{1}{\delta E(c)}-\frac{\lambda}{\delta}E(L)\right)\right)\right)\\ +S_a\left(S_g+\lambda_c\left(S_h-S_d\left(\frac{b(b+1)}{2}\lambda E(L)-\frac{\lambda}{\delta}(1+b)\right)\right)-S_a(\,S_g-\lambda_c(1+b))\right)\end{array}\right)\end{array}}{(1-(b+1)S_a)^2} \quad (32)$$

where $\lambda_c = \left(\pi - \frac{b}{1-b}\right)$

$$S_d = pS_1^{*'}(\delta) + (1-p)pS_2^{*'}(\delta);\ \ S_a = (pS_1^*(\delta) + (1-p)S_2^*(\delta)),$$

$$S_c = p(1-S_1^*(\delta)) + (1-p)(1-S_2^*(\delta));\ \ S_h = \frac{b\lambda}{2}E\left(L^2\right) - \frac{b}{2E(c)}E(L)$$

$$S_e = \frac{\pi\lambda}{\delta}E(R) - \delta;\ \ S_f = \frac{\lambda}{\delta^2} + \frac{\lambda}{2}E\left(R^2\right);\ \ S_g = \frac{b}{2}E(L)(\lambda E(R) - 1)$$

Also, $R^{*'}(0)$ and $L^{*'}(0)$ are the mean repair time and mean vacation time; $R^{*''}(0)$ and $L^{*''}(0)$ are the second moment repair time and vacation time.

7. Rate Arguments

Disasters in the system can occur either before the commencement of a repair period or at the conclusion of a busy period. Consequently, the rate at which disasters occur is expressed as

$$r_d = \frac{\lambda P_0\left(\pi - \frac{b}{1-b}\right)(P(1-S_1^*(\delta)) + (1-P)(1-S_2^*(\delta)))}{(1-(b+1)\left(p(S_1^*(\delta)) + (1-p)\left(S_2^*(\delta)\right)\right)} \quad (33)$$

At the end of a busy period, the server may proceed to take a vacation. Hence, the rate of normal busy period completion is expressed as

$$r_{nbpc} = \frac{z\lambda P_0(\pi R^*(A_z) - H_z)\big(P(1 - S_1^*(\delta)) + (1 - P)(1 - S_2^*(\delta))\big)}{z - \big(pS_1^*(A_z + \delta) + (1 - p).S_2^*(A_z + \delta)\big)(zbL^*(A_z) + 1)} \tag{34}$$

Every busy period is initiated either following the conclusion of the previous busy period or after the occurrence of a disaster. Accordingly, the rate of initiation of a busy period is given as

$$r_{sbp} = \lambda P_0(P(1 - S_1^*(\delta)) + (1 - P)(1 - S_2^*(\delta))) \left(\frac{z(\pi R^*(A_z) - H_z)}{z - \big(pS_1^*(A_z+\delta) + (1-p).S_2^*(A_z+\delta)\big)(zbL^*(A_z)+1)} + \frac{(\pi - \frac{b}{1-b})}{(1-(b+1)\big(p(S_1^*(\delta)) + (1-p)(S_2^*(\delta))\big)} \right) \tag{35}$$

A customer leaves the system either after his first essential service or second optional service. Therefore, the rate of customers leaving the system (due to service completion) is given as

$$r_{clsc} = \frac{\lambda P_0\left(\pi - \frac{b}{1-b}\right)(p(S_1^*(\delta)) + (1 - p)(S_2^*(\delta)))}{(1 - (b + 1)\big(p(S_1^*(\delta)) + (1 - p)(S_2^*(\delta))\big)} \tag{36}$$

If a customer suffers disaster only during the first essential service, therefore, the rate of customers leaving (due to disaster) is given as

$$r_{cld} = \lambda\left(E(c) - P_0 \frac{\left(\pi - \frac{b}{1-b}\right)(p(S_1^*(\delta)) + (1 - p)(S_2^*(\delta)))}{(1 - (b + 1)\big(p(S_1^*(\delta)) + (1 - p)(S_2^*(\delta))\big)} \right) \tag{37}$$

8. Numerical Illustration

Numerical technique was applied to compute the queue size distribution for various states in the illustrated real-life situation that exist in textile production. Parameters μ, r, v are assumed to be distributed in exponential. The numerical parameters were chosen as illustrative values to highlight the behavioral impact of service choice, vacations, and disaster–repair dynamics. Real industrial datasets that jointly capture all these features are not readily available, but the selected ranges are consistent with those used in related queueing studies.

In a textile manufacturing unit, the arrival rate of fabric rolls to the manufacturing unit is λ, where they choose between standard finishing or advanced finishing services based on their specific needs. Standard finishing involves basic chemical treatments aimed at enhancing fabric durability, with a processing rate $\mu_1 = 5$, while advanced finishing includes high-tech processes like waterproofing, anti-bacterial coatings, or UV curing for wrinkle resistance, processed at a rate $\mu_2 = 6$. Both services are susceptible to disasters; standard finishing faces machine malfunctions due to wear and tear, and advanced finishing encounters high-tech failures such as UV curing machine breakdowns at a disaster rate δ. After a disaster, the machine undergoes a repair phase at a rate r before resuming operations. Additionally, during periods of low workload, the machine may enter a Bernoulli vacation state for maintenance with a rate v.

To analyze the described textile production system, the tables below summarize the key parameters, and the graphs represent the impact of these parameters on the performance metrics. These visualizations provide a clear understanding of the system's behavior under different scenarios, highlighting the effects of disasters in different service.

From Table 2 and Figure 1, it is evident that as the probability p of opting for the standard finishing service of the first kind increases, the idle time of the fabric rolls decreases, while the queue length and expected waiting time increase. This occurs because the service rate for standard finishing μ_1 is lower than that of advanced finishing μ_2.

Table 2. Performance measures with $\lambda = 2$ and $\delta = 3$.

p	P_0	$E(Q_L)$	$E(W_T)$
0.2	0.0675	8.033	4.017
0.4	0.0520	11.585	5.792
0.6	0.0356	18.683	9.341
0.8	0.0183	39.965	19.983

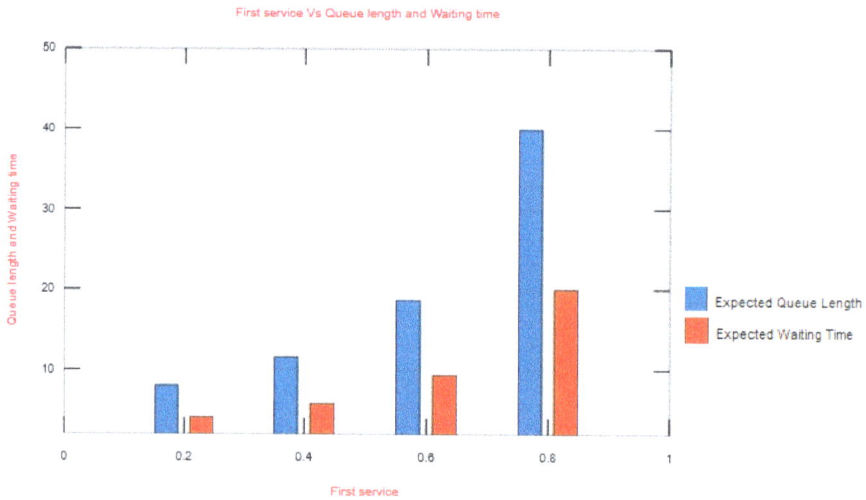

Figure 1. Prob. for first kind service vs. queue length and waiting time.

From Table 3 and Figure 2, it is clear that an increase in the arrival rate of fabric rolls leads to a rise in both the queue length and expected waiting time, reflecting the added workload on the system. Conversely, when the disaster rate increases, as also shown in Table 4 and Figure 3, the queue length and expected waiting time decrease, indicating reduced service continuity due to frequent interruptions requiring repairs.

Table 3. Performance measures with $\delta = 4,\ p = 0.25,$ and $b = 0.5$.

λ	P_0	$E(Q_L)$	$E(W_T)$
3.0	0.0974	1.2013	0.4004
3.2	0.0898	1.6357	0.5111
3.4	0.0831	2.0700	0.6088
3.6	0.0772	2.5032	0.6953
3.8	0.0719	2.9353	0.7725

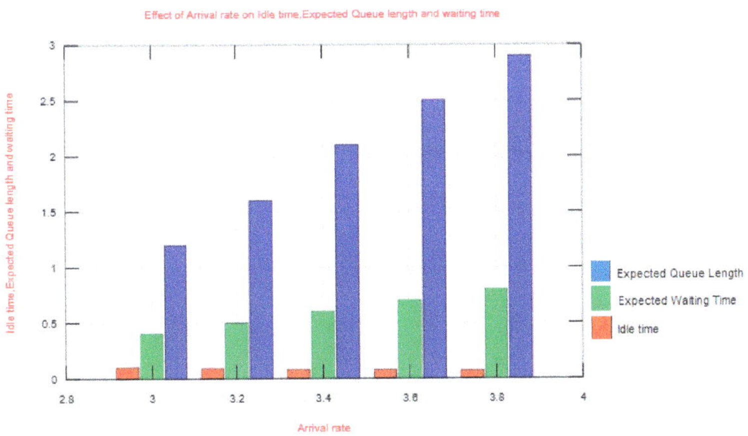

Figure 2. Arrival rate vs. idle time, queue length, and waiting time.

Table 4. Performance measures with $\lambda = 2$, $p = 0.25$, and $b = 0.5$.

δ	P_0	$E(Q_L)$	$E(W_T)$
3.0	0.0227	31.453	15.727
3.2	0.0537	10.161	5.080
3.4	0.0823	4.566	2.283
3.6	0.1087	1.877	0.938
3.8	0.1332	0.228	0.114

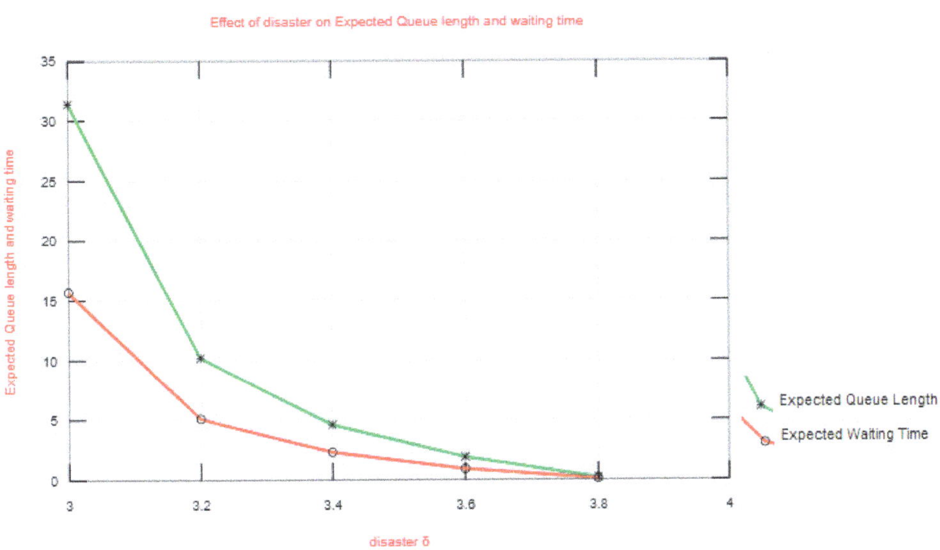

Figure 3. Disaster rate vs. queue length and waiting time.

Although the model is motivated by textile manufacturing operations, empirical datasets that jointly capture bulk arrivals, heterogeneous services, Bernoulli vacations, and disaster–repair behavior are not currently available; therefore, the numerical results presented here serve as theoretical illustrations, with analytical correctness verified through consistency with known $M^X/G/1$ special cases.

9. Conclusions

In this article, an $M^X/G/1$ queueing model with two heterogeneous services and a Bernoulli vacation schedule is examined in the context of disasters and repairs within the textile manufacturing industry. We derive the queue size distributions for various steady states, along with quality metrics, using the supplementary variable technique. Numerical examples are provided to illustrate the approach, demonstrating the disaster, impact waiting times, and queue lengths for the two service types in textile production. The numerical analysis reveals key insights: as the arrival rate and the probability of opting for the service increase, both the server's busy period and customer waiting times also rise. Conversely, when the disaster rate increases, leading to more frequent system interruptions, the server's busy period and customer waiting time decrease. These findings highlight the critical role of managing service options, machine downtime, and operational disruptions in optimizing production efficiency and minimizing delays in textile manufacturing.

Author Contributions: Conceptualization, methodology and validation, L.B. and S.J.; writing—original draft preparation, L.B.; writing—review and editing, S.J., L.B., V.D., and S.A.; visualization, L.B.; supervision, L.B. and S.J. All authors have read and agreed to the published version of the manuscript.

Funding: This research received no external funding.

Data Availability Statement: Data is contained within the article.

Conflicts of Interest: The authors declare no conflicts of interest.

Appendix A. Notation and Mathematical Remarks

Appendix A.1. Summary of Symbols and Variable Definitions

The key variables used throughout the analysis are summarized below for clarity:

- m: Number of customers in the system.
- n: Number of customers in the queue.
- λ: The average rate of customers entering the queue system.
- μ: The average rate of serving customers per server.
- ρ: A measure of traffic congestion for single server system, which is defined as $\rho = \frac{\lambda}{\mu}$.
- N_t: Number of customers in the system at time t.
- $S_{i,t}$: Elapsed service time for i $= 1, 2$ at time t.
- R_t: Elapsed repair time at time t.
- $L_{j,t}$: Elapsed vacation time for $j = 1, 2, \ldots$ at time t.
- S_1: Random variable representing the essential service with mean service time $E(S_1)$.
- S_2: Random variable representing the optional service with mean service time $E(S_2)$.
- P_0: Probability that at time t, there are no customers in the system, and the server is idle but available in the system.
- $P_n^{(e)}(x)$: Probability that at time t, the server is providing the first essential service, and there are n customers in the queue.
- $P_n^{(o)}(x)$: Probability that at time t, the server is providing the second optional service, and there are n customers in the queue.
- $R_n(x)$: Probability that at time t, the system is inactive due to system repair while there are n customers in the queue waiting for service.

All PGFs, LSTs, and auxiliary functions appearing in Sections 4–6 are analytic in the unit disk and are defined at their first use in the text.

Appendix A.2. Notes on Mathematical Transitions

To maintain continuity in the derivations, we summarize the main transitions used:

1. Applying PGFs: Whenever the steady-state equations involve the number of customers in the system, we apply the probability generating function by multiplying with certain powers of z and summing it over n. This converts recursive balance relations into algebraic equations in z, enabling closed-form expressions.
2. Applying Laplace–Stieltjes transforms (LSTs): Service-time distributions and repair-time distributions are introduced through their LSTs to simplify convolution expressions and waiting-time relations. All transform steps correspond directly to the integral definitions of the involved random variables.
3. Differentiating PGFs: Derivatives of PGFs at z = 1 are used to obtain the mean queue length and mean waiting time.
4. These steps follow standard queueing-theoretic procedures and are applied consistently across Sections 4 and 5.

Appendix A.3. Dimensional Consistency

All performance measures have been verified for dimensional consistency:

- Arrival rate carries dimension time.
- Service times and repair time carry dimension time.
- Quantities such as queue length, loss probability, and utilization are dimensionless.

References

1. Afanasyev, G.A. On the Busy Period in Queuing Systems with Vacations. *Theory Probab. Its Appl.* **2025**, *70*, 418–424. [CrossRef]
2. Afthab Begum, M.L.; Fijy Jose, P.; Bama, S. $M^X/G/1$ queue with disasters and working breakdowns. *Int. J. Sci. Res. Publ.* **2016**, *6*, 2250–3153.
3. Arumuganathan, R.; Jeyakumar, S. A Non-Markovian bulk queue with multiple vacations and control policy on request for re service. *Qual. Technol. Quant. Manag.* **2011**, *8*, 253–269. [CrossRef]
4. Barron, Y. A replenishment inventory model with a stock-dependent demand and age–stock-dependent cost functions in a random environment. *Asia-Pac. J. Oper. Res.* **2022**, *39*, 2150035.
5. Choi, D.I.; Lim, D.E. Analysis of a Markovian Queueing Model with an Alternating Server and Queue-Length-Based Threshold Control. *Mathematics* **2025**, *13*, 3555.
6. Choudhury, G.; Paul, M. A two phase queueing system with Bernoulli feedback. *Int. J. Inf. Manag. Sci.* **2005**, *16*, 35–52.
7. Choudhury, G.; Deka, M. A single server Queueing system with two phases of service subject to server breakdown and Bernoulli vacation. *Appl. Math. Model.* **2012**, *36*, 6050–6060. [CrossRef]
8. Fu, G.; Jiang, M.; Zhan, W. Optimization Decisions with Bounded Rationality in Customer-Intensive Services Under Gumbel Distributions. *Axioms* **2025**, *14*, 309. [CrossRef]
9. Guendouzi, A.; Bouzebda, S. Cost Optimization in a GI/M/2/N Queue with Heterogeneous Servers, Working Vacations, and Impatient Customers via the Bat Algorithm. *Mathematics* **2025**, *13*, 3559. [CrossRef]
10. Jeyakumar, S.; Logapriya, B. Production analysis of manufacturing industry in a single vacation policy under disaster. *Math. Models Eng.* **2023**, *9*, 198–207.
11. Jeyakumar, S.; Logapriya, B. Modelling $M^X/G/1$ Queueing System with Optional Second Service under Disaster and Repairs with Non-Terminating Vacation. *Indian J. Nat. Sci.* **2024**, *14*, 69871–69878.
12. Jeyakumar, S.; Logapriya, B. Mathematical analysis on production control in manufacturing units under disaster and repair with compulsory vacation. *OPSEARCH* **2024**, *62*, 532–549. [CrossRef]
13. Jeyakumar, S.; Senthilnathan, B. A study on the behaviour of the server breakdown without interruption in $M^X/G(a,b)/1$ queuing system with multiple vacations and closedown time. *Appl. Math. Comput.* **2012**, *219*, 2618–2633.
14. Jingjing, Y.E.; Liu, L.; Jiang, T. Analysis of a single server queue with disasters and repairs under Bernoulli vacation schedule. *J. Syst. Sci. Inf.* **2016**, *4*, 547–559.
15. Kadi, A.; Boualem, M.; Touche, N.; Dehimi, A. Modeling and optimization of an M/M/1/K queue with single working vacation, feedback, and impatience timers under N-policy. *Discret. Contin. Model. Appl. Comput. Sci.* **2025**, *33*, 10–26. [CrossRef]
16. Ke, J.C.; Pearn, W.L. Optimal management policy for heterogeneous arrival queueing systems with server breakdowns and vacations. *Qual. Technol. Quant. Manag.* **2004**, *1*, 149–162. [CrossRef]
17. Kim, B.K.; Lee, D.H. The $M/G/1$ Queue with disasters and working breakdowns. *Appl. Math. Model.* **2014**, *38*, 1788–1798. [CrossRef]
18. Kumar, B.K.; Arivudainambi, D. The transient solution of $M/M/1$ Queue with catastrophes. *Comput. Math. Appl.* **2000**, *40*, 1233–1240. [CrossRef]

19. Madan, K.C. On a single server queue with two-stage heterogeneous service and deterministic server vacations. *Int. J. Syst. Sci.* **2001**, *32*, 837–844. [CrossRef]
20. Madan, K.C.; Al-Rawi, Z.R.; Al-Nasser, A.D. On $M^X/(G1,G2)/1/G(BS)/Vs$ vacation queue with two types of general heterogeneous service. *J. Appl. Math. Decis. Sci.* **2005**, *3*, 123–135.
21. Mahanta, S.; Choudhury, G.; Ling, N. On queue with two types of general heterogeneous service with Bernoulli feedback. *Cogent Math. Stat.* **2018**, *5*, 1. [CrossRef]
22. Mytalas, G.C.; Zazanis, M.A. An $M^X/G/1$ queueing system with disasters and repairs under MAV policy. *Nav. Res. Logist.* **2015**, *62*, 171–189. [CrossRef]
23. Niranjan, S.P.; Latha, S.D.; Vlase, S.; Scutaru, M.L. Analysis of Bulk Queueing Model with Load Balancing and Vacation. *Axioms* **2024**, *14*, 18. [CrossRef]
24. Palaniammal, S.; Kumar, K. A bulk queue's analysis with two-stage heterogeneous services, multiple vacations, closedown with server breakdown, and two types of renovation. *Math. Model. Eng.* **2024**, *10*, 49–64.
25. Park, H.M.; Yang, W.S.; Chae, K.C. Analysis of the $G1/Geo/1$ Queue with disaster. *Stoch. Anal. Appl.* **2009**, *28*, 44–53. [CrossRef]
26. Sasikala, S.; Indhira, K.; Chandrasekaran, V.M. A study on $M^X/G^B/1$ retrial Queueing system with Bernoulli vacation schedule and variable server capacity. *Int. J. Knowl. Manag. Tour. Hosp.* **2017**, *1*, 263–277.
27. Singh, C.J.; Jain, M.; Kumar, B. $M^X/G/1$ unreliable retrial queue with the option of additional service and Bernoulli Vacation. *Ain Shams Eng. J.* **2016**, *7*, 415–429. [CrossRef]
28. Xie, X.; Sun, W.; Wang, H.; Li, S. Equilibrium and Optimization in a Multi-server Queue with N-policy, Heterogeneous Information and Reneging. *Methodol. Comput. Appl. Probab.* **2025**, *27*, 85. [CrossRef]
29. Yechiali, U. Queues with system disasters and impatient customers when system is down. *Queueing Syst.* **2007**, *56*, 195–202. [CrossRef]
30. Zhu, S.; Wang, J. Strategic Joining in a Single-Server Markovian Queue with Bernoulli Working Vacations. *J. Syst. Sci. Complex.* **2025**, *38*, 1683–1706. [CrossRef]

MDPI AG
Grosspeteranlage 5
4052 Basel
Switzerland
Tel.: +41 61 683 77 34

Axioms Editorial Office
E-mail: axioms@mdpi.com
www.mdpi.com/journal/axioms

www.ingramcontent.com/pod-product-compliance
Lightning Source LLC
Chambersburg PA
CBHW041945260926
51850CB00018B/896
9783725876877